INFLUENCING PEOPLE IN ORGANIZATIONS

CONCEPTS AND CASES

THE DRYDEN PRESS SERIES IN MANAGEMENT

INFLUENCING PEOPLE IN ORGANIZATIONS

CONCEPTS AND CASES

Harry Wilkinson

Rice University

The Dryden Press
Harcourt Brace Jovanovich College Publishers

Fort Worth Philadelphia San Diego New York Orlando Austin San Antonio
Toronto Montreal London Sydney Tokyo

Editor in Chief	Robert A. Pawlik
Acquisitions Editor	Ruth Rominger
Project Editor	Cheryl Hauser
Assistant Project Editor	Matt Ball
Production Manager	Mandy Manzano
Book Designers	Sue Hart and Paula Goldstein

Address for Editorial Correspondence
The Dryden Press, 301 Commerce Street, Suite 3700, Fort Worth, TX 76102

Address for Orders
The Dryden Press, 6277 Sea Harbor Drive, Orlando, FL 32887
1-800-782-4479, or 1-800-433,0001 (in Florida)

ISBN: 0-03-097257-4

Library of Congress Catalog Number: 92-73430

Printed in the United States of America
3 4 5 6 7 8 9 0 1 2 067 9 8 7 6 5 4 3 2 1

The Dryden Press
Harcourt Brace Jovanovich

PREFACE

Influencing People in Organizations: Concepts and Cases is intended to be a graduate level, case-oriented, organizational behavior textbook for use in masters programs in business, public administration, and engineering management. It is also intended for use in university-sponsored or in-company executive development programs. With supplemental reading materials, such as "Managing People and Organizations" from Harvard Business School Publications, as well as some adaptation in teaching approach and use of the case studies, this textbook may be used at the upper class levels in more pragmatic undergraduate programs.

The news media and many successful executives have expressed criticism of many MBA programs for their failure to provide graduates with the essential interpersonal skills necessary to be good team players and function effectively with their peers, managers, and subordinates when they enter the work force.[1] This textbook assumes these criticisms have some validity and attempts to address these concerns by placing a primary emphasis on the development of interpersonal skills through the *application* of concepts rather than acquisition of knowledge alone. Indeed, some faculties have begun to move toward a more pragmatic, application-oriented approach to courses such as organizational behavior, power and influence, organizational development, individual self-assessment, and engineering management.

This book makes four assumptions about all those who will use it. First, they have at least three years of job experience; second, they have seen people functioning in organizations and have some basis for assessing that functioning; third, they either are or aspire to be managers; and fourth, they want to develop knowledge and skills that will be useful to them immediately in improving their on-the-job performance. This textbook attempts to give those who fit these assumptions the maximum opportunity to develop the essential interpersonal skills they will need to be truly effective in their jobs.

There are at least two pitfalls to be avoided in approaching the development of effective interpersonal skills . The first pitfall is the tendency for many managers and students to want quick, easy answers to complex people problems because of the severe time pressures under which they work. Unfortunately, in real-life situations there are seldom quick and easy answers. Many individuals and organizations eagerly buy into quick fixes because they initially see the "Hawthorne effect,"[2] but since the results are not sustainable, they may buy into one quick fix after another. This textbook intentionally does not cover many of the quick fix approaches that are so popular and appealing because they are a substitute for the in-depth understanding and analysis necessary to deal with complex situations. In short, focusing on panaceas inhibits the acquisition of effective interpersonal skills.

A second pitfall in the acquisition of effective interpersonal skills is the focus on basic research that has not yet reached the point of useful application.[3] This type of research may be very useful in the long run and may be of great interest to academicians but to those who are, or aspire to be, managers it may be seen as a diversion of time and energy from developing the essential interpersonal skills through application of demonstrably useful concepts. In this textbook, considerable effort has been expended to avoid these two pitfalls. Neither quick fix approaches nor good research not yet proven useful to practicing managers has been included. Also excluded are some concepts that may have found some limited usefulness in the past but which, for one reason or another, are no longer used. An attempt has been made, however, to include those concepts with considerable historical significance that executives may need as background for future concepts not yet developed. Of course, what to include and what to exclude is a matter of judgment. Some instructors may prefer a bit more academic rigor while others may prefer a bit more practical emphasis. For this reason, instructors may wish to omit some concept chapters or supplement those they do use with other readings from academic or practitioner journals, videos, or books such as "Managing People and Organizations" suggested earlier.

This textbook aims to provide skills in all three of Sternberg's forms of cognitive functioning: componental (linear), experiential (non-linear), and contextual.[4] It is divided into two main parts, Part 1—the concept chapters, which deal primarily with linear intelligence and knowledge, while Part 2—the cases, gives the user the opportunity to build all three types of skill: linear through case analyses; non-linear through a series of case experiences and discussions to build judgment; and contextual or street smarts through the necessity of reading the environment in each case to reach a reasonable solution. It is anticipated that most instructors will spend the bulk of seminar time on the cases in Part 2 that can give experience in applying many of the concepts in Part 1.

This textbook derives from the work and experiences of many people since 1960 in MBA programs, management consulting, and executive development during which the initial drafts of all the concept chapters and cases were researched and written, mostly at client expense (except for the student-initiated cases).

Only the more successful concepts and cases are presented here. This original work was done by many different members of University Affiliates, Inc., staff and copyrighted by the firm. They are used here with the permission of University Affiliates, Inc.

It should be noted that all the cases in this book are derived from field research, including interviews with the executives actually involved in the situation. They have been written as crisply and concisely as was considered feasible but contain all the information the manager had which he or she felt was significant, including his or her feelings about the information. They also include any information the case writer may have felt was critical even if the manager did not; but the desire to keep the cases short resulted in the omission of some color or information which might have been interesting but not central to the situation as the manager saw it.

In disguising the cases I have tried to use easy to pronounce, often one-syllable names so that neither foreign nor U.S. students would be distracted by difficult names. There are fewer women and members of ethnic groups in managerial positions in the industries described in the cases than some people might like to see, but that is the current reality. Since I feel it is more important for students to acquire the skills to deal with the world as it is, including all its biases, I have tried to preserve reality rather than fictionalize the cases to describe the way some may feel the world ought to be. Therefore, I have included sexist and racist viewpoints and preserved ethnicity and gender whenever these were important. In a few cases, I have made a manager female or used an ethnic name when this would not change the analysis in order to add, however slightly, more diversity reflecting the ever-evolving reality of the workplace.

Most cases are multifaceted as they were in the actual situations, requiring the manager, or student, to deal with these interdependent issues with incomplete, often distorted or misleading information. They have been selected for this book because

a. they concern first or second level managers facing problems and issues that are typical at those levels,
b. it is anticipated that those who use this book will soon be, are, or recently have been in similar positions, and
c. the difficulty of translating from the case study to on the job performance is made easier by (a) and (b) above.

There is *no* one-to-one relationship between the concept chapters and the cases and indeed, some concept chapters are intended for future use on the job rather than for immediate skill building with cases (see Chapter 3). The cases are *not* intended to illustrate concepts; very seldom in organizational life does a situation occur that illustrates a single concept and even more rarely do these situations have much significance. Each case is intended to be an experience that adds to the readers non-linear base or intuitive judgment (see Chapter 2) . Each case is intended to give the reader practice in looking at and adjusting to the environment to build contextual skills or street smarts as well as the analytical or linear skills.

ACKNOWLEDGMENTS

This textbook could not have been put together without the assistance, inputs, and support of many people . Those members of the staff of University Affiliates, Inc. (UAI), to whom I am especially indebted include Robert Benfari, now a senior lecturer at Harvard University; James Burns, now Dean of Business at San Diego University; and Charles Orth, now retired. Others whose contributions deserve recognition include Charles Hampden-Turner; Jack Aber; many of the executives in client organizations who are too numerous to mention and who, for the most part, would prefer to remain anonymous; and all of the support staff, especially Nina Drouilhet, Linda Lewin, and Debbie Neal.

I am further deeply indebted to the faculty and administration at the Jesse H. Jones Graduate School of Administration at Rice University for welcoming me as a colleague and providing me with the encouragement and resources necessary to bring this project to fruition. Thanks are also due the staff at the Jones school for assistance in word processing and administrative tasks. Special thanks to my research assistant Tracy Poirier who not only assisted with the research but also with the references, editing, and word processing and to Jennifer Rawlings who also assisted with editing and word processing.

Special thanks are also due to Mary Fischer who was the first person in the publishing industry to share my enthusiasm for this project; Scott Isenberg who nursed the book through its early phases; and Butch Gemin and Ruth Rominger who brought it to final publication.

No set of acknowledgments would be complete without thanking the students at the Jones School whose use of materials prior to publication resulted in significant improvements as the textbook evolved through several drafts. Thanks also to the many participants in the executive development programs UAI taught for many clients over the years and whose questions provided the inputs to innumerable revisions and rewrites of various materials used in this book.

Finally, I acknowledge my debt to my teachers and mentors at the Harvard Business School particularly "Fritz" Roethlisberger, Bob Merry, George Baker, and later, "Chris" Christensen who

a. instilled in me a belief in the strength of the case method,
b. enlightened me about the art of case writing and the art of leading case discussions,

c. nurtured and encouraged my intellectual curiosity and interest in practical research, and

d. led me to have the highest regard for those who teach and learn with the case method.

Whatever strengths there are in this book, I owe to them; whatever weaknesses there are are mine alone.

FOOTNOTES

1. Deutschman, Alan. "The Trouble with MBAs." *Fortune* July 29, 1991: 67–73. Linden, Dana Wechsler, Jody Brennon and Randall Lane. "Another Boom Ends. " *Forbes* January 20, 1992 .

2. The term "Hawthorne effect" derives from the initial experiments conducted at the Western Electric Company, Hawthorne Works in Chicago by a group including a number from Harvard University. This research was reported in the book *Management and the Worker*, by F. J. Roethlisberger and William J. Dickson, Harvard University Press, Cambridge, MA, 1946. One of the things they concluded is that attention from management and others, by itself, can have a significant impact on performance. The "Hawthorne effect" is specifically discussed in the book *Counseling in an Organization*, by the same authors, F. J. Roethlisberger and William J. Dickson, Division of Research, Harvard Business School, Boston, MA, 1966.

3. Fielden, John S. and Jean D. Gibbons, "Merit Myopia and Business School Faculty Publications." *Business Horizons*, March–April 1991. Sowell, Thomas, "Beggars in Tuxedos", *Forbes*, April 27, 1992.

4. Sternberg, R. J. (1985) *Beyond IQ: A Triarchic Theory of Human Intelligence*, NY: Cambridge University Press.

Contents

x   Contents

PART 1

CONCEPT CHAPTERS

CHAPTER 1

INTRODUCTION

Professional managers face challenges every day. Often these are complex and frustrating. The professional manager must study situations and people, analyze incomplete data, and reach decisions that he or she feels makes sense. Very seldom are there nice, neat, precise "textbook" solutions for managerial problems. If no "textbook" answers can be learned for the managerial problems, what can the manager who wishes to develop the ability to deal effectively with the situations he or she faces do? What can he or she study? Which skills should be developed?

Should we be concerned about organizational behavior and interpersonal skills including the acquisition and use of power? Many books and articles have been written extolling Japanese management and threatening dire consequences for the U.S. economy if we do not improve our managerial skills as a nation. Paradoxically, *The Art of Japanese Management* by Pascale and Athos seemed to suggest that what the Japanese did to create their "miracle" was to look at the best companies in the industrialized West, take what they learned back to Japan, adapt it to their unique culture, and spread it throughout their economy.[1] *In Search of Excellence* by Peters and Waterman,[2] which was based on a study of U.S. firms that grew out of the earlier study of Japanese firms by Pascale and Athos, identified 50 U.S. companies that were said to demonstrate consistently good management. Both the Japanese and the best U.S. companies are very "people oriented." Much attention has also been given to the quality of Japanese products compared to those made in the United States, and "Total Quality Management" (or TQM) has become a set of buzz words popular in the Defense Department, the aerospace industry, and some other organizations as well.[3] Those who espouse TQM argue that many U.S. organizations will require a "culture" change to become "people oriented" enough to be successful (see Chapter 22). In short, interpersonal skills have been recognized as essential for success in today's international and domestic organizational environments and are becoming increasingly important.

Many of the managerial mistakes that can be observed in organizations are caused by too narrow a definition of interpersonal problems. As a very simple example, a manager may conclude that one of his or her subordinates performs poorly because that subordinate is just fundamentally bad. A conclusion like this is dysfunctional for two reasons. First, it is rarely correct; the world is just more

3

complex than that. Second, it precludes the possibility of solving the problem. If management has concluded that Joe is bad, then there is little reason to understand his value systems, to attempt to find ways to motivate him, to structure his job so that it is more satisfying to him, or to allow him to find outlets and satisfiers for his needs. If Joe is bad, one must protect oneself from him. The organization becomes a battlefield. The same type of example can be drawn from other employment situations, such as departments with which one must work or the environment within which one must function.

Some theorists in the field of organizational behavior divide schools of thought into two areas: the atomistic and holistic theories. Atomistic theories assume that a single cause can be found to explain the behavior or pattern of behavior of employees in organizations. The quickest example of this type of theory that comes to mind is the experiment involving Pavlov's dogs.[4] A bell is rung and the dog is fed. After enough repetitions of this phenomenon, the dog salivates with the ringing of the bell, whether or not food is present. One will probably say that no manager could believe or accept such a simple explanation for individuals' behavior in organizations. Many articles have been written and arguments conducted about the right style of leadership for organizational effectiveness.[5] Other articles have discussed the personality traits of "good" managers.[6] If we think about it, these are atomistic theories. One assumes here that behavior is the result of one variable: leadership styles or personality traits.

Holistic concepts assume that a person's behavior is really the result of many different forces operating simultaneously. At the very minimum, behavior depends on

- one's personal history, including one's relationship with superiors, subordinates, and peers;
- one's expectations of the roles that superiors, subordinates, and peers should play;
- one's skill in doing the job and one's confidence in that skill; and
- one's values, needs, motivations, and other factors that may be important at the time.

Another way of looking at the holistic concept of behavior is that one's total set of life experiences and genetic makeup leads to the evolution of one's personal attributes or characteristics, while the sets of expectations or psychological contracts formed when one becomes a member of various groups,[7] such as a church, community, profession, or organization, and various environmental factors, such as economic and social conditions, contribute to the evolution of one's self concept or self-image and finally one's own analysis or rationalization of one's behavior. Any one or all of these factors may influence behavior under certain circumstances.

Why is one executive a good "people person" while another is not? What does it take to have good interpersonal skills? Experienced executives are aware of the many different theories about human behavior but often feel that few of them work all the time. Yet successful, people-oriented executives have learned *when* the various concepts from psychology and organizational behavior are useful and when they are not. Consciously or intuitively, they use the concepts that work in the various situations they face. This book attempts to include in Part I those concepts which have proved useful, presented in a short, concise, practitioner oriented manner.

Successful, people-oriented executives appear to have at least a few things in common. They are knowledgeable in the technologies involved in their jobs but are also knowledgeable in the currently useful concepts of psychology and organizational behavior that are applicable in the situations they face. Their intuition and judgment are good and correctly identifies which concepts will be successful in specific situations. They are empathetic; they care about, listen to, and understand the people with whom they work. They are sincere; they believe in what they say or do and do not pretend or play games. They are ethical, honest, and fair; they tell it like it is, but do so with tact and concern. They focus on those things that are positive more than on those that are negative. They reinforce positive achievements and do not labor over failures; their focus is on "how do we fix it?" rather than on "who is to blame?" Finally, they are enthusiastic about their achievements as well as those of the people around them, and they demonstrate that enthusiasm even for small achievements.

As the reader will see in Chapter 2, there are three different types of what can be described as cognitive functioning, mental processes, intelligence, knowledge, or skills. These are componential, that is, linear thinking or what is taught in school and measured in IQ tests; experiential, that is, nonlinear, intuitive thinking, judgment, or what we derive from experience; and contextual, what is sometimes called "street smarts" or the ability to read our environment and adjust to it.[8] These are related to, yet different from, the older and perhaps more familiar technical, conceptual, and human skills described by Katz in 1955.[9] One way of relating these factors is given below.

FACTORS OF COGNITIVE FUNCTIONING

Compotential	Experiential	Contextual
Linear	Nonlinear/integrative	"Street smarts"
IQ	Experience	Reading environment
Analysis	Synthesis	Adjustment/compromise
Textbook	Intuition/judgment	Judgment/politics
Technical/factual	Conceptual	Human/empathetic
Problem solving	Problem finding	Opportunity finding
Case analysis	Case experience	Case environment

Successful, people-oriented managers have learned that interpersonal skills require an integration of all three of these types of cognitive functioning. In this book, the concept chapters provide a knowledge base while the cases in Part II offer the opportunity to acquire linear skills through analysis, nonlinear skills through discussion to build judgment, and contextual skills through the necessity to evaluate the environment in each case in order to determine which of the alternatives are achievable. Nonlinear and contextual skills are very different from the linear skills, which are the basis of most college courses. Nonlinear and contextual skills are related to judgment acquired by experience over many years.

What can we do to acquire and effectively use interpersonal skills that require linear, nonlinear, and contextual skills? Just as we cannot acquire body tone or the ability to swim or ride a bicycle by reading a book or listening to a lecture, the same is true with interpersonal skills. To acquire body tone requires strenuous exercise and to maintain it requires strenuous exercise on a continuing basis. The same is true with interpersonal skills; we must work hard to acquire them and continue to work hard to maintain them. You learn to swim by getting in the water and thrashing about until you acquire the skill through experience. You learn to ride a bicycle by getting on the bike and trying different ways until you succeed in acquiring the skill. In the same way, you can begin to acquire interpersonal skills by trial and error. But since learning on the job can be very costly in terms of your career, you can begin to acquire interpersonal skills by actively participating in class discussions of real organizational case studies. Trying to acquire interpersonal skills passively has the same effect as being in the water but not trying to swim. The case studies in Part II allow you to use the concepts and your prior experience to experiment, to try new approaches, and to begin to develop your interpersonal skills. When you are trying to build body tone, early and continuous exercise throughout the program improves the tone your body will achieve. In a like manner, early and consistent participation during the course increases the level of skill you will acquire and be able to demonstrate by the end of the course. If you are starting an aerobics program from scratch, you obviously will not reach a high level of body tone in a short time. In the same way, you are unlikely to acquire a high level of interpersonal skills in a one- or two-semester organizational behavior course. Building and maintaining interpersonal skills, like body tone, is a continuous endeavor throughout your lifetime. This book is intended to start you off in this process.

Interpersonal skills are critical to success on the job, particularly in middle management or if you aspire to a leadership position. But as noted in the preface, the news media and many successful executives have criticized many MBA programs for their failure to provide graduates with the essential interpersonal skills, specifically nonlinear and contextual skills, necessary to be good team players and function effectively with their peers, managers, and subordinates when they enter the work force.[10] This book gives you the opportunity to learn practical, useful concepts that will help you build your linear skills. Through repeated experiences in multifaceted case analysis and discussion, you will have the opportunity to build your linear and nonlinear (or intuitive judgment skills) and improve your ability to read and adjust to your environment. Thus, you will learn useful concepts, apply these to behavioral issues, develop your intuition, hone your empathy, deepen your sincerity, clarify your ethics, amplify your focus on the positive, and expand your enthusiasm as other successful managers have done. By putting all these together in the *process* of case analysis and discussion, you will begin your journey on the long road to acquiring and maintaining the interpersonal skills so necessary to career success. After this, it is up to you to continue to build and maintain your interpersonal skills throughout your working lifetime.

QUESTIONS FOR REFLECTION AND DISCUSSION

1. What are the differences between knowledge, wisdom, judgment, and intuition?
2. How does one acquire wisdom, judgment, and intuition?
3. How does one teach or evaluate wisdom, judgment, and intuition?
4. How does one build and maintain interpersonal skills throughout one's working lifetime?

NOTES

1. Richard T. Pascale and Antony G. Athos, *The Art of Japanese Management* (New York: Simon & Schuster, 1981).
2. Thomas J. Peters and Robert H. Waterman, Jr., *In Search of Excellence* (New York: Harper & Row, 1982), pp. 21–22.
3. Richard Schonberger, "Total Quality Management Cuts a Broad Swath—Through Manufacturing and Beyond," *Organizational Dynamics*, Spring 1992, pp. 16–28.
4. Calvin Hall and Gardner Lindzey, *Introduction to Theories of Personality* (New York: John Wiley & Sons, 1985), p. 468.
5. Bernard M. Bass, *Bass & Stogdill's, Handbook of Leadership*, 3rd ed. (New York: The Free Press, 1990).
6. David Keirsey and Marilyn Bates, *Please Understand Me* (Del Mar, CA: Prometheus Nemesis, 1978); and Robert Benfari, *Understanding Your Management Style* (New York: The Free Press, 1991).
7. *Expectations* is a term often used in management literature; see, for example, "Pygmalion in Management," by J. Sterling Livingston, *Harvard Business Review*, July/August 1969, which was originally derived from *Pygmalion in the Classroom*, by Robert Rosenthal and Lenore Jacobson (New York: Holt, Rinehart and Winston, 1968). *Psychological contract* is a term often used in psychological literature and, more recently, management literature; see, for example, *Managing Human Assets*, by Michael Beer, Bert Spector, Paul R. Lawrence, D. Quinn Mills, and Richard L. Walton (New York: The Free Press, 1984). The term apparently originated as a psychological extension derived from A. H. Croust's article, "Origin and Meaning of the Social Compact Doctrine as Expressed by Greek Philosophers," *Ethics*, October 1946.
8. R. J. Sternberg, *Beyond IQ: A Triarchic Theory of Human Intelligence* (New York: Cambridge University Press, 1985).
9. Robert L. Katz, "Skills of an Effective Administrator," *Harvard Business Review*, January/February 1955, pp. 33–42.
10. Alan Deutschman, "The Trouble with MBAs," *Fortune*, July 29, 1991, pp. 67–73; and Dana Wechsler Linden, Jody Brennon, and Randall Lane, "Another Boom Ends," *Forbes*, January 20, 1992, pp. 67–68.

CHAPTER 2

INTELLIGENCE
AND MANAGEMENT

June was hired by a high-tech, *Fortune* 500 company after graduating from an engineering program at an Ivy League university. Her grade-point average was 3.86, and her recommendations were excellent. June was welcomed into the company with great expectations. In her first year, she performed at a high level in a job that involved individual contribution and little need for teamwork with other engineers or groups. At that point her boss decided to promote her to a first-line supervisory position and assigned her to a group working on a subunit of integrated systems. This large, multimillion-dollar program involved all functional departments in the company. Since the company was organized as a matrix structure, many tasks had to be coupled across work groups. Teamwork was not only necessary within June's own work group, but also with other groups in the organization.

Six months after June was given her new responsibilities, her boss, John, received a number of complaints about June's behavior and performance. She was brilliant at her specialty, but she displayed many irritating and dysfunctional behaviors. She was described as self-centered and was accused of hoarding her results, being uncooperative outside her group, remaining insensitive to her people, and lacking awareness of the big picture. One of her peers stated, "She just doesn't have street smarts."

John attempted to remedy the situation by talking to June about these problems. This only exacerbated the situation, however. After another six months of frustration and failure in trying to deal with the situation, her boss finally wrote June off as a failed promotion.

The scenario and its consequences are not uncommon in organizations. The exact rate of this type of failure is unknown, but it is high enough that the case

Note: This chapter is reprinted (with minor modifications) from *Business Horizons*, May/June 1988, Copyright 1988 by the Foundation for the School of Business at Indiana University, and is used with permission.

cannot be treated as an isolated one. What went wrong? For one thing, June received the promotion on the basis of data that was inadequate for predicting future job performance. Her grade-point average and references reflected past performance in areas that do not predict performance in jobs requiring multiform skills. Other factors that contributed to this failure lie in several of the areas we will explore in this chapter. With careful study, potential managers will be given an understanding of the factors that can lead to a higher level of organizational effectiveness.

In this case, there are several possible explanations for what went wrong:

1. June was a bad choice and did not live up to expectations.
2. The job was beyond her capabilities.
3. The system did not apply the right yardsticks when it selected employees.
4. The system did not develop June's potential.
5. The system did not know what skills are needed for effective performance in an interactive task environment.
6. A combination of the above.

If we analyze the situation from an organizational perspective, the blame shifts away from the hapless employee and we can see what is needed for organizational effectiveness. Three interrelated factors hold the key to obtaining organizational effectiveness:

1. Knowing what the job's skill requirements are, including technical, conceptual and human skills.
2. Knowing your strengths and weaknesses as a manager.
3. Knowing the strengths and weaknesses of others (subordinates, peers, and bosses).

The manager must then apply this knowledge to the selection, development, and influence of others in the organization.

In order to give a broader perspective, we have organized this chapter into the following sections: the relationship between academic performance and job performance, the conceptual skills of a manager, power skills, understanding oneself, others, and the environment, and measuring and developing practical intelligence.

ACADEMIC PERFORMANCE AND JOB PERFORMANCE

A manager's performance on the job is not related to his or her performance in school or on aptitude tests. This was first discussed in a 1971 *Harvard Business Review* article by J. Sterling Livingston.[1] More recent research by Yale psychologist Robert J. Sternberg corroborates the earlier dictum.[2] The typical school focuses heavily on developing componential IQ and actually uses tests of componential IQ for admittance. The result is an overrefinement of one aspect of the big picture. This development of componential IQ to the detriment of the other two subforms (experiential and contextual) probably accounts for the lack of relationship between standard tests, grade point averages, and job performance. Sternberg points out that by the time people are weeded out through the many hurdles of educational life, the range of IQ is very restricted—110–150 for executives. If one takes the whole range of IQ, from 40 to 150, and correlates the scores with performance, there might be a relationship, but there does not appear to be one within the higher range by itself. Livingston and Sternberg agree that graduate school does not prepare a student for a job's practical tasks. Sternberg calls this aptitude practical intelligence and adds that the usual paper-and-pencil tests, such as the GRE (Graduate Record Examination) and IQ tests, measure only one part of the global concept of "intelligence."

From these two complementary studies of educational performance and job performance, two factors emerge. Standard tests do not measure the whole range of the components of practical intelligence, and colleges and graduate schools teach only some of the skills needed to be effective on the job.

A MANAGER'S CONCEPTUAL SKILLS

Sternberg has isolated three subforms of intelligence that have practical implications for performance of everyday tasks. The first factor is called *componential intelligence*. Componential intelligence relates to how we think and process information internally—what IQ tests measure. It is basically analytical skill (and in this book we will refer to this as linear skill). When a job needs this type of thinking, an individual with these skills will perform very well. On the other hand, when a job demands different skills, such as combining disparate experiences and insightful thinking, componential intelligence does not help. Sternberg calls the subform of intelligence needed in this situation *experiential thinking* (and in this book we will refer to this as nonlinear, integrative, or intuitive thinking). The person with this skill will be good at linking past experience with new experience and combining these situations into creative insights. Some people have both componential and experiential intelligence, while others are high in only one. The individuals high in only one subform will perform very differently in jobs that require different skills.

The third subform of intelligent behavior involves the capacity to interact with the environment and to read correctly the requirements in the situational context. Sternberg calls this form *contextual intelligence*. People who have this intellectual skill are usually labeled "street smart." They may not possess a very high level of componential IQ or experiential IQ, but they learn to play the game very well and to manipulate the environment effectively.

Most jobs require the application of a combination of the three forms of intelligence. Livingston makes the point that a manager's job involves very little of the strict application of analytical (or linear, componential IQ) skills and a heavy application of the conceptual (or nonlinear, experiential IQ) skills. He states that the effective manager must be able to identify problems and opportunities as well as solve problems.

Opportunity Finding

The pertinent question is not how to do things right, but how to find the right things to do. An elegant solution to the wrong problem wastes valuable resources and limits the effectiveness of all involved. Opportunity finding is the ability to scan the environment, see the areas in which the most can be gained, and focus on the opportunities.

Opportunity finding is probably a mixture of experiential and contextual skills. It can only be developed when a person interacts with the environment. Some people are born with the ability to look for opportunities, but it can be developed with the appropriate training. Most of the emphasis on entrepreneurial development that one sees in the business literature is directed at setting up organizational climates to foster opportunity finding.

Problem Finding

Problem finding is a separate management skill from problem solving. It involves different cognitive processes and is probably more experiential (nonlinear) than componential (linear). A problem finder must have an acute sensitivity to the environment, the subtle signs of change in that environment, and their relationship to future events. The problem finder uses more intuition than data. The facts are used in the context of the situational changes to corroborate trends and tendencies, not as the basis of analytical problem solving. The development of problem-finding skills depends largely on the person's opportunity to apply these skills through firsthand experience. This does not mean that it cannot be taught. Quite the contrary, competence skills can be improved by training, as advocated by McClelland.[3] Using this approach, the navy carried out a competency-based training program that resulted in improved operational effectiveness.[4]

Problem Solving

To be a good problem solver, one must analyze the facts, relate them to the current situation, classify the problem, seek alternative solutions, find one solution based upon trade-off analysis, and then take action. Problem solving involves a mixture of (linear) componential IQ and (nonlinear) experiential IQ. Livingston says that most people are trained in the analytical portion of the process but fail in the trade-off (relationship to reality) and execution (action) parts. He maintains these are not taught in the usual academic environment.

The application of these cognitive skills does not ensure that a manager will perform effectively. Management style and motivation interact with cognitive capabilities to round out the picture. A person can be high on all three factors of cognitive functioning (componential, experiential, and contextual), and therefore have the native capacity to find and solve problems and seek opportunities, but fail to execute as a manager because his or her motivational profile does not fit the requirements of the managerial job.

The most effective managers are those whose personalities and previous experiences fit well with their organization and position. In a more general sense, effective managers are usually motivated to influence people (power skills), understand themselves and others (perceptive and intuitive skills), and they have an ability to understand and influence the environment. In short, they integrate good leadership skills with good administrative skills.

POWER SKILLS

A successful manager should be aware of the role of power in effective performance (see also Chapter 8).[5] Achievement by itself does not make an effective manager, only a competent employee. The manager must influence people to participate, get people to accept various roles, build liaisons across the organization and networks for effective communications, and get on with the job of managing. All of these roles demand the effective use of power. Recent research on the characteristics of effective managers shows that most effective managers possess a high need for power. This implies that the high performers use a variety of power bases to influence people and the environment. People can develop their capacity to use power effectively. The critical point is that this motivation, whether inbred or developed, is an essential component of the managerial makeup.

UNDERSTANDING ONESELF, OTHERS, AND THE ENVIRONMENT

Wagner and Sternberg, like Livingston, have a three-category system for classifying practical intelligence skills for professionals and managers: tacit knowledge about managing oneself, managing others, and managing a career.[6] These three categories do not appear different from Livingston's three categories (a) the need to manage, (b) the need for power, and (c) the capacity for empathy, in that they are extensions of similar concepts. The power skills are clearly part of managing others and a career. Management of oneself is not directly isolated by Livingston, but is mentioned as a requisite for being an effective manager.

According to Wagner and Sternberg, *managing self* refers to knowledge about how to manage oneself on a daily basis to maximize one's productivity. The emphasis is on one's personal assessment of the goals and objectives of the job, the priorities of the tasks, knowledge about the effective and efficient means of accomplishing the end result, and knowledge of what motivates oneself. The focus is on the person's approaches to getting the job done. Self-knowledge about motivation and other aspects of one's management style is critical. The roles of achievement and power motivation come into clear perspective in this scheme of practical intelligence.

Managing others refers to knowledge of the work habits, the strengths and weaknesses, and the goal orientation of both subordinates and colleagues. One could add that managing others should include understanding one's boss. This category is directly related to Livingston's power-skill concept. Managing others takes into account all of the interpersonal skills needed to get people to coordinate and accomplish task activities and to maximize both performance and satisfaction.

Managing a career refers to the ability to know what the reward structure is, what will gain recognition within the organization, and how reputations are established. This category has a high degree of organizational specificity; each organization or career pathway has unique characteristics that may not be transferable to other organizations or careers. Therefore, knowledge about the organization's culture is imperative if one is to truly develop the skills needed to manage one's career.

Another area of tacit knowledge concerning the organization's culture is not mentioned by Wagner and Sternberg. It seems to be needed to define fully practical intelligence for managers. *Managing the environment* refers to knowledge of the value system, the conflict style, and the orientation to interpersonal issues within the organization. The value system defines the organization's dos and don'ts, its perception of the role it plays in the external environment, its perception of the hierarchical structure (loose or strict), its approach to job enrichment and self-development, its view of the reward structure (monetary or other), its preferred communication channels, its view of the role of delegation, and even its dress code. All of these elements add up to a gestalt that defines the specific culture of a given organization. Without this knowledge, the most brilliant contributor can fall prey to invisible forces that can hinder a career. It appears that this aspect of practical intelligence should stand as a separate practical skill.

MEASURING PRACTICAL INTELLIGENCE

Componential (linear) intelligence can be measured by the usual battery of standardized IQ tests. Practical intelligence, on the other hand, cannot. But students of practical intelligence have defined three alternative approaches to the problem: the motivational, the simulation, and the critical-incident method.

The Motivational Approach

The motivational approach focuses on the motive patterns needed to manage successfully. These motive patterns—the need for achievement, power, and affiliation—correspond to the group of motives that McClelland and Livingston each found to be related to superior performance in large samples of middle- and upper-level managers.[7] The similarities between the concepts of McClelland, Livingston, and Wagner and Sternberg are depicted below.

MANAGERIAL SKILLS AND MOTIVES

Wagner and Sternberg	Livingston	McClelland
Management of Oneself	Need to manage	Need for achievement
Management of others	Need for power	Need for power
Management of a career	Need for empathy	Need for affiliation

Motive patterns may be measured using two methods: direct and indirect. The direct method uses a self-report questionnaire that can be scored in a standardized fashion and requires very little training to administer and score. The indirect, or projective, method demands extensive training for the people who administer and score the stories given by the participants in response to a set of pictures. Participants can fake answers to look good if the direct method is used. The projective method is less prone to this distortion.

The motivational approach to assessing practical intelligence can be used to select managers or to counsel them on their respective needs and their relationship to a given job. It seems to be more beneficial to use the motivational approach as part of a development program instead of as an entry measure. For example, the need for power has been cited as an important aspect of the manager's competence. On the other hand, the person who is higher in achievement and affiliation can develop, through skills training, influence techniques that would enhance these power skills. The measurements in this instance are used to alert the manager to possible pitfalls. The manager may or may not choose to develop new skills, depending on her or his level of desire and commitment. The interpretation of the combinations of motive patterns can be complex, since—using three strength levels, low, medium, and high—there can be 27 such combinations. The analysis becomes more complex but enriched when other need patterns, such as need for autonomy, deference, and recognition, are added.

The assessment of motive patterns has been found to have a low but reliable relationship to performance in industrial, government, and academic organizations. The low but significant relationship is expected, since management performance is made up of many skills and motivation is a necessary, but not sufficient, component. One aspect of the assessment of practical intelligence should be the motivational approach. Combined with other assessments, it can give a better picture of the manager's strengths and weaknesses. It must be emphasized that measurement should be used as a part of a development program aimed at increasing skill levels. When the assessment of practical intelligence is used in this fashion, the problem of faking disappears *if* the participant is truly interested in improvement. Direct measures can then be used. The participants should be advised that the tests are for their use only and faking will only fake oneself. The goal is self-knowledge that can be used by the participant to build greater competence.

The Simulation Approach

The simulation approach has been used in many contexts for many years. The Germans used the simulation technique in World War I to assess potential for espionage. During World War II, the Americans, under the guidance of "Wild Bill" Donovan and Henry Murray, used similar methods to assess candidates for the Office of Strategic Services, the forerunner of the Central Intelligence Agency.[8] A recent use of the method was the development of the assessment-center approach by Douglas Bray for AT&T.[9] The program, a longitudinal study of managers, eventually led to the institutionalization of assessment centers for the selection of managers and communication consultants.

The method consists of observing participants in situations that have been set up to simulate job performance. The key to the simulation approach is to have a good conceptual model of the specific and general aspects of the job. The observer can then focus on a few important variables during the simulations. The participants are rated based upon performance in the simulations; the simulations are the vehicles for determining the ratings on the variables; and the variables are the components of practical intelligence needed for the job. The list can be lengthy or short. The pattern of the variables is used to give feedback to the participants. The AT&T assessment centers were used to check whether a candidate had the potential to do the job, and the observers had to integrate the pattern of the variables to come up with a rating. An assessment team adjudicated the ratings of the variables and overall rating.

Some specific simulations are the in-basket technique, group problem solving, individual problem solving, presentations, and interviews. Each technique samples job-related behavior. The key to the success of the simulation approach is job knowledge. This leads to the definition of the job variables, which in turn leads to the selection of the specific simulations that will sample the critical job variables. Selecting simulations without defining the key variables leads to vacuous observations.

The simulation approach demands a high level of job knowledge. One must construct the list of variables, design simulations, train a staff to make reliable judgments, and integrate the relationships of the variables. The setup time for this approach is long and costly, but the results can be very impressive. The combination of the motivational approach and the simulation approach is an advanced method of assessing practical intelligence.

The Critical-Incident Technique

The critical-incident technique is strongly supported by Robert Sternberg. In this procedure, people respond to critical incidents. The results are then analyzed qualitatively to see which skills are highlighted. When using the critical-incident approach, it is important to use a valid sample of critical incidents that relate to the skills needed for successful performance. Case material can be gathered through interviews with successful middle- and senior-level managers.

The critical-incident technique is similar to the simulation method in that a set of variables must be constructed to evaluate the responses to the cases. This method is less costly and labor-intensive than the simulation approach, but it does not give the in-depth observation of actual behavior, only an "as if" demonstration.

Wagner and Sternberg take the critical-incident technique one step further in what they call the knowledge-based approach. In this approach, knowledge gathered from experts and novices is used to find the essential skills.[10] The premise is that experts differ from novices in the amount and organization of their knowledge about the situation or task. The advance by Sternberg lies not in the specific methodology of the knowledge-based approach, but in the application of his classification of the three knowledge areas discussed earlier (supplemented, in our view, by knowledge of the organization's culture). The system, combined with the motivational and simulation approaches, appears to be the state of the art in the measurement of practical intelligence.

The measurement of practical intelligence differs considerably from the assessment of scholastic and traditional intelligence. Practical intelligence is skill in dealing with pragmatic events in a real-world context. It is a form of intelligence that is not directly taught in the typical school's curriculum and has an informal element to it. Some people, through the luck of the draw, have the intuitive capacity to be outstanding performers. Others with the gift of standard intelligence perform brilliantly in their school years and burn out when the situation calls for practical intelligence. The measurement of practical intelligence serves best when it is used as a self-learning tool for individuals who want to increase their capacity to perform or who want to find job situations that best fit their strengths and minimize their weaknesses. Both approaches are valid, and the choice depends upon the person's goals.

DEVELOPING PRACTICAL INTELLIGENCE

The critical issue in the development of practical intelligence is the skills on which to focus. The three that recur in the research on practical intelligence appear to be influence skills, conceptualization skills, and interpersonal skills. In all the studies that look at the superior performance of managers, these three areas are repeatedly cited as the ones that distinguish superior managers from average performers. It is apparent, then, that any training or development program should include these three skill areas.

The first step in the program should be the assessment of the baseline skill level for each of the three areas. This can be attained by using the three assessment methods cited earlier. The three skill areas must be broken down into defined components, however, before the program can go forward.

Influence skills should be defined as the relative use of the eight power bases (see Exhibit 2-1 and Chapter 8).

Klemp and McClelland distinguish four types of influence skills: concern for influence, directive influence, collaborative influence, and symbolic influence.[11]

EXHIBIT 2-1

INFLUENCE SKILLS

Authority power
Coercive power
Reward power
Information power
Affiliative power
Expert power
Referent power
Group power

These categories seem to be higher-order variables that require the application of various combinations of the eight power bases. For example, the exercise of collaborative influence requires the combination of referent power, group power, reward power, and (possibly) expert power.[12]

The methods for developing the specific influence skills include self-analysis of strengths and weaknesses, critical-incident analyses, role playing of specific scenarios, and imagery rehearsal. The emphasis should be on the development of specific skills using practical situations.

Some interpersonal skills are cited in Exhibit 2-2. These specific skills, like the influence subset, can be developed by the use of such behavioral techniques as role playing, imagery, rehearsal, and case analyses.

Conceptual skills (see Exhibit 2-3) can be developed by using critical-incident techniques, cases designed to focus on specific conceptual skills, and exercises that demonstrate the behaviors that need to be shaped.

Practical intelligence *can* be defined in subunits that have relevance to effective management functioning. These skills *can* be developed by the use of various behaviorally oriented techniques. It is vitally important, both for the organization and the budding manager, that the test for practical intelligence be made.

Postscript

It should be noted that most university courses focus dominately, if not exclusively, on componential intelligence, where answers are clear and definite. Thus, ambiguity and uncertainty may not have played much of a role in the previous academic experiences of many users of this book. Reading a book or listening to a lecture is an effective way of acquiring componential, linear knowledge. However, it is critical to recognize that experiential and contextual skills are like wisdom or body tone—they can be acquired through real or simulated experiences but not learned by reading a book or listening to a lecture. Case analyses and discussions can be the simulated experiences whereby one can begin to acquire experiential and contextual wisdom.

EXHIBIT 2-2

INTERPERSONAL SKILLS

Communication skills (listening and expressing)
Sensitivity to other's needs
Knowledge of self (motives, preferences, and values)
Knowledge of others
Ability to handle stressful situations
Ability to handle difficult people
Social responsibility
Social adaptability
Ability to use positive reinforcement
Ability to make critical statements on a conditional basis
Tolerance of uncertainty and ambiguity

EXHIBIT 2-3

CONCEPTUAL SKILLS

Planning and priority setting
Decision making (problem solving)
Diagnostic information seeking (problem finding)
Synthetic thinking (opportunity finding)

As stated in Chapter 1, this book is intended to give the user the opportunity to add to his or her componential, experiential, and contextual skill bases through case discussions. During the discussions the focus should be on

1. building problem-solving, problem-finding, and opportunity-finding skills;
2. enhancing one's understanding of oneself, others, and the environments in which one functions;
3. developing and/or honing one's power and leadership skills; and
4. assessing one's own practical intelligence in order to begin the process of growth in this area.

QUESTIONS FOR REFLECTION AND DISCUSSION

1. What should June's manager have done to help her avoid the failed promotion?
2. What are the differences and similarities between opportunity finding, problem finding, and problem solving?
3. What are the differences and similarities between managing oneself, others, and a career?
4. What are the differences and similarities between the motivational approach, the simulation approach, and the critical-incident technique?

NOTES

1. J. S. Livingston, "Myth of the Well-Educated Manager," *Harvard Business Review,* January/February 1971.
2. R. J. Sternberg, *Beyond IQ: A Triarchic Theory of Human Intelligence* (New York: Cambridge University Press, 1985).
3. D. C. McClelland, "Testing for Competence Rather Than Intelligence," *American Psychologist* 28, 1973, pp. 1–14.
4. U.S. Department of the Navy, "A History of Leadership and Management Education and Training" (Washington: Naval Military Personnel Command, 1984).
5. J. P. Kotter, *Power and Influence* (New York: The Free Press, 1985).
6. R. K. Wagner and R. J. Sternberg, "Practical Intelligence in Real World Pursuits: The Role of Tacit Knowledge," *Journal of Personality and Social Psychology* 48, 1985, pp. 436–58.

7. D. C. McClelland and R. E. Boyatis, "The Leadership Motive Pattern and Long-term Success in Management," *Journal of Applied Psychology* 67, 1982, pp. 737–43.

8. H. E. Murray, *The Assessment of Men* (New York: Rinehart, 1948).

9. D. W. Bray, "The Assessment Center and The Study of Lives," *American Psychologist* 37, 1982, pp. 180–89.

10. R. K. Wagner and R. J. Sternberg, "Tacit Knowledge and Intelligence in the Everyday World," in *Practical Intelligence*, ed. R. J. Sternberg and R. K. Wagner (New York: Cambridge University Press, 1986).

11. G. O. Klemp and D. C. McClelland, "What Characterizes Intelligence Functioning Among Senior Managers" in *Practical Intelligence*, ed. R. J. Sternberg and R.K. Wagner (New York: Cambridge University Press, 1986).

12. R. C. Benfari, H. E. Wilkinson, and C. D. Orth, "The Effective Uses of Power," *Business Horizons*, May/June 1986.

CHAPTER 3

THE CASE METHOD OF LEARNING[1]

Effective management development programs and many pragmatic MBA programs use the case method of learning in a manner similar to that used in law schools. A case is an accurate historic portrayal of an actual, usually multifaceted, situation with which a manager in a real organization had to cope. A case may deal with the total organization or with a specific segment, such as a branch office. Some cases may be concerned with overall, very complex policy problems, such as diversification, merger, restructuring, or human resources management. Other cases may focus dominantly on problems and issues in one or two functional areas, such as organizational behavior or marketing. Most cases involve the use of linear, nonlinear, and contextual skills (see also Chapters 1 and 2) to some degree in order to analyze and reach a reasonable solution to the problems presented. Most cases parallel real life in that all the information the manager might like to have before making a decision is almost never available. The great strength of the case method in developing managerial skills stems from the fact that it forces one to take an active role in analyzing real organizational situations. Further, it requires one to participate directly in achieving workable courses of action.

It might be added that there are no simple, sovereign, or classroom solutions to most case studies, but one can go from active experimentation in order to solve a concrete case problem to the formulation of more basic principles. A useful guide to the problem-solving cycle would involve four interrelated steps from the Learning Styles Inventory by Kolb, et al.:[2]

1. The encounter with a concrete set of experiences; that is, the data in the case
2. Reflective observation; that is, standing back and assessing the concrete situation in a functional manner, neither making premature value judgements or fixing blame
3. Abstract conceptualization of the problem; that is, drawing upon one's knowledge base of the relevant theories and concepts in order to place the data in a conceptual framework and put boundary limits on the problem
4. Active experimentation; that is, developing and testing one's hypotheses, leading to making and implementing a decision

The case method is a simulated *experience* that permits one to run through this four-step problem-solving cycle. The *process* of analysis, discussion, and skill development is paramount in the case method, *not* particular solutions.

The more useful organizational behavior cases are often described as a "slice of life," since they generally contain all of the information available that the manager in the real situation or the case writer thought was important. These are generally written as if seen through the eyes of one of the managers involved. It includes facts, opinions, biases and sometimes misleading information that the manager had to face in real life. Everyone perceives with their own senses, which can be distorted, but each one must deal with that perception, even when it may be different from "reality." Effective managers learn to take account of the way biases, personality characteristics, expectations, and previous experiences may distort data as well as opinions. Thus, one must learn to deal with case situations, as well as real-life situations, through one's limited senses but fine tune one's senses to adjust for possible distortions. If a case in this book contains a statement in quotation marks, it is safe to assume that this is what was actually said. On the other hand, if a statement is not in quotation marks, it should be assumed that this is what the person from whose point of view the case is written understood it to be and that this understanding may be distorted, just as it might be in real life.

On the basis of the information presented in the case, each participant analyzes the situation individually or in small groups, makes assumptions to provide for missing data, assesses the impact of biases and other distorting factors, examines alternative explanations for the behaviors described, deduces the limitations imposed by the environment, and works out an approach that will provide a reasonable course of action to be taken under the conditions as they are understood. Active class participation is necessary in the case method; the greater the participation, the more each participant gains from the perspectives, approaches, and proposed actions of peers, and the more he or she adds to his or her nonlinear and contextual skill base.[3]

In the case method, the participant's role is transformed from passive observer, as in the lecture method, to active contributor. The instructor's role is transformed from lecturer to discussion moderator. As Christensen observes, "A discussion class is a *partnership* in which students and instructor share the responsibilities and power of teaching and the privilege of learning together."[4] Each participant contributes to group understanding, responds to the contributions and arguments of others, and, finally, learns to communicate with peers. This calls for effective listening skills as well as open-mindedness and receptivity to the ideas of others.

Julie Hertenstein described participation very well indeed.[5]

> A good listener builds on the contributions of others, relating comments to, but not repeating, previous statements. When a question is asked, the careful listener answers it instead of moving in a different direction. He or she can support good arguments, challenge assumptions, point out inconsistencies, and probe weaknesses in the analysis. The careful listener knows when and how to synthesize and summarize the comments of previous speakers, and when to shift the discussion to new ground.

In addition to listening carefully, students must present information effectively. They should identify important points, organize them logically, and state them succinctly while noting important assumptions. Students must provide supporting evidence and persuade others to accept their positions. They must be willing to answer questions, respond to criticism, and consider new evidence, modifying an earlier position when warranted.

Frequent participation is not necessarily good, particularly if the student's contributions are mediocre. Infrequent participation is not necessarily bad; in fact, the most effective contributors are often students who carefully choose their opportunities. They avoid wasting 'air time' on mundane comments; when they do speak, consequently, fellow students recognize that an important insight is likely and listen attentively.

Respect for all participants in a discussion is an essential ingredient and precludes personal attacks, which are disruptive and do nothing to further the acquisition of skills in any event. On the other hand, a quest for the acquisition of skills requires each participant to question what is not clear or to challenge those arguments with which he or she disagrees. Each participant should analyze the situation, adopt an explanation for the events that occurred in the specific environment in which they took place, evaluate alternatives, propose specific action steps, and present these thoughts during the discussion, *but* each participant should also maintain an open mind as other data, explanations, and proposals are made. Flexibility to revise the analysis and proposed actions is part of the learning process in the case method that adds to the individual's nonlinear and contextual skill bases.

The aim of the case method is to increase the managerial effectiveness of each participant in his or her current as well as future job. To increase effectiveness, the behavior of each participant must positively change. Yet, Carl Rogers observed, "the only learning which significantly influences behavior is self-discovered, self-appropriated learning."[6] Thus, through self-discovered, self-appropriated learning, the case method assists each participant to

- develop better technical, human and/or conceptual skills,
- build better linear, nonlinear, and contextual skills,
- detect and adjust for possibly distorted data,
- better understand themselves and others,
- nurture their communications skills to better convey their own thoughts and decisions both orally and in writing,
- learn to listen more effectively, and
- improve their spontaneous and reflective responses. Spontaneous responses are instinctive and instantaneous while reflective responses are those which occur *after* thinking about the situation. (See Chapter 4.)

In this way each participant *can*, through each person's own efforts, acquire the skills necessary to make positive changes in his or her own behavior.

The instructor's role is that of discussion moderator, coach, mentor, and partner. The participant's role is that of analyzer, presenter, listener, decision maker, and partner. Herein lies a problem in the early stages of case discussion.

People tend to search for the "correct" solution when, in fact, there is often no single correct solution to some problems. An important benefit of the case method is that in time, participants discover that there may be several ways to solve a given set of problems. They find that only the most thorough analysis applying the most relevant concepts and lessons from previous experiences leads to the more reasonable solutions. Therefore, the first requirement of case study is rigorous analysis and exploration of the problems and issues rather than concentration on a course of action. Case analysis is not a "quick fix"; it calls for a thorough understanding and evaluation of the facts, environment, perceptions, opinions, behaviors and interdependencies presented in the case.

Many cases are interesting because in real life the manager did not grasp the multifaceted nature of the problems and issues or identified a few symptoms rather than the whole set of problems. Other cases are interesting because the "obvious solution," usually based on assumptions not validated, is only superficial and led the real life manager into trouble. Consequently, thorough analysis requires an evaluation of the backgrounds and behaviors of the significant people, deduction of the limitations imposed by the environment, questioning of assumptions, consideration of alternatives, and a weighing of pros and cons of each possible action before deciding on specific actions.

One efficient way to prepare for a case discussion is to first read the case very quickly to obtain general impressions. At this stage, some questions should suggest themselves. In dealing with behavioral cases, one must consider the people involved, including their experiences, biases, background, motivations, power bases, interdependencies, and roles in the organization. It is often essential to examine the context or environment in which the people are functioning, including the way results are obtained, measured, and rewarded. By asking these and similar questions, one is starting to put oneself into the situation described by the case.

After having read the case once quickly, it is useful to read it again carefully. Many participants find a highlighter marker useful to identify more significant data for later review and further study. In examining behavioral cases, one must be careful not to accept things at face value without considering other possibilities. For example, organization charts may not reflect status, organizational level, power, or the actual lines through which the organization functions. Many participants have found it very valuable throughout their preparation to bring to bear their own nonlinear skills or knowledge of how organizations function, to listen to their judgment and insights for useful clues, particularly for subconscious behaviors, motivation, or anything that does not quite "feel" right. The further in advance this preparation is done, the more time the subconscious mind has to process the information and thus yield the often critical insights. It is important to relate the theories and concepts one knows or has learned to the case data, and to look for interdependencies. One must examine in depth the people, environment, and situations described. Although Levinson observed, "we as adults are little aware of why we behave as we do,"[7] by carefully examining the background and behavior of the people and taking note of any biases or other influences that may be distorting their perceptions, we, as outsiders, may be able to deduce, at least partly, why people behave as they do. One should look for differences between the behavior described and the behavior that one would have expected given the case data and one's own experiences. Alternate explanations for these differences should be developed as well as an assessment of them. It may be useful in building one's contextual skills and understanding to think of the organization as a living organism of many interacting parts in order to see the interdependencies and environmental limitations in better perspective.

Other important factors to include are the work being done and the technology involved, the size of the organization and/or group involved, the informal and formal structure, the resources in both money and people, the strengths and weaknesses of the group and individuals involved, and the organizational and/or group culture, which is an important yet often overlooked factor. Organizational and individual objectives as well as any conflict between them may be important also.

A number of cautions should be considered in both oral and written case analyses and discussions as well as in real life situations:

1. Avoid overstatements, emotionally laden words, and premature value judgments that may cloud one's perceptions, such as "He's a poor manager" or "She's always unreasonable."
2. Avoid dealing with broad generalizations or policy issues rather than the specifics in the case. For example, don't say "management should . . ."; rather say "Ms. X should. . . ."
3. Avoid impractical statements, such as "He should be more sensitive," that would require a personality change, or "the customer should not demand . . . ;" they do or will go elsewhere.
4. Don't be superficial; go beyond the obvious, examine alternatives, think carefully, and look for clues or nuances that may suggest other approaches or directions to examine.
5. Avoid *quick fix* actions or using *common sense* on obvious problems before thoroughly analyzing the case. Because the U.S. culture puts so much emphasis on short-term results, it is all too easy, even for experienced and successful managers, to fall into this trap.
6. Avoid looking for someone to blame; instead, try to understand why people behaved as they have. Real life has very few villains or heroes but rather good, well-intentioned people doing their best, as they see it, with the tools they have. Focus on understanding the basis for what is described.
7. Avoid the temptation to fire someone, reorganize, or form a task force. These things may prove useful after analysis, but are more often used as a means for avoiding needed analysis.

Remember, organizations, like people, are neither all good nor all bad. Look for what is strong as well as what is weak in the organization and in the significant people and groups described in the case. Remember also that in real life one has to deal with situations as one sees them and work through the difficulties with the skills one has at the time. The case method helps to build and improve those skills. It is this *process*, including the case discussion, that offers each participant the opportunity to build his or her linear, nonlinear, and contextual skills thus laying the foundation for improved interpersonal skills. It is analogous to getting into the water and thrashing about after reading a book on how to swim rather than relying on the book alone. One must have the experience of swimming to really know how. The answers derived from a case discussion are less important than the *process* used to get there. It is the *process* and the experience derived from it that lays the foundation for improved people skills—*not* a focus on correct answers.

Malcolm P. McNair, when he was professor of Business Administration at the Harvard Business School, captured the essence of the analysis required in an excerpt entitled, "Tough-Mindedness and the Case Method":[8]

> William James, a great teacher of psychology and philosophy at Harvard during the early years of this century, made the useful distinction between people who are tough-minded and people who are tender-minded. These terms have nothing to do with levels of ethical conduct; the toughness referred to is toughness of the intellectual apparatus, toughness of the spirit, not toughness of the heart. Essentially, it is the attitude and the qualities and the training that enable one to seize on facts and make these facts a basis for intelligent, courageous action. The tough-minded have a zest for tackling hard problems. They dare to grapple with the unfamiliar and wrest useful truth from stubborn new facts. They are not dismayed by change for they know that change at an accelerated tempo is the pattern of living, the only pattern on which successful action can be based. Above all, the tough-minded do not wall themselves in with comfortable illusions. They do not rely on the easy precepts of tradition or on mere conformity to regulations. They know that the answers are not in the book.

Many people find it useful to get together in small groups to prepare cases. Working with a group of compatible people may improve one's analysis and understanding of the case; however, the group is not a substitute for individual responsibility. Group work may sharpen the awareness of the serious participants, but it does not help those who wish to coast. One doesn't develop one's own skills by watching others develop theirs. Finally, whether preparation is done individually or in a group, one should build on what others have contributed, but be sure to add to the discussion. People get from the case method only as much as they put into it. After all, it is each participant's linear, nonlinear, and contextual skills that are being built or not built and interpersonal skills cannot be improved without this foundation.

A case discussion may start with the identification of the significant problems and issues or the significant data and/or the background of the significant people. It may then center around the way different participants have analyzed the case and the basis for the differences. Conclusions may be derived and finally, the discussion may end with action recommendations. The role of the instructor during the discussion is that of moderator, but as Glover and Hower have noted,

"On occasion (usually when asked) he (or she) will put forth ideas of his (or her) own; but he (or she) will do so with the explicit understanding that his (or her) ideas are to be scrutinized, discussed, criticized, accepted, or rejected with the same freedom that is accorded those of anyone else in the class—even the wisest instructor has no monopoly on ideas."[9] Thus the instructor is a *partner* in the process of acquiring skills but is *not* an expert as might be the case in the lecture method.

If you are preparing a written analysis, make it easy for the reader. Begin by defining the problems and issues you think are significant and indicate why you think they are significant. Then present your analysis of the case data as concisely as you can. Use the theories and concepts you have learned to explain what has happened and reach conclusions about the problems and issues you have identified. The length of the analysis may be minimized by attaching a highlighted copy of the case study with appropriate references in the analysis to show the reader what data was thought to be significant. Some readers may prefer this data integrated into the analysis. Ask the reader what is preferred. Finally, make *specific* recommendations concerning *who* should do *what*, when, where, and how to solve the problems and deal with the issues.

Many different theories and concepts may be applicable to any case. It is seldom that any single theory or concept will appear vital to every participant, just as it is difficult to find any case which is of vital interest to every participant. This does not reduce the importance of the theory, concept, or case as a part of the total program. It may be that you will find most of the material intriguing or that only some of it will be so. Whatever your reactions, there are valid reasons for reading all of it, but with varying degrees of thoroughness, depending upon your current knowledge, interest, and needs.

Since most seminar time will be devoted to case discussions, it is essential that all cases be analyzed thoroughly. The concept chapters contain the theories and concepts for which all participants will be held responsible. The time it is necessary to spend on each chapter will vary greatly depending on your prior knowledge and experience, the complexity of the material, its relevance, and your interest. Some concept chapters are included for information, to let you know that something is available, or that people are writing in a particular field. Some chapters are intended to be provocative, not definitive. Some should aid in gaining understanding of a situation, an idea, or a concept already presented. Others should be read for general information, still others for content that will help in analyses of specific problem areas and/or to make decisions based upon the theory or concept presented, but not all concept chapters will find application in the cases.

Some chapters and cases will be given different interpretations by different readers, again based upon each reader's own knowledge, interest, and needs. Many, but not all, of the concept chapters are included to be of use with the cases. The theories and concepts covered frequently facilitate understanding some of the case issues or provide an analytical framework that can help you establish a viewpoint toward the case. The choice of time and effort spent on each chapter and case is yours.

QUESTIONS FOR REFLECTION AND DISCUSSION

1. How are the roles of student and instructor different in a case discussion compared to a lecture?
2. What is good participation in a case discussion and how can it be evaluated or measured?

3. What can each participant do to maximize the probability of improving her or his interpersonal skills and on-the-job performance?
4. What are the differences and similarities between understanding another person's background and personal characteristics and stereotyping that person?

NOTES

1. Andrew Towl, *To Study Administration by Cases* (Boston: Harvard Business School, 1969); Kenneth R. Andrews, ed., *The Case Method of Teaching Human Relations and Administration*, (Cambridge: Harvard University Press, 1953); and C. Roland Christensen, *Teaching by the Case Method*, (Boston: Harvard Business School, 1981) and *Teaching and the Case Method* (Boston: Harvard Business School, 1987).

2. David A. Kolb, I. M. Rubin, and J. M. McIntyre, *Organizational Psychology: An Experiential Approach* ("Learning Styles Inventory"), 2nd ed. (Englewood Cliffs, NJ: Prentice Hall, 1974).

3. R. J. Sternberg, *Beyond IQ: A Triarchic Theory of Human Intelligence* (New York: Cambridge University Press, 1985).

4. C. Roland Christensen, David A. Garvin, and Ann Sweet, eds. *Education for Judgement: The Artistry of Discussion Leadership* (Boston: Harvard Business School Press, 1991), p. 15.

5. J. H. Hertenstein, "Patterns of Participation," in *Education for Judgment*, ed. C. R. Christensen, D. A. Garvin, and A. Sweet (Boston: Harvard Business School Press, 1991), p. 180.

6. Carl R. Rogers, *On Becoming A Person* (Boston: Houghton Mifflin, 1961).

7. Harry Levinson, "Fads, Fantasies and Psychological Management," *Consulting Psychology Journal*, Winter 1992.

8. Malcolm P. McNair, *The Case Method at the Harvard Business School* (New York: McGraw-Hill, 1954), p. 8.

9. John D. Glover and Ralph M. Hower, *Some Notes on the Use of the Administrator*, (Homewood, IL: Richard D. Irwin, 1950).

CHAPTER 4

SPONTANEOUS AND REFLECTIVE BEHAVIORS:

AN INTEGRATION OF SOME PSYCHOLOGICAL AND PROCESS MOTIVATIONAL CONCEPTS

THE PROBLEM

A manager's function is to influence people to perform with optimum efficiency and effectiveness in the achievement of organizational goals and objectives. But some managers in today's environment are frustrated when the people around them behave in ways the manager did not anticipate. This frustration is increased when the motivational and psychological concepts that the manager found useful a few years ago no longer seem to help very much today. To some managers, their employees often appear to behave erratically in response to a wide range of disparate influences.

As managers observe the decreasing usefulness of motivational and psychological concepts, they also see the increasing difficulty and complexity of successfully influencing others. In *Power and Influence*, John P. Kotter observes that our organizational environments are becoming increasingly complex, resulting in considerable interdependence between a wide range of people having considerable diversity with respect to "goals, values, stakes, assumptions and perception."[1] In *Power and the Corporate Mind*, Zaleznik and Kets de Vries observe, "People are products of experiences they have never relinquished. Personal history will always make its claim even though it operates silently, and paradoxically, usually beyond the individual's awareness."[2] As the diversity in people's personal history increases, so does the difficulty of understanding and influencing those people.

A few managers seem very adept at understanding and influencing the behavior of those around them, and we can learn from these managers' experiences. Let's look at an example of unanticipated behavior and the successful actions taken by a senior manager to influence a subordinate and thereby correct the situation.

Joe Reed, a division manager in a progressive high-technology company, was having a stressful day. He had had an argument at home, he had a very tight schedule, much incoming paper work, and several important decisions to make under severe time pressure. One decision was which of his subordinate managers to recommend for a career enhancing three-month assignment at a distant location. In his rush to get on to other things, Joe nominated Art White for the job, even though he felt Kay Cook was more qualified. Both Art and Kay had families, but Joe felt that Kay would not want to leave her children and therefore would be reluctant to accept the assignment.

Vice-president Dan Stone had worked with Joe Reed for many years. When Joe's nomination of Art White hit his desk for approval, he was puzzled. His first reaction was to telephone Joe and ask why he had not nominated Kay. After reflection, he decided on a less direct approach. It was Dan's style to "manage by walking around,"[3] and later that morning he stopped in on Joe Reed and asked, "How are things going?" During this informal discussion, Dan learned of the pressures Joe felt and was able to deduce that Joe's nomination of Art was influenced by these pressures. Had Joe been under less pressure, Dan felt, he would have nominated Kay, the more qualified person. Dan sensed, however, that if he brought this up directly, Joe would become defensive and rationalize his recommendation of Art. Dan wanted to correct the situation and decided on an indirect approach to give Joe time to think. Late that day, at the end of a regular meeting with all of his division managers, Dan spent several minutes reemphasizing the company's policy of promoting and offering assignments to the best qualified individuals regardless of race, age, sex, or seniority. He did not mention any specific instances.

The next morning, Joe called to suggest that Kay Cook be offered the assignment instead of Art White. Joe said he did not expect Kay to accept but would be glad to make the offer to her. Dan approved the change, Joe offered Kay the job, and, to his surprise, she accepted with obvious delight.

ANALYSIS

In this case, Dan Stone successfully influenced Joe Reed to reconsider and make a more functional decision. Apparently Stone understood that people may not always respond as those around them anticipate. Although neither psychological concepts (such as personality types,[4] operant conditioning,[5] and so on) nor motivation concepts (needs,[6] expectancy,[7] or equity theories,[8] for example) by themselves seem to explain the observed behavior, some insight can be gained by combining parts of these concepts with recognition that a person may respond to any situation with one of two general types of behavior: spontaneous, which implies instinctive and/or instantaneous behavior, or reflective, which occurs after taking time to think before taking action. Henry A. Murray first described these behaviors as *reactive* and *proactive*, but these terms have recently acquired meanings not consistent with our usage,[9] and therefore we adopt the terms *spontaneous* and *reflective*. Thus, in our increasingly complex environment, people may be spontaneous or reflective in response to both psychological and motivational influences. To gain insight, managers need to understand these psychological and motivational influences as Dan Stone apparently did.

From the management and psychological literature and the organizational observations that we have made over the last 25 years, we have identified two sets of influences on reflective behavior and one set of influences on spontaneous behavior. Reflective behavior is influenced by the *expectations* the individual *perceives* that others in the organization have of him or her, and vice versa. In other words, the "psychological contracts" that an individual has with others in the organization relate to the expectancy theory of motivation (endnote 7)[10] and the individual's self-concept,[11] including his or her belief systems (which are related to the equity theory of motivation referred to in endnote 8). Spontaneous behavior is influenced by an individual's personal attributes, "usually beyond the individual's awareness" (Zaleznik), which derive from psychological concepts, such as genetic and environmental forces, personality (Hall and Lindzey), and the totality of the individual's life experiences (personal history), including education, cultural background, early childhood experiences, and acquired biases. Individuals tend to be spontaneous when under time pressure or stress and reflective when they have the time and inclination to think before acting. Realistically, individuals cannot always consciously think before they act any more than they can always consciously think before breathing or blinking their eyes. There will be situations, perhaps many situations, when a person will be spontaneous.

These sets of influences help the executive understand, as Vice-president Dan Stone did, that actions derive from multiple, not singular, influences and that an individual's (such as Joe Reed's) behavior may be either spontaneous or reflective depending on which set of influences, and even which influences within the set, are dominant at the time. From the executive's point of view, the response of an individual derived from one set of influences may not be the one most in line with organizational goals and objectives. By understanding the three sets of influences unique in each person, and the probable spontaneous or reflective behavior deriving from them, executives can assess which behavior is likely to be most in line with organizational objectives and can then chose a strategy to act in ways to maximize the probability of eliciting the most appropriate behavior.

The remainder of this chapter will

1. explore the three sets of influences as derived from the literature and observation, namely, expectations, self-concepts and personal attributes;
2. examine the spontaneous and reflective behaviors that originate from these three sets of influences;
3. present the three types of predictions a manager can make regarding spontaneous and reflective behaviors and the six strategies that a manager can use to influence behavior;

4. look at examples of managers using these six strategies to influence reflective and/or spontaneous behavior more effectively; and

5. discuss how a manager can use these concepts (as Dan Stone did) to predict likely behaviors and then choose a strategy to maximize the probability of positively influencing people to act in ways that maximize their contribution to organizational goals and objectives.

Sets of Influences Explored

Expectations

When an individual enters into a relationship with another individual, or joins a group or organization, a set of expectations is formed by each of the parties with respect to their own actions as well as the actions of the other party. Individuals who accept employment with a new group or organization accept what they understand to be their new manager's expectations of them as well as the group's values, culture, and norms. In addition, they have expectations of their manager's and the group's or organization's behavior toward them. People accept employment in order to receive the rewards of affiliation and consciously try to conform to their manager's expectations of them—that is, they behave *reflectively*. Described in terms of the expectancy theory (endnote 7), people accept employment because they perceive that their efforts will yield an adequate level of performance and that the rewards they receive will justify the effort (motivation = probability that effort will yield performance × the probability that the performance will be rewarded × the value of the reward expected). Managers should recognize that performance-related rewards as described in expectancy theory are important, but that the other rewards of affiliation are also important.

Thus, managers can enhance their ability to influence reflective behavior by making their expectations in a relationship as explicit as possible and verifying what they understand to be the other parties expectations of them. Unfortunately, a clear understanding of expectations is seldom achieved initially because both parties to the relationship usually make implicit and unverified assumptions. When there is a congruence of common social or cultural experiences those assumptions may be accurate, but where there is a diversity in backgrounds they may not be.[12] Since diversity in organizations is increasing (Kotter), important inexplicit expectations may not be mutually understood.

As time passes, expectations in a relationship change as a result of the evolving environment or from the changes in one or both of the parties to the relationship. In the absence of explicit renegotiations, differing assumptions may lead to differing expectations. To maximize their ability to influence, effective executives need to renegotiate mutually acceptable expectations periodically or whenever they sense possible changes.

Even so, mutually agreed upon expectations may not always yield the reflective behavior expected. Individuals have many relationships in organizations, some with conflicting sets of expectations, and conforming to a manager's expectations is often different from conforming to the expectations of a spouse, subordinates, peers, or other superiors. For example, when a manager promotes a member of a group to head that group, the manager expects the new supervisor to act in ways that conform to the role of "supervisor" (the manager's expectations). However, the remaining members of the group may still expect that individual to continue to behave as a peer and see the new behavior as unwarranted and insensitive (the peers' expectations). These conflicting expectations may lead the new supervisor to make compromises. Managers should recognize that these opposing relationships may sometimes cause an individual to compromise, yielding a reflective behavior that falls somewhere between the conflicting expectations.

Self-concept

All individuals have a *perception* or *mental picture* of themselves. This self-concept (Combs and Snygg) includes belief systems, self-expectations, intrinsic motivations,[13] and concepts of fairness and equity that have evolved over time. Self-concept influences reflective behavior when relationships change or the individual's belief systems are involved. Examples of when this may happen include joining or leaving an organization, forming or ending a relationship, job changes, promotions, or relocations. Belief systems come into play in situations involving career development activities, or some kind of trauma or crisis involving perceived competence, ethics (such as honesty, fairness, justice, and equity), or legal issues. Although these kinds of situations do not occur on a daily basis in organizations as do routine situations that are more directly influenced by expectations, they are usually important when they do occur. Therefore, in situations involving these issues or changes, the ability of executives to negotiate mutually acceptable expectations and obtain the desired performance is enhanced by understanding the self-concept influences of those concerned.

Once the set of expectations involved in a new or changing relationship is accepted, small changes may occur over time that result in actions inconsistent with the individual's belief system. When this happens, the individual usually modifies his or her self-concept to fit the actions.[14] For example, in the late sixties and early seventies, the belief systems of some young people led them to oppose the Vietnam War. As a result, some of them refused to accept work for defense contractors because they would be expected to do work that directly or indirectly would support the Vietnam War. Others accepted such employment and after a period of time modified their belief systems to do work which they had previously thought they would not do.

Personal Attributes

Psychologists have argued for many years over the extent to which people's behavior is influenced by genetics and environment. While differing on the degree, most psychologists today acknowledge that both personality and previous experiences have an influence on the way people behave. An individual's personality in an organization is relatively stable and leads that individual to display specific personal characteristics (for example, a tendency to be outspoken or quiet, practical and observant or intuitive and imaginative, logical and cold or empathetic and warm, adaptive and flexible or organized and decisive).[15] At the same time, individuals learn from, and are influenced by, the people around them, their environment, and their culture. Rewards or pleasure are reinforcing experiences that tend to influence the individual to act in ways that gain additional rewards or pleasure (Skinner). Conversely, punishment or pain are inhibiting or displacing experiences that tend to influence the individual to act in ways to avoid the punishment or pain. Effective executives are cautious in using punishment since the actions taken by the individual to avoid punishment may not be those desired. For example, subordinates punished for being rude to customers or peers may avoid further punishment by avoiding contact with customers or peers, rather than learning to be more polite.

Personal attributes developed from childhood experiences may exert a powerful influence on some people. For example, an only child of busy parents who gave in to the child's tantrums may still throw tantrums as an adult in the work environment. A child who was "framed" by other children to look guilty of various offenses over a long period may have a strong tendency to be suspicious and guarded in his or her work relationships. Children often use one parent as a role model; thus, a child of a very demanding father may be very demanding of those around him or her at work.

The culture that was dominant when and where a person grew up may exert a powerful influence on personal attributes. For example, a person experiencing deprivation may respond as Scarlet O'Hara did in *Gone With the Wind* when she vows to do anything to avoid being hungry again. Much has been written of the effect the Vietnam era had on those who grew up at that time. Jokes about the fast-paced New Yorker or the relaxed Southerner are indicative of the geographic influences that may exist. Other powerful influences might include membership, years earlier, in a highly valued club or organization; an inspirational coach or teacher; a close friend or colleague in an earlier era; a strong role model or mentor; an accident or trauma; or military service. Beyond these, subconscious biases may have been acquired that may be negative (such as those against competitors or people of different ethnic groups or gender) or positive (such as those toward graduates of specific schools or people from a certain geographic area or a preferred socioeconomic class). The resulting behavior may lead to self-fulfilling prophecies, such as a positive or negative performance appraisal that might not otherwise have been deserved (Livingston). Any or all of these influences may be evident in the individual's spontaneous behavior at various times.

Spontaneous responses are usually dominant when managers are under time pressure, as in the Joe Reed case. But, people seldom think they are spontaneous, because if their actions are questioned, they feel attacked, become defensive, and rationalize their actions to be consistent with either their self-concept or perceived sets of expectations. Joe Reed's manager, Dan Stone, recognized this and used a nonthreatening situation (the meeting) to reassert his expectations (company policy) with all his managers, thus giving Joe the opportunity to reconsider his recommendation in a reflective way, without feeling attacked or being put on the defensive.

An individual's personality and life experiences may or may not be suitable for the job or situation. Truly effective executives whose jobs have behavioral requirements that are suited to the executives personalities and life experiences make excellent decisions spontaneously, using their intuitive judgments.[16] However, even when an executive's personal attributes are generally suitable for the job, special situations may arise in which his or her personality and life experiences might not be suitable. In these situations effective executives switch to become reflective. Thus, many busy and successful executives will put certain issues aside in order to have "more time to think," as a mechanism to avoid dysfunctional spontaneous decisions.

Reflective and Spontaneous Behaviors

Exhibit 4-1 represents one way of visually depicting how spontaneous and reflective behaviors derive from the three sets of influences—expectations and self-concept yield reflective behavior, and this reflective behavior becomes part of life experiences, which are part of personal attributes that yield spontaneous behavior.

For example, a young marine officer controls his or her actions to conform to very high group expectations and rather quickly adopts the self-concept and high esprit of "being a marine." After twenty years, the colonel's actions are spontaneous (habit) and based on experiences he or she no longer thinks about very often. Even in civilian clothes, the colonel's posture, bearing, and other clues suggest "marine" to an astute observer. In the same way, other organizations or groups impress, to varying degrees, a set of behaviors on those who remain in them for long periods. For example, review the behavior of the employees of organizations

EXHIBIT 4-1

BEHAVIORS DERIVED FROM THE SETS OF INFLUENCES

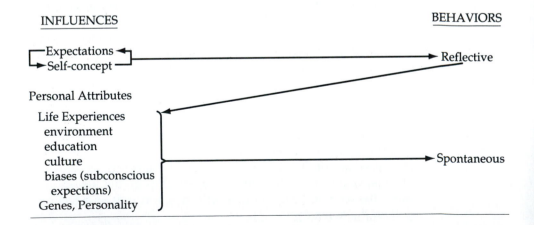

like Marriott Hotels, IBM, or Hewlett Packard as described in *In Search of Excellence* (Peters and Waterman).

The difference between reflective and spontaneous responses can be seen by comparing the way people speak with the way they write. Typically, the difference is not only in vocabulary but also in the way in which they express themselves. Writing takes time, which the brain can use to reflect on what is being written. When people speak, they have far less time to reflect on what they are saying. Generally, writing is reflective while speaking is spontaneous, except when speeches are prepared in advance.

Another example of the difference between spontaneous and reflective responses can be seen when managers change jobs or move up the ladder in professional organizations. Normally, they want to act in ways that conform to their understanding of what is expected of them, given the organizational culture and power structure. Therefore, they are reflective in ways that are congruent with these expectations, but when under stress they are sometimes spontaneous in ways that seem more congruent with past actions and previous life experiences. Thus, the reflective behavior deriving from the expectations and self-concept influences of people can shift rather quickly with changes in status while spontaneous patterns often lag behind, changing more slowly as new experiences derived from reflective responses can counterbalance previous life experiences. An exception to this would be a major traumatic experience, such as being fired or divorced, which may be so powerful an experience that it has an immediate influence on a person's spontaneous behavior.

Predicting and Influencing Behavior

A manager can make three possible predictions regarding spontaneous and reflective behavior:

1. Spontaneous behavior derived from personal attributes is predicted to be at least acceptably in line with organizational objectives.
2. Reflective behavior derived from expectations and/or self-concept is predicted to be at least acceptably in line with organizational objectives.
3. Neither is predicted to be acceptable in terms of organizational objectives or a more desirable outcome is thought to be feasible through renegotiation of new or revised expectations.

Based on the above predictions, a manager might choose from six general kinds of influence strategies:

1. Influence an individual to be reflective in accordance with existing expectations when reflective behavior derived from expectations is predicted to be acceptably in line with organizational goals and objectives. One way this may be achieved is to interact with the individual when he or she is *not* busy and discuss expectations first.
2. Influence an individual to be reflective in accordance with that person's self-concept when that reflective behavior derived from that person's self-concept is predicted to be acceptably in line with organizational goals and objectives.

One way this may be achieved is to interact with the individual when he or she is *not* busy and discuss career, ethical, or legal issues first.

3. Influence an individual to be spontaneous when that behavior is predicted to be at least acceptably in line with organizational goals and objectives. One way this may be achieved is to interact with the individual when he or she is very busy and under time pressure.

4. Renegotiate expectations and then influence the individual to be reflective in accordance with the new expectations. This influence can be facilitated by interacting positively as coach or mentor to reinforce the new expectations and thus enhance the probability of the desired reflective behavior.

5. Over a longer period, initiate management development, career development, coaching, or other programs to encourage the individual or groups of individuals to reevaluate their self-concepts.

6. Also over a long period, provide positive feedback on desirable reflective behavior thus creating life experiences that have the effect of positive reinforcement (Skinner) until this behavior becomes spontaneous.

Executives can choose one or a combination of these strategies and control their own actions in conformity with them to maximize the probability that an individual will behave in the desired way during the manager's interaction on a specific issue.

Examples

Managers can use these strategies in many different situations. Vice-president Dan Stone used a combination strategy based on strategies #1 and #4 and behaved accordingly to influence Joe Reed to reassess reflectively a situation in which Joe had already behaved spontaneously. As a result, Joe changed his decision. Three other examples of executives predicting behavior and choosing a strategy to influence it are a sales situation, an organizational unit, and peer group meetings.

A Sales Situation

Executives who leave people-oriented companies often fall into one of two categories. The first category includes long-time, successful employees who, though fully imbued with the culture and strongly affiliated with others in the organization, are offered outside employment that is "too attractive to turn down." The second category is made up of employees with less time and success in the organization who feel they have not received the recognition or advancement due them, are disgruntled, and seek outside employment "to better themselves." In both categories, the new employer expects the new executives to make decisions that are in the best interests of their new organization and not based on positive or negative biases toward their previous employer. If these new executives are given the opportunity to buy products manufactured by their previous employer, the spontaneous response of the first group would be to buy from the previous employer, while the spontaneous response of the second group would be to buy from someone other than the previous employer. Executives from both groups would rationalize their decision to convince themselves and their new employer that they have made the best decision (and a good salesperson will provide that rationalization). Therefore, a salesperson from the previous employer's organization will have a higher probability of a sale if he or she is able to meet an executive from the first category when that executive is spontaneous (strategy #3) and with those from the second category when they are reflective (strategy #1), while the situation is reversed for salespersons not from the previous employer's organization. Effective salespeople recognize this, sometimes intuitively, and develop influence strategies that include appointments when the individual is very busy and likely to be spontaneous, or conversely, when the individual is likely to have time and inclination to be reflective.

An Organizational Unit

Executives can influence large groups of subordinates to improve total performance by taking actions directed at each of the three influences (strategies #4, #5, and #6). A striking example of this occurred when a new general manager took over a manufacturing operation with instructions to "straighten it out or shut it down." After several months on the job, the new general manager concluded that many subordinate managers (approximately 100) were reacting in negative, self-fulfilling ways to most situations. They felt corporate management expected them to be second-rate, neither understood nor cared about their contributions, and had sent in a new manager to put them out of work.

The new general manager chose to influence both spontaneous and reflective behavior by addressing each of the three sets of influences. With respect to expectations (strategy #4), he set new but reasonable and attainable goals and objectives, both with groups and individuals, and negotiated high but realistic expectations for the achievement of those goals and objectives. He "managed by walking around" to help his people stay reflective to the maximum extent, reinforce his expectations, and offer encouragement.

To raise their self-concept and skill levels, he established a management-development team building program for all his managers, including himself (strategy #5). He also established a career development program that required his managers to think and write about their own future development opportunities and career alternatives, as well as those of their subordinates. This required an examination of career goals and objectives, and thus the managers' self-concepts. A manager for career development reporting directly to the new general manager was appointed to enhance the process and ensure top level involvement. This provided further effort designed to encourage managers to be reflective.

To address personal attributes, he posted targets and achievements wherever reasonable throughout the plant for small work groups, departments, and the plant as a whole to provide positive feedback and reinforcing experiences (strategy #6). He implemented a system of rewards for individuals and groups for a wide range of desired behaviors as another means of providing positive success experiences.

Thus, he was positively affecting expectations, self-concepts, and personal attributes leading to improvements in both reflective and spontaneous behaviors. The results were swift and substantial. The plant turned around in less than a year and within three years had become one of the top performers in the company.

Peer Group Meetings

Executives can influence peer relationships as was done at the Naval Air Development Center.[17] After a series of senior management meetings on alternatives to improve the current organizational structure and performance, top management designated a group of executives (who reported directly to top management) to develop a proposed new structure or "straw man" to provide a basis for further discussions at future management meetings. Each of the appointed executives agreed with the desirability of improving the structure and performance—including improved coordination, communication, and resource allocation—and each had self-concepts of being able to achieve this goal. At the same time, each of the appointed executives was highly competitive, parochial, jealous of his or her "turf," and behaving spontaneously in a defensive manner, as if in win–lose situations. The chairman of the group, a peer of the others, quickly observed the spontaneous behavior of group members in their tendency to squabble and blame each other for a wide range of past performances.

The chair concluded that so long as the group remained spontaneous, little would get done. Therefore, he decided to maximize reflective behavior (strategy #2). He opened each meeting with a restatement of the goals and objectives that each member of the group accepted as within his or her competence to achieve. During the meeting, he frequently intervened to ask how a particular point being discussed contributed to the goals and objectives of the group. A facilitator was added to the group to assist the chair and the group in maintaining a reflective approach to their work. The level of dysfunctional spontaneous behavior declined sharply and the group was able to put forth a proposed new structure in a few weeks. This was accepted with only minor modifications at a subsequent senior management meeting and was later implemented.

SOLUTION

What Executives Can Do

It is critical to remember that people are *not* puppets to be manipulated. What executives *can* do is manipulate their own behavior in the hope of enhancing the probability of positively influencing another person. To the extent that these efforts have greater positive effects than other efforts, they are worth using. But, there are *no* panaceas. Executives must be realistic and recognize that, of course, they cannot know or influence, let alone control, all the factors that may lead people to behave in ways that are not completely congruent with organizational goals and objectives (for example, executives cannot change someone's personality). But executives can learn to think more carefully about and manage more effectively the margins they do have. For example, executives can renegotiate expectations and thus influence reflective behavior in a relatively short time and over longer periods executives can establish individual or group development programs to encourage higher self-concepts. They also can reward, or positively reinforce, desirable behavior, thus providing a series of successful experiences to influence personal attributes. By understanding and using these concepts managers can improve their ability to anticipate reflective and spontaneous behavior more accurately by predicting the probable responses of individuals, groups, or organizational units to the various actions an executive might take. Thus, they can choose one or several of the six general strategies to enhance the probability of positively influencing individuals, groups, or organizational units to achieve organizational goals and objectives.

Executives can predict probable reflective responses of people if they understand the expectations influencing those people. Negotiating and periodically renegotiating expectations gives the manager an improved ability to predict how people will respond when they are reflective and controlling their actions to conform to those expectations. Similarly, managers can improve their ability to predict probable reflective responses derived from the individual's self-concept, including belief system. Managers can deduce the more significant influences by listening to what the individual may say directly or indirectly, to them or to others, which may give clues to his or her belief system—including goals, objectives, norms, ethics, and values—and from observation and analysis of the individual's responses when changing relationships, discussing career objectives, or facing potentially traumatic situations involving ethical or legal issues. From these deductions, managers can infer the probable reflective responses when the individual's self-concept influences are dominant.

To predict probable spontaneous responses an executive can use integrative and intuitive thought processes, melding previous observations of the spontaneous responses of other people with knowledge of their background and a "feel" for their personalities. Many people-oriented, effective executives regularly, without apparent thought or effort, predict probable spontaneous responses of those around them whom they know well, as in the examples given above. Other executives have acquired an ability to predict spontaneous responses of others after short periods of listening and observing them when they are spontaneous and then deducing at least some of their personal attributes (Kotter's diversity). Again, executives need to listen carefully to what the individual may say directly or indirectly to them or to others that may indicate personality or personal history, such as previous experiences, cultural factors, or education. For example, a naval officer with 25 years of operational service may have had so many experiences in that hierarchical and often autocratic environment that he tends to spontaneously behave that way himself; that is, he may subconsciously behave like his role models, particularly when under stress. He may spontaneously behave this way even when his self-concept yields reflective behavior that is sensitive and participative. Regardless of what level of people skill an executive has acquired, he or she can learn to predict probable spontaneous responses better by trusting and accepting his or her own intuitive judgment (Simon, et al.) and focusing whatever sensitivity and understanding he or she has in that direction. This is what Dan Stone did with Joe Reed.

The executive must remember, however, that this form of stereotyping will always result in some degree of error. As time passes, executives should expect to refine their ability to predict as more data about an individual becomes available. This refinement is necessary not only because inevitable stereotyping errors, but because more life experiences are occurring to everyone every day and both the executive and the other person will be different people with expanded life experiences as time goes on. Once managers understand these sets of influences and focus on them, they can predict the probable spontaneous and reflective response of other individuals to each of the alternative actions that the managers may take. They are then able to evaluate which responses are at least acceptably in line with organizational goals and objectives and choose a strategy or combination of strategies to interact in a manner and at a time when the desired responses are most likely. For example: the more time pressure (very busy) or stress a person is under the more likely he or she is to be spontaneous; conversely, the more pensive a person is and the lower the time pressures, the more likely he or she is to be reflective. It should be noted that managers are usually under time pressure themselves and may not be able to take the time to understand an individual when a problem situation arises. To use these concepts effectively, managers should apply whatever people skills they have to understand those around them *before* problems develop.

Of course, executives can spend whatever time they choose on developing and refining their ability to predict probable reflective and spontaneous responses before problems arise, but predicting spontaneous behavior is usually more difficult and more time consuming. For particularly important or difficult individuals (such as a senior manager or a very complex peer or subordinate upon whom the executive may be critically dependent for the achievement of organizational objectives), more time may be justified. If so, the executive can gather background data on a particular person from company announcements, records, or other sources. Then he or she might choose a quiet period, such as "down time" on an extended business trip with the other person, to reminisce about his or her own past, including education, previous work experience, family, and so on. This often elicits similar information from the other person. Executives can also use their skill as observers to determine when another person is spontaneous (that is, under some kind of time pressure or stress) and then observe both the actions and the context of the situation in which the actions occur. It is often useful to write down these observations as an objective journalist might, including the background data collected and the observed reactions or responses of others. Only after completing the objective observations does the executive step back and begin his or her analysis. This analysis focuses on deducing those personal attributes, such as perceptions, assumptions being made, motivations, problem solving decision styles, biases, and personality, which help explain what was observed. Some executives in both private and government organizations, for example, members of the U.S. Senior Executive Service, have learned about the Myers-Briggs character and temperament types (Keirsey and Bates). With this understanding, the executive can deduce which type he or she is observing and his or her ability to predict may be substantially enhanced thereby. By reiterating this observation/analysis process, the executive can become more proficient in understanding and predicting probable spontaneous responses.

Many people respond to certain words or phrases that "flip" them from spontaneous to reflective behavior or vice versa. For example, many people become spontaneous when the word *taxes* is mentioned. In like manner, many people become reflective when the phrase "what are the legal and ethical implications of this proposal" is used, or when expectations are brought up for renegotiation or discussion. The impact of these words and phrases derives from each person's life experiences. Hence, different words or phrases may be necessary for different people and, indeed, the same word or phrase may have opposite effects on different people. For example, use of the word *audit* leads many executives to be spontaneous, but many accountants to be reflective. Executives must determine which words or phrases have the desired effect for each person they wish to influence. The executive may then incorporate the use of these words as part of his or her strategy of optimizing the probability of either spontaneous or reflective responses.

Beyond this, executives need to know what to do if neither the predicted reflective nor spontaneous response is acceptable in terms of organizational goals, or if they face a situation involving people new to the organization or people they have not yet been able to understand. For example, if an executive wishes to influence a person or group to improve performance beyond what is currently expected, the set of expectations in their relationship must be renegotiated, as in the plant manager example given earlier, to make the necessary modifications concerning performance, and then the executive needs to coach that person or group so as to maximize the probability that they will be reflective in ways that are consistent with the new expectations. Over time, the behavior derived from the new expectations provides new life experiences, which influence spontaneous responses, which may become habitual, as in the marine colonel example given earlier.

It should be noted, however, that the response being solicited must be in the best interest of the organization, as it was in all the examples in this chapter. When the response elicited is later perceived to be based only on the self-interest of the influencing individual, then the process is viewed as manipulative and may have a negative or destructive impact on the relationship. Conversely, when the response is in the best interest of the organization, no one views the process as manipulative. Rather, the influencing individual is seen as being sensitive to the needs and feelings of the other person or group. People do not object to the process when they look good as a result. In the Joe Reed case, Joe is not likely to resent Dan Stone's intervention because Joe made a better decision and looks good as a result.

Summary

Human behavior is very complex indeed and the approach described in this chapter is not a panacea. It is one tool that executives can learn to use to better predict and influence the actions of others. This may lead to the development of more effective working relationships in the organization, and for some executives and organizations, the results have been dramatic.

Executives can improve their ability to influence the key people around them, including their senior managers, peers, and subordinates, by

1. developing an understanding of spontaneous and reflective behaviors that derive from expectations, self-concepts, and personal attributes;
2. developing clear, explicit sets of expectations with other people and listening carefully to the expectations other people express, not only with respect to the executive but also with respect to all other relationships they have;
3. understanding other people's self-concepts by forming a deduction based on listening for clues to their belief system during career discussions as well as observation and analysis of their responses to changing relationships or potentially traumatic situations involving ethical or legal issues;
4. understanding other people's spontaneous responses intuitively by focusing on them, by observing people in situations where they are clearly being spontaneous, by knowing or learning about their personality and background, and by deducing those personal attributes that explain what is observed;
5. using the above understanding to better predict the probable spontaneous and reflective responses of other people to the various actions the executive might take;
6. determining which of the predicted responses is likely to be most in line with organizational goals and objectives; and
7. choosing a strategy, including the time and method of interacting, to enhance the probability that the behavior derived from that interaction, either reflective or spontaneous, is the one most likely to yield the best response in terms of organizational goals and objectives or renegotiating expectations, and through coaching enhance the probability of reflective responses.

QUESTIONS FOR REFLECTION AND DISCUSSION

1. What are the differences and similarities between expectations, self-concept, and personal attributes or characteristics?
2. How can someone tell when another person is behaving reflectively or spontaneously?
3. What can managers do to enhance the probability of positively influencing another person?
4. What potential problems might arise when a manager tries to influence another person?

NOTES

1. John P. Kotter, *Power and Influence,* (New York: The Free Press, 1985).
2. Abraham Zaleznik and Manfred F. R. Kets de Vries, *Power and the Corporate Mind*, 2nd ed. (Chicago: Bonus Books, 1985), p. xii.

3. Thomas J. Peters and Robert H. Waterman, Jr., *In Search of Excellence* (New York: Harper & Row, 1982).

4. Calvin S. Hall and Gardner Lindzey, *Theories of Personality*, 3rd ed. (New York: John Wiley & Sons, 1978).

5. B. F. Skinner, *Contingencies of Reinforcement* (New York: Appleton-Century-Crofts, 1969); *About Behaviorism* (New York: Vintage, 1976); and *Beyond Freedom & Dignity* (New York: Alfred A. Knopf, 1971).

6. Douglas McGregor, *Leadership and Motivation* (Cambridge: The MIT Press, 1966); *The Human Side of Enterprise* (New York: McGraw-Hill, 1960); Abraham Maslow, "A Theory of Human Motivation," *Psychological Review* 4, 1943, 370–96.

7. Victor H. Vroom, *Work and Motivation* (New York: Wiley, 1964); and Edward Lawler, *Motivation in Work Organizations* (Monterey, CA: Brooks/Cole, 1973).

8. J. S. Adams, "Toward an Understanding of Inequity," *Journal of Abnormal and Social Psychology* 67, 1963, 422–36.

9. Edwin S. Shneidman, ed. Endeavors in Psychology: *Selections from the Personology of Henry A. Murray* (New York: Harper & Row, 1981); Henry A. Murray, *Explorations in Personality* (New York: Oxford University Press, 1938); and Peter M. Senge, *The Fifth Discipline* (New York: Doubleday, 1990), pp. 20–21.

10. *Expectations* is a term often used in management literature. See, for example, "Pygmalion in Management," by J. Sterling Livingston, *Harvard Business Review*, July/August 1969, which was originally derived from *Pygmalion in the Classroom*, by Robert Rosenthal and Lenore Jacobson (New York: Holt, Rinehart and Winston, 1968). *Psychological contract* is a term often used in psychological literature and, more recently, management literature. See, for example, *Managing Human Assets*, by Michael Beer, Bert Spector, Paul R. Lawrence, D. Quinn Mills, and Richard L. Walton (New York: The Free Press, 1984), p. 75. The term apparently originated as a psychological extension derived from A. H. Croust's article, "Origin and Meaning of the Social Compact Doctrine as Expressed by Greek Philosophers," in *Ethics*, October 1946.

11. Arthur W. Combs and Donald Snygg, *Individual Behavior: A Perceptual Approach to Behavior* (New York Harper & Row, 1959).

12. Carl R. Rogers, *On Becoming a Person* (Boston: Houghton Mifflin, 1961).

13. B. M. Straw, *Intrinsic and Extrinsic Motivations* (Morristown, NJ: General Learning Press, 1976).

14. Leon Festinger, "A Theory of Social Comparison Processes," *Human Relations* 7, 1954, pp. 117–40.

15. David Keirsey and Marilyn Bates, *Please Understand Me: Character & Temperament Types* (Del Mar, CA: Prometheus Nemesis Books, 1978). Discusses the Myer-Briggs Type Indicators derived from Jung's theories.

16. Herbert A. Simon, "Making Management Decisions: The Role of Intuition and Emotion," *Academy of Management Executive*, February 1987; Weston H. Agor, "How Top Executives Use Their Intuitions to Make Important Decisions," *Business Horizons*, January/February 1986. Orlando Behling and Norman Eckel, "Making Sense Out of Intuition," *Academy of Management Executive*, February 1991. This article is critical of the role of intuition in decision making; Thomas J. Peters and Robert H. Waterman, Jr., *In Search of Excellence* (New York: Harper & Row, 1982).

17. Harry Wilkinson, Robert Benfari, and Charles Orth, "Planned Organization Change at the U. S. Naval Air Development Center—A Case History," *Journal of Management Case Studies* 3, 1987, pp. 320–34.

CHAPTER 5

CONTENT MOTIVATION THEORIES:
AN INTEGRATED OPERATIONAL MODEL

In this chapter, we attempt to minimize the frustration that many managers feel due to the many content motivation concepts or theories, each of which seems to have some validity in some situations and not in others. We modify a number of content motivational concepts and theories in order to unify them in an integrated model that will help managers see the interrelationships among them. Next, we show how the model can guide managers to effective action, leading to improved performance.

THE EVOLUTION OF MOTIVATION THEORIES

Although motivation theories began with simple approaches to the relatively simple work environments of the time, Chapter 4 noted that in the complex organizations and society of today it seems apparent that people are motivated by multiple influences, including their perceptions of the expectations others have of them and their own expectations, self images, and self concepts yielding reflective behavior,[1] and their personalities and life experiences yielding spontaneous behavior.

In the less complex era of the early 1900s, motivation theory assumed that the employer essentially bought or exchanged the purchasing power of his or her wage dollars for the worker's time, interest, effort, and contribution. This kind of reward/exchange theory was probably the first widely accepted motivation theory.

Note: This chapter is based on an article with the same title by Wilkinson, Orth, and Benfari, which first appeared in the *SAM Advanced Management Journal*, Autumn 1986, and is used here with the permission of the *SAM Advanced Management Journal*.

It was the foundation on which Taylor built his concepts of scientific management, efficiency, and work simplification.[2] At that time, it seemed to accurately describe workers' responses to existing environments.

As time passed it became clear that monetary rewards, including the plethora of incentive wage and bonus plans, did not by themselves buy interest, commitment, and motivation. In the post–World War II era, new motivation theories were evolved by the behavioral sciences in response to the changing environment of the time. Especially noteworthy were the conceptual contributions of Douglas McGregor,[3] Abraham Maslow,[4] Frederick Herzberg,[5] David McClelland,[6] and John Morse and Jay Lorsch.[7]

McGregor's Theory X and Theory Y

The Taylor, or classical, school of management is a straightforward one emphasizing the need for formal, well-established lines of authority, clearly defined jobs, and sufficient authority to meet responsibilities. It remains more dominant in the less skilled, blue-collar, labor-intensive organizations, such as the assembly-line manufacturing of simple products. (Some of these products are now made in the less complex environments of developing countries.) McGregor postulated that there was a second approach more suited to some organizations. This second approach is often called the participative school of management. Its focus is on involving organizational members in the decision-making process to increase motivation, to give them a clearer picture of the factors involved, and to make them potentially capable of performing more effectively in their jobs. This approach appears to be more dominant in professional or creative organizations, such as research and development laboratories, high-tech manufacturing and sales, hospitals, advertising agencies, or consulting firms. It also appears to be the approach used by the companies identified in *In Search of Excellence*[8] and by the Japanese.[9]

McGregor identifies the psychological assumptions, generalizations, and hypotheses about human nature and behavior that underlie these two approaches. He names them Theory X (classical) and Theory Y (participative). While Theories X and Y are the underlying beliefs and are not themselves managerial strategies, they have become synonymous with styles of management. They represent two ends of a spectrum; most organizations function near the center of the spectrum, slightly to one side or the other.

Theory X

The assumptions that characterize the Theory X view of human behavior include the following:

1. The average human being has an inherent dislike of work and will avoid it if possible and because of this, most people must be coerced, controlled, directed, and threatened with punishment to get them to put forth adequate effort to achieve organizational objectives.

2. The average human being prefers to be directed, wishes to avoid responsibility, has relatively little ambition, and wants security above all.

To some degree these assumptions characterize organizations that specify rigid standards of work behavior, that have stringent rules and regulations that are rigorously enforced, and that tend to follow Taylor's concepts of scientific management. Historically, there has been some evidence of at least limited confirmation of these underlying assumptions in the day-to-day affairs of industry, or else these notions would no longer be around. McGregor, however, believed that many aspects of human behavior are incompatible with the Theory X assumptions.

Theory Y

The other end of the spectrum proposed by McGregor is predicated upon the following assumptions:

1. The expenditure of physical and mental effort in work is as natural as in play or rest and the average human being learns, under proper conditions, not only to accept responsibility but to seek it.
2. People will exercise self-direction and self-control in the service of objectives to which they are committed and this commitment is a function of the rewards associated with their achievement.
3. The intellectual potential of the average person is only partly used in organizational settings and the capacity to exercise a relatively high degree of imagination, ingenuity, and creativity in the solution of organizational problems is widely, not narrowly, distributed in the population.

McGregor concluded that his Theory Y approach to behavior is the best one for managers to follow. Many managers have observed that in some companies and situations, a management style leaning toward the "Taylor" approach (Theory X) works while in others it fails miserably, and, conversely, a management style leaning toward Theory Y, while having successful application in some situations, does not always work well in others.

In trying to resolve this difficulty, Morse and Lorsch developed a contingency theory based on the nature of the task or work. They propose that managers "must design and develop organizations so that the organizational characteristics fit the nature of the task to be done." They further state

> Enterprises with highly predictable tasks perform better with organizations characterized by the highly formalized procedures and management hierarchies of the classical approach. With highly uncertain tasks that require more extensive problem solving, on the other hand, organizations that are less formal and emphasize self-control and member participation in decision making are more effective.[10]

To test their contingency theory, Morse and Lorsch conducted a study involving four plants or organizational units. Two of these performed a relatively certain task: manufacturing standardized containers on high-speed, automated production lines (Akron plant and Hartford plant). The other two (Stockton labs and Carmel labs) performed the relatively uncertain work of research and development in communications technology. One of each pair was evaluated by that company's management as highly effective (Akron and Stockton) and one as less effective (Hartford and Carmel).

In brief, they found that the more effective manufacturing plant (Akron) tended toward a more formalized and controlling organization (Theory X), while the less effective plant (Hartford) tended toward a less formalized and controlling organization (Theory Y). In the research and development organizations, however, just the opposite was true. The more effective research and development organization (Stockton labs) tended toward a less formalized and controlling organization (Theory Y), while the less effective (Carmel labs) tended toward a more formalized and controlling organization (Theory X). Thus, the successful organizations were different in character (one tended toward Theory X the other Theory Y), but the management style of each organization apparently fit the requirements of its task very well.

Morse and Lorsch concluded that the task-organization fit is simultaneously linked to both individual motivation and effective unit performance. The implication for managers is the selection of an appropriate set of actions that will move them toward a task-organization fit. The proper question is not "Should we choose Theory X or Theory Y?" but "What organizational approach is most appropriate, given the task and the people?" (See Exhibit 5-1.)

MASLOW'S NEED HIERARCHY

The Taylor theory of motivation presented a view of people as motivated to restore equilibrium. Satisfaction and inactivity were regarded as people's normal state (McGregor's Theory X). But for Maslow, the satisfaction of a need did not imply satiation and quiescence. Maslow postulated that people are continuously in a motivated state but that the nature of the motivation is fluctuating and complex. Further, Maslow theorized that human beings rarely reach a state of complete satisfaction except for brief moments. He regarded activity to satisfy ever changing needs as the normal state. He put it this way

> Gratification of one need and its consequent removal from the center of the stage brings about not a state of rest, but rather the emergence into consciousness of another, higher need.[11]

As one desire becomes satisfied, another takes its place, and as this desire becomes satisfied, still another replaces it. This sequence of emerging needs formed the basis of Maslow's *hierarchy of needs*, which are listed below:

1. Physiological needs (food, air, water)
2. Safety needs (order, stability, rules)
3. Social needs (affiliation, love)
4. Ego needs (status, respect of peers)
5. Self-fulfillment needs (self-actualization)

Maslow hypothesized that these sets of needs are arranged in a hierarchy starting with the physiological needs at the bottom, progressing through safety needs and

EXHIBIT 5-1

AN INTEGRATED MOTIVATIONAL MODEL

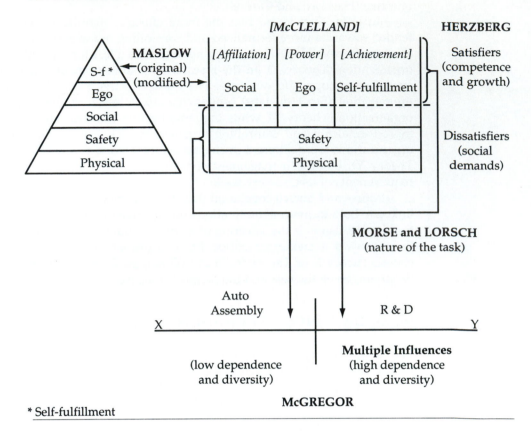

* Self-fulfillment

so on, to the need for self-fulfillment which stands at the top. According to Maslow, the lower needs in the hierarchy must be satisfied before the higher needs can emerge. In other words, one will experience the ego needs only after physiological, safety, and social needs are met.

Nevertheless, in highly professional organizations such as R&D groups, many people seem to be motivated by social, ego, and self-fulfillment simultaneously. Some people appear to have these needs to a degree that can never be fully satisfied. Thus, it seems reasonable to modify Maslow's concepts so that the three highest needs operate in parallel and are open ended. Both the original and modified Maslow concepts are shown as part of Exhibit 5-1.

HERZBERG'S TWO FACTOR THEORY

Herzberg postulated that "the factors involved in producing job satisfaction (which produces motivation) are separate and distinct from the factors that lead to job dissatisfaction (which produces hostility)." The two feelings of satisfaction and dissatisfaction are not opposites of each other but separate and distinct: "The opposite of job satisfaction is not job dissatisfaction, but rather NO job satisfaction; and similarly, the opposite of job dissatisfaction is not job satisfaction but NO job dissatisfaction."

Contemporary society is seen to guarantee satisfaction of the lower needs, Maslow's physiological and safety needs, and at least a small increment of satisfaction in the higher needs. Thus, the purpose of work behavior is not to satisfy these lower needs: "The best types of feelings that such (lower) need fulfillment can lead to is job attitude neutrality." However, if management should interfere with the otherwise assumed fulfillment of these lower needs, such as might be the case under arbitrary layoff and firing procedures, then not having these "hygiene" needs fulfilled leads to dissatisfaction as expressed by hostility, conflict, and/or crisis.

The other set of needs, "satisfiers," relates to higher human nature: Maslow's social, ego or self-esteem, and self-fulfillment needs. Since contemporary society does not guarantee fulfillment of these needs, the purpose of work behavior is to do so. Thus, Herzberg postulates that when a job presents the worker with opportunities to satisfy these higher needs, he or she will be motivated to better work performance. Here again, Herzberg postulates, if the job does not offer opportunities to satisfy these higher order needs, it will not lead to job dissatisfaction but rather to job attitude neutrality and no motivation.

Herzberg argues that satisfiers are the motivators by which to obtain commitment and drive; therefore, management should provide jobs that offer opportunities for achievement, recognition, challenge, growth, responsibility, and accomplishment. At the same time, management must prevent what Herzberg calls the "hygiene" factors (Maslow's lower level needs)—company policy and administration, supervision, interpersonal relationships, working conditions, salary, status, and security—from becoming sources of dissatisfaction, leading to hostility.

To the question "How do you motivate employees?" Herzberg has but one answer: "The only way to motivate the capable employee is to give him (or her) challenging work for which he (or she) can assume responsibility" and thus derive at least partial satisfaction of his or her higher needs. The best of all possible job *contexts* or job environments can only remove any dissatisfiers. To promote job satisfaction and motivation, one needs to provide a good job *content*. Herzberg's concept can be viewed as a special application of Maslow in a highly complex industrialized society, in organizations having tasks and people more appropriate to McGregor's Theory Y.

McClelland's Needs for Achievement, Affiliation, and Power

David McClelland developed a theory of motivation based on the relative strengths of the needs for achievement, affiliation, and power. Although he was originally most concerned with his belief that the need for achievement was central to effective managerial behavior, McClelland later became convinced that the need for power was equally important and that, in fact, the relative strengths of all three needs (in effect, a motivational profile) had to be analyzed in the context of the kind of organization the individual was managing.

The need for achievement governs an individual's orientation to tasks he or she faces in the organization. Is the person motivated by the rewards for a job well done? The needs for affiliation and power govern an individual's interpersonal relationships. Does the person seek friends, strive for leadership, is he or she warm and friendly? By examining Maslow's upper three levels in a totally different way and redefining them, they can approximate McClelland's power, achievement, and affiliation needs. McClelland's affiliation needs are analogous to Maslow's social needs and his achievement needs appear related to Maslow's needs for self-fulfillment. Power needs appear to embrace some social and self-fulfillment needs, but seem more related to ego needs since power puts us "above" others and gives us status. (See Exhibit 5-1.)

MULTIPLE INFLUENCES

Chapter 4 identifies three interdependent sets of influences: expectations, self-image or self-concept, and intrinsic factors (personal attributes). The degree to which these sets of influences are different appears to be related to (1) the amount of dependencies and diversities inherent in the organization as suggested by the level of ambiguity, uncertainty, and complexity, and (2) the number of different experiences that have occurred in the individual's past as suggested by (a) cultural background, (b) education, (c) professional achievements and status, and (d) organizational achievements or position in the hierarchy of the organization. The greater the dependencies, diversity, and number of experiences, the greater the apparent degree of difference. The first of these seems to correspond with the Morse and Lorsch task-organization fit and both fit with Kotter's dependencies and diversities. This suggests that in complex organizations where a Theory Y style is effective, the multiple influence model will have greater application than in those that are less complex where a Theory X style is more effective.

INTEGRATION

The results of integrating and summarizing these various theories of motivation as revised and reformed, can be expressed diagrammatically (Exhibit 5-1). Note that Maslow's lower level needs are allied to Herzberg's hygiene factors or "dissatisfiers" and that these, in turn, are the motivational factors most often observed operating in organizations tending toward McGregor's Theory X style of work and management. Conversely, Maslow's higher level needs, analogous to Herzberg's "satisfiers," are the dominant motivational factors observed in organizations tending toward a Theory Y style. McClelland's affiliation, power, and achievement needs are a somewhat different amalgam of Maslow's three higher level needs.

Industrial societies as a whole are becoming more ambiguous, uncertain, and complex. Levels of education and diversity of background are increasing, and larger numbers of people view themselves as professionals who must depend on each other for the achievement of organizational goals and objectives. This suggests that in these complex societies the midpoint on the Theory X–Theory Y spectrum is shifting to the right while the dotted line between satisfiers and dissatisfiers in the Herzberg scheme is moving upward.

We can draw the following conclusions:

1. Herzberg's dissatisfiers are similar to Maslow's first two levels of need plus some small increment in each of the top three needs in his hierarchy.
2. These dissatisfiers tend to be related to the autocratic structured management style of Taylor or McGregor's Theory X.
3. Morse and Lorsch have identified this autocratic style as more effective for routine tasks.
4. Herzberg's satisfiers are similar to Maslow's top three levels of need.
5. McClelland's achievement, power, and affiliation needs are a different mix of Maslow's top three levels of need.
6. These satisfiers are related to the participative management style described by McGregor as Theory Y.
7. This style, according to Morse and Lorsch, appears more effective for tasks with high levels of complexity.
8. The nature of the people and of the tasks being performed in the U.S. economy results in higher and higher levels of dependency, diversity, uncertainty, complexity, education, and professionalism. This, in turn, leads to a greater observed difference between spontaneous and reflective behavior, and a greater applicability of multiple influences. Thus, in the U.S. economy, sensitivity to spontaneous and reflective behavior deriving from multiple influences is an increasingly important managerial tool.

As a result of modifying these motivational concepts in order to tie them together in an integrated model, the manager is able to see relationships among them. This integrated model provides an analytical framework for any supervisor or manager trying to improve the performance of individuals, groups or the entire organization.

THE INTEGRATED MOTIVATIONAL MODEL IN USE

Many, if not most, managers tend to believe that they should study motivation to better understand what influences or motivates their employees. While this focus can be helpful in understanding the behavior of individuals or groups, no simple theory or model addresses the two most important tasks of the manager: first, building and using relationships to achieve organizational goals and objectives, and, second, designing work systems and developing an organizational climate that motivates most employees toward higher levels of performance.

HUMAN RESOURCES MANAGEMENT

The integrated motivation model is an important contributor to decisions on fundamental policies affecting the management of the organization's human resources. It simplifies the manager's task by demonstrating that, while each of the theorists embraced by the model have made specific contributions, there is no essential disagreement among them but rather a different application, depending on the people and environment in each situation.

It seems clear, for instance, that the assumptions about human behavior associated with McGregor's Theory Y and supported by the higher level motivational needs of Maslow, McClelland, and Herzberg all point toward design of work systems emphasizing the responsibility, participation, and commitment of workers at all organizational levels. This approach is most appropriate in our highly complex society in organizations with high levels of interdependence and diversity (Kotter).

In *Managing Human Assets* the authors present two alternate work systems, Model A (the traditional work system) and Model B (the high-commitment work system).[12] Model A is based on Theory X assumptions and lower level needs of the theorists (effective in organizations with low levels of interdependence and diversity or in less complex societies). Model B is based on Theory Y and higher level needs. While acknowledging that the traditional work systems have been applicable to blue-collar and clerical workers while high-commitment work systems have been reserved for professional and managerial systems, the authors note that successful experiments have been conducted recently, especially in new organizations, applying Model B to all levels, including blue-collar and clerical. They project increasing reliance on Model B to achieve optimum performance in our increasingly high-tech society which, in turn, is consistent with increased sensitivity to spontaneous and reflective behaviors derived from multiple influences as described in Chapter 4.

Examples

Two specific examples, both involving clerical personnel, demonstrate the use of the integrated model. In most organizations in our highly complex society, a manager has a high dependency on his or her secretary and there is often a high level of diversity between their backgrounds and experience. Thus, the relationship between them can be strengthened by a Theory Y, multiple influence approach in behavior. Beyond this, the manager can use a Model B approach (high commitment work system) in modifying the secretary's job to include greater opportunities for increased contribution, responsibility, participation, and personal competence. This will lead to greater mutual respect, less status differentiation, high levels of mutual affiliation, and referent power (reciprocity) and therefore higher levels of performance.[13]

On the other hand, if the manager does not see or accept the high dependency and diversity and approaches the secretary in a Theory X manner as an extension of a typewriter or word processor and uses a Model A (the traditional work system) approach to define the secretary's job, the integrated model tells us that the secretary's motivation, performance, and job satisfaction will be minimal.

Another example of the utility of the integrated model is the typing or word processing pool. In a Theory X approach by managers who assume low levels of dependence and diversity and use the traditional Model A to design the work of the pool, people will be placed in single skill, simple positions for which they are already qualified or can be easily trained. The usual result of this approach is low motivation, low performance, and low job satisfaction leading to low morale, high turnover, and excessive training costs. What does the integrated model tell us about this situation? It tells us that the plus values of the traditional highly structured and supervised pool organization are not really plus values in our complex society.

If we shift our assumptions in the Theory Y direction, we can see that the integrated model gives us a different orientation. We see the need for relatively small, self-directed teams of word processors highly interactive with a small group of managers. In this way, strong cooperative relationships are built and the word processor teams gain status and job satisfaction; they accept tasks as a team and gain acceptance and rewards as an effective self-governing and evaluating team. Using the integrated model in organizations with high levels of dependency or diversity tells us that the high commitment work system (Model B) reinforced with a positive Theory Y management style incorporating sensitivity to spontaneous and reflective behaviors derived from the multiple influences described in Chapter 4, leads to high motivation, productivity, and the real cost-effectiveness of a secretarial or word processing pool.

The integrated model tells the manager how to adjust managerial style to the realities of human motivation in the work place and how to proceed in developing work systems, given the social and organizational environment and the nature of the people.

QUESTIONS FOR REFLECTION AND DISCUSSION

1. What is *motivation* and how does a manager motivate another person?
2. What are the differences and similarities between the content theories of Maslow, McClelland, and Herzberg?
3. What are the differences and similarities between the psychological and process concepts in Chapter 4 and the content concepts in Chapter 5?
4. What are the differences and similarities between human resources management and interpersonal skills?

NOTES

1. Arthur W. Combs and Donald Snygg, *Individual Behavior: A Perceptual Approach to Behavior* (New York: Harper & Row, 1959), pp. 126–44.
2. Frederick W. Taylor, *Scientific Management* (Hanover: Dartmouth College, 1912).
3. Douglas McGregor, *The Human Side of Enterprise* (New York: McGraw-Hill, 1960).

4. Abraham H. Maslow, *Motivation and Personality* (New York: Harper & Row, 1964).

5. Frederick Herzberg, *Work and the Nature of Man* (New York: World Publishing, 1966).

6. David C. McClelland, *The Achieving Society* (New York: D. Van Nostrand, 1961).

7. John J. Morse and Jay W. Lorsch, "Beyond Theory Y," *Harvard Business Review*, May/June 1970, pp. 61–68.

8. Thomas J. Peters and Robert H. Waterman, Jr., *In Search of Excellence*, (New York: Harper & Row, 1982).

9. Richard T. Pascale and Anthony G. Athos, *The Art of Japanese Management* (New York: Warner Books, 1981).

10. Morse and Lorsch, "Beyond Theory Y," p. 62.

11. Maslow, *Motivation and Personality."*

12. Michael Beer, Bert Spector, Paul R. Lawrence, D. Quinn Mills, and Richard E. Walton, *Managing Human Assets*, (New York: The Free Press, 1984), pp. 164–75.

13. Robert C. Benfari, Harry E. Wilkinson, Charles D. Orth, "The Effective Use of Power," *Business Horizons*, May/June 1986, pp. 12–16. Reproduced as Chapter 8.

CHAPTER 6

PERCEPTION IN ORGANIZATIONS[1]

Managers make decisions based on how they perceive, that is, sense and understand, the events, people, and things around them. Yet most of us have had experiences in which our perceptions were clearly erroneous and the events, people, and things around us were not what they appeared to be. While more accurate perceptions should obviously provide a stronger base for decision making, some managers may argue that problems resulting from inaccurate perceptions are infrequent and often minor. Of course, most of us *do* perceive reasonably accurately most of the time, but effective executives know that, as in sports or any other professional field, the difference between top and mediocre performance is often measured in millimeters and microseconds. Since most managers strive to be that little bit better than their peers, they must seek to understand the perceptual process better in order to develop the skill to perceive more accurately and thus have a better base for making decisions.

A person receives a constant stream of data from his or her senses. In the manager's world, the data about a situation or an event usually involves another person or persons in some sort of organizational setting surrounded by desks, machines, reports, and other "things." Why do managers "see" some things and not others? How do managers filter what is relevant and what is not? What kinds of filters screen, obscure, or distort "reality"? What kind of conclusions, inferences, or judgments do managers reach from the data that passes through their filters?

Like manufacturing, perception involves a process leading to a product output. In psychology these two are usually called perceiving (the process) and percept (the product) respectively. The product is composed of the conclusions, inferences, or judgments we reach about an event or situation while the process involves all the steps that take us there.

The human brain is bombarded by massive amounts of information gathered by our senses, only some of which can be processed, usually spontaneously, without reflective thought. Individuals seem to spontaneously expect and look forward to events or inputs that conform to their personal characteristics,[2] personality, and life experiences that have been rewarded or punished in the past.[3]

55

These usually subconscious expectations are like hypotheses that such-and-so will occur or should occur. For example, a supervisor who has a high opinion of, a liking for, and high performance expectations of a particular person may "see" higher performance than would an outside, objective observer. Conversely, a supervisor who has a low opinion of, a dislike for, and low performance expectations of another person may "see" lower performance than would an outside, objective observer. Thus, every person has built up in his or her mind certain, usually subconscious, assumptions, expectations, and hypotheses about the world in which he or she lives, which profoundly influence how the person perceives events. These expectations, assumptions, and hypotheses do not spring up in isolation but derive from the same set of influences that lead to spontaneous behaviors, namely previous life experiences and ongoing encounters with the environment, including culture, education, biases, and motivations. They also may derive from the same sets of influences leading to reflective behaviors, namely the more recent sets of expectations from the many relationships one may have and from one's self concept, including norms from the organizations, departments and groups with whom one interacts and the ethical, legal, and cultural factors in one's value system. These expectations, assumptions, and hypotheses define what our senses lead us to perceive or not perceive in the environment. We see what we expect or want to see.[4] All perception occurs in a rich, dynamic, ongoing context, and a thorough understanding of the perceptual process demands that we understand the roles of expectations, assumptions, and hypotheses, which, taken together, constitute what may be called a person's assumptive world.

Based on this assumptive world, the individual selects those relevant bits of sensory data from the immediate environment, which he or she has found from previous experience to be useful in some way. This selection process works negatively as well to filter out of a situation those "realities" (bits of sensory data) that the individual's previous experience suggests are not useful. For example, a boss may consciously or subconsciously identify an employee as being very similar to another person the boss has already judged to be incompetent. This association may generate subconscious expectations in the mind of the boss that leads him or her to accept as relevant only evidence of the employee's incompetence. The same boss may identify a secretary as being very similar to a favored son or daughter thus generating positive subconscious expectations and filtering out as not relevant evidence of the secretary's incompetence. In effect, the boss's expectations of performance are affected by earlier judgments of others, including their biases, which thus become part of the boss's assumptive world but have little or nothing to do with actual performance in the particular situation he or she is observing. This contributes to the "self-fulfilling prophecy" or "Pygmalion effect"[5] discussed in Chapter 4. An obvious conclusion: it is dysfunctional when biases overly influence what is accepted or rejected as relevant.

Our perception of relevance determines our focus in our perceptual field. We narrow our field of view and focus on what we believe is relevant. This might be called "spotlight perception" or tunnel vision.[6] When we broaden our field of view to encompass other aspects in a situation, however, we can be said to be using "floodlight perception." In order to obtain accurate perceptions, managers must both spotlight and floodlight. We focus on what we perceive to be relevant but must recognize that our assumptive world may cause us to filter out aspects of a situation others may perceive to be highly relevant. During this relevance processing, a manager can add to or subtract from the available sensory data, and narrowly or broadly attend to the situation or event. In short, we perceive our environment selectively.

An example of the relevance filter is the Sherlock Holmes stories. Most of us who read the stories spontaneously filter out the critical clues as not relevant while the great detective is able to avoid filtering out that data by perceiving reflectively and is ultimately able to put the pieces together to solve the mystery. Indeed, new detectives must consciously control their perception in order to perceive reflectively and thus avoid filtering out what may later prove relevant and important.

Managers process and evaluate what has passed through their relevance filters into their perceptual field in order to reach the final structuring of a conclusion, inference, or judgment (percept), which is usually done spontaneously. The manager may then use this percept, however accurate or inaccurate, to make decisions. When we evaluate, we are testing previously held assumptions, expectations, and/or hypotheses derived from our life experiences against the sensory data from our field of view as filtered by our assessment of the relevance of these data. This testing and checking is the analyzing and synthesizing process by which tentative assumptions and sensory input are structured into percepts and, again, this is usually done spontaneously. In other words, we check our current hypotheses about what is going on against our past experience. This hypothesis may change spontaneously several times before we are relatively sure about what we perceive; confronted with ambiguous input, our current perceptions may vacillate repeatedly. If the latest, best hypothesis does not "check" reasonably well against past experience, then the perceivers will try other hypotheses until the percept is structured to their satisfaction or may become reflective and require further sensory information.

To avoid the many problems associated with percept distortions, managers must consciously and reflectively withhold evaluative judgments as long as feasible while they set about trying to obtain additional sensory data. It is only when managers observe the organized pattern into which these events fit that they can begin to understand the situation. This reflective effort is called "taking a functional point of view."[7] Taking a functional point of view requires the manager to

1. withhold evaluative or attributive judgments until the pattern of relationships is clear or until verification has been accomplished to the extent feasible; and
2. avoid taking sides or imposing premature application of his or her own assumptive world and filtered perceptions until all the information from others is in, while recognizing that the information received is always filtered and probably slanted or distorted by the expectations, self-images, and biases of ourselves as well as others.

If the perceptual processing is done accurately, our percept may match what is happening. If it is not done accurately, the final percept may be in error. In other words, a distortion or distortions may be introduced into the perceptual processes. These distortions may be more likely when we are perceiving spontaneously, depending on the fit of our previous life experiences and personal attributes with the situation being perceived. Several major characteristics contribute to perceptual distortion:

1. We structure our perception to fit immediate wishes, biases, needs, and expectations. We see what we expect, or hope, to see.
2. We may allow our emotions to influence the perceptual process by either intensifying or interfering with it. For example, our feelings of love, hate, happiness, or anger may amplify and/or distort either the relevance of an incident or the positive or negative judgments we make about it.
3. We may not be aware that our spontaneous perception of reality is distorted by such factors as our defensiveness (such as when we are challenged at work or elsewhere) and our subconscious biases.
4. Our inner determinants involving personal attributes, such as memory, emotion, wishes, and personality characteristics and perhaps subconscious self-concept factors, including needs and/or ethics derived from cultural factors, will carry more weight than our outer determinants, which include the psychological contracts we have with others and our environment.
5. Previous experience with positive or negative reinforcement in similar situations may have generated strong biases that influence current perceptions, such as big business is bad, or management exploits labor.
6. Life experiences and traditions in our culture, the college we attend, and the organizations for which we have worked or are working can influence how information is processed, particularly spontaneously when we interact with a different culture or organization.

To make effective decisions a manager must not only perceive but understand other people.[8] The process by which we perceive people and the causes for their behavior is called *attribution*. We attribute a person's behavior to some cause or causes. We infer whether the causes for a person's behavior are internal or external to the person, and stable or unstable over time and in different situations.[9] Attribution permits us to perceive people and their behaviors as structured, stable, and meaningful. Although people will act in diverse ways in different situations, we will still perceive stability in these cases because of the inferences we make about their intentions or motives. In this way, we tie their behavior to some common threads, either in the environment or the person or both. We also use attribution when we attempt to understand the unexpected ("he meant to . . . ," "she had to . . . ," and so on). Attribution is the process by which we see people as actors rather than objects. Because of this, two people will often have quite different explanations for why a particular behavior has occurred. Therefore, in order to understand more accurately the behavior of another person, we must reflectively test our attribution thus entering the testing and checking stage of perception. In Chapter 4 we saw an example of reflective testing before attribution: Vice-president Dan Stone was surprised by Joe Reed's recommendation of Art White instead of Kay Cook but he went out to *test* the situation before *assuming* anything or attributing motives to Reed.

We are all biased observers. Everyone has had life experiences that have generated individual needs, expectations, and belief systems that determine how we perceive people, objects, and events. Sometimes these individual characteristics get in the way of making accurate attributions and/or predictions about people, objects, and events. People with high affiliation needs, for instance, may see the world and other people in terms of love, hate, rejection, and acceptance and will judge others, including subordinates, peers, and bosses on these dimensions. More importantly, these inner needs may preclude the individual from attributing other important characteristics to a person. In a similar fashion, strong needs for achievement or power may also bias our attributions. We may perceive very differently when we spontaneously respond compared to when we take time to reflectively respond.

The ability to develop differentiated perceptions of others is a mark of an effective manager. In other words, effective managers tend to perceive reflectively and more accurately, with fewer distortions, the differences among their peers, subordinates, and bosses. They can make more accurate attributions and judgments about the strengths and weaknesses of those around them.

PERCEPTUAL DIFFICULTIES

Effective managers have a better view of reality because they tend to recognize the following characteristics of human perception:

1. Everyone is biased by his or her life experiences both positively and negatively.
2. Everyone constructs his or her perceptions to meet his or her needs and assumptions about the world.
3. Perceptions serve the purpose of explaining the world, and also defending ourselves (self-image) from other explanations.
4. Perceptions often serve the function of reducing uncertainties and may become "reality," rather than possibility, in the eyes of the individual concerned.
5. Untested perceptions create self-fulfilling or circular perceptual processes. We continue to selectively perceive what we want to perceive to prove our hypotheses; we wall ourselves off from competing information.
6. Our assumptions and beliefs lead to behavior on our part that will be congruent with these perceptions. We create a self-fulfilling prophecy.

HOW TO PERCEIVE MORE ACCURATELY

You as a manager can take a number of steps, to the extent of your ability, that will assist you in perceiving reflectively and more accurately:

1. Perform a thorough self-analysis to understand your own motives, needs, beliefs, and biases. (See "Perceptual Issues We Need to Examine" below.)
2. Perform a thorough analysis of others to understand their spontaneous and reflective behaviors deriving from their personal attributes (including

history, motives, needs, and biases), their self-concepts (including beliefs and values), and the psychological contracts they have.

3. Construct situations where hypotheses and perceptions can be tested and confirmed or discarded reflectively.

4. Reflectively create a climate of openness between yourself and others in order to be able to discuss the undiscussable.

5. Reflectively generate valid information, avoid premature attribution, and focus on the particular behavior in the situation.

6. Listen to your intuitions, which are guides to your feelings, needs, and motives.

7. Scrutinize these intuitions so you understand them.

8. Seek feedback from others on your perceptions; how do they see the situation.

9. Take responsibility for your perceptions; you should put statements in the form of "I think," "I feel," and "I believe."

10. Give feedback to others about your perceptions. But be sure the feedback is intended to be and is phrased to be helpful and *not* intended to boost your own ego.

11. Broaden your perspective by reading about, listening to, and observing people, things, and events. Look at, and learn at least a little bit about, literature, art, politics, behavior, humanities, ethics, science, and so on, as opposed to looking only at our area of specialization or interest. This broadens your life experiences.

12. Accept the anxiety involved in dealing with uncertainty. We all have the same feelings about uncertainty; we differ in how we handle our anxieties over uncertainty. Acceptance of the universality of the situation will allow you to go on with the task of confirming or discarding your dysfunctional attributions, assumptions, and perceptions.

13. Do not make the task of evaluating perceptions into a win–lose situation. Any perceptions, right or wrong, are "reality" for the person who has them. Premature judgments may create defensiveness and close the learning loop between individuals.

Another way you, as a manager, can improve your reflective "functional perception" is to verify or validate your perceptions. You can do this by sharing your perceptions with others while they share theirs with you. To do this, you must examine a number of issues that may give you insights into your perceptual filters on both relevance and evaluation.

PERCEPTUAL ISSUES YOU NEED TO EXAMINE

1. Uniqueness. What makes me different from others? What makes the other person different from me?

2. Image of self. How do I see myself? What do I like best and least about myself?

3. Image of others. What yardsticks do I use most to evaluate others?

4. Past experience. What are the most important past experiences that made an impression on me?

5. Mood. Am I consistent and stable or am I likely to fluctuate in my moods? What are my mood states?
6. Learning. What are the important things I have learned? What are my belief systems?
7. Values. Do I know what values I cherish? What possession, tangible or intangible, would I surrender last?
8. Familiarity. In what area of activity am I most familiar and secure?
9. Wants. What one thing would I most want to be able to do?
10. Emotions. Do I handle my emotions openly or defensively?
11. Focus. To what activity do I give most of my attention on the job?
12. Motivation. What are my most salient needs: power, achievement, or affiliation?
13. Attention. What do I look for most when I meet a person for the first time?
14. Completion of the incomplete. Do I communicate the whole story?
15. Simplification or complication. Do I look to simple or complex explanations of people, events, and things?

Although the perceptual process is a very difficult and complex one, managers who understand it and develop the skills to improve the accuracy of their perceptions have a stronger base for decision making and thus have that critical small edge over their peers and competitors.

QUESTIONS FOR REFLECTION AND DISCUSSION

1. What factors influence how our relevance filters operate?
2. What factors influence how our evaluative filters operate?
3. What are the differences and similarities between spontaneous and reflective perception?
4. What can managers do to improve their ability to perceive more accurately?

NOTES

1. Michael W. Levine and Jeremy M. Shefner, *Fundamentals of Sensation and Perception*, 2nd ed. (Pacific Grove, CA: Brooks/Cole, 1991); and Edward E. Jones, *Interpersonal Perception* (New York: Freeman, 1990).
2. Abraham Zaleznik and Manfred F. R. Kets de Vries, *Power and the Corporate Mind*, 2nd ed. (Chicago: Bonus Books, 1985).
3. B. F. Skinner, *About Behaviorism* (New York: Vintage, 1976).
4. Harold J. Leavitt, *Managerial Psychology*, 2nd ed. (Chicago: University of Chicago Press, 1964).
5. J. Sterling Livingston, "Pygmalion in Management," *Harvard Business Review*, July/August 1969.
6. Arthur W. Combs and Donald Snygg, *Individual Behavior: A Perceptual Approach to Behavior*, (New York: Harper & Row, 1949).

7. Alexander H. Leighton, *Human Relations in a Changing World* (New York: E. P. Dutton & Co., 1949), pp. 156–61.

8. Jean M. Bartunek, "Why Did You Do That? Attribution Theory In Organizations," *Business Horizons*, September/October 1981.

9. Harold H. Kelley, "The Processes of Casual Attribution," *American Psychologist*, February 1973.

CHAPTER 7

EFFECTIVE COMMUNICATIONS

SENDING AND RECEIVING MESSAGES

When things go awry in organizations (as evidenced by poor performance, mistakes, or bad decisions, for example), after-the-fact analysis often comes up with an easy diagnosis: poor communication. Unfortunately, this simple answer seldom prevents recurrence of the same or similar situations. Poor communication is frequently a symptom of a problem but seldom a cause. It is a gross generalization of a highly complex series of interactions between organizations, groups, or individuals requiring both the knowledge and learned skills of those attempting to communicate effectively.

All communication requires a transmitter (or sender) and a receiver. If both the transmitter and receiver are tuned to each other, operating properly and without noise or distortion in the system, the message gets through, or at least this is normally true when we are transmitting and receiving electronically. When human beings are involved, however, there is almost always noise and distortion bedeviling the interactive process, often caused by unrecognized differences in spontaneous responses derived from life experiences, lack of knowledge (especially cross-cultural knowledge), failure to interpret correctly available clues, inaccurate perception, biases, or failure to differentiate between what someone said and what he or she meant.

A number of hefty books have been written about the communication process in organizations. In this chapter, we will not attempt to cover all the bases nor deal with the total complexity of the process. Written communication takes time on the part of both the sender and receiver and thus is usually undertaken when we are reflective. Written communication is susceptible to some of the same problems and difficulties that affect verbal (that is, spoken) communications, but perhaps to a lesser degree. We will focus on communications that are usually spontaneous, specifically on the three important elements of knowledge and/or skill that are of particular concern to managers who hope to communicate more effectively:

1. Sending/receiving/responding verbally, especially skillful listening.
2. Sending/receiving/responding physically (body language).
3. Dealing with cultural differences, particularly those involving space, time, and things.

VERBAL COMMUNICATION

The Power of Listening[1]

Typically, our education has afforded us the opportunity to study grammar, rhetoric, public speaking, expository writing, or other related skills. However, these *output* skills of communication alone do not prevent problems of communication, for communication is a two-way street involving *input* as well. Most of the preoccupation with communication has focused on output, and we still find a broad range of courses in composition, effective speaking, and the arts of plain and fancy talk. Not surprisingly, experts writing about communication have begun to see that a large part of the problem is caused by faulty listening. As the noted general semanticist S. I. Hayakawa stated some years ago, "It does not avail the speakers to have spoken well if we as listeners have failed to understand, or if we come away believing them to have said things they didn't say at all."[2] Listening is a problem when ineffective and a source of power and a leadership skill when effective. Improvement in our ability to listen effectively will go a long way in improving communication.

It goes without saying that listening means not just maintaining a polite silence while you rehearse in your mind the speech you are going to make the next time you can grab a conversational opening. Listening also means more than just hearing words. In order to understand someone, you often must make an effort to know what the speaker means in terms of his or her spontaneous responses derived from his or her perceptions and life experiences, and not just in terms of your own spontaneous responses. In his article, "How to Listen to Other People," Hayakawa writes

> Listening means trying to see the problem the way the speaker sees it—which means not sympathy, which is feeling for him, but empathy, which is experiencing with him. Listening requires entering actively and imaginatively into the other fellow's situation and trying to understand a frame of reference (life experiences) different from your own.[3]

Carl Rogers and F. J. Roethlisberger, in their treatment of "Barriers and Gateways to Communication,"[4] reiterated the importance of empathetic listening, saying that in order to communicate with understanding you have "to see the expressed idea and attitude from the other person's point of view, to sense how it feels to him, to achieve his frame of reference [based on his life experiences and perceptions] in regard to the thing he is talking about."

Recognizing the Speaker's Frame of Reference (Understanding the Speaker's Perceptions and Life Experiences)

The first item of importance to be derived from this concept of effective listening is this: we must occasionally remind ourselves that a speaker may have perspectives quite different from our own and that what he or she means by a statement might be very different from what we would mean if we used the same words. Our common language is such that ordinary words mean different things to different people. It is an unreasonable demand on the part of the listener to expect everyone else to use words with the precise meaning he or she would use were he or she speaking. To listen effectively, we must listen reflectively and with empathy.

Thus far we have said that communication may be impeded if we fail to allow for the possibility of a speaker having different experiences and perspectives from our own. Empathetic listening requires a sensitivity that goes beyond the speaker's words to get at the meaning behind the words. If we fail to understand the speaker's frame of reference and insist on hearing everything he or she says in terms of our own, the reason may be our mistaken assumption that words, independent of the people who are using them, have unambiguous meaning. It is the listener's job to understand what the speaker means, not what the words mean.

The Problem of Evaluating in Terms of Our Own Frame of Reference

Rogers and Roethlisberger proposed that a "major barrier to mutual interpersonal communication is our very natural tendency to judge, to evaluate, to approve (or disapprove) the statement of the other person or the other group." They illustrated the point as follows:

> Suppose someone, commenting on this discussion, makes the statement, "I didn't like what the man said." What will you respond? Almost invariably your reply will either be approval or disapproval of the attitude expressed. Either you respond, "I didn't like it either; I thought it was terrible," or else you tend to reply, "Oh, I thought it was really good." In other words, your primary reaction is to evaluate it from your point of view, your own frame of reference.

This is an example of your spontaneous perceptual evaluative filters—derived from your life experiences and perceptions—in action.

By evaluating in this manner, the listener has only brought his or her spontaneous response derived from his or her frame of reference to bear on the matter. Instead of communication with understanding, the interaction consists of two ideas, two feelings, two judgments missing each other in psychological space and in this situation the psychological distance between the two remains unbridged. In the instance noted above, for example, the evaluative response has failed to inform the listener why the person did not like the discussion or what the discussion apparently meant from his or her point of view.

Here is another example of how spontaneous responses or frames of reference and consequent evaluations can influence the ability to receive messages with minimal distortion. A senior manager, born during the Roaring Twenties and raised during the depression of the 1930s, is interacting with a subordinate born during the post–World War II baby boom and raised during the affluent fifties. Concerned with security and husbanding resources, the boss says, "We can't afford that new equipment." Through the filters of his life experiences and perspectives, the subordinate's evaluation is "the old tightwad won't listen to reason." The boss, from his point of view, believes the subordinate is a "materialistic spendthrift." Neither party is likely to be able to deal effectively with the other or "hear" the other's analysis of the "facts." Each "listens" to the other through his own life experiences, his own filtered and less-than-insightful evaluations. Lacking understanding of where the other is "coming from," each party to the flawed communication distorts the messages being sent and received, and an effective analysis of the "facts" gets lost in the process.

In order for communication to flow rather than break down, we must be able to understand what the speaker means, and this often means making an attempt to understand his or her spontaneous responses (life experiences and perspectives) rather than evaluating his or her statements by using our own spontaneous meanings or definitions, derived from our own life experiences and perspectives. Among other things, this implies that listening does *not* mean waiting alertly for the flaws in the other fellow's arguments so that later you can cut him down. In regard to the tendency to evaluate rather than listen empathetically, Hayakawa suggests a general rule:

> Refrain from agreement or disagreement with a speaker, refrain from praise or censure of his [or her] views, until we are sure that we thoroughly understand what those views are.

Pathways to Better Communication

The point has been made that good listening is reflective, empathetic listening; that is, listening with an awareness that the speaker may be operating with different life experiences and perspectives leading to a different set of spontaneous responses or frames of reference, and trying to understand those experiences and perspectives and that set of spontaneous responses or frames of reference in order to glean the speaker's meaning. This does not imply that we have to agree with a speaker; rather it suggests that we have to see reflectively and empathetically his or her meaning through his or her eyes before we can agree or disagree. Writers on the subject of effective communication have suggested certain procedures for improving understanding:

1. A good listener does not merely remain silent; he or she asks questions. However, these questions must avoid all implications, whether in tone of voice or in wording, of skepticism, challenge, or hostility; that is, we must avoid putting the speaker in the position of defending his or her perspectives. Our questions

must clearly be motivated by curiosity about the speaker's views and perspectives. Such questions, which may be called "questions for clarification," usually take the form, "Would you expand on the point about . . . ?" or "What exactly is your recommendation again?" or "Would you mind restating the argument about . . . ?"

2. Rogers and Hayakawa both suggest the following procedure: before commenting upon a statement, the listener can try to restate to the speaker's satisfaction what the speaker has just said. Hayakawa writes, "Perhaps the most useful kind of question at this stage is something like 'I am going to restate in my words what I think you mean. Then, would you mind telling me if I've understood you correctly?'" Or, if talking with someone of more recent vintage, try "Hey man, let's see if I got that."

Rogers suggests that, as an experiment, the next time you expect to get into an especially difficult or heated argument with someone, institute this rule for your behavior: "I can speak for myself only *after* I have first restated the ideas and feelings of the other speaker accurately and to that person's satisfaction." If this is done sincerely, in a true effort to understand not only what the other person says but what he or she feels and what his or her perspectives are, the usual response is that the other person begins to make some effort to understand your point of view. Rogers continues

> Can you imagine what this kind of an approach would mean if it were projected into larger areas? What would happen to a labor/management dispute if it were conducted in such a way that labor, without necessarily agreeing, could accurately state management's point of view in a way that management could accept; and management, without approving labor's stand, could state labor's case in a way that labor agreed was accurate? It would mean that real communication was established, and one could practically guarantee that some reasonable solution would be reached. And in addition, after an agreement was reached, there would be a higher probability that both sides understand to what they have agreed.

These techniques in themselves will not guarantee effective listening, but they should help the listener to avoid some of the terminological tangles resulting from incongruent or conflicting spontaneous responses derived from the unique life experiences and perspectives of the speaker and listener that are at the root of poor communication. Recognizing and respecting the speaker's frame of reference, Rogers and Roethlisberger point out, can help sidestep the hostilities, resentments, and defensiveness that arise through misunderstanding.

Improvement in the quality of listening can go a long way toward avoiding the misunderstandings that often are the basis for ineffective communication. Effective listening is reflective, empathetic listening. Before responding to a statement, a listener is advised to be certain he or she has reflectively understood the statement in the speaker's terms. This requires a sensitivity to the speaker's life experiences, perspectives and frames of reference, which may be quite different from the listener's. The listener must be able to see things through the eyes of the speaker in order to be sure he or she has understood.

Listening empathetically, however, may not be as easily achieved as it might sound. Writers on the subject have noted that, in addition to a willingness and the necessary skills, empathetic listening requires *courage*. As Rogers writes

> If you really understand another person in this way, if you are willing to enter his private world and see the way life appears to him [or her with his or her life experiences and perspectives] without any attempt to make evaluative judgments [based on your own life experiences and perspectives], you run the risk of being changed yourself [you may modify your own frame of reference]. You might see it his [or her] way; you might find yourself influenced in your attitudes or your personality [and your perspectives].

Rogers's point above, that good communication can seem too dangerous, suggests the curious turn of thought that misunderstandings and poor communication, in some circumstances, might be functional for preserving intact our intrinsic perspectives and biases. Writers on the subject of communication typically adopt the point of view that poor communication is a problem everyone laments, and that, as far as everyone is concerned, we would be better off with communicative clarity. There are some writers, however, notably Charlotte Kursh, who suggest that it is a mistake to view good communication as a panacea. In her article, "The Benefits of Poor Communication," she challenges the assumption that better communication will necessarily reduce strife and conflict. She writes

> A better understanding of the situation might serve only to underline the differences rather than to resolve them. Indeed, many of the techniques thought of as bad communication were apparently developed with the aim of bypassing or avoiding confrontation, and some of them continue to be reasonably successful in this aim.[5]

Kursch's point is that the assumption that the attainment of maximum clarity as measured by some more or less objective standard is always in the interest of at least one of the parties to an interaction, and often of both, may not always be correct. The heated rhetorical clashes, with all their implied misunderstandings of each other's position, such as between the Arabs and the Israelis for example, may prove quite functional. The speakers might not be at all interested in understanding each other; rather, suggests Kursh, they have their eyes on "pleasing the crowds" that are their constituents. As a further illustration of this point, Kursh writes

> The fuzziness, the lack of clarity, the meaninglessness of the ordinary political speech can be an important tool in getting a working majority—and a consensus, however arrived at, may be vital for the well-being or even existence of a nation.

The possibility that poor communication may be functional is raised not with the purpose of advocating it; rather, it is raised to point out the importance of recognizing that the cause of misunderstanding and poor communication may go far beyond the problems of speaking and listening well, to the fundamentally different life experiences and intrinsic values of the individual, group, organization, or nation, thus yielding quite different spontaneous responses. In these circumstances, there is not a problem in communications but a fundamental conflict in deep-rooted life experiences, cultures, and perspectives. Where good communication and understanding is called for, skillful reflective listening without making evaluative judgments will go a long way toward accomplishing it. "Managers who overcome the language barrier in their own organizations will find their interactions . . . vastly more productive."[6]

NONVERBAL COMMUNICATION[7]

Body Language—Conflict or Congruence between Verbal and Physical Signals[8]

If we are even minimally sensitive, most of us have some skill at interpreting the many sets of signals (often called *constellations*) we receive from facial expressions, hand movements, and other body movements people exhibit. What people mean, as contrasted with what they say, is often most explicitly revealed through these complex sets of body language signals. Most of us, within our own culture, are able to interpret correctly obvious examples of these *constellations*:

• Male-female "magnetism," which results in a complex set of signals that may or may not be consistent with the words spoken.
• An authoritarian boss, "taught" to be a participative manager, signals through grimaces, frowns, changes in eye contact, folding arms, or other body language whenever a subordinate, whose ideas he or she does not respect, ventures one.
• One person involved in an intense conversation with another notices that the other party signals that the psychological distance, and sometimes even the physical distance, between them has increased through the loss of eye contact, expressions of annoyance, changes in posture, and other signs.

All of these are examples of complete sets of clues that some of us "read" accurately and others, less sensitive to physical manifestations influencing communication, hardly notice.

Body language talks, sometimes more clearly than the words we say. If you have ever tried to communicate with someone who does not speak your language and were forced to get your message across through gestures and facial expressions, you understand the power of body language. Or if you consider telephone conversations, in which each party cannot see the other's expressions (with the consequent miscommunication), or the blind, who have to receive all their signals through the interpretation of voice inflection, then you will recognize the importance of physical accompaniments to verbal signals.

Body language is one means of communication; it is one language among others, including the language we speak, and the language of space, time, and things. It is also largely unconscious and spontaneous. We usually do not particularly notice it, in ourselves or others, and therefore we often miss an important element of the total communication process.

These nonverbal messages may either confirm or deny the verbal messages accompanying them (or be neutral, unintended, or misinterpreted). As an important part of the total communications package, we need to learn to "read" the complex sets of physical elements in messages sent and to resolve any conflicts we perceive between the physical and verbal signals.

A complication exists, however: sets of nonverbal signals vary immensely, not only between individuals but between cultures and in connection with the context of the total communication. Take this ubiquitous symbol in the American society:

A smile. What does it mean when it is

a. accompanied by a gun in your ribs and the admonition to "stick 'em up"?
b. accompanied by the phrase "have a nice day," said routinely by the supermarket checker?
c. preceded by the message from your boss that you have just goofed badly and need to watch your step?
d. exhibited by a used car salesperson trying to sell you a clunker?

To complicate matters further, what does a smile mean in different cultures, to say nothing of different kinds of smiles, such as a thin-lipped smile from a Texas rancher, a toothsome smile from a Japanese businessman, an indulgent smile from a Boston Brahmin dowager, a diffident smile from a shy Pakistani woman, or an eye-twinkling smile from an Irishman?

These signals are given in interrelated sets or constellations and, in context within our own culture, may be easily "read" by most of us if we pay attention to our spontaneous intuitive responses. Single signs or small sets of other facial and bodily signals are easily misinterpreted, especially if we are unfamiliar with the individual's background and life experiences. Eye contact is an especially difficult aspect of body language to read across different cultures. In her paper, Jane Lyman Holtz of the Harvard Business School focused on this problem:

> How we look and how we are looked at has a lot to do with our needs for approval, acceptance, trust and love—and we usually react accordingly. Looking is a non-tactile way to "touch" another. Looking away or not looking at all is a clear-cut sign of disinterest—of distancing oneself from another. Avoiding eye contact is a way of hiding true feelings, especially discomfort or guilt. People who feel insecure about themselves will avoid eye contact in a threatening situation but seek it when the situation is to their advantage. In such a way, characteristics of self-concept can be expressed through body language. The meanings of eye contact and avoidance differ across culture and social class. Albert Scheflen describes the differences he has observed between middle class Americans and working class Blacks and Puerto Ricans, and the misunderstandings that can arise from a lack of awareness or understanding: "In an interaction, Black males do not look at each other's faces as often as white middle class males do. By cultural prohibition, eye-to-eye gazing is considered rude. As a consequence of having used their gaze in this way for a lifetime, Blacks tend to avoid face-to-face gazing when they are talking with whites. Sensitive whites will often

respond by dropping their eyes also. Puerto Rican boys are taught to look down as a gesture of respect. We have seen middle class teachers try to force a lad to look them in the face. In one case, a Puerto Rican boy who was treated in this manner fled from the school in panic."[9]

Many other sets of clues are available to the astute observer; we express feelings with our hands, arms, legs, and total body posture. Once again, it is important to emphasize that these clues can be correctly interpreted only in context and only in constellations or large sets. As Holtz puts it, "No position, expression, or movement can be considered in isolation. Communication is a 'multi-channel' system. Body language is but one channel, interdependent with our use of time, space, things, and verbal language."

For the manager concerned about more accurate communication and the consequent better judgments and decisions, awareness of and increasing skill in interpreting body language appears to be an appropriate and useful adjunct to the tool kit.

COMMUNICATING WITH TIME, SPACE, AND THINGS

How Different Cultures Use Time, Space, and Things Differently

In the early 1960s, applied anthropologist Edward Hall published a classic book entitled *The Silent Language*, followed five years later by another, *The Hidden Dimension*.[10] In these books (highly recommended reading for managers), Hall demonstrated graphically how people inhabiting different cultures use time, space, and things to communicate messages and how people in those cultures, lacking knowledge of the differences, often miscommunicate. Dealing particularly with the American society, he demonstrated the many ways we send messages nonverbally, and in subsequent years a number of authors have extended his insights and applied them to management. We can learn two important lessons from Hall and others who have built on his ideas:

1. People around the world view time very differently than we do; they are equally or even more sensitive to spatial discriminations, and things carry many different messages to people in other parts of the world than they do for us.
2. Different parts of many countries, such as the United States, and different people in the same country often view time, space, and things differently. Managers from Texas have almost as much of a problem communicating with Bostonians as with Brazilians. A British multinational manager may have more difficulty communicating with a British "punk rocker" than with another manager in his own company from another country.

The Many Dimensions of Time

Professor Anthony G. Athos has noted that we have many ways of talking about time: "We have time, keep time, buy time and save time; we mark time, spend it, sell it and waste it; we kill time, pass time, take time and make time."[11] In the world of business and industry, we are concerned with overtime and flextime. We speak of "banker's hours" and consider the implications of the four-day work week. We worry about workaholic managers who spend too much time on the job and about malingering workers who spend too little.

In many parts of the United States, and particularly in connection with work, junior managers are very concerned about being "on time." And how we handle on-timeness communicates a good deal about an individual's relative status. An executive who has summoned subordinates to a meeting expects them to be on time for the meeting, but is not overly-concerned about keeping them waiting if he or she is busy. The subordinates, on the other hand, will often arrive ahead of the time set, even if it means they will cool their heels in the boss's waiting room until he or she is ready for them.

Managers of equal status sometimes will use time in somewhat subtle ways to communicate relative status. One manager calls another and asks him or her to be in his office at 10:00 A.M. for a conference. Whether or not he or she has a legitimate reason, the second manager, without explanation or apology, shows up ten minutes late. Nothing has been said, but a message has been given and received.

The amount of time we are willing to give another person also communicates a message, sometimes positive, sometimes negative. Consider the manager who interacts frequently with subordinates in their offices in a friendly or supportive way, contrasted with the manager who rarely leaves her or his office and only calls people in to critique their work. Or a boss who spends many hours coaching a subordinate, but gives little time to anyone else in the office. A signal has been given, and it has positive connotations for the recipient of the manager's time and negative connotations for everyone else.

The way different cultures and subcultures deal with time is often affected by elements peculiar to the culture. In Spain and Latin America, most work stops for at least two hours in the heat of the afternoon while people enjoy siesta. To make up for the hiatus, work continues until late in the evening and the dinner hour is advanced to 10:00 P.M.

When visitors from cultures where a much more relaxed attitude toward timeliness prevails come to the United States, their U.S. hosts may escort them on tightly scheduled visits that fit the hosts' concept of maximizing the effective use of time. The visitors often find it difficult to understand why it is necessary to be on time for appointments and find themselves exhausted at the end of a day of rigidly scheduled visits.

Lack of sensitivity to other people's ways of viewing time can trap us into inappropriate behavior toward them. Professor Athos recounts an interesting example of this:

> Using time to manipulate or control others is common, even if we who do so are unaware of it. I once hired a Mexican-American gardener on a monthly contract to care for my yard. When we were discussing the arrangements, I felt somewhat uncertain that he would do all I wanted done or do it to my satisfaction. My feelings of mistrust were expressed by focusing on time. I wanted to know precisely what day of the week he would come and how many hours he would stay. He seemed to understand and said, "Thursdays. Four hours."

Well, he actually did come on Thursdays once in a while but he also came on every other day of the week except Sunday and Monday. He never to my knowledge stayed four hours even when I happened to be home. I was sure I was being "taken" until it occurred to me that the yard had never looked so good and that everything really needing to be done was done.

The gardener apparently thought in terms of planting and cutting and fertilizing cycles. He felt his duty was to the yard, not to me. He sent me bills about every three or four months and then he often had to ask me what I owed him. He trusted me completely to pay him what he deserved. He worked in terms of seasons of the year, and I was trying to pin him down to an hourly basis. My attempt to replace my mistrust with the brittle satisfactions of controlling another person, in time, would eventually have led him to quit or me to fire him. I was lucky to see what was going on and I left him alone. We got along fine.[12]

Clearly the ways we handle time communicate many different messages about how we feel, and, not infrequently, unconscious and unintended messages account for many of the problems in communication between people.

The Hidden Language of Space

We communicate a good deal about ourselves and how we feel about others by how we use space. The best example of this, apparent to all who work in organizations, involves the strong values connected with the size and locations of offices. Although ambiguities are sometimes caused by the purposeful or accidental flouting of the basic values, almost anyone can walk into a plant or office for the first time and accurately estimate the relative status of those working there by observing the circumstances of the individual workplaces.

Borrowing heavily from Edward Hall's work, Athos has identified five basic values that most of us assume when concerned about work space:

1. *More is better than less.* Many a battle has been fought by executives over the size of their offices. While the acute concern felt by most people about office size has its amusing aspects, most organizations have found it expedient to be sure that office size accurately reflects the rank of the person occupying it.
2. *Private is better than public.* In general, secretaries work in open spaces, junior managers often work in cubicles enclosed only by room dividers or in offices with several other inhabitants, while senior managers have private offices where doors can be closed.
3. *Higher is better than lower.* Senior executives usually have their offices in upper floors of office buildings. When people speak about the "seventh floor," in the U.S. State Department offices in Washington, D.C., they are referring to the offices of the secretary and undersecretary. In other organizations, "Let's go upstairs with this" means "Let's go see the boss." Being "kicked upstairs" means an ineffective manager is being given the boot from a sensitive operating position to the implied (but false) status of an empty office in the executive suite.
4. *Near is better than far.* At a large government laboratory, the executive offices are referred to as "Mahogany Row." The director's suite of offices is at one end of

Mahogany Row, the associate director's office is next in line, and the rank of other executives is directly related to how near their offices are to the director's.

5. *In is better than out.* We speak of the "in group." An executive's office may be located, for business reasons, far from the seat of power or even, in large organizations, in another city. However, when visiting headquarters, if she or he sits near the boss at the conference table, that executive is "in."

While much of the above noted uses of space and the values connected with them are similar to those of other cultures, the needs, values, and customs connected with *interpersonal space* vary considerably from one culture to another. Hall has identified the often fascinating cross-cultural differences, and indeed the differences between people from the same culture, in regard to their feelings about and behavior regarding what he calls their "bubble of personal space." Degrees of tolerance for closeness to others varies tremendously between individuals and are sometimes related to race or ethnic factors, sometimes to status or social position, and sometimes to both.

The phrase "keep your distance" is germane to this phenomenon. While Latin or Arab males frequently embrace or talk nose-to-nose, British and Nordic males prefer to converse, even intimately, at a "respectable" distance. When those of one persuasion intrude on the "territory" of those who feel differently, sometimes amusing and sometimes tragic or dysfunctional results can be observed. In the United States, an insecure manager usually prefers to keep a desk or equivalent space between himself and a subordinate, while that same manager might be perfectly comfortable with closer contact with peers.

So, communication can be facilitated or can break down as a consequence of sensitivity to the "proper" uses of space and time.

Things Signal Status

People of high status sometimes try to lessen the manifestations of their higher levels in their society by downplaying the importance of things; people of lower status rarely do so. In most cultures, the possession of (more, bigger, expensive, unique, beautiful) things connotes status, wealth, education, and taste; all in contrast to (less, smaller, cheaper, common, ugly) things possessed by those less fortunate. Some relish and even flaunt the former; others feel guilty about or wish to hide their good fortune.

Those who possess less sometimes want to signal more than they have to the world, for example, the economically deprived individual who drives a Cadillac. Or, we see the opposite, for example, the wealthy individual who prefers a modest home and a compact car.

In summation, like time and space, things emit signals that are part and parcel of the complex communication process. Managers who wish to communicate effectively need to pay as much attention to these signals as to those received from effective listening to verbal messages and knowledgeable observation of sets of clues from body language. Managers who operate in subcultures of the United States and in cultures other than their own need to recognize the difficulties in expression verbally, physically, and with regard to time, space, and things. People everywhere are extraordinarily sensitive to the values embodied in their cultures. An effective manager takes all the facets of communication into account when interacting with individuals and groups and when making important decisions.

QUESTIONS FOR REFLECTION AND DISCUSSION

1. What can managers to do improve their listening skills?
2. What can managers do to improve their ability to send and receive nonverbal signals?
3. What can managers do to improve their sensitivity to the way others perceive time, space, and things?
4. What can managers do to improve their communications skills?

NOTES

1. R. N. Bostrom, *Listening Behavior: Measurement & Application* (New York: Guilford, 1990); and J. Brownell, *Building Active Listening Skills* (Englewood Cliffs, NJ: Prentice-Hall, 1986).
2. S. I. Hayakawa, *Symbol, Status and Personality* (New York: Harcourt Brace Jovanovich, 1956).
3. Hayakawa, *Symbol, Status and Personality*, pp. 32–33.
4. Carl Rogers and F. J. Roethlisberger, "Barriers and Gateways to Communication," *Harvard Business Review*, July/August 1952, reprinted November/December 1991, pp. 105–11.
5. Charlotte Olmstead Kursh, "The Benefits of Poor Communication," *The Psychoanalytic Review*, 1971, pp. 189–208.
6. Richard D. Massimilian, "The New Language Barrier: Closer to Home Than You Think," *Business Horizons*, July/August, 1990.
7. Robert Rosenthal, ed., *Skills In Nonverbal Communications: Individual Differences* (Cambridge, MA: Oelgeschlager, Gunn & Hain, 1979).
8. C. L. McKenzie, and C. J. Oazi, "Communication Barriers In The Workplace," *Business Horizons*, March/April, 1983.
9. Jane Lyman Holtz, *Communication: The Use of Body Language* (Boston: Harvard Business School, 1973).
10. Edward T. Hall, *The Silent Language* (Westport: Greenwood Press, 1980), reprint of 1973 edition; and *The Hidden Dimension* (Garden City: Doubleday, 1966).
11. Anthony G. Athos and R. E. Coffey, *Behavior in Organizations: A Multidimensional View* (Englewood Cliffs, NJ: Prentice-Hall, 1968).
12. Athos and Coffey, *Behavior in Organizations*, pp. 70–71.

CHAPTER 8

THE EFFECTIVE USE OF POWER[1]

Acquiring and using power effectively is necessary for survival in organizations, for managing relationships, and for individual fulfillment.[2] The manager's sense of self-esteem, desire for self-fulfillment, and competence is enhanced by his or her ability to use power effectively. While power can be an attribute of political systems, organizations, and groups as well as individuals, this chapter will focus primarily on power as individual managers use it in social relationships within organizations. The one important exception to this emphasis on individual power is a discussion of ways that group power can be used to solve problems.

A simple but conceptually correct definition of power is the *capacity to influence the behavior of others*. Power in this sense is value-neutral. We can only judge the effectiveness of the use of power by observing the context of the social relationships involved and the outcomes of attempts to influence.

For individuals, power exists on two levels:

- as a motive;[3] and
- as behavior.[4]

The need to feel in control, to influence, to organize groups, to become, and to grow are examples of power on the motivational level. At this level, power is latent or potential. When these motives are translated into action, power is manifested in behavior. This chapter deals with the action-oriented, behavioral aspects of power.

In organizations, the potential power of the individual manager is embedded in the networks of social interactions that are part of the work setting. In power interactions, the one who exercises power attempts to influence a recipient. In some interactions, the attempts to influence will be reciprocal, and the recipient and the exerciser of power will exchange places.

Note: This chapter is reprinted (with minor modifications) from *Business Horizons*, May/June 1986, Copyright 1986 by the Foundation for the School of Business at Indiana University, and is used with permission.

One-sided relationships have only one recipient and one wielder of power. The behavior of the one who exercises power can be perceived by the recipient as negative (P–) or positive (P+). The behavior is considered negative when the recipient perceives it as exploitation, manipulation, or win-lose competition. The person on the receiving end is always in a losing position in these situations. Recipients see power positively when they benefit from the situation. That benefit may be economic, symbolic, or personal. When the person on the receiving end perceives power as positive, the interaction takes on a win-win character. The recipient senses support, increased motivation, and ego enhancement.[5]

THE BEHAVIORAL BASES OF POWER

Theoretical and empirical studies of organizational behavior have defined eight behavioral bases of power that can be used to influence another person or group. Anyone can develop the skills to use most of these power bases in order to maximize individual effectiveness in forwarding the goals of the organization. The eight bases of power we will examine are

- reward;
- coercion;
- authority;
- referent (charisma, reciprocity, and track record);
- expert;
- information;
- affiliation; and finally,
- group power.

Reward Power

When managers give a positive stroke, some form of remuneration, awards, or any symbolic gesture that is seen as a compliment, they are exercising reward power. The behaviors involved are either verbal or nonverbal interactions with those on the receiving end.

By definition, reward power is P+. Its magnitude depends, however, on the recipient's perception of the meaning of the behavior. A promotion or a sizable bonus has more positive power than a complimentary letter. Personally appearing at the employee's work site to deliver a compliment has more positive power than a phone call.

Coercion Power

The manager demonstrates coercion power by injuring another person physically or psychologically. Coercive behaviors are verbal and nonverbal put-downs, slights, symbolic gestures of disdain, or actual physical attacks. A demotion, an unwanted transfer, or the withholding of needed resources are more extreme forms of coercion power. Coercion power is perceived as P–.

Authority Power

The legitimate right of a manager to control and the concomitant obligation of others to obey confirms authority power. This power base has both positive and negative aspects. The increased use of reward power under the appropriate circumstances usually results in higher motivation and loyalty. The overuse of authority power, however, can have negative consequences.

Authority power is best used as a potentiality rather than an actuality. Behaving as "the boss" too often may be seen as P–. Recipients can short circuit authority power in subtle or undetected ways. The manager may be buying short-term compliance at the expense of long-term commitment. But in times of crisis or need, the exercise of leadership based on authority normally will be perceived as P+ (see Chapter 10).

Referent Power

Referent power is in the eye of the beholder. Managers have referent power when someone identifies with them. The identification can be based upon personal characteristics that are seen as charismatic, but the perception of charisma is totally dependent upon the recipient who envies or feels a need to be identified with these somewhat mystical powers. One doesn't build charismatic power; either it's there or it isn't. The identification can also be based on "track record";[6] people want to be associated with a winner.

A more common form of referent power, one that anyone can acquire, is reciprocal identification, which sometimes means friendship. In this case the referent power is developed through associating with another individual, sharing personal information, or providing something of value to someone else. Managers can build on common interests, values, viewpoints, and preferences to allow other people to get to know them. This process, when used with rewards and information, leads to a reciprocal relationship. Either person can call on the other in time of need; in effect, each has IOUs out that can be called in. In this context, referent power or reciprocity in an organizational setting is very similar to reciprocity in a social setting. When someone invites us to dinner, we feel an obligation to return the favor by inviting him or her to dinner. The same sense of obligation operates for favors given in an organizational setting. We try to repay favors, invitations, and other positive strokes.

Because of the identification factor, referent power is usually seen as P+.

Expert Power

When managers have specialized knowledge that is valued by another person, they have the potential for expert power. When the need arises, this power can be exercised to help another person or group. When expert power is solicited and given, it is perceived as P+. However, the unsolicited use of expert power can be seen as an unwanted intrusion and therefore is P–.

Expert power used by itself is a very limited power base. Its continual use can put barriers between a manager and others that may be difficult to remove.

The way expert power is delivered is critical in forming the perceptions of the recipient. Expert advice given in a condescending or authoritative manner will be seen as a put-down. Such power will be perceived as P–, as will withholding expertise in time of need.

Information Power

The information power base depends upon access to information that is not public knowledge. Managers may have access to this information because of their position or because of connections within the organization. For example, they may have used referent power to build reciprocal relationships that give them information through informal channels.[7]

Information power can exist at all levels of the organization. It is entirely possible, in some closed organizations, that executives at the top have less information about what is going on within the organization than the people in the middle or even the lower levels.

A secretary to a senior executive has information power. Not only is there access to information, but there is also the ability to control the flow of information to and from the senior executive.

Affiliation Power

Affiliation power is borrowed from an authority or leadership source with whom a person is associated. For example, executive secretaries and staff assistants reporting to high-level officers can manifest affiliation power by acting as surrogates for the authority figure. If they are acting according to the wishes of the person who actually has the authority, this is a legitimate and appropriate use of power. On the other hand, if it is apparent to recipients that the exerciser of this power is acting out of self-interest, it is clearly P–. Another example of negative affiliation power occurs when critical interfaces in the organization are used to obstruct or block performance. For instance, when the wielder of power interprets accounting or personnel policies rigidly, borrowing authority from his or her interpretation of rules and regulations, those on the receiving end usually perceive it as P–.

Group Power (See also Chapters 15 through 19)

Group power involves a number of individuals interacting in problem solving, conflict resolution, or creative brainstorming. This power base can be considered P+ only when the group resolution of the problem or situation is greater than the individual contributions—when the group reaches a synergistic solution.

This result requires careful design and management of the group process. When this end is accomplished, however, individuals will have a greater commitment to problem solving and action than would have been possible if one or two members had dominated the proceedings. When a few people dominate, the usual result is groupthink which is P– (see Chapter 17).[8]

STEPS FOR BUILDING REFERENT POWER

Many executives seem unaware of or unskilled in the acquisition and use of referent power. Although it has the most potential, it is the least used base of power. Organizational power seems comparable to that in a storage battery, which is draining even as it sits on the shelf. Acquiring referent power is one of the easiest and quickest ways for effective executives to keep their batteries charged.

Some people have found these guidelines helpful in building referent power:

- *Get to know your colleagues.* Apply your knowledge about motivations, preferences, values, past history, and interests. This insight is important in order to understand their spontaneous behavior.
- *Build your relationship on shared interests, motivations, and goals.*
- *Respect different interests.* This will include goals and values; do not attack or disdain another person's style.
- *Use reward power and positive reinforcement.*[9] Giving positive strokes, when deserved or needed, is the cheapest and easiest way to build a relationship. Remember, the key to motivation is the need to be competent. When you affirm the competence of another person, they value you.
- *Invite reciprocal influence.* Show that you respect and want the perceptions, opinions, and information others have to offer.
- *Give your expertise and share information.* This is especially important when you don't stand to benefit by the results of your interventions.
- *Minimize status concerns.* Other than its charismatic aspect, referent power is based on reciprocal identification. People tend to relate to equals, not to superiors. You do not need to abdicate your authority or responsibility, but you should put the trappings of office in their proper place.
- *Become an expert communicator.* People value straightforward and noncontradictory messages. Develop both your verbal and nonverbal channels of communication for both transmitting and receiving or listening.
- *Get to know the informal political structure of the organization.*[10] The formal structure does not tell the whole story. In some instances, you may be able to build relationships without regard for the formal authority structure. In other cases, you may have to go through channels. By reading the environment, you can avoid some embarrassing incidents.
- *Get to know how people react to stress and crisis.* Trying to negotiate requests when another person is under stress may doom your attempts.

Some organizations, for example, defense contractors with several very large projects, use a matrix structure (see Chapter 21) where clear lines of authority are not always present. Work is performed not by order or edict, but by the functional organization on a negotiated basis with the program office. In such systems, using various power bases effectively is essential. Because of multiple programs and limited resources, conflict is an everyday occurrence. The key to conflict resolution is the ability to negotiate workable psychological contracts with colleagues who have no formal reporting obligations. The use of threats (coercion power) or appeals to higher authority can lead to long-term conflict. The party under siege can, at some time in the future, make use of affiliation power to retaliate.

Acquiring and using referent power effectively is important not only to managers in matrix organizations, but to all managers at any level in any organization. Effective managers either intuitively or reflectively develop preventive measures for lessening the impact of short-term conflicts over resources. Because most managers are not natural politicians, they have to develop behavioral and conceptual skills to effectively negotiate their needs.

CREATING CONDITIONS FOR GROUP POWER

In the day-to-day operations of an organization, the manager regularly and inevitably will either lead or participate in problem-solving groups. Usually participants in these groups leave the meetings with a feeling of frustration or futility. They tend to ask themselves, "Why do we waste our time this way?"

The reason for their frustration is quite simple: the group process was not understood and managed. When leaderless groups are left to develop on their own, they generally end up being controlled by the most vocal and power-oriented individuals. If the group contains individuals with different status levels, the high-status individuals can dominate the proceedings. On the other hand, groups directed by an appointed person with organizational status and authority run the risk of drifting into the groupthink mode.

Effective group problem solving needs to draw on positive group power, GP+, in order to be synergistic. This involves a reflective orientation on the part of the leaders and the participants in the group. The following steps are some behavioral guidelines for develop-ing GP+.

1. Ensure a climate of openness to opinions, perceptions, conflicts, and possibilities.
2. Use positive reinforcement to reward the contributions of others.
3. Ban the use of negative criticism toward individuals.
4. Clarify the objectives of the meeting. Is the agenda intended to find opportunities? To solve problems? To evaluate or implement? To inform? Is the meeting to result in consensus, plurality, simple majority decision, or no decision at all?
5. Divide the group process into four phases:
   a. The generation of opinions, perceptions, and alternatives.
   b. The development of criteria for judging alternatives.
   c. The trade-off phases, where the criteria are applied to the alternatives.
   d. The identification of action steps for implementation.
   These phases can take place in one session or over many meetings, depending upon the complexity of the problem.
6. To get the most contributions and reciprocal influence, manage the group process by assigning roles to individual group members:
   a. *The gatekeeper.* Tries to involve all participants in the problem-solving process, minimizes the use of premature evaluations, and brings hidden conflicts to the surface.
   b. *The clarifier.* Restates the opinions, perceptions, and attributions of others;.
   c. *The critical evaluator.* Analyzes and evaluates potential decisions at the end of any phase of the group.

7. Make creative use of the different styles in the group. By identifying the range of differences in the group, the potential biases are brought out in the open. The gatekeeper can use an understanding of these differences to elicit maximum contributions and to prevent conflicts over style rather than substance.

8. At the end of each meeting, set some time aside for the group to evaluate the process that took place at that meeting.

In groups or in other relationships, the manager who has developed referent power widely and who uses reward, expert, and information power effectively will almost certainly be able to influence the behavior of others in positive ways. The other power modes—coercion, authority, affiliation, and group—may be useful from time to time. But the manager who uses referent, reward, expert, and information power skillfully can contribute substantially to forwarding organizational goals.

QUESTIONS FOR REFLECTION AND DISCUSSION

1. What are the differences and similarities between authority and power?
2. What can managers do to improve their ability to acquire and use power more effectively?
3. What potential problems are there in the acquisition and use of power?
4. What kinds of situations have you seen in which power was abused? When was it used effectively?

NOTES

1. Jeffrey Pfeffer, *Managing With Power: Politics and Influence in Organizations* (Boston: Harvard Business School Press, 1992).

2. Robert N. McMurry, "Power and the Ambitious Executive," *Harvard Business Review*, November/December, 1973.

3. David C. McClelland and David H. Burnham, "Power is the Great Motivator," *Harvard Business Review*, March/April, 1976.

4. Abraham Zaleznik and Manfred F. R. Kets de Vries, *Power and the Corporate Mind*, 2nd ed. (Chicago: Bonus Books, 1985).

5. Rensis Likert and Jane Gibson Likert, *New Ways of Managing Conflict* (New York: McGraw-Hill, 1976), pp. 269–75.

6. John P. Kotter, *Power and Influence* (New York: The Free Press, 1985).

7. Robert E. Kaplan, "Trade Routes: The Manager's Networks of Relationships," *Organizational Dynamics*, Spring 1984.

8. Irving Janis, *Groupthink: Psychological Studies of Policy Decisions and Fiascos*, 2nd ed. (Boston: Houghton-Mifflin, 1982).

9. Robert D. Shaffer, "Things I Have Learned the Hard Way," *Consulting Psychology Bulletin*, Winter/Spring, 1991.

10. Abraham Zaleznik, "Power and Politics in Organization Life," *Harvard Business Review*, May/June, 1970.

CHAPTER 9

DELEGATION: A PROCESS AND A MANAGEMENT SKILL

To delegate, according to a dictionary definition, is "to commit powers or functions to another as agent or deputy." Around this seemingly simple concept, however, basic issues of management are frequently argued and a good many myths and stereotypes have developed. Some theorists have suggested that a person be granted authority commensurate with the responsibilities assigned.[1] In real organizations with individuals and groups increasingly interdependent,[2] we can never have authority over all those upon whom we are dependent to fulfill our assigned duties. Neither authority nor power can be fully delegated, but must be earned by both the delegator and the people to whom he or she delegates. Other theorists have suggested that after delegating a task, the delegator should leave the delegatee alone to finish the task. Again, in real organizations it does not work that way. Effective delegation is not abdication and requires checks on progress.[3]

Every manager delegates; it is virtually impossible for an individual to do all of the work of the organizational unit he or she manages. Indeed, "an executive who attempts to do everything usually winds up accomplishing nothing."[4] In professionally oriented organizations in particular, he or she frequently knows less than the subordinates about the details of the tasks assigned to the unit. What is delegated and the degree to which a manager delegates may vary widely from manager to manager and organization to organization.[5]

THE PROCESS OF DELEGATION

Fundamentally, the manager delegates work: an activity, a task, or an objective that someone else is expected to carry out. Once delegated, these become "duties" of the person to whom the work was delegated. Typically, an effective manager identifies all of the work that needs to be done, decides to do some portion of it him or herself, and divides the remainder among other people in the unit. The duties delegated can be defined in two ways: as *functions* or activities, or in terms of the *results* expected.[6] The manager can say, for instance, that a certain engineer is accountable for the performance of particular kinds of tests or that a draftsman is to draw design sketches for a certain product. Or, the manager can tell the engineer that an analysis of all test reports is required by 4:00 P.M. each day. In the former instances, functions are assigned; in the latter, certain results are expected.

Along with the assignment of duties, the delegator expects the delegatee to acquire the power necessary to carry out the duties assigned. The engineer must have or acquire the materials, instruments, and space needed to conduct the tests. If necessary, others must be willing to help in order to get all the tests done in time to have the reports ready when required each day. The acquisition of power is not a simple matter; there are a number of restrictions on the amount and kind of power at the manager's disposal (see Chapter 8).[7]

When we delegate in terms of expected results, we are managing by objectives (see Chapter 14).[8] We are saying to a subordinate, "I am holding you accountable for these end results and will evaluate your work in terms of your ability to meet the objectives implied." In addition to the assignment of duties and the acquisition of power, delegation involves an assumption that the delegatee will feel obliged to make his or her best effort to carry out the duties assigned. That is, they will feel responsible for completing the assignment.

The interrelationships among these three elements of delegation—duties, power, and responsibility—are apparent. Delegation is not real unless all three are present. Duties must be assigned as clearly as possible, some measure of power must be acquired, and responsibility must be assumed.

In trying to delegate effectively, managers run into trouble in all three of these areas. They may fail to spell out duties and objectives clearly enough or may themselves take on more of the activities of their organization than they can possibly accomplish. They may fail to recognize the limits of the power available to them or others. They may make assumptions about the abilities of their subordinates that are unrealistic; that is, they may delegate to people who do not have the motivation or skills necessary to assume the responsibilities for duties delegated to them. Delegation is, in fact, a managerial skill and like all skills, it can be and needs to be acquired.

In assigning duties, for instance, the effective manager soon learns the advantages of several specific kinds of behavior. He or she learns that assigned activities must be as specific as possible, but also learns that the process of making them specific can range from telling a subordinate exactly what to do and when to do it, to participating with the subordinate to decide what activities need to be accomplished to achieve these objectives. In both cases, delegation has taken place, but the motivation and job satisfaction of the subordinate will be greater when he or she participates in the process than when he or she is told what to do, as we learned from Chapter 5.[9]

Delegation is, in fact, a complex *process*. It is influenced by cultural factors in the organization and the individual. It is dependent on the kind and degree of power exerted and the ability and willingness of individuals to assume responsibility for assigned duties and eventual results. The process of delegation demonstrates the function of these and other variables in organizational dynamics. We can construct a model based on these variables that serves to integrate much of what we have said earlier or will cover in later chapters about culture, power, motivation, and management by objectives. Diagrammatically, the model would look like this:

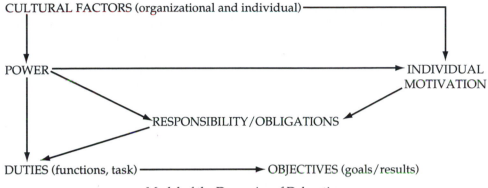

Model of the Dynamics of Delegation

This model can be superimposed on any organizational structure. It illustrates the essential dynamics of delegation in a functionally organized system, a project-oriented organization, or even a matrix organization, which combines the functional and project systems. The relative importance of the various elements of the model will vary somewhat depending on the particular structure to which it is applied, but the fundamental dynamics are the same.

People and their behavior are incorporated into this model by implication; culture influences both the way power is used and the individual's motivation, which in turn influence feelings of responsibility and the resulting behavior in carrying out assigned functions and tasks and in achieving desired objectives. Finally, pressures from forces external to the organization that may influence the delegation process are also incorporated in the model by implication and such pressures might influence any or all of the factors.

Skillful managers of professional people therefore need to look at delegation from a number of points of view as they try to evaluate their own ability to delegate effectively. Managers need to understand the cultural influences on themselves and on other people. They need to assess the influence of the particular organizational and subgroup structures, methods of operation, and environmental forces. They need to understand the influence of expectations, self-image, and personal attributes on themselves and those to whom they delegate in order to predict the kinds of behavior that may emerge from the delegation process.

CULTURES AND SUBCULTURES

The way cultures and subcultures influence delegation can be observed in any organization whose work is based on professional or technical expertise, such as medicine, law, accounting, science, or engineering. Almost all of the professional people, whether they be managers or members of the technical staff, have been educated in, and received many of their basic cultural or value orientations from, the technical disciplines. The Ph.D. scientist has not only learned about physics, chemistry, or electronics while working for his or her degree, but has also, and perhaps more importantly, learned the difference between good and bad research. The scientific method is a discipline in itself, and it carries with it a system of values different from, and in many ways in conflict with, the values normally embraced by those whose careers are directed toward learning how best to manage people and organizations. However, most managers of research and development were scientists or engineers first; they chose to move from science to management and from one system of rewards to another.

Consider the manager who was educated as a physicist and from experience reflects a science orientation. Since this manager's more recent aspirations, self-expectations, and experience are oriented to management, he or she also reflects a managerial orientation. When this manager seeks to delegate to R&D staff people who retain primarily the *subculture* of science, two kinds of conflict emerge: first, the manager has both a science and managerial orientation that must be reconciled or rationalized; second, the R&D staff people involved may be far less willing to bend their scientific subculture than is the manager. These differences in subcultures may result in ineffective delegation and, sometimes, in dysfunctional behavior on the parts of those who may perceive some kind of threat to their culture. Consciously or subconsciously, the scientist may refuse to accept responsibility for the duties delegated.

Operationally, this sort of situation, variations of which are seen in almost any organization employing significant numbers of professional people, requires the manager to diagnose accurately the cultures and probable behaviors derived therefrom. It is particularly important that the manager recognize the vital role of the higher order motivators to professionals: they will respond to delegation based on reward, referent, or expert power but will tend to reject assignments based on formal authority or coercion.

DELEGATION, ORGANIZATIONAL STRUCTURE, AND POWER

Regardless of the structure of a particular organization, the intelligent use of power is at the heart of the delegation process. We have said earlier that some measure of support needs to be given by one who delegates, but we have also suggested that real power is informal and is generated by factors other than the position of the delegator or delegatee on the organizational chart and also is not dependent on the particular structure of a particular organization. We have noted further that power is difficult or impossible to delegate because it is a result of the power base established by each individual.[10]

To illustrate, we can observe two different organizational structures inhabited largely by professionals and see how the alternative uses of power influence the process of delegation in each. One is the familiar functional organization characterized by a hierarchy of positions in top and middle management and a line and staff divisional/departmental structure. The other is the matrix organization with a project management structure superimposed on the functional organization and characterized by the importance of peer relationships (see Chapter 21).[11] The first is governed by a functional subculture, the second by a "coordinative" subculture. If we observe what actually happens in effective organizations of both types, we will notice that the main differences occur at the middle management (or project director) level, and that these differences have more to do with power than delegation.

DELEGATION AND EXTERNAL PRESSURES

Different kinds of organizations differ considerably in the degree to which they respond to external pressures, or even in regard to the extent to which they are ordinarily subjected to such pressures. They differ even more in how the delegation process is affected by pressures from outside of the organization.

Some government agencies, staffed primarily with high-level civil servants, are influenced very little by changes in administration or funding. Others are turned upside down every few years as politics, policies, and people turn over. Some businesses and industries are cyclical—they experience boom and bust periods with attendant changes in morale, staffing, and profit. Others maintain a moderate but steady growth no matter what happens to the economy. Some industries are subject to heavy pressures from residents in the communities where they operate while others never hear from their neighbors. Some organizations experience a steady, moderate influence to change while others appear to be subject to a constant stream of emergencies.

The process of delegation within the organization is not impervious to these external pressures and influences. In organizations with a low tolerance for mistakes or errors, a crisis may lead people to be less willing to assume responsibility for duties delegated. Conversely, if the organization encourages risk taking and views mistakes or errors as learning experiences, a crisis may lead people to be more willing to assume responsibility for duties delegated. Frequently observed tendencies in the organizations with a low tolerance for mistakes include more reliance on formal authority, tougher controls exerted from the top down, and changes in policy that filter down slowly through the organization and preclude real delegation until absorbed at lower levels. In the more far-sighted organizations that view errors as learning experiences, management and the organizational culture buffers individuals in the organization against at least some of the external pressures and emergencies. Where this occurs, the delegation process, especially if it is an effective one, remains intact.

DELEGATION AND BEHAVIOR

Given these internal and external influences on the process of delegation, the actual behavior of managers and subordinates is subject to a number of obstacles to effective delegation, which have been spelled out by Newman, Summer, and

Warren.[12] They list a number of possible reasons why a boss may fail to delegate, as follows:

1. The executive has gotten trapped in the "I can do it better myself" fallacy.
2. The executive lacks the ability to direct.
3. The manager lacks confidence in subordinates.
4. An absence of sensitive controls that might warn of impending difficulties.
5. Finally, the manager has a temperamental aversion to taking a chance.

On the other side of the fence, they have also identified several obstacles to a subordinate's accepting responsibility for the duties delegated:

1. The subordinate often finds it easier to ask the boss than to decide for himself or herself how to deal with a problem.
2. The subordinate fears criticism for mistakes.
3. The subordinate believes that he or she lacks the necessary information and resources to do a good job.
4. The subordinate lacks self-confidence.
5. Inadequate incentives are provided.

None of these obstacles are absolutes. Their removal occurs when the skilled manager responds to the model of the process of delegation we have postulated. Thus, by being sensitive to and understanding of those around her or him, an effective manager delegates properly, monitors progress, and thus ensures a more productive organization.

QUESTIONS FOR REFLECTION AND DISCUSSION

1. What are the differences and similarities between assigning specific activities and specific objectives?
2. How can managers determine when another person has the ability and motivation to acquire the power they need to successfully complete a job? How can the manager help?
3. What can managers do to improve their sensitivity to the cultural and subcultural forces influencing delegation?
4. What can managers do to improve their effectiveness as delegators?

NOTES

1. William H. Newman, *Administrative Action* (Englewood Cliffs, NJ: Prentice-Hall, 1951).
2. John P. Kotter, "Power, Dependence, and Effective Management," *Harvard Business Review*, July/August 1977.
3. Rosabeth M. Kanter, *The Change Masters* (New York: Simon & Schuster, 1983), p. 250.
4. Edward J. Mayo and Lance P. Jarvis, "Delegation 101: Lessons From the White House," *Business Horizons* September/October 1988.
5. Glenn H. Matthews, "Run Your Business or Build an Organization?" *Harvard Business Review*, March/April 1984.

6. Robert H. Schaffer, "Demand Better Results—And Get Them," *Harvard Business Review,* November/December 1974.

7. Jeffrey Pfeffer, *Managing With Power: Politics and Influence in Organizations* (Boston: Harvard Business School Press, 1992).

8. Peter F. Drucker, *The Practice of Management* (New York: Harper & Brothers, 1954).

9. John F. Donnelly, "Participative Management at Work," *Harvard Business Review,* January/February 1977.

10. John P. Kotter, *Power and Influence* (New York: The Free Press, 1985).

11. Stanley M. Davis and Paul R. Lawrence, "Problems of Matrix Organizations," *Harvard Business Review,* May/June 1978.

12. William H. Newman and Charles E. Summer, Jr., *The Process of Management: Concepts, Behavior and Practice,* 2nd ed. (Englewood Cliffs, NJ: Prentice-Hall, 1967), pp. 84–95.

CHAPTER 10

LEADERSHIP

On page 173 of the January 18, 1988, issue of *Fortune*, Warren Bennis says

> The difference between managers and leaders is fundamental. The manager administers, the leader innovates. The manager maintains, the leader develops. The manager relies on systems, the leader relies on people. The manager counts on control, the leader counts on trust. The manager does things right, the leader does the right thing.

He also notes that "America's vast industrial empire had been built by leaders . . . [but] inevitably, they were replaced by managers."

The tendency for the management literature to differentiate leadership and management is not new; Zaleznik made the point in 1977.[1] Given the current emphasis on leadership and the apparent decline of the U.S. industrial base compared to the Japanese and Germans, one may wonder why the leaders that built America were "replaced by managers," to use Bennis's words. It is particularly puzzling that America's industrial leaders were called "managers." What happened? Why are today's managers not leaders? One hypothesis might be that because of the emphasis given to systems analysis and linear thinking for the last several decades and the attempts, most notably exemplified by former Secretary of Defense Robert McNamara, to make management more "scientific," the words *manager* and *management* have evolved from the forties to the nineties and now have a different connotation: that of *administrator*, or worse, *bureaucrat*. Certainly, early writers in the field, such as Chester Barnard,[2] seemed to equate leadership of an organization and management. If Bennis is correct in stating that earlier generations of those called managers were also leaders, then it may well be possible that the current difference between the two is a function of an overemphasis on scientific management and linear thinking to the exclusion of nonlinear and contextual thinking essential to the more intuitive functions of leadership. The role of intuition, judgment, and contextual thinking is beginning to reappear in the management and leadership literature as evidenced by Peters and Waterman,[3] Simon,[4] Agor,[5] and Rowan,[6] among others. John Kotter notes "management and leadership are not mutually exclusive . . . the two are complementary and sometimes overlap."[7] If the word *manager* now connotes administrator and bureaucrat, perhaps our culture would be better served reverting to the earlier meaning as used by authors such as Barnard to include leadership as an essential skill.

If we consider the rapidly changing and increasingly complex technological, social, economic, and political environment in which most organizations in the world now must function, then it takes only a short step to conclude that an *effective* manager must be a good leader even when required to be a good administrator or bureaucrat. The examples of successful American companies used by Peters and Waterman seem to support this conclusion as does the increasing interest in intuition as a *managerial* skill.[8] Although in some organizations such as the military it may be possible to be a leader without having administrative skill, it is beginning to become apparent to at least a few observers that managers without leadership skills are not very effective, particularly at senior levels. If our society seems to be stuck with the word *manager* connoting administrator, perhaps we can overcome this problem by defining an *effective* manager as having both leadership *and* administrative skills.

If effective managers need to be good administrators *and* leaders, then what is a good leader and how can you become one? Are leaders born or made? This question has been asked for decades, if not centuries, and is still with us today. It is a question of genes or environment. Even those who favor environment are split over whether leaders can be trained. Whatever portion of leadership that is derived from either genes or environmental factors not susceptible to training is beyond the control of the practical executive, who, therefore, focuses his or her attention on what *can* be influenced.

The number of courses on leadership being offered by the military, industry, and consultants strongly suggests that some skills *can* be taught. Kouzes and Posner state "leadership is an observable, learnable set of practices" or behaviors.[9] But in every field of endeavor, whether in sports or in organizations, the level of skill achieved depends not only on the innate abilities inherent in the individual, but also on such factors as the motivation to excel, the extent of training, and the quality of coaching.

Although a cursory look at the current literature reveals a host of vague, sometimes contradictory definitions of leadership, a common component is the skill to influence others. In essence, an effective leader is able to influence other people to do those things that the leader desires. (In Chapter 4 we observed that it was "a manager's function to influence people." Indeed, the name of this book is *Influencing People in Organizations* and thus, in a very real sense, this whole book is about leadership.) For our purposes, a manager exerts leadership within an organizational framework consisting of a structure, cultures, and subcultures, individuals and groups, a set of tasks in support of goals, various measurement systems, and probably many other factors that facilitate or inhibit various behaviors.

Historically, among the earliest concepts employed to look at leaders and managers was the trait approach, which tried to identify the common individual characteristics that those identified as leaders seemed to possess. In an early study, Tead reported that the traits of an effective leader were nervous and physical energy, a sense of purpose and dedication, enthusiasm, friendliness, integrity, technical mastery, decisiveness, intelligence, teaching skills, and faith.[10] Barnard stated that the significant traits that distinguished leaders from their followers were physique, technical skill, perception, knowledge, memory, imagination, determination, persistence, endurance, and courage. Many other studies of leadership traits followed and these have been examined as a body by scholars such as Bass and Stogdill,[11] Yukl,[12] and others, while more recent successful leaders have been looked at by people such as Bennis,[13] Conger,[14] Kirkpatrick and Locke,[15] Peters and Waterman, and Kotter. Since most definitions of leadership include some element of influencing others and we have looked at Kotter's work on this subject in Chapter 4, let's look at what he has to say about the personal requirements or traits of successful leaders.

Kotter lists six personal requirements:

1. *Broad knowledge of the industry and the company.* This requirement is industry and company specific and therefore, an effective leader in one company or industry may not be an effective leader in another company or industry.
2. *Broad set of solid relationships in the firm and in the industry.* This trait describes effective "networks."
3. *Excellent reputation and a strong track record in a broad set of activities.* This requirement provides a source of power.
4. A *keen mind* (moderately strong analytical ability, good judgment, capacity to think strategically and multidimensionally) a*nd strong interpersonal skills* (the ability to develop good working relationships quickly, empathy, the ability to sell, sensitivity to people, and human nature). This requirement describes linear, nonlinear, and contextual skills, (see Chapter 2) and the interpersonal skills that are the focus of this book.
5. *High integrity.* This trait includes ethics and honesty.
6. *A high energy level and a strong drive to lead.* This trait derives from determination, motivation, and confidence.

An individual's traits do not seem sufficient by themselves to explain effective leadership. To a practicing executive it seems obvious that an effective leader's behavior is a critical factor and will depend not only on his or her own innate personal attributes including ethics and his or her own acquired skills but also on the situation, people, and tasks involved. It is not the purpose of this chapter to trace the historical evolution of the theories of leadership; they are many and varied and *Bass & Stogdill's Handbook of Leadership* covers most of them for those interested.

Within this context, two approaches to leadership have found some favor with both academics and managers: the transformational and situational approaches. Tichy and Ulrich made a significant contribution to the transformational approach by asserting that management has to perform three steps to transform an organization: 1) create a vision, 2) mobilize commitment, and 3) institutionalize change.[16] Bass describes the characteristics of the transformational leader as charisma, inspiration, intellectual stimulation, and individual consideration.[17]

The situational approach includes Tannenbaum and Schmidt's look at autocratic and democratic styles,[18] and Fiedler's contingency model focusing on task-oriented and relationship-oriented situations.[19] Blake and Mouton elaborated on this basic approach with their managerial grid approach,[20] and Hersey and

Blanchard added the followers maturity as a factor.[21] In essence, four leadership styles are in the Hersey and Blanchard model:

1. Telling—high task and low relationship behaviors with low follower maturity.
2. Selling—high task and high relationship behaviors with moderate follower maturity.
3. Participating—high relationship and low task behaviors with moderate follower maturity.
4. Delegating—low relationship and low task behaviors with high follower maturity.

One of the most useful and popular "models" of effective leadership, based on extensive field research and that seems to incorporate much of the earlier literature, has been put forth by Kouzes and Posner. They list five fundamental practices and ten (two each) commitments:

I. Challenging the process.
  1. Search for opportunities (including those presented by subordinates, see Chapter 11).
  2. Experiment and take risks.
II. Inspiring a shared vision.
  3. Envision the future.
  4. Enlist others.
III. Enabling others to act.
  5. Foster collaboration.
  6. Strengthen others.
IV. Modeling the way.
  7. Set the example.
  8. Plan small wins.
V. Encouraging the heart.
  9. Recognize individual contribution.
  10. Celebrate accomplishment.

Within this "model," the behavior of leaders may vary considerably depending on their own unique set of skills as well as the specific skills of the other people involved, the nature of the tasks to be performed, the environment and cultures involved, and a host of other factors, only some of which may be identified.

Kouzes and Posner also observe that "leadership is inextricably connected with the process of innovation." Therefore, since innovation can occur at any level in an organization, so can leadership. Kanter describes three steps middle managers take in the process of innovation: 1) define (and redefine) the project, 2) build a coalition, and 3) take action to handle interference and maintain momentum.[22] These various approaches to leadership seem more similar than different. Kanter's step 1 looks like a combination of Kouzes and Posner's steps 1, 2, 3 and 4. Her step 2 could be a combination of their steps 4, 5, and 6, and her step 3 could be a combination of their steps 7, 8, 9, and 10.

Although we would all like to find the quick-and-easy, step-by-step textbook answers to complex issues, a blind reliance on crutches such as checklists, someone's panacea, or an all-inclusive leadership theory or model seems counterproductive. Indeed, Senge argues that effective "leaders are designers, teachers, and stewards . . . [with] the ability to build shared vision, to bring to the surface and challenge prevailing mental models, and to foster more systematic patterns of thinking."[23] Clearly, this is a time-consuming, complex process, *not* a quick fix. Using models such as those developed by Kotter or Kouzes and Posner may provide potentially useful tools, but those who wish to be *effective* administrators and leaders need to develop an understanding of themselves, their innate characteristics, values, background, strengths, and weaknesses to the extent possible. They must develop the drive, motivation, and determination necessary for the hard work of honing their interpersonal sensitivities and skills and exercising their linear, nonlinear, and contextual capabilities. They need to find a coach in some form who can help them develop more rapidly and to a higher level than might be possible otherwise. They need to take advantage of every opportunity to gain the kind of experiences that will build confidence and shape future success. They need to use the models of leadership to remind themselves of some of the things that need to be done, and they also need to use their own skills and capabilities to build upon these models to identify other actions or behaviors that will contribute to the success of their leadership effort. They need to accept risks and shun complacency by recognizing that "failure teaches leaders valuable lessons, but good results only reinforce their preconceptions and tether them more firmly to their 'tried and true recipes or biases.'"[24] But *how* they should go about doing these things must be decided by each individual for herself or himself. As in all walks of life, reaching the highest levels in one's chosen profession requires hard work with few, if any, shortcuts or easy paths.

Whatever our personal attributes may be, we can improve our leadership skills by understanding and by work. How far any of us may go is limited by many factors including our personal attributes, but we *can* improve. It's up to us.

QUESTIONS FOR REFLECTION AND DISCUSSION

1. What are the differences and similarities between administrators and leaders?
2. What are the differences and similarities between the "trait" and "behavioral" theories of leadership?
3. What types of power do effective leaders acquire and use?
4. If both leaders and managers influence people, how can they do so more effectively?

NOTES

1. A. Zaleznik, "Managers and Leaders: Are They Different?" *Harvard Business Review,* May/June 1977.
2. C. Barnard, *The Functions of the Executive* (Cambridge, MA: Harvard University Press, 1938).
3. Thomas J. Peters and Robert H. Waterman, Jr., *In Search of Excellence* (New York: Harper & Row, 1982).

4. Herbert A. Simon, "Making Management Decisions: The Role of Intuition and Emotion," *Academy of Management Executive*, February 1987.

5. Weston H. Agor, "How Top Executives Use Their Intuitions to Make Important Decisions." *Business Horizons*, January/February 1986.

6. R. Rowan, *The Intuitive Manager* (Boston: Little, Brown and Co., 1986).

7. J. Kotter, *The Leadership Factor* (New York: The Free Press, 1988).

8. R. Rowan, *The Intuitive Manager* (Boston: Little, Brown and Co., 1986). See also endnote 15, Chapter 4.

9. J. Kouzes and B. Posner, *The Leadership Challenge* (Washington: Jossey-Bass, 1987).

10. O. Tead, *The Art of Leadership* (New York: McGraw-Hill, 1935).

11. Bernard M. Bass, *Bass & Stogdill's Handbook of Leadership*, 3rd ed. (New York: The Free Press, 1990); and "Leadership: Good, Better, Best." *Organizational Dynamics*, Winter 1985.

12. G. Yukl, *Leadership in Organizations* (Englewood Cliffs, NJ: Prentice-Hall, 1981).

13. W. Bennis, "The 4 Competencies of Leadership," *Training and Development Journal*, August 1984, pp. 14–19.

14. J. Conger, "Inspiring Others: The Language of Leadership," *Academy of Management Evecutive*, February 1991.

15. S. Kirkpatrick and E. Locke, "Leadership: Do Traits Matter?" *Academy of Management Executive*, May 1991.

16. N. M. Tichy and D. Ulrich, "The Leadership Challenge—A Call for the Transformational Leader," *Sloan Management Review*, Fall 1984.

17. Bernard M. Bass, "From Transactional to Transformational Leadership: Learning to Share the Vision," *Organizational Dynamics*, Winter 1990.

18. R. Tannenbaum and R. Schmidt, "How to Choose a Leadership Pattern," *Harvard Business Review*, May/June 1973, pp. 162–80.

19. F. E. Fiedler, *A Theory of Leadership Effectiveness* (New York: McGraw-Hill, 1967); and "The Leadership Game: Matching the Man to the Situation," *Organizational Dynamics*, Winter 1976.

20. Robert R. Blake and Jane S. Mouton, *The Managerial Grid* (Houston: Gulf Publishing, 1964); and *Building a Dynamic Corporation Through Grid Organization Development* (Reading, MA: Addison-Wesley, 1969).

21. Paul Hersey and Ken Blanchard, *Management of Organizational Behavior: Utilizing Human Resources* (Englewood Cliffs, NJ: Prentice-Hall, 1969); and *Management of Organizational Behavior* (Englewood Cliffs, NJ: Prentice-Hall, 1982).

22. R. Kanter, "The Middle Manager as Innovator," *Harvard Business Review*, July/August 1982, pp. 95–105.

23. P. Senge, *The Fifth Discipline: The Art and Routine of the Learning Organization* (New York: Doubleday Currency, 1990).

24. D. Miller, "The Icarus Paradox: How Exceptional Companies Bring About Their Own Downfall," *Business Horizons*, January/February 1992.

CHAPTER 11

MANAGING CREATIVITY

Effective managers, which we define as effective administrators and leaders, know their organizations need creativity and innovation to grow and prosper. But, as Rosabeth Moss Kanter points out in her book, *The Change Masters*,[1] and in her *Harvard Business Review* article and the video based on the article,[2] implementing a creative or innovative idea is hard work. A creative idea may derive spontaneously from the individual's intuition or judgment but its implementation will require a great deal of reflection and well-planned, tactful behavior.

Managers have many different attitudes toward creativity and how it should be managed. The problems differ depending on the nature of the goals and objectives of the organization involved. A research and development laboratory must obtain a constant flow of creative ideas to achieve its primary mission, while an assembly line operation may not be able to afford creative ideas because of the disruption they would cause. In order to clarify the difficulties of managing creativity, it may be useful to look at views from opposite ends of the spectrum. The view of the hard-nosed industrialist taking the production organization's perspective is probably best represented by Levitt in his article "Creativity Is Not Enough."[3] The permissive view of creativity is exemplified by those who ponder the way the world ought to be rather than the way it is. Our purpose here is to contrast these two views and try to tie them together and reconcile their arguments to help the effective manager cope with his or her own perspective of the problems of managing creativity.

THE PRODUCTION ORGANIZATION'S PERSPECTIVE

Levitt suggests that what is commonly construed as creativity "is not the miraculous road to . . . growth and affluence that is so abundantly claimed these days." Levitt argues that the organization's sometimes cold response to novel suggestions is understandable, if not in fact commendable. Noting that writers or experts in the social sciences (who are not managers, as Levitt takes great pains to point out) generally saddle the boss with the blame and responsibility for maintaining an environment that is unsympathetic to creativity. Levitt suggests why:

> Organization and creativity do not seem to go together while organization and conformity do. Advocacy of a "permissive environment" for creativity in an organization is often a veiled attack on the idea of the organization itself. This quickly becomes clear when one recognizes this inescapable fact: One of the collateral purposes of an organization is to be inhospitable to a great and constant flow of ideas and creativity.
>
> Whether we are talking about the United States Steel Corporation or the United Steel Workers of America, the U.S. Army or the Salvation Army, the United States or the U.S.S.R., the purpose of organization is to achieve the kind and degree of conformity necessary to do a particular job. . . . Without organization there would be chaos and decay. Organization exists in order to create that amount and kind of inflexibility that is necessary to get the most pressingly intended job done efficiently and on time.
>
> Creativity and innovation disturb that order. Hence, organization tends to be inhospitable to creativity and innovation, though without creativity and innovation it would eventually perish.

Why Doors Are Closed on Creativity

Most senior managers are extremely busy people trying to husband their time for the essential task of strategic long-range planning, but they are constantly drawn into the task of controlling the organization. Consequently, managers become involved in day-to-day operations and must constantly fight to relieve themselves of unnecessary burdens. There are always far more problems than managers are capable of handling personally, and they delegate the less significant problems and establish control systems to ensure that significant issues, out of line with planned expectations, are brought to their attention. Managers are constantly battling to keep their time free and to force decisions on problems to lower levels in the organization. As Toffler notes, many executives are required to make an ever-increasing number of decisions that are often dealing with less and less tangible factors and, indeed, some may be approaching their decision-making limits.[4] A bright young man or woman with a new creative idea on how the organization can do things better is frustrated by the resistance encountered. The reason, according to Levitt, is easy to understand. "But, as anyone who knows anything about any organization knows only too well, it is hard enough for a manager to get things done at all, let alone to introduce a new way of doing things no matter how good it may seem."

An important reason for an organization's lack of receptivity to creative ideas is that creativity in its most prevalent form often does not actually help. As Levitt sees it, advocates of creativity have failed to distinguish between the relatively easy process of being creative in the abstract and the infinitely more difficult process of being innovative in the concrete. A useful distinction can be drawn between the creative idea as an abstraction and its possible implementation in the real world. A novel idea may be interesting, but without an accompanying suggestion concerning how it might actually be implemented it might also be useless. Creativity, if it is to be of use, must go beyond the novel idea stage and also involve the ability to put ideas to work. Ideas must be translated into meaningful action.

As Levitt notes

> The major problem is that so-called creative people often (though certainly not always) pass off on *others* the responsibility for getting down to brass tacks. They have plenty of ideas but little businesslike follow-though. They do not make the right kind of effort to help their ideas get a hearing and a try.
>
> All in all, ideation is relatively abundant. It is its implementation that is more scarce. . . . Ideas do not implement themselves—neither in business nor in art, science, philosophy, politics, love, war. People implement ideas.

Without suggesting how his or her idea can be implemented—even with only some modest ball park suggestions of the risks, the costs, the manpower requisites, the time budgets, and the possible payoff—the person with the naked idea, however novel, has little of practical value to offer. Since organizations are uniquely "get-things-done" institutions, creativity without action-oriented follow-through is a strikingly barren form of individual behavior in Levitt's view.

Thus, from the point of view of the production organization, the problem with creativity is not entirely a matter of establishing a permissive environment for creativity. Furthermore, second thoughts can be formed about shifting the blame to the boss. The problem of creativity, considering the nature of organization, is that it often occurs in an unusable form. The creative person must present ideas responsibly and in a manner that includes suggestions for practical implementation.

Many social scientists could maintain that creativity is a unique and fragile talent and that imposing the burden of practical analysis, costs, risks, payoffs, and alternative means of implementation could destroy or inhibit it. As Levitt notes

> This is probably true. But this could be salutary, both for him and for the company. Ideas are useless unless used. The proof of their value is their implementation. Until then they are in limbo. If the executive's job pressures mean that an idea seldom gets a good hearing unless it is responsibly presented, then the unthrottled and irresponsible creative man is useless to the company. If an insistence on some responsibility for implementation throttles him, he may produce fewer ideas, but their chances of a judicious hearing and thereafter being followed through are greatly improved.

It has been said that managers ought to make an effort to communicate with the creative individuals in their own language. What Levitt suggests is that the creative person would do well to learn to address the manager, in the manager's language, in ways that are helpful to the organization.

Despite an organization's resistance to creativity, innovation is necessary in business—and innovation begins with somebody's proposal.[5] What is the answer for the person with a new idea? The creator must make the idea useful. To do this Levitt offers two suggestions:

1. *He must work with the situation as it is.* Since the executive is already constantly bombarded with problems, there is little wonder that after a while he does not

want any more new ideas. The "idea man" must learn to accept this fact of life and act accordingly.

2. *When he suggests an idea, the responsible procedure is to include at least some minimal indication of what it involves in terms of costs, risks, manpower time, and perhaps even specific people who ought to carry it through.*

Levitt goes on to say,

This is not to suggest that every idea needs a thoroughly documented study before it is mentioned to anyone. Far from it. What is needed will vary from case to case, depending on four factors:

1. *The position or rank of the idea-originator in the organization*—How "responsible" a man needs to act for an idea to get a hearing clearly depends on his rank. The powerful chief executive officer can simply instruct subordinates to take and develop one of his ideas. But when the ideas flow in the opposite direction—upward instead of downward they are unlikely to "flow" unless they are supported by the kind of follow-through I have been urging.

2. *The complexity of the idea*—The more complex and involved the implications of an idea, and the more change and rearrangement it may require within the organization or in its present way of doing things, then obviously the greater is the need to cover the required ground in some responsible fashion when the proposal is presented. . . .

3. *The nature of the industry*—How much supporting detail a subordinate should submit along with his idea often depends on the industry involved and the intent of the idea. . . .

4. *The attitude and job of the person to whom the idea is submitted*—Everybody knows that some bosses are more receptive to new ideas than others. Some are more receptive to extreme novelty than others. The extent of their known receptiveness will in part determine the elaborateness of support a suggested new idea requires at its original stage.

In short, a new creative idea creates more problems for the busy manager. What managers and their organizations need are more solutions and fewer problems. A new creative idea is more likely to receive a fair hearing when it has been thoroughly thought out before presentation and includes a full assessment of its probable costs, risks, and payoffs together with some alternative plans of implementation. In this way the idea becomes a potential solution and not just another set of problems for the manager.

THE PERMISSIVE VIEW OF CREATIVITY— THE INDIVIDUAL'S PERSPECTIVE

Thus far we have been looking at the problems creativity presents to the manager and the production organization. We have put considerable burden on the creative individual and indeed that is most probably where the primary burden belongs. Yet creativity is essential to the continued survival and growth of professional organizations and its absence is as likely to result in the slow strangulation of the organization as is the absence of strong, positive leadership.[6] Indeed, in Chapter 10 we saw that challenging the process by searching for, and presumably finding, opportunities is a function of an effective leader.

Most effective managers in professional organizations recognize not only the desirability of some creativity but their responsibility to establish an environment as conducive to creativity as organizational constraints will permit.[7] Let us then take another perspective. Let us look at the management difficulties of establishing an atmosphere conducive to maximum individual creativity.

From the point of view of the potential innovator in an organization, the source of frustration and bitterness lies in the organization's response—or lack of response—to creativity. Many social science experts who have studied creativity in the abstract assert that what places the greatest hindrance on creative activity in organizations is not so much a lack of creative individuals, but rather a lack of managers who comprehend and reward creative work. While commonly viewed as the brainchild of moments of isolation and solitary thought, creative activity is also an interpersonal process—it is nurtured by supportive and understanding interactions with other people. As William James noted long ago, "The community stagnates without the impulse of the individual; the impulse dies away without the sympathy of the community."

Because of the nature of creativity,[8] the creative activities of an individual may seem worthless at first, if not bizarre. According to Arthur Koestler in *The Act of Creation*,[9] creativity involves taking two previously unassociated ideas—ideas from two unrelated systems of thought—and putting them together in a meaningful and useful combination. An elementary act of creativity can be performed by a talented monkey faced with the problem of obtaining a banana placed beyond its reach, outside its cage. If there is a bush within its cage, and if the monkey's previous life experiences include playing with a stick, then it can sometimes visualize the solution to its problem. The monkey extracts from the "bush system of thought" the element of "stick" and extracts from its "play system of thought" the idea of pushing or raking at objects. The monkey then combines these two into a novel action that it has neither done nor seen before: the monkey breaks a branch from the bush and retrieves the banana. This is a creative act—a novel synthesis of two separate ideas that by themselves would not have been sufficient to solve the problem.

The invention of the printing press resulted from an essentially similar problem. Gutenberg had seen playing cards stamped with inked wooden blocks, and he had seen a winepress in operation squeezing grapes. He combined the principle of inked blocks with the operation of a press, forming a novel synthesis: the printing press. Originally, the creative elements employed here were unrelated. What do playing cards have to do with a winepress? The behavior of a creative individual may strike the average person as being quite odd. Only when the creator has proven the value of this seemingly disconnected intuitive activity will his or her worth be appreciated.

The manager of a creative individual plays an important role between the inception of a novel idea and its possible implementation. According to some social science writers, the manager can promote creative activity by

1. Permitting the creative activities, even though they may seem irrelevant;
2. Understanding the needs and motivations of creative people;
3. Recognizing the risks and anxieties creative people may feel; and
4. Providing helpful feedback to creative people.

The amount of creativity that flourishes in an organization depends, in part, on the capability of at least a few managers to nurture it.

Permitting Creative Activities

Most managers are expected to keep close to budgets and schedules and to justify expenditures of time and money. They are rewarded by higher managers for keeping on top of things, and being able to explain exactly what is happening, why, and when results are likely to be forthcoming. Consequently, the manager is under pressure to direct or control subordinates, including the creative ones, by telling them where to look, what to produce, and when to produce. This emphasis may inhibit creativity.

Suppose a manager sees an employee flying a kite. An average manager would expect that employee to have his or her mind on the job—a job that probably does not include kite flying. But had someone prevented Ben Franklin from indulging in his pastime, we might still be lacking electric light bulbs, can openers, and razors, not to mention lightning rods. Creative people may be criticized for what appears to be useless daydreaming and irrelevant activity.

The logic of creative developments is often not apparent until seen retrospectively. Their worth as well might not be perceived during the developmental period. It is often only after completion and implementation that a creative innovation validates itself. Old validating criteria may not apply to the new development. What this means for managers is that they cannot know whether a creative person is about to succeed by applying the rational criteria developed from previous discoveries. There is no way for managers to predict success or failure unless they can share to some extent the thought processes of their creative employees. If they can get inside the employees' world and see through their eyes, then the adventure of creative search can not only be shared, but also help inform the managers about the likelihood of a payoff.

The difficulty of permitting the creative act to go on is complicated by the identification of who are the creative people. Creativity seems unrelated to good grades and high IQ (see Chapter 2). But creativity is essentially new knowledge and fresh ways of perceiving combinations. Creative children may actually "throw away" high grades by thinking for themselves instead of giving the teacher what the teacher expects. Children who do not conform to the teacher's expectation are seen less favorably by their teachers.[10] The creative child may ask offbeat questions that embarrass the teacher in front of the class. Teachers prefer to be confirmed as good teachers, and the docile, obedient, high I.Q. children who memorize what they are told and repeat it, word perfect, are the ones who often earn the teacher's affection, gratitude, and high grades.

Understanding the Needs and Motivations of Creative People

Having thought of a new idea or system, the creative person may want to share the conception with someone else. The British inventor of the cinematograph rushed out into the street at night, seized a policeman, and almost dragged him into his laboratory to watch his movie. Merely combining ideas may not be enough; the combination must be perceived as meaningful, and this may require confirmation by others. A manager who understands the needs and motivations of creative employees may be able to share their unconventional visions.

This kind of understanding may not be easy to acquire. Managers trying to understand creative employees may feel uncomfortable if their self-image relates status to contribution and if the employee lectures them on the subject saying in effect, "no, you haven't grasped my point, try again!" Unless a manager is mature, self-confident, and secure, this process of studying the perspectives of subordinates may evoke various defense mechanisms. It may be difficult to understand creative employees whose life experiences and subcultures may be quite different. Creative employees may seem preoccupied with their own activities, which may seem unrelated to the goals and objectives of the organization.

Recognizing the Risks and Anxieties Creative People May Feel

Creative people may be subject to anxiety resulting from bucking the status quo. Other people may not understand them, perhaps in part because they are unable or unwilling to communicate clearly. Other people may refuse to relinquish their accustomed ways of doing things, their frames of reference, and their usual criteria of evaluation. Hence creative people may doubt themselves. Do other people ignore and reject them because of resistance to change, or is there some basic fault in the idea or worse, in the creative person?

Providing Helpful Feedback to Creative People

Won't a creative person confirmed by many people become an "insider"? And will his creative abilities then atrophy? This situation may occur when the creative genius suddenly finds everyone fervently embracing him. He is no longer critical of the status quo; he now has a reputation to lose if he takes a risk or makes a fool of himself. He is in the public gaze, so he spends the rest of his career elaborating on his basic ideas, safely respectable at last, and in the bosom of the organization. Lack of support may inhibit creativity, but success in the form of a large salary and public recognition may result in the cessation of creative ideas.

Creative people may find few people whose opinions they respect in whom they can confide. It is these people who can help the creative person to greater achievements. In the privacy of a trusted relationship with a manager, for example, the creative person can be given the freedom to experiment without loss of public face. The effective manager can promise to confirm what he or she truly understands and admires, but that failure to understand some things is inevitable and will be admitted frankly. Effective managers will also criticize quite fearlessly that which they feel is erroneous. The relationship is valuable because the opinion of one honest person is worth more than the cheers of a thousand who are ready to jump on the bandwagon. Henry VIII threatened Sir Thomas More with execution, and finally killed the "man for all seasons" because he wanted the confirmation of "an honest man." The chorus of approval from self-serving courtiers did not calm Henry at all. He needed an honest man to tell him he was right, an independent opinion, and he was murderously angry when he could not get it.

The creative person is often complex, many-sided, and difficult to understand. It may not be easy or without risk to invest in creative people, but it may be rewarding. If a creative idea is to enter an organization and be put to effective use, the manager of the creative employee will be the entryway. When effective managers and leaders support a proposal, they share the risks, the anxieties, and the communication problems that were once their subordinate's alone. In addition, they may be gambling for higher stakes than their subordinates. If they persevere nonetheless, they might find that there are vast treasures to be discovered and great opportunities that will enlarge their horizons. They are learning to mine the most undiscovered, unresearched territory in the world—the capacity of the human mind to create.

SUMMARY

The production view and permissive view of creativity seem to raise a paradoxical question. As Levitt notes

> If conformity and rigidity are necessary requisites of organization, and if these in turn help stifle creativity, and furthermore if the creative man might indeed be stifled if he is required to spell out many of the details needed to convert his ideas into effective innovations, does all this mean that modern organizations have evolved into such involuted monsters that they suffer the fearful fate of the dinosaur—too big and unwieldy to survive?
>
> The answer to this is *no*. First, it is questionable whether the creative impulse would automatically dry up if the idea man is required to take some responsibility for follow-through. The people who so resolutely proclaim their own creative energy will scarcely assert that they need a hothouse for its flowering. . . . [Organizations'] capacity to distribute risk over a broad base and among the many individuals involved in implementing newness are significant. They make it both economically and, for the individuals involved, personally easier to break untried ground.
>
> What often misleads people is that making big operating or policy changes requires also making big organizational changes. . . . The boat can and may have to be rocked but one virtue of a big boat is that it takes an awful lot to rock it. Certain people or departments in the boat may feel the rocking more than others, and to that extent strive to avoid the incidents that produce it. But the built-in-stabilizers of bigness and of group decision making can be used as powerful influences in *encouraging* people to risk these incidents.

The problem of creativity in the organization goes beyond the presence or absence of a permissive environment for creativity: It depends on a balanced view of the goals and objectives of both the organization and the individuals in it; it depends on effective managers and their ability to perceive their subordinates functionally and their skill in listening; it depends on their ability to motivate and their ability to analyze the interpersonal behavior of their people; and it depends on their ability to act in such a way that their organization will respond appropriately and accommodate both creativity and attention to the managerial and operation control issues such as costs and schedules. Finally, As Howell and Higgins assert, "someone must take the creative idea, guide it through the trying period when resistance is at a peak, and persevere until it becomes an innovation. In short, every idea needs a champion."[11]

QUESTIONS FOR REFLECTION AND DISCUSSION

1. What are the differences and similarities between how creativity is viewed by the line manager and how it is viewed by the creative individual?
2. What is creativity and how do managers identify and measure it?
3. What are the advantages and disadvantages of creativity? When are these important?
4. What can managers do to effectively manage creativity?

NOTES

1. Rosabeth Moss Kanter, *The Change Masters* (New York: Simon & Schuster, 1983).
2. Rosabeth Moss Kanter, "The Middle Manager as Innovator," *Harvard Business Review,* July/August 1982; and The Harvard Business Review video of the same title.
3. Theodore Levitt, "Creativity Is Not Enough," *Harvard Business Review,* May/June 1963, pp. 72–83.
4. Alvin Toffler, *Future Shock* (New York: Random House, 1970).
5. Don Frey, "Learning the Ropes: My Life As a Product Champion," *Harvard Business Review,* September/October 1991.
6. Stratford P. Sherman, "Eight Big Masters of Innovation," *Fortune,* October 15, 1984.
7. Andrall E. Pearson, "Tough-Minded Ways to Get Innovative," *Harvard Business Review,* January/February 1988.
8. Emily T. Smith, "Are You Creative?" *Business Week,* September 30, 1985.
9. Arthur Koestler, *The Act of Creation* (New York: Macmillan, 1964).
10. Robert Rosenthal and Lenore Jacobson, *Pygmalion in the Classroom* (New York: Rinehart and Winston, 1968).
11. Jane M. Howell and Christopher A. Higgins, "Champions of Change: Identifying, Understanding, and Supporting Champions of Technological Innovations," *Organizational Dynamics,* Summer 1990.

CHAPTER 12

THE MANAGER'S ROLE AS COACH AND MENTOR

Many effective managers at all levels recognize the need to develop the employees they supervise. By helping staff members expand their capabilities and improve their performance, managers can gain more time to improve their own capabilities and performance. Further, by building a reputation for developing employees, managers can enhance their chances for promotion. Even more important, they can create a lasting source of power through mutually beneficial relationships with the employees they have helped.

Managers who are most effective at developing employees have incorporated the skill of coaching into their management style.[1] These managers display behavior and skills that are very similar to the behavior and skills of an athletics coach. Although coaching is an important aspect of every effective manager's job, it is especially important when a manager is a mentor.[2] Employees who have been fortunate enough to have had a mentor, particularly early in their careers, usually find their careers enhanced by the experience and frequently incorporate coaching into their own management styles.[3]

In *The Change Masters*, Rosabeth Kanter argued that all companies that want to achieve excellence should encourage managers to become mentors to their employees.[4] In *Power and Influence*, John Kotter agreed that mentors, sponsors, coaches, and role models can be especially important in helping young people early in their careers. He stated, "Virtually all of the successful and effective executives I have known have had two or more of these kinds of relationships early in their careers. Some have had upwards of a dozen people they were able to rely on for different needs—some provided important contacts, others gave key information in specific areas, and still others taught them certain valued skills."[5]

Note: This chapter is reprinted (with very minor modifications), by permission of the publisher, from *Organizational Dynamics*, Spring 1987, © 1987 by the American Management Association, New York. All rights reserved.

If many managers in an organization would adopt a coaching style, thereby creating an organizational culture that reflected their coaching relationships, the probable result would be stronger management teams at all levels, enhanced management performance, and a less stressful environment for all employees. Many of the personnel problems that occur in an overly competitive organizational climate might be prevented. Teamwork and mutual support among employees would be nurtured, while power struggles and infighting would be reduced. Competition would be directed outward instead of within the organization.

Despite these potential benefits, coaching remains a neglected management function in many organizations. As Kotter noted, "Although almost all large corporations, and many small ones too, acknowledge the importance of mentoring, coaching, sponsoring, and role modeling for the development of their next generation of leaders, few seem to do a very good job in this regard."

Why is coaching so often neglected? From the manager's perspective, at least three factors inhibit greater practice of coaching as a management style. First, many organizational climates are not conducive to coaching,[6] and managers are not rewarded for developing employees. As a result, managers have few incentives or role models in this area. Second, lacking role models, managers do not recognize the benefits, to themselves and to their employees, of a management style that emphasizes coaching. Third, time, training, changes in attitudes, and sometimes frustrating practice are needed to develop coaching skills and to incorporate these skills into a person's management style.

THE ROLE OF COACHING

To be effective as a mentor, a manager must be very skilled at acquiring and using power, building and using relationships, and teaching and coaching others.[7] Coaching, however, should not be confused with career counseling (which usually is the responsibility of human resources professionals) or performance appraisal (a periodic, usually annual, evaluation of performance). Although coaching is related to both those activities, it differs in that it is a day-by-day, hands-on process of helping employees to recognize opportunities that improve their performance and capabilities. As such, it resembles on-the-job training, but it requires managers to have skills beyond those of a trainer, including the ability to analyze ways to improve employees' performance and capabilities, plan mutually acceptable action, create a supportive and helpful climate, and influence employees to change their behavior.

A manager's job really encompasses three distinct roles: manager, evaluator, and coach. The role of manager includes the responsibility for developing and communicating performance goals and expectations. The role of evaluator includes the responsibility for conducting periodic performance appraisals—evaluations of performance against the goals and tasks that have been developed and communicated. The role of coach includes the responsibility for helping employees improve their capabilities and performance on a day-to-day basis as well as over the long term.

Performance improvement can be viewed as a positive modification of behavior (from behavior modification and reinforcement theory). Changing behavior, however, can be difficult since it is the product of a person's life experiences, self-image, and perception of the expectations that others have of him or her. People tend to use their past successes as proof that they are doing things the right way. When they achieve less than complete success, they tend to blame other factors, such as the environment, the marketplace, their boss or other organizational units, or the lack of needed resources to get the job done. To increase motivation, expand capabilities, and develop new and better ways of accomplishing desired results, employees must first recognize that these efforts to improve performance by changing behavior are desirable. Of course, a mentor should not discount all "excuses"; some of them may be valid, in which case management action is needed to remove blocks to performance.

Generally, people are disposed to expand their capabilities and improve their performance (that is, change their behavior) when they know that these actions are expected and when they perceive that change will be nonthreatening and in their own self-interest. The development of an explicit set of expectations between supervisor and employee or between organization and employee is therefore a vital step in the coaching process.[8] When properly developed, mutually understood expectations lead to specific performance goals, enabling the mentor to observe actual performance and provide helpful feedback when performance does not meet the goals.

In most instances, expectations should be renegotiated as often as necessary, usually several times a year. Either the mentor or the employee can initiate the process when either perceives that circumstances or the environment has changed or that old expectations are no longer as useful as they might be.

CREATING THE PROPER CLIMATE

Climate, orientation, and behavior are considerably different when mentors function as an evaluator and when they function as a coach. They therefore must carefully differentiate between these two roles when interacting with employees. As an evaluator, mentors express judgments about performance against previously agreed upon goals and objectives. As coaches, mentors must express concern for helping the employees develop to their fullest potential. (This positive oriented mind-set can also be carried forward to performance appraisal, as we will see in Chapter 13.)

To play the latter role effectively, mentors must temporarily suspend judgment, listen empathetically,[9] probe for concerns related to an employee's self-assessment, and be ready to offer specific suggestions regarding training and self-development opportunities that would help the employee achieve career goals as well as the objectives of the organization. If an employee's career goals are not in line with the organization's objectives, the matter should be discussed as part of the coaching interaction.

For the coaching process to be effective, the mentor must create a climate that contributes to a free and open exchange of ideas and that is perceived by both mentor and employee to be a growth environment. Some characteristics of this kind of environment are described below:

- Since coaching is intended to help an employee, a mentor should never use words or actions that imply a threat. Expressions such as, "If you want to succeed in this job you had better . . ." or "If you know what's good for you, you will . . ." are to be avoided. People generally respond to implied or overt threats with denial, flight, anger, or aggression. These reactions will have a negative effect on the coaching process.
- Coaching requires a positive relationship between employee and mentor; the employee must respect the mentor's integrity and capability as a leader and the mentor must respect the employee's integrity and capacity to do the job.
- A mentor develops trust by demonstrating an honest interest in an employee and fostering open and candid two-way communication. The mentor listens, tries to understand, is supportive of the employee's efforts, and respects the employee's individuality.
- A coaching session should be free from interruptions or distractions. The location should ensure privacy and be conducive to a frank exchange of views. For example, a coaching session should not be conducted at lunch, on a plane, or in a hallway. An employee's office or workplace, if privacy can be ensured, may be an appropriate and nonthreatening location.
- Timing can greatly influence whether coaching sessions will be effective. For example, before a coaching session is held, sufficient time must be allowed to permit an employee to learn new skills or acquire added capabilities. Timing is especially important after an event in which intense emotional feelings are involved, such as after a critical presentation to upper management. An employee may not be ready to accept feedback or coaching right away. On the other hand, the coaching session should not be delayed to the point that it is difficult to recall details of the event.
- During a coaching session, an employee must clearly recognize that his or her mentor is functioning as a coach, not as an evaluator. As a coach, the mentor should be seen as supportive rather than judgmental, as one who provides helpful feedback rather than criticism.[10]

Four Critical Skills

Most managers are not born coaches. Just as an athletics coach needs to learn how to coach through experience, observation, and training, so does a manager. Some of the skills needed are implicit in the establishment of the proper climate for coaching (which was discussed above). In addition, managers need to develop four critical skills that are related to the coaching session itself and to the manager's preparation for it.

Observational Skills

A mentor must be able to monitor an employee's performance against established goals and expectations. Long before having to evaluate performance during a formal appraisal session, the mentor should spot opportunities for the employee to expand capabilities and improve performance and should take prompt action to help the employee do so. Mentors must therefore observe their employees' behavior and performance on a day-to-day basis.

Some data can be accumulated by direct observation (for example, the manner in which a meeting was conducted or a presentation made or an employee's relationships with other employees). Other data can be acquired indirectly from the mentor's network of relationships with other employees. Still other data can be obtained by studying an employee's reports (such as special or routine assignments, memos, and letters) or through control devices (such as expenses incurred versus those budgeted).

Analytical Skills

Mentors must have two types of analytical skills: they must be able to identify opportunities for employees to expand their capabilities and improve performance, and they must be able to determine when coaching is the action needed to help employees improve performance and/or expand their capabilities. The process of deciding when coaching is or is not needed entails analysis of the factors influencing an employee's performance (behavior). This step-by-step analytical process is outlined in Exhibit 12-1.

Identifying opportunities for employees to improve performance requires a somewhat different analytical process based partly on the data mentors have gathered from their own and other's observations of an employee's behavior and partly on interviews with the employee. Several questions will need to be answered: How was the work performed? What was done well? What could have been improved? What other strategies or approaches might have been used? What specific improvements would make it easier for the employee to perform at an optimal level?

Interviewing Skills

A mentor must be able to ask employees the right questions the right way and listen actively. Essentially, there are three types of questions that can be used by the skillful interviewer: the open-ended question, the closed question, and the reflective question. Each is used for a specific purpose to accomplish a desired result.

Open-ended questions are used to encourage the respondent to rethink the problem, think of things that he or she has not considered previously, achieve insight or understanding, or draw his or her own conclusions. For example, when discussing a problem involving an opportunity for an employee to improve performance, a mentor should not respond to the employee's proposed solution by saying, "It won't work, we've tried it before. Try this approach." Instead, any of

---

EXHIBIT 12-1

THE ANALYTICAL PROCESS OF COACHING*

ANALYTICAL QUESTIONS		ACTION STEPS
Does employee know performance can be improved?	———NO———▶	Let employee know.
Does employee know what is expected of him or her?	———NO———▶	Reinforce applicable performance standards.
Are there obstacles beyond the employee's control?	———YES———▶	Remove obstacles or revise standards.
Does the employee know how to improve?	———NO———▶	Train employee and/or provide practice or demonstration.
Do negative consequences follow good performance?	———YES———▶	Change the consequence.
Do positive consequences follow poor performance?	———YES———▶	Change the consequence.
Could the employee make the improvements if he or she wanted to?	———NO———▶	Consider reassignment, transfer, other action.
	———YES———▶	Redirect subordinate's behavior through coaching.

---

*Adapted from *Coaching for Improved Work Performance* by Ferdinand F. Fournies, Van Nostrand Reinhold, New York, 1978.

the following open-ended questions, among others, might be asked: What other approaches have you considered? What are the advantages and disadvantages of your approach? What have others done when faced with a similar problem?

Closed questions are used to guide a discussion into a specific area or to get specific information when a discussion is producing too many generalities. For example, a mentor might ask an employee: Who in the section has been responding to your requests for information? How much additional time do you think you need to get the job done in a superior manner? Have you had a chance to talk with other people about their concerns?

Reflective questions restate, in question form, a statement a person has made. They are used to prevent misunderstanding and to communicate concern about and/or interest in what the person has said. For example: if an employee says, "The system just isn't working," the mentor might ask "You mean it isn't running at all?" If an employee says, "I can't get Ann to do anything I ask," the mentor might ask, "She refuses to follow your directions?" Or if an employee says, "There isn't enough in the budget to handle current training requirements," the mentor might ask, "You think we didn't forecast very well?"

Real listening, active listening,[11] is a skill that most managers need to learn. People tend to be too concerned about what *they* want to communicate next instead of listening for sometimes buried ideas, feelings, or beliefs that the other person is trying to communicate. To signal employees that they are really listening, mentors can use nonverbal behavior, such as obvious attentiveness, smiles, nods, eye contact, or verbal behavior like making accepting statements, paraphrasing what the employee has said, and asking probing questions to elicit more information or opinions.

Feedback Skills

If a mentor's feedback to an employee causes defensiveness, withdrawal, anger, or intimidation (that is, it has a negative orientation), the feedback has not been given effectively and is not likely to produce the desired changes in behavior. Employees should perceive feedback as being helpful to them in their efforts to expand their capabilities or improve their performance. Some guidelines for delivering feedback are discussed below:

- *Be specific, not general.* For example, telling an employee that he or she is abrasive is not helpful. Instead, a mentor should provide details, such as "Jack was visibly angry with you for cutting him down at the team meeting yesterday. What can you do to repair your relationship with him?"
- *Be descriptive, not evaluative.* For example, telling an employee that he or she "handled that situation very badly" is not helpful. A better approach would be to say "When you made your presentation yesterday, if you had focused more attention on your audience you might have sensed their impatience and kept your explanations shorter."
- *Take both your own and your employee's needs into account.* Feedback can be destructive when it is self-serving and fails to be sensitive to the needs of the person receiving the feedback. For instance, a mentor needs to be careful not to give feedback when angry or tense. The temptation to relieve one's anger or tension by assailing the employee may be hard to resist.
- *Be sure the feedback is directed toward behavior that can be changed.* A mentor will only generate frustration by identifying a shortcoming over which an employee has no control. The following scenario provides an example of skillful coaching:

> Mentor: You seem to be falling behind on your inspection schedule.
> Employee: I've been asked to do a lot of other things.
> Mentor: There are always other things to do but until recently you managed to keep up with your inspections.
> Employee: In the last month, your boss has given me two special assignments that I thought you knew about.
> Mentor: I didn't know. I guess I have a problem. What were the assignments?

Employee: (Gives details.)

Mentor: I'm glad we've identified the real problem here. One thing, hereafter if my boss gives you assignments, don't assume that I know about it. Come and tell me.

In the example above, the mentor did not assume that the employee was slacking off. Instead, she attempted to discover an explanation for a problem that she had observed. She quickly learned that the problem was not the employee's but her own—a problem involving her relationship with her boss. At the same time she was able to take the first step toward solving the problem by asking the employee to report any special assignments given to her.

- *Be sure the feedback is well timed.* Feedback should be given as soon as possible after an action (or lack of action) *unless* a cooling-off period is indicated. When emotions are strong, an employee may not listen to or make effective use of feedback.
- *Make sure that you and the employee have clearly understood each other.* There are too many filters in the normal communication process to guarantee mutual understanding of what is said.

A WAY OF MANAGING

Coaching is a management technique that is based on knowledge about how and under what conditions employees improve and grow and on specific skills that managers need to practice, develop, and incorporate into their management style. These skills are not those of a psychologist, psychiatrist, or analyst; they are management skills. Once learned, coaching becomes an integral part of any manager's way of managing. Coaching is *not* a way of solving one-time problems. It is a way of helping employees, over time, to improve (change) their performance (behavior and results) to outstanding levels or at least to the highest level of which they are capable. As such, the development and practice of coaching knowledge and skills can and should result in improved performance, for all who are exposed to it.

SELECTED BIBLIOGRAPHY

Power and influence skills are a critical part of the set of tools a mentor needs to use as well as instill or develop in those he or she is trying to help. John Kotter's *Power and Influence* (The Free Press, 1985) is an excellent source of information on the general approach to the acquisition and use of power in organizations. He also discusses network building and the role a mentor can play in helping young employees develop these skills. His earlier articles, such as "Managing Your Boss" (*Harvard Business Review,* January/February 1980) and "Power, Dependence and Effective Management" (*Harvard Business Review,* July/August 1977), are useful as well. Rosabeth Kanter's book *The Change Masters* (Simon & Schuster, 1984) also discusses the important role of mentors in organizations that want to achieve excellence.

For a more specific discussion of power and influence skills, see our article "The Effective Uses of Power" (*Business Horizons,* May/June 1986) (see Chapter 8) and our monograph *Influencing People in Organizations* (University Affiliates, Inc., 1986) (see Chapter 4). In *Beyond Freedom and Dignity* (Bantam Books, 1971), B. F. Skinner, among others, discusses the importance of positive reinforcement as a way of influencing behavior. Other books by B. F. Skinner on behavior modification and reinforcement theory may also be of interest such as *Contingencies of Reinforcement* (Appleton-Century-Crofts, 1969) and *About Behaviorism* (Vintage, 1976).

QUESTIONS FOR REFLECTION AND DISCUSSION

1. What can a person do to find and maintain a mentor?
2. What can managers do to find people worthy and willing to be mentored?
3. What are the differences and similarities between an effective manager and coach?
4. What can managers do to become more effective coaches?

NOTES

1. Dan Hurley, "The Mentor Mystique," *Psychology Today,* May 1988.
2. K. E. Kram, *Mentoring at Work: Developmental Relationships in Organizational Life* (Glenview, IL: Scott, Foresman, 1985).
3. Franklin J. Lunding, George L. Clemente, and Donald S. Perkins, "Everyone Who Makes It Has a Mentor," *Harvard Business Review,* July/August 1978.
4. Rosebeth M. Kanter, *The Change Masters* (New York: Simon & Schuster, 1984).
5. John P. Kotter, *Power and Influence* (New York: The Free Press, 1985).
6. Clinton O. Longnecker and Dennis A. Gioia, "The Executive Appraisal Paradox," *Academy of Management Executive,* May 1992.
7. Beverly J. Bernstein and Beverly L. Kaye, "Teacher, Tutor, Colleague, Coach," *Personnel Journal,* November 1986.
8. J. Sterling Livingston, "Pygmalion in Management," *Harvard Business Review,* July/August 1969.
9. Carl Rogers and F. J. Roethlisberger, "Barriers and Gateways to Communication," *Harvard Business Review,* July/August 1952; reprinted November/December 1991.
10. B. F. Skinner, *Contingencies of Reinforcement* (New York: Appleton-Century-Crofts, 1969); *About Behaviorism* (New York: Vintage, 1976); and *Beyond Freedom & Dignity* (New York: Knopf, 1971).
11. J. Brownell, *Building Active Listening Skills* (Englewood Cliffs, NJ: Prentice-Hall, 1986).

CHAPTER 13

PERFORMANCE APPRAISAL

In spite of the best efforts of well-intentioned managers and a large volume of material written about performance appraisals, most managers and employees approach the process with trepidation.[1] Why do so few people look forward to and benefit from performance appraisals?[2] The observable problems are caused by (a) the manager who uses the review as an opportunity to criticize the employee about what he or she has done wrong or not done at all and to recount all of the employee's mistakes (often for the first time); (b) the employee who is constantly "selling" by regularly announcing why he or she should receive a higher rating, a raise, or promotion; and (c) the manager and employee who fence over whether the review is fair or not. Even the so-called sandwich approach, in which a manager tells the employee good things at the beginning and the end of the appraisal while the discussion of weaknesses is sandwiched in the middle, does little to ease these problems. In the end, too many appraisals are seen as discouraging to employees, while the manager is placed in the position of defending his or her viewpoint. Little wonder that performance appraisals can lead to a breakdown in communications, negative feelings on both sides, and a dip in performance rather than an upswing.

What has gone wrong? The focus is negative rather than positive. Whether the appraisal is based on the management by objectives approaches that we will discuss in Chapter 14 or any of the other commonly used approaches, including behaviorally anchored rating scales,[3] they may include some discussion of what management perceives to be the employee's "weaknesses." Most performance reviews focus on looking back at what has been done wrong, what mistakes were made, what has not been done, and what should have been done rather than looking forward to what can be done. Unfortunately, too many performance reviews dredge up the past to explain what must be fixed instead of using past

Note: This chapter was written by Harry Wilkinson, Rice University, and David Kreischer, Citibank Illinois, F.S.B. It was copyrighted in 1991 by the authors and is reproduced here (with very minor modifications) with their permission.

accomplishments to demonstrate what is working well for the employee. By focusing on what must be fixed or what is wrong, the reviewer leaves the interviewee feeling devalued ("I'm OK except for this fatal flaw"), and discouraged ("I'll never be effective enough"),[4] or angry ("I'll get even"), in which the interviewee takes discouragement on the offensive by looking for opportunities to knock down or knock out the cause of the discouragement (which is usually seen as the reviewer or another person or persons) rather than the performance.

This focus on weaknesses tends to make both the employee and the manager defensive raising the levels of spontaneous anxiety and minimizing any benefits that might have accrued from the process. Peter Drucker said

> The effective executive makes strength productive. He knows that one cannot build on weakness. . . . [One] cannot, of course, overcome the weaknesses with which each of us is abundantly endowed. But [focusing on strengths] can make them irrelevant. . . . [The] task is to use the strengths of each [person] as a building block for joint performance.[5]

Even though these words were printed in 1967 by one of the top business consultants, many organizations today still *require* managers to identify and discuss weaknesses with their employees.

This negatively focused performance appraisal model with its emphasis on weaknesses, in which the reviewer is judge and the reviewee is judged, has contributed to the loss of competitiveness of many organizations. Robert Schaffer said

> In company after company, I have asked managers to estimate how much more their organizations would produce if overlapping functions were eliminated, if units began to work more in sync with each other, if people worked more closely to their real potential, and if they dissipated less energy in political hassles, self-aggrandizing behavior, useless meetings, and projects that go nowhere. Not surprisingly, almost everyone has selected the "25 to 50%" and the "over 50%" categories.
>
> . . . the principal reason is that "few managers possess the capacity—or feel compelled—to establish high performance-improvement expectations in ways that elicit results."[6]

The important phrase for our purposes is "in ways that elicit results." We know that positive reinforcement tends to yield more of a desired behavior.[7] Thus, if we focus on and reinforce strengths and the enhancement of those strengths, people will work more closely to their real potential. If, at the same time, we set "high performance-improvement expectations" *and* express our sincere confidence that the person can achieve them,[8] then we can improve individual and organizational effectiveness.

To achieve this, we need to use a performance appraisal process similar to the coaching process described in Chapter 12 in which both parties form a partnership to achieve greater success in the future. Most people feel they *can* improve their performance. What is needed is an approach that helps them to identify opportunities to improve and that does not generate the kind of defensiveness that a focus on weaknesses creates. In this "focusing on strengths" process, both participants together look at the value added by the reviewee's contributions to the team and the organization. Using contributions as the basis, they explore what strengths (with specific behavioral examples) have led to these achievements. Then the discussion can turn toward how these strengths can be used to make further contributions. In addition, the discussion should include what other strengths and talents the individual possesses or can readily acquire that might help expand his or her ability to contribute. It is obvious that to do this a manager *must* know his or her people well enough to recognize their existing and potential strengths and talents; the manager must know what the employees have done, are doing, and are capable of doing, not only by reviewing the personnel files but by individually discussing these issues with each person. Some managers at Citibank Illinois are experimenting with this process, and thus far, have found participants are encouraged by it. They feel valuable and motivated to add their value more often and in more ways, which leads to greater productivity and impact on the company's business.

In the more traditional performance appraisal process, people tend to become focused on weaknesses or what's lacking (called a deficiency model), which results in thinking that something must be "fixed" to get better or to be of value. The process presented here assumes the person is valuable so both parties can explore what strengths distinguish the individual and plan for enhancing and applying those strengths more frequently or with greater impact to contribute more effectively to organizational goals and objectives. Citibank Illinois's experience with this process indicates people look forward to reviews and ask for feedback more often and from more people because, after all, the name of the game is enhancing what is already strong.

The process of focusing on strengths is distinguished as much for what is *not* included (a weakness-oriented mind-set) as for what *is* included (a positive, forward looking mind-set). There are two prerequisites for a performance review that focuses on strengths. Both the supervisor and the employee must be equally responsible for bringing examples of strengths to the review and explaining how these strengths were used or could be used to contribute to organizational objectives. In addition, it is helpful to agree beforehand on what achievements will be discussed (for example, behavior improvement goals, tasks assigned, contributions since the last review, or progress against performance standards). If we take the approach used in the Citibank Illinois effective people management workshop and modify it based on the company's initial experiences, then we will have a suggested six-step process for a performance appraisal review that focuses on strengths. (See also Chapter 12 for the section on creating a climate for coaching.)

THE SIX STEP PROCESS

Step 1

Set the stage by emphasizing that the review is a shared responsibility for discussing strengths, how these strengths were, or could be, used to contribute to organizational objectives, and how these strengths, and other strengths or talents the individual has or can easily acquire, can be used to achieve further contributions.

But when do we discuss what *did* go wrong? Too late! The time to address a problem is when the problem occurs (such as right when a person gets stuck and has some difficulty figuring out how to progress on a task), and ideally resolving the problem as part of the coaching process described in Chapter 12. Otherwise, the person or team is in jeopardy of being unable to make progress and be productive. Thus, it makes no sense to wait for a review to reestablish a productive direction. The purpose of focusing on strengths is to create a partnership aimed at building on a person's strengths or talents. The importance of this review is emphasized by conducting it in private without interruptions.

Step 2

Discussing what has been accomplished is the second step. The interviewee should be encouraged to offer his or her thoughts first. The goal here is to overcome modesty. Toward this end, the interviewer should look for opportunities to add accomplishments or clarify the interviewee's favorable impact on the team and the organization. Being specific is also important so that the interviewer and interviewee can easily recognize the contributions as genuine and more readily work with the contributions to determine what practices (strengths) led to them. The experience at Citibank Illinois showed that there are always enough accomplishments to discuss as long as you stick with specifics both in terms of what has been done and with what effect. However, the discussion flows more readily if both parties have prepared for it in advance; prior preparation also demonstrates mutual respect. Discussion may center on the accomplishments attained, such as achieving the behavior improvement goals, completing assigned tasks, meeting objectives agreed upon, reaching or surpassing standards, and carrying out job description duties, or it may simply center on the most significant things done since the last review. The discussion serves as the basis for identifying keys to success (strengths): it is, therefore, an exercise in encouragement.

Step 3

Discussing specific situations in which the interviewee made valuable contributions is the third step intended to identify the strengths the interviewee adds to the team or organization. It is essential to pinpoint what a person says or does that results in making a contribution (achieving success). Identifying talents is probably the most challenging aspect of the interview process. Modesty or reticence is an obstacle (so is boastfulness), but sometimes a person does not know clearly what strengths he or she has used that led to success. If the person does not know, it may be necessary to identify the strengths specifically so that they can be used repeatedly? A useful tool in drawing out successful practices is to concentrate on the consequences in terms of how specific actions favorably affected the situation. A good barometer for understanding consequences is to recognize how you, the interviewer, were affected by specific behaviors or actions of the interviewee. If you enjoy a person's sense of humor, the person may be able to use his or her humor favorably with others. Or you might start with the effect or consequences and ask, "How do you think you were able to have such a favorable impact in that situation?" The listing of strengths or talents need not be exhaustive, but often the interviewee settles for too few. Since the goal is to demonstrate added value, the interviewer should be thorough so the interviewee is encouraged to bring as many talents to the task, and each successive task, as possible.

Step 4

Assisting the interviewee in identifying opportunities to enhance his or her strengths is the fourth forward-looking step. How can the individual more effectively use his or her talents to address the tasks at hand? Are there different or bigger tasks where these talents can be applied? What can be done to complement demonstrated talents to build a stronger basis for contributing (for example, strengthening existing facilitation skills to add to excellent presentation skills as a way of contributing more as a trainer, sales person, or manager). A frank discussion of limitations related to the use of talents should also be included, but this review should *not* focus on weaknesses. The application of strengths may suggest limitations, such as an unused or hidden talent that can be developed, or the potential for misapplying a strength. For example, if a person is a particularly strong presenter, he or she may be less proficient and/or interested in listening. If that person talks too much (abuses his or her strength), he or she may not understand the other's position (for lack of listening) and as a result, the presenter may be less convincing no matter how much talking is done. However, the strong presenter may be willing and able to build listening skills, so what has gone unnoticed or undernourished until now becomes a potential strength. But what if the person cannot or will not build listening skills? Is that person deficient? Fatally flawed? In need of "fixing"? No! However, the interviewer and interviewee should look for opportunities to compensate, such as adding to the team someone with good listening skills who is highly respected by the team and who will act as interpreter when appropriate, or the interviewee may schedule pauses to avoid nonstop talking and to ask for and encourage questions. This leads naturally to a discussion of what talents others may have to offer, as well as what talents the interviewee can offer to his or her teammates.

Step 5

Career development planning is the next step in looking for opportunities to enhance demonstrated strengths to permit even greater contributions. The motive here is to seek the opportunities for the employee to assume more complex responsibilities within the current job or team or to take on a new assignment (or perhaps even a promotion) that gives greater range to the interviewee's strengths. In discussing career directions, it is important to talk about how demonstrated strengths can be improved and applied as well as what other existing strengths or talents can be improved and applied that would add value when tackling a new assignment or responsibility. A person should be encouraged to take on assignments or responsibilities that will use his or her strengths and stretch and develop those strengths, but there is little sense in trying to "correct" weaknesses. No good football coach would say to a good, lithe, thin wide receiver that he was weak as a defensive lineman and set out to correct this "weakness." The good football coach (and the good manager) looks for ways to enhance strengths—ways to make the wide receiver a better wide receiver and either help the existing defensive lineman become better or hire new talent. In the same way, a good manager looking at an introverted, task-oriented, and very good engineer, should not try to correct that engineer's perceived weakness as a people manager *unless* a careful analysis of the demonstrated or potential talents the engineer possesses match those needed by a manager.

Step 6

Asking, "How can I help?" is the vitally important final step in the process of focusing on strengths. It binds the partnership in an *ongoing,* constructive way. By volunteering to help, the interviewer commits to contributing to the interviewee's continued improvement. Again, it is important that the interviewee be as specific as possible regarding what would be helpful. Is career advocacy needed now? Job enrichment? More coaching (see Chapter 12)? Greater or more frequent recognition and/or feedback? Finally, there should be agreement regarding the next steps and when the parties will meet again to discuss how to further enhance strengths for even greater contributions. The Citibank Illinois experience suggests people will look forward to these interviews and may ask for them more frequently.

SUMMARY

In summary, the process of focusing on strengths is as important for what is not included as for what is included. What is missing is an emphasis on weakness (that is, what must be "corrected") and, sometimes, rankings (how much sense would it make to rank all the members of a football team and how stable would that ranking be?).

People do not need to be fixed (the deficiency model). They need to know how to use and enhance their talents. If someone is stuck and unable to advance in completing a task, the time to address it is when he or she is stuck. To resolve the problem, management can change or modify what practices are being used to tackle the task, change the task, add needed talent to the team, or, if a recurring pattern exists (where a person gets consistently stuck and cannot make progress on the tasks assigned), help the person change assignments to one requiring the strongest talents the person has, thus enabling him or her to contribute at a level closer to his or her real potential. For example, if a good professional football coach recognizes that the talents of a particular college quarterback are more suited to those of a wide receiver in the pros, he may encourage him to become a wide receiver when the college player becomes a pro, thereby maximizing the player's ability to contribute to the team.

Finally, no one likes to be ranked unless they are ranked number one. And no one remains number one for very long. A fairer way to distribute compensation or rewards is necessary. Why not base rewards on what the *team* contributes and its usefulness, that is, utilize gainsharing, a team-based reward system.[9]

In any case, the goal of performance appraisals is to look forward to achieving greater contributions. To this end it is "important for the organization that its executives focus on strengths and work on making strengths productive in their own group and with their own subordinates."[10]

QUESTIONS FOR REFLECTION AND DISCUSSION

1. What do people like and dislike about performance appraisals? Why?
2. What are the differences and similarities between appraising performance and coaching?
3. Under what circumstances might a manager or a coach withhold appraisal information from an appraisee?
4. What are the potential problems of a positive performance appraisal?

NOTES

1. B. Rice, "Performance Review: The Job Nobody Likes," *Psychology Today,* September 1986.
2. Clinton O. Longnecker and Dennis A. Gioia, "The Executive Appraisal Paradox," *Academy of Management Executive*, May 1992.
3. P. C. Smith and L. M. Kendall, "Retranslation of Expectations: An Approach to the Construction of Unambiguous Anchors for Rating Scales," *Journal of Applied Psychology* 47, 1963.
4. Paul H. Thompson and Gene W. Dalton, "Performance Appraisals: Managers Beware," *Harvard Business Review,* January/February 1970.
5. P. Drucker, *The Effective Executive* (New York: Harper & Row, 1967).
6. R. Schaffer, "Demand Better Results—And Get Them" (Retrospective Commentary), *Harvard Business Review,* March/April 1991.
7. B. F. Skinner, *Contingencies of Reinforcement* (New York: Appleton-Century-Crofts, 1969; *Beyond Freedom & Dignity* (New York: Alfred A. Knopf, 1971); and *About Behaviorism* (New York: Vintage, 1976).
8. J. S. Lingston, "Pygmalion in Management," *Harvard Business Review,* July/August 1969. See also Chapter 4.
9. Edward J. Ost, "Team-Based Pay: New Wave Strategic Incentives," *Sloan Management Review*, Spring 1990.
10. Drucker, *The Effective Executive*, p. 92.

CHAPTER 14

INDIVIDUAL PERFORMANCE AND ORGANIZATIONAL OBJECTIVES

Organizations, their various subgroups, and individuals all need a sense of direction and a vision of future possibilities—where are we going and how will we get there? Ideally, this need involves a process, with *planning* at one end of the continuum and *performance leading to desired results* at the other. In between, the critical phases of the process involve determining organizational goals and defining subgroup and individual objectives that stem from those goals. In actuality, managers must deal with a set of interdependent relationships.[1] The problem really is, "How do we integrate organizational goals with personal goals to achieve both short-range objectives and, at the same time, focus on tomorrow's opportunities, creative achievements, and challenging goals?" For many years, managers have been looking for ways to improve both profitability and productivity and, more recently, to improve product quality and market share as well. Any managerial tool is only as good as the *linear*, *nonlinear*, and *contextual* skills of the people or organization that tries to use that tool.[2] It is important to emphasize that it is the human beings in the organization that are doing the important work of conceptualizing both the long-term and short-term goals of the organization based upon environmental feedback, including an assessment of creative breakthroughs and future opportunities. In this context, a useful managerial tool must fit in with the values of the organization, subgroups, and individuals in order to be a viable, workable tool.

One evolving managerial tool that has been the subject of considerable controversy over its use and misuse is called management by objectives (MBO).[3] Like any other managerial tool, it has advantages and limitations.[4] Those who became fervent advocates of MBO as a cure-all for organizational problems were the ones who most frequently became disillusioned and cynical when it became apparent that MBO wasn't the panacea they thought it was. The terms *goals* and *objectives* were often used interchangeably, which contributed to the early disillusionment. For our purposes, goals are defined as long-term expressions of organizational strategy and objectives are defined as short-term targets for implementing organizational strategy.

MANAGEMENT BY OBJECTIVES

MBO has gone through a series of evolutionary stages since it was first introduced as a managerial concept in the fifties. In the early stage, it was seen as a means of fostering more objective performance appraisals based on specific achievements rather than on trait-centered approaches. At that time, it seemed to be a step forward from a highly subjective and intuitive system that measured the personality traits of the inner person rather than the person's achievements. MBO was considered fairer to the individual manager or subordinate and did motivate people to higher personal accomplishments as a result of setting objectives and generating a knowledge that they would be measured against them. At that time, the ideal process was envisioned as follows:

1. Clarify both the job to be done and the expectations of accomplishment.
2. Foster the increasing competence and growth of the subordinate.
3. Enhance communications between the superior and the subordinate.
4. Relate individual performance to organizational goals.
5. Use the performance rating system as a device for organizational control and integration.
6. Stimulate the subordinate's motivation.
7. Measure and judge achievement.
8. Use these achievements as a basis for judgments about salary and promotion.

According to this model, the process would follow in five steps: (1) individual discussion with the superior of the subordinate's description of his or her own job, (2) establishment of short-term performance targets, (3) establishment of checkpoints to measure progress, (4) meetings with the superior to discuss progress toward targets, and (5) discussion between superiors and subordinates, at the end of a defined period, to assess the results of the subordinates' efforts.

In spite of the rational orderliness of the process, a basic deficiency in this approach to MBO eventually became apparent.[5] The individual manager was concerned with appraising only the short-term performance of the subunits and consequently could not integrate into the longer range organizational effort. These managers could not set objectives that would ultimately contribute to the more comprehensive organizational goals. Many managers never considered this potentially dysfunctional consequence and proceeded with a system that focused on the individual rather than the organization as the foundation for goal definition and achievement. Several additional factors involved in the use of MBO as an organizational goal-setting device also began to emerge:

1. The total situation in which the supervisor and subordinate were operating, including those factors over which neither exercised any control, sometimes made feedback to the subordinate misleading or unfair.
2. The establishment and evaluation of internally consistent and realistically achievable objectives required far more interaction among different levels of an organization than had been assumed, and therefore it required more time than had been allowed.
3. Since every organization is, in part, a social system involving a network of interpersonal relationships, a person could do an excellent job of meeting short-term objectives but fail in the long run as a partner, subordinate, superior, or colleague. These are human skills that have both hidden costs and profits for organizations, but these costs and profits are not measured in the short-term technical performance of jobs.
4. Individual managers often sacrificed critical but unmeasured long-term goals to obtain short-term but measurable objectives, such as when a manager substantially reduces R & D expenditures to achieve current year profitability objectives.

Thus, it became clear that MBO as an isolated tool for appraising management performance had many undesirable side effects that needed to be taken into account.[6] A final major problem, in addition to the ones listed above, appeared to be that the impetus for MBO came from personnel officials and not from line management or the chief executive of the organization. In other words, it was a system that started from static job descriptions and personal goals at the bottom and the side (staff) of the organization rather than from top management, with its view of the organization as a whole.

A reemphasis of MBO in the 1960s shifted from individual goal setting, as the initial step, to organizational goal setting. This consisted of a series of events, as follows:

1. Objectives were set by the office of the chief executive, the chairman of the board, and the president. All subsequent levels of the organization's objectives emanated from this set of overall organizational goals.
2. Objectives were prepared within the planning-budgeting cycle and time period. This meant that the objective-setting process became much more an iterative process and time was provided for these iterations.
3. Communication channels between activities were opened to discuss overlapping responsibilities and to identify missing as well as marginal activities. Gaps were plugged, overlaps minimized, and marginal activities strengthened or dropped. Frequently, organizational structure was modified to reflect these changes.
4. Measurements of achievement began to recognize factors beyond the control of individual managers.

At this point, managers tended to become committed to organizational objectives and see the whole picture rather than just part of it. Organizational values became more widely accepted and expectations,[7] which constitute psychological contracts, more explicit. Individual managers and subgroups began to perceive more functionally their roles and relationships within the organization.[8] For example, engineering and production groups both began to see their different value systems and behavior patterns as contributing to the commonly accepted larger organizational values and culture. When goals are set from the vantage point of clearly understood and commonly accepted environmental constraints or pressures upon an organization, and then are filtered down to the subunits, an organization gains in functional perception.

The integration of MBO into the organization evaluation system and the shift away from the individual trait ratings were vast improvements for the organizations that adopted this approach. A number of disadvantages still remained, however. MBO was still short-term oriented. MBO programs aimed at better performance appraisals and the integration of the individual manager's objectives; the objectives of the organization normally focused on the next year. In many ways, next year's performance is predetermined by the internal inertia that has already been built up in the past or by external factors. To that extent, short-run objectives may add little to short-run performance. The argument, then, is that if managers are going to lead and make an impact on the organization, they must set longer term objectives and plan the way to achieve them.

Integration with long-range planning is part of the current evolution of management by objectives. The objectives that ultimately are set for the organization and the individual managers in it, and the action plans supporting the objectives, represent the fruits of an extensive analysis of a wide variety of possible objectives and constraints upon the organization.

MBO began with limited objectives (a focus on the individual and his or her personal goals), continued with an effort to integrate organizations with mostly short-run individual goal setting, and finally recognized long-range planning as the critical missing link. Although MBO evolved in this fashion, it is clear to many organizational and behavioral scientists that the effective way of implementing MBO is to start first with long-range planning; second, to integrate long range plans with the immediate operations; and finally, to integrate immediate operations with individual goals and objectives. This is a complete reversal of the historic evolution of MBO and puts the responsibility on top management and the strategic planners in the organization. Environmental analysis, technological forecasting, the identification of opportunities for innovations, the evolution of a vision for the future, and the establishment of priorities become the essential features of the goal-setting operation. From these various data bases come the operational goals, programs, and objectives. In one sense, they derive from the commonly accepted overall value orientations or culture of the organization. Like individual value orientations, they can be congruent or incongruent with the environment or with themselves. Much of the resistance to objective and goal setting at the middle and lower levels of management is due to 1) an unclear picture by top management of the overall values (or organizational culture) and goals that it should foster or 2) incomplete feedback through various communication channels regarding what the values and goals are perceived to be and why they are important.

INTEGRATING INDIVIDUAL GOALS AND OBJECTIVES

Once organizational goals are set and commonly accepted, the talents, strengths, goals and values of the individual must be considered. At this point, given the organization's priorities, missions, goals, and programs mentioned above, the organizational task becomes one of first understanding the person's goals, values, talents, and strengths and then assessing, with that person, how well his or her talents and strengths can be used in the organization so that progress can be made toward the person's goals without compromising his or her values.[9] Thus, the optimum contributory individual behavior arises when there is congruence between first, the individual's strengths and talents and the organization's needs and desires, and second, the individual's goals and values and those of the organization. In this case, the requirements of both mesh, interrelate, and become synergistic. If these factors do not mesh, the individual must exert considerable effort to reach acceptable compromises, covert or overt, between his or her own goals and those of the organization. This not only takes away from the effort expended to accomplish the work but may result in work that is less than optimum.

This conflict of personal goals and values with organizational goals and values is sometimes due to lack of clarity on the part of the organization in articulating its expectations. This conflict is curable through dialogue and the establishment of psychological contracts involving mutually understood expectations between top management and the critical individuals. Such an assessment by all groups should be a means of providing each with constructive feedback. The group discussion should examine organizational and environmental obstacles to goal achievement. If an individual believes his or her personal goals cannot be met in the framework of a clearly articulated set of organizational goals, some form of arrangement for transfer or change would seem in the best interests of all concerned.

As described to this point, the assessment of goals and values of both the organization and the individual takes place after the fact, and in this case one is then faced with the problem of undoing the existing misunderstanding. The functional approach to the problem of goal setting and the assessment of individual strengths is a recurring process of dialogue, environmental assessment, and changes on both the organizational and individual levels. This form of cycling and recycling of information at all levels of the operation ensures against the abrupt realization, for both the individual and the organization, that something is going off in the wrong direction. Taken in this context, MBO is not just a means for individual appraisal but is a tool used at all levels in the organization, especially at the top level. In this case, no one is the appraiser or the appraised—it is a two-way street. Somewhere along the line, both the organization and the individuals in it must negotiate a program of action that fits in with the overall missions and goals of the organization and the talents and strengths of the individuals.

Management by objectives is a basic management tool that needs to be integrated into the overall operations of an organization with specific emphasis upon the long-range and strategic planning of upper management. It is not an isolated tool, but rather it is a dynamic concept that demands full attention and participation at all levels in the organization. To be truly effective, today's objectives must be redefined in light of changes and opportunities forecasted for tomorrow.[10] At the interpersonal level, MBO cannot be used as a punishment system that hamstrings managers on short-term objectives that are self-defeating in the long run. The integration of MBO in an organization can be facilitated by examining the psychological assumptions underlying the objectives (organizational culture and its harmony with environmental priorities) and by matching the talents and strengths of the individual with the needs of the organization to realize the goals and values of both.

QUESTIONS FOR REFLECTION AND DISCUSSION

1. What are the advantages and disadvantages of MBO?
2. Under what circumstances might it be desirable to modify organizational and/or individual goals *after* they have been set?
3. How can the long- and short-term objectives of both the individual and organization be balanced?
4. What are the potential problems in balancing long- and short-term objectives?

NOTES

1. John P. Kotter, "Power, Dependence, and Effective Management," *Harvard Business Review*, July/August 1977.
2. R. J. Sternberg, *Beyond IQ: A Triarchic Theory of Human Intelligence* (New York: Cambridge University Press, 1985).
3. Peter Drucker, *The Practice of Management* (New York: Harper, 1954); G. S. Odiorne, *Management by Objectives* (New York: Pitman, 1965); and S. J. Carroll and H. L. Tosi, *Management by Objectives: Applications and Research* (New York: Macmillan, 1973).
4. Harry Levinson, "Management by Whose Objectives?" *Harvard Business Review*, July/August 1970.
5. Michael Beer and Robert A. Ruh, "Employee Growth Through Performance Management," *Harvard Business Review*, July/August 1976.
6. Harry Levinson, "Appraisal of *What* Performance?" *Harvard Business Review*, July/August 1976.
7. J. Sterling Livingston, "Pygmalion in Management," *Harvard Business Review*, January/February, 1971.
8. Alexander H. Leighton, *Human Relations in a Changing World* (New York: Dutton, 1949).
9. G. P. Latham and E. A. Locke, "Goal Setting: a Motivational Technique That Works," *Organizational Dynamics*, Autumn 1979.
10. J. P. Muczyk and B. C. Reimann, "MBO as a Complement to Effective Leadership," *Academy of Management Executive*, March 1989.

CHAPTER 15

MANAGING STRESS

Many commentators on the topic of stress assert that we live in an age of stress. The pressures caused by our occupations, the volatility of the economic market, and the uncertainties of life in general all contribute to the stress syndrome. Also, a variety of dissimilar situations—emotional arousal, effort, fatigue, pain, fear, concentration, humiliation, loss of blood, and even great and unexpected success—are capable of producing stress. Dr. Hans Selze identified three stages of stress: alarm, resistance, and exhaustion.[1] He called these three stages the general adaptation syndrome, or GAS. Stress prepares us for fight or flight. The body produces adrenaline, and blood pressure increases. Managed stress may enhance performance,[2] but repeated episodes of elevated blood pressure without any exercise to relieve the symptoms may have long-term negative effects such as permanently high blood pressure or even heart attacks or strokes.[3] The implications for the over-worked executive are obvious. No one escapes the inevitable consequences of the stress reaction. The key to adaptation is managing the process and the consequences.[4]

The agents or demands that evoke the patterned response are referred to as stressors. Stressors, it should be noted, are not exclusively physical in nature. Emotions—love, hate, joy, challenge, and fear—as well as thoughts, also call forth the changes characteristic of the stress syndrome. In fact, psychological arousal is one of the most frequent activators.

KEY CONCEPTS FOR STRESS MANAGEMENT

Many behavioral techniques can be applied on the individual level in order to manage stress. These techniques depend on developing specific behavioral skills to match the stressor. But before you can maximally apply these techniques, you must accept two key assumptions about behavior change: the responsibility assumption and willing/action.

Responsibility Assumption

Sartre stated that "one is entirely responsible for one's life, not only for one's actions but for one's failure to act." Linked to this assumption is the statement that we also perceive the world around us and give significance to it (see

Chapter 6). We see what are the important elements for us as individuals. Both of these levels of personal responsibility have enormous significance for behavior change. To perceive the world and to be responsible for one's plight may be a deeply frightening insight. These assumptions put the monkey on our backs and, paradoxically, open up opportunities for controlling ourselves in relation to our environment.[5]

Willing/Action

To know and not to act is not to know at all
—Japanese proverb

Awareness of responsibility is only the first step in the process of change. In order to change one must commit oneself to some action. The word *responsibility* itself denotes the capability: *response* and *ability*—that is, the ability to respond. Once an individual fully experiences a wish (to lose weight, control a spontaneous temper, learn a new skill), he or she is faced with a decision. A decision is the bridge between wishing and action. Decisions can be made with a full sense of deliberate, reflective effort.

Irrational Beliefs

The way in which we perceive events shapes our responses to them and, unfortunately, much of our perception is spontaneous; our personal attributes and belief systems may lead to faulty perceptions and, in turn, to stress. For example, believing firmly in how things "should be" or "should be done" or how people "should behave," may lead us to get ourselves into unwanted emotional states that may take a terrible toll on our health and well-being. If we believe traffic jams should not occur, our spontaneous perception of a traffic jam may lead us to anger and stress unnecessarily.

If you recognize this as a tendency in yourself, you can choose to adopt a more pragmatic attitude toward life in general. Your task is to decide which events in your life you can truly exert any control over and which are impervious to influence by you. We can avoid many unnecessary instances provoking the stress response by switching from spontaneous to reflective perception. When we perceive reflectively, we can recognize that there is nothing we can do about traffic jams and thus avoid seeing them as stressors.

Injustices occur in life, we know, and people do act badly toward one another. Our ability to influence such events is, at best, limited. By changing to reflective perception we can avoid the stress response.

Managing Stress—Problems and Suggestions[6]

Problem: You are doing more and more in order to pile up accomplishments and win more and more approval, yet you are feeling dissatisfied and perhaps resentful.

Suggestion: Ask yourself what your own needs and wants are. What would you really like to do? Get off by yourself somewhere and think about what would really give you pleasure, without considering whether it would beat out or, conversely, please someone else.

Problem: You interrupt others while they are talking, imposing your own opinions on them and talking in loud tones for emphasis.

Suggestion: Listen to yourself. Stress-prone personalities (type As) have a tendency to talk too much, too loudly, and too aggressively in tone.[7] If you sound like a know-it-all to yourself, imagine how you sound to others! Build a habit of taking a deep breath each time you start to interrupt other people while they are speaking; in the moment it takes you to breathe, concentrate on what *they* are saying. When the speaker is finished, ask a question instead of immediately taking up the discussion yourself.

Problem: You think about several things at once, doing more than one thing at a time.

Suggestion: Deliberately stare off into space or out the window while waiting for a call to go through, for example, instead of trying to write a memo while waiting. Line up your priorities, writing down your goals in life. What, exactly, would you enjoy accomplishing? Stress-prone individuals often have trouble doing this. They have a tendency to put as much time in on unimportant things as on important things. Listing priorities along with what has to be done to achieve each goal is very good discipline for such individuals. Checking back frequently, of course, is essential.

Problem: You run out of time frequently.

Suggestion: Once again, a list of priorities is important. What can you delegate? What can you eliminate altogether? For those tasks you *must* accomplish, allow yourself more time in the planning stage so that you don't fall behind when an attack of "hurry sickness" hits you. Also, build in time for the relaxation response and quiet reflection when planning your day's activities.[8] You set your own schedule, so make it reasonable for yourself. This may mean saying no to some people, handing off some responsibilities to others, not taking nonessential phone calls, and all in all, dominating things less and less. When you can handle all that, you will have modified typical stress prone (type A) behavior in a very important way. Also, consider how much of this sense of time urgency you're bringing on yourself. Insecurity about your ability to succeed at something can lead to procrastination, and putting things off inevitably leads to a sense of urgency.

Problem: You are in or are surrounded by chaos.

Suggestion: Do what you can to change your environment. Instead of living in the disorder and frenzy that often surrounds typical stress-prone people, make your work and living areas pleasant, soothing, and beautiful. Also, as much as possible, surround yourself with the people who give you some pleasure. At least limit your involvement with the people you *know* arouse anger or tension in you.

You may not be able to change your personality, but taking control of your environment and your own behavior can be entirely consistent with the typical stress-prone personality.[9] In addition to establishing patterns of response like those listed in the above prescriptions, stress-prone people are encouraged to exercise regularly, allow for periods of rest and relaxation, eat wholesome foods, and reduce or eliminate smoking and the drinking of alcoholic beverages.

WORK-RELATED STRESS[10]

Here are some stressors together with suggestions for ways to handle each one. As you look at them, think of a personal confrontation with this type of stressor in your life. How did *you* handle it? What was the outcome? What options do you see now?

Problems and Suggestions

Problem: Too much to do.
Suggestions:

- Delegate those tasks which can be done by others.
- Evaluate your time management. Is your time being used to the best advantage? You want to allow enough time for each task without crowding your schedule so that unexpected interruptions will throw everything off completely.
- Share your entire workload. It may be that a parallel position needs to be created. At the very least, you may need an assistant.

Problem: Too little to do.
Suggestions:

- Make sure your superiors know that you are available for additional tasks by telling them, pleasantly but firmly, that you are ready and able to handle more work.
- Switch tasks with coworkers. Divide your work with another who can handle it; take some of that person's tasks on if you can perform them well. Find diversions on the job that relate to the job.
- Innovate. Maybe you can find new areas within your job to expand, change, or develop. You will certainly gain the respect and trust of your employer if you can come up with new ways to accomplish more.

Problem: Ambiguity or rigidity in relation to one's work.
Suggestions:

- Clarify. Make sure you get a clear statement of your responsibilities and review it periodically with your immediate superiors.

- Show a rigid supervisor how using you in more flexible ways will improve his or her productivity. Remember the doctrine of selfish altruism.
- Communicate. Keep lines open to your boss; don't let resentments pile up until you explode. He or she might not even realize that details have not been made clear to you with regard to the work you are expected to do.
- Don't wait until the annual performance appraisal to have a job discussion.

> Problem: Extreme role conflict or too little conflict.[11] Is the fit right for the job?

Suggestions:

- Here you might start with self-talk. Sit down and think out what you want from the job, clarifying your role responsibilities and deciding for yourself if job and personal roles come into conflict. Put them in priority order. Are you in role conflict because you are afraid of taking risks? Then approach others in your life who are involved—coworkers, spouse, employer, and so on—and come to some arrangement that will serve the needs of all. Role switching with mates with regard to tasks assigned to each, for example, might be a big help in easing the day-to-day tension that you find building up.
- Is there so little role conflict in your life as to deny you the diversity of experience necessary to grow, adapt, and change?

> Problem: Too much responsibility, particularly for people, or no responsibility at all.

Suggestions:

- The stress is greater, of course, when there is responsibility without control. If this is your situation, try asserting yourself by demonstrating your ability to assume greater control or at least your right to participate in decision making.
- If you have no responsibility, show your boss how giving you more responsibility will make him or her a better manager. Point out that the higher a manager goes, the greater the need to delegate responsibility. He or she can "practice" on you.
- Ask for more responsibility that is tied to control of the situation. Explain that it is more difficult to maintain responsibility for people or tasks when you have little or no control over what is involved.
- Perhaps you can make a greater effort to adapt to the other personalities involved, making sure that you do not in any way threaten your colleagues (particularly your immediate superiors). Often, just getting along better with people leads to increased trust, and from there, more participation in management.

> Problem: Negative competition—"Your job stinks but mine is very good."—or no competition at all.

Suggestions:

- Always compliment your competitors on their efforts; never downgrade their work. Look for its good points and praise them.

- Positive competition can be very stimulating. It can work for you, motivating you and keeping you interested in your job. When it becomes negative, however, with comparisons being made to one's advantage or another's, it is not useful. Label negative competition when you confront it. Call for a more adaptive option—positive competition—and seek out others who will go along with you, getting the group to agree on things.
- Seek out mentors and support networks (groups of persons with similar problems). Use them. They'll love it and so will you.
- Cultivate and enjoy the feeling of being above it all when it comes to negative competition. Watch others get stuck while you remain free.

Problem: Constant change and daily variability, or deadening stability.
Suggestions:

- This is another situation that calls for cooperation between worker and supervisor. Try discussing the problems of doing the same work all the time and, together, seek out solutions. For example, it may be possible to trade for a short period each day with another worker who is longing for a break in routine, too. On the other hand, if your work is constantly changing and has you constantly moving from one place to another or if you never have a chance to see your work through to completion, you might propose to management the idea of alternating tasks—doing one job one day and another job the next—instead of racing around to finish everything in one day or, again, trading with a coworker to see how far your skills will take you.
- Find ways to unwind, to relieve the tension that builds up in these situations. A brief period of physical exercise is very helpful.
- Get away from the office, even if just for a five-minute walk each day, preferably in the middle of your day.

Problem: Stress carriers at your job: individuals who are demanding, highly anxious, or workaholics; indecisive individuals who cannot provide the leadership or support needed from them; or individuals who are chronic complainers or depressives.

Suggestions:

- Provide what support you can, but assuming you cannot really help such a person to change his or her behavior, make every effort to get off by yourself as much as possible. Once alone, do any relaxation technique that works for you. Remain in repose for a few minutes before returning to the stress-producing situation.
- Remind yourself that you are not in control of your stress-carrier's personality. Reaffirm your belief in yourself and take responsibility for what you can control.
- If you are in this situation or if you find yourself completely isolated in your work, it is extremely important for you to develop other social contacts that are rewarding to you. A balanced, satisfying life outside the work environment is a great help.

Problem: The atmosphere at your company discourages the expression of individual emotional reactions and encourages identification with the organization, even at the cost of family life.[12]

Suggestions:

- Let go of your anger when appropriate and do so in an appropriate manner. The assertive style, combining directness, honesty, and respect for others' feelings, is usually the most adaptive way of doing this. Certainly, care must be taken not to say or do anything so damaging that you sever relations with the organization; still, it is harmful to you to suppress the hostility you may be feeling. It will raise your stress level and ultimately harm the company as well through your lowered productivity or absenteeism. Finally, in passive, obstructionistic ways, you might begin to jeopardize your job.
- Engage in tension-releasing activities, such as physical exercise, private walks on breaks, or even yelling if you can find a place to do it where you won't be too conspicuous.
- Remind yourself from time to time that you are not the organization. You have your own identity and a full life away from the job. Define yourself accordingly. Don't permit anyone to define who you are.
- Share your own definition with your employer when it comes to your work life.

Problem: Friction in the interaction of career opportunity and management style.

Suggestions:

- Assess and evaluate your own career and make sure, by reevaluating from time to time, that you are being supported in your aspirations by managers, supervisors, or others in charge of your progress.
- Make a plan for your career and if you find that management is not responsive to your plan, do what you can to discuss your frustrations with the appropriate persons. If you are still dissatisfied that your needs are being met, begin seeking out other job opportunities. Learn how to do this most effectively.

Problem: Many tedious or burdensome details associated with corporate life: meetings, deadlines, business lunches, and so forth.

Suggestions:

- Develop skills of time management so that you don't feel overwhelmed by the sheer numbers of things to be done, appointments to be kept, and so on.
- Decide which tasks are most valuable to you. Having a business lunch every day, for example, might not be a true necessity. Some of these appointments may be important; others not so important that you couldn't delegate them to other people or eliminate them altogether by doing business by phone.
- Try to find enrichment in the unwanted or tedious tasks you must do. Often, by looking at things from a new angle or getting a new person involved with you, you can freshen up the whole procedure so that it is not so burdensome to you.

- Try to make your contribution, in anything over which you do have control, enlightening, meaningful, fun, and appropriate.

All of these occupational stressors apply to managers as well as subordinates. In fact, management-level people must be aware of the effects of these stressors on themselves as well as the people whom they supervise. Be aware of the role you may be playing in raising the stress levels of your staff, and try using the alternatives listed above—or your own suggestions—in dealing with them on a day-to-day basis.

QUESTIONS FOR REFLECTION AND DISCUSSION

1. What are the differences and similarities between our reflective and spontaneous perceptions of a situation?
2. What are the differences and similarities between work-related and nonwork-related stress?
3. What kinds of situations create stress in you? Why?
4. What can managers do to optimize stress (and performance) and minimize the risks of excessive stress?

NOTES

1. Hans Selze, *The Stress of Life*, 2nd ed. (New York: McGraw-Hill, 1976); *Stress Without Distress* (New York: J. B. Lippencott, 1974).
2. David W. Ewing, "Tension Can Be An Asset," *Harvard Business Review*, September/October 1964.
3. J. M. Ivancevich, M. T. Matteson, and E. P. Richards III, "Who's Liable for Stress on the Job?" *Harvard Business Review*, March/April 1985.
4. K. Albrecht, *Stress and the Manager: Making It Work for You* (Englewood Cliffs, NJ: Prentice-Hall, 1975).
5. M. T. Matteson and J. M. Ivancevich, *Controlling Work Stress* (San Francisco: Jossey-Bass, 1987).
6. Donald Meichenbaum, *Stress Innoculation Training* (New York: Pergamon, 1985).
7. M. Friedman and R. Roseman, *Type A Behavior and Your Heart* (New York: Knopf, 1974).
8. Herbert Benson, *The Relaxation Response* (New York: Morrow, 1975).
9. J. E. Bishop, "Prognosis for the Type A Personality Improves in a New Heart Disease Study," *Wall Street Journal*, January 14, 1988.
10. J. L. Quick and J. D. Quick, *Organizational Stress and Preventive Management* (New York: McGraw-Hill, 1984).

11. R. L. Kahn, D. M. Wolfe, R. P. Quinn, and J. D. Snoek, *Organizational Stress: Studies in Role Conflict and Ambiguity* (New York: Wiley, 1964).

12. D. T. Hall and J. Richter, "Balancing Work Life and Home Life: What Can Organizations Do to Help?" *Academy of Management Executive*, August 1988.

CHAPTER 16

MANAGING CONFLICT

The human being is enormously complex, and his or her world of immediate experience simultaneously contains many needs, desires, values, goals, choices or options, and both positive and negative features of his or her surroundings. Organizational complexity, diversity, and the interdependencies between individuals and groups are increasing.[1] All these lead us to experience conflict in one form or another. The degree of conflict ranges from the scarcely perceptible to the utmost of paralyzing stress. It is important to note that conflict can exist within the individual, between individuals, and among groups. The problem of intrapersonal conflict as an important determinant of behavior has been covered by the material on functional perception in Chapter 6 and will not be dealt with here. The focus here will be on interpersonal conflict,[2] group conflict,[3] and their relationship to organizational behavior.

Although conflict may be either functional or dysfunctional depending on the particular situation and the way the conflict is managed,[4] many of us assume that conflict implies mutual opposition or aggression. We observe conflict around individual or group goals, roles, status, rewards and limited resources.[5] When individuals or groups perceive they are in competition with other individuals or groups, conflict may result, but it may also arise whenever a strongly motivated individual feels his or her self-image (or self-esteem or self-expectations) is threatened or is frustrated by another. Some people have argued that conflicts have a biological basis, presumably in the form of innate aggressiveness, and evidence suggests that some forms of conflict may result from the frustration of basic needs or values.[6] Various cultures have evolved different views of handling conflict. One viewpoint is consistent among behavioral sciences, and that is that some situations call for competition while others call for integrative or cooperative actions. Conflict can exist in both of these situations when individuals, because of their different behavior patterns, clash with each other over goals and the means of reaching these goals.

Because conflict has many dysfunctional aspects to it, most of the concern over conflict has been with the resolution or smoothing operations necessary to dispel the negative side effects. The human relations movement in the 1930s devoted its efforts to fostering cooperation and group cohesiveness through conflict resolution. Like many elementary approaches, it overshot its mark. In the zealous attempt to resolve conflict the reformers missed one point: conflict is both inevitable and normal. Without conflict one does not have the variety of opinion necessary to determine the means of achieving a goal or the priority of the goals themselves. In this sense, conflict, if it is related to the means or the goals themselves, can be functional in that it fosters divergent thinking rather than conformity or consensus based on the mean level of thinking.

If conflict is managed, it can become a creative force. The way it is managed—rather than suppressed, ignored, or avoided—contributes significantly to the effectiveness of individuals or groups.[7] The adoption of this new appreciation of conflict shifts the focus from a value-laden assumption that conflict is always bad, to a more functional view that takes into account when conflict is likely to arise, when it is appropriate, and how it can be managed so that it is functional rather than dysfunctional. In any given situation, individuals may choose either to compete, cooperate, or ignore others. These choices, to some degree, are determined by the situation. In a serious poker game, one would not consciously want to cooperate with fellow players and disclose one's strategy. This kind of a situation is commonly called the *distributive* or *zero-sum* game (when one person wins, the other must lose). On the other hand, suppose a group of two or more people are working as a team to piece together a jigsaw puzzle; as they work against the clock or against another team, they may exemplify a *cooperative* or *integrative* approach to each other. Conflict could emerge in this situation over strategies, but is clearly task-oriented and not aimed at reducing the other person's status or prestige. Discussions with a fellow member of a research team may be largely an integrative process but may contain some strains of healthy conflict over the means of meeting various goals.

This form of conflict in an integrative situation is functional. It is very different from conflict in a distributive situation, which sometimes becomes aggressively hostile, as in a war. Because we are human and suffer from blind spots and misconceptions, we may have difficulties in reading the environment and assessing when we are in a distributive situation versus an integrative one. Reality being what it is, we generally have a mix between these pure types. For example, we may be working on a task force to solve a given problem while, at the same time, competing with our peers for promotions or recognition. The latter situation, because of its very nature, has the highest potential for latent or hidden conflict. This situation has been labelled the "prisoner's dilemma"—damned if you do and damned if you don't.

The critical factor involved is awareness of the situation and what is the appropriate behavior. In organizational life we are often told that we are in a cooperative situation and that coordination is the watchword. Yet, in spite of exhortations, admonitions, and threats from superiors, peers, and consultants, we find ourselves in the midst of conflict. Some of this conflict arises from personal misconceptions that then lead people to play a distributive game when an integrative one is more appropriate. On the positive side, the conflict may have legitimate roots based on different life experiences or due to differences of opinion with regard to the goals or means to an end. Managing by consensus, in the latter situation, is very dangerous in that it submerges the conflict and maintains it on a hidden level, ready to reemerge when the opportunity presents itself.

Realistic conflict over issues needs to be resolved on both the task level and the group maintenance level.

People have tendencies to respond to situations in a rather stable, consistent fashion and usually respond very slowly to changes in the environment. People's spontaneous behavior derives from their personal attributes, which have evolved over their lifetimes (see Chapter 4). People who react to every situation as if it were a distributive game are likely to transform a discussion into a debate. Because of their personal characteristics they see life as a Darwinian struggle of the survival of the fittest. These personal characteristics color all of their perceptions and situational interactions.

Other people may have personal characteristics that lead them to approach most situations as if they were integrative games. They intrinsically feel that people should work together to make a better world to the point where they may let a used car dealer bilk them in a deal. Those who are able to stand back from a situation and determine what it is all about reflectively would tend to follow a different strategy based on the contingencies. This is not a new approach but rather the old plea for behavioral flexibility, a trait most of us do not exhibit to a large degree.

MANAGING CONFLICT

We must be aware of two different situations when we attempt to deal with conflict: conflict that is overt and conflict that is hidden or covert. These forms of conflict have different sources and solutions.

Overt Conflict

We can make three possible diagnoses:

1. We may examine the logical aspects of the situation and discover that no real conflict of goals or competitive reward structure exists. These apparent conflicts may arise due to such factors as misunderstandings, differing assumption, or complementary perceptions. This presents an opportunity for new integrative attempts.
2. The parties involved already recognize that there is no real goal conflict but that different management styles, behavior patterns, and the resultant interpersonal relations between them prevent collaboration on the means to move toward a common goal or goals. Here, one must work directly on improving interpersonal relationships, clarifying differences in approach and creating mutual trust and concern. This implies not avoiding the conflict, but actually confronting the issues in a face-to-face manner.[8]
3. We may discover that an apparent conflict in goals is significant and real. There are two possible solutions: a) focus on the goal conflict or b) play a distributive strategy. The latter strategy tends to escalate the conflict and results in one party with higher status and more power dominating the other.[9] Usually the dominating party is the one who had the "bulge" or the big guns in their favor

(most likely, the boss). A more realistic approach is to open up a dialogue over the differences and see where the divergence is really serious. Once a dialogue is opened on a fair and equal basis, the game shifts from a zero-sum to a cooperative venture to seek points of communality and alternatives for both sides. This strategy does not mandate a compromise, but open discussion of the divergent goals and the consequences for both parties in continuing to follow a rigid pattern often leads to an acceptable compromise.

A good example of this form of conflict is the battle over basic research or advanced development in an R & D organization. Scientists will adhere to the position that the goals of the organization should center around basic research, while some managers and engineers will take the position that application is the ultimate goal of the organization. In reality, the pressure to do basic or applied research is dependent upon the constraints from the environment. Either extreme exists only in the eye of the beholder. In practical reality, it is a matter of emphasis and responsiveness to environmental demands. One camp cannot survive without the other, in spite of their extreme positions. The end or goal conflict can only be resolved by focusing on the internal value orientations and the demands from the external environment.

Hidden, Suppressed, or Covert Conflict

Individuals may have subconscious personal characteristics that lead to spontaneous behavior indicating hidden conflict. Delays, avoidance of direct face-to-face interactions, or perhaps even feigned or real illness may indicate hidden conflict. The conflict deriving from subconscious personal characteristics can be understood only by understanding the individual's life experiences, which have formed these characteristics. They can be dealt with by taking those steps outlined in Chapter 4 to get the individual to behave reflectively and thus avoid the hidden conflict.

Chris Argyris has pointed out that one of the most common observations in organizational studies is that managers lack awareness of their own spontaneous behavior patterns as well as the negative effect of their behavior on others' spontaneous behavior.[10] He has isolated two common patterns of group decision making, labelled Pattern A and Pattern B. These patterns represent different styles of hidden or covert conflict over goals and means in the decision-making process. For example, Pattern A behavior is thoughtful, rational, and mildly competitive. This was the behavior pattern most frequently seen in group decision meetings. It is a form of zero-sum one-upmanship that focuses on the concern for ideas in order to shoot them down in an impersonal fashion. People would gain information about the others' points of view so as to politely discredit them. Pattern B behavior is competitive first, thoughtful and rational second. In this pattern, conformity to ideas replaces concern for ideas as the strongest norm. Also, antagonism to ideas is higher than receptivity. This relatively high antagonism indicates high competitiveness and a great degree of pent-up feelings.

In both of these patterns, managers are rarely seen

- taking risks or experimenting with new ideas or feelings;

- helping others to own up, be open, and take risks;
- using a style of behavior that supports the norm of individuality and trust as well as mistrust; or
- expressing feelings, positive or negative.

Both of these patterns, although different in style, represent a closed-minded approach to conflict. Pattern A is the polite dismissal of another's viewpoint, while Pattern B is the hostile dismissal. In both cases, they can be viewed as dysfunctional forms of handling conflict. They are zero-sum games in different disguises.

Argyris and others believe that personal characteristics like basic values are the determinants behind this common approach to handling conflict. In both cases, the conflict is submerged rather than confronted in an authentic, open fashion. The personal characteristics that are important to these patterns are

1. a belief in "scientific reasoning based on fact" and avoidance of the discussion of feelings, emotions, or opinions;
2. a belief in the effectiveness of unilateral action versus meaningful participatory discussion; and
3. a belief that conflict is always destructive (hostile) and will interfere with the achievement of organizational objectives.

These personal characteristics lead to various action patterns on the part of managers and subordinates. One such action pattern is restricted commitment by all members. There tends to be less than open discussion of the issues and commitment of the personnel tends to be less complete, although they may reassure themselves that they are wholeheartedly involved. Another behavior pattern is called *subordinate gamesmanship*. In this type of game, negative information is not fed upwards; only positive or "look good" information is passed upwards. The dynamics behind this behavior is the fear of reprisal from the upper levels and a withholding of necessary information from top management. A system that reflectively and functionally looks at problems will encourage risk-taking where individuals discuss both negative and positive inputs.

These two defensive spontaneous behavior patterns of managers, at all levels, tend to generate distrust and antagonism rather than healthy functional conflict. We have observed that those behavior patterns leading to ineffectiveness tend to operate most strongly during the important decision-making meetings. Another interesting finding is that more effective and more committed executives tend to be upset about these behaviors within themselves on a self-image basis, whereas the less effective, less committed managers tend simply to lament them on a verbal level. They also tend to take on an "I told them so" attitude (a form of self-justification).

The basic question is, "What can be done to reverse this situation of covert conflict in order to create an atmosphere of reflective functional problem-solving?" As with most complex situations, there are no simple solutions to this issue. For starters, however, the manager can strive to be aware that he or she is programmed with a set of personal characteristics and values which may lead to spontaneous behavior that is not always helpful to others. Managers can also strive to uncover, through careful questioning, the effect of their behavior on others. They can advantageously use feedback from typical dysfunctional meetings actively to uncover the binds, the blind spots, and the hidden behavior that took place in the session. The most basic step, however, is to realize that conflict has both functional and dysfunctional aspects. When conflict is hidden or covert, we can expect spontaneous behavior patterns similar to the ones described above. By keeping the individuals involved reflective in their responses (see Chapter 4), the hidden conflict can be avoided or perhaps converted to overt conflict. Overt conflict can be handled and turned into an asset. The reflective reiterative process of creating a group climate that includes openness, individual risk-taking, and personal awareness is the best preventative of dysfunctional conflict.

SUMMARY

Conflict is not only inevitable in any structured situation, but also desirable, in optimal amounts, as a motivator and catalyst for adaptive change, particularly in creative, professional, innovative organizations. Not all organizations have the same values, goals and perceptions, and just as there is diversity in the organization, so is there diversity among the different subunits and among different individuals within each subunit. As Kelly observed, "The way conflict is managed—rather than suppressed, ignored or avoided—contributes significantly to a company's effectiveness."[11]

Successful problem solving requires not merely that the final solution be presented but that all possible alternatives be made available for consideration. Consensus, or conflict avoidance, will not facilitate optimum problem solving; functional conflict is vital. Work requires open, functional conflict in order to help define and clarify all options available.

QUESTIONS FOR REFLECTION AND DISCUSSION

1. Under what circumstances might conflict be functional? Dysfunctional?
2. What are the differences and similarities between overt and covert conflict?
3. What can managers do to manage conflict more effectively?
4. What are the potential problems in managing conflict?

NOTES

1. John P. Kotter, *Power and Influence* (New York: The Free Press, 1985).
2. A. C. Filley, *Interpersonal Conflict Resolution* (Glenview, IL: Scott, Foresman, 1975).
3. R. R. Blake, and J. S. Mouton, "Overcoming Group Warfare," *Harvard Business Review,* November/December 1984.
4. R. Caffasella, "Managing Conflict: An Analytical Tool," *Training and Development Journal,* February 1984.

5. S. P. Robbins, *Managing Organizational Conflict* (Englewood Cliffs, NJ: Prentice-Hall, 1974).

6. R. N. McMurry, "Conflicts in Human Values," *Harvard Business Review*, May/June 1963.

7. Joe Kelly, "Make Conflict Work for You," *Harvard Business Review*, July/August 1970, pp. 103–13.

8. A. S. Grove, "How to Make Confrontation Work for You," *Fortune*, July 23, 1984.

9. R. E. Walton, *Managing Conflict: Interpersonal Dialogue and Third Party Roles* (Reading, MA: Addison-Wesley, 1987).

10. Chris Argyris, "Interpersonal Barriers to Decision Making," *Harvard Business Review* March/April 1966, pp. 84–97; and "Double Loop Learning in Organizations," *Harvard Business Review*, September/October 1977, pp. 115–25.

11. Kelly, "Make Conflict Work for You."

CHAPTER 17

GROUP BEHAVIOR AND TEAM BUILDING

Every organization has a number of groups that perform significant tasks that contribute to the accomplishment of its goals and objectives. Increasingly, modern management practice includes a considerable amount of interpersonal contact in small work groups. As tasks become more difficult and complex, technical specialization and differentiation occur. At the same time, the successful completion of tasks requires an increasing amount of integration and coordination among individuals and groups.[1] Tasks are most often carried out in small work groups, their purpose being to prepare products or services, solve problems, analyze alternatives, exchange information, resolve differences of opinion, and make decisions. These groups may be formal or informal, long-lived or short-lived, and responsible for a specific task or series of related tasks. Each group's effectiveness depends upon the members' collective ability to behave in each instance as an effective team and to manage the process of completing tasks.[2]

A work group is composed of a number of people usually with diverse personalities, skills, motivations, interests, and backgrounds.[3] In most organizations the tasks assigned a work group establish interdependencies with other groups or individuals, require a variety of functions or activities to be performed within a specified time and budget, and specify the quantity and quality of the output. The people in a work group must perform the assigned tasks within the constraints imposed by the organization, including such things as the reward systems, formal procedures for measurement and control, the organizational structure, a hierarchy of status and reporting relationships, and the physical environment in which the group must function.

The work group functions within a larger corporate culture derived from the history of the organization, the external constraints imposed by society and various stakeholders, and the purposes now served by the organization.[4] As the work group functions, it evolves a group culture, which includes the social roles various members are expected to play, the values, sentiments, and norms of behavior to which members are expected to adhere, and the social interaction patterns that are expected.[5] Manifestations of this group culture include the language it uses, the stories it tells, and the rituals that evolve. All of these factors affect the productivity of the group and the satisfaction the individuals in the group obtain, including their sense of competence and growth.[6]

To improve the effectiveness of a small work group, the manager or member of the group needs to understand what he or she can do (what action he or she can take or what behavior he or she can exhibit) that will have a positive effect as well as what might have a negative effect. It seems clear that the selection of people for the group, the physical setting in which the group must function, the tasks that the group is asked to perform, and the constraints imposed by the organization will, over time, influence the group culture which in turn influences productivity. It is critical for managers to understand which of these factors they can influence and to what effect. To do this, managers must understand the way groups behave in order to build a more effective working team.

All groups and the members thereof have tasks to accomplish or goals to reach. These task-related issues are the *content* of interpersonal contacts, group meetings, and discussions. Equally important is the group interaction *process*, which occurs simultaneously with the content interactions. The process includes the way individual members interact or behave toward one another. This can result in an open environment with cooperation and trust or a closed suspicious environment with antagonisms, competition, and distrust. Clearly, the process can have a positive or negative effect on the content output of the group.

Interaction is more than simply the verbal or written exchange of information between people (see Chapter 7). It may also include body language signals, such as gestures, glances, nods or shakes of the head, pats on the back (literal or figurative), frowns, caresses, or slaps, and any other way in which meanings can be transmitted from one person to another and back again.[7] *Interaction* refers to communications in its broadest sense and covers all the various ways in which people can and do express themselves in face-to-face meetings.

We all participate in small work groups and it is essential that we understand both the process and the content of such groups. By devoting particular attention to how (process) a group performs its tasks (content), we may gain insight into both our own past behavior in groups and ways we might make future group behavior more effective.

Every work group functions on two levels:

1. It has something to do (purpose or task orientation), which gives rise to a set of required activities, procedures, methods and formal structure.
2. It must be kept running in order to do it (maintenance function or process orientation), which gives rise to a group culture or set of emergent activities, procedures, methods, and informal structure that is related to the process and not to the task.

These twin functions require continual attention. Groups deal with their purpose or task orientation by establishing, explicitly or implicitly, a set of task-related expectations for such things as work assignments, work flow, procedures, rules, and followership or leadership roles. These task orientations are part of the essential nature of small work groups. A set of process-related expectations evolves for the maintenance function. Both sets of expectations taken together form the core of the group culture.

Groups vacillate back and forth between task and process functions, that is, between interactions dealing directly with the task and interactions dealing with emotional or social relations and structures among the members. The former tend to create tensions within the group because the tasks require solving difficult problems that raise anxiety levels and the latter tend to reduce tension and achieve harmony. Both tendencies apparently need to be satisfied in all small work groups engaged in performing some task.

To be an effective group leader or participant one should be aware of the processes within groups and the concomitant problems that can develop in small work groups. To shape our own behavior and the behavior of others, we must become alert but nonintrusive observers of the interaction in small groups. If one is able to observe and analyze the interaction in the group process, one is in a position to diagnose what is happening and predict what will happen. One is then in a position to proceed with the business of the group or take corrective steps.

OBSERVING THE GROUP PROCESS

Observing the group process means focusing on the "here and now": how are the various group members behaving in this group situation? Does the group stick close to the main purpose or topic? Do certain members characteristically play certain roles in the group? How effective is the leadership of the group? Are members cooperative? Supportive? Antagonistic? Do they trust each other? Do they feel free to express what's really on their minds (are they leveling with one another)? The effectiveness of the group in reaching its goals or accomplishing its task depends in large part on the answers to these questions. It is via the group process that the content gets accomplished.

Just as there are many questions about group behavior, so there are many possible guides and scales for observation. Some managers have found three types of observations particularly useful for collecting three different kinds of information: who talked to whom, who makes what kinds of contributions, and what happened in the group.

Who Talked to Whom?

If the network of communication channels within the group is accurately observed, it can tell a great deal about the informal structure within the group. Do individuals address most of their comments to one person? Are there balanced communication networks? Are separate coalitions formed or forming within the group? Are there initiators and/or reactors? Are there isolates within the group? Every conversation is an interaction (or a series of interactions), but the many nonverbal communications or contacts are equally valid as interactions. In observing interactions, it is usually important to note by whom they are initiated and whether two or more people are simultaneously involved.

Who Makes What Kinds of Contributions?

As we have already suggested, some interactions are task- or content-related and some are process- or maintenance-related. The task-related interactions generally serve either to offer, or solicit from others, solutions or opinions. They can lead to raises in tension or emotional levels, requiring some immediate attention. The maintenance interactions take over in order to deal with the level of tension and restore some sense of stability before tasks or task-related discussion can be resumed. These roles involve either positive or negative reaction to remarks made by other members.

Many groups obviously suffer because the contributions of members do not complement each other. A well-balanced group will have perceivers, doers, coordinators, critics, confirmers, and integrators. For instance, one member may have excellent insights into the group's character and needs; another may initiate new ideas based on these insights; a third may welcome and reward the ideas of others; a fourth may expose the weaknesses of certain ideas; a fifth may be skilled at reconciling viewpoints, and the sixth may be the group's historian or ideologist, clarifying the conclusions the members have reached and enunciating the rules by which they live.

The group with equilibrium has either a member for each of these roles or it has skilled members who are able to shift from one role to another as the need arises. Other groups, however, may have an abundance of initiators who refuse to listen to each other's ideas or may be dominated by assertive initiators notable more for being energetic than for exercising good judgment. Often those members with a capacity to solve problems find themselves overruled by other, less well-informed members who are willing to support one another, but unwilling to initiate. They may accurately perceive their problems but fail to correct them. Rather, their sometimes painful insights are an excuse for contemplation and inaction. They suffer from "analysis paralysis." Another type of group may act too compulsively with little perception or premeditation. It may permit such wide divergencies in behavior that coordination collapses. Or, it may insist upon such close coordination that individuality is stifled.

An alert manager will ask himself, "What does this group need?" It may be lacking insight. It may be short on risk-taking, on assertiveness, or on the capacity to reach its more deviant, though creative, members. It may need someone willing to listen and confirm, a synergist able to reconcile viewpoints, or a chronicler able to summarize and integrate the group's progress. If a group can be rebalanced, it will often develop more productive and satisfying relationships.

What Happened in the Group?

In most successful groups, the process tends to move through time from a relative emphasis upon the problems of orientation (who are we, how should we relate to one another, why are we here) to problems of evaluation (discussion of the agenda, resolving conflict, dealing with dissonance) and subsequently to problems of control (firming up the leadership/followership patterns or sticking to the course of action agreed upon by the group members). As a group grows through time, both positive and negative interactions become more frequent. This natural process occurs as individuals get to know one another, open up, and take personal risks with each other. These phases in group interaction are common to all groups, but when and how they occur can be important. Forcing control or evaluation too early in the growth cycle of a new group may have significant adverse effects because the process or maintenance functions have been neglected or shut off. If a group is allowed to progress in a natural way, it is more likely to grow and become more cohesive, more productive, and more capable of helping its individual members in specific ways.

Both the effectiveness of the group and the satisfaction of its members are increased when the members see their personal goals as being advanced by the group's goals, that is, when the two are perceived as being in harmony (see Chapter 14). When individual members push personal goals that are not in harmony with group goals, both satisfaction and group effectiveness decline.

This kind of consideration gives rise to the notion of the "hidden agenda" in groups—what each, or at least some, of the members are after given their particular experiences, aptitudes, and expectations. By contrast, the "open agenda" is what the group is supposed to be doing—solving a problem, designing or producing a product, organizing itself for action, and so on. The hidden agenda consists of what is intrinsically motivating its members—relative power, higher achievement or competence, increase in prestige, desire for promotion or recognition, and so on. The stronger the hidden agenda, consciously or unconsciously pursued by group members, the less effective the group will be at achieving its stated purpose. Some people believe that every group has its hidden agenda and that a wise leader will be guided by that as well as by the open agenda.

GROUP PERSONALITIES

We have looked inside the small work group. Now let's look at the small work group as an entity in itself with which the manager must deal. That groups may be said to have personalities in the same way as human beings do is implied by the fact that individuals adopt and accept a psychological contract or set of expectations among members of a group concerning the group culture that will govern their day-to-day interaction.[8] This is closely analogous to the manner in which an individual evolves his or her various self-expectations. We define group culture as the values or norms that lead to a set of expectations among group members that certain kinds of behavior are to be encouraged and rewarded while other kinds of behavior are to be discouraged and punished (see also Chapter 19). A manager needs to consider the probable influence of actions he or she might take on the culture of the group and its resultant productivity. A change in the physical layout in which the group functions could have a positive, negative, or neutral effect. The same can be said for changes in the reward system, the type of tasks assigned, and even the addition to or subtraction from the group of specific people. Obviously, the strengths of the group's culture will influence the level of response the group may have to the various actions a manager might take.

The extent to which group culture influences the behavior of members is a measure of cohesiveness, or affiliation. The greater the degree of cohesiveness the greater the degree to which individual behavior conforms to group values. Cohesiveness derives from the strength of the desire of members to remain members. Members of a football team, fraternity, sorority, or executive group may take pride in their membership and be strongly motivated to maintain group membership. Groups that perceive themselves under some kind of external threat or siege may be cohesive because group survival is threatened. Examples would include an army platoon or a naval unit under combat conditions. The threat may be psychological and not physical. For example, a small sect that believes that the earth is flat may be cohesive because outside the group there is nothing but the disconfirmation of conflicting opinion. A civil rights group will tend to be cohesive to the extent that it anticipates ridicule and opposition, and the same applies to radical groups attempting to change the status quo. Such groups must draw their nurture from within, since the world outside is often hostile.

In some situations cohesiveness may be related to the skills and/or maturity of the group's members. People with poor linear, nonlinear, and contextual skills may need a great deal of mutual guidance, mutual interaction, and the psychological support of being able to judge themselves and others by group standards.[9] By the same token, they may be rather afraid of the outside world because they do not perceive that they have the skills to operate in that uncertain environment. Therefore, they may huddle together for psychological support. Examples that readily spring to mind are street gangs, some native tribal peoples, and groups of tourists. For example, the cohesiveness of strangers is often increased by the introduction of anxiety (such as a lack of language skills) or fear (such as the fear of being lost or separated from the group).

Inside organizations, groups consisting of several different professional specialists such as engineers, scientists, and so on may be very low on cohesiveness. This may be influenced by the perceived mobility of the specialists and the resultant reduced effect of external or organizational threats to the group. Members may feel confident of moving on to other groups easily. In addition, most professional specialists have strong affiliations with other groups outside the organization, such as family, professional groups, churches, fraternal groups, and alumni groups. Many of these other groups have value systems to which the professional specialist has given allegiance. These are called reference groups and their effect is to limit the extent to which the culture of small work groups in the organization can deviate from those of the reference groups, particularly in nontask related areas. This in turn limits the psychological contracts between the group members and with the organization. This often results in a high tolerance for widely different values among individuals in the group (diversity), particularly with respect to emergent, informal, or process-oriented behavior. Low cohesiveness gives the manager far more flexibility, but increases the complexity of dealing with the group, while high cohesiveness may lead to dysfunctional cultural norms if not managed carefully.

GROUPTHINK

When a highly cohesive group begins to behave in a concurrence-seeking manner to such an extent that conflicting opinion is stifled, it is exhibiting a form of dysfunctional behavior labeled *groupthink*. The term *groupthink* is used as a quick and easy way to refer to the mode of thinking in which people behave in ways that tend to override realistic appraisals of alternative courses of action. The term refers to a deterioration in mental efficiency, reality testing, and moral judgments as a result of group pressure.

The symptoms of groupthink arise when the members of decision-making groups become motivated to avoid being too harsh in their judgments of the leaders' or their colleagues' ideas. They adopt a soft line of criticism, even in their own thinking. At their meetings, all the members are amiable and seek complete concurrence on every important issue with no bickering or conflict to spoil the cozy, warm, "we-feeling" atmosphere.

In Irving Janis's studies of high-level governmental decision makers, he notes:

> The more amiability and esprit de corps there is among the members of a policy-making in-group, the greater the danger that independent critical thinking will be replaced by groupthink, which is likely to result in irrational and dehumanizing actions directed against out-groups.[10]

Janis identifies eight main symptoms of groupthink shared by most if not all of the members of the group:

1. *Invulnerability*. They possess an illusion of invulnerability that provides for them some degree of reassurance about the strength of their position in spite of clear warnings of such risks, which leads them to become overoptimistic and willing to take extraordinary risks.
2. *Rationalization*. They collectively construct rationalizations in order to discount warnings and other forms of negative feedback that, taken seriously, might lead the group members to reconsider their assumptions each time they recommit themselves to past decisions.
3. *Morality*. They believe unquestioningly in the inherent morality of their group, which inclines the members to ignore the potentially negative ethical or moral consequences of their decisions.
4. *Stereotypes*. They construct stereotyped views of the leaders of "enemy" groups; opposing groups are perceived as being so evil that genuine attempts at negotiating differences with them are unwarranted, or they are seen as too weak or too stupid to deal effectively with whatever attempts the group makes to defeat their purposes, no matter how risky the attempts are.
5. *Pressure*. They apply direct pressure to any individual member of the group who momentarily expresses doubts about any of the group's shared illusions or who questions the validity of the arguments supporting a policy alternative favored by the majority. This gambit reinforces the concurrence-seeking norm that loyal members are expected to maintain.

6. *Self-censorship.* They avoid deviating from what appears to be group consensus; they keep silent about their misgivings and even minimize to themselves the importance of their doubts.

7. *Unanimity.* They create an illusion of unanimity within the group concerning almost all judgments expressed by members who speak in favor of the majority view. This symptom results partly from the preceding one, and these effects are augmented by the false assumption that any individual who remains silent during any part of the discussion is in full accord with what the others are saying.

8. *Mindguards.* They sometimes appoint themselves as mindguards to protect the leader and fellow members from adverse information that might break the unanimity they shared about the effectiveness and morality of past decisions.

When a group of executives frequently displays most or all of these interrelated symptoms, a number of consequences are likely:

1. The group limits its discussions to a few alternative courses of action (often only two) without an initial survey of all the alternatives that might be worthy of consideration.

2. The group fails to reexamine the course of action initially preferred by the majority after they learn the risks and drawbacks they had not originally considered.

3. The members spend little or no time discussing whether there are nonobvious gains they may have overlooked or ways of reducing the seemingly prohibitive costs that made rejected alternatives appear undesirable to them.

4. Members make little or no attempt to obtain information from experts within their own organizations who might be able to supply more precise estimates of potential risks and rewards.

5. Members show positive interest in facts and opinions that support their preferred policy; they tend to ignore facts and opinions that do not.

6. Members spend little time deliberating how the chosen policy might be hindered by bureaucratic inertia, sabotaged by political opponents, or temporarily derailed by common accidents. Consequently, they fail to work out contingency plans to cope with foreseeable setbacks that could endanger the overall success of their chosen course.

Managers who wish to avoid the pitfalls of groupthink can take a variety of steps to minimize the risk:

1. The manager or leader of a group should encourage and *solicit* conflicting opinions. To facilitate this process the manager may assign the role of critical evaluator to each member, encouraging the group to give high priority to openly airing objections, doubts, and conflicting opinions. This practice needs to be reinforced by the leader's willingness to accept criticism of his or her own judgments in order to discourage members from soft-pedaling their disagreements and from allowing their striving for concurrence to inhibit criticism.

2. The manager should avoid stating preferences and expectations about possible solutions and remain as neutral as feasible. The leader should encourage open inquiry and impartial probing of a wide range of alternatives.

3. The manager may set up two or more subgroups to look at the same issue from different points of view to minimize insularity.

4. The manager should periodically ask each member to discuss the group's deliberations with associates in his or her own unit of the organization, assuming that those associates can be trusted to adhere to the same security regulations that govern the policy-makers, and then to report back their reactions to the group.

5. The manager should invite one or more outside experts to each meeting on a staggered basis and encourage the experts to question the views of the core members.

6. The manager should encourage at least one member of the group to play devil's advocate, functioning as a good lawyer would in challenging the testimony of those who advocate a specific position.

7. The manager should ask the group to survey all warning signals from any source including any rivals and develop alternative responses should any of these warnings come to fruition in terms of the behavior and/or intentions of people outside the group.

8. After the group has reached a preliminary consensus about what seems to be the best decision, the manager should hold a "second chance" meeting at which every member expresses as vividly as possible all residual doubts, and rethinks the entire issue before making a definitive choice.

By the steps above, a manager can minimize the probability of experiencing the negative consequences of groupthink and make the cohesiveness of the group a positive force contributing to organizational effectiveness.

TEAM BUILDING[11]

Just as a competitive sports team has to practice to develop and maintain its effectiveness as a unit, so also do management teams need to sharpen their skills in working together not only to avoid negative influences such as groupthink discussed above, but to build greater positive influences to maximize achievement of the goals and objectives for which the group was formed. The essence of team building involves, first, an acceptance of the tasks assigned to the team; second, developing an understanding of the goals, roles, procedures, and interpersonal relationships of the group (as discussed earlier in this chapter) as they relate to the assigned tasks; and third, developing the skills of team members that will enable them to function effectively within the group. Unless these critical variables receive attention, the effectiveness of the group may suffer. Developing these understandings and skills takes practice and explicit attention.

Although team building can and does take place on the job, there is usually a strong tendency for the team to focus on the assigned task (content) to the exclusion of the process skills and understandings that would enable the team to achieve its assigned tasks far more effectively. Therefore, on-the-job team building may not be as productive a method for developing the understandings and specific process skills for managing a task team as a two or three day off-site workshop staffed by external facilitators who understand the organization and its managers. An external facilitator can plan the agenda and process of the workshop groups to provide an appropriate learning experience for the development of needed skills.[12] When the teams have developed these skills, they can be practiced and maintained on the job.[13] A typical team-building session would include, in addition to work on the assigned task, an analysis of the goals, roles, procedures, and interpersonal relations of the group, time allowed to work through problems identified in each of these areas, and practice of individual skills for dealing with such problems on the job.

Goals

The effective coordination of a team's resources rests, in part, on the ability of the group to set mutually agreeable and specific goals and objectives for itself that relate to the tasks assigned to the team. These goals and objectives may involve both personal and organizational concerns as well as short- and long-term concerns. If the goals and objectives that relate to the assigned tasks are not explicitly resolved, conflict can be expected around how much time and energy should be devoted to various subtasks. Much energy can be wasted if the goals and/or priorities are not clearly understood and mutually accepted. Different people may have different perceptions of the goals, priorities, and choices that must be made. It is unlikely that the resources will exist in sufficient quantity to do everything at the same level of quality. Therefore, the first step in team building is to address the issue of goals, objectives, and priorities as they relate to the assigned task. Even in a single meeting, confusion over, or lack of agreement on, the purpose of the team can result in overt or covert conflict. For example, a team exploring an issue requires very different participant behaviors than a team engaged in information sharing or education. Yet either or both purposes may be appropriate to the assigned task.

Roles

Related to the inherent ambiguity of goals and priorities is a set of problems having to do with roles. Ambiguities about who should be doing what can only be partially handled by a priori formal job descriptions or agreements. These documents cannot and should not be relied upon to cover the day-to-day contingencies that arise when groups struggle to accomplish a task.

Many problems arise in this area simply because people are not clear and specific about what they expect of each other. Managers on a team seldom negotiate such issues as "Why am I on this team?"; "What can I contribute to the team's tasks?"; "What does each member of the team expect from me?"; "What can I expect from each member of the team?"; or "How do expectations change over time or in different situations?" As a result, role ambiguity can ensue. People are not clear about what to do, which often leads to role conflict where people are fighting over resources and sometimes power.

Another type of problem occurs when the sum total of all the expectations held of a person or a group exceeds what the individual or group can achieve in the time allocated. This leads to overload conflict and often frustration. In short, individual and team effectiveness suffers because those involved do not have the specific skills needed to develop clear and agreed-upon expectations that function as psychological contracts.

Procedures

While the focus on the first two categories is *what* (goals) and *who* (roles), the procedural focus is on *how*. Effective teamwork requires clear and agreed-upon procedures in several areas: "How will decisions be made?"; "How will conflicts be resolved?"; "How will issues and/or problems be identified, explored, and, where appropriate, solved?"; "How often will there be team meetings?"; "Who will attend?"; and "How should meetings be conducted, and what specific skills do we need to manage our meetings effectively?" Generally, procedures are mechanisms for acquiring, sharing, exploring, and processing information, identifying alternatives, and making recommendations.

Interpersonal Relations

Another area for potential problems can be traced to people's intolerance of other people's personal style. The recognition of the existence of differences among individuals can lead to greater insight of oneself and the creative use of personal preferences for more effective functioning of the team. One hears references to such vague terms as a *personality clash* or *bad chemistry*. These attributions are symptoms of the lack of understanding of personal differences and their potential as positive rather than negative qualities. One important difference between people involves the type of data with which we prefer to work. Some people are more comfortable with concrete, fact-oriented data, while others prefer more abstract conceptualizations. Neither preference is more appropriate than the other; the task at hand will govern which view is more functional. Another difference is how we handle judgments. Some individuals prefer generalized, principle-based approaches while others prefer a case-by-case approach. The way a person prefers to think is still another style variable. Some people rely exclusively on linear or *rational* thinking while others recognize the value of integrative or *intuitive* thinking. Unless these and many other differences are understood, the psychological gap between individuals may never be bridged. Effective teamwork depends upon the development of productive interpersonal relations, based on an understanding of and appreciation for different personal styles.

The four-factor framework (goals, roles, procedures, and interpersonal relations) can help in building teamwork in two ways: first, it can help to provide a conceptual base for how an organization may function more effectively. The framework can develop conceptual clarity so that the specific issue that must be resolved can be isolated and treated. A role-related problem should be addressed in a different manner than a goal-related problem. Second, there are behavioral skills involved in all of the categories. These skills can be developed and implemented for higher individual and organizational effectiveness. The team-building experience, carefully organized and monitored by experienced professional facilitators, can contribute substantially to both of these outcomes while avoiding traumatic confrontations or personal attacks that can destroy team effectiveness.

SUMMARY

With greater awareness of group process, including role behavior, the manager and members of his or her group can more effectively accomplish the content that is the primary concern of the group. With more and more time being devoted to interactions in groups, we cannot afford the luxury of ignoring these process phenomena. The manager, by understanding the influence of reference groups as well as the culture of the small work group, is better able to understand the behavior he or she observes and predict the probable response to various actions he or she may take with respect to those things he or she can influence and the impact those actions may have on the group culture and productivity.

QUESTIONS FOR REFLECTION AND DISCUSSION

1. How does a group or corporate culture evolve?
2. What can managers do to better understand the way a group functions?
3. What can managers do to avoid *groupthink*?
4. What can managers do to conduct teams or groups more effectively?

NOTES

1. Paul Lawrence and Jay Lorsch, *Organization and Environment: Managing Differentiation and Integration* (Homewood, IL: Irwin, 1967).
2. L. N. Jewell and H. J. Reitz, *Group Effectiveness in Organizations* (Glenview, IL: Scott, Foresman, 1981).
3. J. P. Kotter, *Power and Influence* (New York: The Free Press, 1985).
4. E. H. Schein, "Coming to a New Awareness of Organizational Culture," *Sloan Management Review*, Winter 1984.
5. M. E. Shaw, *Group Dynamics: The Psychology of Small Group Behavior*, 3rd ed. (New York: McGraw-Hill, 1981).
6. J. R. Hackman and G. R. Oldham, *Work Redesign* (Reading, MA: Addison-Wesley, 1980).
7. R. Rosenthal, ed., *Skills in Nonverbal Communications, Individual Differences* (Cambridge, MA: Oelgeschlager, Ginn & Hain, 1979).
8. *Expectations* is a term often used in management literature, for example, "Pygmalion in Management," by J. Sterling Livingston, *Harvard Business Review*, July/August 1969, which originally derived from *Pygmalion in the Classroom*, by Robert Rosenthal and Lenore Jacobson (New York: Holt, Rinehart and Winston, 1968). *Psychological contract* is a term often used in psychological literature and, more recently, management literature, such as *Managing Human Assets*, by Michael Beer, Bert Spector, Paul R. Lawrence, D. Quinn Mills, and Richard L. Walton, (New York: The Free Press, 1984), p. 75. The term apparently originated as a psychological extension derived from A. H. Croust's article, "Origin and Meaning of the Social Compact Doctrine as Expressed by Greek Philosophers: in *Ethics*, October 1946.

9. R. J. Sternberg, *Beyond IQ: A Triarchic Theory of Human Intelligence* (New York: Cambridge University Press, 1985).

10. Irving Janis, "Groupthink," *Psychology Today,* November 1971.

11. W. G. Dyer, *Team Building: Issues and Alternatives* (Reading, MA: Addison-Wesley, 1977).

12. E. H. Schein, *Process Consultation: Its Role in Organizational Development* (Reading, MA: Addison-Wesley, 1969).

13. W. G. Bennis, *Organizational Development: Its Nature, Origins, and Prospects* (Reading, MA: Addison-Wesley, 1969).

CHAPTER 18

MANAGING CHANGE

The views expressed by Paul R. Lawrence toward change in organizations can be thought of as an example of classical human relations: he focuses on the psychological needs and personality of the actors at all levels of the management process, but in particular is concerned with the interaction between staff people, such as accountants, and line people, such as a small work group of machine operators, who are carrying out specific sub-tasks when a small but important creative innovation is to be introduced.[1] Lawrence's main point is that resistance is not aimed at the creative innovation itself but rather at the accompanying disruptions that usually occur in the stable social relationships or group culture. His major concern is to show how resistance to change can be eased so that adaptive innovations can be facilitated.

Specifically, Lawrence takes issue with the popular notion that participation can help reduce resistance to change. When members of a group such as machine operators are consulted in only a token manner, such as when plans were actually made in advance, no true feedback takes place, the pseudo-participation will be recognized as manipulation, and resentment and increased resistance will ensue. On the other hand, when staff members genuinely respect the members of the group for what they can contribute to solving the problems associated with innovation, there exists real psychological participation and change is facilitated. Thus, Lawrence is not arguing against genuine participation but against its abuse as a psychological gimmick.

The presence of resistance, Lawrence notes, is not something that has to be muscled out but rather a diagnostic sign, like pain in a medical patient, that something is wrong and further examination is in order. Probable causes may be the failure on the part of the staff to understand the point of view of members of the work group or a lack of respect for them.

Informal patterns of relationships or group culture may provide much of what is satisfying in work (see Chapter 16). When these patterns are upset by the imposition of new techniques or procedures, individuals may feel threatened and may fight back overtly or covertly. Recognizing these relationships and going along with them makes organizational change easier. Sources of trouble in organizational change include self-preoccupation and self-righteousness on the part of staff people, lack of respect for the genuine skill and potential contribution of the members of a group, and an over-enthusiastic interest on the part of staff in their own special area of competence. Naturally, these categories tend to overlap a good deal.

The staff person charged with the task of introducing or implementing an innovation is highly dependent on the members of the group on at least two counts. First, the members will be familiar with practical operational difficulties that the specialist, from his or her more theoretical position, may either ignore or fail to recognize. Second, the members are bound to have a real feeling for the informal social networks in which the outside staff person probably does not participate. Thus, the staff person must establish a psychological contract of mutual collaboration between him or herself and the members of the group. He or she must communicate in the language of the group to get points across and must help the group members make sense of the new procedure. Using fancy language (jargon) or refusing to explain the new techniques at all on the grounds that it is too complex will probably be interpreted as an insult and thus evoke hostility.

The staff person must remember that introducing an innovation takes time because new skills cannot be learned immediately. If the staff specialist becomes impatient and communicates that he or she feels the group is resisting change deliberately, the group may oblige by behaving just that way.

To minimize resistance to change, managers should encourage the development of better understanding throughout the organization by facilitating functional perception and communication between individuals and groups with different cultures and points of view. This approach will not eliminate the structural conflict in subgroup cultures in an organization; indeed, increasing specialization is increasing the probability that different subgroup members of the same large organization are actually living in worlds with very different cultures and points of view.

While Lawrence's work focuses on the pitfalls to be avoided in managing change in small work groups, Greiner has concentrated on studying successful change patterns, so that he provides a positive model for managing change in larger groups and/or organizations.[2] Greiner tends to focus on broader kinds of alterations than the ones studied by Lawrence but he relies in part on Lawrence's earlier findings.

GREINER'S SIX-FOLD PATH (SEE ALSO CHAPTER 19)

In surveying specific changes in eighteen organizations, Greiner developed a model of change that helped him describe much of the positive adaptation that he found. He suggests the following six phases as common to managing the kinds of change with which he is concerned:

1. *Pressure and Arousal.* Top management begins to feel that change in themselves and their staffs would be desirable. This state of affairs is usually brought about only by simultaneous pressures from the outside (public pressures, slumping sales, competitor breakthrough, stockholder discontent) and from the inside (labor disputes, low morale, interorganizational conflict, high costs, low

productivity). Top management feels that this state of affairs reflects on its ability and seeks expert assistance from the outside.

2. *Intervention and Reorientation.* The outsider selected to help the organization is accepted as an equal by top management and respected for the person's skills and reputation for helping improve organizational functioning. Rather than prescribing specific solutions for particular problems, this "change agent" encourages top management to begin to examine past practices and start identifying specific problems for themselves. The key process here is the reexamination of underlying assumptions and traditional practices.

3. *Diagnosis and Recognition.* The reexamination process begins to spread throughout the organization. Information is assembled. Individuals genuinely collaborate in seeking to identify problem areas and their causes. Power is shared among the consultant, top management, and the rest of the organization, so that topics once considered taboo begin to be discussed. If this phase succeeds, it paves the way for further development by indicating to all subordinates that upper management is itself willing to change, that previously ignored problem areas are being acknowledged and faced squarely, and that ideas from lower levels are being accepted and valued higher up. (If, at this stage, top management acts unilaterally to define problems by decree or passes the buck by delegating the search effort to lower levels in order to avoid participation, then organizational confidence in the process will be lost and the change effort will fail.)

4. *Invention and Commitment.* Having suspended traditional practices and diagnosed problem areas, the organization must now search for and identify appropriate solutions. If the work of the previous phases has been successful, this will be a collaborative effort in group problem solving. A variety of specialized techniques are available to train organizational members in group dynamics and creative interchange.

5. *Experimentation and Search.* Before tentative solutions can be introduced on a large scale, they must be tested out. Here both the validity of the specific solutions and of the concept of shared power is carefully examined. Small changes are introduced at all levels of the organization and the results noted. The changes are regarded as experimental only. Signs of positive results are sought.

6. *Reinforcement and Acceptance.* If the solutions selected have been adaptive, this should be a phase of consolidation. There is an improvement in the accomplishment of organizational tasks and goals. These positive results bring support for the changes from all levels of the organization; in addition, the practice of shared power gains wider approval. It is hoped that the process will begin to snowball so more problem areas are identified and creative solutions developed. This pattern of recognition and response to difficulty becomes accepted and taken into the organization's regular way of doing things. The organization can now carry on by itself, and the consultant recedes from view.

It should be noted that these steps put forth in 1967 are similar to those of Kouzes and Posner put forth in 1987 (described in Chapter 10) and applied at the organizational level, the main difference being the use of outside experts to facilitate the process. It may be that in 1967 the trend toward emphasizing linear thinking to the exclusion of the nonlinear and contextual thinking essential to good leaders (discussed in Chapter 10) had progressed to the point that outside facilitators were necessary to compensate for the lack or at least reduced levels of nonlinear and contextual skills.

Essential to Greiner's model is the concept of shared power. The problem-solving task must involve collaboration between all levels of the organization. If decisions are announced from on high, be this by decree, replacement of key managers, or pointed changes in the formal structure, collaborative problem solving will not be possible. At the other end, if top management delegates authority completely and remains aloof from the problem-solving process, a lack of commitment will be felt and subordinates will be wary of making innovative recommendations.

In line with this concept, Greiner makes four basic points:

1. Organizational change is a slow, collaborative process. It cannot be imposed from above on a group either by top management or by a consultant.
2. The responsibility and capability for organizational change resides in all levels of the organization.
3. Too much emphasis in organizational change is still given to unilateral and delegated change approaches; in a dynamic and rapidly changing organizational situation, the shared power approach is much more responsive.
4. Exchange of ideas and concepts across vertical and horizontal organizational lines would probably help generate more innovative solutions and more tools for solving organizational problems.

Transformational leaders focus on a larger organizational entity as did Greiner,[3] but they develop their own vision of the future more in line with the Kouzes and Posner model (see Chapter 10).[4] They manage change through personal enthusiasm, which they are able to spread throughout the organization. Lee Iacocca at the Chrysler Corporation is an example of a transformational manager.

More recently Nadler observed, "Change management requires an understanding of how organizations function as well as an appreciation of the peculiar dynamics of transitions."[5] This clearly suggests understanding individuals and groups in terms of both spontaneous and reflective behaviors as well as understanding how they can be influenced to change. Further, Brannen notes, "For change to work, organizational culture must support the innovation."[6] She also notes that culture is "shaped by the ongoing interactions of the people in the firm. . . ." But these interactions derive from the spontaneous and reflective behaviors of the people. Finally, Goodstein and Burke acknowledge, "We are only beginning to understand the nature of change and how to manage the process involved, especially with respect to organizations."[7]

In summary, a manager must remember that change cannot be imposed by edict.[8] Change involves human beings who have ideas, perceptions, values, and concern for their competence, status, and security. Change itself has the propensity to upset the delicate equilibrium of systems that individuals and organizations

\

tend to set up.[9] One of the pitfalls the manager of change must avoid is believing that change can take place by attending only to the rational aspects of the situation. One should recognize that human behavior and values are diverse and complex; humans have a spectrum of concerns and needs that must be satisfied. The individual's actions to satisfy these needs depend on many things: willingness to take risks, the actual situation, perceptions of the situation, and past successes or failures in finding satisfaction. Some of these perceptions may be distorted or idiosyncratic, so a person may not respond to rational pleading for a given change.

The awareness of these interactive forces is one of the important first steps in understanding any change program. What is needed is not merely the willingness to confront change, but a commitment to go beyond changes in structure and procedures—to become sensitive to the human forces and to act to make them congruent with the objectives of the change being contemplated.[10]

QUESTIONS FOR REFLECTION AND DISCUSSION

1. Why do people resist change?
2. What are the differences and similarities between leadership, creativity, and the management of change?
3. What can managers do to conduct change more effectively?
4. What are the potential problems of managing change?

NOTES

1. Paul R. Lawrence, "How to Deal with Resistance to Change," *Harvard Business Review*, May/June 1954, pp. 49–57.
2. L. E. Greiner, "Patterns of Organization Change," *Harvard Business Review*, May/June 1967, pp. 119–30.
3. N. M. Tichy and D. Ulrich, "The Leadership Challenge—A Call for the Transformational Leader," *Sloan Management Review*, Fall 1984, pp. 59–68.
4. J. Kouzes and B. Posner, *The Leadership Challenge*, (Washington: Jossey-Bass, 1987).
5. David Nadler, "The Effective Management of Organizational Change" in *Handbook of Organizational Behavior*, ed. Jay Lorsch (Englewood Cliffs, NJ: Prentice-Hall, 1987).
6. Mary Yoko Brannen, "Culture as the Critical Factor in Implementing Innovation," *Business Horizons*, November/December 1991.
7. Leonard Goodstein and Warner Burke, "Creating Successful Organizational Change," *Organizational Dynamics*, Spring 1991.
8. R. M. Kanter, "The Middle Manager As Innovator," *Harvard Business Review*, July/August 1982.
9. R. M. Kanter, *The Change Masters*, (New York: Simon & Schuster, 1983).
10. J. B. Quinn, "Managing Innovation: Controlled Chaos," *Harvard Business Review*, May/June 1985.

CHAPTER 19

ORGANIZATIONAL DEVELOPMENT

In *Future Shock*, Alvin Toffler predicted that the increasing pace of technological and social change would profoundly effect our way of life in the latter years of the twentieth century.[1] In 1983, the British inventor responsible for a number of technological changes, Clive Sinclair, told a British television audience that "the 1990s will differ from the 1970s as profoundly as the 19th century from the 18th." With the advent of the silicon chip and the robot, he continued, society is on the edge of economic transformations comparable to those made by the automobile, telephone, and airplane.

The capacity of our organizations and institutions to predict and respond effectively to these external changes with appropriate transitions in the internal systems, processes, relationships, and skills has, in the United States and much of the Western world, lagged far behind the need for such transitions. This, in spite of demonstrations by organizational development (OD) professionals, especially in the past fifteen years, that organizational transitions can be managed successfully.[2] The reasons for this reluctance to change or inability to manage effectively the change process in organizations are as complex as the pressures for change that have developed in the external environment. In recent years, these pressures have increased even more rapidly and intensely than Toffler predicted and, faced with the need to respond to competition from countries such as Japan who have not only benefited from low labor costs but who have innovated their technological and organizational systems to deal with the changes in the external environment, many companies in the United States and Europe are now playing catch-up; they are investing time, effort, and funds in carefully orchestrated organizational development programs.

Perhaps because of the recent emphasis on scientific management and the evolution of managers into administrators or bureaucrats, as discussed in Chapter 10, there appears to be a shortage of effective managers such as Lee Iacocca who have the leadership skills required to transform or change organizations in response to rapidly evolving technical and environmental forces.[3] Probably because of the shortage of strong leadership skills, organizational development (OD) specialists emerged to facilitate the change process.[4] This chapter looks at OD from that perspective, but it should be remembered that effective managers can use OD techniques with or without outside facilitators.

The literature on OD is vast, as is that on planned change (transitions). Gordon Lippitt has defined these two terms as follows:

> Organization Development: any planned, organization-wide effort to increase the effectiveness and health of an organization through various "interventions" in the organizational processes using behavioral and management sciences technologies.
>
> Planned Change: an intended, designed, or purposive attempt by an individual, group, organization, or larger social system to influence directly the status quo of itself, another organism, or a situation.[5]

Planned organizational change is therefore a specific series of interventions in organizational processes designed to influence the status quo in the direction of greater organizational effectiveness, efficiency, and health.

Based on Lewin's pioneering three-step procedure (unfreezing the present situation, moving to new behavior patterns or levels, and refreezing at the new, desired level),[6] Greiner has described a distinct pattern in the evolution of successful change in organizations.[7] (A similar pattern or series of steps was proposed earlier by Lippitt, Watson, and Westley).[8] We will here describe these steps and interweave more recent insights, models, and experience of other OD professionals as appropriate.

Step 1. The organization, and especially top management, is under considerable external and internal pressure for improvement long before an explicit organization change is contemplated. Performance and/or morale are low. Top management seems to be groping for a solution to its problems.
Beer has described the impetus for change as a lack of "fit" or congruence between one or more of four internal variables and the external environment:[9]

I. The Organization
    a. People
    b. Internal Environment
    c. Process
    d. Culture

II. The External Environment
    a. Competitive Market Environment
    b. Technical Environment
    c. Social Environment
    d. Government Regulation Environment

Beer defines the four organizational variables as follows:

a. People—the members of the organization, their competence (especially the competence of key managers), values, and needs.

b. Internal environment—the organizational design of formal mechanisms to shape behaviors, such as the structure, control systems, policies, job structures, reward systems, and accountability systems.

c. Process—the behavioral interactions in the organization. Process is some function of people and internal environment/structure. It includes leadership, conflict management, planning, and goal setting.

d. Culture—the shared perceptions that members have about what kinds of behaviors and attitudes are valued in the organization. Culture is a function of people, internal environment/structure, and process. Culture is difficult to change without working extensively with the other three variables.

Steps 2–4. A new person, known for his or her ability to introduce improvements, enters the organization either as the official head of the organization or as a consultant who deals directly with the head of the organization. An initial act of the new person is to encourage a reexamination of past practices and current problems within the organization. The head of the organization and immediate subordinates assume a direct and highly involved role in conducting this reexamination.

The "new person" described here is known variously as an external change agent, an OD practitioner, or a change process facilitator. While the role of the external change agent (working closely with at least one internal change agent who is either a top manager or internal OD practitioner) has been perceived as critical to the success of organization change efforts in the past, the need for, the role of, and the focus of the change agent's efforts have all come into question in recent years. Margulies and Raia have expressed these concerns succinctly:

> In the formative years, the theory of planned change placed special emphasis on the role of the agent of change. Normally, such agents were considered to be external to the client system and in possession of the specialized expertise required for social system diagnosis and change. In the last decade or so, the reliance on external change agents has been reduced. Managers in all types of organizations are better at organizational diagnosis and have a much better grasp of change methods and technology. In addition, many more organizations are training internal people in the skills and art of the change process. . . . Our point is that now the processes are followed and performed less by external people and more by internal people than ever before.

Thompson, however, believes the role of the external OD practitioner should be to prepare managers actively to create and manage change.[10] Margulies and Raia continue:

> Second, we are concerned that the models are change-agent oriented. The process generally describes those activities performed by a change agent in conjunction with a client system. High emphasis is placed on the role of the change agent in the process. . . . Very little emphasis is placed on the client's role, necessary client skills, guidelines for use of external resources, proper selection of change agents, and so on.
>
> Third, we are concerned that planned change has developed a rather narrow focus. For the most part, those involved as practitioners and empiricists in this field have been behavioral scientists, primarily psychologists and sociologists. Planned change has assumed a thrust, a technology, and an image which deals with only one of the major subsystems of organizations. Criticisms of the overemphasis on the human relations or people approaches, or on the sociocultural dimensions of organizations are justified. . . . Very little is documented on interventions of a systemic and holistic nature, those involving structural, technological, and managerial innovations.[11]

The above critique of the role and focus of the change agent, published in 1978, has more recently been specifically addressed and confirmed by other OD practitioners. Lippitt's *Organizational Renewal*, published in 1982, is subtitled *A Holistic Approach to Organization Development* and suggests that a systemic approach to change should address such managerial policies and practices as long-range planning, operations research, financial systems and budgeting, human resource accounting, flextime, and union negotiations and contracts. Beer notes that most OD practitioners do not deal with the variables he has listed under "internal environment," do not concern themselves with the external environmental variables and the need for fit between internal and external variables, and do not ask such questions as

- In what business is this organization engaged?
- What is its strategy?
- How is it doing relative to competitors?
- What difficulties is it having with its external environment?
- What internal variables are causing those difficulties?

Step 5. The new person, with top management support, engages several levels of the organization in collaborative, fact-finding, problem-solving discussions to identify and diagnose current organization problems.
This is the vital diagnostic stage of the change effort. Planned transitions are almost, by definition, data-based. Two important questions about the diagnostic process stand out.

1. *Who gathers what data*? Beer has stated that the primary need is to improve the fit between the organizational variables and external environment variables, and that the purpose of diagnosis is to develop a strategy—a plan for improving the fit. "When OD is rooted in the strategy of the organization, OD will have saliency and importance. OD will not be just team-building or some other OD technology, but an overall effort to bring alignment between the organization's key variables and important changes in the external environment." Data must be gathered, therefore, not only about the people, internal environment, process and culture of the organization, but also about the external environment, including both current and prospective changes in the external environment. Given the dimensions of this task, all the knowledge and skills available should be devoted to it. Organizational management is obviously best equipped to deal with the external environmental data—especially the competitive and technological environments. Internal and external OD practitioners are probably better able to gather organizational data, particularly the potentially sensitive data about and from the people and internal environment.

2. *Who owns the data*? The need to involve people at all organizational levels in the change process and to share the power inherent in decision-making, problem-solving, and the evolution of strategy has been stated by OD practitioners for many years. As a practical matter, people tend to resist changes if they have not been involved in the planning process from the outset. The fact that they have contributed to the data bank is only the beginning of real involvement; they also need to be involved in the use of the data to solve problems and devise appropriate strategies. Typically, the data is analyzed by OD practitioners and fed back to all organizational levels, starting at the top and working down to the lowest levels who have contributed to the data.

The remaining steps in Greiner's pattern of success in changing organizations deal with how the data gathered is used to plan and implement change.

Since more recent experience has contributed considerably to this phase of the change process, we will look to the work of others to complete this review.

The systemic approach to OD intervention and particularly to the planned change process has been an important and relatively recent trend. Beer notes that there are three important concepts related to this perspective of the organization:

1. *Organizational efficiency* describes the quality of the fit between the four major internal variables: people, internal environment, process, and culture. It is possible for there to be a high degree of organizational efficiency but for that efficiency to be irrelevant to the external environment.
2. *Organizational effectiveness* describes the quality of fit between the organization and the environment. It is only when organizational effectiveness drops that it becomes important to examine the internal variables.
3. *Organizational health* describes the organization's ability to adapt to external and internal changes.

These concepts are important for the manager initiating and directing change and for OD practitioners implementing the change process to understand because, as Beer states:

> The traditional role of the OD practitioner has been to improve organizational health. Starting with a normative position about conditions that foster participation and readiness to change, the practitioner would use a number of technologies to increase confrontation, openness, etc., in the organization. This early focus on health does not seem relevant to managers who are bleeding to death on efficiency and effectiveness issues. It would take a very secure and powerful chief executive to be able to sponsor a long term program to improve organizational health. Health issues are crucial and must be part of many interventions but they are not the way to start. The OD practitioners (internal and/or external) need to start out with effectiveness issues and understand them, then move to understanding the efficiency issues causing the problems in effectiveness. It is only then that a program to improve organizational health becomes relevant.

The profound implication of this statement, says Beer and others who favor the holistic and systemic model of planned change, is that managers need to learn OD skills and OD practitioners need to have solid grounding in marketing, strategy formulation, and other management skills. This prescription applies to both internal and external OD practitioners and to managers at upper levels of organizations who may find themselves in change agent roles.

For effective managers concerned about the need for change in their organizations, therefore, here are three final pieces of advice:

1. If you are hiring an internal OD practitioner or contracting for the services of an OD consultant or external change agent, look for not only background and skills in OD and the applied behavioral sciences, but also individuals and firms who have knowledge and experience in general management.
2. As effective managers in a position to initiate or influence a process of planned organizational change, you need to acquaint yourselves with enough knowledge about leadership as well as the OD field to enable you to make intelligent

decisions about the particular change process that makes sense for your organization at a certain time and under certain circumstances. At the very least, this means selective study of the admittedly vast leadership and OD literature.

3. Whether you use an internal or external OD specialist, be sure to spell out in as much detail as feasible what you expect from the specialist, what the boundaries or limitations to the project are, and what the specialist can expect from you. In short, a good psychological contract will avoid misunderstandings.[12]

QUESTIONS FOR REFLECTION AND DISCUSSION

1. What are the differences and similarities between managing change and organizational development?
2. What are the differences and similarities between organizational efficiency, effectiveness, and health?
3. Under what circumstances might a manager want to undertake organizational development?
4. What can managers do to conduct organizational development more effectively?

NOTES

1. A. Toffler, *Future Shock* (New York: Random House, 1970).
2. W. G. Bennis, *Organizational Development: Its Nature, Origins, and Prospects* (Reading, MA: Addison-Wesley, 1969).
3. N. M. Tichy and D. Ulrich, "The Leadership Challenge—A Call for the Transformational Leader," *Sloan Management Review,* Fall 1984, pp. 59–68.
4. E. H. Schein, *Process Consultation: Its Role in Organizational Development* (Reading, MA: Addison-Wesley, 1969).
5. Gordon L. Lippitt, *Organization Renewal*, 2nd ed. (Englewood Cliffs, NJ: Prentice-Hall, 1982).
6. Kurt Lewin, *Field Theory in Social Science* (London: Harper & Row, 1951).
7. Larry E. Greiner, "Patterns of Organization Change," *Harvard Business Review*, May/June 1967, pp. 119–30.
8. R. Lippitt, J. Watson, and B. Westley, *The Dynamics of Planned Change* (New York: Harcourt Brace Jovanovich, 1958).
9. Michael Beer, "A Strategic Perspective of Organization Development," Paper presented at 1980 ASTD Conference and included in *Organzation Development Strategies for the Future*, ed. Kris Schaeffer, ASTD (American Society for Training and Development), 1981.
10. John T. Thompson, "Helping Line Managers to Be Change Agents," *Training and Development Journal*, April 1981, pp. 52–56.
11. Newton Margulies and Anthony P. Raia, *Conceptual Foundations of Organizational Development* (New York: McGraw Hill, 1978) pp. 51–52.
12. R. Wagner Boss, "Contracting and Successful Organization Development Consultation," *Consulting Psychology Bulletin*, Winter/Spring 1991.

CHAPTER 20

VISION, ORGANIZATION, AND CHANGE

Creating a vision of what is possible for an organization in terms of future opportunities is essential for effective managers.[1] The successful management of change through creative innovation, especially technological innovation, is a major part of the process involved in implementing an organization's vision. Aside from basic product improvements, innovation is triggered by the recognition of an environmental signal. The signal may be a new opportunity to the organization or it may be the availability of a new technology. Thus, a key step in the process of creating a vision is the development of the ability among many people in the organization to sense the environment accurately and completely enough for the organization's needs—a contextual leadership skill that effective managers possess.

It is essential in today's highly complex, diverse, and interdependent organizations to involve many different people in the evolution of a shared vision to ensure commitment throughout the organization.[2] But this shared vision will derive more from nonlinear than linear thought processes, for as Zaleznik observes: "Vision, the hallmark of leadership, is less a derivative of spreadsheets and more a product of the mind called imagination."[3] At the same time, if the organization is to filter and organize these signals, information must be developed and made available specifying the organization's capacities and strengths (ideally, an appraisal of the organization comparable to that described in Chapter 13 for individuals).

The product of this environmental search and internal audit is the vision and resulting strategy of the organization. The process of formulating a vision requires, among other things: 1) an assessment of the internal strengths and potential of the organization, 2) the design and implementation of a program for innovation (see Chapter 11) to ensure a flow of creative ideas and opportunities, 3) an assessment of what is unique about the organization and what differentiates it from other organizations, and 4) a realistic estimate of which creative opportunities offer the greatest use of organizational strengths. Implementing the vision includes the design or modification of downstream coupling systems for the organization together with the design and implementation of effective integration (or coordinative) activities.

Two key elements are needed to formulate a vision: a determination of environmental opportunities and an assessment of the organization's unique strengths. If these are effectively meshed, a strong vision can be developed. The problem is that these two parts are dynamically linked in the organization. We do not independently look at the environment and then assess our unique strengths. Our strengths dictate which portions of the environment are to be searched. To some extent, this has been the case for those firms operating in the aerospace business. This includes both private organizations and government laboratories.

For several decades after World War II, most organizations that were technically adequate could be assured, in most cases, of a steady stream of business. In several cases they were even able to pick and choose among the business opportunities that interested them. In this phase of their history many organizations failed to develop effective marketing systems tuned to many sources of business and to the trends toward quality products evident in other countries.[4] These just were not needed in the eyes of many U.S. senior managers. As the business picture changed, not only did they lose business in a growing market, but in many ways the demands of these markets were fundamentally different. In a very real sense, organizations in the United States were still reading the elements of their environment that had been important in the past. While they concentrated on doing the same things, they missed the trends in the international marketplace and some did not even realize that they *were* dealing in an international marketplace. They were tuned to what was important in the past but were missing what was important at that time and what would be important in the future. One can only hope that U.S. executives today are no longer so myopic.

Fundamentally the environmental sensors of many United States organizations are designed to focus on what was important in the past, rather than what will be important in the future. When we speak of sensors we are obviously speaking about people in various work groups. It is difficult, but essential, to establish market- and customer-oriented groups to focus on market and customer trends that may be important in the future.

INTERNAL PATTERNS OF ORGANIZATION

Ted Levitt observed that organizations needed to define broadly, rather than narrowly, the businesses in which they were engaged.[5] Once the organization did this, they were in a position to develop their internal patterns of organization to take advantage of the future opportunities that could be identified. Lorsch and Lawrence described this as differentiating themselves.[6] In its simplest form this means establishing organizational units to deal with specific segments of the firm's environment that offered future opportunities and units to deal with specific current elements of the primary task of the organization. At a very basic level this means organizing units to focus on the future while other units focus on the production tasks, the financial and record keeping functions, and so on.

As we view a large organization, the coordination tasks become extremely complex. Many different organizational units are formed to deal with the complex environment the organization faces. Some of the factors affecting organizational complexity are the number and types of technologies employed, the size and complexity of the markets and customers served, the product life cycle, the size of the organization, and the turbulence or stability of the critical areas in its environment. Let us now look at each of these individually.

Technologies Employed

Organizations operating at the leading edge of the state of the art in technologies that are changing rapidly have extremely difficult tasks in monitoring developments in their fields and transmitting them inside so others can use them. The organization manufacturing glass bottles thinks it is dealing with a very stable technology. In most cases it does little to monitor this environment. It may feel that the time rate is such that it can afford to sit back and react to new innovations when necessary. If this firm saw itself in the container business rather than the glass bottle business it might not be so complacent.

The high technology and/or market driven organizations cannot sit back. They may find competitors running away with their business even when they are working intensively in the technology and the marketplace. They need to look at their customers, the life cycles of their products, the size of their organization, and the stability of their environment.

Customers Served

Staying "close to the customer" is one of seven variables listed in *In Search of Excellence*[7] and *The Art of Japanese Management*.[8] Maintaining a close relationship with customers and the marketplace is essential but time consuming and costly. It provides the organization with information crucial to the identification of new opportunities essential to an effective vision of the future. One of the most difficult customers to serve is the federal government and its agencies. The sheer size of the government creates many organizational levels and many coordination points. The nature of this customer is such that many approval levels have been established as safeguards. Auditing, evaluating, policing, and investigating are fundamental pieces to the system. They can be justified only because of the large number of dollars involved. What we are concerned about is the complexity that results and the need for the organization to differentiate itself in terms of the demand of the future and the demands of the past and present.

Product Life Cycle

The product life cycle has two effects on organizational differentiation. First, when life cycles are short, the organization usually must be working on several projects at a time to ensure an even flow of work. Otherwise the firm would eventually find itself out of work and facing high overhead due to nonproductive time. Few organizations wish to come to a complete standstill at any time.

Secondly, when cycles are short individuals must change jobs frequently and in many cases be working on several tasks managed by different superiors at the same time. This greatly complicates the organization. This complexity shows up most clearly in matrix organizations.[9] It manifests itself by the necessity for power and influence skills,[10] building networks of informal relationships, and negotiating.

Size of Organization and Environmental Stability

The size of the organization has an effect on organizational complexity in two ways. First, it tends to increase the levels of management just to allow managers to deal with reasonably sized groups of subordinates. Above some level this does not seem to have much further effect because of the tremendous number of people that can be organized in five or six levels. Secondly the size of the organization influences the ability of individuals to conceptualize and maintain a knowledge of the organization's activities.

The stability of the environment determines the time rate of feedback required by the organization. If the environment is relatively stable, time delays in obtaining information about changes will have little effect on the organization. If the environment is rapidly changing, the organization must have individuals and organizational units monitoring it carefully. Time delays in feedback can be devastating. This problem becomes especially critical when there are changes in the environment that affect the relative rate at which the environment is changing. This relates to what we have said about the changes in the customer system served by those involved in technical or market driven work. Feedback from that sector is now critical.

Considering these factors, the firm must develop a pattern of internal differentiation that is consistent with environmental forces, the tasks selected, and the technologies employed.

THE INTEGRATION OF ACTIVITIES

If the organization is to implement its vision effectively, it is not enough to develop the appropriate organizational pattern; it must also find an effective way to link or integrate all of these elements together. In the process of change and innovation it must especially develop systems for the downstream coupling of idea generation to useful products. The more complexly differentiated an organization is, the more difficult it will be to integrate.

As Jasinski has specified, the critical relationships in most high-technology organizations are not the vertical ones but the horizontal ones.[11] Breakdown between peers in different departments are much more common and much more damaging than breakdowns between superior and subordinate. At these points, there are conflicts in goals, roles, time orientation, and interpersonal styles (see Chapter 15). Within vertical relationships, these factors tend to be very similar and therefore they do not interfere with effective communication and coordination. A clear example of this tendency can be seen in the relationship between production and sales in the glass container business. Production has as a goal increased efficiency and reduced costs. Sales has as a goal customer satisfaction. If it could operate independently, production would attempt to produce a year's supply of one size and shape, then change to a second size and shape and produce a year's supply of it, and so forth. If sales were given a free rein, it would attempt to respond to every customer's need and would ask the factory to change continually from one size to another to suit the customer's needs. In this situation, the integrative device is the production schedule and because the organization is relatively simple, superiors in the hierarchy can resolve conflicts and manage integration. In highly differentiated organizations with many conflicts and many decisions to be reached, the hierarchy breaks down and the organization becomes poorly integrated. Several techniques have been developed to deal with this problem. These are the use of integrators,[12] the establishment of integrative units, and the development of integrative devices.

The Integrator

Integrators are used throughout most large organizations. They are referred to by various names, such as liaison engineers, project managers, lead engineers, work package coordinators, and task leaders. Whatever the name, their task is the same. They are to help effect sound functional relationships between two or more organizational units. People in these roles must develop an understanding, even an empathic one, of those in the units they coordinate if they are to be successful.

Integrative Units

Committees are examples of integrative units. As the organization becomes more complex and the need for integration increases, it develops more permanent units. First, it has standing committees, then such units as project offices, product line groups, task management offices, and others. These units do not do the work themselves; they integrate the activities of others who design its products, produce them, and sell them. In effect, they take over the general management tasks for a specific piece of the organization's business. Many factors help these groups to be effective, but it seems most important that they clearly understand that their goal is integration and not the actual task of designing or building a product. An integrative device that has become widespread in its use and especially important in matrix organizations is the program or project office. Its primary task is to achieve integration of organizational efforts to complete a specific task.

Integrative Devices

In our earlier example, we said that a production schedule was an integrative device. Many other devices exist that can help management in this task. Some of these are the control system, the reward system, the physical layout, and delegated authority. Control systems can be designed to measure the degree of integration. Management can measure the time frame for development and marketing of products. It can monitor changes after the product is designed. It can measure the time rate of communication. Reward systems can be established to reward integration. Group incentives, joint evaluation of integrators, and promotion policies are all examples of these. Physically locating people close to each other tends to facilitate integration. Separating them tends to block effective integration. The amount of authority delegated to integrators facilitates integration in two ways. First, it directly helps the integrator to obtain help by increasing his or her power. Secondly, it increases the integrator's status so that the person can obtain informal help.

SUMMARY

The process of creating and implementing a vision begins at the boundary of the organization. The environment is monitored, needs and opportunities are identified, and resources of the organization are utilized. The organization must monitor those elements of the environment that are currently critical and those that are likely to become critical. Once an opportunity is identified that matches unique organizational strengths, a vision can emerge that will determine the nature of the organization in the future. The nature of the task will push the organization toward a certain structure. Once this pattern is determined, the organization must find ways of effectively integrating activities. In general, during the innovative process this task of integration is the most difficult for the organization. People, organizational units, and devices must be developed to accomplish that task.

QUESTIONS FOR REFLECTION AND DISCUSSION

1. What can managers do to optimize the probability that opportunities in their environment that match the organization's strength are identified?
2. What can managers do to avoid the complacency that often derives from success?
3. What can managers do to optimize a "close to the customer" attitude within their organization?
4. What can managers to do optimize the probability that the necessary integration will get done in their organization?

NOTES

1. J. Kouzes and B. Posner, *The Leadership Challenge* (Washington: Jossey-Bass, 1987).
2. Peter M. Senge, *The Fifth Discipline: The Art and Practice of the Learning Organization* (New York: Doubleday, 1990); and "The Leader's New Works: Building Learning Organizations," *Sloan Management Review,* Fall 1990.
3. Abraham Zaleznik, "Managers and Leaders: Are They Different?—Retrospective Commentary," *Harvard Business Review,* March/April 1992.

4. Theodore Levitt, *The Marketing Mode* (New York: McGraw-Hill, 1969).

5. Theodore Levitt, "Marketing Myopia," *Harvard Business Review,* July/August 1960, p. 167.

6. Paul R. Lawrence and Jay Lorsch, *Organization and Environment* (Boston: Harvard Business School, 1967).

7. Thomas J. Peters and Robert H. Waterman, Jr., *In Search of Excellence* (New York: Harper & Row, 1982).

8. Richard T. Pascale and Anthony G. Athos, *The Art of Japanese Management* (New York: Warner Books, 1981).

9. C. A. Bartlett and S. Ghoshal, "Matrix Management: Not a Structure, a Frame of Mind," *Harvard Business Review,* July/August 1990.

10. John P. Kotter, *Power and Influence* (New York: The Free Press, 1985).

11. Frank J. Jasinski, "Adapting Organizations to New Technology," *Harvard Business Review,* January/February 1959, pp. 79–86.

12. Paul Lawrence and Jay Lorsch, "New Management Job: The Integrator," *Harvard Business Review,* November/December 1967, pp. 142–51.

CHAPTER 21

COORDINATIVE ORGANIZATIONS

An organization is a multivariate system that consists of tasks, informal social structure, technology, and formal organizational structure. All four components are highly interdependent and must mesh together in order to meet the demands of the external environment. Most people are familiar with the traditional vertical functional organization that develops specialties within the given functions, such as engineering, research, accounting, and personnel. This traditional type of organizational structure has proved to be successful in stable situations involving relatively well-defined and/or routine tasks.[1]

However, when the nature of the tasks to be performed is very complex and uncertain, such as those in highly creative professional organizations, the traditional structure appears too rigid and inflexible. This has been especially true in the past several decades during which we have witnessed rapid change in technology, products, services, and markets. For example, the aerospace research and development organizations were called upon to meet large-scale demands for highly complex new products or projects that demanded integration and coordination across many technical disciplines. To meet this challenge, a new form of organization within an organization evolved. This type of organization has been variously called "matrix,"[2] "project,"[3] "multidimensional,"[4] "coordinative,"[5] or "integrative" by organizational theorists.[6] The need for coordinative management is illustrated by the activities associated with task management in a research and development organization. These are the people assigned the tasks of reducing various new technologies to practice. Yet, with many different such tasks on hand, it is extremely difficult for the functional manager of engineering to cover both the special demands of specific tasks and the regular demands of the stable, day-to-day operations within engineering. Covering both aspects creates a strain on the existing organization in the sense that responsibilities and loyalties are divided.[7]

Conflicts between coordinative management and the traditional functional structure occur at the upper management level as well as at the middle and lower levels. One of the sources of conflict is that the whole process of coordinative organizations and, more basically, the need for their existence may not have been fully explained or communicated in most organizations. Coordinative management sometimes develops in a spontaneous rather than in a reflective, planned, coordinated fashion. In one sense, such a development can be described as the result of poor communications, yet it seems that more than communications are needed.

The philosophy of top management needs to be in line with the cultural requirements of the new approach, that is, a new set of expectations or psychological contracts may need to be developed explicitly between the organization and its employees, resulting in modified formal procedures or instructions. Many top managers have made their way to the top through the traditional functional organizational structure and feel that this is the only way to run the show. Task or coordinative management to these types of managers is often seen only as an expedient that must be tolerated. When that attitude is perceived, many of the people involved in coordinative management become unsure of their place in the organization. It can also result in the reward system remaining consonant with the old functional organization and not giving equal weight to the performances of the coordinative managers, that is, the organizational culture is not congruent with the reflectively understood need for a coordinative organization. These conflicts inhibit effective coordinative management.

In dealing with the concept of task or coordinative management, one must understand the framework of the environment, which points up the salient differences between the roles of the task or coordinative manager and the traditional functional manager. While these differences may be polarized in theory more than in reality, they do influence the manager's behavior. Group and individual conflicts will probably develop when both functional and matrix structures exist in a single organization. Awareness of the essential paradoxes is the first step toward conflict resolution and the achievement of a balance between those value systems that will optimize achievement of overall organizational goals in both the short and long run. Senior executives can easily jeopardize the success of the task by lack of awareness, unnecessary or unbalanced intervention, or personal whim based on personal values.

A few general guidelines can be offered that will facilitate the transition from the traditional functional form of organization to the coordinative form:

GUIDELINE 1—DEFINE THE OBJECTIVE

Those involved in achieving the task are performing unfamiliar activities at a rapid pace and can easily get off the right track or fall short of meeting their commitments; as a result, many steps of their work may have to be retraced. To minimize this risk, management should clarify the objective of the task well in advance by

1. defining management's intent in undertaking the effort;

2. outlining the scope of the task, including the identification of the departments, units, functions, and staffs involved and the approximate degree of their involvement; and

3. describing the end results of the effort and its permanent effects, if any, on the overall organization.

GUIDELINE 2—ESTABLISH A TASK ORGANIZATION

For a functionally-organized company, successful coordinative management means establishing, for the duration of the effort, a workable compromise between two quite different organizational concepts. The basic ingredients of such a compromise are

1. the appointment of one experienced, competent manager to coordinate the task full-time;
2. the organization of the task management function in terms of responsibilities;
3. the assignment of a limited number of people to the task team; and
4. maintenance of a balance of power between the functional heads and the coordinative manager.

GUIDELINE 3—INSTALL TASK CONTROLS

Special task controls dealing with scheduling, deadlines, cost, and quality are normally superimposed upon the existing reporting structure for the duration of the effort. Then they are discontinued. These controls vary widely in their accuracy, timeliness, and use, but they can be of significant help to organizations making the transition to coordinative management. In particular, the crucial relationship between time control and cost control must be recognized so that cost, schedule, and performance are fully integrated.

These three guidelines suggest how top management can achieve organizational clarity when it organizes a coordinative management team. The important point to be emphasized is that complementary management organizations can exist within the operations of an organization: the vertical, traditional organization (concerned with the development of specific professional specialties within departmental functional lines, which is necessary for the long-range survival of the organization) and the horizontal, coordinative organization (concerned with specific tasks or efforts that require coordination and integration across functional lines, which is necessary for the timely achievement of short-range tasks). The resulting organization will not consist of a single matrix and a single functional organization, but rather of many matrices, even a hierarchy of matrices. Such a structure reflects the impact of rapid change in professional specialties on the organizational structure and its functions. Moreover, it points up the need to provide a management structure around a specific task with commensurate lateral and horizontal relationships.

FORMS OF COORDINATIVE MANAGEMENT

There is no single form of coordinative or integrative management but rather a spectrum or continuum involving varying degrees of authority and power,[8] the number of subordinates, and the nature of the task. Generally, as the task becomes more complex and requires more and more cross-discipline interaction, organizations tend to give the coordinative manager more status, authority, and people reporting to him.[9]

PERSONAL QUALITIES OF A COORDINATIVE MANAGER

The typical manager who is handed his or her first coordinative management assignment finds adjustment to this anomalous new role painful, confusing, and even demoralizing. Lacking real effective line authority, the coordinative manager must lead, persuade and influence peers by the acquisition and use of power (see Chapter 8) through a trying period of time. In the same way that top management must recognize the importance of setting the stage for the acceptance of coordinative management, the coordinative manager must understand the critical difference between the exercise of power and influence as opposed to authority.

Power is the ability to influence the behavior of others, regardless of the basis for that ability. Authority is one form of power that is legitimately attached to an organizational position; it is delegated by job descriptions, organizational titles, standard operating procedures, and related policies. Other forms of power, on the other hand, are acquired without the legitimacy of organizational position. An individual may exercise power in one's environment simply because of knowledge and expertise or a network of contacts that have been built up over time. In essence, these are forms of power that can be applied across horizontal lines in the organization. These combinations of power and influence emphasize the coordinative manager's modus operandi and determine personal effectiveness. The coordinative manager almost never has unilateral authority in the task effort; he or she frequently negotiates with the functional managers. This relationship may be described as a *deliberate conflict*, in which the coordinative manager determines the when and the what of the activities required by the task, whereas the functional managers, in supporting many different tasks in the organization, determine how the support will be given. Unilateral authority is inaccessible to the coordinative manager in this interface between task and functional units.

If the guidelines suggested earlier are followed and an explicit understanding or psychological contract has been negotiated between the various levels of management, the interface can result in a successful problem-solving approach rather than a hostile conflict between polarized positions. Negotiations between equally balanced value systems provide an opportunity to achieve tradeoffs that maximize the objectives of the task and still maintain relative autonomy for the functional groups. Effective relationships in the coordinative environment depend on manifestations other than the exercise of legitimate authority.[10] The most effective working arrangements are seldom autocratic, but rest on the manager's ability to build reciprocity in his or her environment, to create and maintain political alliances and to resolve conflict between functional managers. Unilateral decisions, dogmatic attitudes, and appeals to authority in a hierarchical position are inconsistent with the analysis of specialized knowledge that is called for in a professional environment. Instead, the coordinative manager's job is to identify points of agreement and conflict, to use constructive criticism, to think reflectively about alternatives and only *then* to take a leadership position, based on the quality of the manager's knowledge. This is the true exercise of expert, referent, and reward power.

One can ask why coordinative management within organizations is necessary. The simple answer is that the environment is changing and, in turn, making greater and more diverse demands upon traditional organizations. Old-line bureaucracies are ineffective in dealing with the transitional states in which some organizations, especially high-tech organizations, find themselves today. Yet, there are no simple or sovereign solutions to the problems that organizations face. Managers must be content to live with essential paradoxes that have to be resolved by rational, lucid decision making. An organization cannot abandon its traditional functional units because basic knowledge is generated within those professional specialties.

Carried to an extreme, functional departmental structure results in parochialism and conflict of interests based on stereotypical points of view. Coordinative organizational structures carried to their extreme lead to short-range solutions that may be destructive to the long-range survival of the organization. These are paradoxes that we must learn to live with. The solution, complex though it may be, is to develop coordinative organizations that depend on the conceptual integrative skills of the manager and de-emphasize the manager's allegiance to purely personal or purely disciplinary needs.

On the one hand, a base for professional expertise must be generated, which is usually done most effectively in functional departments. On the other hand, these specialties must be applied to solving general problems, which is usually done most effectively in the interdisciplinary coordinative organizations. It is an historical evolution that first involved the formation of organizations along bureaucratic lines to ensure efficient operation. However, the old-time bureaucracy with strong centers of authority is not suited to modern professional problem solving. What is needed is a coordinative structure that maximizes the application of professional specialties across functional lines.[11]

The means of effectively meeting these needs are still embedded in the human equation. People must work together. They work together best when they understand the overall vision of the organization and the resulting mission, objectives, goals, and subgoals, and when they resist inclinations to do work the way it has always been done. Paradoxically, people find themselves having to overcome resistance to change in spite of the functional need for change. Clarity of the organization's vision and goals at all levels in the organization is one step toward the elimination of dysfunctional conflict that degenerates into hostility. Another step is the recognition by all individuals that they are parts of a network of mutual interdependencies that require linear, nonlinear, and contextual skills to maximize the positive effect of functional conflict.

QUESTIONS FOR REFLECTION AND DISCUSSION

1. What are the differences and similarities between a matrix and a functional organization?
2. What can managers do to minimize dysfunctional conflict and optimize functional conflict in a matrix organization?
3. What can managers do to optimize the effective acquisition and use of power in a matrix organization?
4. What can managers do to *coordinate* more effectively?

NOTES

1. J. J. Morse and J. W. Lorsch. "Beyond Theory Y," *Harvard Business Review*, May/June 1970, pp. 61–68. Also see Chapter 6.
2. S. M. Davis and P. R. Lawrence, *Matrix* (Reading, MA: Addison-Wesley, 1977).
3. J. R. Galbraith, "Matrix Organization Designs," *Business Horizons*, March/April 1971.
4. W. C. Goggin, "How the Multidimensional Structure Works at Dow Corning," *Harvard Business Review*, January/February 1974.
5. D. T. Cleland and W. Munsey, "Who Works With Whom?" *Harvard Business Review*, September/October 1967.
6. J. R. Galbraith, *Organization Design* (Reading, MA: Addison-Wesley, 1977).
7. S. M. Davis and P. R. Lawrence, "Problems of Matrix Organizations," *Harvard Business Review*, May/June 1978.
8. J. L. Brown and N. M. Agnew, "The Balance of Power in a Matrix Structure," *Business Horizons*, November/December 1982.
9. J. M. Sinclair, "Is the Matrix Really Necessary?" *Project Management Journal*, March 1984.
10. C. A. Bartlett and S. Ghoshal, "Matrix Management: Not a Structure, a Frame of Mind," *Harvard Business Review*, July/August 1990.
11. J. R. Gordon, L. S. Corsini, and M. L. Fetters, "Restructuring Accounting Firms for Better Client Service," *Sloan Management Review*, Spring 1985.

CHAPTER 22

WHY DON'T MORE COMPANIES IMPLEMENT TQM— SUCCESSFULLY?

ABSTRACT

Impressive benefits have been achieved by some U.S. firms using Total Quality Management [TQM].[1] The Japanese apparently use this approach with consistent success.[2] But even when initial results are impressive, some U.S. firms find further gains elusive. The secrets of long-term success are cultural. In the United States, we stress individualism and competitiveness; many believe that it is those qualities that have made us strong. But this belief often creates organizational cultures and subcultures fostering specialization and parochialism that may, at times, impede multifunctional cooperation. Top management *can* transform its organizational culture so as to maintain its strengths and still achieve impressive benefits from a TQM program over the long term. Such a transformation requires commitment; vision; a people-oriented philosophy; sufficient analysis to determine existing cultures, desired cultures, and alternatives to get there; carefully planned interventions implemented incrementally over a sustained period; and continuous follow-up. By taking this surefooted approach, numerous pitfalls are

Source: This chapter, copyrighted by University Affiliates, Inc., in 1989, was first published as one of a collection of technical papers presented at the First National Total Quality Management Symposium held in Denver, Colorado, November 1–3, 1989. These papers were printed by the American Institute of Aeronautics and Astronautics, Inc., in 1989. In this context, TQM means an effort to enlist *everyone* in the organization to focus on making every product and process the very best it can be in terms of value to the customer and without any defects.

avoided, the culture makes the transition to greater harmony, and the TQM program incubates to mature success.

INTRODUCTION

The potential gains from TQM are generally acknowledged to be very high indeed,[3] as evidenced by remarkable achievements in Japan. But Japan is not the United States and as Pascale and Athos observed in *The Art of Japanese Management*, "Most of the practical solutions to our problems are not to be found in Japan but right here at home".[4] We know that impressive initial results have been achieved by some U.S. organizations using multifunctional teams and other TQM approaches.[5] How-to guides have been written, including one prepared by the Department of Defense. But if the gains are so great and we know how to do it, why hasn't TQM already been instituted throughout the U.S. economy?

A FREQUENT DIFFICULTY—EXISTING CULTURE

Based on our observations of organizations over the last thirty years, we feel the answers lie, in part at least, in the evolution of most organizational cultures in the United States today. It seems clear that "the shift to Total Quality is a revolution in the way we operate organizations,"[6] *Business Week* said in its July 10, 1989, issue. The article continued "evidence suggests strongly that the old system of assumptions, beliefs, and practices relating to work has been disproved." But it is those assumptions, beliefs, and practices that are an integral part of organizational cultures. Our emphasis on individualism and competitiveness has made us strong in many ways but has also fostered specialization and parochialism, which sometimes inhibits trust, teamwork, and full cooperation. Multifunctional teams (for example, consisting of people from many functions including research, engineering, production, marketing, and sales) are essential to an effective TQM program. But multifunctional teams are not fully effective in a culture that inhibits trust, teamwork, and cooperation. This kind of culture tends to make long-term gains from TQM elusive, even when short term gains are achieved.

On the positive side, some U.S. companies have evolved cultures that foster cooperation *and* competition, individualism *and* teamwork, and they have achieved long-term success with multifunctional teams. Some of these were described in Peters and Waterman's *In Search of Excellence*.[7] But while that book came out in 1982, few organizations have adopted the approaches described in the book. Perhaps one of the reasons more firms are not moving rapidly to embrace TQM is the same reason ship captains don't want to sail through uncharted shoals—it's risky. Regrettably, some managers who recognize that sustainable organizational culture transformation is required for long-term TQM success also see it as a high-risk endeavor that takes too much time, money, and effort.

Some organizations have achieved significant *short-term* results from efforts that fall under the TQM umbrella including multifunctional teams, quality circles, and other forms of employee participation. For these firms, the gains more than offset the short-term costs. Managers and behavioral scientists have known for years that intense management attention and effort with a group of employees *can* yield significant short-term effects. This was first observed during the Harvard Business School study of Western Electric's Hawthorne Works in the late twenties, now often referred to as the "Hawthorne effect."[8] Any intense management effort can benefit from this phenomenon, including TQM. Even so, some managers view sustainable, long-term gains as elusive and costly.

In our judgment, short, intermediate, and long-term gains from a TQM program *can* be achieved in a cost effective manner *if* implemented properly. But that requires managing cultural transformation. We all know that organizational cultures evolve over time.[9] The only real questions are whether or not that evolution is managed and what direction it takes. Managers can *influence* and *accelerate* the way their organizational cultures and subcultures evolve and change.[10] Peters and Waterman observed that for the excellent companies "the process of shaping cultures . . . [is] the prime management role." In short, the excellent companies manage their cultures.

WHAT MUST BE DONE?

General

The Department of Defense noted in its draft guide for implementation of a total quality management program that step one must be to "establish the TQM management and cultural environment" that this *does* require a "long-term commitment," and that both management and employees must realize that some results will be immediate, but others will take four to seven years of commitment to achieve in support of a never ending improvement process. Thus, the Defense Department contends, and we agree, that employee involvement with strong management attention and support can yield short-term results but intermediate and long-term results can be achieved only by careful analysis and implementation of a step-by-step program that includes long-term commitment and significant culture change.[11] We think this process can be accelerated by effectively managing the cultural transformation process and recognizing that 1) every organization is different, 2) what works for one organization may be different from what works for another, and 3) even within one organization, functionally and geographically separated units will have different subcultures.[12]

From our observations and experiences in a variety of organizations and our analysis of the management literature, we conclude that there are five steps necessary for the successful transformation of organizational cultures.

1. The organization's past and present must be examined in depth to determine what are the unique existing organizational cultures and subcultures, both functional and geographic.
2. A careful determination must be made of the kinds of cultures and subcultures that will preserve existing organizational strengths but also yield the d(

TQM results in the organization as a whole and in each functional and geographic subunit.

3. A thorough examination must be made of a wide range of alternative paths of evolution, from existing to desired organizational cultures and subcultures, recognizing that these will be unique in each organization and each subunit therein.

4. These alternatives must be analyzed to determine which are most likely to be acceptable and successful and the time and resources that each may require.

5. An integrated set of interventions must be skillfully planned and implemented in small increments over a sustained period.

This last step must include establishing and communicating an overall organizational vision and a people-oriented set of values and philosophy. It will probably require revisions in group and individual goals and objectives, organizational structure, practices, procedures, and reward systems. Participative, employee involving activities, such as skill development programs and multifunctional team building efforts, are also essential. It should be obvious that each organization will require different approaches to suit the specific situations that exist therein. So-called "packaged" programs or "cookbook" approaches are not likely to work without substantial modification that recognizes the unique aspects of each functional and geographic subunit as well as the organization as a whole.

Specific

Our experience while functioning as facilitators and external change agents in a wide variety of organizations has suggested several critical elements of the cultural transformation process that we do not find emphasized in the literature or observed in common practice. These elements reduce or eliminate resistance to the cultural transformation process and thus enhance the probability of positive improvements in organizational cultures and subcultures. In our opinion, there are five critical elements:

1. A sufficient level of information must be collected and analyzed to permit completion of the five general steps listed earlier.

2. The focus must be on cultural transformations that are acceptable and desirable to the organization and its functional and geographic subunits as well as to most of the individual managers and employees.

3. Skill development programs must be provided that the individual employees, first-line and middle managers as well as top management, deem most appropriate to assist each person in acquiring those skills needed for the successful implementation of a TQM program.

4. There must be long-term, strong top-management involvement and support to maximize the probability of achieving the desired transformations.

5. Outside, professional, third-party facilitators are needed not only for the expertise they bring but because they can minimize the effects of the competitiveness, lack of trust, and parochialism that is often a part of the existing organizational culture. In addition, they perform functions that managers and employees

would otherwise have to do, thus minimizing the time diverted from regular operating functions.

WHO CAN HELP DO IT?

Employees

Employee acceptance and participation is essential for an effective TQM program. The first critical element in the cultural transformation process, therefore, is to involve the largest number of people economically feasible. This involvement should begin with the information-collection effort and should include interviews within all functional and geographic groups. We have found that cultural transformations tend to be more successful when they focus on what the organization and the individuals in it perceive as most in line with their own self-interest, namely, facilitating improvements in their current performance as individuals as well as the performance of the organization as a whole. Therefore, a series of interviews need to be conducted that focus on how to maximize the opportunities for each person to further improve his or her individual performance in light of the changing environment in which the organization functions and along lines that will improve the effectiveness of the organization as well. Since most people feel there are opportunities to do better, this approach does not generate the covert resistance that a perceived focus on weaknesses or needs sometimes does. The interviews should be nondirective, to avoid the preoccupations or concerns of top management or the biases so frequently found in structured questionnaires and to maximize the possibilities for individuals to contribute what they feel is most significant.

This positive approach gives those interviewed a chance to become involved in contributing success-oriented and often creative insights and ideas about the TQM program and the cultural transformation process. This approach not only yields highly useful information but creates a perception among many people that the TQM program is open, nonthreatening, potentially career enhancing, and individually beneficial.

Management

Absolutely essential to long-term success is strong and continuing top-management leadership, involvement, and support of the organizational development process that leads to cultural transformations (and support of the external facilitators who help bring it about). We have seen top managers initiate one fad after another and after some initial success, delegate the continuing effort to subordinate managers. The usual result of this delegation is the death of the fad. Of course, senior managers are *very* busy and must be very selective in the use of their time but the gains from cultural transformation leading to successful TQM certainly justify a long-term commitment. The first, and probably most important, task of top management embarking on a cultural transformation process is the establishment and communication of a revitalized corporate vision and people-oriented philosophy. But this vision and philosophy must be lived in the corporate offices and nurtured as it filters down. Good intentions, and "lip service" are not enough. If people in the organization perceive that this is the extent of management's commitment, the program will achieve little. Another important step is recruiting and empowering a number of enthusiastic and concerned individuals at all levels to function as advocates for cultural transformation and TQM. It is then necessary to maintain open lines of communication between management and these advocates, including the outside facilitators. Top management also needs to communicate to everyone involved the role the facilitators have as information collectors and analyzers, advisors to the organization, and process planners and implementers. Reassuring, developing, and protecting first-line and middle managers may be necessary since they may feel threatened by more employee involvement and fear a loss of control followed by punishment from senior managers. As the cultural transformation process progresses, additional top-management involvement will be essential; the specific nature of this involvement will depend on events at the time and cannot be delineated in advance.

Facilitators

As the captain of a ship usually engages the services of a pilot when entering a navigationally difficult area, foresighted top managers usually engage the services of facilitators when embarking on cultural transformations. In both cases the quality of the people engaged is critical to success. Based on our experience and observations in various organizations, and our analysis of the management literature, we conclude that five factors are necessary for facilitators to be successful in assisting organizations in cultural transformations:

1. They must have in-depth, substantive competence in the behavioral and management sciences at a level equivalent to a doctoral degree in order to bring a high level of expertise to the organization.
2. Experience as line managers is essential to bring a practical rather than theoretical approach to the task.
3. Experience working with similar organizations is another essential factor in order to avoid previously identified pitfalls.
4. They must have a background in whatever technical disciplines are organizationally important or experience in dealing with similar people in these disciplines in order to effectively communicate in the language of the organization and with the people in it.
5. Finally, they must have demonstrated skill in a) being effective facilitators, b) providing counseling support and assistance to executives and employees, and c) planning, implementing, and following up similar integrated cultural transformation programs.

The facilitators advise top management on their leadership roles and tasks, conduct the interviews, analyze the information obtained, communicate the results to all those interviewed and to the larger organization, participate with top management in the planning and implementation of an integrated set of interventions, assist in the evaluation and redirection of these interventions, when and if necessary, and finally, assist in planning and implementing training for the advocates to carry out long-term follow-up activities.

During the interview phase early in the cultural transformation process, curiosity will be aroused. It is important that the interview information and analysis be fed back to the organization by the facilitators. Doing so builds trust and raises expectations of eventual benefits to the organization and individuals and minimizes any potential resistance. This feedback is made initially to the top management and staff. This group discusses implications of the information, alternatives for action, and decides on a preliminary action plan. After this initial feedback to top management, the same information, including the preliminary action plan, is conveyed to all those who participated in the interview process and often to the entire organization. The top manager often participates in the feedback session(s) to demonstrate his or her commitment to the program, to answer questions about the preliminary action plan, and to encourage suggestions for improvements in this plan. The support generated during the feedback session(s) leads to greater impact from the interventions when they are initiated.

PITFALLS TO BE AVOIDED

General

Independent research has shown that people have a tendency to resist any kind of change, including cultural transformations, except when six conditions are present:[13]

1. Managers and employees must feel that they have the knowledge of what individual and organizational performance improvements and cultural transformations are desirable and why (feedback of the interview results usually provides this perception) as well as the substantive knowledge necessary to make these changes.
2. They must perceive that they have, or can gain, the skill to use this knowledge to operate effectively during and after the cultural transformations.
3. The cultural transformations must be seen as being in their individual self-interest, for example, enhancing their individual opportunities for satisfaction or rewards. Again, many people perceive identification of needs or weaknesses as reducing opportunities.
4. The cultural and subcultural transformations must be seen as being in the self-interest of the group or organization with which they identify, that is, they should make the group or organization more effective in fulfilling its basic goals and objectives.
5. There must be both internal and external environmental forces requiring cultural and subcultural transformations for the TQM program. Internal forces must include the desire of both the top management team and the employees to be more responsive to cultural and economic changes. External forces include recent governmental requirements, social trends, and public pressures.

6. There must be both internal and external catalysts and facilitators, namely, internal catalysts at the top of the organization, who give their full and complete support to the cultural transformations leading to a successful TQM program, and external nonthreatening facilitators to assist the individuals in reducing any risks they may perceive to be associated with the transformations.

To minimize resistance, these six conditions must be considered by the facilitators and management while planning an integrated set of interventions. The way these interventions are planned and implemented is critical in minimizing resistance to organizational culture and subculture transformations. By focusing interventions on those opportunities open to individuals to significantly improve their performance, their individual self-interest can be addressed. At the same time, these interventions can be focused on those opportunities open to individuals that are consistent with improving organizational effectiveness through the TQM program, without reducing the effectiveness of functional or geographic groups. In this way, the individual's perception of the benefits of the TQM program to the group or organization with which they identify is improved. Increasing participants' awareness of the internal and external forces that are pushing for the TQM program can be enhanced in many ways, such as through discussion groups, guest speakers at company functions, articles in company or community newspapers, selected readings and informational materials in skill development programs, and by management announcements and meetings. By involving top management whenever possible in all aspects of the TQM program, top managers demonstrate their commitment and quickly become identified as internal catalysts, while the outside facilitators' roles continue to be structured as risk reducing, nonthreatening external catalysts.

Specific

We have identified seven specific pitfalls that often inhibit the transformation to organizational cultures supportive of TQM:

1. Management's (especially first-line and middle manager's) unwillingness to share real power with their employees can subvert the cultural transformation effort.
2. The sometimes adversarial attitudes between labor and management can make building trust and cooperation more difficult.
3. Reward systems designed to achieve strong functional specialization often fail to recognize the need to achieve real understanding, cooperation, and trust between these groups and, therefore, can be counterproductive.
4. If people perceive that team building of any kind is a threatening win/lose game with high risks, then these activities will yield few, if any, positive results.
5. Substantial costs for training, development, team building, and other such activities may be perceived as excessive.
6. Lack of long-term commitment and overreliance on quick-fix approaches can cripple cultural transformations.

7. Failure to give consideration to the ideas and concerns expressed by people in the organization may be perceived as a lack of the people-oriented values and philosophy necessary to a successful TQM program.

The type of cultural transformation necessary to a successful TQM program can best be achieved when top management openly addresses all of these pitfalls in a carefully planned cultural transformation program implemented through an integrated set of interventions in small increments over many weeks.

Finally, our experience has shown that the kind and degree of performance improvement obtained from cultural transformations correlates more with calendar time than clock time. That is, people usually improve their performance in small increments over rather long periods of time. The extent of the improvement seems to depend, to a large degree, on reinforcing the successful experiences that have led to incremental improvements. For this reason, we normally recommend spacing out interventions so that incremental improvements in performance can be made over as long a period as is economically and logistically reasonable. At the same time, we also recognize that time is critical and unnecessary delays are counterproductive. Therefore, a balance needs to be struck between the need to demonstrate tangible TQM progress to the whole organization and the time necessary to transform the organizational culture.

SUMMARY

In conclusion, a well-planned and implemented TQM program can achieve short-, intermediate-, and long-term maximum success when the cultural transformation process is well-handled by top management and external facilitators.

- This includes addressing those factors that may lead to resistance, as well as those elements contributing to success.
- It requires significant involvement of the organization's top management, as well as subordinate managers and employees, in the identification of opportunities for cultural and subcultural transformations contributing to TQM program effectiveness.
- It requires the participants' continued involvement in planning and implementing of an integrated set of interventions in small increments over as long a period as is logistically reasonable that will still show steady TQM progress.
- It requires a never ending set of reinforcing activities.
- It requires top management investment in a significant career development program as part of the TQM program. This also signals positive top management support to people throughout the organization.

In this way, the organization preserves the strengths derived from individualism, competitiveness, and specialization while at the same time transforms the culture to emphasize cooperation, trust, a customer orientation, and a growing sense of comradeship as well. Thus, long-term TQM success requires a high-level effort to manage cultural transformations.

QUESTIONS FOR REFLECTION AND DISCUSSION

1. What are the potential risks and benefits of a TQM program?
2. What sort of culture change is desirable for a TQM program?
3. How can this culture change be made effectively?
4. What can managers do to implement a TQM program effectively?

NOTES

1. K. R. Thompson, "A Conversation with Robert W. Galvin," *Organizational Dynamics,* Spring 1992.
2. E. H. Schein, "Does Japanese Management Style Have a Message for American Managers?" *Sloan Management Review,* Fall 1981.
3. R. J. Schonberger, "Total Quality Management Cuts a Broad Swath—Through Manufacturing and Beyond," *Organizational Dynamics,* Spring 1992.
4. Richard T. Pascale and Antony G. Athos, *The Art of Japanese Management* (New York: Simon & Schuster, 1981).
5. D. A. Garvin, "How the Baldridge Award Really Works," *Harvard Business Review,* November/December 1991.
6. Tom Lane, "The Will To Lead," *Consulting Psychology Bulletin,* Fall 1991.
7. Thomas J. Peters and Robert H. Waterman, Jr., *In Search of Excellence* (New York: Harper & Row, 1982).
8. F. J. Roethlisberger and William J. Dickson, *Counseling in an Organization* (Boston: Harvard Business School, 1966).
9. E. H. Schein, "Coming to a New Awareness of Organizational Culture," *Sloan Management Review,* Winter 1984.
10. W. Ouchi, *Theory Z: How American Business Can Meet the Japanese Challenge* (Reading, MA: Addison-Wesley, 1979); and C. W. Joiner, Jr., "Making the 'Z' Concept Work," *Sloan Management Review,* September 1985.
11. S. P. McCormack, "TQM: Getting It Right the First Time," *Training & Development Journal,* June 1992.
12. H. Schwartz and S. Davis, "Matching Corporate Culture and Business Strategy," *Organizational Dynamics,* Summer 1981.
13. John P. Kotter and Leonard A. Schlesinger, "Choosing Strategies for Change," *Harvard Business Review,* March/April 1979, pp. 106–14; Herbert E. Meyer, "The Science of Telling Executives How They're Doing," *Fortune,* January 1974; Paul R. Lawrence, "How to Deal with Resistance to Change," *Harvard Business Review,* January/February 1969, pp. 4–12; and Chris Arguris and Donald A. Schon, *Theory in Practice: Increasing Professional Effectiveness* (Washington: Jossey-Bass, 1974).

CHAPTER 23

An Integrated Approach to Understanding Behavior

Previous concept chapters have attempted to show that over a period of time the manager can improve his or her linear, nonlinear, and contextual skills in dealing with specific situations.[1] A manager can learn which behavioral concepts work under which circumstances. A manager can improve his or her conceptual, human, and technical skills in diagnosing problems.[2] He or she can learn to use models, which help in analyzing diagnostic data. He or she can become aware of the personal characteristics and expectations of others that relate to the problems they face and thus develop empathy with and sympathy for them.[3] He or she can develop a better understanding of his or her personal characteristics, values, ethics, and specific strengths. He or she can learn to maintain reflectively a positive and enthusiastic approach to managerial issues. Finally, a manager can develop an understanding of the leadership processes by which change occurs in an organization. In a real sense, the manager's primary task is to influence people in organizations to make positive change that benefits them and the organization in both the short and long term.

Individual Behavior

Some aspects of organizational and individual behavior seem especially important to the manager. We have examined how expectations (psychological contracts including organizational goals and objectives and/or expectancy theory),[4] self-image (including individual goals and objectives and/or equity theory),[5] and personal characteristics (including personality and life experiences)[6] influence the behavior of people. We have also examined how perception, communication, and content theories of motivation (including power)[7] influence the behavior of people. Now we will integrate these concepts into an approach useful to managers as they try to understand the behavior of those around them and attempt to answer the question: "Why do individuals behave as they do and what can be done to influence that behavior?" This integrated approach may be diagrammed as follows:

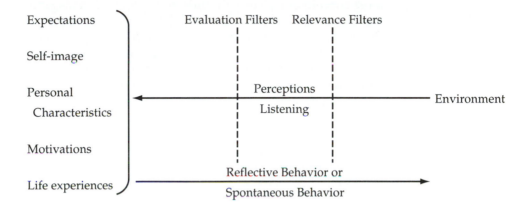

Briefly, the individual "sees" the environment; filters out what is not relevant; evaluates the remainder; processes this data through the individual's own self-image,[8] sets of expectations, personal characteristics, motivational factors, and life experiences; and then responds with reflective or spontaneous behavior.[9] Both the relevance and evaluation filters are products of the individual's self-image, expectations, and personal characteristics and life experiences. Let's look at a brief example of this sequence: On a dark night, we have to take a walk through a rather run-down section of town. As we round a corner, we come face-to-face with a very large, muscular, unshaven, disheveled man in tattered dirty clothes. At the very least, our behavior might include a rather uneasy feeling and a little shrinking away from this man. Let's analyze this sequence. The actual event to occur in our environment was the appearance of a man of a certain description in a certain situation. Because his particular appearance startled us, our relevance filters immediately passed this data on. Because we had already evaluated these particular surroundings, our perception was somewhat biased and we evaluated or perceived him as a potential threat. Among the factors influencing our behavior was a need for security and a desire to stay out of harm's way. Therefore we began a spontaneous behavior pattern to deal with the environment—we backed up a little and got the adrenaline started.

This is a very basic example. Most of the situations in the managerial world involve many things occurring in the environment at once. Complex sets of perceptions, and the many factors influencing the individual's behavior are all operating at once. An important thing to keep in mind is that any behavior is a function of the perception of the individual, and not necessarily what is occurring in the environment. We still do not know if the man we met was a threat to us or not.

TWO-PARTY RELATIONSHIPS

The next natural extension from our integrated approach to individual behavior is the interaction between two individuals. While we could examine many different two-party relationships, probably the most important from our point of view are the ones between the manager and the people with whom he or she must work. We must concern ourselves with three basic types of managerial relationships: 1) the superior to subordinate relationship; 2) the relationship between the manager and his or her peers or specialists who help accomplish the work; and 3) the relationship between the manager and his or her boss, which is probably the single most important relationship influencing the performance of the manager. Although the relationship of the manager with his or her superior could be viewed as just another superior-subordinate relationship, its importance justifies a separate category.

If we expand our integrated approach to understanding behavior in a two-party relationship, it is necessary to recognize that individual A is part of individual B's environment and vice versa. If an understanding of individual behavior is difficult, an understanding of the interactions between two people is exceedingly more complex.

We can diagram a two party relationship as follows:

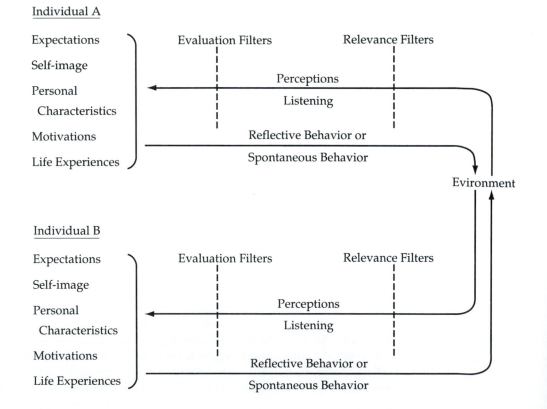

We might say that perfect communications would be the transfer of a concept or image from the mind of individual A to the mind of individual B, without distortion. Although perfect communications may occur where the concept or image is highly technical and both individuals are thoroughly trained experts in that field, it occurs less often in the more intangible managerial aspects of interpersonal relations. The words individual A uses or the behavior he or she exhibits are based on his or her personal characteristics and life history. Individual B, on the other hand, using his or her own personal characteristics and life history, might mean something quite different when using those words or exhibiting that behavior. Hence, the difficulty of communication.

If both individuals understand the various factors influencing the other's behavior and want to understand and be understood, then the channels of communication may be opened wider and a freer flow of information with a minimum of distortion is more likely. We are all aware of the many efforts of management to communicate with employees. Employee manuals, company newspapers, letters from the president, and all of the forms and reports that are generated in organizations are designed to obtain similar perceptions among employees. We have already seen that the communication problems that face the manager in relationships both with subordinates and with specialists who support the manager are frequently caused by ineffective listening by focusing on what the words or behavior meant rather than what the *communicator* meant.[10]

Now that we have, at least to some extent, described the interaction between two individuals with our integrated approach, we will explore some of the implications of this for the manager as he or she operates within the organization. Two especially important factors are the set of skills and understanding that the manager brings to bear and the style of behavior the manager exhibits. It is essential for the manager who wishes to be effective to take the initiative in clarifying the perceptions between him or her and either the specialists, the boss, or the subordinates involved. If we think about what a manager does, to a very large extent he or she manages relationships between himself or herself and others to positively influence the others' behavior. The manager concentrates on getting individuals to behave in functional ways. The specific behavior selected or used can only be evaluated in terms of the way in which it influences getting the job done.

One of the major problems faced by the manager is that the relationships with others may demand conflicting behavior modes: superiors may expect the manager to be forceful and directive with subordinates; specialists may expect the manager to be technical and logical; subordinates may expect him or her to be warm and human. Our integrated approach may be expanded to include as many relationships as the manager needs to examine.

To this point, we have been talking about the relationships faced by any manager. When we look at an individual manager, can we use our integrated approach as it is, or must it be expanded and used differently? One factor that complicates our integrated approach is the degree to which people in organizations hold allegiances to groups that are not departments of the organization (for example, their allegiances to professions, such as physicist or diplomat, or to outside organizations, such as a church, fraternity, or family). Sociologists call these *reference groups*. In a very real sense, the fact that many of the members of the organization may be part of another organization or group to which they have strong attachments complicates our integrated approach. Members of such powerful reference groups may have different subcultures than do other members of the organization. The existence of such powerful reference groups outside the organization with which we are concerned makes the individual manager's job more difficult.

INTERGROUP COOPERATION

In one sense, we can study the interaction between work groups in much the same way as we study the interaction between two individuals. If we take our integrated approach for the individual and for the interrelationship of two individuals and expand it for a group, we can diagram it as follows:

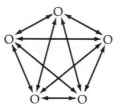

Actually, our diagram would have to be much more complex. Each individual is perceiving each other as an individual, and in sets of two, three, or more. At the same time, each person's behavior is directed toward these same numbers. Few, if any, managers have either the time or the need to consider all of these relationships at one time. To make the integrated approach useful to the manager, we will attempt to treat the group as a separate entity, having an identity and characteristics similar to an individual. We will try to describe those factors that are important to us as managers.

If we are to analyze any group, especially a group within a larger organization, it is important to keep in mind that there are two ways of viewing the group. Many different names have been used to identify these viewpoints, the most familiar being *formal* and *informal*. The formal derives from the reason for the group to exist or the actions required by the task. This is often referred to as the *required system* (or task-related content interactions), and it includes those activities and interactions that the group must carry out to remain a member of the larger organization and to enjoy its benefits. As an example, a department utilizes a certain technology to provide a product or service to the rest of the organization, for instance, the machine shop must use cutting tools to provide machined parts for the fabrications department. This required system, coupled with the subcultural factors that evolve in the group over time as well as the sets of factors influencing the behavior of the specific individuals who make up the group, leads to informal patterns of behavior often called the *emergent system* (or process-related interactions). Most of us have relatively little difficulty in identifying the parts of the formal or required systems and their relationships to each other, but the informal or emergent system is often more difficult to discern.

Refer back to our initial diagram. If we think of a group as an entity, then the same diagram applies to the group as it does to an individual. A group will filter and evaluate (perceive) data relevant to the group's tasks and subculture and this will affect its behavior. Conversely, it will filter *out* data it does not see as relevant and will thus not have a behavior toward this aspect of its environment. Let's look at the ways in which the group behaves in terms of the integrated approach.

The major factors affecting an individual's perception of his or her environment are his or her self-image, sets of expectations, personal characteristics, motivations, and life experiences. When we start to analyze the group, it becomes obvious that similar factors affect the perceptions of the group. The many factors shared by the group include expectations, experiences, norms or values, sentiments, required and emergent activities, roles and social ranking, and the way the group sees itself. From all of these factors emerges a group culture,[11] which has a potent impact on perception and resultant behavior.

We said that as individuals, each of us has a set of factors that influence our behavior in a manner consistent with our perceptions of the environment and these factors. The factors influencing a group may be different than the factors influencing the individuals that make it up, but certainly the cultural factors of the group influence individual factors and vice versa. At the very least, there seems to be a need for a group to survive and prosper. A philosophical argument as to whether or not the group as an entity can have any influencing factors apart from those of the individuals who make it up, however, is not germane to our discussion. The group obviously operates to satisfy dominant subcultural factors that are important to members, and the degree to which it does this will influence the closeness or unity of the group. We call this *cohesiveness*.

One final factor with which we must deal is social or informal structure. When two people get together they begin to develop a social structure. Even when not formally required, leaders emerge, a ranking of members occurs, and subgroups develop. Anyone who wishes to understand a group and to influence it must deal with these elements. Therefore, if we are to expand our integrated approach from the individual to the group, we must add group subcultural factors, group cohesiveness, the group's ability to satisfy individual members' dominant factors, and the informal internal social structure.

When we wish to look at intergroup relationships, we must analyze differences in social structure, subcultural factors, and cohesiveness within and between the groups, to see if they are compatible or likely to lead to conflict. Let's look at one fairly typical example. Research groups tend to expect decisions to be reached in accordance with scientific knowledge, and the one with the most technical knowledge in a specific area makes the decision. Production organizations, on the other hand, tend to expect decisions to be made by the person highest in the hierarchy. In their view, "You can offer your opinion, but the boss is the boss." It is easy to see the conflict likely to occur when a young research scientist is sent to a meeting of production managers and the group is required to solve a processing problem. The scientist expects to have substantial influence because of his or her technical skills, while the production people see a person who is not even a manager trying to tell them what to do.

Let's again expand our integrated approach and consider the interaction between two departments. Obviously, individuals have the perceptions and respond with the behaviors; what they perceive and the way they behave is greatly conditioned by the cohesiveness, social structure, and subcultural factors of their groups.

We have developed an integrated approach to the study of individual behavior, the manager's role, and intergroup cooperation. As we progressed from each level to the next, we found that the same basic kinds of variables had to be considered, but we had to simplify and group our variables. If we were to analyze a group of eight people with our integrated approach to individual behavior, we would end up with so much information it would be almost impossible to organize it. As we look at the organization as a whole, we will again simplify and expand.

THE TOTAL ORGANIZATION

Until now, we have dealt almost entirely with the human element in organizations. There are many more elements than just the human one. If we are to develop a total integrated approach, we should deal with some of these. Again, it is important to keep in mind that our total organization is in contact with an environment and that it is influenced by and influences that environment. Let's expand our diagram to include the total organization:

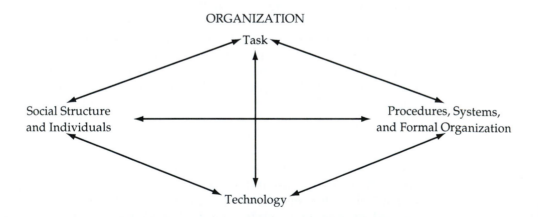

What do we mean by the terms used in the diagram?[12]

Task refers to the organizational raison d'être. The production of goods and the generation of all types of services is included. In many cases, we are talking about intermediate services or goods that go into a final product. In-process inspection is an example of such a task.

Procedures, systems, and formal organization refers to all of the formal systems designed and implemented by management to organize and control a firm. Included are the formal hierarchy or authority, information systems, pay systems, work shifts, and most formal personnel policies.

Technology includes all of the tools and techniques used by members of the organization to complete their tasks. Computers, tape-controlled machine tools, and cash registers would all be included in this category. In addition to physical tools, techniques such as PERT, Markov chain analysis, linear programming, and stochastic analysis are included.

Social structure and individuals refers to all the individuals, groups, and emergent informal structures discussed earlier.

It is almost impossible to overstress the interdependence of the above categories. If a firm is in the business of selling programming services to industrial firms (task), it will usually be formally organized into small teams (formal organization), which will use high-speed digital computers (technology). The individuals will feel that technical excellence should be rewarded and that the informal leader of the group should have the most skill (social structure). Similar examples can be developed using organizations with other specific tasks. A major problem with this is that many modern organizations are extremely complex and are simultaneously completing many tasks that are significantly different, demand different formal organizations and technologies, and have different informal social structures.

The most important task of top operating management is to determine how the total organization should be differentiated into units that can deal with all of the tasks of the firm. After this has been done, management must then find ways to integrate all of these diverse units into an effective, functioning organization.[13] We are all familiar with the fact that modern organizations face complex, rapidly changing environments and must manage transitions, innovations, and change effectively if they are to grow and prosper. It therefore becomes quite important, if we are to complete our integrated approach, to find a way to include the environment of the firm, and to discuss how effective managers can bring about change in complex organizations.

THE ENVIRONMENT AND CHANGE

When we are discussing the environment, we must first decide what are its critical components. That is, what are the important parts that management must closely follow and analyze? The answer to this question varies with the particular industry or firm being studied, but we can develop a general list that has wide applicability.

For purposes of discussion, let's select a major segment of a large organization, say, a production plant, rather than the total organization, as our unit for study. We can diagram the relationship as appears on the following page:

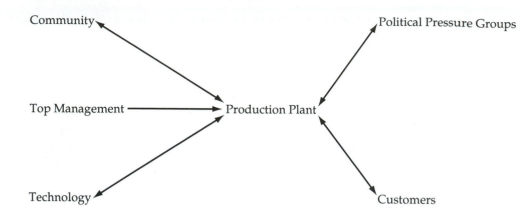

It is important to keep in mind that everything we have discussed up to this point is included within the items shown. Some of the impacts of these factors are very straightforward and easy to understand. Almost everyone is aware of the tremendous impact of *technology* on the organization. It is important to keep in mind, however, that technology has not only led to new products, and therefore changes in task, but has also had an impact on the formal organization (for example, coordinative organizations) and the informal social structure (for example, the highly mobile engineer or scientist whose primary allegiance is to his or her profession rather than the organization). The pressure of environmental elements in other areas is almost as obvious. The problems of the inner city (*community*) are becoming an increasingly strong influence on business. *Customers* with increased sophistication are becoming much more demanding. *Political pressure groups*, leading to such changes as credit disclosure, safety and pollution control devices, and benefit programs, are becoming more pervasive and powerful. All of these pressures are coming to bear on the organization and are demanding change. The production plant faces exactly the same set of factors as the organization as a whole, but it must also deal with a *top management* group that applies additional demands.

We could spend a great amount of time dealing with the problems of measuring these forces and forecasting future ones. However, it is more important to say that the production plant must formally organize in terms of these critical areas to ensure an awareness of the direction of the change and to guarantee responsiveness. Once management determines that change is needed, what techniques are available to effect that change?

Any effort to change a firm must deal with our four primary interdependent variables: task, technology, formal organization, and informal social structure. Let's take the last of these first. We can change social structure by three basic techniques: we can train people, we can provide external or internal consulting assistance, and we can do research to provide the organization with data to facilitate change. However, it is important to note that in all cases we can only help. People within the organization bring about change in this area. Our other three categories are more straightforward and easier for managers to handle.

Management can select and assign new tasks, it can set up alternative organizations, and it can introduce new technologies. This may be the reason management often changes these variables, even when it is not very efficient, and then deals with the problems of informal social structure.

In summary, what has been provided here is a road map that, in a sense, explains where we are trying to go. New concepts have been introduced but at the center of our integrated approach is the fundamental concept that if managers are to be successful, they must understand what makes an individual do what he or she does, that is, what causes an individual's behavior. We have shown that this is a very complex question and we have no simple, atomistic answer. We must use concepts to lead our thinking into the analysis of complex systems and ultimately improve our inherent response in managerial situations.

QUESTIONS FOR REFLECTION AND DISCUSSION

1. What are the differences and similarities between the behavior of individuals, groups, and organizations?
2. What are the differences and similarities in expectations, self-image, and personal characteristics between the behavior of individuals, groups, and organizations?
3. What are the differences and similarities in the roles of external and internal environments on individuals, groups, and organizations?
4. What can managers do to influence individuals, groups, and organizations more effectively?

NOTES

1. R. J. Sternberg, *Beyond IQ: A Triarchic Theory of Human Intelligence* (New York: Cambridge University Press, 1985).
2. Robert L. Katz, "Skills of an Effective Administrator," *Harvard Business Review*, January/February 1955.
3. *Expectations* is a term often used in management literature; see, for example, "Pygmalion in Management" by J. Sterling Livingston, *Harvard Business Review*, July/August 1969, which was originally derived from *Pygmalion in the Classroom* by Robert Rosenthal and Lenore Jacobson (New York: Holt, Rinehart and Winston, 1968). *Psychological contract* is a term often used in psychological literature and more recently, management literature; see, for example, *Managing Human Assets* by Michael Beer, Bert Spector, Paul R. Lawrence, D. Quinn Mills, and Richard L. Walton (New York: The Free Press, 1984), p. 75. The term apparently originated as a psychological extension derived from A. H. Croust's article, "Origin and Meaning of the Social Compact Doctrine as Expressed by Greek Philosophers" in *Ethics*, October 1946.
4. Victor H. Vroom, *Work and Motivation* (New York: Wiley, 1964); and Edward Lawler, *Motivation in Work Organizations* (Monterey, CA: Brooks/Cole, 1973).
5. J. S. Adams, "Toward an Understanding of Inequity," *Journal of Abnormal and Social Psychology* 67, 1963, pp. 422–36.

6. Calvin S. Hall and Gardner Lindzey, *Theories of Personality*, 3rd ed. (New York: John Wiley & Sons, 1978).

7. David C. McClelland, *The Achieving Society* (New York: D. Van Nostrand Co., 1961).

8. Arthur W. Combs and Donald Snygg, *Individual Behavior: A Perceptual Approach to Behavior* (New York: Harper & Row, 1959), pp. 126–44.

9. Edwin S. Shneidman, ed., *Endeavors in Psychology: Selections from the Personology of Henry A. Murray* (New York: Harper & Row, 1981); Henry A. Murray, *Explorations in Personality* (New York: Oxford University Press, 1938; and Peter M. Senge, *The Fifth Discipline* (New York: Doubleday, 1990), pp. 20–21.

10. R. N. Bostrom, *Listening Behavior: Measurement & Application* (New York: Guilford, 1990); and J. Brownell, *Building Active Listening Skills* (Englewood Cliffs, NJ: Prentice-Hall, 1986).

11. E. H. Schein, "Coming to a New Awareness of Organizational Culture," *Sloan Management Review*, Winter 1984.

12. This diagram derives from the one put forth by H. J. Leavitt in *Managerial Psychology*, 3rd ed. (Chicago: University of Chicago Press, 1972), p. 264.

13. Paul Lawrence and Jay Lorsch, *Organization and Environment: Managing Differentiation and Integration* (Homewood, IL: Irwin, 1967).

PART 2

CASES

SECTION 6

CASE WRITING PROJECT AND ACTION EXERCISES

SECTION 7

CLASSIC CASES BY OTHER AUTHORS

ALPHA-OMEGA, INC. (A)

Alpha-Omega, Inc., (AO) is a very large multinational corporation selling a full spectrum of computers and related products. In every country in which AO has a significant operation, it has established a wholly owned subsidiary in accordance with the laws of that country. AO Claytonia, Ltd., is such a subsidiary. Claytonia is a moderately large, highly industrialized country whose capital is Bridgeton.

AO recently reorganized to fully integrate its operations. In most countries the company headquarters is fully unified with central staff functions. Marketing is divided into two divisions, one for specifically identified very large customers, the Large Accounts Marketing Division (LAMD) and the other for all other customers, the General Marketing Division (GMD). Prior to this reorganization, Bridgeton had fifteen marketing branch offices, each with a set of products and territories. The territories of a branch selling one set of product lines were duplicated in other branches selling other product lines.

A year prior to the reorganization, Bill Brown was one of several marketing managers in the Suburban II branch in the Greater Bridgeton area selling small and medium-sized computers. After the reorganization, he was marketing manager in the new marketing division devoted to all but the very large accounts. Bill Brown was born forty years ago and graduated from a large, well-known university with a degree in mathematics. After graduation, he served in the Claytonia Air Force as an electronics engineer for two years and was then employed as an electronics engineer in the development laboratories of XYZ Computer Company for two years. He then became a computer sales representative for QRS, Ltd., a competitor of AO's, for three years.

Brown joined AO as a sales trainee thirteen years ago and was a salesperson on quota for nine years. He exceeded his quota in eight of those years, received country recognition in four years, and received international recognition in two years. He was promoted to staff manager four years ago and to his present job two years ago. His unit had exceeded its quota one month before the end of the marketing year in both those years. His branch manager had twice commented favorably on his people skills. (Bill Brown grew up in a lower middle-class, small-town environment. His father was a very scholastically oriented man, an amateur archeologist, who lived a happy and contented life. Brown's father was not interested in high economic achievement and neither were his two brothers.)

Shortly before the new marketing year was to begin, Bill Brown had been notified that there was to be a reorganization of the company and that he would lose three of his six salespeople (all of whom had made their last year's quota and seemed assured of making their quota in the coming new year). He was to have three other salespeople assigned to his unit. Before the reorganization actually took place, Brown set about learning as much as he could about each of the three new men to be assigned to him. The following excerpts are from files on each of the three that Brown considered significant:

Lou Grant was to be reassigned from the Suburban I branch where he had been moderately successful. He was 29 years old and had been with AO for four years. He had made his quotas in the first two years he had been assigned one. He had a university degree in civil engineering and had worked for several years in that area, which is where he became involved and interested in computers and their technical applications.

Bill Brown's manager told him that Lou Grant had a "personality conflict" with his marketing manager in the Suburban I branch and had asked the branch manager to move him to a unit with a different marketing manager even before the AO reorganization had been announced. Indeed, he seemed to have had quite a few "personality conflicts." Unfortunately, it was apparent that he would miss his quota for the current year, and seemed to be carrying a "chip on his shoulder." (His brother, who is older by five years, is a branch manager with the Digital Equipment Corporation.) The personnel records verified that Grant's AO product education had been limited to small computers and related equipment. One item in his file that puzzled Brown was a comment made by Grant's previous manager to the effect that Grant "lacked the breeding to be a sales representative at the upper end of the AO product line."

George Grey was to be transferred from the Midtown branch, which was an experimental branch in which customers came to a central location to see the midsized and smaller computers. Grey was 35 years old and had joined AO only two years ago. He had formerly been a very successful salesperson and then sales manager for Burroughs, the latter

position being comparable to an account manager in AO rather than a marketing manager.

Last week it was announced that the Midtown unit from which Grey was being transferred was being abolished with the reorganization. It was not surprising then that Grey did not seem likely to make his six-month quota. Grey's unit manager at the Midtown branch had told Brown that Grey had a wide range of personal problems, including his recent divorce from a very attractive former model who ran off with a movie producer, as well as surgery for cancer, which seems to have been fully cured. Grey had been educated in the "school of hard knocks." When he was a child, he witnessed his mother being seriously abused by his father. His father left without providing support for him or his mother. Grey was sent to boarding school by an uncle and was very active in athletics, even though he was small in stature. He did a tour in the army infantry and then held a number of odd jobs until he became interested in electronics. He worked for two electronics firms before joining Burroughs.

Based on this background it was not surprising that Grey's Midtown unit manager described him as sometimes moody or depressed, and sometimes vitriolic. However, the Midtown unit manager also observed that, from a personality standpoint, Grey was a "natural salesrep," though at times a bit arrogant and somewhat of a prima donna. The Midtown manager felt that Grey appeared to be a bit careless or sloppy about what he sold or what the customer needed as well as about paperwork. Grey was described as the type of salesperson who might sell a piece of equipment without being sure it was the best for the customer's particular demands. In short, he had the potential to be an outstanding salesperson but needed close supervision and much "tidying up" after him.

Sam Fry was to be reassigned from the Large Accounts–West branch and would be bringing several accounts with him that were not designated for the specific Large Accounts Division. These accounts were to make up about two-thirds of his quota for the coming year. He was 47 years old and had been with AO for 18 years. During almost all of that time he dealt with large computers and large accounts, first as a systems engineer (SE) for eight years and then as a sales representative. He had made his quota eight years, won international recognition two years and country recognition one year. Prior to joining AO, he was an accountant (with the Claytonia equivalent to the CPA) with a major accounting firm. He is a senior sales representative, with a correspondingly higher quota.

Fry was described by the Large Accounts–West manager as a man of very good breeding with a good, private education. He is very well-spoken, lives in a grand house and has three brothers-in-law who are high-level executives in major Claytonia companies. Like Lou Grant, Fry had requested reassignment prior to the announcement of the AO reorganization because his marketing manager upset him. He was also scheduled for routine surgery early in the first month of the new marketing year which would keep him from reporting to his new unit in Suburban II for several weeks, perhaps a month.

As Bill Brown reflected on his soon-to-be new organization, he anticipated that his three present salespeople would continue their solid performances. He had good relations with all three and had already begun discussing their work and quotas for next year with them. He expected no management problems from any of them. His three new salespeople presented a different situation. He suspected they might all be difficult to manage in one way or another and, indeed, they may have been assigned to him because that was the case.

QUESTIONS

1. If you were in Bill Brown's position, what additional information would you want to obtain about your three new salespeople? Where would you get it?
2. Develop a strategy for managing the three new salespeople for the coming year.
3. Describe in detail your objectives and behavior on your first meeting with each of the three new salespeople.
4. If you were in the position of Lou Grant, George Grey, or Sam Fry, what additional information would you want to obtain about your new marketing manager? Where would you get it?
5. Develop a strategy for managing your new boss for the coming year.
6. Describe in detail your objectives and behavior in your first meeting with your new boss.

ALPHA-OMEGA, INC. (B)

Alpha-Omega, Inc., (AO) is a very large multinational corporation selling a full spectrum of computers and related products. In every country in which AO has a significant operation, it has established a wholly owned subsidiary in accordance with the laws of that country. AO Claytonia, Ltd., is such a subsidiary. Claytonia is a moderately large, highly industrialized country whose capital is Bridgeton.

AO recently reorganized to fully integrate its operations. In most countries the company headquarters is fully unified with central staff functions. Marketing is divided into two divisions, one for specifically identified very large customers, the Large Accounts Marketing Division (LAMD) and the other for all other customers, the General Marketing Division (GMD).

Prior to the reorganization, Sam Fry was a senior sales representative in the Large Accounts–West branch where he successfully marketed large computers and dealt almost exclusively with large accounts (see Alpha-Omega, Inc. (A)). As a result of the reorganization, Sam Fry was assigned to a marketing unit in the Suburban II branch of the General Marketing Division. Fry had brought along several of his accounts that were not designated for the Large Accounts Marketing Division. In addition, Fry had been assigned a number of small and medium sized accounts by his new marketing manager, Bill Brown. Fry soon concluded that these newly assigned smaller accounts were less sophisticated in their knowledge of data processing capabilities and more reluctant to make decisions based on rational financial analyses than the larger firms with which he had worked.

Fry was particularly frustrated by the Capstone Breweries account, which he had taken over. He had read the file notes left by the previous salesperson, including the results of an AO survey of the Capstone account (see Exhibit 1). He had met with the head of management services at Capstone (see Exhibit 2 for a partial organizational chart of Capstone Breweries), whom he judged was technically competent. In addition, he had met briefly with the financial director whom he found to have a keen mind and would likely be very demanding for factual data to justify an AO recommendation.

In an effort to acquire some insights into his newly assigned small accounts, Fry asked George Grey, another salesperson in the same marketing unit who had had several years' experience with smaller accounts, to have lunch and discuss the Capstone Breweries account. A summary of the information that emerged from this discussion is given below:

Capstone Breweries is a traditional, family-owned business that has grown to employ over 200 people by taking over several independent small breweries in Claytonia over the years. It has approximately 2,500 wholesale customers and 2,700 product lines. Last year

EXHIBIT 1

EXCERPTS FROM AO MARKETING FILES ON CAPSTONE BREWERIES

Business Problems Recognized by the Customer

1. Coding errors. Order forms frequently came in with handwritten words that had to be accurately coded to reflect the product.
2. Order form. Nine-part form required extensive handling and filing.
3. Data preparation. Six order-takers at machines were costly, not very effective, and used enormous amounts of overtime during peak seasons.
4. Postal costs. Costs were inflating rapidly.
5. Cost of resolving errors. Many customers paid no bills whatsoever until errors had been cleared.
6. Inflation on the cost of credit. The credit cost was hurting end-of-year results.

Business Problems Discovered by Alpha-Omega Survey

1. No central buying.
2. No central stocking policy. Multiple depots were slow in reporting their stock situations, resulting in inefficient inventory maintenance; for example, some items were understocked while others were overstocked.
3. Depots were autonomous and run by people with varying abilities and motivation. For example, two depots didn't sell Capstone beer at all but sold competitive brands only.
4. Management information on depots was far too late, inaccurate, and poorly presented. Management tended to look at turnover by customer rather than profitability by customer.
5. Outstanding debit problem was increasing. Credit controllers were trying to do a job with information that was so old that it was impacting their performance markedly. For example, the controllers spent three weeks investigating an outstanding debit on a statement that was three months old only to discover that the customer had paid it.

it had gross sales of just over $16 million. Its prime business is selling and distributing its own beer, competitive beers and lagers, specialty wines, and spirits. It has a multilocation distribution setup in which beer is produced at a central point and stocking depots are located at another five locations. It has been public for some years now, but 60 percent is owned by four of the directors, country-type gentlemen whose involvement has been very close because of their family ties (see Exhibit 3 for a description of key family members at Capstone and their ownership). Capstone has recruited a Scottish financial director to use his business acumen to address the problems of a company its size whose sales turnover has grown only by inflation and whose profitability has become increasingly small. He makes all the decisions involving numbers and although his recommendation is crucial for board of directors approval, he does not himself vote on the board.

Six years ago, Capstone recognized the need to mechanize some of its accounting systems, so it brought in an outside consultant who advised the firm on what to choose by way of a computer. At that time, Capstone chose an MDQ Decade 10, implemented with the assistance of some programming from the firm's consultant. The company also recruited

EXHIBIT 2

CAPSTONE BREWERIES—PARTIAL ORGANIZATION CHART

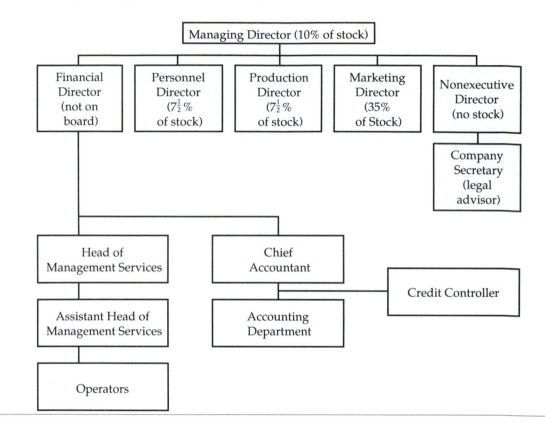

two data processing people after the order was placed. The head of management services seems competent, open-minded, and has a good understanding of where data processing is going in the company. The head programmer appears to have very little ambition or drive. The information demands six years ago were small and the business was run by the various depots, and the company inevitably made some profits. It also owns over 600 pubs in Claytonia and these contribute to profits as well.

Apparently, after the Decade 10 had been running for about five years, the Capstone people had discussions with their MDQ supplier to try to remedy a problem that was growing worse. They were obtaining orders by telephone selling, filling these orders by loading vans, and giving a delivery note to the salesperson who delivered to the customer. The customer then took what was delivered, sometimes picking and choosing volumes and quantities of the total delivery, and returned empty kegs and barrels, which might have had residual quantities of beer in them, for which the customer received an allowance. Paperwork went back with the salesperson at the end of the day and had to be put through the system; eventually, an invoice was produced. This system led to a high number of errors due to incorrect invoices, partial deliveries, and, by the head of management services' own

EXHIBIT 3

Managing Director—Owns 10 Percent of Capstone Breweries Stock

- Age: early 5Os
- Family: married, three children, one son and two daughters, ages unknown
- Education: Eaton and Cambridge
- Background: elder son of a member of House of Lords; independently wealthy—very visibly so, lives in large country house on estate that includes 1,400 acres for farming
- Other: numerically blind; was embarrassed in recent AO executive course when instructor asked him to add a short column of figures and he was unable to do so. First managing director of a company that I know of who was unable to manipulate figures.

Marketing Director—Owns 35 Percent of Capstone Breweries Stock

- Age: about 55
- Family: unknown
- Education: Eaton and Cambridge
- Background: very wealthy but not titled; cousin of the managing director; 20 years of army service, retired as colonel; patron of archeologic expedition in Greece and spends Thursday and Friday of *every* week on site assisting in this project
- Other: at work no more than three days each week (Monday through Wednesday); spends most of his time in company pubs drinking with customers, therefore, Capstone Breweries' marketing force seems neglected and misdirected

Production Director—Owns 7 1/2 Percent of Capstone Breweries Stock

- Age: about 50
- Family: unknown
- Education: Eaton and Cambridge
- Background: moderately wealthy; cousin of managing director; older brother of personnel director, chair of local football club
- Other: seems reasonably competent but seems to view his primary interest as the football club, sometimes neglects Capstone

Personnel Director—Owns 7 1/2 Percent of Capstone Breweries Stock

- Age: about 45
- Family: unknown
- Education: Eaton and Cambridge
- Background: moderately wealthy; cousin of managing director, younger brother of production director, active in local football club (like his brother)

- Other: probably put in personnel so he would not do any harm; lots of problems with strike of drivers; gives workers two free pints per day

Outside Director—Owns no stock in Capstone Breweries

- Age: mid-70s
- Family: father of managing director
- Education: Eaton and Cambridge
- Background: member of the House of Lords; large estate with manor house
- Other: function on Board of Directors seems to be to minimize arguments among other members

Financial Director—Owns no stock in Capstone Breweries

- Age: about 45
- Family: married, two daughters
- Education: Edinburgh University
- Background: Scottish; only nonfamily member of management; widely experienced in both large and small companies, all in financial area
- Other: seems to be highly regarded but not on board, his recommendation is crucial but may not be sufficient; for all practical purposes he makes all day-to-day decisions involving numbers; has an acute, clear mind; very demanding for facts to prove business case; "You will have to give me convincing arguments (facts) on why I should change suppliers (of computers)."

Head of Management Services—Owns no stock in Capstone Breweries

- Age: 38
- Family: married, two children
- Education: Thames School of Accounting
- Background: employed as accountant before moving to data processing at age 24, 10 years ago had very favorable experience with AO equipment at another company, member of City Council
- Other: very active in community activities; open, receptive mind; enthusiastic and hard-working when committed

admission, a rather confused invoice numbering system. Disputes arose about paying invoices and the outstanding debit was growing every day.

Discussions were held with MDQ about alternative ways of handling data in an attempt to speed up the system and improve accuracy. MDQ recommended moving to an on-line system, which only meant bypassing the PC to input directly into a computer workstation and then into the computer. The head of management services felt that this was not totally satisfactory, so he contacted AO as well as others to look at alternative systems with him. The financial director is aware of the head of management services' inquiries but has by no means given his authorization to proceed. The other directors aren't aware that other computer companies have been contacted.

Grey informed Fry that six months ago he had sold a system to the Fawcett corporation, a small brewery with somewhat similar problems to Capstone's. Grey suggested that Fry consider arranging a visit so that the Capstone people could see the Fawcett operation, since it had proven to be an effective and profitable operating system. Grey felt sure that a demonstration carried out by the Fawcett Brewery would be very useful in gaining support for an AO proposal to the Capstone financial director and board of directors. Grey went on to describe the system and outlined several basic advantages that Fry might want to relate to the Capstone people: 1) the Fawcett installation was demonstrably successful, which made comparable installation at Capstone a very low risk; 2) it offered reciprocal training, which made conversion to a new system much simpler; and 3) it would allow for faster system implementation, since Fawcett Brewery's software could be used. Fry agreed that this seemed like an excellent idea.

QUESTIONS

1. What are the differences between marketing computers to large accounts versus small and medium-sized accounts?
2. If you were in Sam Fry's position, what additional information would you want to obtain? Where and how would you get it? What would you do with it?
3. If you were in Sam Fry's position, what would you do now? What strategy would you follow in order to influence the decision makers at Capstone? How would you go about implementing your strategy?
4. What sort of financial rationalization or justification do you feel is appropriate in this case?

ALPHA-OMEGA, INC. (C)

Alpha-Omega, Inc., (AO) is a very large multinational corporation selling a full spectrum of computers and related products. In every country in which AO has a significant operation, it has established a wholly owned subsidiary in accordance with the laws of that country. AO Claytonia is such a subsidiary. Claytonia is a moderately large, highly industrialized country whose capital is Bridgeton. AO recently reorganized to fully integrate its operations.

Late one Friday afternoon, Bill Brown, marketing manager (see Exhibit 1), was preparing to review with his branch manager, Bob White, what appeared to be the loss of an account. The Acme Company had been a stable and consistent AO customer since Brown had become a marketing manager several years ago. Since neither the salesperson nor Acme ever brought an issue to Brown, he had tended to leave a good situation alone

EXHIBIT 1

ABBREVIATED ORGANIZATION CHART FOR AO-CLAYTONIA

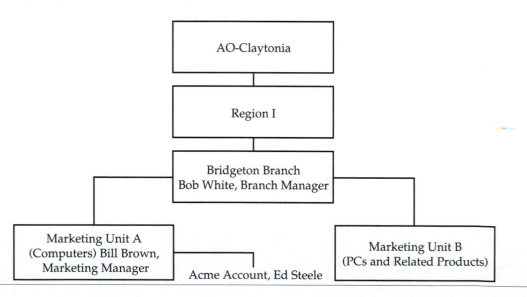

and had had only superficial contacts with Acme managers.

Last year, the first negative signals had arrived. Brown had received a telephone call from Acme's vice-president of finance, Tom Wood, stating that they had terminated the employment of their corporate data processing manager (DPM) and had just hired someone new, Brad Cook, to replace him. Wood requested that a new salesperson be assigned to work with Cook so that a fresh start might be achieved. During this telephone discussion, two points had emerged: (1) Acme management considered their former DPM insufficiently qualified for his post, and (2) Wood felt that the AO salesperson assigned to Acme was much too close personally to the former DPM and therefore wanted a different salesperson. Wood also suggested that the new salesperson should develop contacts with each of the DPMs in the four subsidiary operations of Acme— not only with the corporate DPM as had been the case.

In discussing the situation with the salesperson assigned to Acme, Brown had been told that indeed there was a very close relationship between the salesperson and the former Acme corporate DPM. Under the circumstances, it was agreed that a new salesperson should be assigned. Brown also learned that almost all sales contact with Acme had been with the corporate DPM, who had been very favorably inclined toward AO and the AO salesperson. Contact with Tom Wood, the financial director who had jurisdiction over data processing, was cordial but infrequent. *[It is strongly suggested that the reader refer frequently to Exhibit 2, "Partial Acme Company Organization Chart," in order to keep the people and titles of those in Acme or its subsidiaries clear.]*

The former Acme corporate DPM had purchased a GB computer system for one of the manufacturing subsidiaries, Atwood Manufacturing Company, to replace a smaller GA system which had been used for accounting and manufacturing applications. This had been an easy sale by the AO salesperson to the former Acme corporate DPM, without any contact with the Atwood DPM or the data processing staff at Atwood who would use the equipment. The systems engineer (SE) assigned by AO to assist Atwood during the installation had told the AO salesman that "the only problem is, the Atwood data processing people seem to have expectations for the GB computer system that are far too high...and completely unreasonable." The salesperson concluded that there did not seem to be any commitment from the Atwood data processing staff to try to make the GB computer system work and that, therefore, complaints were being received that "the computer system doesn't work." The AO salesman had dismissed these after discussions with his SE. In reviewing the situation, Brown wondered whether the Atwood difficulties and complaints, which the salesperson was convinced were of their own making, had anything to do with the termination of the Acme corporate DPM.

After considering everything that was then known, Brown, with the approval of his boss (Bob White, branch manager), assigned Ed Steele, a salesperson with a highly analytical, businesslike style, to the Acme account. This style contrasted sharply with the personal and involved style of the former salesperson and therefore Brown thought Steele most likely would be fully acceptable to Acme's vice-president of finance, the new Acme corporate DPM, and the DPMs of the four subsidiaries (two manufacturing subsidiaries, Atwood and Sunfield, one Sales and Distribution Company subsidiary and one Service Company subsidiary).

Steele had demonstrated himself to be a very effective AO salesperson during the four years he had been with the company. Steele was 33 years old. Prior to joining AO, he had

EXHIBIT 2

PARTIAL ACME COMPANY ORGANIZATION CHART

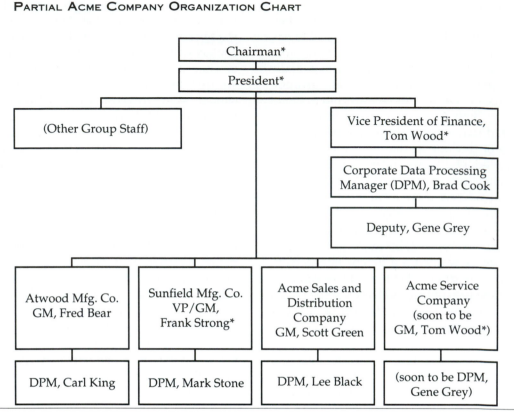

*Also on the Acme Board of Directors

spent eight years selling advertising space, rising to manager, and handling 23 different magazines. His previous experience also included one year at a major Claytonia bank and one year at an international news-gathering agency. He had no university education but since his father was a military officer, he had grown up at various Claytonia military bases around the world.

Immediately after being assigned to the Acme account, Steele had embarked on the task of acquainting himself with the Acme organization and the key people with whom he would interact (again, see Exhibit 2). He also set about understanding the data processing requirements of each of the four subsidiaries as well as the thinking of Brad Cook, the new Acme corporate DPM. Further, Steele had strongly urged his boss, Bill Brown, the marketing manager, and the branch manager, Bob White, to establish relations with senior managers in the Acme subsidiaries and the corporate offices. White had begun to develop these relationships right away. Brown had felt that too much attention to the Acme account by AO personnel might be counterproductive, so he encouraged White and Steele to develop and maintain relationships with the important people at Acme headquarters and at the subsidiaries.

Steele had learned that all four Acme subsidiaries had AO computing equipment. In all four subsidiaries, larger computing equipment was needed, probably built around a GD computer system with substantial amounts of peripheral equipment, such as printers, terminals, and so on, some at remote locations. Steele also learned that Brad Cook, the Acme corporate DPM, felt that Acme had an urgent need for stand-alone PCs for word processing and he passed that information on to the marketing manager of Marketing Unit B, responsible for PCs and related products.

Over the next several months, a number of personnel changes occurred at Acme's subsidiaries, which were apparently influenced by Brad Cook: the Sunfield Company DPM (again, see Exhibit 2) was replaced by an outsider with considerable experience at another company in managing AO computer equipment and very positively biased toward it; the DPM at the Sales and Distribution Company was also replaced by an outsider with considerable experience in data processing, who seemed highly analytical; the DPM at the Service Company was terminated and Brad Cook's recently hired deputy was slated to take that job in a few months. Exhibit 3 summarizes what Steele learned about Brad Cook and each of the subsidiary DPMs.

Three months after taking over the Acme account, Steele had defined the requirements of each of the subsidiaries and noted that growth in all four would soon overtake existing computer equipment. He had made presentations to the general manager and DPM in each of the subsidiaries and felt that his presentations had been well received at all but Atwood, where their expectations were far beyond what Steele felt was realistic. Steele had told both Fred Bear, the Atwood general manager, and Carl King, the Atwood DPM, that he would *not* make a formal proposal for new computing equipment because their expectations were unrealistic, but that he would be pleased to do so if they brought their expecta-

tions and resulting requirements down to reality.

During the next four months, Steele had maintained contact with Acme and its four subsidiaries largely through telephone calls, and felt that "everything is on hold—nothing seems to be happening except the problems caused by the lack of capacity, which I had predicted."

Meanwhile, Bob White, the AO branch manager, had made calls on the general managers of the subsidiaries and had established very good relations with Frank Strong, vice-president and general manager at the Sunfield Company, and Tom Wood, the Acme vice-president of finance. Wood had confided that the reason he wanted the AO salesperson to have direct contact with the DPMs in Acme's subsidiaries was not only to avoid "breakdowns in communications like that which had created the problems at Atwood," but also because the Acme President had recently made some decisions that would, in time, make the subsidiaries far more autonomous and trim corporate overhead substantially by reducing the staff and functions at that level. It was not yet clear how this would effect specific corporate staff functions, such as data processing, but the overall trend was clear.

Wood had also explained that he was soon to be named general manager of the Service Company in addition to retaining the title and functions of vice-president of finance for the Acme Company. It was for this reason that Wood had used his influence to have the Acme corporate deputy DPM assigned as the Service Company DPM. In closing, Wood also noted that Acme was attempting to sell off the Atwood Company to a foreign company in the same product line that wanted to establish a business base in Claytonia. Wood had said he expected this information to be reported in the financial news media momentarily, and indeed, a few days later the financial news did report that such negotiations were proceeding. Exhibit 4 summarizes what

---

EXHIBIT 3

SUMMARY OF THE BACKGROUNDS OF THE ACME SUBSIDIARY DP MANAGERS AS
SEEN BY ED STEELE, AO MARKETING REPRESENTATIVE

Carl King, DPM at the Atwood Manufacturing Company

King is about 30 years old, married, has two children, and no university education. He has
six years' prior experience as manufacturing manager in an electronics defense systems
operation. In this previous job, he was responsible for the installation of a QRS computer
for manufacturing control applications. He was apparently highly successful in this job,
which led to his being hired by Atwood. He has had no previous data processing training
and consequently has little data processing skill. He strongly resisted attending two short
AO computer seminars, but finally went. He seems to service users of the Atwood GB
system very well and they seem quite happy, but he does not seem able to assess the time
requirements to implement user requests. This creates difficulties, which he blames on AO
or the GB equipment, which he does not seem to understand. He and his staff seem to
resent the fact that the equipment was pushed on them by the former corporate DPM
without any input from them. Carl King is pro-competition.

Mark Stone, DPM at the Sunfield Manufacturing Company, Ltd.

Stone is about 43 years old, a family man, conservative, a low reactor, and not a schemer.
He graduated from one of Claytonia's finest business schools (the same one attended by
his boss, the general manager). Has had fifteen years' prior experience in data processing,
and rose to data processing (DP) manager after a few years. Most of his experience is with
AO equipment, although he has experience with some other equipment also. He still has
very strong ties with AO people at his previous job, particularly one who was originally
trained by him and was then hired by AO as a systems engineer (SE) and recently promoted to AO staff in manufacturing support. Bill Brown received a telephone call from his
counterpart handling the territory including Mark Stone's previous employer. He was told
Stone is very friendly to AO and has had excellent relations for many years. He has a very
clear picture of his objectives including a GD system, but feels Brad Cook is pushing the
competition.

Lee Black, DPM at the Acme Sales and Distribution Company, Ltd.

Black is about 24 years old, still single, a university graduate in data processing, and has
one year of prior experience with DA system. He apparently was recruited by Brad Cook,
who expected Black to be his prodigy, but Black is now very independent. Far more
technically competent than Brad Cook, whom he views as mildly incompetent. Black has a
very serious and analytical personality; he is somewhat cold.

Gene Grey, deputy corporate DPM, soon-to-be DPM of the Acme Service Company, Ltd.

Grey is about 33 years old, and information about his education and family is not known.
His previous experience includes four years as DP manager with a large, multinational
electronics (noncomputer) company. He had jurisdiction over several GB systems and had

a very good reputation for a job well done with his former employer. Grey also was recruited by Brad Cook and appears more technically competent. Friendly, Grey seems pro-AO.

Brad Cook, corporate DPM

Cook is about 35 years old, married, has two children. He is a university graduate who applied for a job with AO and was turned down. He worked for Honeywell for a couple of years and several other firms as well. Prior to joining Acme, Cook spent four years as an analyst and project leader for QRS Computer Company. He made a very big jump to Acme Corporate DPM. Seems to be good on details but poor on forward planning. He appears isolated from his boss as well as DPMs and GMs in the subsidiaries. He seems insecure and needs attention.

the branch manager, Bob White, learned about each of the general managers of the subsidiary companies.

Several months later, in mid-October, Bob White had read in the financial section of the *Bridgeton Times* that discussions regarding the sale of the Atwood subsidiary of Acme had been suspended indefinitely. He telephoned Tom Wood to confirm this information and was advised that indeed it was true and that Atwood would remain an Acme subsidiary for the immediate future. Wood also told White that Fred Bear, the Atwood general manager, and his DPM, Carl King, were actively investigating competitive computing equipment. White arranged to visit Atwood and see the general manager.

At this meeting, early in November, the Atwood general manager told White that they had basically the same requirements they had had four months ago but that they now had "more realistic expectations." He acknowledged that they had been investigating competitive computing equipment but observed that changing manufacturers at this stage looked difficult. Therefore, he wanted AO to propose a solution to his requirements, probably built around a GD computer system. White agreed to have Steele submit a proposal before the end of the year.

Three weeks later, White received a call from the marketing manager of Unit B, responsible for PCs and related products, saying that he had just received a call from Brad Cook, their Acme customer, for PCs. According to the Unit B marketing manager, Cook had said, "AO has messed up the Atwood installation; now the entire PC deal is off." After further discussion, White was able to piece together what had happened: shortly after being notified by Steele that Acme was a PC prospect, the Unit B marketing manager had assigned a salesperson to call on Brad Cook, who they assumed was "Mr. Data Processing" at the Acme Company. Through Cook, a special PC seminar was scheduled for Acme executives. At this seminar, most Acme executives were favorably impressed, except Fred Bear and Carl King from Atwood, who were the only ones already using PCs (Apple) and did not want to make a change.

At this meeting, Brad Cook seemed very influential and powerful; the driving force behind the acquisition of stand-alone PCs. Shortly after this, Cook signed an order for eight WP-10s for delivery in ten months. These were to be trial units which, if successful, would lead to further purchases and, ultimately, a network tied into the central computer. The problem was long lead time for delivery, and Cook demanded three WP-4s (not compatible with the WP-10) immediately to provide an interim capability. The AO people from Marketing Unit B argued against this with Brad Cook, but

EXHIBIT 4

SUMMARY OF THE BACKGROUNDS OF THE ACME SUBSIDIARY GENERAL MANAGERS
AS SEEN BY BOB WHITE, AO BRANCH MANAGER

Fred Bear, GM, Atwood Manufacturing Company

Bear is in his mid-30s, and information about his education and family is not known. He is highly independent and resentful of guidance from corporate staff. Bear has three years at Atwood and formerly was an executive in one of the largest Claytonia manufacturing companies. He depends heavily on his own staff. The potential sale of Atwood by Acme has made him even more independent and less willing to listen to corporate staff.

Frank Strong, GM, Sunfield Manufacturing Company, Acme Vice-President, and Member of the board of directors

Strong is about 37 years old and is very closed-mouthed about his background, therefore little is known. He is a graduate of one of Claytonia's top business schools and very proud of this accomplishment. He has had three years with Acme, two at Sunfield. He has prior experience as a manager in production engineering in one of the largest Claytonia manufacturing companies. Strong has a good reputation as a firefighter; he is a strong and decisive manager.

Scott Green, GM, Acme Sales and Distribution Co.

Green is about 38 years old, a university graduate, and his family data is not known. He has worked with Acme for about one year, all as GM at the Sales and Distribution Company. His prior experience includes four years as a manager in special products engineering and modification in one of the largest manufacturing companies in Claytonia. He has earlier experience in both manufacturing and engineering.

Tom Wood, Acme Vice-President of finance, Soon-to-Be General Manager of the Acme Service Company, and Member of the board of directors

Wood is about 32 years old, a university graduate, and his family history is not known. Extremely bright, Wood served four years with Acme as vice-president of finance. He has previous experience in the financial department of one of the largest manufacturing companies in Claytonia; his other experience is not known. Wood seems very friendly and open toward me and favorably inclined to AO.

finally agreed because a conversion kit (WP-4 to WP-10) had been announced for delivery in ten months also. One of the WP-4s had gone to Atwood to replace the Apple equipment, over the strong objections of Bear and King. The other two subsidiaries did not seem anxious to do much with the WP-4s, but did not object to them.

Five months later, Unit B was notified that WP-10 deliveries could begin in two months if customers so desired. They notified Brad Cook who had said yes and the training of the Acme people to use the WP-10 had begun. Unfortunately, the Unit B people did not think to tie in the conversion kit, which was not to be available for three more months. The salesperson knew that Atwood was the only one actively using the WP-4, and that they had a large set of files on it. On a routine call to Atwood, the Unit B systems engineer had mentioned that the conversion kit would not be available for three months, and the general manager and DPM exploded. They called Brad Cook and demanded withdrawal of the WP-4 and cancellation of the WP-10s. They also demanded the reinstallation of the Apple equipment they had been using. Cook had capitulated and had then called the Unit B manager with his statement that AO had "messed up." The Unit B manager had then called White.

After some further discussion, White had suggested that the Unit B manager call Tom Wood, the Acme vice-president of Finance, and go see him, which was done. On returning from this meeting with Wood, the Unit B manager again called White to say that when he went to see Wood, Brad Cook was in the office also. At the meeting, the Unit B manager had reiterated AO's original arguments that the WP-4s should not have been installed. Wood had agreed with this, to Brad Cook's obvious consternation. The Unit B manager had agreed that all of Atwood's WP-4 data would be converted to the WP-10 by AO personnel. Cook telephoned the Atwood general manager with this information and was told it was too late: they had ordered the Apple equipment on their own and they wanted the AO equipment out. Cook again capitulated. Finally, it was agreed that the other three subsidiaries could use all eight of the WP-10s originally ordered, and the installations could proceed.

Bill Brown had wondered what impact all of this would have on his unit's proposal to Atwood. He spoke with Steele about what had happened and suggested that Steele call on the DPM at the Sunfield Company, who seemed favorably disposed to AO, to see what he could learn about the inside situation in Acme with respect to the data processing function.

Today, immediately after returning from his meeting with Sunfield's DPM (Mark Stone), Steele came to Brown's office. Stone had told Steele that Brad Cook had signed a letter of intent with a competitor for two computer systems for the manufacturing subsidiaries, one for Atwood and one for Sunfield. Apparently, according to Stone, Cook still wanted GD computer systems for the marketing and service companies but wanted competitive equipment for the manufacturing companies. Stone still wanted the GD system and had made a presentation recommending this to the Acme board, but Brad Cook had recommended the competitor. After this meeting, Frank Strong, the vice-president and general manager of Sunfield, told both Stone and Cook that he wanted a common solution. Stone told Steele that right now, the competitor looked better even to him, but he expected AO to be able to come up with something significantly better in the near future.

Since White was out of the office, Brown telephoned King, the Atwood DPM, and was told that they had indeed ordered competitive equipment before they had received the AO proposal because the PC fiasco was "the last straw." Steele was convinced that a hard-nosed letter to the Acme president or vice-president of finance was called for, insisting that they make up their minds. Steele felt he had already spent more time there than was justified, and Brown was inclined to agree. Brown knew that White would return to the office on Monday and that he and Steele would have to brief him on what had happened and recommend a course of action.

QUESTIONS

1. Evaluate the various Acme political forces acting upon Brad Cook. Determine how power has been acquired and used and by

whom since Cook arrived (look particularly at Cook, Bear, and King at Atwood). How has Cook's behavior been affected by these changing power relationships?

2. What should Bill Brown have done differently? When?
3. What strategy should Bill Brown and Ed Steele recommend to Bob White?

ALPHA-OMEGA, INC. (D)

After Bill Brown, the marketing manager, and Ed Steele, the salesperson, had briefed Bob White, their branch manager, regarding the Acme Company account, White asked them not to write a hard-nosed letter to Brad Cook, the Acme corporate DPM. White wanted to arrange a lunch with Tom Wood, the Acme vice-president of finance and soon-to-be general manager (GM) of the Acme Service Company, and also with Frank Strong and Scott Green, the GMs of the Sunfield Company and the Acme Sales and Distribution Company.

After the luncheon with Wood had been scheduled, White received a letter from Brad Cook that stated that no AO personnel, including White, Brown, and Steele, should contact any of the Acme GMs or DPMs except through him. The letter noted that copies were sent to all the GMs and DPMs at Acme. A few days later, White telephoned Tom Wood to confirm their luncheon arrangement. During this conversation, White mentioned the letter he had received from Brad Cook. Wood indicated that he had not received a copy of it nor heard anything about it and that White could certainly ignore it as far as he was concerned. White then telephoned Frank Strong, the Sunfield GM, to arrange a luncheon with him. He, too, indicated that he had not seen the Cook letter and that White could ignore it as far as he was concerned also.

After being briefed on the Cook letter and the response of two of the Acme subsidiary GMs, Steele decided to call three of the DPMs (all except Atwood) over the next week or so. None had received a copy of the Cook letter and all three urged Steele to ignore it insofar as their relationship with him was concerned.

The luncheon Bob White had with Tom Wood was very useful but Wood had asked that White *not* discuss their conversation with *anyone*. White then arranged a luncheon with Brad Cook and told him that his AO business responsibilities were such that he would have to continue to see whomever in Acme he deemed necessary but that he had no objection to keeping Cook informed after the fact. Cook's response was weak and he agreed that this would be fine for all AO personnel.

The first clue that Bill Brown had about those luncheon conversations came during a strategy meeting between White, Brown, and Steele. At this meeting, it was decided that the proposals for GD computer systems at the Sales and Distribution Company and the Service Company should be pursued vigorously by both Brown and Steele. White would also help if that seemed desirable. The strategy toward the Sunfield proposal for a GD computer system would be to encourage them to, as he put it, "wait and see how the Atwood installation goes. They may have trouble; you want to keep your options open. Besides, they are only putting on existing applications; new ones are a year away." White would pass this message

221

along at his upcoming luncheon with Frank Strong, and Brown and Steele should push it with the Sunfield DPM, Mark Stone, who wanted the GD computer system anyway.

The second clue came when White asked if either Brown or Steele knew that Brad Cook had had his employment terminated in two of his previous positions. Brown guessed that White had obtained this information either in his luncheon with Tom Wood or Brad Cook. It was possible, of course, that White had known this information for some time.

Two months later, as part of the strategy of pushing the Sales and Distribution Company and Service Company proposals, Brown and Steele made a courtesy call on Brad Cook. Cook seemed very depressed and casually observed, "I feel very isolated. Since Tom Wood has taken over as general manager at the Service Company, I report directly to the president. I've only had five minutes with my boss in the last two months [since Tom Wood left]." Brown suggested that perhaps it would be helpful to Cook's image if he arranged a meeting between his boss, himself, and the AO branch manager, Bob White, with Brown and Steele also included. Cook was enthusiastic about this idea and agreed to set it up.

Later in the meeting, Cook observed, "Your competitor tells us what direction they are going in and what their future plans are for manufacturing applications. Paper tiger, maybe, but they are good promises. We can see their whole manufacturing plan ahead and it looks very good. AO, on the other hand, won't tell us anything—we have no idea what you may be planning."

In a meeting with Mark Stone, the DPM at Sunfield, Steele found him receptive to the AO wait-and-see strategy. Stone observed, "The competitive equipment and promised manufacturing applications look much better than the GD computer system and its announced manufacturing applications. But I'm betting that AO will come out soon with additional announced manufacturing applications that will make yours the best proposal."

A month later, the Acme Service Company signed the order for a GD computer system. Two months after that, the Acme Sales and Distribution Company did the same.

QUESTIONS

1. What should Ed Steele have done differently? Bill Brown? Bob White?
2. What should Ed Steele do now? Bill Brown? Bob White?

ATLAS DEVELOPMENT LABORATORY (A), PART 1

Bob Quinn was sitting at his desk at the Atlas Development Laboratory (ADL) late one Friday afternoon, reflecting on the problems that seemed to leap out of the notebook he had been keeping since his arrival at ADL six weeks earlier. He noted with particular interest that Department A in the Special Engineering Lab seemed to be the target for criticisms he had heard from three other groups at ADL. He had been careful not to draw any conclusions from this data since he knew he was scheduled to work for Dr. Ted Stone, manager of Department A, on Monday.

After graduating with a BS and MS in Engineering Physics from Purdue University, Bob Quinn had joined a U.S. government laboratory where he had reached a senior engineer level working for six years in a variety of technical assignments. Budgetary cutbacks and lack of opportunity had made him begin to look for other employment. After a one year search, he accepted a position as a technical coordinator with ADL.

When he reported for work, Quinn had been taken to the office of the ADL general manager, Dr. Frank Hart. Hart explained that there were many places at ADL where Quinn's talents could make a contribution, and to facilitate his getting on board as quickly as possible, Hart had arranged for Quinn to be rotated through each of the five major laboratories at ADL, spending four weeks in each. After this orientation, he would be permanently assigned to whichever laboratory seemed to be able to use his skills most effectively. Hart went on to explain that ADL was an academically dominated, scientifically oriented organization and was substantially different from the government environment to which Quinn had become accustomed. Hart observed that Quinn's ability to generate a favorable personal chemistry with the senior scientists would not only determine his future assignment at ADL, but would undoubtedly influence his ability to work productively. A partial organization chart for ADL is shown in Exhibit 1.

Quinn had already enrolled in an evening MBA program at a nearby university, since he felt that management skills would be valuable to him at ADL and would become an increasingly important requirement for promotion. He had already observed a correlation between his work at ADL and his MBA program. In last evening's class he was assigned to write a paper on communications due the following week. Quinn wanted to

EXHIBIT 1

ADL Partial Organization Chart

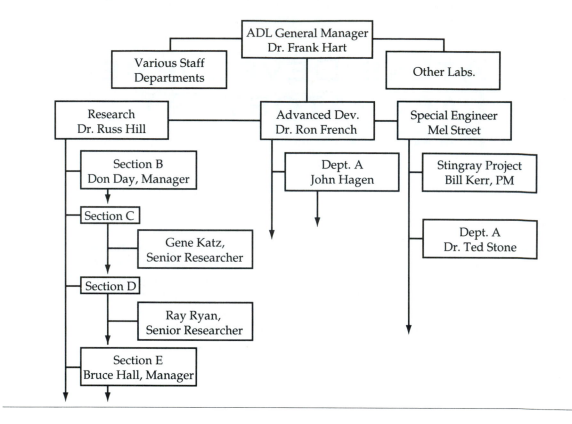

write on communications at ADL, and he thought his working notebook could provide the basic data.

His first four weeks at ADL had been spent in the research lab, where he worked in each of the five departments and most of the sections within these departments. He had enjoyed this experience and found most of the people friendly, helpful, and obviously very intelligent and dedicated to their special fields of interest. He had started his notebook immediately, thinking that he would be exposed to considerable information that would be of value, and he felt the notebook would provide a reasonable means of saving and cataloging this data.

As he reviewed his notes for data useful in writing his communications paper, four incidents, all from his first four weeks in the research lab, seemed of particular interest.

THE ALPHA MEASUREMENTS

The first incident, involving communications with Stone's department, occurred on Quinn's third day in the research lab at ADL. In a discussion with Quinn, Senior Researcher Gene Katz described the incident as typical of the lack of communications between the research and special engineering labs at ADL. Katz had been engaged in making basic alpha measurements for over six months when he discovered from his boss that Dr. Stone's department had contracted with an outside group to make very similar measurements. Katz felt that his work could have been readily adapted to get the data Stone's people needed. Katz acknowledged that Stone's people apparently did not know about the work he was doing, though he felt they should have known. Further, so far as Katz knew, there were no communications at any level between the two labs regarding these measurements. Katz expressed the opinion that, short of the detailed and often voluminous papers written to report *completed* research, there was simply no easy mechanism for feeding information about the work currently being done in research to the people in engineering, nor was there any simple mechanism for research to learn the information needs of engineering, hence there was no real cross-fertilization between the labs at ADL. Katz went on to explain that the only reason he found out about this contracted work was that his boss happened to attend an ADL senior management review meeting that included a progress report from the contractor Stone's group had hired.

THE SUPERIOR COMPONENT

Quinn was told about the second incident, involving communications with Dr. Stone's department, a week later while working in Dr. Don Day's section of the research lab. Day described the incident as an example of engineering's parochialism and lack of willingness to use the better components being developed by his group. According to Day, his group had recently perfected a substantially superior component that would have resulted in a 30 percent improvement in the effectiveness of a product being developed in Dr. Stone's department, had Dr. Stone or his people been willing to undertake the necessary testing and redesign. In fact, Day understood that

a 40 percent improvement was actually achieved in another product being developed by a different department that, Day felt, was not quite so parochial.

In discussing this incident with several people in the research lab, Quinn had been able to obtain the following opinions:

1. The superior component might be 75 percent more expensive than the one it would replace, but would probably add only a 5 percent increase in the total cost per unit to achieve a 30 percent increase in overall product effectiveness.
2. Engineering would have to incur some additional costs, not only for testing and redesign, but also for quality control.
3. Day's section had a national reputation in the technical field related to this component, and this was well known by other groups throughout ADL.
4. Day's group published technical reports on virtually everything they did and circulated these widely to all groups at ADL, universities, private organizations, and government laboratories and agencies that might be interested.
5. The reports from Day's group contained analytic computations of the increases in capability to be expected in various applications of their work.

Quinn had received the general impression from Day and his people that they took considerable pride in their work and the national recognition it received. They felt their work spoke for itself and that it was not their "burden to rub other people's noses" in their data. They had no inclination to "take engineering people by the hand and do a Madison Avenue job on them," but rather felt that if an engineer had a problem involving their work he should first consult the literature and then come and talk to them. They, too, expressed the opinion that there was no simple mechanism to find out what was going on currently throughout ADL, no booklet or catalogue of available skills, capabilities, or work being done.

THE CASUAL CONVERSATION

As Quinn went through his notebook he ran across another incident that related to interlab communications. Dr. Bruce Hall and his small section of the research lab were located about two miles away from the main ADL building in a modest but comfortable building leased by ADL. Hall told Quinn that he felt this distance created communications problems and kept the informal channels of communication from working. Hall felt that if it were not for old friends and his own concerted effort to find reasons to be in the main ADL building, he and his group would quickly become cut off completely from the mainstream operations.

As an example, Hall mentioned a luncheon conversation he had with an old friend from the advanced development lab in the cafeteria in the main ADL building. The friend casually mentioned a problem on which two engineers in nearby offices had been working for three months. After a few questions, Hall determined that his group had solved this same problem a year ago. After lunch, the necessary information was passed to the two engineers who were delighted to receive this unexpected help. Still, six man-months of effort had been expended because of a lack of communications.

Hall speculated that a monthly *Technical Highlights* publication from the general manager, with a list of tasks on which people were working along with a one-line description, would be a valuable aid in keeping track of what was going on at ADL. In addition, he felt that research people needed to think in terms of applications and to see that data got to the proper people, not just publish a paper and wash their hands of it. Hall also complained about the lack of a secretary to answer telephones when someone in his group was out of his office. Hall was confident that calls were missed and the callers became discouraged by unanswered calls.

THE INSENSITIVE DEVICE

Quinn reviewed still another incident from his notebook and remembered quite vividly the discussion he had had with Ray Ryan, a senior researcher in Section D of the research lab, regarding some devices Dr. Stone's people had wanted to purchase to make measurements for the Red Baron program. Ryan had been visibly angry in describing the incident. He had maintained that Stone's group was interested only in supporting its own people and not in whether worthwhile technical results could be produced in this manner. Stone's people, Ryan thought, were unwilling to cooperate across laboratory lines, even when another group like his own was clearly more competent. Beyond this, Ryan felt that Quinn should understand several other factors that he, Ryan, thought were very significant in this instance.

1. Dr. Hill, research lab director, was asked by the general manager to review a $140,000 contract that Stone's group wanted to award an outside firm for the purchase of some devices. (It was policy for the general manager to approve all contracts and purchase orders over $50,000, but he often asked others to review these before he approved.) Dr. Hill delegated this assignment to Ryan.
2. After insisting on seeing the program plan describing how the devices were to be used, Ryan wrote a memorandum (see Exhibit 2), which he was sure was the reason for the cancellation of the proposed contract.
3. The general manager asked Dr. Hill to prepare a proposal to do the work. Dr. Hill again delegated this to Ryan, and he prepared the proposal shown in Exhibit 3.

EXHIBIT 2
ADL

MEMORANDUM

From: Ray Ryan
To: Dr. Russ Hill
Subject: Comments on the R&D Contract for Design & Production of a Three-Component Device

1. As requested, the following quick look comments are made on the subject contract.

2. The proposed contract calls for the design and production of a device with the objective of evaluating its usefulness under the task outlined in reference (a). It is proposed to carry out measurements of the background noise as well as specific signals from designated sources.

3. Of immediate interest are the specifications relating to frequency band width and sensitivity.

4. The author's previous experience and a few simple calculations reveal the following:
   a. The planned sensitivity is not sufficient to measure anything in the proposed environment.
   b. A simple calculation shows that to be detected at the planned frequency, the designated source would have to produce signals far beyond anything known to exist, and at one-tenth the planned frequency detection is barely within the realm of possibility, though not likely.

5. The above considerations lead to the following conclusions:
   a. Consideration of this device can reasonably be limited to very low frequencies for the foreseeable future.
   b. Measurements should be made with a device of 100 times greater sensitivity to be of any value.

6. The device as described in the contract, while it is the best general purpose instrument currently available and does possess many desirable features, is not capable of meeting the program requirements.

7. It should be possible to design and build *in-house* a three-component device which would provide the necessary sensitivity for approximately one-fourth of the cost of the proposed device. The necessary analyzing equipment is already in-house.

8. It is my opinion that a feasibility study requires instrumentation capable of making measurements with the greatest possible sensitivity. This then allows a quick evaluation of possible sensors that could meet the size and power requirements.

9. I will pursue the subject further and forward a specific proposal for the construction of the in-house device and the gathering and analysis of pertinent data as soon as time permits.

10. In closing, a review of the past history of this technology would not lead to expectations of successful development.

11. As a result of conversations with Johnson (the writer of the contract specifications) in the past few days, I think he is also convinced that investigations in the upper frequency band will prove fruitless.

EXHIBIT 3

ADL

Memorandum (excerpts)

From: Ray Ryan
To: Dr. Russ Hill
Subject: Proposal for Field Measurements

1. Calculations have shown that it is possible to construct a three component device. The desired sensitivity can be achieved. The low weight of the device will relieve the dependence of the measurement program on extensive support facilities. . . .
4. Tape recording and signal analysis facilities already exist at ADL that have capabilities exceeding the requirements of this program. We do not anticipate any major expenses, other than manpower, for data reduction and analysis. By preserving the signals on tape it will be possible to amass a body of data that can be subjected uniformly to a variety of signal processing techniques as desired.
5. Since nothing in the design and construction of the device requires state-of-the-art techniques, this phase of the program should proceed straightforwardly. A second device could be constructed simultaneously with the first at a somewhat lower unit cost. Experience has shown that having a second unit available will often save expensive field test time.
6. Data of the type required for this program can probably be obtained in any of a number of locations. The choice of a test site will depend on the availability of suitable sources, environmental factors, and the support facilities available. Since some aspects of the device may be tailored to meet requirements of a specific test site, some thought should be given to potential sites as early as possible. An adequate data base for initial analysis should be acquired within six months with an active data acquisition program. We would estimate that approximately two months will then be required for completing the data analysis and planning subsequent phases of the program.
7. During the next budget cycle the program outlined here should provide an adequate base on which to project the feasibility of contemplating developments in this area. If

Ryan was convinced that his proposal had been forwarded through the general manager to Dr. Stone, but so far as he knew, neither Dr. Stone nor anyone in Department A had responded to this proposal.

4. It was Ryan's understanding, however, that Dr. Stone did modify an existing contract to purchase the desired devices. Stone thus avoided the requirement for the approval of the general manager.
5. Ryan then wrote a memo to Dr. Hill, trying to stop Stone's group from making the measurements (see Exhibit 4). Ryan was not sure how far this memo went.

6. Ryan understood that Dr. Stone's people had made measurements, but based on what information he could find out, Ryan felt they had little to show for it.
7. At several meetings between research and special engineering personnel, Ryan had displayed considerable irritation and had lived true to his espoused philosophy: "Especially in technical areas, if a man is wrong, tell him so in no uncertain words, face-to-face, no matter who is present."

Before leaving his assignment in the research lab, Quinn had discussed these four measurements can be made with the anticipated sensitivity it should also be possible to estimate the technological advance required before feasibility can be demonstrated if it is not immediately achievable. The total expense of the program including the construction of two devices, data collection, and data analysis is estimated at $239,000, as shown below. We would be willing to undertake such a program in support of the overall efforts of Dr. Stone or to provide whatever level of assistance Dr. Stone may require in this area.

Time and Manpower Estimates for Device Construction

ACTION	TIME REQUIRED	MANPOWER REQUIRED
Device design study	2 weeks	2 man-weeks
Mechanical and electrical design	3	3
Fabrication	8	4
Construction and testing	3	3

Device Cost Estimate (one)

Manpower	$25K
Shopwork	13K
Materials	6K
Total device cost	$44K

Program Cost Estimates

Device construction (two devices)	77 K
Data collection (manpower—1 man-year)	100 K
Field test and travel expenses	27 K
Data analysis and publication	35 K
(Manpower—1/3 man-year)	
Total cost	239 K

incidents with Tom Kane, the technical coordinator assigned to the research lab. Kane thought it likely that there were motives that neither he nor Quinn could see that may have contributed to the generation of these lacks of communication. Quinn had written in his notebook several factors that Kane felt might partially account for the incidents about which he had been told:

1. The man making the choice believes he has done a good job of surveying all possible principles, or devices, or whatever. He actually looks at the in-house device and finds that it has deficiencies or is too expensive, and he chooses another device, believing that he is right in so doing.

2. Cost is a major factor the engineers must consider these days. One can even have a difference of opinion regarding the costs to apply to this new development versus the manufacturing costs in full-scale production.

3. The in-house source of information may not have been as complete and sexy as the commercial advertising.

4. Introduction of something new into a developing product means taking a chance. There are several possible reasons for

EXHIBIT 4

ADL

Memorandum (excerpts)

From: Ray Ryan
To: Dr. Russ Hill
Subject: Measurements in Support of the Red Baron Study Program

1. Johnson came to my office to discuss some ideas for conducting measurements in support of the Red Baron study program. As I understand this plan, a product will be developed containing devices capable of making unattended measurements.

2. While the problems involved in the design of such a product are appreciable, they are not insuperable. One might reasonably question the suggestion by Johnson that this approach would be less costly and more flexible than alternative devices.

3. From our discussion, it would seem that the proposed product will be used to study signals from designated sources. Beyond the well-known equations for the signal attenuation, one can straightforwardly conclude that typical signal strength *will fall below* the sensitivity of the product and will therefore not be recorded.

4. With respect to designated Q sources, the situation is not quite as clear but certain statements can be made.
   a. If one is to interpret the Q signals in terms of actual source strength, some reasonably accurate control must be maintained over the relative positions of the source and the measuring system. The resultant test program must necessarily be complex and costly.
   b. It is, therefore, unlikely that useful data will be obtained in this manner.
   c. Therefore, it makes little sense to design special equipment and undertake a difficult test program to obtain data that could be obtained quite reasonably from a much simpler system.
   d. It is unrealistic to suppose that any appreciable number of Q sources could be made available for a test program of this complexity now or in the immediate future.

5. There is no reason to suppose that results of a comparable nature could not be obtained in laboratory tests. Indeed, since the problems of control and monitoring are much less complicated in the laboratory, it is not unreasonable to expect that superior results may be achieved there.

6. In summary, there is no justification in my opinion for the conduct of any measurements in support of the Red Baron program unless product sensitivities can be improved by at least two orders of magnitude and it can be demonstrated that simpler laboratory measurements will not provide an adequate result.

---

failure. The scientist who originates the new development may not have solved all the problems associated with its manufacture and use. This may mean it costs more to incorporate it, or it may mean total failure of the new idea and/or delay of the product development. The engineer must take a chance. Some do, some do not. Some do when the risk is low and the advantage is great. All possible intermediate situations can arise.

Quinn was convinced that these four incidents and Kane's comments would provide the basis for his paper on communications and he resolved to discuss this with Dr. Stone on

Monday to get the views and perspectives of the people in the special engineering lab.

QUESTIONS

1. What do you think of Tom Kane's explanation for the communications gap?
2. What part do you think such nontechnical factors as status, who gets credit, ego involvement, "not invented here," and personalities, played in the three incidents involving the research and the special engineering labs?
3. How do *you* explain the four incidents? Which elements are similar? Which are different?
4. How would you improve communications at ADL if you were the general manager? What else might you do?
5. If you were Quinn, what would you say to Stone when you reported on Monday?

ATLAS DEVELOPMENT LABORATORY (A), PART 2

At 8:00 A.M. Monday morning, Bob Quinn reported as assigned to Dr. Stone. During their conversation, Quinn stated that he needed to write a paper on communications for one of his evening MBA courses, and that he had planned to use four incidents he had picked up in the research lab, three of them involving people in Dr. Stone's department. Quinn expressed a desire to talk with these people, since he was sure that their perspectives of each incident would differ sharply from those of the people in the research lab.

After determining which incidents were of interest to Quinn, Stone stated quite emphatically that none of the three incidents involving his department was a problem in communications; that research knows what he is doing and he knows what research is doing; that in each incident it was a matter of feasibility and technical judgment and *not* communications. Beyond this, Stone stated that he thought politics and competition between labs at ADL were very healthy things and should not be questioned or diminished. He insisted that the incidents were sour grapes because the research lab had not been funded very well recently. He stated further that his group and the research groups actively compete for the same customers, for the same dollars, and give presentations to the same people on the same day.

Stone said that although he could not keep Quinn from writing about these incidents, he certainly did *not* want him to do so, that they were very minor incidents, that he did *not* want old wounds reopened, and that under no circumstances would he permit Quinn to discuss these incidents with his people. The meeting ended with the suggestion from Stone that Quinn focus his attention on "what's right at ADL" and "avoid petty issues that are dead anyway."

QUESTIONS

1. How does Dr. Stone's response affect your answers in Part 1?
2. How do you explain Dr. Stone's response?
3. If you were Quinn, what would you do now? What, if anything, should he say to Mel Street, manager of the special engineering lab?

ATLAS DEVELOPMENT LABORATORY (B)

Bob Quinn, one of several technical coordinators at the Atlas Development Laboratory (ADL) [see Atlas Development Laboratory (A)] had an 8:30 A.M. appointment with Bill Kerr, project manager for Stingray. The appointment had been suggested by Mel Street, manager of the special engineering lab at ADL. After the usual introductions and amenities, Quinn explained briefly that, as part of his ADL orientation, he had been asked to spend a month or so in each of the functional departments. To date, he had spent one month in the research lab and two weeks in the special engineering lab. Mel Street had suggested to Quinn that a few days in each of several project offices would benefit him considerably. The Stingray Project was of particular interest because of its importance to ADL and to special engineering. Quinn especially wanted to learn how Kerr solved the knotty problems that arose during the development of new products.

Kerr said, "Stingray isn't a typical development program and we manage it so as to avoid problems. I'll be happy to tell you about all the positive things we are doing on this project, but for problems you'll have to look elsewhere, because we just don't have any."

Quinn said that while he was in the research lab he had met Dr. Kurt Steele, chief of the Kappa Sensors Section, who had told him that the Kappa sensor selected for Stingray was causing serious problems and that an ad hoc ADL committee had been set up to investigate it.

Kerr smiled and said, "It is *not* a problem. Kurt Steele is mad because we didn't fund him to do additional basic research leading to the development of an advanced sensor. Of course he is going to say it won't work. His only interest is in developing new theories and writing esoteric papers for publication. He's not interested in meeting our requirements within any reasonable limits on time and money. If we gave it to him, it would take five years to do the job.

"As far as the committee is concerned," Kerr continued, "it is an interesting approach, and I'm curious to see if they can come up with any helpful suggestions. But I have to be realistic. No committee is going to be able to evaluate my decision to use the Kappa sensor or be able to predict whether or not we will get it to work as we want it to. It is a technical judgment. I made it; I'm responsible for it; I've got to live with it. Frankly, I don't like being second-guessed by people who have no responsibility to make it work. We have some of the best people in special engineering devoting most of their time to the sensor. They are attacking it from many angles, including consulting with outside contractors and the Kappa sensor specialists from the Delphi research lab.

Developing it to its full potential will take some time—all new developments do. But it works now and it will work better as we make improvements. It's *not* a problem. What else do you want to talk about?"

Quinn responded, "I would like you to give me the background on the Stingray Project as you see it, and fill me in on any unique situations involving Stingray that you feel are of special interest. In addition, I'd like to have any broad spectrum documentation you may have that I can study on my own. Then, with your permission, I'd like to talk with several members of your staff as well as some of the other people in the lab who are involved with Stingray. After that, I'll stick to looking over people's shoulders and asking an occasional question."

"Now, wait a minute. We don't have that kind of time," Kerr said. "Each of my people is working at 150 percent of capacity. All eight of them have tough deadlines to meet. Even I had to steal the time I'm giving you now. And I have another appointment at 9:30, so we better move quickly. I'll try to condense the Stingray background into the time we have left.

"The concept for the Stingray Project has been actively pursued at ADL for about ten years now. The concept was first developed as a Zortech product, but we have always felt that it was feasible to use it as a Simblat product as well. Originally, the Simblat idea didn't have much support so it had only discretionary funding with occasional direct funding in small amounts. It stayed in the early development stage until about a year ago. At that time, one of our big customers got very excited about the potential for Stingray, particularly its multiple purpose uses. We gave him a ballpark estimate for total cost, and then the lab was promised some big funding starting this year.

"It was in early July last year that the customer finally decided that Stingray should be a high priority program and gave ADL the sole responsibility for both management and technical development. This means taking Stingray through the research, development, and advanced engineering leading to production engineered designs. In addition, we have the responsibility for selecting the manufacturing company. Like other labs, we have plenty of experience selecting companies for small products, subassemblies, special parts, and other hardware or services, but this is the first time I have been involved in selecting a major manufacturing company.

"The organization for this particular project is rather complex. Tom Vickers, senior vice-president of our customer, has been designated as the coordinating representative. The chairman of the Q department at the university has been assigned to monitor the program. ADL and the Q department at the university are actually at the same organizational level, in an advisory relationship with each other. Both report directly to the customer. The more usual relationship is that ADL is the supplier of services and the university is our customer.

"You will note that, in effect, I have three bosses. I report to Tom Vickers, to Dr. Hart, the general manager here at ADL, and to Mel Street, manager of the special engineering lab. On a day-to-day basis I don't see much of Vickers or Hart, but I do work very closely with Mel Street since the special engineering lab has been given primary functional control responsibility for Stingray. In addition, I spend a good deal of my time at the university or with the customer coordinating with various interested officials. This project represents a real opportunity for us if we can manage it properly and, of course, that's what we are going to do. I will have to spend considerable time in learning how to select a major manufacturing company since I haven't had much experience in this area. On the whole, though, I think it is much easier to make competent purchasing people out of engineers than it is to make engineers out of purchasing people."

Quinn said, "I think I understand what you've said so far, but what are the highlights of the internal management structure for Stingray? What is the basic project organization? How are work assignments made? How will you control costs, schedules, and technical performance?"

Kerr went on, "Actually, there is no organization chart in the classic sense. There are no rigid lines of authority. Everything is on a special relationship basis, and I have to do a lot of improvising as I go along. There are lab-wide guidelines for managers of ADL projects, but in my judgment, they are not worth the paper they are written on. They were written *by* line managers, *for* line managers. I don't pay any attention to them. They make the project manager a coordinator and you just can't manage a project like Stingray that way."

"I see," said Quinn. "There's one thing I want to understand, though. I gather that you, as project manager, have no direct authority over the line or functional people here at ADL, right?"

"Right," agreed Kerr.

"How then," continued Quinn, "do you get anything accomplished?"

Kerr smiled. "There is really no one way," he said. "Actually, this position requires technical know-how plus a good deal of persuasiveness. I am a man of many faces and many moods. I can be easygoing or hard-nosed; flexible or rigid. I can plead and cajole, or bluff and threaten. I use whatever approach I think will work. In other words, I play the game by my rules only. I make up those rules with just one objective in mind—to get Stingray completed on time and within budget."

"Is persuasion really enough?" asked Quinn. "Does it always produce the results you want?"

"Not always," admitted Kerr. "However, when the chips are down, I have plenty of power. For example, if a lead engineer in Department X gives me a hard time on cost, time, or specs, I can always threaten to take that particular assignment away and give it to an outside company."

"Have you ever actually taken such a step?" asked Quinn.

"No, but I would if I had to," answered Kerr. "But these days there is apt to be a lot of unallocated professional manpower around, so most of the functional people toe the line pretty quickly if they are faced with losing billable work. Sometimes I've had issues that go right up the line to Dr. Hart. I have been on the winning side most of the time at this level. I'll have to admit that in this job you must maintain top management support."

Kerr glanced at his watch. "It's 9:30, Bob, and I have to go. I'll ask my secretary to pull some materials you may want to review from the files. We'll give you what help we can, but don't press us too hard."

Later that morning, Quinn stopped in to see Stu Holden, the technical coordinator for the special engineering lab. He had been in this job for about two years and was to be promoted to associate engineer in the engineering development department the following month.

Quinn began, "You know, Stu, I've just been talking with Bill Kerr, trying to get some orientation on Stingray. He gave me a brief rundown on some of the formal details of the project. However, I still don't have any feel for the day-to-day, people-to-people problems of controlling a project the size of Stingray. You have been in the special engineering lab for some time; what do you see as Kerr's major problem areas?"

Holden nodded understandingly and said, "Kerr has plenty of headaches. I wouldn't want to be in his shoes. One of his major problems is dealing with some of the people at the university who don't like ADL's role as *the* program manager for Stingray. ADL's position of potential power vis-a-vis Stingray seems to be resented by some. Kerr gets a lot of informal and divergent "suggestions" from some very high-level people. In addition, the university people may tend to forget that they do not have any direct authority over Stingray. Many of these conflicting suggestions concern the technical side of Stingray. But they also zero in on Kerr's lack of experience in selecting a manufacturing company for a major program. When he wanted to make some changes in the manufacturing specifications, someone representing the university came into the picture with some untimely suggestions and managed to delay things for a couple of weeks. Kerr has locked horns with these guys a number of times. The general atmosphere is a little strained.

"Much of the trouble may be Bill's own fault. It seems to be pretty hard to establish rapport with him. For example, I haven't seen him give any evidence that he recognizes his own lack of expertise in the purchasing area, but I have seen him make it very embarrassing for a purchasing type who did not have the technical sophistication of an experienced engineer. Mel Street often intervenes to help resolve an issue that Kerr should have been able to handle. Occasionally, Mel even has to side with the university people.

"Another thing that has hurt our relations with the university and our customer is that we don't document what goes on during Stingray meetings; there is no formally distributed record of what was discussed and the points that were agreed upon. I have tried without success to have Bill arrange for an accurate and comprehensive set of minutes."

"Thanks. This is the kind of data that helps clarify things, Stu," said Quinn. "There is one specific incident I'm curious about. When I was with Bill Kerr this morning, I tried to get him to talk about the Kappa sensor for Stingray, but he preferred to pass over it pretty lightly. What can you tell me?"

Holden grinned. "Ah yes. 'The Case of the Inadequate Sensor'! It is becoming well known around the lab. I can't give you all the details but I know some of the highlights. Earlier in the Stingray Project, it became ap-

parent that there would be a need for a Kappa sensor with considerably greater sensitivity than ever before required. Kerr asked Kurt Steele, the ADL expert on Kappa sensors, to see if such a sensor with sufficient sensitivity was available commercially and, if not, what it would take to design one based on existing technology. Steele, after an unsuccessful search of commercial sources, told Kerr that the highly sensitive Kappa sensor would have to be started from ground zero. No design using existing technology could meet the sensitivity requirement. Furthermore, the estimated cost and time required for the development was far beyond what Kerr had available. Steele tried to explain this by noting that the laboratory had not seen fit to support adequate levels of research in Kappa sensors. As a result, when a specific project like Stingray came along, it was necessary to start with the type of basic research that should have been in the pipelines right along. Kerr was in too much of a hurry to be interested in this line of reasoning. He told Steele to forget it, and then went into the open market to find and contract for a Kappa sensor that would meet the rigid specifications needed for Stingray.

"Kerr worked with the Oracle Research Laboratory and the National Corporation and has come up with a Kappa sensor designed from existing technology that he believes can be improved until it meets the Stingray specs. Steele said flatly that its basic design precludes it from ever meeting the specs. Kerr appears to be furious. Rumor has it that he actually threatened Steele in the hall and called him an obstructionist who was unresponsive to the needs of Stingray. Steele responded by showing the results of some tests that he had run four years ago. Actually, there are probably a number of technical problems. A very serious one, in my opinion, relates to excessive background 'noise'. If this is not solved satisfactorily, it could be detrimental to the success of the entire Stingray Project.

"As I see it, this situation reflects a difference in technical judgment between Kerr and his staff and Steele and his people. In the meantime, word of the 'Inadequate Kappa Sensor' reached the ears of Street and Hart. The latter had previously asked Street to set up an independent committee to make technical evaluations as the Stingray Project progressed. Therefore, this committee was asked to evaluate the Kappa sensor, and to come up with specific recommendations. Street had appointed the committee and made Frank Wolf, his deputy, its chairperson. It is fairly well known at ADL that Frank Wolf and Kurt Steele are old friends, and some people wonder how objective the committee is going to be."

Holden shook his head. "It's really sad. It is my personal judgment that if Steele had been given the green light and the level of funding he requested six or seven years ago, there would be no Kappa sensor problem today. I think also that Kerr viewed Steele—perhaps unjustifiably—as a mere theorist. He probably visualized a significant amount of the Stingray funds down Steel's drain and maybe no usable Kappa sensor to show for it within the time available. As I see it, both Steele and Kerr are strong willed, very articulate, and have utterly different temperaments."

Quinn was intrigued by what appeared to be a serious difference in technical judgment between the project manager and Steele, the scientist, who was apparently the most qualified person at ADL in the area of Kappa sensor technology. He decided to discuss the matter with Frank Wolf, chairperson of the ad hoc committee investigating the problem. However, when Quinn talked to Wolf on the phone, the latter refused to see him or to talk about the situation, saying that a judge never discusses a trial until it is over.

QUESTIONS

1. Evaluate Bill Kerr's style of project management.
2. Considering the opinions expressed by Stu Holden, what, if any, problems do you foresee?
3. Analyze Kerr's handling of the Kappa sensor situation. What might he have done to forestall the situation that developed?

ATLAS TELEPHONE EQUIPMENT COMPANY

Fiber-optic switching equipment is viewed by some as still a bit of black magic. Each installation requires a tailor-made design of both hardware and software. Very tight tolerances in a super clean environment are necessary during manufacturing. Software for each system must be tailored to the unique requirements for which it has been designed. Then each element must be tested both independently and as part of the integrated system before being shipped to the location where it is to be installed.

Since the technology is moving so rapidly, each new system is designed by the scientists at the Atlas Laboratories in New Jersey and built in a specially constructed new plant in rural Tennessee. All critical modules are manufactured in the "clean" portion of the plant and moved to the assembly area to be combined with parts supplied by other Atlas plants or vendors throughout the United States. Each system is completely assembled and tested before being shipped. Once at the installation site, the various units would be reassembled, checked, and put in operation at the proper time.

When Atlas first began to manufacture this equipment, each new system developed many problems that began to surface at the time of each new installation. The scientists at the New Jersey laboratory blamed poor inte-gration and software testing done by the Tennessee plant engineers for the problems. The Tennessee engineers blamed basic design flaws as the root of the problems.

In the highly competitive and rapidly moving technological environment in which the Atlas Company operated, continuation of these problems could be devastating to the company's market position. Therefore, top management directed the vice-president of the laboratories, Dr. Lou Compton, and the plant manager, Gene Blake, to find a way to quickly solve these problems. In consultation with Dr. Greg Prince, chief software scientist at the Atlas Laboratories, it was decided to permanently assign a software scientist to the Tennessee plant to supervise the integration and software testing prior to shipment. Previous efforts at loaning a New Jersey scientist to the Tennessee plant had been unsuccessful. The plant engineers had viewed these loaned scientists as spies and interlopers. Frequent arguments and hostile behavior did little to solve the problems.

Dr. Prince decided that Dr. Ian Silk was the best person for this assignment. Silk had come to the New Jersey laboratories from England three years ago. He was born and educated just outside Oxford where his father had been a professor. The eldest in a family of four children, two boys and two girls, he had shown an early aptitude for math. After receiving his Ph.D. in Computer Sciences, he worked in two English laboratories largely on software projects. He was in his mid-thirties and married with two boys. Although very friendly and affable, he was a no nonsense type person on software issues. Prince felt that Silk's outgoing personality and technical expertise made him an ideal choice to assign to the Tennessee plant.

In discussing the new assignment with Silk, Prince pointed out that this challenging assignment in a manufacturing environment would give Silk the breadth and insights that laboratory management felt were necessary for those aspiring to senior laboratory management positions. Prince predicted that after a few years of successful experience in Tennessee, Silk would begin the climb up the laboratory management ladder. He also explained to Silk that he was convinced the recent problems were due entirely to inadequate and/or improper integration and software testing. Silk would be assigned to the Tennessee plant for administrative and payroll purposes with the nominal title of senior software specialist, but in reality he would continue to be a senior software scientist in Prince's department. Silk was expected to make frequent visits to the New Jersey laboratories and maintain frequent telephone communications with Prince. "Even though you will be physically located in Tennessee, you will still be a member of my team and I will continue to look after your career," Silk was told by Prince.

When Silk arrived at the Tennessee plant several weeks later, he was greeted warmly by Gene Blake, the plant manager, who said, "I'm delighted that management has finally given me the technical expertise I need to keep these fiber-optic switching systems going out of here on schedule and without technical glitches." Blake explained that Silk would be an independent technical specialist on his staff reporting directly to him. "If you need anything or have any problems, my door is always open to

my staff." Blake then took Silk on a plant tour, during which he introduced Silk to Jim Burns, the manager of the Software Engineering Section, and to Mike Mead, the manager of the Integration Engineering Section. Blake observed that each switching system went through final assembly and testing under the general direction of these two sections. Each new system had a supervisor and group of engineers from each of the two sections more or less permanently assigned to monitor that system from early manufacturing to final shipping. Blake told both Burns and Mead that Silk would be his expert on all integration and software testing. He stated further that he expected them and their supervisors and engineers to cooperate fully with Silk in all such testing.

At the end of the plant tour, Blake took Silk to the personnel office and waited for Silk to get his plant pass and for the administrative processing. Blake and Silk returned to the front office area where Blake showed Silk the office he had assigned him. It was across the hall and several doors down from Blake's corner office and directly across the hall from both Burns's and Mead's offices.

In describing these events to his wife, Silk said he felt very awkward as the man in the middle. On the one hand, he had been told by Dr. Prince that he was still on his team but, on the other hand, Blake clearly felt that Silk was now on the plant team. Silk felt the better part of valor was to keep his mouth shut and let the relationships upon which he was dependent develop in as near a normal manner as possible.

As Silk started work on the integration and software testing for the next fiber-optic switching system in the pipeline, it became apparent that the dominant priorities for all plant personnel were schedule and cost in that order. "That's how we're measured," snapped one of the engineering supervisors when Silk raised the issue. As the shipping date neared, more and more emphasis was given to getting the system out the back door (shipping dock). When the supervisors felt Silk's tests were not being run fast enough or might delay the shipping date, they urged him to take shortcuts. Typical comments included "Those lab guys over design and over test everything"; "Those tests are way beyond what is necessary to insure the system works"; and "Those scientists haven't the foggiest idea how the system really functions in actual operations after installation; if they did, they wouldn't require all that unnecessary Mickey Mouse."

Silk's friendly, affable manner seemed to have little impact when the supervisors were under stress. Silk found it necessary in several instances during the first few weeks to insist that his approach to the integration and software testing be adhered to rigidly and threatened to take the matter immediately to Blake if this was not done. Reluctantly and with considerable animosity, the supervisors would back down muttering such things as "Cry baby"; "Who does he think he is?" and "Makes himself look good at our expense."

About a month after arriving, Silk and his family moved into a house on the south side of town near the country club. This area had been suggested to Mrs. Silk by Mrs. Blake, who extolled the schools in that part of town. In addition to Mr. and Mrs. Blake, several other plant executives and their families lived in this little enclave including Mr. and Mrs. Burns. As a result of this proximity, Silk began to ride to work with Jim Burns and two other plant executives. It was the practice of this group, and several other groups as well, to stop at the country club on the way home from the plant for a little exercise, a libation or two, and general camaraderie with the other plant executives who lived nearby, including Gene Blake. The families of these executives shared in the camaraderie through dinner parties and a variety of functions at the country club and at each others' homes. After a few weeks, it became apparent to all that Ian Silk and Jim Burns had become good friends.

The supervisors who worked for Burns quickly observed this growing friendship and began to be noticeably more circumspect and deferential in their dealings with Silk. Silk in turn took advantage of this change in behavior to try and change their attitudes. To overcome the natural resentment they might feel at their loss of status due to Silk's taking over some of their former responsibilities, Silk began to ask these supervisors their opinions on a variety of issues as a means of giving them "positive strokes." Since they seemed genuinely pleased, Silk quickly extended these "strokes" to Mead's supervisors. These strokes and Silk's friendly and affable manner began to have an increasingly positive effect.

A few discrete inquiries led Silk to discover that Mike Mead was not a member of the country club, and indeed Mead and his family lived on the north side of town. Silk's relationship with Mead was friendly but distant. Although Mead did not seem very sociable himself, Silk wondered if there still might be some resentment on Mead's part at being left out of the business-related conversations that frequently occurred during social occasions at the country club or in the homes of other executives.

As Christmastime approached, there was a brief break in the schedule for shipping new systems. Silk took advantage of this slack time to take his family to visit his relatives in England. Blake had approved the vacation and wished a pleasant trip to Silk and his family. Unfortunately, during this vacation, a fire destroyed one of the fiber-optic switching systems of a major customer. This necessitated changing and accelerating the schedule of deliveries so that this customer's system could be replaced as soon as possible. In Silk's absence the system was shipped without Silk being able to supervise the integration and software testing. As a result, the system was installed and put in service with a number of serious technical glitches. It took the installation engineers several months to get all the bugs out of the system, which resulted in user complaints.

Atlas management was pleased with the quick response to a customer emergency but was disturbed that the plant supervisors did not seem able to run the integration and software testing properly in Silk's absence. Blake was directed to straighten out the situation. As a result, Mead suggested that his senior engineer, Hal Swan, assist Silk and learn the intricacies of the integration and software testing processes. Mead observed, "This plant cannot afford to be so dependent on one person!"

When Silk returned from vacation, Blake told him what had happened and informed him that he had decided to assign Hal Swan to assist Silk. He said he hoped Silk could teach Swan everything necessary before Silk had to be away from the plant again. During the next several weeks, as work on the next system progressed, it seemed to Silk that Swan was openly hostile and arrogant. Gradually, Silk's friendly, affable manner and gentle cajoling seemed to win over Hal Swan. Swan's hostility lessened and seemed to shift away from Silk and toward Mead. This resulted in Mead formally reprimanding Swan for insubordination. This action by Mead seemed to alienate Swan still further.

Thereafter, Swan began to confide to Silk that Mead seemed to be "power hungry" and resented the close relationship that Silk and Burns seemed to have with Blake. Swan also alleged that Mead was attempting to build alliances with other plant executives. Silk was not sure how to evaluate these confidences until he observed Mead as a guest of several plant executives at the country club on several occasions. Silk concluded that Mead's attempt to participate in the activities at the country club were manipulative at best. After all, Mead lived on the other side of town at some considerable distance from the country club and it just did not seem natural for Mead to travel all that distance without some ulterior motive. Silk suspected that most of the other executives felt the same way since he overheard several comments identifying Mead as a "phony."

After returning from one of the many conferences at the Atlas Laboratories two weeks later, Silk was surprised when Mead came into his office with a smile and a "good morning." Mead announced that he had obtained four tickets for the annual open house of a distillery producing one of the finest whiskeys in Tennessee. He asked Silk and his wife to join him and his wife as their guests for this open house to be followed by dinner at the Mead residence on the way home.

During this outing, Mead spoke frequently of the outstanding work Silk was doing and how the technical problems attributable to integration and software had virtually disappeared since Silk's arrival. After sampling the famous product of the distillery, Mead boldly suggested that Silk might be even better off as the assistant manager of the Integration Section with a group of engineers reporting directly to him. In this way, Mead said, Silk would no longer be dependent on the cooperation of supervisors and engineers who reported to other managers. Silk acknowledged that he had no line authority and that Mead's suggestion would provide it.

On the way home that evening, Silk told his wife he was alarmed by this power play of Mead's. Not only would he become subordinate to Mead, but Mead would surely see to it that his ties to the New Jersey laboratories were severed permanently. He feared this would have a negative effect not only on his career at the labs, but also on his ability to get cooperation from both the software scientists at the labs and the software supervisors and engineers reporting to Jim Burns.

The next morning, Silk stopped by Blake's office to suggest a racketball game at the country club after work with the loser buying the drinks afterwards. Blake accepted the invitation with a smile and noted it would be a pleasure to have Silk buy him a few drinks.

After the game, which Blake conveniently won, Silk explained to Blake that he was still considered a member of the laboratory software department by the people there. He went on to explain that this arrangement contributed significantly to his ability to get design modifications from the scientists there which, in turn, contributed greatly to the positive results he had achieved at the Tennessee plant. He went on to explain what Mead had suggested and observed that should this suggestion be implemented it could have a very adverse effect on his ability to get the systems out with an absolute minimum of technical glitches in the integration and software areas. Blake listened attentively and said anything that would inhibit Silk's effectiveness was not a step forward. Blake also admitted that he was one of those who viewed the integration and software area as a "bit of black magic." Since he was not technically qualified in those areas, he would have to depend on Burns and Mead as well as Silk and Swan for future success. Then he told Silk that Mead had requested a meeting with him and Silk to discuss "a suggestion for further improvement in our testing program." Blake assured Silk that because of what had been discussed between them that evening, no organizational change would be made.

The next day Blake invited Burns to attend the meeting with Mead and Silk saying that "Software Engineering is vitally concerned with the whole integration and software testing program." To start the meeting, Blake asked Mead to present his suggestion. Blake then asked Burns and Silk to present their views. Both argued against the suggested change. Blake then said he wanted to encourage any and all ideas that might be beneficial to the plant and thanked Mead for his thoughts and initiative. He went on to state that in this instance, he felt the arguments against the change were somewhat more persuasive to him and therefore, there would be no change.

QUESTIONS

1. What do you think are the most important facts and incidents in this case?
2. What types of power did Silk use in each of the incidents you identified in Question 1 above?
3. If Silk were transferred back to the laboratories and you were assigned from the laboratories to replace him at the Tennessee plant, what specifically would you do? Describe the steps you would take to build relationships with the key people on whom you would be dependent.

BETSY CARR

As she looked back on the ups and downs of her career in the past four years, Betsy Carr wondered if there might have been more ups and fewer downs if she had done things differently. Certainly, there was nothing she could do about the first down, in fact she felt she had been lucky to find her first job in the Missiles Division of Amalgamated Industries after she and the 18 aeronautical engineers she supervised were laid off at another division of Amalgamated Industries after the cancellation of a government contract.

Carr had been an engineering manager at the other division, and while the engineering analyst job in the X Project Office at the Missiles Division involved a two-level drop in salary scale, she retained her salary (near the top of the current scale compared with near the bottom on her previous scale) and was a lot better off than many of the engineers she had supervised who had to accept much lower salaries with other companies or within Amalgamated Industries. Her new job employed many of the skills she had developed in her previous positions, and she was particularly pleased when she learned she had been selected from a pool of 165 eligibles.

Carr had been selected by Ruth May, the deputy project director. Unfortunately, soon after Carr reported to her new job, May was promoted to project director and Paul Turk was appointed to the deputy director position. Another unlucky event prevented Carr from developing an early relationship with her new boss: because of her special skills, she was temporarily assigned for three months to a project at another division of Amalgamated Industries. While she phoned Turk at least weekly, she was not physically present on a day-to-day basis while Turk was settling into his new job.

When she returned from the temporary assignment, she was puzzled by Turk's apparent attitude toward her. He simply refused to give her any meaningful assignments. He seemed to spend most of his time with two male engineers who had been working in the Missiles Division for eight to ten years, and most of the analytical assignments went to them. "They were the keepers of our institutional memory and I guess Paul felt a need to pick their brains," Carr said years later.

Carr appealed to Ruth May and began to get not only assignments from her but assignments that were generally regarded as high priority. May told Carr she had asked Turk why he was not assigning work to her and Turk responded that he had reviewed one of her assignments and found it seriously flawed, reflecting her lack of knowledge about the special requirements of the Missiles Division among other things. May had told Turk that the assignment in question was the first one Carr had done when she came to the division.

As her immediate supervisor, Paul Turk was obliged to submit Carr's performance appraisal after her first four months on the job, three of which had been spent on the temporary assignment to a project in another division. He commented on four assignments she had done, three of which were high priority and were assigned to Carr by Ruth May, and noted that all had been completed satisfactorily. He gave Carr an "excellent" overall rating (in her previous job she had received consistent "outstanding" ratings) and in substantiation of this rating, commented in part as follows:

> Ms. Carr's efforts during this appraisal period clearly demonstrate the professional qualities she brings to the job. She approached every task and project with vigor and determination and she was able to produce quality work in difficult circumstances.
>
> This report covers a period in which Ms. Carr was just arriving in the Missiles Division, in which she had a change of supervisors since her supervisor moved up to become her boss's boss, and in which she was called away for a period of three months to assist in a vital project at another division. Furthermore, because of the unique nature of the systems used at the Missiles Division, a very long adjustment period is usually required of even the most experienced engineers. Despite this turmoil and need for adjustment, Ms. Carr fit right into the structure of this Project Office. She began to learn the system on her own and was quickly familiar with many of the more esoteric aspects of the Missiles Division's systems. She brought sage advice and perspective to the analytical work of the office and she undertook her projects not just as learning efforts but as challenges . . .
>
> Ms. Carr's absence from the Missiles Division for the final three months of the year was sorely felt here. I am glad she was called upon to participate in this important project, but I'm doubly glad to have her back.

In the section on performance improvement, Turk commented as follows:

> Ms. Carr still needs to learn more about the Missiles Division. Our unique and different systems are unlike any other in Amalgamated Industries and Ms. Carr's most valuable

contributions will be in her analysis [of these systems].

Ruth May added several pages of her own to the formal appraisal in which she commented:

> I concur in general with this performance appraisal and believe it to be a fair and accurate assessment of Ms. Carr's work. Ms. Carr was considered the best of approximately 165 people eligible for her position. She brings a great fund of knowledge of aeronautical engineering as well as management to the job.
>
> Her first major task was to complete an analysis desired by the vice-president for Programs. It was a difficult assignment to analyze correctly and for which to locate appropriate data, but Ms. Carr achieved her goal with excellence.
>
> Just as she was about to begin other major tasks, members of another division insisted on her being assigned to them for at least three months to work on a particularly urgent project for which she was eminently qualified. She returned only at year's end. We are all anxious to make full use of her many engineering and management talents during the course of the next year.

Betsy Carr decided not to add any employee statement even though company policy provided for it and there was a space on the form for it. She simply signed the appraisal, indicating that she had seen it.

During the following year, a number of incidents involving her relationship with Paul Turk occurred that bothered Carr. Soon after her return, the Project Office was involved in a discrimination suit involving a black engineer of Caribbean decent. Carr, concerned about Turk's attitude toward blacks, remonstrated with him. To her surprise, she discovered that Turk had not realized that she was black (Carr was light-skinned).

Another incident involved one of the two long-term male engineers in the office (and Carr observed that Turk continued to spend most of his time with these two and continued to give them most of the meaningful assignments). At one point during the year, this man virtually invited himself to Carr's home. Carr and her husband, a partner in one of the largest and most prestigious law firms in the United States, had a substantial combined income and no children; they had a lovely home and obviously lived well. The self-invited colleague reported on this, and in fact constantly talked about it back in the office, and Carr was informed that Turk was overheard commenting that he didn't understand how she, a "mere senior engineer," could live so well. (Turk had four children, three in college, and his home and life-style could not compare with that of Carr and her husband.) Turk was also overheard to say that Carr was overpaid (still receiving her salary from her previous job even though she was near the top of the scale for her current position).

Early in the year, one of Carr's assignments was heavily revised, in her absence, by other staff members at Turk's direction. Although she had been completing comparable assignments for many years without criticism, Carr enrolled in and successfully completed a Missiles Division course on the special techniques of technical analysis required by the division.

Also early in the year, one of the other engineers in the office suggested to Turk that since Carr was new to the Missiles Division, he might send her on a trip to one of the launching test sites so she could get some hands-on experience with how people functioned in an operational environment and the problems they faced. Paul's response was: "Oh yeah, small chance."

A final incident particularly disturbed Carr. During a time that she was working on several projects at once, Turk told her to stop working on one of them and said, "Sit on it and it will go away." Later, Ruth May asked where the analysis on this project was and Turk denied he had ever told Carr to stop working on it.

In spite of these incidents, Carr was shocked when she received her second perfor-

mance appraisal report; Turk had rated her down to "Satisfactory." He had again discussed only four projects Carr had worked on, only two of these being designated as high priority; all were completed satisfactorily. In justifying his evaluation, Turk had written:

> Ms. Carr has continued to develop her knowledge about the Missiles Division's systems. She came to this position fully qualified in all aspects of analytical work, but without comprehensive knowledge of the Missiles Division's unique structure and methods."

He then commented favorably on two of the projects Carr had completed, noting however that on one that "her written report was revised in her absence by myself and other members of the staff."

The final paragraph of his commentary read as follows:

> The projects described above indicate a steady and solid progress toward full participation in the analyses of this Project Office. The very long read-in time required for work in the Missiles Division milieu meant that at first Ms. Carr could not know where to begin looking for data or how to recognize what she had found. Thus, at the end of this rating period, she was able to easily locate and compile data that would have required significantly longer time at the beginning. She accepted with considerable grace and maturity the editing of her . . . project, and she produced a second project that required no editing. She has begun to feel comfortable in this environment and feels now she can solicit advice and assistance from other staff members who are more familiar with the Missiles Division's systems. This should help her to continue to improve her assignments as she lets her considerable engineering skills shine through. Betsy is a very bright and energetic person who brings extensive background and experience to this job. She is developing her knowledge of the Missiles Division and is working to reach her potential as a fine engineer.

Under the section called " Performance Improvement Opportunities," Paul stated:

The narrative above alludes to difficulties in the preparation of Ms. Carr's final written reports on her assignments. Her reports at the outset lacked focus and were prepared in a more scholarly style than that to which Missiles Division people are accustomed. She has attended an advanced technical methods seminar and has worked closely with colleagues on the preferred Missiles Division's technical writing style.

Ruth May, added the following comments:

With each assignment she completes, Ms. Carr gains in self-confidence and her analyses are organized and presented more like traditional Missiles Division products. Consequently, while there have been some ups and downs over the past year, I am confident that Ms. Carr has now passed through the traditionally difficult apprenticeship phase and is ready to bloom in terms of depth, speed, and style of her engineering analyses.

The relationship between her and her boss has been thoroughly correct and professional, and both are working to build and solidify their team relationship so that it enhances all individual projects within this Project Office.

This time, Carr completely filled the space provided for an employee statement. What she wrote is reproduced verbatim below (including misspellings and grammatical errors), less a listing of six projects she had completed during the year:

This is to discuss my own assessment of performance during my tenure with this office. It is my impressions that I have either volunteered or been assigned to projects of significant magnitude in terms of difficulty, requiring originality, ingenuity and self direction. I am of the impression that this has provided me with an extensive wealth of information about the Missiles Division and has accelerated my learning curve process by a large degree. However, one must chose. There are frequently disadvantages to pursuing such an activist course where ones natural learning

prosesses (which generally include making mistakes for various reasons including not yet being the expert on topics) becomes clear for all to observe. The non-doer is not likely to be criticized if he/she has no record to demonstrate things that he/she does or does not know. There obviously is nothing profound about this, but it is an important fact to bear in mind when performance is being assessed. In this light, I feel that, while my performance appraisal is accurate, other things could have been said. For example, the number of projects that I have undertaken as a relatively new person, I feel, have been somewhat extrodinary. They include: (six projects listed)

I also learned to use the Engineering Work Station to assist in my data base compilation and analysis. I am without reluctance to state that each and every one of the projects listed above were extensive efforts. Of course, there have been other short-term ad hoc projects as well. It should be borne in mind that all of these projects have been completed in a 19 month time period, 3 months of my tenure were spent at another division working on yet another effort.

Finally, my main objective is to continue to improve in my work and to be respected as a person who is well competent to carry-out a diverse number of activities in support of the goals of the Missiles Division.

During her second year on the job, Carr experienced a further deterioration of her relationship with Paul Turk. She noticed that he continued to associate most closely with the two male engineers, and that he related much more easily with the other two women in the office, one a junior engineer and the other a senior clerk who, in Carr's estimation, did not produce but spent a lot of time talking with Turk.

One incident that occurred even caused her to think seriously about filing a formal grievance. At one point during the year, Paul Turk obtained approval for an engineering manager position in the Project Office. Carr wanted to be considered for the promotion but Turk said no. He told her frankly he had created the position because he wanted to promote one of the two male engineers he had spent so much time with since he took office.

Carr talked with the personnel department but the man Turk wanted was selected. Carr went to Ruth May and asked her if she should file a formal grievance. May told her some things she already knew: that grieving rarely enhanced a career, and that Turk was about to be transferred and that she would get a fresh start with a new supervisor in a few months.

When Turk left (his new assignment was with an academic program at a university), he wrote performance reviews on all his people. He ranked everyone in the office except Carr as "outstanding" (including even the female Carr had evaluated as a "do-nothing"). He rated Betsy once again as "satisfactory." She asked him why he did not mention the improvement in her technical writing skills. His response was: "If there's no problem, why mention it?" He also told her he was surprised she was able to bounce back from the first satisfactory rating. As Carr told the casewriter, "He thought I would fold."

In spite of the opportunity to work for a new supervisor, Betsy Carr decided, following her second successive "satisfactory" rating in her first Missiles Division job with Amalgamated Industries, that her best career move would be into another position in the division. She perceived herself a technical generalist and manager with skills beyond the special ones that had secured her the job in Ruth May's Project Office, and hoped another opportunity would present itself. It did.

Soon after Paul Turk departed and before his successor arrived, Carr convinced Ruth May to nominate her for an engineering manager's job in another project. One month later she was promoted to this manager's job. The new job made use of her management skills over and above those technical skills she was called upon to use in Ruth May's Project Office, but did not involve a lot of technical report writing. (It should be noted that in the Missiles Division, unlike other divisions of Amalgamated Industries, the Personnel Department plays a more significant role in the selection of engineering managers.)

A few weeks after she had started work in her new position, Carr met Paul Turk in the corridors of the Division. He put his arm around her, congratulated her on her promotion, and apologized for having been a poor supervisor.

QUESTIONS

1. Should Betsy Carr have done anything differently to improve her career advancement opportunities?
2. Should she have remained in the job and taken her chances with a new supervisor?
3. What impact on her career has resulted from the two successive "satisfactory" ratings?
4. Considering all that has happened to Betsy Carr over the past few years, do you feel she has mismanaged her career? Why or why not?
5. How do you interpret Paul Turk's apology to Carr?

MISSILE PRODUCTS CORPORATION (A)

In October, the director for Research and Engineering in the Office of the Secretary of Defense had disapproved navy recommendations. The navy had wanted to proceed with the engineering development and acquisition of the SURTAC (Surface-Tactical) missile system with the Missile Products Corporation (MPC), a subsidiary of the Matrix Development Corporation, as the principal development agent. The director did not object to the selection of MPC, but felt that the navy had not accomplished all the objectives of system definition. The director clearly wanted MPC to work on an advance development hardware feasibility contract. It was also clear that the advance development effort would be funded at a reduced level, representing a stretch-out of the SURTAC system development. A contract was negotiated late the next year, directing MPC to fabricate the agreed upon subsystems and to perform feasibility tests demonstrating the necessary operational capabilities.

The SURTAC system was an advanced surface-to-surface tactical missile for multipurpose use in limited war that had grown out of the development of an earlier missile designed for use against enemy ships and selected ground targets. The new SURTAC system was based on a state-of-the-art advance in a homing device to guide the missile after launching it from the ship or small craft that located the target. The original required operational capability was amended to include attack on sophisticated radar systems and to apply the SURTAC to interdiction-type targets, such as trucks, tanks, and supply trains.

Sam Roberts, project manager for the missile guidance subsystem, was very concerned about the MPC organizational traditions. As a result of his discussions of the project with the SURTAC program manager, Stan Jones, and the general manager of MPC, Dick Nolan, it was agreed that a significant amount of reorientation of traditional MPC project operations was necessary to attain the goals of the project. Nolan felt that the SURTAC missile guidance project should serve as a model for refining the lead engineer concept at MPC (see Exhibit 1 for a partial organization chart of MPC). Sam Roberts decided that he should set up a reporting structure for the SURTAC guidance project consisting of lead engineers from the functional organization and project engineers from the project office thus, hopefully providing a balance in the power between the two of them to facilitate optimal decision making.

From the conversations in the past few months with the navy, three guidance subsystems in the SURTAC missile and one guidance subsystem for the ship or other platform would require feasibility demonstration tests

EXHIBIT 1

PARTIAL ORGANIZATION CHART OF MPC

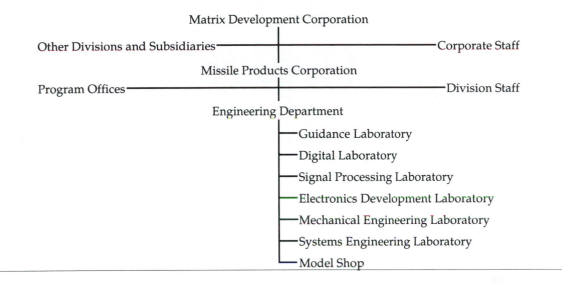

Matrix Development Corporation

Other Divisions and Subsidiaries —————————— Corporate Staff

Missile Products Corporation

Program Offices —————————— Division Staff

Engineering Department
- Guidance Laboratory
- Digital Laboratory
- Signal Processing Laboratory
- Electronics Development Laboratory
- Mechanical Engineering Laboratory
- Systems Engineering Laboratory
- Model Shop

(a partial end-item tree for the SURTAC system is presented in Exhibit 2). The critical subsystems for the missile guidance project are the intercept computer, the sensor, and the electronic countermeasures (ECM) and mode selection logic. The critical guidance subsystem for the ship is the signal receiving subsystem.

Based on his analysis of the project, Sam Roberts made his choice of lead engineers. Three of the six design departments would play a major role in the feasibility demonstration. They were the system engineering department, the digital department, and the signal processing department. Roberts decided that he would draw his lead engineers from these sections and from the technical staff. He designated Gene Mack, one of the department managers in the signal processing department, as the lead engineer for the ship signal receiving subsystem. Mack had previous experience as a design engineer, lead engineer, and section manager. It appeared to Roberts that Mack had the technical scope plus a talent for organizing and controlling any program. He would

interface with Pete Johnson as the project engineer for shipboard equipment in the program office. Pete Johnson was also the chief engineer on the SURTAC guidance project.

Roberts permitted Mack to select three of his section managers to be lead engineers for the antenna, receiver, and processor subsystems of the signal receiving system. They were

1. Carl Willey, the junior person in charge of the antenna. This was his first job as a lead engineer (LE) since joining MPC five years ago as a new BSEE. His experience had all been related to antenna design and development.
2. John Haskins, the receiver lead engineer. This was his third LE assignment within a year. Haskins, a former major in the air force, had spent most of his ten-year military career as an electronic countermeasure (ECM) specialist before joining MPC six years ago.
3. Bill Jenkins, the processor LE, had only recently joined MPC but had over ten years'

EXHIBIT 2

PARTIAL END-ITEM BREAKDOWN OF **SURTAC**

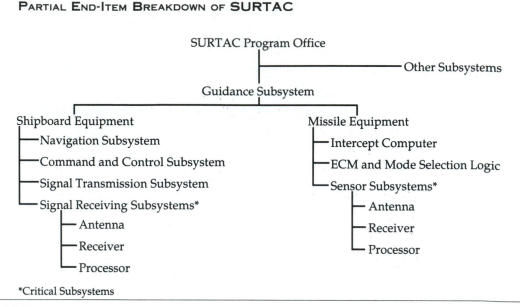

*Critical Subsystems

*Critical Subsystems

experience in the electronics industry as a design engineer and as a development lab manager with a small New England R & D corporation.

Sam Roberts felt that these appointments took care of the signal receiving subsystem that was an integral part of the shipboard equipment, but that he also needed a lead engineer for each key missile guidance subsystem (three in all). In making the choice for the lead engineers, Roberts felt the need for the flexibility to modify the subsystems as more data came in from the design groups and as navy thinking progressed.

Roberts felt that the three subsystems pertaining to the missile should be broken out into five subsystems: 1) intercept computer, 2) sensor antenna, 3) sensor receiver, 4) sensor processor, and 5) ECM and mode logic. He then selected five individuals to be lead engineers for the various elements of the missile hardware. Each of these people would report

directly to Dick Miller, the project engineer in the program office, who was in charge of the guidance portion of the SURTAC missile. The lead engineers were as follows:

1. Herb Olson, a section manager in the digital department who would be the lead engineer for the intercept computer. Olson was young and relatively new to MPC but was technically sophisticated in regard to digital concepts.
2. Bob Taylor would be the lead engineer for the ECM and mode selection subsystem. Taylor was a section manager in the systems engineering department. Roberts felt that Taylor would have to lean heavily on the digital and signal processing departments for most of his work. In the past, he had demonstrated both a skill and an interest in managing technical projects and had worked well with the department engineers.
3. Ed Smith, who was one of the technical staff consultants, would be the lead engineer for

the sensor antenna. Smith was considered to be one of the outstanding authorities on antennas in the country. He had recently returned from a year's teaching at Stevens Institute of Technology and was currently available for a 100 percent effort.

4. Scott Harple, a section manager in the signal processing department, was to be lead engineer for the sensor receiver. Harple had a lot of experience and had been with MPC for almost ten years, working on a variety of systems. Almost all the sensor receiver work would be performed in the signal processing department. No other projects were scheduled for his department during the projected six months.

5. Finally, Dan Long, who was also a technical staff consultant, would be LE for the sensor processor. This would not take 100 percent of his time and he had worked with both analytical and experimental groups easily.

The final reporting structure of the SURTAC lead engineers and MPC program office is depicted in Exhibit 3.

QUESTIONS

1. What do you think about Sam Roberts's overall decisions on the choices of lead engineers? What about departmental involvement at this point? What do you think about the respective candidates?
2. What do you think about the task analysis of the overall project? Do you agree with the task breakouts? What conflicts do you foresee based on Roberts's overall decisions?
3. Do Roberts's decisions fit the power balancing purpose for the lead engineer concept?
4. Predict the behavior of the lead engineers in the next phase of the project.

EXHIBIT 3

REPORTING STRUCTURE WITHIN THE **SURTAC** GUIDANCE SUBSYSTEMS

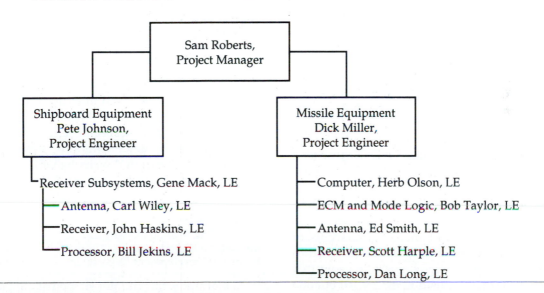

MISSILE PRODUCTS CORPORATION (B)

Early in the spring, Sam Roberts called the first management meeting of all the lead engineers on the SURTAC guidance project for a status report. Present at the meeting were the nine lead engineers and two of the department managers. A number of problems surfaced at this meeting.

Bob Taylor, lead engineer for the ECM and mode selection subsystem, was not sure that there was enough data to corroborate the validity of the basic integrated system design. He felt that systems engineering should be doing extensive trade-off analyses and he should monitor all the SURTAC guidance design efforts and should redirect subsystem design according to these analyses. Roberts reminded Taylor that they had a contract to build hardware and test feasibility.

The next comment came from Ed Smith, the technical staff consultant who was the lead engineer for the sensor antenna. "I've got absolutely no control over the people who are going to work on the sensor antenna," he complained. "I mean, since I've been back, I've observed some pretty medieval concepts of design and fabrication around here. I tried to get some sharp young fellows who've written theses on target acquisition theory. All but one of them are on special assignments to the marketing manager. They're out jawboning while I've got an antenna to build!"

At this point, the department manager for systems engineering wanted to discuss another topic. His department's contribution to the intercept computer subsystem had been drastically slashed from what was originally planned. Herb Olson, the lead engineer for the intercept computer subsystem and a section manager in the digital department, had originally planned to allocate work and funds on the computer as follows:

Digital Department	40%
Systems Engineering Department	30%
Mechanical Department	20%
Electronic Development Department	10%

This allocation was based on the assumption that MPC would be funded for full-scale engineering development. When MPC was funded only to perform specific hardware subsystem feasibility demonstrations, funds for the intercept computer were halved. Olson recast the allocated work and funds as follows:

Digital Department	70%
Systems Engineering Department	5%
Mechanical Department	10%
Electronic Development Department	15%

Naturally, this did not sit well at all, particularly with the manager of the systems engineering department who argued that 50 percent of his workload forecast and manloading projection for the next six months was SUR-TAC work.

"In effect," he concluded, "this redirection is going to make six of my systems engineers available for six months. Furthermore, Herb just arbitrarily reduced our 30 percent share of the computer work to 5 percent so he could take care of his own people. He has the lion's share now and he's assuming the major part of the systems engineering tasks that by rights belong to us." What followed was a heated argument between Herb Olson and the manager of systems engineering.

Sam Roberts was forced to close the meeting at this point because he was due in Washington for a week's visit to the Office of the Secretary of Defense (OSD). He decided that another progress meeting should be scheduled within the month.

One month later, several new problems came to the surface. These were revealed at the next meeting of the group. Roberts had asked each lead engineer to make a presentation on the progress of the subsystems during the past month. Gene Mack, LE for the shipboard signal receiving subsystem, made the first presentation. He stated that although the shipboard signal receiver was on schedule and within cost, the breadboard, which was ready for program management office signoff, had not been approved by Pete Johnson, chief engineer on the SURTAC guidance project, because he was at Dahlgren discussing a navy-recommended change in the signal band width. Mack knew about the recommendation and had discussed it with his engineers. Fortunately, only the long-lead items had been ordered and Mack was not concerned over the impact of the change on either his schedule or his budget.

The reports from the missile guidance subsystems lead engineers were not as encouraging. All the missile guidance subsystems were behind schedule and the sensor antenna was below nominal specification and overrun in cost. Ed Smith, LE in charge of the sensor

antenna, was not overly concerned about the antenna because he felt it was too early to achieve nominal spec performance.

After three hours of discussion of the problems, Roberts sketched out a tentative action plan for the future. The engineering department managers were called in and briefed, and their concurrence with the revised priorities required by the plan was obtained. Before closing the meeting, Roberts announced that the MPC general manager, Dick Nolan, had asked him for a progress report on the use of the lead engineer concept in the SURTAC guidance project. Specifically, Nolan wanted to know what kind of management styles were adopted in order to get things done. Roberts then set the date for another meeting within the week to discuss this topic.

At the next meeting, the nine lead engineers were asked to describe their management techniques to the group. Gene Mack was first to present. "I planned to have three of my section managers as lead engineers for portions of the signal receiver. We got together to think the work through in great detail and plan our course of action. As far as relations with my lead engineers, they are informal. This way we have pretty good communications. I'm rarely in the dark and because they keep me informed, I can monitor progress continuously and we have a perpetual replanning effort.

"I've got a planning syndrome I'm really preoccupied with. At the outset, we define the work in detail and then little deviations from that plan can easily be identified and coped with. I've found that by thinking the job through at the beginning, the implementation usually works and reflects our trade-off analyses, although sometimes the trade-offs are intuitive."

Willey, Haskins, and Jenkins were nodding in agreement. Jenkins stated, "The successful manager has to be able to view the project as a whole. He has to see how the different organizations depend on each other and how changes by one affect the others. The success of a decision depends on the manager's ability to sell its across-the-board impact.

"I never tolerate an impasse," he continued. "When I see a problem on the horizon, I pull out all the communication stops and broadcast the circumstances to the project engineer, the department manager, and anyone else who would be an interface if that problem materialized."

"In my opinion," offered Carl Willey, "a manager of a technical performing organization should personally be proficient in the specific disciplines of his charter. Success requires being in charge from the first gun and getting your people with you from that first minute. You have to know all the contract provisions. You have to define and authorize all task assignments; conduct all design reviews, beginning with the initial subsystem block diagram; and endorse all action-item directives. The thing to avoid is being exposed to just half the problem. That's tantamount to knowing just enough to be dangerous."

John Haskins had a somewhat different outlook. "When problems occur within my area of responsibility, it's my job to resolve them with whatever resources I can beg, borrow, or steal. Going topside for help is an admission that I can't cut the mustard and this isn't going to get me bigger and better future assignments. It's difficult enough to insulate myself from the SURTAC project office when everything's going *right*. If I go back to them or my boss in the department for help, it certainly won't improve the interference problem. The project office just won't let go if they know you've got a problem."

Roberts then called on Herb Olson to discuss his management style. Olson stated that he was discouraged. It seemed to him that the lead engineer just couldn't win: if he was a dictator, he got nowhere, and if he tried to use a cooperative leadership approach, the work still didn't get done. Olson felt that a lead engineer was asked to perform and then was

given as much control over the departments or engineers as he had over the tides.

Roberts asked Olson to be more specific. Olson stated that the basic problem was that two-thirds of the work on the intercept computer was performed outside his section. As section manager, he had control over the tasks performed within his section, but work in other sections and departments had been falling behind schedule. Olson first became alarmed about a month after work had started. As part of his informal control procedures, he had been chatting with an engineer performing a subtask that involved designing a component of the intercept computer. This work was being done in another section and Olson found out that the man was really devoting most of his time to a different project. Olson was surprised. "How come?" he asked.

"I had to finish up another job that was already overdue," the engineer explained. "This intercept computer subtask was just starting and I knew I could make up a delay on it in a week or two. Besides, I'm already putting in a 54-hour week and I'm not paid for overtime."

Olson decided to mention the situation to the engineer's section manager, Joe Ellis, to make sure that there had not been confusion over manloading and scheduling. When asked, Ellis was rather abrupt in responding to Olson and asked him how he expected his workers to perform if they were continually bothered. Olson agreed to talk directly with Ellis and left believing that the schedule had been agreed to.

Olson stated that two other serious problems had come up that prevented him from performing his role as lead engineer. Don Muller, one of the staff scientists reporting directly to the general manager of MPC, called Olson and stated that the design approach for the intercept computer was, in his opinion, inferior. Prior to the start of work, the design as presented in the proposal had been reviewed by Olson, the engineers who would be building and testing the computer, and Joe Ellis, manager of the section making a principal component. Other approaches considered at that time would have required additional systems engineering with regard to interfaces and would have jeopardized both dollars and schedule for the program. Therefore, Olson, along with Ellis and the engineers, had decided to proceed with the original concept.

Olson called an informal design review with Muller, Ellis, the engineers, and Dick Miller, the project engineer. By the end of the meeting, they agreed that the spec could be met with the original concept although the growth potential of the principal component would be limited. Muller had found in Dick Miller a sympathetic ear to his alternative approach, which was, in fact, superior. Olson stood firm on the decision but he was generally unhappy with the results of the meeting. Although Dick Miller had not said so directly, he was clearly questioning Olson's capability as lead engineer, and both Ellis and his engineer left feeling that their technical competence had been challenged.

The second problem concerned a change of design on a module that eliminated some extra margin that he had worked hard to maintain. When he investigated, he was told that the signoff box for release of shop drawings contained a space for the draftsman's signature, his section manager's signature, and a program office signature—but not the lead engineer's signature. The drafting section manager had noticed the extra margin and had talked it over with Dick Miller. After agreeing that it was not necessary, he had modified the drawing to eliminate the margin and then released the drawings to the model shop. Olson was able to redline the shop fabrication drawings but time was lost and additional material had to be used.

At this point, Roberts decided to call a halt to Olson's presentation and to open the problem for discussion by the group.

QUESTIONS

1. Why don't the shipboard equipment (signal receiving) projects have the same problems as the sensor antenna projects?
2. What role should the project engineer play in this case?
3. If you were Herb Olson, what style would you adopt to get the job done?
4. Discuss an alternative overall plan for the SURTAC guidance project, involving the program office, lead engineers, project engineer, and the departments.

MISSILE PRODUCTS CORPORATION (C)

THE LEAD ENGINEER CONCEPT FROM VARIOUS PERSPECTIVES

Hardy Ames, head of Industrial Relations at Missile Products Corporation (MPC), was pursuing a reappraisal of the functional operation of the lead engineer concept at the request of his boss, Dick Nolan, general manager of MPC. Hardy Ames had been one of the principals in the early stages of the development of the lead engineer concept six years earlier. He had had numerous meetings with top management and outside consultants, examining both the benefits and costs of a complex matrix organization and, especially, the decision to establish the lead engineer position.

Both Dick Nolan and Hardy Ames agreed that now that the lead engineer system had been operating for five years, reappraisal was in order. It had been clear to both of them and to top management as well that the concept was a viable one but that some intimate knowledge about the perceptions of the role was necessary if misconceptions were to be clarified and if certain problems that had cropped up were to be addressed.

The MPC Background

MPC, a subsidiary of the Matrix Development Corporation, depended upon government con-tracts for both large and small equipment development for a major portion of its current business. In the early years, MPC was organized along functional or departmental lines. At that time, the primary objective was to advance the state of the art technically, leading to the development of very advanced, sophisticated hardware. Responsibility for many of the early projects was centered in the engineering laboratory and the projects required little interface outside that department. Funding was provided through advanced development government contracts, sometimes on a cost sharing basis. During these years, many new concepts and designs were generated and patented.

As time went by, top management at MPC recognized that the Department of Defense (DOD) was putting more emphasis on the cost of new equipment and less on sophisticated technical breakthroughs. This resulted in a shift away from advanced development (sometimes level of effort) contracts and toward tight performance specified contracts, with a corresponding shift toward a strong project orientation. Projects were growing in size and scope and their detailed requirements were increasingly determined by various agencies within DOD. Like many other organizations in the same situation, MPC evolved into a matrix organization. The equipment development effort was visualized as flowing through an organizational structure that featured both horizontal and vertical interfaces.

As the number and complexity of programs grew, Dick Nolan, the general manager, designated people to be program managers, reporting directly to him and acting in his name on all program matters. These program managers formed small staffs (program management offices) to carry out their responsibility to organize, plan, and direct the activities required to achieve and manage the programs. The functional organizations within MPC maintained technical skill centers for performance of engineering tasks within the context of the program plans generated by program management.

To some people in the organization, this seemed like the erosion of authority, responsibility, and status of the technically strong functional groups and, therefore, they resented the change. On balance, however, it seemed as if the matrix concept was the only way to go in view of the present and future environment. DOD was increasingly requiring a matrix organization as a condition of contract award. In addition, DOD was also requiring tighter controls in cost, schedules, and technical performance through the use of such tools as work breakdown structures, configuration management, reliability standards, value engineering, and total quality management (TQM). The program office expanded to handle these contractual requirements and to exercise the necessary control over any given program or project. The controls from the viewpoint of the program office were necessary to meet the minimum requirements of the contract.

As the matrix concept evolved at MPC, the program offices began to become increasingly dominant and functional managers more harassed. The increasing number of project engineers dealing with a single functional manager became an unwarranted burden on the latter. To restore the balance between the program offices and the functional departments, the manager of the engineering laboratory established the position of lead engineer, who would act in a quasi-staff capacity to his functional manager in the same way that the program manager acted in a staff capacity to the MPC general manager. Thus, the lead engineer and project engineer became the critical links in the interface between the program office and the functional departments. The lead engineer would take a work package (task) from the project engineer (program office) and manage it within the functional departments.

The formal role of the lead engineer was described in the operations manual (OPMAN) for MPC. The planning, concept design, detailed design, documentation and release, fabrication and assembly, and system integration and test responsibilities were formalized in writing. The systems analysis portion of the lead engineer's role as it related to his work package became clear and precise.

Review of the Lead Engineer Concept

Despite the clarity and precision of the systems analysis aspects of the lead engineer's role as described in OPMAN, other elements appeared to make for less than harmonious interactions among the lead engineer, the project engineer, the program office, and the functional departments.

Hardy Ames recalled that the lead engineer concept was tried first in programs that were small and isolated. Few problems were generated. As the concept spread to programs of increasing complexity and scope, more and more resentment toward the lead engineer developed. Part of this resentment, Ames recognized, came about because the lead engineer's responsibilities had grown but his authority had not. He became very visible and sometimes very irritating to the functional organization when he acted more as a representative of the program office than the functional organization.

Hardy Ames pictured the program offices and the functional departments as two sets of forces or vectors interacting with each other. Too much program control, he thought, would stifle functional skills and initiative. On the other hand, too many functional prerogatives would reduce contractual control. Ames thought that, in the optimal case, program controls and functional skills would be balanced, resulting in a new vector that would be in line with the demands of the program office, while still using and enhancing the skills of the functional departments.

To give himself a basis for formulating new insights with the lead engineer concept, Hardy Ames interviewed extensively throughout MPC. The following sections represent typical views:

Views from the Program Offices

A Project Manager:

I don't feel that the situation we face today is unique. It has existed for many years, but now that the crunch on dollars and schedules has become really tight, we try to find whipping boys for our problems rather than pinpointing the solutions. The lead engineer concept is basically a good one and we cannot live without it. On the other hand, the problem is bigger than the choice of the right person for the job. After the work breakdown structure is worked out, yielding work packages with detailed task descriptions and schedules, the project manager then turns over responsibility for a group of work packages to the project engineer, who in turn passes them on to the lead engineers. The system requires smooth working relationships between the lead engineer and the project engineer at one level, and the PMO (Project Management Office) and the departments at the next level.

Often, the departments are not responsive to the PMO's overall needs. Let's face it, the departments are organized on a feu-

dal basis of hierarchical power and they lose sight of company objectives. Most department managers are interested in concept design and don't care about the requirements imposed upon the PMO by the government contract. In this case, the best lead engineer is only 50 percent effective. Battles are constantly fought with the department managers who want to keep the money and the control in their departments.

Somewhere along the line, the philosophy of the matrix organization was never conveyed to some people. They all like to do business as usual and deny or repress reality. Look, OPMAN is explicit about the whole system yet we still have the problem of territoriality. Who wants to give up authority? In my relationships with lead engineers, I am a pragmatist. If the job is big and the potential payoff is critical, I work closely with the lead engineers and the project engineers to bring the line managers to heel. Sometimes this backfires, especially when it comes down to the fabrication of the device. My main style is to get the loyalty of the lead engineer and then let him fight it out with the functional departments. The most successful lead engineer is the one who never says die and keeps the pressure on the task engineer and the departments. I realize that this becomes sticky when there is dual reporting responsibility, but the first priority from my perspective is the program office and the customer. The way I see it, the PMO becomes the doer and any other way the tail is wagging the dog.

A Project Engineer:

I have six lead engineers working for me. I encourage the maximal interplay between them and me. Only when this occurs do you get the maximal realization of what can be accomplished with the scope of work. As I see it, one of the potential problems is the lack of empathy of the lead engineers for the values of the program office. The lead engineer has difficulty understanding the project engineer, who is generally more management than technically oriented. Some lead engineers take this lack of emphasis on technical know-how as a weakness, and a potential gulf can develop between the lead engineer and the project engineer as a result. My feeling is that we are all in this together and that some trust and willingness to take risks must be developed between the project engineer and the lead engineer. The PMO has the responsibility to convey the overall philosophy to the lead engineer and to the functional managers.

I have the problem of breaking down the resistance of people who see the program office as usurpers of authority. Although we have a well-written manual of operations, people tend to react on a set of preconceived values and not on a set of idealized instructions. The manual sets the tone but not the behavior of people. In some cases, the manual collects dust on the functional manager's bookshelf and in that case I have to soft sell the principles. One of the biggest mistakes a lead engineer or a member of the program office can make is to think that there is leverage only on the functional departments. Once this message is conveyed to people, they bristle and crouch for a fight.

The lead engineers who realize they are working with a different set of values are the ones who will get the most mileage out of their task engineers and the most cooperation from the functional managers. In other words, I am stressing a balanced approach by the lead engineers. They have to be sensitive to human relations, technically knowledgeable but not to the point of overemphasis, willing to live with uncertainty, and not constantly bucking problems up the authority hierarchy. Following the rules without regard to the interpersonal relationships involved can be a serious handicap. Let me emphasize that the lead engineers will not be the savior of the MPC organization, but they are a vital link that needs support from both the program office and the functional departments. Some of the problems they face are outside the realm of their limited role. On the other hand, they must be aware of the dynamics of the situation in order to deal effectively with the tasks that face them.

From the Viewpoint of the Lead Engineer

Hardy Ames called on a number of lead engineers to ask them their perceptions of the lead engineer concept. The first person Ames contacted was lead engineer on a large, complex program involving monitoring five task engineers and a budget of $10 million. He had been on this project for three years and was quick to point out that his role as lead engineer was different from many other lead engineers. Because of the size of his budget and the complexity of the work packages, he had some additional leverage with the functional departments, even though he had no more authority in the organization than any other lead engineer. He stated that he had other responsibilities that went outside the boundaries of MPC in the form of subcontracts to independent vendors. The five task engineers represented five functional departments at MPC. He saw his role as coordinating across the functional lines in order to ensure completion of his work packages within the schedule, cost, and technical specifications of the contract. It was apparent that he was an enthusiastic person who was very involved with his work. On the other hand, he appeared to be very aware of the problems that he faced in the daily operation of his job.

Look, one thing that I have to impress on you is the fact that I am a man in the middle. For one thing, there is friction between the departments. Each department is an empire unto itself. I have to proceed with caution when I deal with the functional managers. I can't give them the impression that I am bulldogging them nor can I take a back seat to their desires. It is a constant tightrope walk. Let me give you a few examples of these problems.

The first problem is one of *performance realism*. The people in each department have their own standards of performance and are unwilling to compromise their technical expertise. Most departmental personnel see themselves as the technical experts who should have the ultimate say on design matters. This problem has to be dealt with by communicating to the task engineers and the department managers the constraints of the contract. Most of the time an informal session on these matters clears the air and the work can then proceed. In some cases, the battle has to be escalated to the level of the engineering laboratory manager, or in extreme cases, to the MPC general manager. This ploy cannot be used more than once or you destroy your hard-earned trust with the functional departments.

The second problem concerns *design inadequacies*. The departments tend to project their feelings of inadequacy onto the program office in order to find a scapegoat. They will usually say that an inadequate set of specifications was drawn up. I see this as another problem in human relations. If you defend the program office, you lose the cooperation of the department. If you let the people in the program office justify every mistake by projecting onto others, they begin to believe themselves and adopt a self-righteous attitude. The lead engineer has to take these problems into account and achieve goals in spite of these human frailties. Don't get me wrong; I am not a paragon of virtue, but I have been on both sides of the fence. I worked in a functional department and spent some time in the pro-

gram office. These experiences have helped temper my values and permitted me to see both sides of the coin. As a result of my observations, I have adopted a position in which I am sensitive to the values of others. My prime goal is to get the job done *through*, not *over* people. At times I have to overlook things. I reject the opinion that I should identify with the program office. This type of reasoning will make friends in the PMO but stop the flow of work at the operational level. Let me say it is easier these days to identify with the program office, especially when your program reflects 30 percent of the present and future revenue of the company.

I get ego satisfaction out of working with people and achieving a goal. My method is to be as straight and as open as possible. Most of the time this works. The exception is with the shops. The shop employees have their own environment and tend to react in fixed ways. Under the present leadership, it is almost impossible to convince them that they should conform to the manual of operations. A control chart to them is just a waste of time and energy. This battle has to be fought on higher levels. The situation with the shops is similar to our relationship with the manufacturing group at Flowertown. Most of the people in manufacturing respond strictly to an authority relationship. If you try to use a little informal persuasion, you are accused of trying to upset the apple cart. I realize that a manufacturing environment demands a different style of management, but when you have some of those people mixed in with a project organization, you have a feud that beats the *Beverly Hillbillies* in winning the Emmy for stupidity.

In spite of these recurrent problems, I feel that I am personally achieving satisfaction and contributing to the company. On the other hand, I can see why some engineers would never be a lead engineer unless their life, or more precisely their job, depended upon it. Some engineers see the lead engineer as the end of their professional career. That may be true if you see your job in terms of advanced concept design rather than in managing systems. I get a big kick out of being where the action is. I thought about it many times and have come to the conclusion that it takes a person who has seen all sides and then comes to terms with his or her professional and managerial career by combining both in one job. Granted, I have a unique lead engineer job; one that has high visibility in the organization. To me, that puts my future in my own hands. If I blow it, well, everyone knows it; if I do a good job, then there is the road to a higher position in the company. But again I have to say that it takes a specialized person who is not bound to the usual organizational hierarchy to want to be a good lead engineer.

Hardy Ames next talked with a lead engineer who managed a modest software development project with a budget of $40,000. This young engineer had been with the company for three years and was only recently assigned to the role of lead engineer. She recited the usual lead engineer creed about responsibility for budgets, scheduling, technical reviews, and all of the other terms found in the MPC operations manual. Her project was limited to six months' work and was described as a form of technical optimization. She was in the second month of her project and she described the progress as slow due to certain technical snags. The one task engineer who reported to her seemed to be going off in a direction that did not coincide with her game plan.

She said:

Basically, I am a technical person who likes to get in on the design myself. All during my professional education I was told that an engineer is someone who designs rather than worries about costs and scheduling; that aspect was for accountants and administrators. The reason I accepted this job is that I can get my feet wet on a small scale and see how it goes. From where I sit, the lead engineer has all the potential of becoming the whipping boy of either the program office or the functional departments. The program office starts withdrawing once the problems rear their ugly heads and that leaves only one person, the lead engineer. Another bad feature is that you are assigned to the task without the necessary supporting people reporting to you. You have to go around like a beggar to get them to do your job. The situation is one of no control, no rewards. If someone wanted to design a system to frustrate someone, you couldn't find a better place to start than with the lead engineer slot.

Right now I have mixed emotions about whether or not the lead engineer job is a helpful one for a young engineer who is trying to find his or her niche in an R & D organization. Some people can cut the mustard as lead engineers and others can't. I am beginning to feel that I am going down the wrong road. In my previous job, I had a great supervisor. He was an old-timer in the business and was very personable with people. He was the kind of a boss who respected me for my technical competence and told me when I did a good job. The need to be respected for my technical expertise is now being blocked in my current role. Don't get me wrong; I see the need for a lead engineer and I am not knocking the concept. I am stating that it may not be the place for me in a professional sense. You have to be too much of a salesperson to get the job done. I know that DOD requires a coordinative organization, but I feel much more comfortable in a functional department where I can design equipment right from the conceptual stage. To be perfectly frank with you, I hope that the present exposure to the lead engineer role has not damaged my career in the company. This goes back to my comment about the lead engineer becoming the convenient whipping boy in the organization. Right now I am hoping the next four months will pass quickly and I will be able to return to my section.

Views of the Functional Managers

Guidance Systems Department Manager:

I am dissatisfied with the program office. As far as I am concerned, most program managers are not technically competent to deal with the internal design problems in the laboratories. The typical PM [program manager] is someone who can deal with the contractors and vendors but has no business interfering with the functional or design departments. As far as I am concerned, the problems are generated on this level and the lead engineer becomes a convenient layer between the program office and the functional departments. Under this system, the functional departments become the scapegoat when promises are not kept; I should emphasize, promises which should not have been made to start with. I am talking about technical requirements, costs, and scheduling. The program office is never willing to accept scheduling delays even though the facts prove their necessity. The lead engineer in most cases identifies rather strongly with the program office and tries to ram unrealistic demands through the functional departments. I regularly have three to five confrontations with various lead engineers interfacing with my department every week. Some of these escalate up to the general manager.

In the beginning, the argument used for program and project management was the press of reality. The program office/lead engineer/functional department interfaces were supposed to introduce a more rational approach to the problem. The way it seems to work is that the program office constantly tries to oversell the customer and then comes back via the lead engineer to extract the pound of flesh from the functional departments. The process should work in reverse. The lead engineer should negotiate with the functional department and then justify the company's position to the customer.

Another problem is the proliferation of lead engineers. Some of these people are managing small budgets that don't require the skills of a lead engineer. Such jobs could be done within the functional departments without the lead engineer interface. A more serious problem is generated when you have a lead engineer who reports to you and to the program office. It is very difficult to deal with disagreements on this level. I guess most of my comments are on the negative side but I think these factors have to be faced by management before a workable solution in the form of the right reporting structure and the right person for the job will result.

The biggest problem is the tendency for the program office to bend over backwards to do whatever the customer wants even if it doesn't make sense. This is a particularly tough problem to resolve in times of tightly specified fixed-price contracts. But I think that to deny the reality of the impact of impossible schedules and budgets upon the functional departments is living with your head in the sand. I could say quite a bit about the problems with the support groups and the problems that this situation generates but I think that you will get that information from the lead engineers themselves.

Signal Processing Department Manager:

If you can understand the system, you can generally make it work. What is lacking most of the time is a road map. Most of the wailing is because we do not know or understand the system. Now I know that the new operations manual covers the basic philosophy and the systems flow, but many people in the functional departments don't pay any attention to it. They look upon it as another encumbrance to their usual responsibilities. As far as I am concerned, the lead engineer concept is still in the evolutionary stage. When it was first introduced, I had a negative reaction to it. First of all, the lead engineer lacked adequate authority. Then, as time moved on, I saw some bright lead engineers function in the capacity of department managers without the title or authority. As I looked at the process more carefully, I saw that it took a special kind of person to be a lead engineer, one who commands and wins the respect of the department managers. It seems to me that most of the department managers have seen that it is a workable concept and have given their support to the concept. The big problem area is in commanding the respect of the support groups. Most of these people respect and react to authority above all. Somehow, we should be able to correct this situation by conferring some sort of authority on the lead engineer. Then again, I may be thinking like a functional manager who is used to dealing with people on an authority level.

I have heard the pros and cons of the lead engineer job as a career path in the company and I have a few views on that issue too. Looking back at the situation, most managerially oriented engineers should take to the lead engineer job because the lead engineer is a "star recognition" system visible throughout the laboratories, giving professional identity and stature that one would not receive as an ordinary design engineer. As a lead engineer, one is not encumbered with the administrative details of a department manager, such as salary adjustments, hiring, firing, absenteeism, and so on; one just complains to the line manager. Now

some people might not be satisfied with that position and want the authority that goes along with being the department manager. As I see it, there are more pros than cons from a purely career development point of view.

When you ask me what makes for a successful lead engineer, I can give three essential qualities: social sensitivity, autonomy, and goal orientation. A poor lead engineer is most likely to be either a person who lacks the human skills in the sense of ignoring others' needs or trying to pull the power play on them. A secondary feature in a poor lead engineer is the commitment to a professional engineering career without regard to the managerial function. I say that this is secondary because some people may espouse the professional value system but on the intrinsic level, really dig the managerial system and its rewards. Sometimes that only comes out after trial and error. From where I sit in the organization, it appears as if the lead engineer is the prototype of the manager of the future, especially in high-technology companies.

Views of the Task Engineers

The tenor of the views expressed by the task engineers was quite different from other groups interviewed. They appeared to be more reluctant to discuss the issues than the other principals.

A Task Engineer in the Mechanical Engineering Department: (Note that this task engineer sat in a crowded office surrounded by blueprints, documents, and company manuals. He shared the office with another colleague who was so absorbed in her own work that she did not even realize that a visitor was present.)

On the whole, the people in the mechanical engineering department are not paperwork types. We have little regard for all the forms and procedures that have been created over the first five years in a futile effort to expedite the work on a project. These policies and procedures often cause unnecessary problems, such as the need for an assembly drawing release before parts can be ordered, thereby causing a six-week delay. Another bone of contention is the qualification and conditioning of relatively new active devices, which sometimes result in up to a 15-week delivery schedule, versus 3 weeks without these encumbrances.

The biggest problem is that the lead engineer and other task engineers up the line generate specifications for a black box that requires nonstandardized parts. This requires a long-form drawing, complex documentation, and finally, verification of the document. Everyone gets into the act. This was not the case five years ago. You have to go through seven people in the specification cycle and a minimum of five people in the approval stage. The whole system is dragging. Once this happens, the lead engineer is on your neck and wants to know why the component is behind schedule. We support people have to bear the brunt of all the snafus in the system. I try to circumvent the system as much as I can, but it is getting tougher and tougher each day. The net result is ulcers for me. Once you have approval for the component, down it goes to the model shop to see if it can be fabricated. Then the fireworks start.

In spite of all the documentation, there is still a communications gap between what the lead engineer wants and what the model shop does. For example, we had a simple problem turned into a three-day fiasco. A joint had to be soldered but the pieces didn't conform to specifications and had to be ground down. The person in the model shop used a sand-blasting technique, which is okay for some cases, but in this situation it left a residue that prevented the solder from taking. Finally, after three days of fussing

around, we suggested pickling the part to take off the silicon residue. Then the soldering took.

Now that may seem to be a minor example, but if you multiply these by the hundreds you see the bind we get into. You cannot do everything by the numbers. When things come down to the mechanical engineering department, they become real time problems and create pressure-cooker situations for the task engineer. Then, in addition to these difficulties, the task engineer is not always given the visibility that the lead engineer gets. I haven't even gone into the problems over finances that most task engineers have to face with the lead engineer. Most of the time, the designs require new technology that demands quick reaction, but the learning curve is never taken into account and we end up on the short end of the stick.

A Task Engineer in the Model Shop:

Many of my colleagues do not share my views, and I am not typical of the opinions in the model shop. As a task engineer, I have grown to believe in the lead engineer concept; it is the only way to operate in the current environment. My involvement with the lead engineer starts as soon as a decision is made to respond to a request for proposal. A good lead engineer tries to get the best estimates of the cost to build a component. When this process becomes one of game playing, the trust between the lead engineer and the people in the model shop is eroded. As far as I am concerned, this could be avoided if both sides would try to see the big picture and not try to pad the package beyond limits. In my experience, this procedure has worked well. The lead engineer and all of the task engineers have to triangulate on the work package. Unless this coordinative effort is achieved, the cost and schedule estimates go down the drain. The OPMAN is a good thing because it gives people the necessary road maps to know where they are going and when to start a reiterative process. The people who want to return to the Stone Age of operations are merely clinging to the nostalgia of the past. I'm not trying to pretend we don't have problems; of course we do. There are significant difficulties with the production facilities at Flowertown where a completely different set of values pervades the organization. I'm in no position to give any solutions to this nitty-gritty problem.

QUESTIONS

1. Analyze and compare the views expressed in this case.
2. What are the value orientations of the various levels in the organization and how do these affect their viewpoints?
   a. program office
   b. lead engineers
   c. functional department managers
   d. task engineers
3. What do you see as the strengths and weaknesses of the lead engineer concept at MPC?
4. Based on the comments in the case and your personal experience, what set of personal qualities do you think a lead engineer ought to have in order to carry out the job?
5. What can be done from an organizational point of view to make project management work more efficiently and effectively with respect to both the task to be performed and the people who perform it?
6. What would you recommend to top management as a result of this reappraisal of the lead engineer concept if you were
   a. Hardy Ames, head of Industrial Relations?
   b. Charles Bertram, the outside consultant?
   c. asked for your own opinion?

A Case of Promotion

It was the end of spring. The weather was perfect. A special kind of southern summer was about to begin. Joe Marconi, a senior engineer at the Eastern Division of the Mammoth Construction Company, sat and reflected over his career. In many ways he thought he might have made serious career errors. He had worked for the Mammoth Construction Company for almost thirty years. Even after the onset of diabetes ten years ago, he had continued to work hard and tried to develop his career. He had a strong feeling that the company system had worked against him. He could still remember the way the company had tried to force him to retire after he was stricken with diabetes because of the difficulty he had in adjusting to insulin and special diets. It seemed like the managers intentionally assigned him to jobs that required that he be away from home where the insulin and dietary regimens were difficult to maintain. He knew they could have given him more office work but for some reason they didn't do this. No one had ever questioned his technical ability.

Seven years ago he decided that the solution might be to get an assignment overseas. It would be a fresh start and it would be easier to get a promotion. He took an assignment in southern Europe as a lateral transfer. It had been a tough assignment but he felt he had done well. After a few years he had been offered a promotion to project engineer in another part of southern Europe. He discussed the job at length with Bob King, the man who was to be his supervisor. It was clear that it was the type of job where he would ruffle some feathers but the technical objectives could be reached. King assured him that he understood this, and if the technical objectives were accomplished, Marconi wouldn't be rated poorly for irritating a few people.

Things had gone reasonably well technically, but apparently a lot of people had been annoyed by his successful work. He had not received any formal negative feedback, but he knew through the grapevine that others had complained to his supervisor. He had received satisfactory performance appraisals and had taken satisfaction in the fact that he had done a good technical job.

After five years he had reached the recommended limit for overseas assignments and he had been requested to file for a transfer back to the United States. In so doing, Marconi wanted to return to the Eastern Division, where he had family roots. Unfortunately, at this time the Eastern Division was overstaffed and Marconi had to accept a position as an associate engineer, a two-level reduction (although his salary was to be maintained at its existing level for two years). Although he knew that an associate engineer job was the minimum he could be offered under company policy, Marconi felt disappointed and was sure that if the people at Eastern Division had *really* wanted to, they could have done better. He knew that twenty-four months later, after his two-year salary continuance ran out, he would have to take a substantial reduction in pay if he was not promoted back to his previous level.

When the reduction in pay actually came, it was a shock since he had always felt that he would be promoted to at least a senior engineer if not a project engineer within two years after his return.

A few months later he found out that there was to be an opening for a senior engineer in his department. At last things seemed to be looking up. There was no one in the department with his background and experience and he was sure he would get the job. Marconi knew it was company policy to fill jobs with the best people based on merit and not on geography, but he also felt that in spite of this, most jobs were filled by local people. Marconi heard through a friend at the corporate personnel office that 47 people had been nominated to fill the job and that he was not even listed among the most highly qualified. He also knew that Eastern Division management had put him among the group of most highly qualified, but he felt this was pro forma. If they had wanted to do something, they could have. Another person was selected. He had a good professional background and was well qualified.

At the time, Marconi's supervisor had explained that one factor that had held him back was that he was not a registered professional engineer. He could have qualified earlier in his career, but it had not seemed important at the time. His supervisor also implied that his past ratings in the interpersonal skills area were not all that hot. Marconi was not sure what that meant, but he decided to contact the Eastern Division personnel office. The

personnel counselor retrieved Marconi's records and showed him the evaluation forms that were prepared by the supervisors when an employee was being considered for promotion. (These were separate and distinct from the annual performance appraisals, and company policy viewed the section on his potential as confidential, but the other part he could see.) He found that his ratings on the so-called interpersonal factors were low, but the evaluation of his technical skills was high. About this time it was announced that there was to be a second opening for a senior engineer in his department. Marconi decided that it would be best to hold off any formal grievance and just apply for the new position. He was sure he would be selected and any static he created now would just make working conditions difficult in the future.

Marconi was nominated by his supervisor and he heard that there were relatively few nominations. He felt confident that he would be selected. At his last annual performance review a week earlier, his supervisor had commented about his fine technical skills. Again he was told by his friend in corporate personnel that he was not on the most highly qualified list. According to his supervisor, he was placed on the list over the corporate personnel office's objections. By this time Marconi was really annoyed but it still did not seem to make any sense to file a formal grievance since he had made the list of eligibles. He decided to wait and see.

About a week later it was announced that Steve Michaels had been selected. Marconi just couldn't understand it. Michaels had only been an associate engineer for a year and a half. In addition, he didn't have anything like Marconi's experience or technical knowledge, and had never held a senior engineer's job before, let alone a project engineer's job. Marconi was furious. He immediately formulated a grievance based on prejudice. "These damn southerners just won't give an Italian a break," he explained to the company EEO (Equal Employment Opportunity) coordinator, Tony Carlucci.

"Look, Joe," Tony responded, "let's be serious about this. There are too many people of various ethnic groups in high places around here for that argument to fly. I know of at least four Italian Americans who are project managers in this organization. You're going to have to come up with something better."

"Well, I know they are just down on me. I haven't been treated fairly," Marconi responded. "Let me think about it for a few days and I'll get back to you. But in the meantime, I want to file a formal grievance based on prejudice."

A couple of days later, however, Marconi had concluded that Carlucci was right and he would not win on the basis of prejudice. He consulted with a coworker in the organization who was known as an expert on company rules and regulations. After some discussion he decided to file his appeal on the basis of age discrimination and supervisor misrating. Before submitting a formal grievance he decided to talk to the personnel manager, Carl Long. He explained the situation and asked that something be done.

The following day, Carl Long held a meeting with two of the three managers involved. Jim Beam was Marconi's current supervisor, but he had not submitted a supervisor's evaluation form concerning Marconi. Beam explained later that if he had submitted one, it would have been very similar to those in the folder. Steve Austin had been Marconi's supervisor in the branch office and it was Austin who had submitted the supervisor's evaluation form. Austin was now also working for Jim Beam. The third manager involved, Bob King, managed one of the major construction departments at the Eastern Division. He had been Marconi's supervisor when they were both overseas and had promoted Marconi to the project engineer position. He had also submitted a supervisor's evaluation for review by the corporate personnel office. Since King was out of town, he could not attend the meeting.

Carl Long began the meeting by explaining his perception of the situation. "You know, the key factor here is the question of Joe's being properly rated or misrated. Steve, why don't you tell us what you think of Joe and his ability."

Steve Austin responded, "Actually it is fairly easy to describe Joe. He is a solid technical man with good experience, but he just doesn't work well with others. He is abrasive and tends to look down on his fellow workers. I can remember one situation when Joe had one of our secretaries in tears because he berated her for being in an inferior profession. He is very hard to work with."

Jim Beam interrupted. "That's exactly right. He does a good technical job, especially when he works alone; but then he will cause trouble because of his inability to get along with others. In many ways he is really a pain in the neck."

Carl Long observed, "One thing that always comes up in these situations is whether or not he was told of his performance so that he could correct his shortcomings. Has Joe been told about his faults?"

Steve Austin answered. "I spoke to him repeatedly about these problems. He just doesn't care."

Jim Beam added, "I can give you specific examples. Joe was assigned to a construction project where the customer was really involved in the project and concerned about the schedule. Well, you know how important our relationship with customers is. Joe told the customer to get off his back and to quit asking dumb questions."

"That's exactly the kind of thing he does," Austin continued. "He has told two engineers in the department, who I know are good men, that they are incompetent. The other men don't want to work with him."

"OK, I think I have heard enough," Carl Long concluded. He then leaned across the desk, pushed the buzzer on his intercom, and asked his secretary to have Mr. Marconi come into his office. He was going to get this straightened out once and for all. Within about five minutes, Joe Marconi arrived at the office. "Joe, I have been discussing your complaint about the recent promotion of Steve Michaels with both Mr. Austin and Mr. Beam. They don't think that there is any real justification for it, but we would like to hear your side of the matter. Would you like to begin by describing your feelings about the many discussions they have had with you concerning your problems in working with others?"

"What discussions?" Joe exclaimed. "Neither one of them ever talked to me about any problems in working with others. As far as I know they both have always been satisfied with my work. There is certainly nothing in any of my annual performance appraisals about it."

With a rather puzzled look on his face, Carl Long turned to the other two men and asked, "Do either of you want to comment on that?"

"Now, Joe," Jim Beam responded, "you know I talked to you about the problem you had with the customer on the Lambda Project."

"Wait a minute," Marconi responded. "I did exactly what you told me to do on that project. You said that the customer was interfering in the project and screwing things up. I was supposed to keep him out of our hair and I did it."

"That's right, Joe," Beam interrupted, "but I meant to do it diplomatically."

"That's a bunch of bull!" Joe exploded. "We both discussed this and agreed that I wasn't going to make any friends on that project. I did exactly as I was told and the work was done on time and within budget. Beyond that, you gave me a good annual performance appraisal."

Austin, in a soothing voice, tried to calm Marconi down by explaining, "Joe, no one is questioning your technical work. That has al-ways been solid. Why, I remember you did an outstanding job on the Sigma Project." Austin went on to recount several examples of Marconi's above average technical work.

"I think we are getting a little off the track," Carl Long interjected. "Let's get back to the poor performance aspects of the supervisor's evaluation." But the two supervisors just seemed to ramble on about technical factors. Most of their statements about Marconi were very complimentary. After 15 or 20 minutes of this, Long concluded that they were not going to provide any specific examples of Marconi's poor performance. After a couple of futile attempts to get them to be specific, he gave up and ended the meeting. Joe Marconi said he wanted a meeting with the other supervisor who had submitted an evaluation. Long set up the meeting. It went very much like the first one. Bob King told Long the same kind of things about Marconi. When Joe was brought into the office, King provided a specific example to demonstrate his point. Marconi responded by saying they both had known it was a difficult assignment that was likely to upset people when he had taken it. He had done exactly as he was told, and when it was over King had commended him and this had been reflected in his annual performance appraisal. King did not deny any of this, but he said he still felt his comments on the supervisor's evaluation form were accurate and he would not change his comments.

At this point Long turned to Marconi and said, "Let's see if we can arrive at a fair solution. There isn't any vacancy for a senior engineer now, so why don't we just say that there won't be any animosity shown by anyone and that you will be seriously considered for the next one available."

Obviously upset, Marconi responded, "No. I don't think that is fair. I want to see the division vice-president".

That afternoon, Marconi filed an EEO grievance. He was within company policy in all respects. He asked the personnel counselor to hold it up until he met with the vice-president. The counselor agreed.

In the meantime he again talked to the coworker who was viewed as something of an expert on company rules and regulations by others in the organization. He heard Marconi out and recommended that he submit a letter to the vice-president claiming that the supervisor's evaluations had not been substantiated, that they differed from his annual performance appraisals, that he was doing the same work as other senior engineers in his department, and that he was entitled to equal pay for equal work.

Two days later he had a meeting with the vice-president. Marconi had asked Carl Long and Tony Carlucci to be there. Marconi was extremely nervous. In his entire career he had never really talked with the division vice-president, and this certainly was not the most pleasant of situations to begin with.

Marconi, sitting very rigid, explained his perception of the situation. The vice-president listened attentively, commented occasionally to try to relax Marconi, and asked some questions. When the explanation was concluded, the vice-president told Marconi, "I will look into this very carefully. I will take corrective action if that is appropriate and there will be no reprisals for any of your actions. You can be certain of that."

The vice-president carefully checked the details of the story and called the three supervisors into his office together with their general manager. After some preliminary questioning, he found out that the general manager had considered himself rather new to the organization, and consequently felt he should stay out of the situation.

The vice-president disagreed with the general manager. "I can't believe a situation like this could occur in your group and you not be on top of it. That is unbelievably bad communication. I expect you to get a better handle on that organization."

The vice-president then turned to the three supervisors. "As for you three, it is clear to me that you don't know a thing about performance evaluation and promotion. If you don't know how, don't do it; find out from somebody else how it should be done."

He continued without interruption, "I want it clearly understood that there are to be no reprisals concerning this man. I am thoroughly disgusted with the management displayed in this situation. That's all." During the entire conversation, no one from the group responded. It was clear the vice-president didn't want any response.

Two weeks later, with the concurrence of all concerned, Joe Marconi was promoted to senior engineer and his complaint was withdrawn.

QUESTIONS

1. What is your evaluation of the line supervisors in this case? What factors are causing their behavior? How effectively did they communicate?
2. How should company policy be changed? What safeguards should be built in?
3. Should Joe Marconi have been promoted? Why?
4. Did Carl Long act in an effective manner?
5. What is your evaluation of the vice-president's action?
6. How could this whole thing happen without the general manager knowing?

EASTERN DIVISION (A)

IMPROVING MORALE IN FACILITIES PLANNING

Ever since the Eastern Division of the Mammoth Construction Company (MCC) moved into an old former textiles factory in the industrial section of the city some years before, a number of employees of the planning department had been unhappy with their office facilities. Housed in large, high-ceilinged, storage-like areas on the top floor in the rear of the building, both the Alpha and Beta Sections were surrounded by windowless walls painted a dingy green. Old gray partitions formed cubicles housing standard old gray steel desks and chairs. Banks of dark green file cabinets, which had seen better days, were piled high with accumulated catalogues and reports. The total effect was shabby and depressing, especially when contrasted with the recently redecorated executive offices on the first floor in the front of the building.

About a year ago, Clay Barnes, the planning department manager from the Central Division of MCC, had paid a visit to Hal Craig, the planning department manager at the Eastern Division. During this visit, Barnes had shown employees of the engineering branch slides of the colorful redecoration just completed at his offices. At about the same time, wall panels and carpeting were installed in the office suite occupied by Hal Craig, Dave Kidd, manager of the Alpha Section, their secretaries, and Mary Knight, the department's program analyst (see the Partial Organization Chart shown in Exhibit 1). These events impelled John Rush, an engineer in the engineering branch, to initiate improvements in the appearance of the branch's work area.

Through the branch manager, Henry Rapp, Rush first inquired about the possibility of getting new desks for the branch. This request was turned down by the financial manager, Brad Doyle, who told Rapp that the budget for office improvements had already been committed to places elsewhere in the building. Rush then asked Rapp if paint and brushes could be made available to employees willing to volunteer to repaint desks, partitions, files, and cabinets. Rapp took this request to the Alpha Section manager, Dave Kidd, who discussed the idea with Hal Craig, the planning department manager. Coincidently, Craig was chairman of the MCC committee charged with planning for and implementing the renovation of the entire building over the next five or six years. Craig was enthusiastic about the idea, feeling that such a self-help project would provide a badly needed boost to departmental morale. He promised to provide the needed materials.

Rush then conducted an informal poll among other employees of the branch to get a feel for a most desired color scheme and to find out how many volunteers would be available to do the work. He drew a color-keyed

EXHIBIT 1

PARTIAL ORGANIZATION CHART: PLANNING DEPARTMENT, EASTERN DIVISION

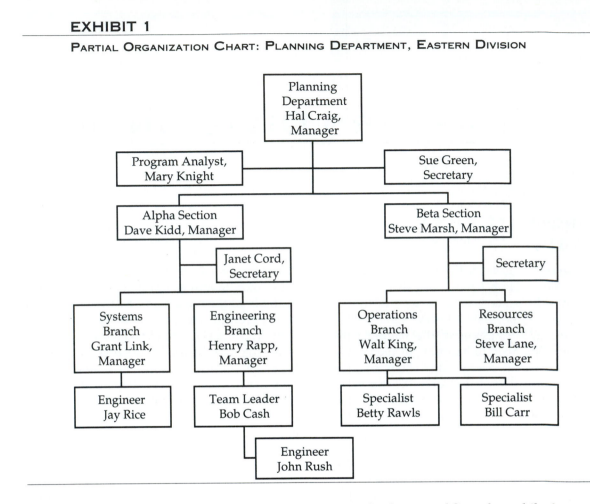

floor plan of the area based on this survey and discovered that nearly a dozen employees of the branch would be willing to come in on Saturdays to paint.

On a Saturday morning in March, a blue-jeaned crew of men and women gathered to begin the project. Hal Craig and Dave Kidd and their secretaries showed up and worked with the engineering branch people. John Rush, who had interrupted renovation of his own home to be there, brought his wife and children with him. At lunch time, several of the group were dispatched to bring in refreshments for the workers, whose labors, while not always expert, were showing colorful results.

On the second Saturday, while the rest of the people continued work in the engineering branch area, Sue Green and Jack Cord, departmental secretaries, concentrated on painting their own desks in the departmental office suite. They were joined by Mary Knight, the program analyst, and her friend Betty Rawls from the Beta Section. It was apparent that everyone was enjoying the work and a spirit of fun and camaraderie prevailed. By the end of a third Saturday's work the total project was three quarters completed.

On the Monday after the third Saturday, Harry Dalton, a union steward, came to see Dave Kidd and asked him if he was familiar with the Fair Labor Standards Act. "You have violated it," he said. "You permitted and caused the nonexempt people to come in and work without compensating them." Considerably upset, Kidd checked with Kate Fry, the personnel manager, who in turn, got the Eastern Division general manager and the manager of the legal department involved and the group spent a considerable amount of time researching the applicable clauses of the Fair Labor Standards Act. They discovered several things:

1. The important parts of the Act had been published in the Eastern Division's employee newsletter several months before.
2. The applicable clause clearly stated that management could not "suffer or permit" nonexempt employees to work overtime without compensating them for their time.
3. Further, exempt employees should be offered compensatory time.

Kate Fry therefore informed Kidd and Craig that the union steward was absolutely correct and that compensation would have to be paid.

Hal Craig called a meeting of affected employees to announce that compensation would be paid. All those who were to receive the payments objected strenuously, saying they had volunteered to do the work and did not expect or want to be paid. On being told that legally they had to be paid, the employees voted to spend the money for plants and prints to add to the decorative scheme of their work places.

Since the work was not finished, Hal Craig decreed that the volunteers could spend an hour and a half of MCC time at the end of the day on Friday afternoons to complete the job. Several people took advantage of this opportunity and by June the job was done; although the high spirits which had existed earlier among the volunteers were considerably dampened. Unfortunately, the walls were still unpainted, but the colorful desks, cabinets, and

partitions at least partly obscured this unpretentious background.

In the meantime, impressed with the improvements taking place in the engineering branch, people in two other branches initiated similar activities with varying degrees of success. Grant Link, head of the systems branch, sent several memos around to his people (see Exhibits 2 and 3) and followed this up with a roster asking for volunteers to paint on Friday afternoons. Of thirteen people responding, only he, a secretary and one engineer volunteered. The order for paint for that branch was canceled (see Exhibit 4) and the systems branch, adjacent to the engineering branch, maintained its gray-green appearance.

Things went a lot better in the operations branch of the Beta Section. There, Betty Rawls, a specialist who had helped in the engineering branch, and who was impressed with the improvements made, went around suggesting to people that some sprucing up would be nice. She received a positive response and asked Steve Marsh, the Beta Section manager, if it would be all right to work on Friday afternoons. He said it would be fine with him if Hal Craig approved. Hal Craig asked to see a plan of what they intended to do.

Rawls consulted with John Rush in the engineering branch, who had developed the plan there and together they drew up a color-keyed floor plan of the entire Beta Section. Betty Rawls took this around to her colleagues in the section for approval, and having received same, submitted the plan to Hal Craig, who also approved it and authorized the purchase of paint and brushes.

Enlisting the aid of her office mate, Bill Carr, Rawls then initiated the "spruce up" in the Beta Section. Rawls and Carr, working on several Friday afternoons, painted their own desks and the partitions around their office space. They then tackled a long row of file cabinets opposite their cubicle. They first removed piles of old reports and catalogues from on top of the cabinets, and

EXHIBIT 2

EASTERN DIVISION

Memorandum

From: Grant Link
To: Distribution
Subject: Painting of Furniture in the Systems Branch

1. We will be faced with the task of painting our area on Friday afternoon in order to complete the engineering branch decorating prior to having the walls painted.
2. Since our area is somewhat larger and more open, it has been suggested that we use only two colors: one color for all file cabinets as common use items and one color for all other furniture.
3. Limiting our area to two colors will retain the open feeling, whereas a multitude of colors would tend to create a clash.
4. Will you please comment on the above and state the two colors you feel would be appropriate to live with five days a week.
5. Please return as soon as possible.

Thank you,

Grant Link

---

after checking with those who knew the history of these documents, disposed of most of this material. Next they cleaned the cabinets to ready them for painting. They discovered that other people from the section passing in the corridor would frequently stop and lend a hand during this operation, and this assistance increased when they began to paint the cabinets. The job on the cabinets took several months of volunteer labor on Friday afternoons.

As the results of Rawls and Carr's work became more apparent, several other people in the operations branch began to work on Friday afternoons painting their own desks and partitions, all according to the plan taped to the partition near Rawls's desk. Although the plan covered the work areas of both branches in the Beta Section, no work was done in the resources branch.

The entire operation got a big lift when the walls of the Beta Section were repainted by a contractor in the early fall. Dingy green became a bright and cheerful off-white, and

Rawls contacted friends in the design department who offered, when funds became available, to help create colorful murals for the walls similar to those in the new quarters of the finance department.

The finance department had, by fall, become the best-looking office area at the Eastern Division, with new, brightly colored desks and partitions and muraled walls (done as part of the building renovation plan by outside professional contractors), accented with many plants and other personal touches in the several branches. Other areas of the large building housing the Eastern Division were temporarily vacant, but it was common knowledge that additional contracted renovation and redecoration was imminent.

QUESTIONS

1. How would you assess the decisions made and roles played by Hal Craig, Dave Kidd, Henry Rapp, Grant Link, and Steve Marsh?

EXHIBIT 3

EASTERN DIVISION

Memorandum

From: Grant Link
To: Distribution
Subject: Painting of Furniture in the Systems Branch

1. By memo last week I asked that each of you express the two (2) colors you would prefer to have used in our area.
2. The majority have expressed very practical and warm colors of light brown and yellow; this means that the common use items, such as all file cabinets and book cases, would be yellow, and all other furniture would be light brown.
3. The paints, brushes, and rollers are purchased from the general manager's discretionary funds.
4. The attached color chips (latex enamel) show the colors we will use; cleanup is relatively easy with water.
5. Jack Cole will advise you when the material is available for painting on Friday afternoons on a voluntary basis.

Grant Link

EXHIBIT 4

EASTERN DIVISION

Memorandum

From: Dave Kidd
To: Grant Link
Subject: Self-Help Painting

1. Attached is your memo with color selection and those interested in improving our work place.
2. Needless to say I am somewhat speechless and amazed. Up until now I thought our people wanted a more decent place to work. Cancel the order for paint.

2. How do you account for the varying degrees to which "self-help" was successful in the engineering, systems, and operations branches?
3. To what degree would you think morale had been improved in the planning department?
4. Was the union justified in taking the action it did? Should management have fought the issue out with the union?
5. What, if anything, might you have done differently if you were Hal Craig? Dave Kidd?

EASTERN DIVISION (B)

FEELINGS AND PERCEPTIONS

Looking back on the events described in EASTERN DIVISION (A), various supervisors and employees of the Planning Department stated strong feelings and varying perspectives.

Dave Kidd, Alpha Section Manager:

It all started in the engineering branch where our creative people are—the artistic types as opposed to the systems types in the systems branch. When Henry Rapp came to us to ask for paint I was delighted. We sent around a note asking who wanted to volunteer and got a real good response. Then, after just a few Saturdays, the union put a stop to it.

I was really upset. We had good esprit de corps going and they had to come to me with this compensation bit. It was discouraging. People were really interested, but having to pay compensation destroyed the esprit. It really floored me. I thought it would be a good thing and we ran into a buzz saw.

Some people think that somebody who didn't want to do the work went to the union. If so, I don't think it was anybody in the planning department. So anyway, we're only half done—the systems branch never got started. The branch manager sent out a memo asking for volunteers, but it kind of died on the vine. We've moved some desks and partitions around there, but that's all.

Of course, now the company is embarked on a building renovation plan and hopefully our area will get some new paint. But it's all done one thing for me as management. It's taught me to be more careful with my people. From now on if someone wants to move a desk four feet, I'll send over to the maintenance department and get them to do it—even if it takes two weeks.

Henry Rapp, Engineering Branch Manager:

I don't know who initiated the idea here, but once it started to get talked up most everybody was enthusiastic. About ten of us came in two or three Saturdays to work. A least one woman from another unit came over and helped. John Rush's wife came in every Saturday we worked. We all worked like hell, but had a good time, too.

Then the union somehow or other got involved. Speculation is that someone in another department didn't want to participate and brought the union in. Anyway, since we were three-fourths done, Hal Craig offered to let us finish up on Friday afternoons. We finished most of it that way, but interest really petered out.

I think the company made a mistake bowing to the union. It was all voluntary; nobody was pressured to come in.

276

Bob Cash, Team Leader, Engineering Branch:

Initially, I was one of the proponents of the volunteer scheme, but then I guess I turned kind of negative on it. One problem was how the color scheme was selected. We had put together a team to select colors. The team included two architects who were best qualified to advise, but the selection was made without them by a civil engineer on the team and John Rush. They didn't get expert advice—we ended up with three or four shades of blue, and blue is described as an accent color in most interior design guides. I would have felt better if an interior designer had been involved.

And then after we got going I was disturbed when I found out Henry Rapp was keeping tabs on who was coming in on Saturday and afterwards people were asked why they weren't there if they didn't show up. It looked like people were being coerced. I must admit, I'm the only one who feels this way—the others I've talked to who volunteered didn't feel they were coerced.

The real reason we got started was we saw people in other divisions getting new furniture—in fact we even traded some of our *very* old stuff for desks and files they discarded. When the union got involved and the whole thing ground to a halt, but we had done most of what we wanted to do.

You know, in a way the fact that the systems branch didn't do anything solidified *them* as a group. Management, from Hal Craig down, was pushing the idea and that branch rejected it. They felt that if the area was to be spruced up, let's go to contract and get it spruced up. I must say at the time I wondered why we were painting and they weren't.

Oh hell, I guess I'd rather have my desk blue than gray and I'm glad I spent the time and I'd do it again.

Jack Cord, secretary to Dave Kidd:

I thought it was a good deal we all got together to do the job. There was a lot of incentive behind it and when we were painting, it was fun. Then later I felt discouraged because people felt hassled about coming in Saturdays. So we had to finish up on Fridays. We *do* have quite a few negative Scrooges who are against everything, but nobody was pressured—if they didn't want to, nobody made them.

Mary Knight, Program Analyst, Planning Department:

I originally felt somewhat pushed by others around here to come in on Saturdays, but I realized they were trying to get something started so I came in. It turned out to be great fun. None of us were aware it would hit back on us the way it did.

I resented the union interfering. Harry Dalton, the union steward, came to me and said, "We are protecting you." I said I didn't want to be protected—that I wanted to do this.

It was too bad about the systems branch. Grant Link sent a note around to his people asking them to volunteer. They were up in arms. Nobody consulted them about the design of the office or colors. The whole thing was initiated in the engineering branch."

Grant Link, Systems Branch Manager:

When I sent around the memo asking what two colors people wanted to paint desks and files, the answer came back light and dark gray, which is what everything already was. I called them all together and questioned whether that's what they really wanted and we came up with light brown and gold. But then nobody wanted to paint.

I think the group is discouraged because other departments are getting new furniture and we are told there's no budget. We've heard our walls are going to be painted like in the Beta Section, but it seems to have fallen through.

To tell you the truth, I don't think our people are particularly unhappy about not having a more attractive place to work. We let them move desks and files around pretty much as they like and that seems to satisfy most everybody.

Jay Rice, Engineer, Systems Branch:

I didn't feel painting was something that was my job to do. I live sixty miles away from the building so Saturdays wasn't an attractive idea for me, and it seems like a waste of money having engineers and managers doing this kind of thing during working hours on Fridays.

I'd like to see the walls painted, but looking out from here over this sea of desks all I see is the tops anyway. I think *people* make working conditions, not paint. It was management who thought it would help morale to spruce up the place—nobody asked us if it would help our morale. And besides, volunteer work makes people into good guys and bad guys and I think we should stay away from that.

John Rush, Engineer, Engineering Branch:

I spend more time in the engineering branch than I do at home and I'd like to come in to a place that's cheerful—not the depressing gray and green dump this was. Look at the other sections where they bought new furniture and have murals on the walls—you feel you're in a nice place. It's discouraging to find out one area has the budget to do these things and we are outcasts with nothing done for us.

So I got involved. First, I tried to see if we could order new furniture and got turned down. We got together and found a lot of us wanted to paint and I made up a scheme of what units would be painted what colors. We got an OK from Hal Craig and from then on it was all strictly volunteer. I brought my wife and kids in and a couple of other guys brought their wives and they were all from the engineering branch except for one woman from the Beta Section. The people from the systems branch weren't involved. We brought in pizza and coke and were having a ball—you should have seen morale go up.

All of a sudden the union got involved. People started saying you are looked on as a nice guy if you come in and looked down on if you don't. And then when we heard they were going to take remedial action and force us to take money it spoiled everything and we quit. A lot of people don't give a damn anymore—they don't want to contribute to causes and don't care about our environment anymore. We even had Henry talked into buying a rug for his office with his own money. He won't do it now—it's not worth it.

Harry Dalton's Side of the Story: Union Perspectives

Harry Dalton, a senior union representative, made the following observations about the events surrounding the self-help redecoration of the planning department area.

A "showing of interest" petition had been submitted by our union four years ago to the Department of Labor regarding the Eastern Division of MCC. An election was subsequently held and professionals and nonprofessionals in Eastern Division voted to be represented exclusively by a local chapter of our professional engineers union. I feel that one of the main reasons for our success in the elections, especially among professionals, was their distaste for the unofficial and unenunciated company policy that professionals were expected to work approximately one extra hour daily without recompense. It got so bad employees were complaining of getting "funny looks" when they left work at the end of eight hours. Of course, the fledgling union was well aware of the situation and during the next eighteen months of negotiating for a contract ensured that a clause prohibiting voluntary overtime was included. In addition, the Fair Labor Standards Act [FLSA] was enacted some months prior to the incident. Of course, the duty for both management and union to consult, confer, and negotiate with each other on items affecting working conditions, et cetera, was well known. Prior to the signing of the union contract and in spite of our feelings about the so-called volunteer work, the union itself suggested to the general manager that volunteers could be used to finish an in-house lunch room. This idea was rejected by management as impractical.

Now to the case at hand. Dave Kidd and Hal Craig were well aware of the union contract and should have been aware of the implications of the FLSA. They were also aware that they had a shop steward in their area, Mary Smith. They never consulted or conferred with her or me, with whom they had dealt before on other matters. I knew that employees were painting, but never dreamed they weren't getting paid. I was approached by a union member who didn't want to volunteer to paint his desk. I said, "Fine. Don't volunteer." He said he didn't want anyone to volunteer. I said that wasn't fair because perhaps the others could use the money. Then he told me they weren't getting paid. I went to Hal Craig with the idea of consulting and possibly negotiating an easy way out for both sides.

Technically, under the law and the contract, management erred and would have to pay the employees if we forced the issue. I told Hal Craig that I had read the FLSA a few months ago but at that time did not consider it in conflict with Eastern Division policy. However, I told him I was aware of volunteers in his area painting their desks and wanted to discuss it. He was incensed and told me to mind my own business and butt out. I told him I realized he had to save face, but that I was sure we could come up with an equitable solution for both sides if we put our heads together. He told me that if I were smart I would drop the case because he wasn't going to see me sabotage the morale in his department. I tried to be reasonable but he used an overbearing tone of voice and made no effort to conceal his feelings of contempt for me. I have dealt with difficult individuals, before but this individual was the apex of arrogance. I told him I would be available for consultation, but if we couldn't work something out within a week he would have to pay the employees. He said he would be damned if he would.

The case went to the general manager and the same attitude prevailed. I was accused of sabotaging the morale of Eastern Division, et cetera, et cetera. I was never asked what solution I would recommend. It happened to be exactly what management finally came up with: let the so-called volunteers paint the last two hours of their shift and get paid. This is the solution management and labor could have come up with in the first place.

Management thinks the union isn't interested in good morale, but we are. The union only wanted people paid for their time and this would have been good for morale. As it developed, morale may have been adversely affected. Some of the disenchantment stemmed from the fact that the finance department got new offices and furniture at company expense. This may have had an adverse impact on the morale of people in the planning department, because they had to do it themselves.

The Financial Perspective

Brad Doyle, as Eastern Division's financial manager, was concerned about all the renovation work going on and planned throughout the headquarters building and the availability of funds to accomplish this work. In this connection, he had been involved with the renovations of office areas in the planning department at several levels.

In November, he perceived that he would be able to make $50,000 available from funds saved in his administration budget for the purchase of office furniture. He asked all department heads to submit their requirements to him and received the following requests: finance department—22 new desks and new executive furniture; operations department—18 new desks, new executive furniture, lounge furniture, and murals; construction department—11 new desks and new executive furniture; planning department—new furniture, carpet, and wall panels for the executive suite, and new colored partitions for the resources branch. The furniture and partitions were ordered before the end of the budget year and a contract was let to do the work in the planning department executive suite. Desks began arriving six months later, although the financial manager's new desk was not delivered until more than a year after it was ordered. The work in Hal Craig's suite was completed in six months. In the fall, the finance department offices, including the new furniture, were finally moved to new space in the building that had been repainted and that featured colorful murals related to the work of the various financial branches. This move had been planned for more than two years.

During the year, the general manager and the financial manager were able to secure an additional $250,000 from MCC headquarters to accomplish major renovation of facilities throughout the building. While only a small portion of these funds had been expended by the end of the calendar year, the financial manager knew that this money was scheduled to be applied as follows: expansion of the construction department and move into redesigned space formerly occupied by the finance department—$150,000; building new corridor—$30,000; renovation of loading area—$10,000; renovation of restrooms—$20,000; painting of the construction and operations Department areas—$30,000; miscellaneous—$10,000; Total—$250,000

The financial manager planned to make another determination this coming November of what funds may have been saved from various parts of his administration budget that could be made available to purchase additional furniture that might be requested by department heads.

QUESTIONS

1. Evaluate the perspectives presented by the union representative.
2. How has your perspective on Eastern Division (A) changed?
3. Would your answers to the questions in the (A) case change in light of the additional data given in this case? If so, how and why?

ROBERT FLEMING

ORGANIZATIONAL INCENTIVES

Robert Fleming was foreman in the transportation department of the Bayview Company Maintenance and Repair Center. The Bayview Company was a subsidiary of Giant Industries, an international conglomerate. Fleming had just received his second Outstanding Performance Commendation from the manager of the Center.

Fleming gave the following account of his accomplishments in the transportation department:

You know, as I think back over the past ten years, I think the company has treated me pretty well; but then, of course, I've treated it pretty well, too.

Six years ago this transportation operation was run by a manager. I was a leadman, back then, reporting to the manager. Then, he retired and I was assigned to run the department. The only thing wrong, though, was that I stayed at the leadman level. I guess I didn't hit it off so well with the company back then. But I was too impatient. It wasn't more than a year after the manager retired when management decided to make my position that of transportation foreman. Well, I was made acting transportation foreman, but after a few months I was finally promoted to the position. I remember the day very well.

Since that time the company and I have hit it off quite well. Two years ago, another allowance of 192 units of equipment was joined to our center's inventory with the accompanying responsibility to support another nearby subsidiary that had given up its allowance. Within the one year after that consolidation, we have reduced the total inventory of equipment by 159 units, without reducing the necessary support to all parties.

By improving methods of assigning and maintaining equipment, I was able to reduce our equipment by 22 percent and the personnel required to perform our Preventive Maintenance Program by 49 percent. This was during the first four years in the job. I accomplished this without any actual reduced workload of assignments. In fact, both the vehicle mileage and hours of usage were greater at the end of this period than they were at the beginning. These improvements reduced costs for maintenance from $886,000 to $605,000. I figure that's about a $30,000 savings for the Company on a monthly basis. Not too bad, eh? [See Exhibit 1.]

I guess the manager of the center thought it was pretty good, too, because he gave me my first Outstanding Performance Commendation [see Exhibit 2]. I also received a "superior" rating in my performance appraisal that year.

I think we've run a good operation here since I took over. We're efficient and the people have a good attitude. I've received several letters complimenting our operations (see Exhibits 3, 4, and 5). Once, I received a letter complimenting me on our operation from the head of one of the units at Giant Industries' corporate headquarters (see Exhibit 3). Yes, I think the company and I get along pretty well together.

EXHIBIT 1

BAYVIEW COMPANY MAINTENANCE AND REPAIR CENTER

Memorandum

To: Manager, Bayview Company Maintenance and Repair Center
From: Transportation Foreman
Via: Operations Manager
Subject: The Results Derived from the Giant Industries Cost Control Program

1. The objective of the Giant Industries Transportation Cost Control Program was to determine the actual cost of maintaining company vehicles and to establish standard maintenance procedures, whereby vehicles would be maintained in good operating condition for their life expectancy and eliminate the possibility of over- or undermaintenance. The control established by this program was standard hours versus actual hours taken from various flat-rate labor manuals used by the automotive industries for vehicle maintenance.

2. Prior to the Cost Control Program, there was no established procedure or control as to the amount of time or money expended for preventive maintenance service and the overhaul of company equipment. In many instances, automotive and construction equipment was being overmaintained with the resultant excess and unnecessary expenditures.

3. The Cost Control Program was established in our area early in its implementation by Giant Industries. The Bayview Company Maintenance and Repair Center was the second activity to go under the program. In June, the Cost Control Program was put into effect in the automotive equipment section, and in August, the material handling and allied equipment was added to the program. This activity pioneered the use of the local cash purchase and the blanket purchase order for repair parts.

4. Our center was used as a model activity by Giant Industries in that other subsidiaries and divisions were directed to visit and establish their Cost Control Programs in accordance with the procedures that were developed here.

5. As of August, there were a total of 1,653 units of automotive, material handling, and allied equipment assigned to our center. These units were the responsibility of my department for preventive maintenance and repair under the program. The people required to service and maintain this equipment include myself, 9 leadmen, and 83 automotive and heavy duty mechanics, for a total of 93. The labor cost for the maintenance of the 1,653 units of equipment for the first month was $39,674.45 for direct labor, and $40,707.30 for overhead—a total of $80,381.75.

6. As of December, the number of units of equipment assigned to the transportation department was 1,256, all of which were being maintained by the transportation maintenance shop. The people assigned to service these units were 2 leadmen, 5 inspectors, 14 automotive mechanics, 5 heavy duty mechanics, 4 automotive equipment servicepeople, and 2 laborers. The cost for the month of December was $28,200.00 for direct labor, and $22,186.84 for overhead—a total of $50,386.84. This shows a monthly savings of approximately $30,000 for labor and overhead during the period that shop labor wages have increased approximately 14 cents per hour.

7. These statistics reveal that there has been a 22 percent reduction in the replacement of units and a 49 percent reduction in personnel for preventive maintenance and overhaul for this activity.

8. This activity requires transportation support for a decreasing proportion of total personnel.
9. These savings are the direct result of the Cost Control Program with other Giant Industries' instructions, such as labor hours and miles per vehicle.

In the late fall, several months after Robert Fleming received his second Outstanding Performance Commendation, he was surprised to learn that the personnel audit group from Giant Industries' headquarters was reevaluating the scope of his duties and responsibilities as transportation foreman.

Fleming's worst suspicions were confirmed when he received a written notice of demotion in December. On February 1, Fleming's title was changed to chief leadman. (See Exhibit 6.)

As a result of this demotion Robert Fleming began to read Giant Industries' bulletins about jobs in overseas and domestic locations. He applied for a position overseas but was not selected (see Exhibit 7).

In mid March, the operations manager called Robert Fleming into his office to congratulate him on his continued high level of performance. Showing Fleming the letters he had received (see Exhibits 8, 9, and 10), he indicated that the great amount of recognition the transportation department, as well as the Bayview Company Maintenance and Repair Center, had received was due to the efforts of employees like Fleming.

After receiving these letters, Robert Fleming continued to read Giant Industries' bulletins and began to call on his network of

EXHIBIT 2

BAYVIEW COMPANY

Memorandum

From: Recorder, Personnel Department
To: Executive Secretary, Incentive Awards Committee
Subject: Robert Fleming: Consideration for Outstanding Performance Rating for the Last Period
Enclosure: (1) Correspondence between the employee's department and the recorder

1. After careful review, the personnel department recommended that the manager of the Bayview Company Maintenance and Repair Center give a performance rating of "outstanding" for the above employee for his performance for the last rating period. Accordingly, enclosure (1)* is forwarded for the convenience of the committee in considering subject employee for appropriate award under the Incentive Awards Program and for forwarding to the Manager of the Bayview Company Maintenance and Repair Center with the committee's recommendation for action.
2. A copy of this memorandum, and of the correspondence justifying the "outstanding" rating, will be placed in the employee's personnel file when action is completed by the manager of the Bayview Maintenance and Repair Center. A copy will also be furnished to the employee.

Thomas J. Dennison

* Enclosure (1) not attached

EXHIBIT 3

Mr. Robert Fleming, Building 543
Bayview Company Maintenance and Repair Center

Dear Mr. Fleming:

I am a senior staff manager from Giant Industries' Headquarters and have just returned from a field trip to your geographic area of responsibility. Last week I spent two days at the Bayview Company and had occasion to travel in your vehicles with your drivers. I found them all to be very efficient in their work and personally interested in my safety and comfort.

I should particularly like to commend to you Mr. John Barrows and Mr. Ernest Hanson. These gentlemen took me on long trips at inconvenient hours, and, by so doing, added much to expeditious use of the limited time I had to accomplish my official duties in your geographic area.

Please accept my congratulations on having people such as these on your staff—people who are obviously interested in performing their duties in such a way as to reflect most favorably on your leadership and on the accomplishment of their duties.

Most appreciatively yours,

Harold B. Lane, Senior Staff Manager
Giant Industries Headquarters

Copies to: Mr. John Barrows and Mr. Ernest Hanson

EXHIBIT 4

BAYVIEW COMPANY MAINTENANCE AND REPAIR CENTER

Memorandum

From: Manager, Maintenance and Repair Center
To: Mr. Robert Fleming, Foreman of the Transportation Department
Via: Operations Manager
Subject: Expression of Appreciation

1. I recently received a letter from the general manager of the Hartwell Subsidiary of Giant Industries located a few miles from here expressing appreciation to me for the loan of several motor vehicles during a recent emergency situation resulting from fire damage. He cited the transportation department of this center for its assistance in the release of these vehicles without jeopardy to the operations of this company.
2. I am indeed gratified to learn that you played an important part in this operation and wish to commend you for your courtesy, cooperation, and understanding attitude in making these vehicles available to the Hartwell Subsidiary.
3. Performing your duties in a manner that made the impression that it did on Hartwell indicates to me that you are well aware of the part which you play in making the total operation of this center a success. Please convey my sincere appreciation to those of your subordinates who may have assisted you in this matter, and accept for yourself my heartiest thanks.

Paul Clark

EXHIBIT 5

BAYVIEW COMPANY

Memorandum

From: Operations Manager
To: Mr. Robert Fleming, Foreman of the Transportation Department
Subject: Expression of Appreciation

Your cooperation with the Hartwell Subsidiary not only reflects credit on you, but it helps greatly in our public relations program. Your consistent attention to your responsibilities is appreciated and you are to be commended for your efforts.

Keith Alberts

EXHIBIT 6

BAYVIEW COMPANY

Memorandum

From: Manager, Maintenance and Repair Center
To: Robert Fleming, Foreman of the Transportation Department
Via: Operations Manager
Subject: Notice of Demotion
Ref: Giant Industries Personnel Audit Group Letter to You

1. By reference (a) you were advised of your proposed demotion based upon a reevaluation of your position, which resulted in a determination being made that the duties and responsibilities performed by and assigned to you were more properly rated at the chief leadman level rather than at the foreman level. You were further told that this determination was based upon a gradual erosion occurring over several years that had reduced the scope of the operations of the transportation department, which you supervise.
2. You were also advised of your right to appeal this action, but to date no appeal has been filed by you. Therefore, your demotion will be effective with the next payroll period.
3. In the event that you wish to formally appeal the determination as to the proper rating for a supervisory level, you should contact the personnel audit group liaison secretary through the Bayview Company personnel department. One of their representatives will give you the information necessary to file an appeal and can explain filing procedures.
4. In view of your many years of exemplary performance, the last eight years of which have been in charge of the transportation department of this center, the necessity of taking this action is very much regretted and is in no way to be considered a reflection upon the manner in which you have performed your duties and responsibilities.

Paul Clark
Operations Manager

EXHIBIT 7

GIANT INDUSTRIES OVERSEAS EMPLOYMENT OFFICE

Mr. Robert Fleming
(home address)

Dear Mr. Fleming:

Although you were seriously considered for the position of transportation foreman at our Maintenance and Repair Center in Munich, Germany, another candidate was selected. The Munich Center and this office appreciate your interest in this vacancy.

We do not expect a similar vacancy in the foreseeable future. Consequently, your application is canceled. If such vacancies do occur, notice will be given in the various Giant Industries publications and we shall be happy to have you resubmit your application at that time.

Thank you again for your interest in Giant Industries' overseas program.

Sincerely yours,

Roger P. James, Recruiter

peers in other subsidiaries to alert him to any opportunities they might know about. As a result, he formally applied for a foreman's job at a West Coast subsidiary.

In September, Fleming was notified that his application for foreman of transportation at a West Coast subsidiary of Giant Industries had been accepted. Shortly thereafter, he noti-fied the operations manager that he would be leaving the Bayview Company Maintenance and Repair Center.

In explaining his action, Fleming said, "I filed applications for job openings for transportation formen that appeared in various Giant Industries' publications because I felt the demotion I received was unfair,

EXHIBIT 8

OFFICE OF THE PRESIDENT, GIANT INDUSTRIES

Memorandum

To: Al Ritter, Vice President Maintenance and Repair

It was most gratifying to read the internal auditor's report pertaining to the repair and maintenance of vehicles and equipment in our corporation. I was particularly impressed with the report's reference to our administrative surveillance of transportation, repair, and maintenance activities, and the efficient methods of evaluating maintenance operations. The standards established in money and man-hours saved through exceptional management practices are in complete harmony with our objectives.

Kindly accept and extend my sincere gratitude to those people responsible for the efficient and effective maintenance procedures in the transportation departments to which you and your staff provide advice and support.

Sincerely,

Andrew Galbraith

EXHIBIT 9

Memorandum

From: Vice-President Maintenance and Repair
To: Manager, Bayview Company Maintenance and Repair Center
Subject: Letter of Appreciation

1. Our internal auditors have submitted a final report to the president of our corporation concerning the maintenance of vehicles and equipment in our corporation. This report was most complimentary to us, and pointed out, among other things, substantial cost reductions being achieved by us in comparison with other corporations.
2. The comments of the president regarding this report are attached. [Exhibit 8.]
3. Your efforts in the continuing development and administration of our Transportation Maintenance Management Program reflect great credit, not only on you, but on our entire corporation as well. I feel privileged to convey to you the appreciation of the president and in adding to it my sincere congratulations and appreciation for a job well done.
4. The report of our internal auditors will, sooner or later, find its way into the hands of our competitors who will attempt to achieve or exceed our results. The leadership of our people will be challenged. Therefore, we must continue our efforts to furnish effective transportation equipment support at minimum cost.
5. It is requested that these comments be passed along to your staff in the transportation department and to other appropriate people in appreciation of their significant contribution toward this achievement.

reflected poor conditions, and involved a loss in wages."

Soon after Fleming announced his intention of leaving the Bayview Company, the manager of the Bayview Company Maintenance and Repair Center decided to exercise his managerial authority and override the recommendation of the personnel audit group from Giant Industries' headquarters and reestablish the position of foreman of the transportation department. He called Fleming into his office. "We do not want you to leave, Mr. Fleming. If you will stay, we will repromote you to your old foreman level. We need your talents, and it would be hard to get along without you."

According to Fleming, "I decided to stay. Not because of the offer, but because my home was in the area where I worked."

Shortly thereafter, the job was reestablished as a foreman-level position and Fleming was repromoted to foreman of the transportation department.

QUESTIONS

1. What effect do you think these events have had on Fleming's job performance and job satisfaction? What actions, if any, should his immediate superiors take?
2. What impact do you think the events described in this case will have on the morale of other foremen at the Bayview Company Maintenance and Repair Center?
3. Has the manager's action established any administrative precedent that will be difficult to overlook in other situations?
4. What aspects of the formal organization affected the motivation of Fleming?

EXHIBIT 10

BAYVIEW COMPANY MAINTENANCE AND REPAIR CENTER

Memorandum

From: Manager, Maintenance and Repair Center
To: Operations Manager
Subject: Letter of Appreciation

I wish to take this opportunity to add my thanks to your transportation department. I feel very confident that you contributed an important portion to the corporation's fine record. I am well aware of the efforts expended by your people in carrying out their assigned responsibilities. Their efforts are reflected in the records, which show that our operations and maintenance costs are among the lowest in this area. It is a pleasure to forward these letters to you.

Please extend my congratulations and the contents of these letters to all the personnel in your transportation department.

5. What influences outside the formal organization affected the motivation of Fleming?
6. What influences on Fleming's motivation are controlled by his immediate superiors?
7. After being rejected for the Munich job what prediction would you have made as to Fleming's subsequent

a. job performance?
b. job satisfaction?

8. What actions, if any, do you think his immediate superiors should have taken and when?
9. Why did Fleming continue to perform as he did?

OCEAN DIVISION (A)

Ed Rice had been general manager of the Ocean Division of Mammoth Construction Company (MCC) for three months. With his appointment had come a firm mandate from MCC headquarters to increase the operating effectiveness and efficiency of the Ocean Division. In view of current budget strains, this mandate was consistent with increased pressure throughout the economy and the construction industry for improving organizational effectiveness and flexibility, while lowering operating costs.

Ed Rice was forty-nine years old, had a bachelor's degree in civil engineering from Cal Tech, and had been through the Advanced Management Program of the Harvard Business School. During his twenty-seven years of service, Rice had earned the reputation of being a creative, progressive executive, who could build effective organizations with a high degree of esprit de corps.

When Rice became general manager of the Ocean Division, he began immediately to acquaint himself with the history and performance of the division. He read all available documents and reports and held in-depth interviews with top and middle managers throughout the organization. He then personally familiarized himself with the operation by taking extensive field trips, and by talking with personnel at all levels. When he felt sufficiently appraised of existing problems, he decided to hold a series of conferences with his key people in order to confirm his tentative conclusions and to develop plans for meeting the tighter standards of MCC. High on his list of priorities was the major task of increasing the creativity, motivation, and performance of personnel throughout the division.

Within a few days, he called the first conference and invited the following executives:

Keith Pierce, assistant general manager
Lou Reed, acquisitions department manager
Al Will, facilities renovation manager
John Watson, planning section manager
Aretha Bryson, comptroller
Frank Ito, design section manager
Matt Lawson, acquisition projects manager
Joe Stock, construction section manager
Cynthia Andrews, utilities section manager

In conversations with these executives, Rice had been impressed by their openness. As a result, he did not set up a detailed agenda for the meeting, but hoped they would be as frank in a group as they had been individually. He indicated his concern over the morale of the Ocean Division and his interest in exploring ways of improving the motivation and performance of personnel.

Following is an account of the general discussion which took place at the conference.

RICE: I believe that the attitudes of people make or break an organization. In the short time I've been here, I've been impressed by the quality of many of our people. Still, I've come to the general conclusion that many people here simply aren't working up to their potential. Under other circumstances this might be tolerable, but as you are well aware, we're now under heavy pressure. In the last MCC review of divisions throughout the United States, we were given only an average rating. As I see it, unless we can come up with some good answers, some creative answers to a number of real problems, the answers will come down to us from corporate headquarters.

I'd appreciate your views on how we can improve the general environment so that we can bring out the best in the people we have and upgrade the motivation and performance of our entire organization. Perhaps we should begin our discussion by expressing opinions as to where we are and where we've been. If we can come to some agreement there, our future direction may become clear. Let me repeat that I'm interested in your real views, no holds barred. Keith, you've been here for almost two years and will be leaving for your new assignment in a month. What do you think?

PIERCE: Mr. Rice, I could talk for the next week about this organization, but I have lots of questions and very few answers. I'd say the prevalent attitude around here is, "Don't rock the boat." Although a lot of people realize we've got to improve just to survive, few are willing to take the initiative. The feeling is that it's better to play it safe than to risk innovation. This attitude discourages creativity since, in my opinion, to be creative is to take risks.

LAWSON: It's easy enough to say that, and I think it accurately describes our situation, but we have to understand how and why this attitude has developed.

PIERCE: I'm not blaming anybody, Matt. It seems to me that most of the people here are accustomed to executing policy determined by the corporation. The whole system rewards those who simply follow existing procedure. Usually, the people who get ahead here are the ones who do as they're told, and who don't ruffle anyone's feelings or upset the top management. They've discovered that the best way to hang onto one's position is to play it safe; these people perform their jobs, as defined, and are duly rewarded with automatic pay increases.

ANDREWS: That's only part of the picture, Keith. Remember, the general manager we had six years ago was an old bulls-of-the-woods type who ran this operation in a way which led to the development of that attitude. It's the bureaucratic and, if I may say so, the authoritarian way this division used to be run.

ITO: I've been here a long time, and that makes sense to me. Mr. Yabowsky, the general manager we are talking about, ran this division with an iron hand, calling all the shots himself. Although it was generally assumed, particularly at MCC headquarters, that our performance had improved, our morale and efficiency were at an all-time low. In my opinion, he killed the initiative of a lot of people; it just wasn't beneficial to take a long-range perspective or try to solve some of our deep-rooted problems. The whole emphasis was on fire fighting and pleasing

Yabowsky. It took this division quite a while to recover after he left. In fact, I'd say many of us still bear the scars of his reign.

REED: I think many of our middle managers fail to realize that the top management of this division has changed style significantly. They still look at us as they looked at the old-bulls-of-the-woods types like Yabowsky. Consider our last general manager, for example. He was very progressive and encouraged more independence and creative planning at lower levels. He attempted to push the decision-making level lower than had ever been permitted before, but few people took advantage of the opportunity. Managers seemed afraid to accept the responsibility for decision making. It's really unfortunate that more people didn't recognize his example or respond to his open and trusting attitude.

BRYSON: It seems to me that we're being too pessimistic. I think we've come a long way. The Management Development Program initiated by our last general manager and the training program for young people out of college are two steps that should do a lot for the vitality of this division. I also think our overall performance in comparison with that of other divisions is pretty good. Isn't it possible that since the MCC rating was a subjective evaluation, it didn't adequately reflect our relative performance?

PIERCE: I don't doubt that, Aretha. You've been at MCC headquarters, and you also have a good feeling for most of the other divisions, but after two years here, I'm discouraged. Maybe my standards are too idealistic, but

I really think we're not performing as well as we could or should.

BRYSON: I'll go along with that. It's just that I don't like seeing everyone take on a completely negative attitude.

RICE: I agree with you, Aretha, but I do want us all to let our hair down during these meetings, even at the risk of overstatement and exaggeration. I think we have a lot to gain by expressing our feelings, negative as well as positive.

ITO: One of the problems that's bothered me for a long time is how to hold on to my best employees. I can think of a handful of topflight people who went as far as they could here, and were then forced to look elsewhere for advancement potential. Many of my best engineers, especially the young ambitious ones, figure the easiest and quickest way to increase their pay is to move around. What's happened is that they learn the ropes here, and just when they're in a position to make a strong contribution to the division, they leave!

ANDREWS: Perhaps that explains why most of our middle management team is relatively old. They make a decent wage, and can see fairly well-defined pay increases until they reach retirement. More important, they have children and roots in the community, and are reluctant to move to a more challenging job elsewhere. It would mean risking a lot of security and having to start from scratch in a new organization.

LAWSON: It's not that tough, Cynthia. You have to realize that we're just one part of a large organization. Most of us know our counterparts in other divisions and at MCC headquarters. Consequently, a move to another organization wouldn't be completely new. In addition to knowing most of the key people around the country, the work isn't that different. Personally speaking, however, I'll admit that I'm not interested in moving. I've adjusted to this particular part of the organization. I know the ins and outs of getting along here and am fairly content, although I do worry when there's talk of consolidation.

BRYSON: Matt has hit the nail on the head. As I see it, most of the people here are pretty happy. Over the years they've developed a sense of mutual trust and cooperation.

WILL: Aretha, I think our present difficulties may well stem from the fact that some of our key people are too happy. They're so secure, so complacent in their attitudes, that I've found it difficult to get this organization moving. The only effective method of propelling them to work seems to be fear. Maybe we should roll a few heads around here to bring the deadwood alive. You have said they moved fast enough when Yabowsky was here!

LAWSON: We all know who you mean, Lois, but I can't believe you really propose going back to the iron-hand method of motivation. That never really accomplishes anything.

ANDREWS: I think we'd all have to agree that although some of our people are competent, they're not up to the demands that have been placed on us recently. Perhaps the easiest way to develop a better spirit here is to bring new outstanding managers into the organization.

STOCK: That's easier said than done. MCC policy and most executives implementing that policy emphasize promoting from within. Furthermore,

it's almost impossible to fire a person with more than fifteen years service without an extremely good reason. In any event, the idea of firing people, even in the cause of more efficient management, is distasteful.

BRYSON: I don't think it's impossible to eliminate deadwood; it's done every day. A number of people left here when Yabowsky made life miserable for them. But I think our first responsibility is to work with the people we have. We've got to make them realize that they're not doing their jobs properly, and then give them an opportunity to shape up and perform. The problem is that very few managers know what they can and can't do, and even if they do know, they rarely avail themselves of all the tools at their disposal. For example, they don't have to give annual increases as if they were automatic.

LAWSON: That's a good point. I've found that many middle managers will look to top management for support before exercising their own judgment. They're reluctant to make decisions themselves, particularly sensitive personnel decisions.

ANDREWS: Talking about personnel decisions makes me think of an exceptional engineer we have supervising the utilities engineering branch. His name is Emilio Santana. Examining his case might help us pinpoint some of the difficulties we've been talking about.

RICE: Excellent idea, Cynthia. It might help us formulate ideas on how to encourage similar motivation and performance among the rest of our personnel.

ANDREWS: I'd just like to mention my personal impressions of Emilio Santana. I was among the group of people that interviewed candidates for his position. During the interview, I was struck by the difference of his attitude in comparison with those of the other candidates. When asked how they'd go about their jobs, the others continually implied that they'd be guided by MCC manuals. Emilio, on the other hand, radiated a great deal of confidence, and indicated that he'd seek to innovate, to introduce the latest methods of doing his job.

WILL: I first encountered Emilio about six months after he'd been on the job. I was impressed with the way he stuck to his guns despite rigorous opposition to some of his new ideas. Furthermore, he supported his arguments with an impressive array of facts and figures. He's one of a rare breed who takes a broad view of his job, and I'd say that a good 25 percent of what he does isn't in his position description.

ITO: I'll go along with that. Emilio has taken quite an interest in our design work, and has made a number of important contributions. I only wish we had his services more often.

LAWSON: The fact that some of his work isn't included in his position description strikes me as unusual. My experience has shown that section managers are reluctant to let their people work for other organizational elements.

ANDREWS: That's true, Matt, but you know as well as I do that once Emilio is involved in a job, it's hard to limit his work, even if we want to. Anyway, I'm happy we've had his assistance on some of our tough problems.

BRYSON: Technically speaking, it is MCC policy that a person's organizational level be determined primarily by his position description; therefore, that description should be updated to include all the work he or she actually does. But with a guy like Emilio, my guess is that we'd have to rewrite his position description every few months. It's hard to limit a good employee. Moreover, I don't think we should try to limit his broad-ranging interests and abilities. A good part of what keeps Emilio going is the challenge of the job, and if we were to remove that challenge, he might become bored very quickly.

PIERCE: I understand that Emilio has applied for a position with the International Development Corporation. That surprises me, Cynthia. Is he unhappy here?

ANDREWS: It surprised me too, Keith. He just recently applied and we had a long talk about it afterwards. It's not a question of being happy or unhappy; I think part of it is money. If he gets the job, he'll get a substantial raise. Moreover, I think, the challenge of the job excites him. I imagine he feels he's gone as far as he can here.

RICE: What do you mean?

ANDREWS: Emilio learns pretty fast. He's covered the waterfront here, and I think he feels there's little opportunity for growth now. It places me in a rough spot. I think he's been treated exceptionally well. Few people get a promotion, two very substantially above average salary increases, and a superior achievement bonus within two and a half years.

PIERCE: That may be true, but the fact remains that he has applied for the new job. Why would he do that if he intended to stay here? I know

Emilio, and my guess is that he's shopping around now. It may be another six months, or even a year, but let's face it, he is looking.

WATSON: Well, another good employee gone!

BRYSON: I don't know about that. I talked with Emilio, and I don't think he's made up his mind yet. But the important thing isn't Emilio Santana; it's people like him. What can we do to keep them, and to encourage others to follow their example?

LAWSON: As a starter, I think we all have to take a greater interest in training and preparing exceptional people for higher positions. Salary increases are neither incentive nor motivation enough for these people.

ANDREWS: Getting back to Emilio for a moment, I can't see where he could go in this organization in the near future anyway. He's in the top level for his position now, and although he can continue to receive good salary increases, that may not be enough for him.

PIERCE: What a shame. Here we have an employee who looks as if he has the makings of a good manager, and our hands are tied.

BRYSON: True. Even though he may not have all the book qualifications, I think he certainly has the potential. He has outstanding conceptual ability and gets along well with people. Do you think he'd be at all interested in a higher management position, Cynthia?

ANDREWS: I don't know. I've always looked upon Emilio as a sharp specialist in his field, and have never thought of him in that light. Isn't he a little young for higher management? Why, he's had only four year's experience with us. Moreover, that experience has been in a limited area.

WATSON: Most of our managers are considerably older, and have had at least ten years experience, but there are exceptions. I can think of a few young ones in other divisions and, for that matter, MCC headquarters also has a number of young executives.

PIERCE: Let's get back to Emilio Santana for now.

BRYSON: If Emilio were interested, it would be possible to give him further training at corporate expense. I'll admit, though, that it's unusual for an employee who has been with us such a short time, but then Emilio appears to be an unusual employee.

LAWSON: What about the possibility of creating a job to fit his particular talents? I could use an assistant to relieve me of some of my burdens, and Emilio may very well be the one who could handle a number of broad-range assignments.

ANDREWS: Now wait a minute. Let's not get too wrapped up in Emilio Santana's future. Before he leaves my division, someone has got to find me a good utilities engineering branch head. They don't grow on trees.

BRYSON: Getting back to your question about creating new jobs, Matt, you all know that for budget control purposes, jobs are defined by position descriptions. To create a new job, we have to put through a deviation request to MCC headquarters and justify the position. Although it isn't easy, it can be done. We can create any new job we want. The problem is that most of the time we don't know what we want.

PIERCE: I'll say "Amen" to that!

RICE: Unfortunately, I have to leave for another meeting now. I think we've covered a lot of ground in our discussion, and a number of pertinent issues have been exposed. As I mentioned at the outset, I've met some sharp people here. I have a lot of confidence in the ability of people to grow when they know it's in their best interest. Somehow, I can't help feeling that top management is equally as responsible as middle management in the continuing job of creating and maintaining a dynamic environment. I'm going to prepare a detailed agenda for our next meeting, related to these issues. I'd also appreciate it if each of you would put your thoughts on paper so that we can begin to explore ways of improving the morale, creativity, and productivity of this division, both over the short term and the long term. Let's adjourn for today.

QUESTIONS

1. Evaluate how effectively Rice has
   a. learned about his organization and its culture,
   b. approached the change process, and
   c. started the senior people thinking about their vision of what the organization might become.
2. How would you describe or characterize the points of view, attitudes, and assump-

tions of the executives at the conference? (For example, considering the background and the approach of Rice, what is his attitude toward improving motivation and performance of people in his division?)
3. From the general discussion, how would you characterize the working environment of the Ocean Division? Is it conducive to creative performance and change? If so, why? If not, why not?
4. From the facts presented, and from your own experience, in what order of importance would you rank the factors motivating people in this division? Why?
5. Where does the initiative, the power to bring about both personal and organizational change and growth, lie (at MCC headquarters, with the general manager, with the section managers, with the individual, or elsewhere)?
6. If you were Rice, what would you do over both the short term and long term to bring about positive change in the morale, motivation, creativity, and productivity of your people?
7. List some of the problems and opportunities created by a change in leadership.
8. What did Rice mean when he said, "Somehow I can't help feeling that top management is equally as responsible as middle management in the continuing job of creating and maintaining a dynamic environment"?

OCEAN DIVISION (B)

During the week following the last top management conference, Emilio Santana was surprised by the unusual attention he received. It seemed as if several of the top executives were all asking him the same questions: Why was he leaving, and what could they do to hold on to him? Within a month, he received word from the International Development Corporation that he had been accepted, and thus gave two weeks notice to his boss.

Matt Lawson, the acquisition projects manager, had talked to Emilio several times in the last month. When he learned that Emilio was definitely leaving, he invited him out to lunch. The following is part of the discussion that took place:

LAWSON: I'm sorry to hear you're leaving, Emilio, though it's no surprise. I figured you would. I hear things in Rio de Janeiro really swing compared to this town.

SANTANA: You are funny, Matt. Though I'm looking forward to Rio, I'll miss the Ocean Division. It's grown on me. But frankly, Matt, I've had it here. Did you know that as soon as I mentioned leaving, everyone from my supervisor to the top management suddenly took a great interest in me?

LAWSON: Well, you're an exceptional guy, Emilio.

SANTANA: I was surprised at first, but then I became annoyed. It strikes me as both stupid and hypocritical.

LAWSON: What do you mean?

SANTANA: I've been here over two and one-half years. During that time, with the exception of my superior achievement bonus, no one has taken an interest in me or my ideas. Suddenly, when I decide to leave, people are swarming all over me. I've been pretty much alone here, particularly when I came up with new ideas that rocked the boat. People talk a good game about creativity and such, but when it comes to the real thing, suddenly there's no support. They get embarrassed, or perhaps frightened, and say "fine idea." but no one has ever really listened to me.

LAWSON: I don't quite follow you, Emilio.

SANTANA: No one stuck his neck out for me until it was pretty safe to do so. No one shared the risks with me, particularly in the early stages of a novel approach. A good example of what I mean is a job I did about six months after I got here. I still remember the gory details. I evaluated a proposed utilities maintenance system and came to the conclusion that the recommendations of the client's senior vice-president would have to be drastically revised. I talked to my supervisor, and she didn't understand what I was talking about. After I carefully explained the implications of what I was suggesting, her response was, "I know what I would do, but it's up to you." Frankly, I was confused and upset by that reaction. It placed me in a double bind. I felt that I'd be damned if I did and damned if I didn't. Finally, I decided to trust my own intuition and judgment, and I developed the facts and figures so that eventually I had an airtight case to present to the client. Even so, I waged that battle alone.

LAWSON: I know the feeling well.

SANTANA: It's taken a lot out of me to put across some of my ideas, and most of my suggestions have gone down the drain. After a while, it gets to you. I think this change will be good for me. I'm beginning to grow stale here.

LAWSON: This is the first time I've heard you sound off like that, Emilio.

SANTANA: That's because people only hear what they want to hear and can understand. When I spoke to personnel, the only thing they heard was that I was content with my salary increases and that I liked the freedom I've enjoyed. Besides, what's the point of complaining when you know that nothing can be done about it? I like Cynthia Andrews and most of the other people I've worked with. Still, it's been difficult because they've no real feeling for me or what I can do.

LAWSON: Well, I wouldn't worry about the past, Emilio.

SANTANA: I just don't want to repeat the past, and frankly, it's good for me to blow off steam. When I checked into this job with the International Development Corporation, I did more than consider the salary and the nature of the work. I looked at the people with whom I'll be working. I'm really excited because they appear to be open and relatively secure. I know I'll get a lot more support there than I ever did here.

LAWSON: Let's hope you're right. When you settle in Rio, drop me a line. I'd like to keep in touch.

SANTANA: Sure thing, Matt. Thanks for the lunch.

WESTERN DIVISION (A)

PLANNING FOR CHANGE

The Mammoth Construction Company (MCC) was facing some difficult economic times, which necessitated a look at all possible ways to reduce costs. Several years earlier, the Western Division had made significant savings by consolidating many of the facilities maintenance and repair (FM&R) functions at its various units located within a few miles of each other at one of the units and giving the new organization the name Consolidated FM&R Center. As a result, the company was able to avoid duplication of effort and, therefore, minimize operating expenses. At that time, several maintenance and repair functions and some personnel from these units were absorbed into the new center. No major problems resulted from the creation of the new organization, although some of the personnel became dissatisfied with it and were allowed to return to new assignments in their old organizations. In an effort to explore possible additional savings, MCC asked the general manager of their Western Division to initiate a study to determine the feasibility of further consolidations of the FM&R functions by bringing five outlying units under the Consolidated FM&R Center.

The general manager, in conjunction with the managers of the various units involved, then established a committee to study the reorganization. In addition, a working subcommittee was established with an individual from each unit representing each unit manager. The result was a mixed group of employees and management personnel. The first chairperson of the committee was Lou Tyler, the representative from the general manager's staff. He initiated the study of the proposed consolidation and in a short time established an agenda and developed a program that he personally subscribed to. However, as the study progressed, some committee members were not in agreement with the results or the proposed recommendations. They particularly objected to the proposed statement that further consolidation would result in an estimated yearly operating savings of $750,000.

Shortly thereafter, Diane Best, another member of the general manager's staff replaced Lou Tyler and took over as chair. While recognizing the disagreements within the committee, Best nevertheless attempted to go ahead with the planning for reorganization. A strong minority faction quickly developed and effectively stalled the work of the committee. No additional work on planning for a reorganization and consolidation of the FM&R functions could be carried out.

As a result, several committee members requested that the general manager appoint Craig Lombardi, the newly appointed divisional manager for administration, to chair the committee. To everyone's surprise, Lombardi was able to get the committee to produce a report in a matter of a few weeks. Several days after the report was published, Janet Feeney, the financial manager, got together with Fred Post, the division controller, and Jasper Carter, the assistant division manager, to discuss the results.

FEENEY: Well, Fred, were you as surprised as I was that the report came out so soon?

POST: Yes. I guess we have to give Lombardi credit for the job he did. There were a number of issues that could have developed into serious obstacles. After all, the committee had been at work for over a year and in a matter of a few weeks, Lombardi produced a report.

FEENEY: I understand that the report estimates it could cost almost $300,000 more a year to further consolidate the FM&R Center.

CARTER: That's right, but there was also a minority report from Lowell and Melcher that indicated the annual cost could go as high as $1 million.

POST: I guess that will kill the proposed consolidation. I thought the original conclusion of the committee was that a savings of $750,000 could be expected if the consolidation went through.

CARTER: True, but that was never subscribed to by the committee as a whole. It was basically Tyler's opinion and work, and although I think he did an honest job, he did not have the committee's support. He should have taken more people into the decision-making process. From what I've heard, he was rather arbitrary and didn't care what the members thought. He went ahead on the basis of what he thought was the best approach, not caring if any of the committee members objected. By the time Best took

over, the whole program had stagnated.

FEENEY: And Best was quite different, I understand; a brain stormer with the iron hand in the velvet glove approach that really irritated everyone. The situation degenerated so much that they all ended up shouting at each other to get their points across. There was no real communication at all.

POST: Yes, but there must have been a particular reason for several of the members to come up with a minority report.

CARTER: Well, both Jack Lowell and Gloria Melcher had a lot of experience in this sort of thing. Melcher was involved in the first partial consolidation of FM&R functions a few years ago and worked in the center for a while before going back to her former organization. She and Lowell both felt the consolidated cost estimates were too low.

FEENEY: Well, nonetheless, I certainly do admire Lombardi's ability to work things out. He's the type of person who can inspire people. He's a great talker and philosopher. I'm sure the morale of the committee picked up when he took over. If anyone could get the various members working, he could.

POST: Yes, and the fact that he had more organizational status than either of the previous chairpersons lent more prestige to the position. Also, Lombardi hadn't been here long enough when he took over to be accused of having any bias.

FEENEY: I'd like to drop in on Lombardi and get the full story on how he was able to manage it.

CARTER: Yes, and I'd like to get the general manager's reaction.

Feeney was able to visit Craig Lombardi later that day. The committee chair was quite willing to talk about what had transpired.

FEENEY: I just thought I'd offer my congratulations on the Consolidation Report. Of all the committee chairs, you were the only one able to get the members to agree. Now that it's all over, perhaps you will give me an answer to a question that I've thought about ever since you became chair. I was curious about how you felt about taking over with all the heat that had been generated. Things were red hot, but they seemed to cool off when you took over.

LOMBARDI: Well, I knew there were going to be problems and that it was not going to be an easy assignment. But I saw it as a challenge. I really planned to change the way the committee was functioning. I'll admit that I did not expect that we'd come up with a group consensus. But as we went along, things fell into place and we were able to overcome the objections some of the members had and to take the sting out of the proposal. One of the most important factors was that when they asked me to chair the committee, this indicated that they had confidence in my impartiality and felt I would not try to direct the committee to any particular goal.

FEENEY: But how did you change the way the committee was operating?

LOMBARDI: All I did was to bring more professionalism into committee deliberations. The basic problem with many committees is that they are too informal. Informality is OK for a two-way telephone conversation, but not for a working committee. Formality creates a sense of urgency. I had the advantage of observing Best's problems with the committee, and I wanted to make sure that everyone had an equal chance to speak and be heard. That's particularly important when a committee is made up of people from various organizations.

FEENEY: There's truth to that. Sometimes those who can speak the loudest and have the most status have their say.

LOMBARDI: Right. What I wanted was a voluntary interchange of ideas; the exact opposite of brainstorming. So to be an impartial leader, I had to achieve a degree of discipline. Although feelings were strong, the formal tone of the committee restored the professional relationships between the members so that they were less likely to get out of hand. Formality made it easier for everyone to contribute, and the sense of participation produced dramatic results. When each person had a say, we were able to get somewhere and to produce a report.

FEENEY: Yes, you certainly changed the entire tone of the committee. I think some of them were ready to use knives; particularly Melcher. It's amazing that it only took a month to resolve the various conflicts.

LOMBARDI: Well, all the facts were there. It was just that the information had to be examined and assimilated. Once this was done and everyone had a chance to express an opinion, it was fairly easy to recast the information so that we could get a consensus. In this way, the cooperation of all the committee members was obtained and, although some had been resisting the study, they fell into line.

FEENEY: Was there any reaction from the general manager when you submitted the report so soon?

LOMBARDI: I haven't really heard anything yet. But Carter seemed pleased that it was out so soon; he had impressed upon me the urgency of the matter.

FEENEY: I wonder what the general manager will say about the $300,000 it's going to cost.

LOMBARDI: I don't think that will make much difference at this point, really. The important thing was to get it done.

QUESTIONS

1. Lombardi feels that the committee's asking that he be named chairperson was a major factor in getting out the report. Would you agree?

2. What was Lombardi's concept of the impartial chairperson? How impartial can a committee chair be? How desirable is impartiality? Do you agree with Lombardi's concept of discipline in regard to committee operations? Is this the only approach that could work at this point?

3. What implication is there in Lombardi's statement that the cost is not important at this point?

WESTERN DIVISION (B)

Jasper Carter, the assistant general manager, met with the general manager of the Western Division of the Mammoth Construction Company (MCC), one week after the appearance of the report on the proposed consolidation of FM&R functions of area units.

GM: Come in, Jasper. I wanted to ask your opinion about the results of the report on consolidation. I must admit I'm surprised it came out so quickly after Lombardi took over.

CARTER: Well, when he started I impressed upon him the fact that action was desired as soon as possible.

GM: But do you really think the committee had time to fully weigh the issues and alternatives?

CARTER: I don't know. They'd been hammering away at the problem for quite some time, so there was really nothing new to discuss.

GM: True, but maybe the speed in getting it out sacrificed careful consideration of the issues. When we first got into this, it looked as if consolidation would result in a $750,000 savings, which seems natural, since a lot of duplication and wasted effort could be eliminated. But now it seems it's going to cost from $300,000 to $1,000,000 a year to carry out the reorganization, depending upon whose view is accepted.

CARTER: Well, to tell you the truth, I was curious about this minority report quoting the $1,000,000 figure. It almost seems as if Lowell and Melcher looked at every issue from the most conservative angle possible, and adjusted costs accordingly. They seemed to have placed the maximum cost on every phase. It might be somewhat biased since Melcher came into the FM&R Center when it was originally established. She was dissatisfied from the start and returned to her original organization.

GM: That is exactly what I had in mind. She may have had an honest bias that resulted in cost estimates that are not portrayed accurately. If this is the case, then perhaps the committee report is similarly biased. A lot of bad feelings might have carried through.

CARTER: Then again, Lowell doesn't seem to have any previous connection, so he might honestly think the costs would be increased. On the other hand, he has quite a few people working for him now and if his functions are absorbed, he would be responsible for far fewer personnel.

GM: Yes, but I don't want to accuse anyone of distorting a situation to protect his empire. I guess we should get together with Post to see what he thinks of the cost estimates. You know,

Jasper, I wonder if a new committee would have avoided this sort of thing, since it could have looked at the whole project anew without any bias whatsoever. Maybe the entire committee should have been replaced, not just the chair, and the study started over again from scratch.

CARTER: Perhaps, but on the other hand, there's no guarantee that the same situation wouldn't occur with other people. Maybe any result is better than the position we were in.

QUESTIONS

1. Is there any truth to Carter's last statement?
2. Will the review of cost estimates by Post provide any insights to Lewis and Carter?
3. Is there a possibility that when some members of a committee are biased, the entire committee will be affected?
4. Would it have been advisable to have formed a new committee rather than continue with the old one? What problems would have to be met in forming a new committee?
5. What creates difficulty when a committee is constituted of people from various organizations? How can a strong minority faction in a committee be overcome?

WELLINGTON
COMPANY (A)

As Paul Marks boarded the plane that would take him to his new assignment at the Wellington Company, a subsidiary of Giant Industries, an international conglomerate, his first impulse was to begin reading the file on his new job. He had been so preoccupied with clearing up loose ends at the Paxton Laboratory construction site that he had barely scanned the materials. Instead, however, he considered the three years he had already spent with Giant Industries.

Paul Marks had just recently become acquainted with the responsibilities and problems of on-site construction of new facilities for Giant Industries, and he was somewhat hesitant as he approached the new and different assignment. He reflected, though, that he had been successful in his last job, for which he had had no special training. More than likely, this one would work out as well. His first position after completing his MBA had been as an engineering management trainee where he had quickly learned the meaning and value of the unending paper work and the value of working with subordinates, superiors, and peers. His first performance appraisal on his year as a trainee had been a good one.

From there, Marks had been assigned to the Paxton Laboratory construction site as assistant manager for construction, where he shared responsibility for several projects, and

was given primary responsibility for coordination of planning and construction of an extreme vacuum test facility for space research. He learned basic supervision principles, and had five inspectors under his jurisdiction. He felt that this assignment had been a success, in a qualified manner, and that he had learned a good deal. The Paxton Laboratory assignment had been vital, challenging, and interesting. He had responsibility for many aspects of several projects, and had learned the risks and rewards of using unique methods and materials in a basically new, one-of-a-kind structure. He had to deal successfully with contractors and designers and handle a variety of legal and management problems. The major shortcoming at the Paxton Laboratory site had been his immediate superior, the supervisory construction engineer. From all appearances, this man had made no attempt to understand the management requirements of the job. His favorite gibe had been, "We engineers keep this business running so that you managers can waltz through and learn how things really get built." It seemed as if he often leaned toward the thinking of the contractor when differences of opinion arose rather than what might be best for Giant Industries.

Several hours later, Marks settled down in his motel and reviewed the material about his new assignment. He came across a partial organization chart of the maintenance department of the Wellington Company, which showed that he would have three supervisors reporting to him: Fred Kildow, shops supervisor; George Hague, supervisor of maintenance control; and Savannah Park, supervisor of administration and budget.

After studying the chart, he re-read the notes he had taken during a conversation with his predecessor, Lloyd James. In summary they said there were no major problems. He added that the president likes the maintenance department because the department got things done. James had briefly sketched the president of the Wellington Company and two of the three people Marks would be managing. The notes contained these remarks:

Moyer W. Latham, president of the Wellington Company: He is an old-timer who has been with Giant Industries for over 35 years. He works well with people including fifty managers and approximately five hundred workers. He always works well with those of us in the maintenance department. He seems overly attached to Fred Kildow, the shops supervisor, but frankly, Kildow gets the work done that the president wants done. Minor irritant is the president's habit of sidestepping the office of the maintenance manager; but he is happy with our work. He sometimes seems unimpressed with Giant Industries minimum maintenance standards, though.

Fred Kildow, shops supervisor: He is an old-line maintenance type, maybe the premier "scrounger" in Giant Industries. Difficult to control at times, but his friendship with the president is a valuable asset. You may have to close your eyes to some of his activities.

George Hague, supervisor of maintenance control: He is doing two jobs, is loyal, honest, and devoted. His papers are always in order, his plans and estimates accurate (but sometimes hard to live with), his reports concise. Keep him and Kildow apart; they don't see eye to eye on anything.

The next day, Marks reported for work, was escorted to the personnel office where he received his badge, and filled out the necessary papers. He had a brief visit with the President and was shown to the maintenance department manager's office. He then introduced himself to his staff and looked over the stack of work that had accumulated.

The first weeks went along smoothly, and Marks felt that he would soon grasp the job at hand. His relations with his staff and with the president seemed to be progressing adequately.

Three weeks after Marks arrived at the Wellington Company, George Hague, manager of the maintenance control, came into his office and began the following exchange.

HAGUE: Mr. Marks, we have a problem here that I may as well bring out into the open right now. The president has been after me to schedule a refurbishing of the executive dining room, but we have neither the time, nor money, nor equipment to do it. Yet the president says that Fred Kildow not only promised to get it done, but promised to complete the job before Thanksgiving. This is without any consultation with me or with Savannah Park. Now I like Fred, I wish I could get along as well as he does, but . . .

MARKS: Wait a minute, wait a minute. I really haven't yet learned the detailed procedures around here, so tell me just what's wrong with refurbishing the executive dining room.

HAGUE: Well, here's what's wrong. My job is to aid in establishing a budget and to plan and estimate maintenance requirements within the framework of the budget, and to write appropriate job orders for accomplishment by the shops. Since the president came here three years ago, our budget has not increased and we're not getting things done properly. The president and Kildow have gone behind my back and have ignored a lot of maintenance, but anytime the president wants something, Kildow gets that done. And some of the methods he uses! His scrounging has got us a whole warehouse full of junk, and it looks to some people like he's saving a lot of money. That's why our material budget is at $110,000, when it should be a lot higher. We're letting things go!

MARKS: What is it specifically that you're upset about? Is it the priority on the executive dining room job, or are we really missing out on getting some important things done?

HAGUE: If you'll come with me for a few minutes, I'll show you what's been overlooked in the last three years.

MARKS: Why don't you just tell me about it?

HAGUE: OK, but I do want you to look at one building.

They rode in Hague's car to what apparently was a warehouse. Inside Marks saw engines, parts, sheet metal, old air conditioners, chairs, desks, wall partitions, lumber, kegs of nails, and enough unidentifiable material to establish a small junkyard.

MARKS: (laughing) Well, it's all here. I'd guess that the inventory system is less than adequate, and that much of this stuff should have been written off years ago.

HAGUE: That's the point, Mr. Marks. All this material, even this building, is Kildow's private property. He's gotten it here by God knows what means and when the president wants something, here it is, to be reworked outside of budget and put at the president's disposal. This old warehouse was scheduled for removal two years ago, but the president has let Kildow keep his junk in it.

As they returned to the office, Hague pointed out roofs that needed repair, gutters that needed painting, fences that needed fixing, and the employee's parking lot that needed work. Marks was doubtful; he could not fathom the reasons behind this apparent neglect. He pulled out the budget, and asked Hague, "Where do we stand?"

HAGUE: Well, you'll note that there is no entry here for much of the painting and resurfacing that's needed. I pointed all this out to the president and to Mr. James, but they just ignored me. Now, let's take a look at our priorities. If you will notice, we're in the midst of repairs to the main entrance driveway, we're just completing extensive work on the visitors' parking area lighting system, and were replacing the entire hot water system in the main building executive offices. The progress is slow. Remember that all this has been scheduled, approved by Mr. James, and handed down to Kildow. But look what he does with it! In seven months we've spent $86,000 of our $110,000 budget, and still the executive dining room to do. We need at least $40,000 to complete these projects and keep the place running, but the President says not to worry, Kildow will find a way. The executive dining room alone will cost $19,000 or $20,000 for a six-ton air conditioner, carpeting, paint, a new hot table, and other items. So far, I haven't scheduled that work; it won't fit into this budget.

MARKS: But how did this come about?

HAGUE: You'll have to talk with the president about that. I'm at my wit's end. And we're going to get into trouble over some of these slipshod ways.

When Marks arrived in his office the next morning, he received a call from the president who suggested they meet the next day to go over the maintenance budget for next year, since it had to be submitted within two weeks. Marks faced the meeting with trepidation. He was uncertain not only of himself, but of his impressions of the Wellington Company, of the president, and of his key staff. As a result, he requested a delay in the meeting, and called Kildow into his office. His first question concerned the private warehouse.

KILDOW: Oh, that? Well, Mr. Marks, I've been in this job for 22 years, and I've learned a lot about cooperation. My job is to keep the company's buildings, machinery, and equipment in working order, to the satisfaction of the maintenance manager, the president, and the annual audit team from Giant Industries. In 22 years, my supply budget has been probably $3 million, and I spend it carefully. I cultivate local business people, various staff people at Giant Industries headquarters, and my contemporaries at other subsidiaries. I know every supplier and disposal yard in the area, and if I do say so myself, I manage my "procurements" rather well. I'd like to show you what I've collected for almost nothing.

MARKS: I've seen it, Fred. What earthly good is most of this stuff?

KILDOW: Well, I guess about half of it is worthless, but I never know which half. However, since it doesn't cost us anything to get or to store, I leave it there. Even the storage building was scheduled to be demolished, but the president let it stand just to store the material.

MARKS: That's great, Fred, but it looks to me as if we may be failing to keep things up the way Giant Industries expects us to.

KILDOW: I don't understand; every one of the last four presidents has been happy, and I haven't seen any maintenance managers get poor performance appraisals. We get very few unfavorable comments from the Giant Industries annual audit teams. I make it our business to keep the president happy and then I'm happy.

MARKS: But are we really maintaining the equipment and property at this subsidiary according to Giant Industries' standards?

KILDOW: I haven't had any complaints yet except from Hague. He always seems to be working at cross purposes with me and the president. He seems to have no concept of what work really needs to be done around here. It would be a lot better if he would spend more time on his job and less time snooping around my shops and interfering with my men.

MARKS: Still, it looks to me as if we're going to need an additional $19,000 or $20,000 this year just to complete the hot water system and the parking lot. And that doesn't even count the work you've promised on the executive dining room.

KILDOW: I'm glad you brought that one up. Several months ago, the president told Hague and Savannah Park, the chief of administration and budget, to put a priority on that job and they never got together. I heard about it, and I will get the job done for about $2,000 cash.

MARKS: How's that?

KILDOW: I've traded and finagled, and if you look in my store out there, you'll find all we need to add is labor.

MARKS: But what about the hot water system and the parking lot?

Paul Marks took Park, Kildow, and Hague with him to the rescheduled budget meeting. Hague and Park had worked all day Saturday to prepare the maintenance department recommendations, and Marks had made notes on work that had to be done. His total budget estimate was for $170,000. Included was $20,800 for completion of the executive dining room job, $15,500 to complete the two major jobs recently started, and $30,000 for deferred maintenance on a rather long list of buildings, equipment, and walkways.

After a brief glance at the major subtotals, the following exchange took place:

President: Paul, I believe we ought to get together. That list of deferred main-

tenance items includes a number of things that are scheduled for replacement, renovation, or removal. Have you seen the internal auditors reports on the backlog of essential maintenance? No, I guess you haven't. I see that the executive dining room job is in next year's budget. Aren't you going to get that done this year, Fred?

Kildow: Well, Mr. Marks here says we can't manage it, even though I've explained how we're going to do it.

WELLINGTON COMPANY (B)

As Paul Marks left the budget meeting, he thought he had learned a great deal in only four weeks on his new job as maintenance manager at the Wellington Company, one of the many subsidiaries of Giant Industries, an international conglomerate. He was concerned about the subsidiary president, Mr. Latham. He didn't want to upset an apparently stable work force, yet he was highly conscious of the need to resolve some of his conflicts. He thought to himself, at various times in the next few days:

I'm not really exercising control of this group or of the maintenance program here. The president knows his needs, the staff knows its job, and I'm sort of a fifth wheel. My engineering skills got me by as assistant construction manager while I learned management; but what's to manage here? And how am I adding to my engineering skill? I'm only a maintenance manager here. If I don't keep everyone satisfied my career at Giant Industries is down the drain. But if I press the president, I've had it, too.

Why did they put me in here? Even James, my predecessor was a far more experienced manager than I am. The employees here have had years to learn the ropes, and I didn't even know what a maintenance manager did until a month ago. I don't even know how to handle the president and the requirements of the job, and do both satisfactorily. What comes first, my responsibilities to Giant Industries or the president's desires?

It'd be nice if I were really needed here. But my boss at the Paxton Laboratories said it, and maybe it's true, "we engineers keep this business running so that you managers can waltz through and learn how things really get built." And here I'm not even learning how things get built let alone keeping up to date in management or engineering.

How was I to know my budget estimate would make the president angry? Was Hague sandbagging me? I'm afraid I looked awfully weak in front of all of them. Why didn't Kildow warn me?

How can I put up with Kildow's methods; even though he seems to get the work done? What happens when we get caught?

I wonder if Hague is really as good as I thought?

But as the months progressed, he felt more at ease in his job as maintenance manager, becoming both tolerant and fond of Kildow, and he was even able to restrain Kildow's wildest efforts. But his relationship with Hague had not progressed as well. He was unable to communicate with Hague, even though he had made many efforts to loosen him up, just as he had succeeded in tightening reins on some of Kildow's schemes.

Although he did not understand some of the president's methods, their relationship had

309

progressed smoothly, and Marks was an occasional dinner guest in the president's home. Over cocktails one evening, Paul Marks discussed some of his concerns with Mr. Latham.

MARKS: Remember last winter when we had the budget meeting, and I came out looking rather foolish?

LATHAM: Yes, I do.

MARKS: I can't remember ever feeling worse. I thought you would be on me for recommending a delay in that executive dining room work. I thought Fred Kildow would never cooperate again. And worse, I was afraid Hague would have apoplexy when you jumped him about trying to make me look bad by withholding information. I know now that was my problem, although he could have helped me. Maybe I never gave him a chance. I can't help thinking that I certainly was green then.

LATHAM: (laughing heartily) I'm not so old that I don't remember going through the same thing once.

MARKS: Yes, but my embarrassment wasn't the end of my concern. At least you were a line manager and knew what you were doing and where you wanted to go, but I'm in a position where the workers do most of the technical work and I'm left with engineering management tasks, whatever they are. I like this assignment and I realize that the work is important, but I'm a mechanical engineer and during the training program I learned to **coordinate** civil engineering jobs—my **first** job **was to be a** civil engineer, and my **present job is** to be a maintenance manager. Frankly, I've had no experience for any of them. I've been considering my future career plans, and I wonder how much longer I can go into

entirely new jobs where the people already on the job know more than I do. I'm honestly thinking of resigning.

LATHAM: We all think that, and it's healthy. But my experience has shown me that every step up the management ladder is difficult. I've held jobs that I swore I'd ruin, but as I look back, every one had its purpose; and best of all, I mastered them.

At Giant Industries, we're trained from the beginning to make decisions in times of crisis. At first, all the jobs are new, but each new move becomes easier because your experience helps bridge the gaps. But Giant Industries won't ease you into a succession of just slightly more difficult jobs. The aim is to make you jump further and higher, so that if crises develop, you'll be prepared to handle them. Years ago, when we were just beginning to grow rapidly, very few of us could visualize the conglomerate that Giant Industries would become, but that early training and growth policy, with all its faults, helped us organize one of the most effective conglomerates in the world. Our entire cadre, small as it was, handled fantastic responsibilities for which we found we had been trained. You're being trained in the same way now.

Every time I change jobs I run into the same doubts and uncertainties, but my experience and training have helped me face up to the old **generic** problems. I find that if I tackle **each job in a** systematic manner, it **works out well enough.**

A few weeks later, Paul Marks attended a policy meeting at Giant Industries' headquarters, and during the conference, he met several young managers who felt as he did about career choices. One of them, 27-year-old Arlene Rogers, was preparing to leave Giant Industries to rejoin her family's firm. In the course of the evening, Rogers showed Marks a copy of a statement she had prepared for her boss.

I had planned to make my career at Giant Industries, not only for the experience, but because I like it. But our family firm needs me rather badly, so I'm leaving. Mr. Charnley, my boss, and I get along well. He asked me for ideas on how I thought Giant Industries could attract and keep more good people. He's very much interested in recruitment and manager development. Here's a copy of a draft of my suggestions. [See Exhibit 1.]

EXHIBIT 1

The young engineering manager with a new MBA wants, and should be given, responsibility. And he should be given it in a situation where he can do something about it. He often cannot (such as when he has an engineering counterpart). That situation dilutes two people. Each uses the other as a crutch.

The young manager must have enough responsibility to assure visible results. There is a need for more and better feedback. Performance appraisals probably serve some purpose, but are not frequent enough to be really useful as feedback.

We tend to assume that young managers all have high morale. This is not a good assumption. They may more easily understand what's going on if they are talked to; it boosts morale just to know you're part of what's going on.

Leadership training of young managers is a *must*! Get them together. Spend some time on their development rather than just on their tasks ("Did you get this done," "that done," and so on). Their advice needs to be sought and listened to.

The project manager concept is good for young managers. It gives them responsibility and freedom to cut across lines: don't restrict them to the formal organization. They are depended upon to make decisions and do the job and report back.

There is need for more formal education, in some format that forces one to think, to give the young manager the opportunity to try something out without committing resources.

There is need for work (engineering) experience before assignment to certain management jobs.

The best bosses understand your lack of experience and respect your willingness to learn. They cool your overenthusiasm without "extinguishing the flame." They listen to your ideas and offer helpful suggestions—as suggestions (for example, "have you considered..." or "You might want to try . . .").

There is an urgent need for continuing learning to avoid technical obsolescence and managerial self-renewal to help all of us develop to our fullest potential, build morale, and so on. The ideal might be to return to a university executive development program for battery-recharging periodically. Include time to reflect on previous assignments and time to prepare for assignments to come.

CRISIS AND CULTURE IN CAMARRA

The International Banking Corporation's branch bank in Newtown, capital of Camarra, was a pleasant but rather small bank, staffed by eight Americans and twenty-one Camerran citizens, two of whom worked as assistants to the loan officer and nineteen others in various capacities from tellers to guards.

Most Camarran citizens were of two distinct ethnic groups; the Banus were traditionally landowners and entrepreneurs. During the colonial period, they took advantage of opportunities to obtain Western education and white-collar jobs, and they were generally more modern and financially secure than the rest of the citizenry. But numerically, they formed a minority of the population.

The Simis were the majority ethnic group. Traditionally, they were farmers and laborers, often migrating to places where they could earn wages to send back to their families in other parts of Camarra. They were slower than the Banus to adopt modern ways, and, as a consequence, illiteracy was high among Simis. Only in the postindependence period had they begun organizing effectively to assert political power through their advantage in numbers.

All Camarrans spoke the same language, but the Banus were more frequently fluent in English and/or French. In the bank, most of the Banu employees were in the better-paying white-collar and supervisory jobs, while most

Simis were semiskilled or unskilled clerks or guards. Ethnic tension between the two groups was a constant reality, especially because the Camarran government had an active policy of encouraging employers to upgrade opportunities for Simis—even with a rough quota system based on population figures. The bank was sympathetic to the Camarran policy even though as a foreign-owned company they were not strictly accountable to the government on the ethnic identification of its employees.

During the early months of their service at the bank, John Star, branch manager, and his deputy, Michael Train, had been critical of Harry Ames, the manager of administration, who spent hours running errands to various government bureaucrats. It seemed to his superiors that these were more appropriate assignments for the high-level Camarran employees who reported to Ames and that he was not demonstrating proper managerial behavior by doing these things himself. When Star or Train remonstrated with him for wasting his own time on such matters, Ames would tell them that he could get things done in hours that the senior Camarran employees couldn't accomplish in days or weeks.

His superiors gradually began to understand that many lower level government bureaucrats were Simis who delighted in giving supplicating Banus from the bank a hard time, but who would readily produce whatever was required if the supplicant were an American. They also began to understand that while local custom assumed that Americans did not have to offer a bribe to secure government services such as a telephone, Camarrans did not have such alternatives available. Invitations to a bank officer's home or to a bank-sponsored film showing or a presentation of books from the bank's library accomplished much. The branch manager told Ames not to tell him how he handled such matters.

A frequent source of difficulty among and between Camarrans working at the bank involved the shortage of transportation facilities in Camarra and the woefully small number of bank vehicles available to them. The "motor pool" consisted of one sedan, used most frequently by the branch manager and his deputy, two banged-up vans of doubtful reliability, a small truck, and a motor scooter. Since the only alternative transport available in Newtown were overcrowded buses running only during business hours, the vans were used to shuttle late-working bank employees to their homes. Like all bank vehicles, they were supposed to be parked in the bank compound overnight where guards could watch them. However, if a supervisory employee (generally a Banu) were to appear at night and tell the Simi guard he needed a vehicle, as sometimes happened, the guard would not argue, even though policy forbade any but assigned drivers to check out bank vehicles, and even clearly stated that bank vehicles were not to be keep out overnight. The Americans, who had their own cars, suspected that this occurred, but given the difficult transportation situation in Newtown and the difficulties of strict enforcement, they did not investigate the situation closely. For their part, the Camarrans involved were always careful to get the vehicles they had borrowed back to the compound before they were

needed the next morning. The bank self-insured the vehicles.

As the holiday season approached, the branch manager and his deputy had been serving together in this third world country for more than a year. The manager of administration, Harry Ames, was on vacation, and the other Americans seemed unconcerned about the events that transpired. The deputy, on the other hand, in the absence of Harry Ames, was acting as the manager of administration and found himself dealing with a major crisis that he believed might have considerable impact on the morale and the current and future effectiveness of the Camarrans employed at the bank.

The bookkeeping supervisor was Dars Gamba, a young, tall, good-looking Banu who was extremely popular among all bank employees, Americans and Camarrans alike. Gamba, in line of duty, was the major user of the bank's motor scooter, and on Thanksgiving eve, having obtained a date with the visiting sister of the American secretary, he took the motor scooter home with him in order to use it to pick up his date and deliver her back to her sister's home afterwards. At 8:00 A.M. on Thanksgiving Day, on his way back to the compound with the motor scooter, Gamba was hit by an electric company truck and died in the hospital four hours later.

The branch manager and deputy, along with other bank personnel, were shocked and saddened by this event. The Americans were particularly concerned, feeling that the rather lax attitude they had evidenced in regard to use of bank vehicles was at least a contributing factor to Gamba's death.

The day after Thanksgiving, John Star, the branch manager, met with his deputy, Michael Train, to discuss action plans following the fatal accident suffered by Dars Gamba. They decided that the regulations governing vehicle use would henceforth be rigidly enforced, and several days later, at a meeting of all the employees of the branch, Star read the new regulation that had been adopted:

> Only personnel assigned as drivers are to use bank vehicles. Each driver will be assigned responsibility for a particular vehicle and must account for any abuses in its use. Every mile driven is to be recorded on trip report forms.
>
> The hours of the duty driver will be extended so that the driver will be available to transport late-working personnel home at night. Only the driver will be allowed to take the (new) motor scooter home overnight.

These measures were given careful follow-up by the Harry Ames, the manager of administration, who returned from his vacation when notified of the tragedy. The new regulations appeared to solve the problem, and there were no further abuses of vehicle use as far as Ames could determine.

Early in December, a group of senior Camarran employees requested an audience with the deputy branch manager. They had been very concerned about Dars Gamba's death and it became apparent to Train as they talked that the morale and effectiveness of all Camarran employees, Banus and Simis alike, had been seriously affected by the incident. As the discussion continued, the major reason they had come to see Train emerged. They wanted to organize a representative group of bank employees to pay a condolence call on Gamba's family who lived near Jeganna, the second largest Camarran city some 150 miles away. Since the rainy season had arrived and the trip involved a four-hour drive over dangerous mountain roads, they requested that a bank van and driver be provided. The only alternative would be to take the overcrowded, accident-prone buses, and given the condition of the roads, the group was reluctant to resort to such an uncomfortable and potentially dangerous trip. In fact, it was stated by several members of the group that unless they could have a bank van, they would not go.

Promising a decision within 24 hours, Train dismissed the group and went to see John Star, the branch manager. He explained the situation to Star and strongly recommended that the group's request be granted. Star was concerned. Not only would the trip remove one of the two available vans from normal and much-needed service for at least a day, but the potential for another accident, this time involving a number of senior Camarran employees, seemed high. He preferred not to take the risk.

Citing the impact on morale of a negative decision and possible damage to the bank's reputation, especially among Banus, when word of the refusal got around, as it surely would in the closely-knit Newtown community, Train argued vigorously for a positive response. John Star finally gave in; looking Train straight in the eye, he said, "OK, you take care of it, but it had better turn out all right."

As it turned out, it took ten days for the group of bank employees to organize the 150-mile trip to Jeganna, where Gamba's family resided. The final group was representative of all bank employees, five Banus and two Simis, or seven people all told. By the time the group was selected and individual schedules worked out, it was Wednesday in the week before the Christmas weekend. Since the Bank's Christmas party for all employees and their families was scheduled for Thursday evening, the group planned to leave for Jeganna early Friday morning (a bank holiday) and return later that same day. Michael Train, the deputy branch manager, identified one of the vans as the vehicle to make the trip and one of the drivers volunteered for the job.

It rained heavily all day Thursday and on into the evening. Both vans were used to provide transportation home from the party for all who needed it. At 7:30 P.M. the driver of the van assigned for the Jeganna trip appeared at Train's home and announced that the van had fallen into a ditch. Train told him to use the other van to pull the first one out. Friday morning, the driver appeared again to tell Train the second van had also fallen into the ditch. This time Train accompanied the bank truck to the scene and a crew of people rescued both vans. By the time the assigned van was cleaned up, it was well into Friday morning and Train authorized the group to stay over night in Jeganna and return Saturday morning rather than negotiate the roads at night.

The drive to Jeganna was uneventful, and the visit with Gamba's family went well, including the presentation of gifts from numerous bank people (Michael Train had sent a gift at his own expense). The group decided to leave for the drive back to Newtown early Friday evening so they could spend Christmas Eve with their families. Unfortunately, a half hour out of Jeganna, the van broke down. The driver, unable to fix it, spent the night with the group in the van, hitched a ride to Newtown the next morning, and appeared at Michael Train's door with the news.

Unable to find the master mechanic, Train, without informing John Star, dispatched the driver with the other van and another driver to rescue the group, who eventually reached their homes late Saturday evening. The bank van was left behind, guarded by the other employee, and on Monday the 26th, Train sent the master mechanic by public transportation to fix it and return it to Newtown.

One of the senior Camarran employees came into Train's office to report on the trip and mentioned that Gamba's father, who was a prominent landowner, had suggested to the group that the nicest thing the bank could do for the family would be to hire Gamba's younger brother as his replacement. He also reported that Gamba's petty cash account was considerably in arrears. Gamba had been in the habit of borrowing from it and replacing amounts borrowed when he was paid, which he had not been able to do before he died. Armed with this new information, Train went to report the weekend's events to John Star, who was almost gleeful on hearing Michael Train's account of the Christmas weekend events. "I told you so," Star said smiling, "I knew you were going to be in trouble." More seriously he went on, "In the long run, we probably lucked out—you may even have done us some good." One easy decision, suggested by Train, was to put a letter of commendation in the second driver's file.

Two ongoing and somewhat tougher decisions were made during Star's meeting with Train. First, they would continue with the risk-taking policy Train had developed by hiring Gamba's brother. He was inexperienced but highly motivated; the extra time and effort the manager of administration, Harry Ames, would have to devote to training him seemed to have a worthwhile payoff potential. (It worked out just that way; the young man performed very well indeed within six months of hiring.) The petty cash problem seemed to be a little more of a dilemma since the amount involved almost equaled the final pay due Dars, and bank regulations did not permit writing the sum off. The bank handled this matter by the book, and the family of Dars Gamba did not protest. Gamba's father said that he trusted the Americans and that he was grateful the bank had agreed to hire his youngest son.

QUESTIONS

1. If you had been Michael Train what would you have done differently? When? Why?
2. How well do you think the bank handled
   a. the father's request that Gamba's younger brother be hired to replace him?
   b. the arrears in Gamba's petty cash account?
3. What factors in the overall situation need to be taken into account in making the decisions noted in Question 2 above?

4. Should Michael Train take any other action as follow-up to the events of the Christmas weekend?

5. Given the cultural conditions in Camarra, as described in this case, what would you predict the impact of Gamba's death would be on

a. Bank personnel, Americans, or Camarrans?

b. the Newtown community?

JOAN DUNN (A)

Joan Dunn, manager of the commercial loan department for the International Banking Corporation (IBC) subsidiary headquartered in Beta, the capital city of Hellena, was wondering what, if anything, to do about Ken Cook, her assistant manager of the department. Dunn had recently been assigned additional duties associated with a study of expansion opportunities for the bank into areas such as credit cards, brokerage affairs, and insurance activities. These duties would take her out of the department frequently. She would have to have someone acting in her job during periods of her absence, and logically, this would be Cook. However, both Dunn and the executive vice-president of the subsidiary felt that Cook was not qualified to handle the responsibilities of her job.

Dunn was disturbed at the seeming inability of the department to function properly during her absence. For example, on a recent ten-day vacation trip, she had received more than a dozen long-distance calls from her office asking her for instructions or decisions. When Dunn returned, she found that the office was considerably behind in its work as a result of waiting for her return in order to get questions answered. Ken Cook, as the senior person in the office, had been acting manager of the commercial loan department.

Cook had worked for IBC for 28 years in various jobs both at home and abroad. He was regarded by all who knew him as a loyal, hard-working person. Cook took pride in his diligence and once told Dunn that throughout his career, he had always followed the practice of reporting to work a half hour early and leaving a half hour after the end of the working day. Cook had an enormous fund of knowledge about commercial loans. His long experience, detailed knowledge and meticulous habits combined to keep the commercial loan department more up to date in its work than was generally true in other IBC subsidiaries. Cook took great pride in his work and rarely made a mistake. His performance appraisals commented on his strengths but for the past several years also recognized that he had reached the limits of his capability and was not suitable for further promotion.

Despite the fact that he was the second in command of the commercial loan department, Cook only nominally supervised the employees in the department who were citizens of Hellena and was not involved at all with the other four employees in the department from different countries. In fact, he showed no desire to supervise others. At the same time, he was proud of the status he had achieved after 28 years of hard work and devoted service. Dunn had noted, for example, that Cook resented and resisted any change in office routine or procedure that might be interpreted as infringing on his position as second-ranking person in the department. He tended to be jealous of the honor, even though he consciously avoided the responsibility. Consequently, Dunn saw herself as caught on the horns of a dilemma. On the one hand, she was reluctant to place "Good Old Ken," as Cook was sometimes called, in her position on an acting basis during the frequent absences she anticipated. On the other hand, she was concerned about the inability of her office to make decisions or exercise judgment when she was away.

In an effort to reexamine what she should expect from "Good Old Ken," Dunn reviewed his job description, which formed the basis for Cook's work. The description stated that he was supposed to direct the work of the employees assigned to him, substitute for the manager of the commercial loan department when necessary, make administrative decisions, initiate plans of action, and render effective judgment. Although Dunn had no complaint with the way Cook did the work that he normally did, it was perfectly apparent that he was not doing everything that his job description called for. If he had been doing the administrative and supervisory work he was supposed to do, the problem of the proper functioning of the office during Dunn's absences would not exist.

Recently, Cook had been the subject of discussion between Dunn and her peers in other sections of the bank. A considerable amount of pressure was often exerted on Cook by senior people at the bank, acting on requests from top executives of client companies or various officials of the Hellena government. They told Dunn that Cook was pleasant in their contacts with him but seemed to be taking a stricter view of the bank's loan requirements than was appropriate. They felt that approving a loan application "wasn't a big deal," and doing favors for client executives or Hellena officials helped build rapport and contacts of considerable value to the bank.

Dunn had discussed this issue with Cook in very general terms, and he had responded by drafting a memo restating IBC's commercial loan requirements, which he wanted her to send to all bank personnel. Although she felt that sometimes, during her absences, undue pressure was applied to Cook, in general, he was less flexible than he might be if he were not so afraid of making a mistake. She did not want to bring the idea of a memo to the executive vice-president, did not feel she could issue it herself, and doubted that it would serve any useful purpose anyway. This incident further convinced her that although Cook was technically competent, his unwillingness to assume responsibility (and risk) severely limited her confidence in his ability to act as manager of the commercial loan department in her absence.

In thinking about the problem, Dunn could see several possible courses of action. She could 1) try to develop some managerial skills and willingness to take responsibility in Cook; 2) try to have Cook transferred to another subsidiary so that she could replace him with a more capable person, although she knew that his shortcomings were generally known in IBC; 3) create two loan sections—one for secured loans, which Cook could run, and one for unsecured loans—and in this way, promote another staff officer who was younger but capable and energetic to head the new section and act in her absences; or 4) allow the situation to continue as it was until Cook's retirement a year and a half hence. She wondered if there were other, possibly better, courses of action she might take.

QUESTIONS

1. What should Dunn do about
   a. the proposed memo?
   b. Ken Cook?
2. If she decides to make any changes, how should she broach the subject to Cook?
3. How can situations like this be avoided?

JOAN DUNN (B)

Joan Dunn, manager of the commercial loan department for the International Banking Corporation (IBC) subsidiary headquartered in Beta, the capital city of Hellena, learned that the department was to be moved from the small main bank building to an adjacent building already partially occupied by the temporary group managing foreclosed property. Several other bank activities then located in scattered offices in Beta were to be moved there along with the commercial loan department. Dunn issued a memorandum to her staff, advising them of the impending move.

During the next few weeks, Dunn sensed a substantial amount of resistance to the prospective change on the part of those employees who were citizens of Hellena. She knew that the new headquarters would be larger and more comfortable than the limited space they now occupied. She was puzzled by the staff's apparent attitude. Dunn suspected that the dislike of her department's permanent Hellena employees for the temporary employees managing the foreclosed properties was the real source of resistance to the move.

As a group, Dunn considered her Hellena personnel unusually efficient and loyal. Most of them were permanent employees, and many had served in the corporate loan department for many years. As Dunn knew, her Hellena staff resented some of the more recent employees temporarily managing foreclosed properties. Some of these temporary employees had been associated with Hellena's former military government and had been hired as a result of considerable government pressure on bank officials. (In view of the deteriorating economic conditions at the time and the threat of government interference in foreign banking interests, IBC officials felt it prudent to yield to this pressure.)

When she questioned her contemporaries at the next bank managers' meeting, Dunn learned from those whose groups were to be moved that the various American personnel involved were not disturbed by the move but a number of the Hellena staff in all groups involved were. To fully examine the reasons for her staff's discontent with the move, Dunn called a meeting of the Hellena employees of her department. When asked, they raised the following issues:

1. Would the move require a reduction in staff?
2. Would the move affect the job security of the Hellena employees working in the commercial loan department? The temporary employees managing foreclosed properties were eligible for considerably fewer employee benefits than the so-called permanent employees in other parts of the bank. These permanent employees were concerned about losing these benefits.
3. In particular, the commercial loan employees worried that the move might affect their medical and/or retirement benefits. Hellena companies were far less generous than foreign owned companies in these areas.

4. As Dunn suspected, a major source of irritation was her staff's attitude toward the "johnny-come-lately" employees managing the foreclosed properties, whose salaries were generally somewhat higher than theirs (presumably to compensate for the temporary status and reduced benefits). At the meeting her staff referred to them as "totalitarians" and implied that their former affiliations made them incompatible with the interests of the bank.

At the meeting, Dunn told her employees that a reduction in staff was unlikely since the commercial loan department did not anticipate a reduction in workload. She deferred the question of medical and retirement benefits. After conferring with the legal officer, other department managers, and the personnel officer of the bank, Dunn issued a memorandum stating that the medical and retirement benefits of the employees would not be affected by the move.

Two months later, the commercial loan department moved to its new headquarters. Shortly thereafter, two other departments of the bank were merged, resulting in a reduction of three Hellena employees. Two of the three were transferred elsewhere within the bank. The transferred employees did not lose their medical or retirement benefits.

During the following month, the two managers of the temporary employees handling foreclosed properties commented to Dunn on the arrogant attitude that the permanent Hellena employees in the commercial loan department had toward their temporary employees. Dunn was reluctant to take action. Ken Cook, her deputy, had already reported to her that employee morale in the commercial loan department had degenerated since the move, and she felt that her people should have time to adjust to their new circumstances before she tried to discipline them.

Her reluctance to act stemmed from two other situations affecting the morale in her department: one involved her own department, the other the public relations department. Prior to the move, there were two Hellena employees who handled the problems associated with the administration of commercial loans to subsidiaries of U.S. companies where those companies, in effect, guaranteed the loans. One of these Hellena employees was a grade level above and informally supervised the other one. The more senior of the two unexpectedly decided to retire, coincident with the move. Dunn felt sure that the individual preferred retirement to adjusting to the move.

After looking at the situation, including the budget constraints of the bank and the projected work load, the personnel officer, the vice-president for administration, and the executive vice-president had urged Dunn not to replace this retiree but to try to get along with the one Hellena employee, supplemented from time to time by other employees of the department when the workload permitted. Dunn had strongly opposed this move but finally felt she had to acquiesce.

Since the remaining Hellena employee would now be required to do the work of the more senior employee as well as his own, Dunn wrote a letter to the personnel officer requesting promotion of the remaining employee at the time of the move. The day before the move, Dunn received a letter from the personnel officer stating that the job of the retiring employee had been overclassified for many years in comparison to comparable positions in other banks in Hellena and, therefore, the personnel officer could not support the promotion. Therefore, Dunn's request was formally disapproved.

Because of the problems associated with the move, a week passed before Dunn was able to discuss the situation with the personnel officer. As a result of this discussion, the personnel officer suggested that Dunn rewrite the job description and resubmit the request. This took considerable effort but was finally done two months later. One week later, Dunn received a letter from the personnel officer again stating that her request was denied because the new job description still did not justify the promotion compared to other foreign banks in Hellena.

Dunn was particularly disturbed by this incident because of another one in the public relations department. The bank published a monthly newsletter for business executives in Hellena in both languages in common use. The translator of Hellena's minority language had also chosen to retire rather than face the move. The job was an important and demanding one since proficiency in three languages was required: the country's minority language, its majority language, and English. None of the other translators in the public relations department could qualify so the bank advertised locally. Ten people responded but only one had the necessary level of fluency. The vice-president for public relations planned to pay the qualifying applicant on the same salary level as the translator who left. The applicant was to be retained on a provisional basis for one year and then become permanent in accordance with standard bank policy.

Dunn was concerned about the effect this could have on the morale and attitudes in her department. The new translator in public relations would have a higher salary scale than all other Hellena employees of the translation section with the exception of the section manager. Dunn understood that all previous translators had entered public relations at a lower salary scale. Dunn felt it was unfair for the new translator to start off with a salary scale that his predecessor had obtained only after many years of service, particularly in view of the problems she was having promoting her employee.

Ms. Dunn realized that the operations of the public relations department would be seriously handicapped without the services of a minority translator, but did not feel their need was any greater than that of her department. She also felt that making the new translator a provisional employee was a mistake and that he would undoubtedly be subject to a certain amount of ill will from the permanent employees. In light of her employees' attitudes and their behavior since the move, this reaction seemed more than likely.

QUESTIONS

1. If you were Dunn, what would you do about
   a. the refusal of the personnel officer to approve the promotion?
   b. the hiring of the new translator by public relations?
2. What action, if any, would you take relative to the attitudes and morale of the Hellena employees in the commercial loan department?
3. If you were Dunn, what could you have done to avoid these problems?

HENRY HALE (A)

Two weeks after arriving as the new executive vice-president of the Karina subsidiary of the International Minerals Corporation (IMC), Henry Hale was trying to decide just how far he should go in solving some obvious managerial problems before bringing them to the president's attention.

This subsidiary of IMC was one of the largest at which Hale had served in his 23 years with IMC. He had come to Karina from a staff position at IMC headquarters. His previous job history with IMC included line jobs in operations, administration, and engineering in various technical capacities. His only previous experience as a manager was in a small engineering department in a European subsidiary mainly concerned with former colonies of the home country.

Before his assignment as executive vice-president, Hale had known the president of the Karina subsidiary, Chris Street, mostly by reputation. Street was sixty-four and had served in various executive assignments at IMC headquarters and at subsidiaries in Latin America and the Middle East. Hale had heard Street described as a "near genius," "erratic but brilliant," and "a superb negotiator with foreign political leaders in protecting IMC interests." Street's handling of a sensitive situation during a political coup in one country was widely recognized for its skill and effectiveness. Hale knew the president would retire in five months when he reached sixty-five.

When Hale arrived in Karina, President Street met his plane and introduced him to key members of the staff. Street drove Hale to the house IMC provided to its executive vice-president, where he talked to Hale for about two hours, filling him in on the major problems of the company, including the important oil refinery construction project that was underway.

"I'll be tied up almost exclusively with this refinery construction project for another couple of weeks," the president had said, "but after that we can really sit down and make some plans. Meanwhile, you just go ahead and work into the company any way you see fit. Keep in touch with me. And don't worry about the staff; they're all good people." When Street left, Hale felt fully informed about the oil refinery construction project, but he wondered how much he would be seeing of the president in the coming months, and even more, he wondered what his own role at the company should be.

The day after he arrived, Hale asked the chief engineer, Jack Lee, to brief him on the various projects in Karina. He listened for almost an hour to what he thought was an extremely lucid and penetrating presentation of the various mineral related projects the company had undertaken in Karina and how these contributed to IMC goals and master plans. Lee described the political situation as it affected IMC interests. The governing party was a coalition of conservative groups, headed by a revered elderly soldier, that encouraged mineral development. Its principal opposition was the recently formed Liberal-Progressive party, which was hostile to what it perceived as "exploitation" and which contained some, as Lee put it, "hot-headed" groups whose behavior was unpredictable at best, if not tending toward violence. Lee spoke of the problems associated with the construction of the refinery and the potential pollution that it might cause. Although the current government strongly favored the refinery, the opposition just as strongly opposed it.

Lee also described sketchily the work of the personnel department in hiring and training Karina citizens to operate the new refinery when completed. He suggested that Hale consult with the vice-president of personnel for a more complete picture of the situation.

After Lee left, Hale asked his secretary to get him all information the company had acquired on the Liberal-Progressive party and its leaders. He suggested that she contact the U.S. ambassador for additional information that might be of value to the company. His secretary returned half an hour later with an armful of folders.

"Here are most of the files we have," she said. "We couldn't seem to find the information we receive periodically from the U.S. ambassador, but the file room people are still looking." Late that afternoon, when the U.S. ambassador's materials had still not appeared, Hale asked Sue Park, the vice-president for administration, to do what she could to find them. The following morning, just before noon, the missing files were delivered to Hale's desk.

After lunch, Hale was briefed by the vice-president for operations, Jeff White, who told him that the personnel department had been working on the hiring and training of Karina employees to operate the refinery for about six months with limited success. Specialists had been trained at refineries owned by IMC in other countries, but the effort had not been as successful here in Karina as had

been hoped. IMC had clearly had considerably more success in hiring and training Karina employees for the production of iron ore for export. White acknowledged the lack of coordination between the operations and personnel departments, but went on to observe that this lack of coordination between departments was common throughout the company and was a reflection of President Street's management style. The president rarely held staff meetings at all, let alone any regular staff meetings. Although Hale's predecessor had held weekly staff meetings to which the heads of all the departments in the company were invited, the personnel department was only rarely represented. Because of expanding requirements of other departments, the personnel offices were moved to a location four miles away from the main company headquarters building, on the other side of the city in closer proximity to the source of Karina employees. Thus, White said, the operations department's only regular contact with the personnel department was through a trainee on his staff, Herbert Smith, who attended the personnel department staff meetings as often as he could and brought back whatever information he could pick up. White observed that President Street took a dim view of the personnel department and the "liberal" policy of hiring Karina employees even when they might be only marginally qualified.

Hale asked White whether he thought any immediate action was necessary on the problems of liaison with the personnel department. White replied that he thought not. He understood that no definite date had been set for operating the refinery with Karina employees, and he suggested waiting until Hale himself had acquired a more complete first-hand knowledge of the refinery project and the general business, economic, and political situation in Karina.

The following day, Hale was studying the company's most recent reports on ore production. He asked for copies of prior years' reports on Karina's ore production. About an hour later, his secretary reported that they could not be found. Hale sent for Sue Park, the vice-president for administration.

"Sue," he said, "this is the second time in two days that I haven't been able to get the files that I asked for from the file room. What's going on down there?"

Park replied, "Well, I don't have much to do with the file room directly. I know we're understaffed. Let me ask Joe Wood..."

"Never mind Wood," said Hale. "Find out what the trouble is and do something about it, will you? And another thing, Sue, would you please try to find out what's holding up the new furniture for this office that was supposed to have arrived last month?"

Park promised to check right away, and left. A few moments later she returned with Joe Wood, the manager whose responsibilities included the file room.

Wood explained that the furniture had arrived over a month ago but was tied up in Customs. He explained further that it was always very difficult to get things through the Customs officials. On the basis of his frequent contact with these officials, Wood speculated that they appeared to resent Americans and all the material things the company had shipped into the country. He added that despite the company policy that forbade gratuities, these would certainly help if they could be given.

Hale asked Wood to try to expedite the furniture and, in the meantime, to get some extra chairs for his office. Park and Wood then left. Hale felt that the delay in Customs was a simple, everyday kind of problem that should have been permanently settled long ago. Was it an individual problem that was really beyond the control of the staff or was it a symptom of more serious trouble? Hale determined to keep his eyes and ears open.

The following week, Hale was visited by an old friend, Paul Carr, manager of the mines at Theta, the major ore producing area in Karina. Carr had joined IMC a year or two after Hale. They had served at the same subsidiary on several occasions and their paths had crossed frequently during various IMC functions. Carr was on vacation and had stopped in to say hello. He expressed hope that with Hale at the subsidiary headquarters, the problems he was encountering at the mines would finally get some attention.

Carr explained that the people at the mines felt isolated, ignored, and even oppressed by the headquarters. They sent regular reports and requests to the headquarters but never received any comments about them, nor any guidance on the kind or quantity of justification data that the headquarters needed. They received information copies of the headquarters' reports to IMC only at irregular intervals, when they received them at all. They had no budgets of their own and they received no financial plans, bench marks, or estimates of the funds they could count on for their operations.

"We have to requisition everything," Carr said, "and we hardly ever get anything. We haven't had any money for tool replacements for about six months now; we keep asking for it, and your budget boy, Scott, keeps turning us down." Carr had tried several times, always unsuccessfully, to get some consideration for the needs of his people at the mines, and he hoped that Hale would be able to do something about it.

The next day, Hale called an informal meeting of four of the department managers. He told them he wanted to bring himself up to date on relations between the headquarters and the various outlying company operations. He asked for a summary of the procedures for dealing with these operations, including the budgeting procedures, the distribution of operational reports within the subsidiary and its outlying operations, the policy and planning guidance that was furnished to the outlying operations, and the number and frequency of headquarters information reports sent to the outlying operations. Both the chief engineer and the vice-president of operations stated that they had no formal budgeting procedures nor list of regular reports for the outlying operations because they felt that the headquarters staff could handle these matters more effectively. The outlying operations had little complexity or variability, they said, and the budgeting and operational reporting was more efficiently handled on a centralized basis at subsidiary headquarters. Neither official was sure what information went from the headquarters to the outlying operations; White thought that his department sent the monthly production reports.

Hale then mentioned a report that he had been reading that morning on the solutions to the difficulties the company had been having with the Karina bureaucracy in the construction of the refinery. He turned to the chief engineer and observed that he thought it was an awfully good report. Lee agreed and said that the writer, Ed Blake, always did a first-rate job. Hale asked Lee to have Blake drop by that afternoon so he could discuss the report with him.

In the middle of the afternoon, Lee himself appeared at the door of Hale's office and explained that she had just found out that Blake was with President Street at the construction site, working on another bureaucratic glitch. Lee explained further that President Street frequently went to the construction site or stayed at home and did his work there.

"Didn't you know Blake was there?" Hale asked.

"No," Lee smiled. "The old man does this every now and then. When he wants someone, he just reaches down and yanks him off whatever he's doing without a word to anyone else. When I found out that he'd taken Blake, I thought I might tip you off about this habit of his, in case you hadn't heard. It's not unusual around here."

"Thanks. Should I try to do something about it?" Hale queried.

"I don't think there's much you *can* do," Lee observed. "That's the way President Street works and we just have to play along. We haven't seen him around here but once in the past two months anyway." Hale remembered that he had not seen the president since he had arrived over ten days before.

On the following Monday, Hale asked for all correspondence between the headquarters and the outlying operations for the past year. The complete set of files was delivered to his office in fifteen minutes. The correspondence seemed to confirm Carr's complaint about tightfisted budget and fiscal policies at the headquarters. The mines office had sent four requests for replacement tool funds in the past year; all but one had been turned down. Hale sent for the vice-president for administration, Sue Park, and asked her to bring Bob Scott, the man responsible for processing budget and fiscal affairs with her.

When the two arrived, Park handed Hale a letter, which Hale scanned. It was a request for the employment of two additional file clerks for the administration department. It also recommended the hiring of an additional engineer for the operations department. The request suggested that the new engineer could be obtained by transferring an engineer from the mining operation to the operations department at the subsidiary headquarters. It was addressed to the IMC personnel department and signed by Park.

"Hold onto this for the time being, Sue," Hale said. "I'd like to talk about it with you. I'm not sure that this is the way to handle the problem. First, let's take up this other thing. I've been looking over our correspondence with the mining operation and I find that we've been refusing funds for tool replacement pretty consistently. Why is that?"

Park seemed surprised. She turned to Scott. Scott said, "I felt the mining operation had been asking for more funds than it really needed. There was only so much money and it could just as well be used for other things."

"What other things?" Hale asked. Then his telephone rang. It was Jack Lee, the chief engineer.

"Something important has come up," Lee said. "I'd like to see you right away."

Hale dismissed Park and Scott. Lee arrived, accompanied by Ed Blake.

"Blake here has just been talking to the local police detective. Tell him what happened, Ed."

Blake said that after discussing a minor problem, the detective mentioned a confidential investigation that posed the probability of the radical left engaging in some form of terrorism to damage the new refinery before it can be completed. Blake learned that the police felt the report was accurate and expected some attempt to be made to damage the refinery within the next few days. This report was receiving wide circulation in the various police departments throughout the country.

Lee pointed out that the report could have serious consequences for the company. The Liberal-Progressive party was fanatically opposed to foreign investments in natural resources and to foreign influence—particularly American—in any form. The political leadership could not lose if an attack were made. It would succeed in destroying or at least delaying the completion of the refinery, or it could use a failed attempt as evidence of how strongly the people were opposed to this type of "exploitation." Furthermore, many of the principal backers of the refinery in the governing Conservative party would not welcome the embarrassment this might cause. It was Blake's conviction that the attack would occur in a few days, and it would almost certainly be used to whip up anti-American sentiment and prejudice which could be turned against IMC.

Hale thanked both Lee and Blake and said he would like to think about it for a few minutes. He promised to call them shortly.

Questions

1. If you were Henry Hale, how would you diagnose the situation in Karina?
2. Which are the most important problems?
3. How would you deal with the situation as it now exists?
4. How would you characterize Hale's management style, to the extent it can be observed?

HENRY HALE (B)

Four months after arriving in Karina, Henry Hale, the executive vice-president of the International Minerals Corporation (IMC) subsidiary there, knew that the subsidiary president, Chris Street, was planning to retire the following month. As the time for his retirement drew near, Street focused all his attention on the completion of the refinery construction project, and increasingly left the responsibility for the management of the subsidiary in the hands of the executive vice-president. Hale had come to Karina as executive vice-president following three years in a staff position at IMC headquarters [see Henry Hale (A)].

Because of Hale's close acquaintance with the IMC headquarters bureaucracy and his numerous personal contacts there, President Street had come to rely heavily on Hale to manage the operations of the subsidiary. Hale frequently telephoned IMC headquarters without consulting Street, and headquarters people called him directly from time to time to inquire about the operational situation in Karina or to advise him on developments at corporate headquarters. Because of Street's complete immersion in the refinery project, as well as his imminent retirement, many matters for which the president was responsible were handled by Hale without consulting with Street. Hale was reasonably sure that the president was generally aware of what was happening, since he had been in Karina for some time. Further, Hale was confident that the president did not feel bothered or handicapped by Hale's independent activities.

President Street successfully completed the refinery project and saw it begin actual operations shortly before he retired. Hale became acting president. Business associates and government officials in Karina seemed genuinely pleased to work with Hale, and over the next six months he was able to establish considerable rapport with most of the senior government officials and his business associates. Hale was deeply involved in many operational problems associated with the new refinery as well as the outlying operations. Hale built up such outstanding relations with IMC headquarters officials that he was sent a letter of appreciation by the IMC vice-president for the region of the world in which Karina was located.

By the time the new president, Frank Stone, arrived seven months later, Hale had already solved virtually all of the problems associated with the operations of the new refinery. On the drive in from the airport to the home IMC provided for its subsidiary president, Hale proudly assured President Stone that the new refinery was one issue with which the president wouldn't have to concern himself. Hale described many of the operational and bureaucratic problems to the president, and assured him that they were all easily solved. During this first talk, Frank Stone smiled frequently but said very little.

Hale had learned from friends at IMC headquarters a few things about the new president. He was fifty-four years old and had just come from another subsidiary where he had been executive vice-president. Before that, Stone had been vice-president of the operations department at two other subsidiaries and had served in various engineering functions at other subsidiaries and in staff positions at IMC headquarters. He had had only one job at a subsidiary in this part of the world, and that was some eighteen years earlier. He was, by reputation, a quiet but highly competent executive.

The next day, Hale met the new president at the main entrance of the subsidiary headquarters building and escorted him first to his office and then around the building, introducing him to the staff. During the next several weeks, Hale made sure that the new president met all the important operating people in the subsidiary, the other foreign business leaders, and the key Karina officials. He often accompanied Stone on these visits. Although Hale believed in delegation and relied heavily on the chief engineer and vice-president for operations, he also believed it important to maintain his own technical skills and, consequently, he sometimes prepared short engineering reports. During the first three weeks of Stone's presence in Karina, Hale submitted two such reports to Stone for his approval. He was pleased when Stone commented favorably on their technical merits.

One morning, Hale received a call from an engineering vice-president at IMC headquarters inquiring about a minor issue involving the new refinery. As Hale was discussing this, he noticed Stone standing by his office door. When he looked up, Stone smiled and walked away. The following day, he received a call from an old friend and former boss who was now a senior official in the IMC personnel department. She had called informally to tell Hale that a close associate of theirs when they were both working in the same department at

IMC headquarters was about to be appointed executive vice-president of the small subsidiary in a nearby country. Again, during this conversation, Hale looked up to find Stone standing by his office doorway, smiling.

During the following week, he received several telephone calls from various high-level business associates and government bureaucrats inquiring about what Hale considered to be trivial subjects. Hale didn't think he should bother the new president with these issues. Hale went to several social events hosted by other senior foreign executives or government officials, including one at which the president of a major competitor of IMC was a guest, as was Frank Stone. He wrote business contact reports on each of these occasions as required by IMC policies and submitted copies of them to Stone.

Late one Friday, Hale's secretary brought in a copy of a memo she thought Hale might want to see right away. It was from President Stone and was addressed to all employees. It stated that the president was IMC's primary official representing IMC in Karina and was charged with the full responsibility for conducting effective operations within Karina and representing IMC in the business community and with officials of the Karina government. It directed all employees to obtain the president's prior approval before contacting any senior business person or government official in Karina or at IMC headquarters. This was to be achieved by the submission of a written request stating the purpose of the contact and the content or intent of the expected conversation.

Hale thought the memo was impractical, ill-advised, and unenforceable. He was disturbed that the president had not discussed it with him before its issuance. If Hale interpreted the memo literally, he would have to submit a written request to go to the dinner being held that night by the manager of the Karina branch of a U. S. bank since he knew that several high-level business leaders and Karina bureaucrats would be there. He decided to discuss it with the president immediately. Perhaps the memo hadn't been distributed yet.

As Hale walked toward the president's office, he could see Stone packing his brief-case, preparing to leave. "About this memo you just sent to all employees...I wish you had discussed it with me before you sent it."

Stone smiled. "Now you know how it feels to be bypassed." Stone stopped smiling and said, "It wouldn't have made any differ-ence if I had discussed it with you. I'm run-ning this show and that's the way I want it. You'd better remember that I'm the one who's responsible for the conduct of IMC's affairs here, not *you*." Hale retorted that he wasn't trying to "run the show," but he thought the memo wasn't enforceable and could damage morale. As he was walking out the door, Stone observed that morale was the executive vice-president's responsibility, as was enforcement of the memo.

Hale was angry. "Just what is he trying to pull?" he thought to himself. Stone hadn't been in Karina long enough to really know the operation functions, let alone build the kind of networks that were essential to operating suc-cessfully in a foreign country, particularly since he lacked any significant experience in this part of the world. Further, Hale thought bit-terly, Stone had made little effort to develop a working relationship with the subsidiary's en-gineering or operations departments or with his executive vice-president.

"This subsidiary has been running as smooth as clockwork since old man Street left," Hale thought to himself. "Why does Stone have to upset the apple cart?"

QUESTIONS

1. Why do you think Stone issued the memo? How do you think the other employees will view it?
2. If you had been Hale, what would you have done differently?
3. If you were Hale, what would you do now?

Henry Hale (C)

Henry Hale, the executive vice-president at the Karina subsidiary of the International Minerals Corporation (IMC), sat stunned as Ira Foss, a management trainee, confronted him over the latest performance appraisal he had been given. Foss demanded that the report be changed and threatened to file a formal grievance if it wasn't. Then he stormed out of Hale's office. Nothing like this had ever happened to Hale during his 26 years with IMC, and he was rather shaken by the experience [see Henry Hale (A) and (B)].

Ira Foss had arrived in Karina almost two years before to fill a vacancy in the operations department. Foss was then thirty years old, a bachelor, rather quiet and unassuming. He had grown up in the Bronx and worked his way through City College of New York where he had earned a prelaw BS degree. During the next four years, he had worked as a messenger in a medium-sized law firm in Manhattan while pursuing his studies at night until he finally got his law degree. After two years as a junior attorney, Foss had applied for and been accepted into IMC's management trainee program. When he had completed the basic management trainee's course (a six-month, intensive management development program), he had been assigned as a trainee to Karina.

When Foss arrived, Hale had interviewed him and had felt some uncertainty about assigning him to the operations department, particularly since he knew nothing of the Karina language and would be in frequent contact with Karina employees. Furthermore, the Karina bureaucrats were becoming increasingly aggressive in involving themselves in the company's affairs. The previous government had been very friendly to IMC and allowed it to function without any interference from government bureaucrats. Unfortunately, this friendly government had recently lost its majority in the Karina parliament and had been forced to form a coalition that included a recently formed right-wing party that drew its support mainly from the old aristocracy, or Royalists, who seemed to resent some activities of IMC that they considered heavy-handed. Hale had asked Foss whether he felt he could handle an operating department vendor liaison assignment.

"I'm not sure," Foss had said, "but I'd certainly like to try. I left my job with the law firm because I felt that it wasn't getting me anywhere. Work for IMC looks a lot more promising."

Hale had then discussed the question of Foss's assignment with Jeff White, the vice-president for operations. They had agreed that because of the urgent need for another person in the department, they should at least give Foss a try in the job.

Foss was accordingly assigned to the operations department and was responsible for the qualification and liaison of Karina vendors and suppliers (most of whom now supported the new right-wing political party). He was also responsible for establishing contacts with potential suppliers and business leaders with whom IMC was not currently doing business (many of whom were the old aristocracy that had, up to this time, avoided doing business with IMC). Hale directed Foss to begin studying the Karina language.

Six months after Foss's arrival in Karina, the annual performance appraisals came due. White brought his report on Foss to Hale's office; he had given Foss relatively high ratings. Hale scanned the report and asked, "Do you really think he's that good?"

"No," White said, "but he's just getting started and I thought this might give him a little incentive."

"Well," Hale responded, "I guess he's working pretty hard and he did a very good job on that contract dispute, but his main business is qualification and liaison with our Karina vendors and suppliers, and he still isn't doing too well at it. Let's call them as we see them, Jeff. You take this back and give him exactly what you think he ought to have, all things considered." White took the report and resubmitted it later with most of the markings in the middle range.

During the next few months, Hale and White found no improvement in Foss's work. After nine months in Karina, he had a good working knowledge of the language, but his efforts still revealed nothing that the two officers felt they did not know themselves from a routine reading of the local business press. Furthermore, they questioned his interpretation of some of the quality issues for which he was responsible. When White asked him about the contacts that he had made with potential new suppliers, Foss said that he hadn't had many opportunities to meet them, and that he didn't feel comfortable with them even though he was able to talk fairly fluently in their native language.

One evening, after a two-week absence from headquarters, White attended a local chamber of commerce dinner and took the opportunity to chat with an old member of the

aristocracy that IMC was now trying to cultivate. He knew that Foss had called on this executive during his absence.

"I believe you met our Mr. Foss while I was away," said White.

"Foss? Foss?" said the executive. "Oh yes, Foss. Yes, he came to see me last week." The executive frowned slightly and changed the subject.

White reported this conversation to Hale. He said that he felt that they had given Foss a fair trial by this time and that he just wasn't working out well in the operations department. Hale agreed. The subsidiary was understaffed, he felt, and everyone had to do his job well. He would try to find another spot for Foss. About a month later, a vacancy occurred in the engineering department. Hale decided to transfer Foss to this assignment where he would have to deal with fewer intangibles and where he might be able to use his legal knowledge more effectively, particularly with repair, renovation, or construction contracts.

Jack Lee, the chief engineer, assigned Foss to prepare the necessary documents for approval by the various Karina bureaucrats before various engineering projects could be undertaken. He arranged for Foss's introduction to the people he would need to know in the Karina government, in local banks, and in the leading engineering and construction companies of interest for his new assignment. Foss began this assignment as he had begun his first one: by collecting a mass of reports, pamphlets, and reference books.

About three months after Foss's transfer to the engineering department and while Lee was away on vacation, Lou Lake, a representative of a large construction company in the United States, visited Karina to talk with Frank Stone, the president of the IMC subsidiary there. His company was interested in bidding on some of the forthcoming construction projects he had heard IMC was considering for Karina over the next couple of years. Frank Stone called Hale and asked him to bring in someone from the engineering department to help Lake with his plans. He added, "This man is important, Henry. We want to give him all the help we can."

Since Lee was away, Hale called Foss. "Come up right away," he said, "Mr. Stone has a big wheel from the States in his office and he wants to talk to you."

When Foss arrived at Hale's office, he was flushed and breathless. "What's wrong?" he blurted. "Was something wrong with that last renovation project?"

"No, this is something about bidding on new projects," said Hale. "Let's go in. They're waiting for us."

During the conversation in Stone's office, Foss was extremely ill at ease. He prefaced his replies to Lake's many questions with apologies and seemed reluctant to commit himself on technical matters. On several occasions, Stone pressed him for more information, and twice Hale had to provide the answers because Foss professed ignorance. Finally, after what was obviously an embarrassing and profitless hour for all concerned, Stone dismissed Foss from the office. When Lake left, he queried Hale at length about Foss's work.

"Well," said Hale, "he is definitely not one of our best."

"Keep an eye on him then," said Stone. "We don't have enough people here to carry any dead wood."

When Lee returned from his vacation, Hale told him about the incident with the construction company representative. He asked Lee to keep a close watch on Foss's work and inform him if he felt that it was unsatisfactory. He wanted to give him a fair trial, but he didn't want any second-rate work being done by this subsidiary.

When the time arrived for the annual performance appraisals, Hale conferred with Lee about Foss's performance in the engineering department. Lee summed up his opinion of Foss's engineering work. His work, he said,

was detailed and thorough; perhaps too thorough. He relied heavily on statistics and second-hand data. He had few effective contacts with the important contractors or Karina bureaucrats in his assigned areas. He worked very slowly and meticulously. The documents he prepared were clear and well written, but they showed little evidence of independent analytical thinking, particularly about the areas of special interest to the various bureaucrats.

Hale suggested that they give him an unsatisfactory rating. Lee hesitated, "Foss isn't very good," he said, "but I don't think he's that bad." He cited in Foss's favor the excellent work he had done in the drafting of preliminary subcontracts that were of considerable help to the company's negotiators in dealing with the various subcontractors the company needed on the Magma project. After some discussion, Hale and Lee agreed that Foss had a number of valuable qualifications, but was not well suited to the engineering department. With Hale's approval, Lee gave Foss a moderately good appraisal and agreed to release him as soon as Hale could find another job for him.

At the next meeting with the department managers, Hale asked about Foss's role at the subsidiary. He was obviously out of place in the operations and engineering departments, principally because he seemed unable to establish any workable personal relationships with the Karina bureaucrats who should form the core of his network of information. On the other hand, he had a gift for detail, and he could assemble a body of impersonal facts into a clear, logical presentation. Further, he had a legal background that ought to be useful. Phil Young, vice-president for External Affairs, pointed out that June Williams, manager of the import/export unit, was scheduled for transfer in three months, and suggested that it might be possible to work Foss in as her replacement. He suggested that the work of the import/export unit might fit Foss's talents better than anything he had done so far, and he added that management would have three months to see how things worked out. Hale and the department managers concurred, and Foss was transferred to the import/export unit to work with Williams for the next three months.

Foss quickly mastered the import and export regulations and Williams reported that when he had to work with a Karina customs official, he conducted himself well. He was courteous, if a little stiff, and he always had the relevant data at his fingertips. Then, three weeks after Foss's transfer to the import/export unit, Williams was suddenly called back to the United States and Foss was left in charge. The staff of the unit, in addition to Foss himself, consisted of three American and seven Karina employees. The unit labored under a chronically excessive workload; it always had a substantial backlog of paperwork and applications.

Since Williams's initial report had been favorable, Hale and Young agreed to leave Foss in charge of the unit, hoping that he would be able to at least hold his own in an obviously difficult situation. In the weeks that followed, the backlog of paper work and applications in the unit grew steadily larger. In casual conversation with one of the staff, Phil Young learned that Foss was doing more of the import/export work personally than any of his predecessors had done. For example, he had directed the two staff people to submit a broad range of specific types of import/export requests, applications, and related documents for his personal review. He rewrote many of the applications himself and he was requesting information and assistance from the IMC staff in the United States at an increasing rate.

After about two months, Young went to Hale. "We're going to have to do something about Foss," he said. "The backlog in his unit is piling up, the list of applications is getting longer, his people are all complaining about

him and still he sits there going over piles of paper. I spoke to him about it the other day and he said he wanted to be absolutely certain about the facts in each case before he submitted the materials to the Karina bureaucrats for action. He said he would have to spend more time working, but I doubt that that's the solution. We'll be getting a complaint from the IMC staff before long. I'm due for a transfer in a couple of months and I don't want to leave this mess for whomever comes in to replace me." Hale told Young to think about the appraisal that he would give Foss at the time of his departure from Karina and, in the meantime, to do what he could to speed up the operations of the import/export unit.

Shortly before leaving Karina for his new assignment, Young submitted to Hale the performance appraisals that he had prepared on the people in the administration department. The report on Foss indicated unsatisfactory performance. Hale agreed with the report. About an hour after Young left Hale's office, Foss requested an appointment and Hale acceded. Foss entered and told Hale that he had just received his performance appraisal from Young as he was leaving for the airport and his new assignment. Foss felt the report and the way it was given was completely unfair.

"If I thought I was that bad," Foss said, "I wouldn't have any self-respect left. I think it's wrong. I just don't see how I could be that bad. I know I'm not the best manager in this subsidiary, but I think there are several others here who aren't as good as I am. I couldn't think anything else and keep my self-respect."

Hale pointed out that he had been given three different positions and that he had been unsuccessful in all three. He added that Foss had been given a fair trial, and while he didn't like to see someone given an unsatisfactory performance appraisal, under the circumstances he felt it was justified. Hale said he would recommend to IMC headquarters that

Foss be transferred to a position where he could make more immediate use of his legal training and his aptitude for detailed work. Personally, he said, he would advise Foss to resign from the IMC.

Foss replied, "Well, frankly, Mr. Hale, I think this is a pretty raw deal. Up until now I've always had good performance appraisals. I thought I was doing fine. Except for a couple of times lately when Mr. Young spoke to me about the backlog in import/export applications, nobody *ever* told me I wasn't doing my work as well as I should have. I thought when you transferred me to the different sections that you were trying to give me some all-around experience in the way a subsidiary functions. I still think I was doing better than some of the others around here. I think you're being very unfair. If I wasn't doing my work properly, someone should have told me so and then helped me do it better. How can I do better if no one shows me how? I think your performance has been unsatisfactory in the way you have handled me. I think that report should be changed, and if it isn't, I intend to file a formal grievance with the personnel department at IMC headquarters."

QUESTIONS

1. Based on your analysis, what are Foss's strengths and weaknesses?
2. If you had been Hale, what would you have done differently in handling Foss? How would you have handled the initial assignments? The first or second performance appraisal? The assignment to engineering? The assignment to the import/export unit?
3. What role should the executive vice-president of a subsidiary have in the career development of American management trainees? What is the role of the department managers? How should these roles be fulfilled?
4. If you were Hale, what would you do now? How do you think Frank Stone will react?

HENRY HALE (D)

Henry Hale, executive vice-president of the Karina subsidiary of the International Minerals Corporation (IMC), was wondering what to do about Kevin Bright, an American management trainee, who consistently failed to follow instructions and whose initiative and abrasive self-confidence had been sources of irritation to some of the staff.

On paper, at least, Bright had considerable potential for making it to the top echelons of IMC. Compared to other American management trainees such as Ira Foss [see Henry Hale (C) and also Henry Hale (A) and (B)], Hale thought Bright was intellectually superior, quite effective personally, ambitious, relatively unflappable, and imbued with a strong sense of social consciousness. Bright had confided to Hale that his moral idealism and strong personal sense of wanting to do something to make the world a better place had led him to join the Peace Corps. For two years he was one of a team of English-language teachers riding circuit in the politically unstable boondocks of Karina. During this period, Bright had developed a fluent command of the Karina language and had cultivated contacts with many dissident Karina citizens. After a two-year stint, he had returned to the United States and pursued graduate studies in management at the University of California at Berkeley Business School and earned his MBA degree with top honors. After graduation, he had applied to IMC, was accepted, and, after advanced training at IMC's Management Development Center, was assigned to the subsidiary in Karina.

Bright didn't seem to require as much attention from Hale as other subordinates of approximately equal rank. However, Hale was grooming Bright for more responsibilities at a faster rate than was usual through shifting assignments. There were objectively justifiable reasons for this special treatment. After all, Bright, by reason of his Peace Corps service, had a more effective command of the Karina language and a more practical knowledge of the Karina culture than any other American in the subsidiary. Moreover, he had an engaging, albeit somewhat condescending, personality, handled himself well in interpersonal situations, and seemed resourceful.

Hale's awareness of Bright's positive qualities, however, was heightened by ill-disguised hints from IMC headquarters that Bright's family had important connections on Wall Street as well as Capitol Hill. Bright's connections became well known to the entire staff of the Karina subsidiary. Hale was proud of his reputation for even-handed, fair dealings with the staff, and he was concerned that his treatment of Bright, if misunderstood, could lead to erosion of that reputation and possibly a decline in morale.

As his first assignment, Hale had made Bright the special assistant to the vice-president for administration. In making this assignment, Hale had several considerations in mind. Since the import/export unit seemed barely able to cope with the fluctuating workload, he felt that Bright might help relieve some of the pressure there during the unit's seasonal peaks. At the same time, he felt that Bright might help improve the operations of the accounts payable unit, which, in Hale's opinion, were deficient—the work was poorly organized and the unit as a whole suffered from too little direction. Further consideration was that Bright's assignment would periodically leave him with a substantial amount of free time. Hale hoped to use Bright's knowledge of the language by assigning him to additional special jobs as the need arose. Hale told Bright that he hoped he would be able to improve the operations of the accounts payable unit and that the special assignment would prove interesting.

During the three months following Bright's arrival in Karina, Hale received several reports on Bright's progress from Al Crane, the newly arrived vice-president of administration. Crane noted on one occasion that Bright had caused some dissatisfaction and unrest in the unit by attempting to reorganize the work flow, but he added that this situation now seemed well under control. Hale thought Crane was being somewhat defensive toward Bright.

Bright was given a number of special jobs during his first three months at the subsidiary. Many were considered routine or even "dirty" jobs by the older members of the staff, but Bright apparently enjoyed them. He said that they gave him an opportunity to exercise some initiative. One example was a personnel problem. An American employee of the subsidiary, a technician, had accumulated a number of small unpaid bar bills, finally leaving his IMC badge and U.S. passport in a bar one evening as security for his bill. Later that same evening, he was taken into custody for drunkenness and disorderly conduct. Several complaints had been lodged in the past

against him. Normally, the matter would have been handled by the company's personnel director, but he was on vacation and Hale suggested that Crane give the job to Bright. During the day, Bright had succeeded in obtaining the technician's release, recovered his badge and passport, and persuaded him to make airline reservations for an immediate return to the United States. Reporting on the case that afternoon, Bright added to his list of accomplishments the completion of his mission "without even having to pick up the tab at the bar where the technician's badge and passport were held."

In June, Terry Gold, the only American assigned to the shipping office in Zeta, suffered a heart attack, was hospitalized for several weeks and then evacuated back to the United States. Gold was not expected to return nor was a replacement likely to be assigned for at least six months. Zeta was a center of Karina dissident political activity, located some 150 miles away. The responsibilities of Gold in Zeta were not substantial. However, as the only IMC American there, Gold was the only current source of reliable information on Karina dissidents and the possible disruptions they might cause in IMC operations not only in Zeta, but throughout Karina. Because of his contacts, Gold had been successful in anticipating changes in dissident behavior and attitudes that might be threatening to IMC interests, and his advice had proven invaluable to the staff of the subsidiary. Gold had an extensive knowledge of the dissident movement in Karina, having lived in Zeta the first eighteen years of his life. He had a fluent command of the Karina language and fifteen years' experience in IMC. For all these reasons, Hale felt that Gold would be an extremely difficult manager to replace.

Faced with the immediate problem of replacing Gold, Hale considered two possibilities: Gil West, a junior manager, and Kevin Bright, still a trainee. While West had several years' experience with IMC, a good basic understanding of the potential threat to IMC's interests posed by the dissidents, and a fair command of the Karina language, Hale felt that he lacked initiative. With the shipping office located 150 miles away, it would not be possible to give West the close supervision and direction that Hale felt he required. Accordingly, he assigned the job to Bright.

In telling Bright about his new assignment, Hale stressed the job's importance in preserving IMC's interests and image. He suggested that Bright study the correspondence sent in by Gold after each contact with leading dissidents. While Gold's correspondence contained a substantial amount of inferences and interpretation, Hale instructed Bright to limit himself, at least at first, to a straight narration of the circumstances leading to his contacts. Further, he was to provide, insofar as he was able, a verbatim report of the conversations that developed. Hale and the vice-president of operations, Jeff White, would then analyze and interpret the narrations submitted by Bright to determine what, if any, action by IMC might be appropriate.

Bright's first letter, submitted one week after assuming his new duties, was almost wholly interpretive in approach. It did not include a verbatim report of his conversations. After reading it, White remarked that the letter showed a good deal of imagination but not much understanding of the basic situation. Hale immediately telephoned Bright and told him that he should, in the future, restrict himself to a narrative report and "leave the interpretation to those with a better understanding of the situation."

During the month that followed, Bright submitted letters about twice a week. On the whole, White and Hale agreed that they were as good as might be expected under the circumstances. While Bright did restrict himself to narrative statements concerning his contacts, the arrangement was not as satisfactory

as having an experienced manager like Gold make the contacts and interpret them in terms of the potential threat to IMC's interests. However, the most important criticism of Bright's work during this month was that his letters were received too late to be of any value had action by IMC been called for. Gold's letters had arrived within 24 hours after an interview, but two or three days might elapse before Bright's letters were received. Hale surmised that the routine work of the shipping office was claiming a large share of Bright's time during these first weeks on the job and that the letters would soon arrive on time. Accordingly, he said nothing to Bright about the matter.

During the second month, however, Bright's letters included more and more interpretation and less and less narrative. They continued to come in late. At the end of the month, Hale felt compelled to call this to Bright's attention.

"Kevin," he said, "we need the transcript of what was said in order to make our interpretation. If you want to add your own thoughts as an appendix to the letter, feel free to do so, but as you know, time is important. Don't hold the letter up just to write your interpretation. If you can't get your thoughts written and get the letter to us within 24 hours of the interview, just send us the letter with the narrative. Do we understand each other?"

"Yes, sir," Bright replied.

One week later White called Hale. "What's going on at the Zeta shipping office?" he asked. "Bright hasn't sent a letter in over a week, and I personally know that he has made three contacts with dissident leaders during that time. With the situation changing as it is, we need all the information we can get and we need it fast!"

Hale felt frustrated and disturbed by Bright's actions. He knew that he would have to take effective action to bring Bright into line, but he wondered if perhaps he had helped Bright off to a bad start somehow. He felt that Bright was better qualified than any other member of the staff and that, with maturity and experience, he would eventually develop into a valuable asset to IMC. Meanwhile, he must keep the rest of the staff from feeling that Bright was being pampered and given more consideration than his talents deserved. He wanted to act fairly and avoid charges of favoritism, yet he wasn't sure how this could be done without hurting Bright.

QUESTIONS

1. Evaluate the way Hale has handled Kevin Bright.
2. If you had been in Hale's position, what would you have done differently?
3. If you were in Hale's position, what would you do now?
4. What role should the executive vice-president of an IMC subsidiary have in the career development of junior staff? What is the role of the department managers? How should these roles be fulfilled?

LES HILL (A)

In May, Les Hill received a telephone call from a friend in the personnel department telling him that he would soon be transferred and promoted to managing business editor at the Tokyo office of the International News Corporation (INC). Hill was very pleased at this prospect. He knew the deputy managing editor, Don Fox, and had worked with Fox at a previous overseas office. Hill, age 38, had been with INC for sixteen years and was near the end of an assignment at INC headquarters in New York. His previous assignments were all general business reporting jobs, mostly overseas. These included assignments in Latin America, Europe, the Middle East, and one previous assignment at INC headquarters. Prior to joining INC, Hill had graduated with an AB in English from Yale University, where he had been an editor of the college daily newspaper. During his previous assignment in New York, he had gone to night school at NYU and obtained a master's degree in business administration.

Hill was anxious to get this job, and he had expressed more than a little interest to his friends in personnel when he found out the job might be available. He had also written a letter to Fox expressing how pleased he would be to work for him again. Hill viewed the job as essential to his career development because it involved supervising a number of other professional reporters. Hill had not had any previous opportunity to gain managerial experience and was anxious to demonstrate his skill and capacity in this area.

Hill knew that Fox was considered to be a top editor who had a reputation for developing his subordinates and working with them to help maximize their performance. Fox was a leader for whom most INC reporters were anxious to work since he encouraged them to use their own initiative and gave them considerable freedom and flexibility in carrying out their assigned functions. Hill had heard Fox described as "an orchestra leader who could play solo on any instrument."

Hill spent several hours with the director for Japanese Affairs and obtained an up-to-date organization chart (see Exhibit 1). Reporting to the managing business editor were a senior reporter on agricultural issues, a senior reporter on Japanese economic policy issues, a senior reporter on labor issues, a senior reporter on import/export issues, a senior reporter on legal issues, one general business reporter, one general business junior reporter, and one reporter trainee.

Hill surmised from his discussion with the director of Japanese Affairs that Fox tended to deal directly with the senior reporters in the business group whenever he felt it was appropriate. Fox apparently maintained an open-door policy and many of the 32 reporters in the Tokyo office took the opportunity to bring some issues to the attention of the deputy managing editor.

Hill also spent at least a half hour with the corporate headquarters counterparts of the specialists in the Tokyo business group, all of

EXHIBIT 1

ORGANIZATION CHART OF THE BUSINESS GROUP AT THE TOKYO OFFICE, INC.

Managing Business Editor
Les Hill

Secretary, Jo Mills

- Senior reporter for agricultural issues, Hugh Gates
- Senior reporter for Japanese policy issues, Saul Pound
- Senior reporter for labor issues, Al Franco
- Senior reporter for import/export issues, Kay Burns
- Senior reporter for legal issues, Frank Kent
- Business reporter, Bill Brown
- Junior business reporter, Tom Ford
- Reporter trainee, Sue Brook

whom were well known by their colleagues. Hill made notes about each of the people he would supervise (see Exhibit 2). His assessment was that the people seemed competent enough in their technical specialties, and the group seemed to be running quite well.

Hill was to replace Jeff White, an older and more senior managing editor, and Hill felt this would enhance his own chances for further advancement. He was convinced he could make his mark on the group, and he looked forward to the opportunity to improve the group's effectiveness. Hill planned to take a four-week vacation before leaving his current assignment at INC headquarters. This gave him about two months to think about his new assignment and develop his own thoughts on how best to work in as chief of the business group. He decided to seek the advice and counsel of two of his previous bosses who were in New York and arranged to have lunch with them.

DISCUSSION WITH DON CARLOS

Don Carlos had served as managing business editor at two offices in Europe and as senior managing business editor at IMC's Chicago office. He was on a special assignment temporarily, but he was expected to be named to a senior position at INC corporate headquarters soon. Hill was sure that Carlos was generally regarded as one of the top business journalists at INC—tough but brilliant. In looking at Les Hill's pending assignment, Carlos had several words of advice:

Don't let this *management* idea throw you. As managing business editor you are first and foremost a news reporter, and don't you forget it. Furthermore, you were selected because you will be the best general business reporter in the office. Naturally, you'll have to devote most of your time to those issues that are most important to the Tokyo managing editor and the deputy managing editor. That means you will have to assign the rest of the work to others and then ride herd on them to see that they do a good job.

This is a very competitive business and your future advancement depends on your personal contribution. If you lead a group that does a good piece of work, be sure you get the credit that rightfully belongs to you. Don't give credit to your subordinates; make them earn their own credit. You've got a fairly large group and one with a few prima donnas in it. You're going to have a tough time controlling them, and for that reason I'd look for an opportunity to let them know who was boss right away. I wouldn't give them any more information than they needed to do their job. It's your job to coordinate the group, not theirs. Beyond this, I think all contacts with senior Japanese businesspeople should generally be made by you as managing business editor while your staff focuses on less senior people and middle level managers.

The Tokyo managing editor and deputy are going to expect you to know what's going on in your group any time something comes to their attention. To do this, you better make your people explain what they're doing to you before you let it go upstairs. If you can't answer the questions from upstairs, you're going to look bad. Focus on your superiors, not your subordinates; it's their job to focus on you.

DISCUSSION WITH CARL MANN

Carl Mann had served as managing business editor twice before being named deputy managing editor in Rome. Mann had served in both general and business assignments and was generally well liked throughout the company. As Les Hill expected, Mann's view of the managing business editor's job in Tokyo was quite different.

You are going to be running a group with several specialists who know more about their areas of expertise than you do, and they will know that. Don't try to be the boss. Let them help you understand their work, but don't try to control them. They are older, more experienced, and certainly more expert than you are. Learn from them. Try to help them if you can; but let them do their job with a minimum of interference from you.

The Tokyo managing editor and deputy don't expect you to know everything, and they will probably tend to deal with the specialists directly anyway. If not, encourage them to do so. You are a generalist, and of course you will focus your attention on those general business issues that are of special interest to the managing editor and deputy. But you can't do everything, and you need the people in your group to get the job done. Give them credit when they do a good job and be sure the managing editor and deputy know they did a good job for you. If you do this, your people will work harder for you.

You are going to be evaluated on your managerial skill as well as your reporting skills.

Remember, the managing editor and deputy are also in managerial positions. Try to learn from their style of management; take your cues from them. You've got a pretty tough assignment. Too bad you haven't had some previous experience or practical INC training in management. Good luck.

Les Hill wondered if these two views might be oversimplified expressions of different philosophies, perhaps growing out of the unique personalities of the two editors. He felt that whatever style or strategy he adopted, it would have to mesh with his own personality. Hill thought of himself as an unusually good business reporter, and his performance appraisals had reflected this assessment. He felt he had done outstanding independent investigative work, wrote well, and had progressed rapidly at INC. On the other hand, he wasn't sure he was going to feel comfortable supervising the work of others, particularly in areas outside his previous experience. Beyond that, Hill's older daughter had experienced considerable difficulty at their last assignment overseas, and his wife was more than a little worried about how she would adjust to another foreign environment.

QUESTIONS

1. If you were Les Hill, what potential problems would you anticipate? How would you minimize them?
2. Develop a strategy you would follow to "work in" as managing business editor.
3. What additional information would you like to have? Why?
4. What are the duties of the managing business editor as you see them? How different are these from the duties Les Hill had performed in his previous assignments?
5. Contrast and evaluate the views of Don Carlos and Carl Mann.

EXHIBIT 2

LES HILL'S NOTES ON THE STAFF IN HIS GROUP

SAUL POUND, SENIOR REPORTER FOR JAPANESE POLICY ISSUES

At age 53, Saul has been in Japan four years. He is a business economist, whose previous experience includes academia, the Federal Reserve System, and two years with the Wall Street Journal before joining INC. This is Saul's second overseas assignment. He does not speak Japanese, but most Japanese government officials speak English. The economic staff at INC headquarters considers him a top reporter technically. A friend in personnel thinks he is a bit quiet and reserved, not very interested in issues outside his area of expertise, and sometimes inflexible. Saul has a good reputation among Japanese government officials but is unknown outside this restricted circle.

HUGH GATES, SENIOR REPORTER FOR AGRICULTURAL ISSUES

At age 48, Hugh has been in Japan one year and has been an agricultural man for 20 years. He has a graduate degree in agriculture, speaks limited Japanese, and spends much time "up country." The agriculture staff at INC headquarters has high regard for him and maintains that he is the "best in the business." Hugh has had at least five other overseas assignments with INC and has received several commendations from INC for exceptional reporting. He has excellent contacts among Japanese agricultural officials at both national and prefecture levels. Hugh tends to operate as a loner, not a team player; he jealously guards his prerogatives.

AL FRANCO, SENIOR REPORTER FOR LABOR ISSUES

At age 58, Al has been in Japan two years and has been active in labor union affairs for almost 40 years. He acquired a bachelors degree in labor economics at night school, enlisted in the infantry and became sergeant before earning a battlefield commission, then used the GI bill at night to get a law degree. He is now active in veterans' organizations. Al rose through the ranks of the United Mine Workers to regional secretary-treasurer and had frequent short-term "special assignments" in the Labor Department. He joined INC eight years ago and this is his second overseas assignment. Al speaks Japanese fairly well and has excellent contacts throughout the Japanese labor movement. His reporting is crisp, illuminating, and accurate earning him an outstanding reputation among IMC labor staff people and among Japanese labor officials. Al is blunt and outspoken—a diamond in the rough.

KAY BURNS, SENIOR REPORTER FOR IMPORT/EXPORT ISSUES

At age 42, Kay has been in Japan a year and one-half. She is a Yale graduate who secured her BA in English. Kay is a naval reserve officer and has held several jobs with large multinational companies. She earned her MBA from Columbia before joining INC 12 years ago. Most of her previous experience at INC is in the advertising and sales function. She requested an assignment in the news-gathering side. This is her first overseas assignment. The import/export staff regards her as a fast-rising comer, but she has limited her contacts to the business community, both American and Japanese, and those Japanese government officials involved in import/export. Kay is thoroughly competent but apparently not broadly interested in news gathering. She learned Japanese in college and speaks it adequately for social affairs, but most Japanese businesspeople speak English.

FRANK KENT, SENIOR REPORTER FOR LEGAL ISSUES

Age 55, Frank earned his BA in history from Dartmouth. He is a former football player, and has been in Japan two years. Frank has experience in several state and federal government agencies, mostly in security or law enforcement He is knowledgeable in legal issues but does not have a law degree. He has learned Japanese well enough to get along with Japanese lawyers, judges, and government officials, and he is responsible for legal issues in Korea, China, and the Philippines as well. Frank shows very narrow interests, but although he is not knowledgeable outside his field, he has a reputation for competence within it. He is very independent.

BILL BROWN, BUSINESS REPORTER

At age 41, Bill has been in Japan one year. He enlisted in the Marine Corps when he was 18 and earned his BA in journalism from the University of Missouri. He worked in banking for one year before joining INC and has had four overseas assignments as a general business reporter and two assignments at INC headquarters in New York. Bill has taken some graduate business courses at NYU. He is quiet, unassuming, competent technically but not outgoing, and is fluent in Japanese, Korean, Chinese and Spanish. His wife is a former Philippine national who has limited contacts with Japanese businesspeople and government officials. She had known Bill from a previous assignment at INC headquarters.

TOM FORD, JUNIOR BUSINESS REPORTER

At age 36, Tom has been in Japan three years. He earned his BS in journalism from Indiana University and served two years with ITT before joining INC. His two previous assignments overseas and two in New York focused on general business. He is thoroughly competent, outgoing, and fluent in Japanese, German, Spanish, and French. I knew him during a previous assignment at INC headquarters. Tom has good contacts and rapport with Japanese businesspeople and government officials.

SUE BROOK, REPORTER TRAINEE

At age 25, Sue has been in Japan six months. She earned her BS and MA in economics from Cornell and served one year in banking before joining INC. This is Sue's first overseas assignment. She is learning Japanese.

LES HILL (B)

In August, Les Hill arrived at the Narita airport outside Tokyo, Japan. He was met by Jeff White, the managing business editor whom he was to replace. Hill and White had known each other from previous assignments, and they discussed old acquaintances as they drove in from the airport. White had arranged for Hill to stay as his guest in the house INC provided for their managing business editor. White was scheduled to depart in two weeks, and Hill and his family would be free to occupy it after that. (Mrs. Hill and the children were not expected to arrive for several weeks.)

During that weekend, White gave Hill a rundown on the people in the group which essentially confirmed Hill's previous assessment. [See Exhibit 2, Les Hill (A).] White expressed considerable confidence in the deputy managing editor, Don Fox, and indicated that Fox left the various group chiefs pretty much alone to run their own shows.

"The deputy tends to handle 'hot' items personally," said White, "but as long as nothing in your group is in that category he will leave you alone. Of course he is always available if you or any of your people has anything they want to discuss. He generally has a short meeting of all the various group managing editors first thing every morning. It normally lasts about twenty minutes and sticks exclusively to intergroup issues. The managing editor and his deputy want the office to speak with a single voice; they want us to be united and face the Japanese and/or INC headquarters together.

"I try to run the group with the same flexibility the deputy uses in running the office. I want to be kept informed, but I generally let the people do their job without much interference from me. There doesn't seem to be any real need for coordination, and I have time to do some creative business reporting on issues that are of particular interest to me. If I don't understand something one of the technical specialists has done, I ask the specialist to come in and explain it to me. It's pretty hard to follow in detail, but then they all seem to be satisfying the INC staff people who screen their reports so I see no need to get very involved."

On Monday, Les Hill attended the deputy's morning meeting with Jeff White and was introduced to the other group chiefs. As the meeting ended, Fox asked Hill to stay for a few minutes. After the usual pleasantries Fox said he thought they ought to talk about what he expected from Hill as managing business editor. As the discussion progressed Fox confirmed what White had already told Hill.

"This is a relatively informal office, and the managing editor and I are comfortable with it that way. If the editor or I happen to become interested in something, we generally go directly to the person working on it. Of course, we expect you to know what's going on in your group and that you will develop the kind of relationships with your people that will encourage them to keep you informed.

"I am sure you are aware that most of the reporters you will be supervising are older, more experienced, and higher in salary level than you. This would suggest to me that you should be especially careful and sensitive in your personal relationships. You are going to need all the human skills you have, and if you need any help, I'm always available."

During the next several days, Hill made the rounds of the other groups to get acquainted with the other group chiefs on an informal basis. He also generally followed what Jeff White was doing, but it was clear to Hill that White was deeply involved in preparing for his departure and wasn't really running the group. White did arrange to take Hill on several formal calls on Japanese business executives to transfer his contacts. On Wednesday afternoon, White suggested that Hill assume responsibility for the group the following day. White wanted to say his farewells to friends in the office and help his wife with final arrangements. With the deputy's approval, Hill took over as managing business editor on Thursday.

Hill had learned early in his career as a reporter to carry a little notebook in his pocket so that he could jot down bits of data or make a note of something to check on later. This had proved to be a very helpful tool in his investigative work, and he was sure it would prove even more useful in managerial areas. In his meetings with other people, he would frequently jot down notes on things he was told. Often he would check on these things several days later to see what progress was being made.

Over the next several weeks, Hill found it very difficult to understand the highly technical news stories that were being sent to him for routine clearance. He felt very strongly that, at least for the first several months, he should not clear anything until he understood it thor-

oughly. He felt confident he could improve the operation of the group once he understood it. As a result, he often found it necessary to delay items until his secretary could get all the backup documentation from the originator and he had had time to understand it.

In addition, he felt the tone of the stories he received left something to be desired and he often made minor changes that he felt conveyed a better tone. Naturally this resulted in a temporary delay in the outgoing work of the group. In an effort to facilitate his review, Hill issued a memorandum to his group directing that "Henceforth, all stories coming to the managing business editor for clearance must have all pertinent background papers attached."

After some initial prodding, most reporters acquiesced to this procedure, but Hill thought there was some unnecessary grumbling on the part of his people. He frequently called in a reporter to find out the reasons certain information had been omitted or to question why some data had been included. In view of the deputy's comments, Hill felt he could not let any of his subordinates feel that he wasn't fully knowledgeable in their areas. Therefore he used specific questions as a way of educating himself. Hill felt that a general question asking in effect "what's this all about?" would have damaged his position and status in the eyes of his subordinates.

There were, of course, frustrations during the ensuing months. Sue Brook, Hill's trainee, was most reluctant to assist Hill's wife in finding adequate household help to care for the children. Tom Ford, who had been out sick the first two months after Hill's arrival, came into Hill's office in late October making jokes to the effect that since all the background information he needed to undertake current assignments was attached to stories buried somewhere in the pile on Hill's desk, he assumed he would not be held accountable. "Or would you just as soon give me the files back?" Ford asked. Hill had examined the files in question, cleared the stories, and returned the files to Ford. This was particularly easy since the files were in the general business reporting area where Hill felt most competent.

A particularly irksome incident that Hill felt showed a lack of dedication to the job was Ford's insistence on taking his scheduled ten days vacation only six weeks after returning from an absence of over three months due to sickness. To make matters worse, the first day of that vacation would occur when both Bill Brown and Sue Brook would be out of the office also, attending an important conference in Osaka. This would have meant that the group would have had *no* general business reporter to cover the office. Ford had made some lame excuse about the trip having been planned for many months and the family going on a prepaid charter flight. Hill was appalled that Ford seemed not to understand the necessity of keeping a general business reporter in the office. Persuasion simply didn't work, and Hill ultimately insisted that Ford postpone his vacation at least the one day. Ford had reluctantly acquiesced.

Another frustrating incident involved the space reallocation made possible by the occupant of adjoining offices moving out and INC's acquisition of the added space. Hill had gone out of his way to discuss the new office space layout possibilities with all the senior reporters, but no one could agree on anything. Hill had called several informal meetings in his office and had not succeeded in getting any agreement. Finally, under pressure from the manager for administration and the deputy, Hill ended the frustrating experience by throwing up his hands, dictating the new office layout, and saying, "That's it. There will be no more discussions. I don't want to hear any more about it." Much to Hill's surprise, his staff seemed relieved at his decision, and as nearly as he could tell, accepted the new arrangements completely.

In February, the office was notified of an impending visit of a very important trade pro-motion committee composed of very senior people from the Labor and Commerce Departments, as well as representatives of private business and labor. The editor and deputy had taken a keen interest in this visit and had assigned both Al Franco, the senior reporter for labor issues, and Kay Burns, the senior reporter for import/export issues to act as liaison officials with the American embassy officials who were scheduling the visit to ensure the committee's visit was covered by INC reporters as thoroughly as possible. Hill had asked for a copy of the notes, correspondence, and schedules for the visitors that Franco and Burns had acquired. One week after his request and only three days before the arrival of the committee, the material was put on Hill's desk. After reviewing it very carefully and analyzing the mission of the committee, Hill felt that there were a number of omissions in coverage of senior Japanese executives who could contribute significant information about the work of the committee. Therefore, he called in Franco and Burns to explain why these executives were not being covered.

Franco had retorted angrily, "What do you take us for, idiots? We've already contacted those executives and they are unavailable during the time the committee will be here."

Hill explained that he was only trying to be helpful. He made several more suggestions regarding other details of the coverage and was met by stony resistance to each point. Finally, sensing that he was not making any progress, Hill said, "OK, do it your way, but it better be good."

In April, Tom Ford's name was on a list of those being promoted from junior reporter to reporter. Hill immediately went to his office to congratulate him, and found Sue Brook and Bill Brown already there. In the few minutes that Hill was in Ford's office several other people either called or dropped by. In May, Tom Ford received notice that he was being transferred to Singapore. He was to be replaced by Fred Case, a business reporter. Hill knew Case only by reputation as a very quiet, somewhat introverted reporter. With this in mind he told Ford that before he left the office Ford should turn over all his contacts with Japanese executives to him. Ford seemed surprised, but did as requested during the next several weeks.

Fred Case arrived two weeks after Ford departed. Case was 38 years old, and had a bachelors degree in history from Arizona State. He had spent two years in the navy and five years in public relations before joining INC 15 years ago. He had completed three assignments as a business reporter in Europe: one assignment as a foreign correspondent with a guerilla group in Afghanistan and two assignments at INC headquarters. After meeting him, Hill concluded that he was indeed quiet, unassuming, and thorough. He doubted that Case could have handled Ford's contacts.

Shortly before Ford left, the deputy announced that he would be leaving in July and that his replacement would be Sam McCarthy. Hill knew little about McCarthy and set about trying to find out about his new boss. A week or so later in a private discussion with Don Fox, Hill learned that McCarthy had a reputation for running a "taut ship" and that Fox thought this might present problems for Hill. He went on to suggest that Hill learn to operate "with a softer touch," that he lead more and direct less, that he give his people "their head" a little more. Fox said he thought Hill was a thoroughly competent reporter in spite of these weaknesses, but perhaps he did not have enough self-confidence. Fox also indicated that he had seen these weaknesses in Hill's performance many months ago and had

planned to give Hill more attention, but that pressing issues had diverted him. Fox went on to say that he thought Hill deserved further advancement and he would write a performance appraisal that he hoped would accomplish this.

Shortly before McCarthy was to arrive, Hill received a letter from a friend in New York stating that rumor had it that McCarthy was already looking for Hill's replacement "as soon as possible." Hill decided that there was no truth to the rumor. "After all," he reasoned, "McCarthy doesn't know me and I don't know him. He wouldn't try to replace me before giving me a chance to perform. Besides," he thought, "if he wants a 'taut ship,' I can give it to him."

Hill wondered just what he ought to do, if anything, in view of his soon-to-arrive "taut ship" boss on the one hand and Fox's comments on his managerial weaknesses on the other. He wondered if these were conflicting bits of data.

QUESTIONS

1. Analyze Hill's behavior as managing business editor. What would you have done differently? Why?
2. What kind of attitudes do the other people in the business group display toward Hill? What should he do about them?
3. How do you evaluate Fox's comments on Hill's weaknesses? If you were Hill, what would you do about them?
4. What should Hill do in preparing for his new boss?

LES HILL (C)

Sam McCarthy, the new deputy managing editor, arrived in Tokyo and officially took the responsibilities of his new office in early July. After the usual introductions and formalities, McCarthy began private conferences with his managers of the various groups. Les Hill was the second to be summoned. McCarthy wasted little time in telling Hill what he expected.

"I've had a long talk with our Tokyo managing editor, Mr. Stone, who said he expected me to manage the internal affairs of the office while he focuses his attention on high-level political investigations and analyses. He promised me a free hand in running it as I see fit. I've heard that this is a very loosely run office, needing better coordination, and I intend to tighten it up. I don't believe in laxity, and I won't stand for people roaming all over the range.

"My philosophy of managing is 'Thinking, planning, and controlling.' I insist on a happy, hardworking *team*. I don't want anyone in this office to think of himself or herself as a 'specialist' even if he or she is. In my office, everyone's primary responsibility is good reporting, across the board. I know that some people with special training and background often chafe under this kind of supervision, but at this office that's the way it's going to be."

"Your group has several people in it who regard themselves as 'specialists,' and I want you to see to it that they all pull together effectively as a happy, hardworking team. I believe in delegation and I expect my group managers to delegate also. I always remember what Walter Bedell Smith said in this connection. He said, 'Delegate, delegate, delegate, but not to a jackass.'"

"I know you have some people in your group with limited competence, and it's your job to get the maximum coordinated production out of them. Some of them may be prima donnas, so don't start out getting them all excited. Treat them as if you were driving turkeys. Don't get them excited or they will fly off in every direction. Get a stick and scratch the ground with it. In this way you can control their direction and movement without getting them too excited."

Les Hill left his first meeting with McCarthy exhilarated. He felt that his new boss was a dynamic, forceful, well-organized executive who knew quite clearly how he wanted the office run. It was certainly going to be in sharp contrast to the more laissez-faire style of Don Fox. As Hill understood it, McCarthy was insisting on forceful leadership with the clear implication that anyone who did not do things McCarthy's way, wouldn't be on McCarthy's team.

Hill immediately resolved to control his group more effectively and to exercise more forceful leadership. Hill prided himself on his loyalty to INC and felt that when he issued an order his people should see it as his order and not something he was passing down from his boss. Hill began to insist on more effective coordination and began to tighten his grip on his group.

Shortly after this Bill Brown sent a story to Hill for clearance. The cover sheet showed that the managing political editor had already cleared it. Hill was angry at this bit of insubordination. Brown should have brought it to him first. It was an example of lax control and Hill resolved to correct it. He called Brown to his office and told him he expected to see all stories that originated in the business group before they were sent to another group for clearance. Brown agreed but seemed unconcerned about the incident. Hill pointed out that all stories were supposed to have a summary. This one did not, and even though it had been cleared that way by another group it reflected badly on the business group.

Brown shrugged and tried to make light of it. "Sorry about that. Guess I just forgot again. I'll have to tie a string around my finger to help remind me."

Hill was angry at this flip attitude. He wanted Brown to take the situation seriously. It was no time for joking around. "Why not put it around your neck?" he retorted. Brown visibly blanched, and Hill therefore assumed that Brown now understood the seriousness of the situation.

Another incident involved Kay Burns, the senior reporter for import/export issues. McCarthy had called Hill during his first week on the job to inquire about a Japanese editorial he had seen speculating on a new trade agreement between Japan and Russia. McCarthy suggested an analysis be made of the potential ramifications on U.S. exports to Japan. Hill indicated that he thought the likelihood of such an agreement was remote, but he would nevertheless have the analysis prepared. Hill telephoned Burns, mentioned the editorial, and then said, "I think you ought to prepare an analysis of the potential impact on U.S. exports that might result if such an agreement were actually concluded. Obviously, the impact would vary depending on the exact content of the agreement, but you can make some assumptions on various alternatives. When can you have it done?"

Burns was very cool in her response. She was emphatic that the probability of a Japanese-Russian trade agreement was nil and therefore any analysis was a waste of time. She also enumerated a list of relatively high priority items on which she was working adding that she simply could not take time in the foreseeable future to do such a report.

Hill was frustrated. Burns, he felt, was being obstinate and uncooperative. Of course Burns had high priority work—everyone in the office did—but that was no excuse for refusing to accept her responsibilities. After some further discussion on priorities, Hill said, "Look Kay, this may not be the hottest item on your desk but I want this analysis done. Get it to me as soon as you can."

In early August, Hill was in the deputy's office reviewing some routine matters with him. When this review ended, McCarthy said, "You know Les, several people in your group appear to be a little agitated. Three of them have taken the opportunity at cocktail parties to express their opinion that the office was running better before you and I got here. They claim they know their staff people in New York and give them what they want. The trouble with the loose control to which they have been accustomed is that they won't do anything other than keep their New York staff people happy. It fosters an attitude that the office is a roof for a collection of independent reporters rather than the integrated office that I want. By the way, where is the analysis of the trade agreement I asked for last month?"

Hill indicated that Burns was working on it but that it had been delayed because of higher priority work.

McCarthy looked at Hill silently for a few moments, then said, "When I ask for something I expect you and your group to move quickly. After four weeks what I asked for ought to be top priority, even if not at first. I don't like surprises, particularly something that no one is on top of. It seems to me that the people in your group are too easygoing about their fields. I want that group to run a lot better than it has been and I expect you to see to it. Is that clear?"

Hill nodded that he understood.

"And another thing," McCarthy continued, "is the question of physical presence. It's very important. Get out of your office. Go to their offices. Don't send memos. Go see them. Get people close to you."

As Hill returned to his office he felt frustrated and chagrined. He had told Burns to do the analysis. Why hadn't she done it? McCarthy apparently wanted him to delegate but at the same time control closely to see that the work was being done properly. He sat down at his desk and wrote a note to himself in his little notebook to jog Burns on the report.

As he looked through his IN basket, Hill came across an anonymous note that referred to INC's policy that spouses and dependents of INC employees were *not* INC employees and should not be asked to perform any functions that might be construed as INC work. The anonymous note went on to give several specific examples of requests by Mrs. McCarthy that seemed to violate this policy and it asked that corrective actions be taken immediately. Hill wondered who had written the memo. His secretary professed to know nothing about it. "Just what am I supposed to do about it?" Hill thought to himself. After further consideration Hill decided that since the memo was unsigned he would do nothing, at least for the time being.

Three weeks later, Hill was shocked to receive a telephone call from the personnel office of INC headquarters in New York advising him, unofficially, that he was to be transferred out of Tokyo in about ten months and would be assigned as the deputy managing editor of the office responsible for reporting on the European Economic Community in Brussels. He would be the second-ranking reporter in an office of considerable importance insofar as U.S. business interests were concerned. In further conversation, Hill was told that the transfer was "definite" and "irreversible," but that it would not be announced or formalized for eight or nine months. Meanwhile, as a courtesy to personnel, Hill was not to discuss it. Hill got the impression from personnel that McCarthy had arrived in New York with a shopping list of things he wanted before he came to Tokyo. Apparently the transfers of several others that McCarthy wanted to get rid of would be accelerated, as his had been.

Hill was stunned. He went to see McCarthy and confronted him with the information given to him by personnel. Hill thought McCarthy was visibly embarrassed. Nevertheless, McCarthy confirmed what personnel had told Hill. McCarthy also implied that he was quite dissatisfied with Hill's performance thus far as managing business editor, and if he couldn't straighten out the group soon, he might find himself sent home a lot sooner than he expected. McCarthy also warned Hill not to discuss the pending transfer. Hill left with the impression that McCarthy wanted to avoid any possible reduction in productivity that might result from anxiety over who would be leaving next if word of his own transfer leaked out. Hill also felt that his own ability to straighten out the group might be impaired if his subordinates learned he had been, in effect, fired. Beyond this he had been in Tokyo only a little more than one year. To leave now would look very bad, but leaving after almost two years would at least be respectable.

QUESTIONS

1. How well has Hill related to his new boss? His group? Analyze and explain his behavior. What would you have done differently?
2. What do you think of the anonymous memo that Hill received? Is it valid? Why? What alternatives are open to Hill? What would you have done about the situation?
3. If you were Les Hill, what would you do now?
4. Develop what you think is an optimum strategy for the next ten months.

LES HILL (D)

Les Hill returned to the Tokyo office of INC on Tuesday after an agonizing three-day Labor Day weekend during which he pondered the situation he was now in. His transfer to INC's EEC Office in Brussels was ten months away and would not be announced for at least eight months. Hill felt he was under severe pressure to tighten up his business group, but he was no longer sure what that meant. He had discussed the situation with his wife in very general terms, but because she was already upset and worried about their older daughter's adjustment to the Japanese environment he had avoided giving her many of the details that were disturbing him. During the weekend he had come to the numbing realization that there was no one with whom he could discuss the situation fully; he would just have to bottle it up and sweat it out as best he could.

He also realized from his conversation with personnel that several other members of his group were in disfavor and would also be transferred out, but he had been unable to find out who these were. He felt torn between his desire to protect his people from damage to their careers or harassment and the necessity, for his own survival, of more tightly controlling the group. A year ago he had been anxious to accept the managerial responsibilities of running a group, but now he felt the burden more severely than he had ever imagined. His responsibilities to the Tokyo office, his boss, his peers, his subordinates, and himself all

seemed to be at least partially in conflict with one another. He was unsure how he should balance these responsibilities.

During the next several weeks, Hill sensed that the deputy editor was increasing the pressure on him to tighten up the group. During several routine private meetings with the deputy, McCarthy had seemed to go out of his way to ridicule virtually all of the people in the business group. His comments were barbed and often belittled the competence of the people in general rather than in specific terms. These comments made Hill feel that he was falling down on the job, but since they were not specific, he felt powerless to deal with them.

Over the next several months Hill sensed that his relationships with his subordinates were beginning to show signs of strain, in part at least because of the pressures the deputy was putting on him, which he did not feel he could pass down. One incident that exemplified this process was the deputy's insistence that Hill survey every reporter in the office and prepare a chart showing all memberships in clubs that were active in Japan. Hill felt this was an onerous, if not nit-picking, task of little value to the office, and he was sure the other reporters would see it that way and some would resent his preparing the chart. Nevertheless, Hill pursued the task with vigor and gave the impression that it was his own idea. Not surprisingly, the chart showed the deputy had the most memberships and McCarthy was pleased by it. Hill was sure some of his subordinates resented it.

A second incident resulted from the deputy's telephoned request for Hill to get Hugh Gates, the senior reporter for agricultural issues, and come to his office at once. Hill quickly discovered that Gates was out of the office, probably on one of his frequent visits to the agricultural areas of the country, but no one seemed to know for sure. Hill immediately went to the deputy's office to see what the problem was. Hill explained to McCarthy that Gates was out but the deputy insisted on knowing *where* Gates was and *exactly* when he would be back. When Hill confessed that he didn't know, the Deputy exploded in anger. McCarthy demanded that from then on Hill know where all of his people were at all times and implied that there would be *no* acceptable excuse for not knowing. (Exhibit 1 shows the memo Hill felt compelled to issue to protect himself.)

A third incident involved an office space reallocation on which the deputy insisted. In view of his earlier experience, Hill decided to simply issue a memorandum giving the new office locations and the details of the move. This time, however, instead of accepting the new layout there was clearly some grumbling and dissatisfaction. Kay Burns had come storming into his office and berated Hill for moving

people around without knowing what they were responsible for. She pointed out the large number of important people who regularly visited her at the office, often in the company of a number of other important people. There was not, Burns maintained, enough room in her proposed new cubicle for everyone to sit down, let alone transact affairs vitally affecting her ability to report on U.S. exports to and imports from Japan. Hill quickly recognized the validity of Burns's position, and after getting the agreement of Hugh Gates, the senior reporter for agricultural issues, Hill switched their offices. He had originally assigned the larger office to Gates because he was more senior, even though he spent much of his time outside the office. Although he had resolved the situation, Hill felt his relationship with Burns had been damaged. This, he felt, was demonstrated two weeks later when Hill asked Burns to attend a luncheon at which a leading business executive's daughter was to receive an award from the U.S. Embassy. The deputy had insisted that someone from the business group should go. Hill had a previous engagement and wanted Burns to represent the group. Burns refused and was adamant. Hill was forced to cancel his other engagement.

A fourth incident involved the visit of a prominent U.S. labor leader to Japan. The deputy insisted that Hill personally be INC's reporter accompanying this labor official

---

EXHIBIT 1

MEMORANDUM

October 10

To: All Members of the Business Group
From: Managing Business Editor
Subject: Hours

Please let me know in advance whenever you expect to arrive in the office significantly after 8 A.M., leave before the closing hour of 5 P.M., or wish to take vacation time.

cc: Deputy Editor

during his visit to Japan. Hill argued that Al Franco, the senior reporter for labor issues, was a more appropriate choice, but the deputy was emphatic in his insistence that Hill do it personally, demanding that Hill accompany the labor official on his visits as well as suggest other activities for him. The deputy made it clear without actually saying so that he did *not* want Al Franco involved in this affair. Hill had reluctantly accepted the assignment. He wanted to explain the circumstances to Franco, but his loyalty to what he perceived to be the INC system and the deputy precluded him from doing so.

Hill felt more comfortable in his relations with the general business reporters. After all, he was senior to them and knew more about their work than they did. But even here strains began to develop. More and more assignments for reporting on general business issues came down from the deputy together with more and more criticisms of the writing style, but only in general terms. Hill passed out the assignments as equally as he could and again acted as though these assignments were his own ideas. He became particularly conscious of the tone of the stories being sent to him for his release and repeatedly made small changes that he felt were important. The deputy would often send the stories back to Hill with instructions to "further improve" them and at other times would delete Hill's changes and send them out as the originator had prepared them. Since Hill found no pattern to these actions, he felt powerless to do anything.

Several months later, the deputy telephoned Hill and stated that he was reviewing a lengthy story that Bill Brown had prepared. He stated that he felt the story was satisfactory and that he would send it out. There was, however, one piece of information concerning a rumor involving three top-level Japanese executives that he thought ought to be reported in a separate story. He instructed Hill to have Brown write the second story. Hill telephoned Brown and asked him to come to his office. When Brown arrived Hill told him that the story he had recently submitted was satisfactory and would be sent on. He also told Brown that he wanted him to write a separate story reporting the rumor contained in the first story. Brown's neck and ears reddened and he said, "That would be unnecessary duplication. The story isn't necessary and I don't think we ought to send it. Besides, I'm already overloaded with a dozen other unnecessary jobs you've given me."

Hill felt his own face flush and a surge of anger well inside himself. He felt that this was inexcusable insubordination but he tried to control his voice as he said, "I'm not asking you what you think. I'm directing you to write that story immediately."

"And I am *not* going to do it," Brown shot back, just as the deputy walked into Hill's office carrying the story Brown had prepared. Seeing the deputy opened the flood gates to an emotional torrent. Brown stated that Hill was persecuting and harassing him, nitpicking his work, inconsistent and contradictory in assignments, being arbitrary and capricious in his dealings, insensitive and inconsiderate in his personal relations, and arrogant, stupid, and incompetent in his work. Brown accused Hill of having a constipated personality and stated quite emphatically, "I cannot and will not work for a man I cannot respect. I want one of us transferred out. If you're not leaving, I want out."

Hill was stunned by this emotional outburst but the deputy broke in and exclaimed, "That's enough." He then delivered a short lecture on the necessity for all reporters to pull together and to get along. He dismissed Brown by saying that he would consider his request for a transfer. After Brown left the deputy berated Hill for not having earned the respect of his people, for permitting such an outburst, for not tightening up the group, and for general malfeasance. "You may be a good reporter, but you certainly can't manage," were the deputy's parting words.

Hill was alone and visibly shaking as he picked up his briefcase to go home for the weekend and ponder the damage that the last several months had done to his career and apparently the careers of several others as well.

QUESTIONS

1. Analyze and evaluate Hill's behavior as managing business editor. What are his strengths and weaknesses?

2. What would you have done about the incidents described in the case?
3. How would you have handled Bill Brown?
4. What would you do now?
5. Considering the likelihood of this outburst becoming widely known throughout the office (the door to Hill's office was open throughout with two secretaries immediately outside). What strategy should Hill follow in his relations with his staff for the next several months?
6. Evaluate the "damage" done to Hill's career.

LES HILL (E)

With four months left to go, Les Hill entered INC's Tokyo office on Monday morning more determined than ever to stick it out, come what may. Hill was reasonably sure that his career had been damaged, but he was not sure how much. His last performance appraisal, written by Don Fox, had been superlative, and he was sure that it was on this basis that he was to be promoted this year to deputy editor in Brussels. On the other hand, he was reasonably sure that the careers of some of his people in the business group had been damaged, perhaps without their being aware of it. Hill resolved to be more sympathetic and understanding with his people.

As he entered the offices, he met Bill Brown in the hall. Hill smiled and said, "Good morning, Bill," and started to raise his hand to offer a handshake, but sensed a cool rebuff as Brown just nodded. "Look, Bill, you and I have not always found it easy to work together, much to my regret, and I am sure yours too. Let's forget what happened last Friday, and for several months prior to that. Let's make a fresh start today."

Bill Brown looked at him penetratingly and then said, "You can't wipe out the past, but we do have to work together. I, for one, will not let anything interfere with my ability to perform effectively."

"Fine," Hill responded. "Say, you're going to the cocktail party being given by the Sony Public Affairs office after work tonight, aren't you? Can I give you a lift?"

"Thanks," Brown said, "but my wife is picking me up."

Hill genuinely regretted the relationship that had evolved between himself and Brown and hoped it could be improved. He considered Brown a thoroughly competent reporter.

During the next month the group seemed to move more quietly. The pressure from the deputy seemed to ease up a bit, and the reporters in the group went about their work in routine fashion, sending Hill copies of their stories. For his part, Hill tried not to telephone or bug his people as much as he had been. Bill Brown, however, chose this time to open a personal crusade to determine the criteria used by the administrative people in the assignment of INC housing and office parking. It seemed to Hill that Brown did not feel abused himself, but that he was doing this as an issue of principle. Hill was reasonably sure that housing and parking were handled on an ad hoc basis depending on pressures from New York and the preferences of the managing editor and his deputy. Brown, he thought, probably viewed his own emotional blowup in front of Hill and the deputy as "standing up like a man," and was using the housing and parking issue to prove to himself that he could do it again.

Hill, on the other hand, viewed Brown's behavior in the same light as he would view the behavior of Don Quixote. If he persisted, it could embarrass the managing editor or his deputy or at least irritate them, thus damaging Brown's career. In late March, one of the senior administrative people complained to Hill about Brown's inquiries and indicated that if they didn't stop he would bring the matter to the attention of the deputy. Hill took the next routine opportunity to discuss the matter with Brown.

"Bill, I'm sympathetic with your point of view on the housing and parking issues, but I doubt that you're going to be able to accomplish very much by your continual probing. Furthermore, I'm afraid you may do yourself harm by continuing to ask these questions."

Brown shrugged and indicated that he knew he wasn't getting very far, that it was just one more example of injustice in the overseas portion of INC. He added that he wasn't trying to change anything but just wanted to know the basis on which housing and parking were assigned. He felt he had made his point about the system and saw no need to push it any further.

A month later, a number of promotions were announced, Hill's among them. As word of the promotion spread, only a few people at the office telephoned or dropped by to congratulate him and these seemed very insincere. Also among those being promoted was Kay Burns. No official acknowledgement of those promoted was made by the office.

Three weeks later, the office received official notification that Hill would be replaced by Ted Hood. Again, only a few people at the office telephoned or dropped by to congratulate him on his move to an office where he would be second in command. Most of them seemed more pleased that he was leaving than that he was going to a good job.

As it came time to start writing performance appraisals Hill was determined to give his people the solid recommendations he felt they deserved. McCarthy gave him the impression that rather negative appraisals were expected on most of the people in the business group. He knew for example that McCarthy felt that Brown's contacts with executives in the Japanese business community were inadequate and ineffective, but Hill thought just the reverse. In preparing to write the appraisal, Hill had several conferences with Brown. During these, the subject of their difficult working relationship was noted as well as the outstanding substantive performance. Hill told Brown, "You're the most honest man I know and you write better than anyone I know."

Shortly before leaving Tokyo, Hill prepared what he considered to be the best appraisal he could write that would get past the deputy. Hill thought it prudent to give Brown somewhat lower markings than he had last year, though all markings were still in or near the outstanding category, and to make the written portion of the appraisal better.

During May and early June, four other reporters were notified of their impending transfers: Saul Pound, the senior reporter for Japanese policy issues, was going back to New York in spite of his desire and request to extend his assignment. Hugh Gates, the senior reporter for agricultural issues, was also returned to New York. Kay Burns had already had her promotion and transfer announced, and Bill Brown was going back to New York assigned to INC headquarters. Several other transfers were imminent. Other groups in the Tokyo office were also hit, but not to the same degree.

Hill was given the typical sendoff, but he again felt it was more form than substance. After being in his new job in Brussels for almost a month, Hill received a letter from a friend in another group in Tokyo who observed that conditions at the Tokyo office were as bad as ever, and the situation in the business group, now being run by Ted Hood was as bad as or worse than when Hill had been there.

QUESTIONS

1. Analyze and evaluate Hill's handling of Bill Brown during his last few months in the Tokyo office.

2. What do you think of the performance appraisal Hill wrote on Brown? Was it fair? Why? What would you have done differently? Why?

3. What damage do you now think has been done to Les Hill's career? To Bill Brown's?

CHARLES MARTIN

Taku is a small underdeveloped nation that for centuries was under the control of one or another of its larger neighbors or a colonial power. In spite of this domination by outside powers, the Taku culture and language has remained intact. The Takulese language is extremely complex, without any traceable origins or similarities to that spoken by nearby nations. Only in the last hundred years has Takulese been put in written form. As an underdeveloped nation they have had no need for technical or scientific words, but very fine distinctions have evolved for natural phenomena. For example, there are twenty words to describe different types of rain.

Most employees of the Taku subsidiary of the Resources Development Company (T-RDC) have had considerable difficulty learning Takulese and have relied on local employees to serve as translators. Conversely, most Takulese officials and major land owners have become fluent in English.

The Takulese social system is characterized by a rigid hierarchy among classes. The upper classes have always provided the senior government officials and major landowners. For the last several decades, the upper classes have taken great pains to educate their children, sending many of them to countries in the industrialized West. More recently, the middle classes have begun to give special emphasis to the education of their children and a few, including children of some modestly wealthy business executives, have been sent to countries in the industrialized West. This has given rise to more than a little dissatisfaction with the slow pace of change in Taku. The result has been the emergence of dissident political groups, particularly among the younger members of the middle classes. T-RDC management decided that it would be in the company's best interest to develop and cultivate relationships with these groups and, if possible, influence them to accept the important role T-RDC can play in the development of the Takulese economy.

Senior management decided that an information bulletin published in Takulese would be an appropriate first step toward building relationships with the dissident groups. To avoid giving the impression of targeting a specific audience, the company decided to distribute the bulletin widely and to publish items of general interest as well as specific information about RDC and its various subsidiaries throughout the world.

Oka Bantu, a member of the upper classes with many relatives who were large landowners of importance to the company or senior government officials, was hired to be the editor of the bulletin. Oka would give the company informal access to these important people should the company ever decide to use it. As editor, Oka would read the various English publications produced by the company and its many subsidiaries, decide which of these might be of interest to the Taku people in general, translate these articles into Takulese, publish them in the bulletin every two weeks, and see to its wide circulation.

Several months after publication of the bulletin had started, Charles Martin was transferred and promoted to become the Manager of Public Relations at T-RDC. Martin had been with RDC for fifteen years, serving in various positions in Asian subsidiaries. Martin was pleased with his promotion and viewed the opportunity in T-RDC as a challenge since he knew neither the language nor culture of Taku.

It was company policy to allow a one week overlap when people like Martin took over a position. Dave Moore, the incumbent manager of public relations, used the time to acquaint Martin with the functions of the job and give him an assessment of the various Takulese and American personnel with whom he would be working. Moore told Martin it was not necessary to learn the language or culture of Taku since all the people important to the company spoke fluent English. Moore also told Martin that he had begun to hear some adverse comments about the bulletin from various Takulese citizens, but had not had a chance to make his own assessment. Moore suggested that Martin should meet with Oka at his earliest convenience and make his own assessment.

On his first day after assuming his new responsibilities, Martin asked Oka to come to his office so that they might become better acquainted and so that Oka could report on the progress being made by the bulletin, its reception by the general public, and his plans for the future of the bulletin. At this meeting Oka was friendly but deferential and assured Martin that the bulletin had made excellent progress, was now being read regularly by a large audience, and that there was no need to plan any changes in the bulletin. Martin chose not to tell Oka about the negative impressions

Moore had until he personally could get more information.

At a supplier's conference, Martin met the Takulese owner of a company doing business with T-RDC who laughed when asked about the bulletin. After some probing, the owner expressed the opinion that the bulletin was both condescending and confusing to the reader. The owner said *he* preferred to obtain his information about RDC from the *English* documents RDC sent to its suppliers. He went on to observe that technical articles were particularly troublesome since Takulese had few technical words. For example, there was no Takulese word that meant drill bit and that in a recent issue of the bulletin it had been translated as "pole with teeth that eats dirt." The owner acknowledged that this was an imaginative approach but doubted that many Takulese understood much of the article. He suggested that Martin substitute a blank space for every technical phrase or word in order to get a feel for how a Takulese might feel reading the article.

This conversation convinced Martin that there were indeed problems with the bulletin. Over the next several weeks, Martin used every opportunity to question the Takulese he met, mostly large landowners, about the bulletin. Like Oka, they were friendly and deferential but distant and seemed to be evasive or noncommittal about the bulletin. Nevertheless, Martin got the impression they were not impressed by it.

Martin again called Oka to his office with the intention of confronting him with this negative information he had obtained. When Oka entered his office, Martin found him to be very friendly, deferential, and enthusiastic about RDC and his work. Based on his experiences in Asia and to avoid any loss of face for Oka, Martin was very tactful and indirect in attempting to convey his negative impressions of the bulletin. Oka nodded his understanding and assured Martin he would do his best to ensure that the bulletin met the high standards of T-RDC.

A few weeks later, a reporter from the local newspaper came by Martin's office on a routine visit to pick up press releases. After some small talk, the reporter confessed that his real purpose in coming to see Martin was in response to a request from the owner of the supply company Martin had talked with earlier. The reporter expressed the same opinions about the bulletin as had the owner. The reporter felt the technical stories were of great interest to the people, but that the local editors were unwilling to print them. Hence the only source of such information was the bulletin. Unfortunately, most people resented being "talked down to," and the Takulese were particularly sensitive on this point. The reporter suggested that the English technical words and phrases be used, but he added that all technical terms should be explained in great detail in footnotes or parenthetical paragraphs. In this way, he felt, the words and phrases would be absorbed into the Takulese language much the same way English technical terms had been absorbed into many other languages. He again reiterated his feeling that the Takulese were very sensitive about their perceived "backwardness" as a nation, and great care would have to be exercised to avoid offending the readers by the way the technical terms were explained.

Martin thanked the reporter for his candor and then summoned Oka to his office. This time Martin did not use innuendo or indirection in explaining what he felt were the shortcomings of the bulletin. Oka sat in stunned silence as Martin proceeded to lay out his criticisms. Martin ended by saying he expected Oka to straighten out the problems and to do so quickly. Oka hung his head and accepted full responsibility for any shortcomings that might exist in the bulletin. He went on to explain that the people he talked with who read the bulletin seemed to understand the articles

very well, but that he would take immediate steps to seek out other views and to add explanatory footnotes as Martin had suggested.

Although Martin could not read the bulletin, he could at least observe that there were footnotes and felt relieved. Six weeks later, Martin received a telephone call from the general manager of T-RDC who told him that he had sat next to the Takulese Minister of Economic Development at the local chamber of commerce luncheon. He went on to tell Martin that the minister had stopped reading the bulletin because of its excessive verbiage. Martin told the general manager about his own investigations of the bulletin and that Oka was working to make the necessary improvements. Martin defended Oka and suggested that Oka be given sufficient time to make the changes. The general manager said it was clearly Martin's problem and he should handle it as he thought best.

Three weeks later, Martin telephoned the reporter who had come to see him and suggested they have lunch. The reporter was very pleased at this invitation and was very willing to discuss the bulletin during the luncheon. He observed that the footnotes had been added but that they had not accomplished much except to make the articles more difficult to read. He felt it would take a most determined reader to wade through the much more lengthy articles in order to derive any understanding. He also felt the nontechnical articles or those with a minimum of technical issues were satisfactory or a shade above but were far from the excellence he expected from RDC. The reporter felt that Oka must be thinking in English and then trying to put the words into Takulese instead of trying to think in Takulese as he wrote the articles. This was typical of the upper classes he observed. Martin again thanked the reporter for his candor.

Martin again summoned Oka to his office and laid out the shortcomings of the bulletin as he saw them. This time Oka was silent but held his head high. Martin was puzzled by this reaction from Oka and asked what Oka intended to do about the shortcomings Martin had just pointed out. In a most formal and aloof manner Oka observed that he had followed Martin's instructions precisely even when he had serious reservations about their appropriateness. He went on to state that if Martin found his performance lacking, he had no alternative but to resign effective immediately. As he started to leave, Oka turned and said perhaps he ought to mention that he had been offered a senior position in the Takulese Office of Economic Development and intended to accept the offer.

QUESTIONS

1. What do you see as the significant cultural differences in this situation?
2. If you had been Martin, what would you have done differently?
3. If you were Martin, what would you do now?
4. In view of the objectives held by the senior managers at T-RDC, how would you evaluate Martin's handling of the bulletin?

GIANT INDUSTRIES, INC. (A)

PERCEPTIONS OF A PURCHASING MANAGER

As purchasing manager for the Metropole Plant, one of the larger manufacturing facilities within Giant Industries, Sam Short was facing all of the problems common to the other twenty-two plant purchasing managers and some additional ones that he felt were caused by relatively weak and unskilled supervisors at the middle management level in his department. During a career of over forty years with the purchasing function at Giant Industries, Short had been employed at a number of different plants. He had come to his present position two years ago from the purchasing managers' job at another high-volume plant where he had served for six years. He planned to retire in eighteen months and viewed this job as his last one but he hoped it would demonstrate the benefits of long experience and effective management.

The purchasing departments in the various plants of Giant Industries are organized in a similar fashion, although the number of employees and volume of purchases handled vary widely among them. Sam Short's purchasing department is organized as shown in Exhibit 1. Due to the seasonal fluctuation in volume of work, part-time or seasonal employees are hired each year to supplement the permanent staff. Reflecting the makeup of the purchasing function as a whole, approximately 70 percent of employees in Short's department were women and nearly 40 percent were from various minority groups. Most of these employees occupy the lower paying clerical positions.

The process of issuing purchase orders requires a series of steps not dissimilar to a production line. In this case, the product is the purchase order and the input to the production process consists of (1) a request for the company to purchase one or more specific items, with supporting documents on need for the item(s) plus an indication of the preferred supplier, and (2) data from a central computer on items or suppliers who, for one reason or another, are on "hold" status. (Seventy percent of the purchase requests are received by internal mail; 30 percent of the requests are hand-carried by the person making the request.) Then there is (3) the purchase order itself—the blank forms need to be turned into a validated purchase order complete with technical specifications and authorized signature. This is done in the processing section.

The purchasing section is staffed with purchasing agents who decide whether the request and supporting documents give proof of need and the preferred supplier is approved or competitive. Purchasing agents at Giant Industries usually start at the entry professional

EXHIBIT 1

PARTIAL ORGANIZATION CHART—METROPOLE PLANT PURCHASING DEPARTMENT

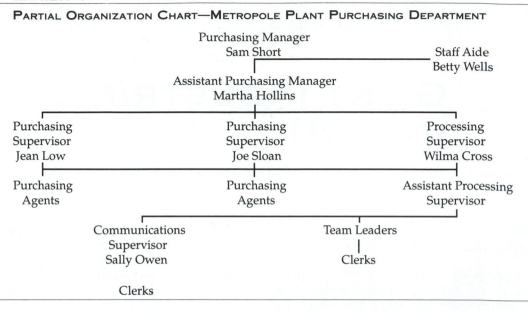

level and have been able to rise two levels. One of the problems faced by Sam Short was a recent corporate personnel instruction that effectively limited the ability of his purchasing agents to rise more than one level. Short believed that the morale implications of this decision, given an already constrained career ladder for his people within Giant Industries, were potentially serious.

Once the purchasing agent's work was completed, purchase requests (in numbered and coded boxes) went forward either to the processing section, if a purchase order was to be issued, or to the communications unit, if additional documentation was required or if a purchase request was to be denied. In processing, the purchase orders were produced and either mailed to the supplier or returned to the person making the request if they wished to pick up the items directly from the supplier. Processing employees were normally recruited at the entry clerical level and could progress three clerical levels, at which point they were required to be able to perform all jobs in the

section. The communications unit was essentially a service unit. Trained operators answered telephone inquiries from suppliers and those requesting purchases or else referred the caller to someone who could answer their questions. The correspondence clerks handled mail inquiries.

Short recognized several long-range problems faced by all the plants and believed he should contribute to their solution from the knowledge and skills gained during his many years of experience. The most obvious of these problems centered on the need for more productivity. Each year the plants had been called upon to handle a higher volume of work with no increases in permanent staff, but with increases in part-time or seasonal staff, and it was expected that this trend would continue. Short believed this was the critical area requiring his attention, and he spent most of his time worrying about the work habits of his people and changes in the process of issuing purchase orders that would lead to greater productivity.

Short felt that successful operations were a product of strict supervision and attention to detail on his part, and typically toured the department twice daily accompanied by Martha Hollins, his assistant. During these tours, he spoke with every supervisor and expected them to tell him what was going on, with special emphasis on any problems that impeded production. While he depended on his assistant, Martha Hollins, to handle purely technical problems, he was usually able to make immediate decisions on most matters and was usually able to spot practices or procedures that were wasting time or money or both. When he did, he would tell the supervisor how to correct the situation and would check during subsequent tours to make sure his instructions were being followed. Short felt that before he took it over two years ago, the department had been in pretty poor shape. Employees were taking far too long to perform their tasks, supervisors were lax on discipline, and many processes were inefficient. Short had instituted a number of changes and was pleased that now, two years later, the department was successfully handling a higher volume with fewer employees.

Short was not happy about the quality of his supervisors and felt that he had to monitor them very closely. His assistant, Martha Hollins, was an experienced technician but could not seem to make decisions, particularly in regard to people problems. She was not a strong leader, and Short doubted she would ever be able to head a plant purchasing department.

Joe Sloan, one of the supervisors in the purchasing section, was Short's main problem. He never seemed to be there when Short wanted him. He did not respect working hours, came in late to work frequently, and was often not in his office when Short came around on his twice daily tours. At least partly because of Sloan's spotty attendance record, Short had established a sign-in and sign-out sheet, which was kept in his secretary's office and which required all supervisors, including himself, to sign in the morning, out for lunch and back in afterwards, and out in the evening. Short felt that Sloan was just not doing his job, and as a result had to be supervised very closely. He had, for instance, noted recently that Sloan's people were often on the telephone, frequently on obviously personal business, and were not tending to their jobs. Short's solution was to remove all but two telephones from the purchasing section. Short felt that if Sloan had been on top of his people he would not have had to make this decision.

Jean Low, the other purchasing supervisor, was something of a rebel. She often seemed to disagree with Short's ideas about how things should be done and was constantly coming up with impractical ideas of her own. She had recently requested that she be allowed to attend an executive development seminar put on by the corporate personnel training office. Short had told her he couldn't spare her and that she needed to spend her time ensuring the productivity of her unit, not attending courses in management.

Short believed that Wilma Cross, supervisor of processing, was probably his strongest middle manager. She was production oriented and kept her people's noses to the grindstone. Her main problem was the high turnover of her employees. Her two unit supervisors were only at the third clerical level and employees in the section were dead-ended at the second clerical level; both unit heads and others frequently left the department for promotional opportunities or permanent positions in other departments within the company. As a result, Wilma was constantly training new people, a task she handled well. Short had encouraged her to take courses in computer and systems applications and felt she was a prime candidate for an assistant purchasing manager's job in one of the other plants. The other supervisor, Sally Owen in the communications section, frequently needed a strong hand from Short to correct inefficiencies.

As Sam Short looked back on the past two years, he was basically satisfied. Although his staff had been reduced by 10 percent in the past three years, his department had successfully processed nearly twice the volume of purchase orders in the current year than it had three years ago. The company auditors who visited his department recently had termed his management style "autocratic," but this didn't bother him. How else would he shape up a department that had fallen into sloppy work habits?

As he looked ahead to his retirement, he was glad he would not have to deal with some major changes in the system of issuing purchase orders, such as the electronic transmission to suppliers, already under way at corporate headquarters, and the shift from the traditional purchase orders to a "credit card" approach, currently being studied by corporate headquarters. These were problems for his successors to worry about.

QUESTIONS

1. Evaluate Sam Short as a manager.
2. What should Short do about Joe Sloan?
3. What should the personnel department do about Sam Short?

Giant Industries, Inc. (B)

Perceptions of the Staff

Sam Short, manager for the past two years of the purchasing department at the Metropole Plant of Giant Industries, was perceived by his middle management group as an authoritarian, an overly strict manager who made all the decisions, criticized frequently, seldom praised or rewarded anyone, reacted emotionally to many situations, and would take action without consulting them or knowing all the facts.

Martha Hollins, the assistant purchasing manager, had been in the department many years, starting as an entry level professional purchasing agent trainee and rising through the ranks to her present position. She had in fact been promoted from her previous job as a purchasing supervisor. She felt that, based on his many years of experience, Sam Short had imposed new ways of doing things on long-term employees and supervisors. This had, she believed, created a good deal of conflict. Short had, for instance, created a number of new, essentially clerical, tasks for the purchasing agents in the purchasing section, which they resented. Martha knew that Joe Sloan, probably at the suggestion of the company auditors, had worked up a flow process chart of a proposed methodology that involved 16 steps to replace the current 27 steps between the pickup of mailed purchase requests and the mailing of processed purchase orders to suppliers.

"What he was recommending was a return to the old process before Sam changed it. Joe didn't get to first base with it," Martha said. "I thought the old way was better myself, but Sam was insistent that we do it his way."

Betty Wells, staff aide to Sam Short, had been an entry level clerk in the processing section before being promoted one level and given the staff aide position. She believed morale in the department was low overall, largely because Sam Short was so strict.

"Under previous bosses, people in purchasing and processing didn't even know what the purchasing manager looked like. They know Sam! He wants to know where everything is and how everyone is doing and people aren't used to it. If you do something wrong, he tells you so in no uncertain terms. And if they suggest a change and he doesn't agree with it, he doesn't let it go. Other bosses would say, 'go ahead and try it,' but Sam has had a lot of experience and knows it's been tried and doesn't work. The production line pressure here creates a lot of stress. It used to be that people took half an hour to accomplish what we allow three minutes for now. We all feel like we're on the firing line."

Joe Sloan was relatively new to the purchasing department (he had come into the job from another department three years before, after 22 years of company service). He believed strongly that the practice of hiring people with college degrees as purchasing agents in the purchasing section was responsible for many of the morale problems in the section. He felt that high-school graduates could do the work and, in fact, believed some of these people were better at it than some of the degree holders. Furthermore, it was a good opportunity for upwardly mobile workers in the processing section to achieve a promotion to a higher level than was possible in processing. This was one of the issues, however, that he felt he could not push strongly, given Sam Short's management style.

"There is a difference in perception between Mr. Short and me on how to do things. I respect him and think he respects me, but we do have our differences. I'm a democratic type of person; he is capable, but he is not democratic. I have not taken steps on this and other issues because I don't feel I have the responsibility and authority. All the decisions are made by the purchasing manager and his assistant. As a result, people, including me, aren't motivated. We get more threats than motivation."

Jean Low, the other supervisor in the purchasing section, was particularly bitter about the way the department was being run. She believed both Sam Short and Martha Hollins had weaknesses that were apparent to the rest of the staff and functioned in ways that made life difficult for the entire middle management group. She characterized the climate of the department as "threatening," and Short as one who made snap decisions based on his emotions of the moment. Martha Hollins, she believed, "clothes herself as a technical specialist. She is very self-protective and puts all the blame on Short for the people decisions she should make and doesn't."

Low noted that there was no clear definition of authority for middle managers. "Short tries to run everything and picks up problems out of context, then takes action without consulting those of us who know." She mentioned one instance in which an inexperienced clerk had put a purchase request in a "refile" box instead of a "to be typed" box. It was soon found and taken to Sally Owen, supervisor of the communications section. Sally decided to consult with Short about it, who promptly decided the whole communications effort was in trouble. Jean asked him if he would like to hear what happened and, when he heard the whole story, Short cooled down. "He just doesn't trust his subordinate managers, and this makes it tough for us to manage. He hits on one or more of us every day about something. He can't stand being told no. He's just a totally authoritarian personality."

Jean told a story that she felt typified the way Sam Short operated. "He told Martha Hollins to meet with Joe Sloan and myself to talk about techniques to improve productivity in our purchasing sections. Martha pulled out all the old techniques she had used when she had been a supervisor there. While we were meeting in Martha's office, Sam was pacing up and down outside the door. Finally, he poked his head in and said it wasn't necessary for all these supervisors to be wasting time in a meeting. He sent us all back to work. He had totally forgotten why we were meeting!"

QUESTIONS

1. Reevaluate Sam Short as a manager in light of the perceptions of his staff.
2. What, if anything, can the subordinates do to improve their working relationships with Sam Short?
3. If you were a senior staff aide to the corporate director of purchasing and the corporate auditors made all this information available to you with the suggestion that you improve the situation, what would you do?

INTERNATIONAL MINERALS CORPORATION

Among those most intimately concerned, perception varied widely about what had happened and was currently happening in the International Cooperation and Liaison Division (ICLD) of the Energy Development Department (EDD) of the International Minerals Corporation (IMC) in early spring. Turnover among professional personnel at all levels in the EDD had been nearly 90 percent in the past year; in fact, even experienced secretaries had left or were about to leave. Negotiations involving the development of energy sources were top priority for IMC worldwide and Paul Ladd, chief of the ICLD for just over six months, realized that his staff of five professionals was, on average, bright and motivated but almost totally inexperienced in the development of energy sources. Ladd himself, in fact, was the only person in the division with any background in the development of energy sources, having come to his present position after two years' service in other divisions of the EDD.

It should be noted that

1. Of the five officers reporting to Paul Ladd, only Bill Evans, who specialized in liaison with the African area, had been in place for more than a year.

2. Ron Craft, assistant chief of the division and liaison officer with European countries, and Marie Wright, specializing in the East Asian area, had preceded Ladd to the division by only two months. They, like Evans and the other two officers, had come to ICLD from assignments in ore extraction or processing subsidiaries located in various countries overseas and had no specific background in the development of energy sources.

3. Four months after Ladd's assignment to the job, the two experienced professionals who had been there when he took over were reassigned and replaced by Jim Larsen and Hal James. Shortly thereafter, the junior of the three secretaries assigned to the division was selected for promotion to another division of EDD. She had not, as yet, been replaced.

4. The two remaining secretaries had been in place for several years and were experienced and knowledgeable. However, Nathan Thomas, Ladd's secretary and manager of the office, had just accepted a promotion to an executive secretary's position elsewhere in the company and was due to leave shortly. Mona Wise, whose main task was as librarian of the extensive and complex library of

documents, reports, and books needed by the division, had already been nominated and was being considered for several promotions into the professional ranks. She expected to hear whether she had been selected for one of these very soon.

5. Each of the professional people reporting to Ladd had two areas of expertise assigned to them and these assignments were based more on tradition than on the skills or interests of the individuals involved. As assistant chief of the division and the second most senior person in the group, Ron Craft was assigned the European area and was expected to be the group's expert on nuclear power as a source of energy. Jim Larsen was assigned to the South American area and also was given the role of public relations expert; he wrote speeches and position papers for Schiff, the department manager, and Harlan, the vice-president, usually on direct request from them. The other assignments were:

Bill Evans: Africa and solar energy
Hal James: The Middle East and oil & gas
Marie Wright: Asia and coal

It should also be noted that Ladd reported to Helen Schiff, who had been promoted into the job as head of the EDD a year before from her former position as manager of the Planning and Policy Division. Her superior, Wade Harlan, vice-president (staff), had only two years ago, held Paul Ladd's job as chief of ICLD. At that time, he was promoted to become head of EDD and a year later he was again promoted to vice-president (staff) under Kate Lamb, senior vice-president. Harlan was regarded by Ladd and all his people as a brilliant engineer and as one the most knowledgeable people in the area of development of energy sources at International Minerals Corporation. Schiff was regarded as highly competent and totally in line with Harlan's beliefs and ideals.

Paul Ladd had graduated from Swarthmore as a civil engineering major and had acquired a masters degree in the same field from MIT two years later. He had joined the International Minerals Corporation engineering staff shortly after graduating from MIT. After serving in several engineering jobs, including as a project engineer at several overseas subsidiaries, he had been assigned to EDD in the Research and Analysis Division. He became manager of the Planning and Policy Division last year when Helen Schiff moved up and six months later was transferred to ICLD as manager of that division. He received this transfer almost ten years to the day after joining the company.

While Ladd was concerned about the relative lack of experience and expertise of his staff, it was the impact of that lack on EDD's ability to influence corporate policy that really worried him. He felt that there was a tendency among his people to try to solve each problem individually and that this undermined the division's efforts to operate at the policy level, especially when the people involved were inexperienced and did not understand what was going on at that level. He believed that a good policy sense was developed by extensive reading, by the day-to-day process of working at it and by consultation with himself, Schiff, and Harlan. When he had first come to EDD, he had sized up the situation and pinpointed the critical skills he believed were needed in the division:

- the ability to analyze
- a firm grip on what is in the company's interest in developing energy resources
- the ability to negotiate with other companies and/or foreign governments
- a good sense of tactics
- most importantly, communication skills

Ladd observed, "Some of my people can't seem to handle the communications process very well. Many of the problems we are called on to deal with have a long history, but we tend to have a short memory and often wonder why our predecessors did what they did. We need to go back in the files, especially on highly technical issues."

Ladd believed, however, that the EDD's real problem had to do with the fact that several other departments had a good deal of clout on corporate policy issues. "In fact," he said, "the real power in this area is in the staff to the IMC president. We are lucky to win half of our battles that involve corporate policy issues. This creates a good deal of frustration among my people and leads to low morale. I just don't know what I can do to correct this."

Ladd's staff group agreed with him on some issues, but they differed with him and among themselves when asked to analyze the current situation of the office. They saw Ladd himself as a brilliant engineer and a superb salesperson, but they found him lacking in both the experience and skill as a manager and in acquiring and using power and influence at senior levels to achieve the department's goals. They agreed with him that the staff to the IMC president and other departments had more clout in regard to corporate policy than EDD had and that, as a group, they were relatively inexperienced, but their concerns and frustrations were influenced more by the behavior of Ladd, Schiff, and Harlan than by this perceived inability to influence corporate policy.

Socially, the group was cohesive and friendly. The three more junior people, located down the hall from Ladd's, Craft's, and Larsen's offices, jokingly referred to themselves as inhabitants of the "lower kingdom" but all five subordinates usually had coffee and lunch together. (Ladd brown-bagged lunch and felt that leaving his office was a waste of time.) Jim Larsen, commenting on the friendliness the professional people enjoyed, said "the congeniality in the office is better than I've seen anywhere—maybe because we're all banded together in our misery."

Several other specific comments about the leadership of the division, the office, and the department made by EDD personnel serve to highlight the issues and problems faced by Paul Ladd and his staff. In some instances, these comments relate to the style of the management group as perceived by their subordinates. Other comments relate to particular happenings that the group believed were relevant to their inability to perform.

The way work was assigned and credit given, for instance, was an issue in the minds of several people. Jim Larsen, the group's public relations expert, believed that Harlan and Schiff were the real experts on the development of energy sources. Larsen said, "Whereas in other departments people might come to us as experts, here we have to go to them and even then they don't always tell us what they want us to do. When they do tell us, we are used as anonymous staff so our ego involvement is minimal. I get shut out of meetings where I have written the position paper, while people at the top of the organization get to go. Too much is concentrated at the top."

On the same issue, Hal James targeted Paul Ladd. "Paul is a superb engineer but not a strong manager. He knows more about some areas I am responsible for than I do, but he is not used to delegating. If Helen Schiff or Wade Harlan say they need a position paper or analysis on such-and-such, he thinks he has been assigned to do it. I've several times called this to his attention when he prepares an analysis or position paper on a subject in my area and I've tried to get him to sit down with me and discuss the way I communicate and particularly the way I prepare analyses and write position papers, but he never seems to have the time."

Bill Evans felt somewhat differently than Hal about Ladd's propensity to do his own analyses and prepare position papers in the other officers' areas of expertise. Noting that he had become the department's expert on solar energy, he pointed out the preferred way of handling potential conflicts. "There is a lot of potential for conflict if we started trying to move into each other's territory. If Ron were preparing an analysis or writing a position paper on European energy problems that involved solar power, he would consult with me. With Paul, it's different. I suppose I could feel upset when he prepares an analysis or writes a position paper on some aspect of solar energy instead of me, but we don't work that way. He accepts my suggestions on the technical side; I accept his on the political side or how to communicate it. He *is* an excellent salesperson."

On a related issue, Hal James noted that the younger people were just not getting the background knowledge about the development of energy sources that Harlan and Schiff had and that Ladd had been able to acquire. "Paul has cut out a substantial position for himself, but his lack of delegation and management skill in general causes problems for the rest of us. He thinks work should come in and the right people will do it. He is satisfied to sit in his office and do his work and hope others will do theirs."

Marie Wright felt much the same way about her apparent inability to acquire technical background. "We are managed fairly closely. I get a lot of direct supervision from Paul; he laboriously reviews everything that goes out of here. His supervision is all directed at the product: especially our written work. On an intellectual level, I am working for a first-class mind, but I don't get a lot of feedback on issues, and I need that to learn what's going on."

In regard to EDD's relationships with other departments and the IMC president's staff, Bill Evans had a somewhat different perspective than most of his colleagues, who expressed considerable frustration at their inability to influence corporate policy and who laid the blame on their lack of expertise. Evans agreed that EDD had no resources other than

the minds of its staff members, but he pointed out that other departments had the same resources and knowledge base and that EDD's problem was to develop a network of relationships with these other departments and the staff people around the company president so they would give EDD the information they needed. "It's all ad hoc—we go to meetings and meet people and start talking to them. Your circle gradually expands. Our job is to have a perspective that takes both company and foreign interests into account. Other departments are concerned only with the company's interests. I need to know how African government leaders think so I can advise our people on how far they can go in attaining IMC objectives. We act as intermediaries or brokers, or in another sense, as geographic experts, giving information about countries in our areas of concern in regard to the development of energy sources. The key to our problem is getting things done through relationships. We can't impose our will on anybody as the staff to the IMC president can."

Ron Craft's analysis was more typical and summed up the basic problem created by management's attitudes and style as seen by most of the people working for Paul Ladd. "The division doesn't seem to work as well as it should given the high quality people here. Paul had to deal with the departures of experienced people and the influx of inexperienced people. He had to run the office, learn the job, and spend a horrendous amount of time in interdepartment meetings. At some point, I took over the job of distributing work, but I had trouble coping too. As a result, people were often not getting work assignments on time, and all this exacerbated the natural tendency of Wade and Helen to think they know what to do and therefore not give us the work we should be doing. Most of us have had the experience of talking with Helen and having the feeling we've been given something to do without knowing what it is. Paul has been trying to get the front office to use us and he's beginning to make an impression, but there seems to be a lack of confidence in our ability to perform and it won't change until they start telling us what they want and trusting us to give it to them."

QUESTIONS

1. How would you describe Paul Ladd's leadership and/or management style? How appropriate is it, given the situation in which he finds himself?

2. Which of the analyses of the problems faced by the EDD do you believe is closest to their actual situation? Why?

3. How does Paul Ladd's analysis of the EDD situation affect his behavior vis-à-vis his subordinates; his supervisors?

4. What, if anything, can Paul Ladd's subordinates do to improve their relationships with their boss?

5. How do you account for the apparent cohesiveness of the group?

THE INTERUNIVERSITY COORDINATING COMMITTEE (A)

INDIVIDUAL VS. ORGANIZATIONAL GOALS

Emma Lu, vice-president for academic affairs of the State University at Metropole (SUM) (one of several universities within the State system), had just returned from a trip where she reviewed progress on a major study in the northern part of the state. The study was a joint program between SUM and the Office of Special Studies (OSS), an independent group within the executive office of the governor.

Lu was dismayed by some embarrassing events that had surfaced during the meetings. It appeared that the OSS had undertaken some independent studies (unknown to SUM) that resulted in the generation of data that conflicted with that contained in SUM reports. The administrators from OSS had used these discrepancies to undermine the joint effort between the two groups and had even intimated that SUM did not have the capacity or willingness to carry out the program. As an isolated instance this would not have disturbed Lu, but she recognized that this was one in a series of events that were resulting in what Lu described as "territorial erosion." She defined "territorial erosion" as a deliberate attempt by

both the administration and the legislature to break up and limit the power of the strong universities and colleges that had developed in the state over the years. For instance, she had also learned from a former college classmate in the Office of the State Comptroller (OSC) that this executive agency was preparing a brief to demonstrate that the various universities in the state were too autonomous and parochial and were not carrying out their missions in an effective fashion. This seemed like an impossible Orwellian dream to Lu. After all, SUM, for instance, was a university that had had a distinguished scientific record since its creation. The growth of its scientific and engineering departments had paralleled and contributed to the growth of the state as a strong industrial region.

Lu was a scientist by profession and a bureaucrat by default and believed in confirming hypotheses by direct observation of verifiable data. She felt that some unbiased opinion from another university in the state system was in order. She set up a luncheon meeting with Harold Wall, provost at the State University at Ruraltania (SUR). SUR and SUM had similar traditions in that they were staffed by highly competent academics, many of whom were scientists interested in generating useful state-of-the-art scientific and engineering data. Dr. Wall was a physicist by training and his career covered 35 years of experience in academia. Lu had many previous meetings with Wall concerning complementary programs involving joint projects by various groups on the two campuses, and though these meetings involved some friction between the two universities, a common sense of purpose usually carried the group over whatever rough waters developed.

After the usual exchange of opening amenities, Lu decided to lay his cards on the table and openly discussed his territorial erosion theory with Dr. Wall. Wall, an open and frank person, confessed that he too was alarmed by the behavior of OSS toward SUR. For example, a study committee in OSS had cited serious overlaps in the work carried out by SUM and SUR. In addition he felt that the previous attempts at reorganization of the state university system were fast becoming a reality. Wall stated that he perceived OSS to be using the tactic of "divide and conquer." He certainly was not against efficiency, but he was greatly disturbed by the disregard for established programs and the continuity of missions and goals.

Lu and Wall recognized that they were in the same rocky boat. In the past, both universities had maintained an arms-length distance and had managed to handle the inevitable underlying conflicts by academic jousting. Now, however, it was becoming clear to both of them that the old game of one-upmanship was going to work against them in this new atmosphere of careful surveillance of university operations by OSS.

Wall, in addition to being a scientist, was interested in philosophy and extremely well read in the dramatic arts. He related to Lu the parable of Karpman's triangle, a device frequently used by dramatists to set up the roles of the victim, persecutor, and rescuer. He suggested that in this situation the persecutor (OSS) was out looking for likely victims (SUM, SUR, and so forth). Wall added that he felt the victims could become their own rescuers by banding together and anticipating the ploys of the persecutor. Lu chuckled at this analogy but recognized that it contained more than a kernel of truth. At the conclusion of the luncheon meeting, both Wall and Lu decided to meet again after each had discussed the overall problem with their respective presidents.

Lu's superior, SUM President George Hahn, was a Ph. D. mathematician and a 30-year career academician. He had served in various capacities in both academic and administrative positions. Although he was very sympathetic to Lu's concerns, he felt that cross-university cooperation was a quixotic dream that usually ended in domination of one university by the other. Despite Hahn's misgivings, Lu did manage to persuade him to attend an upcoming meeting with representatives from SUM.

Dr. Wall's discussion with his president was not quite so fruitful as that of Lu. SUR President Harvey Chopin was a recent political appointee who had come to SUR after retiring from the army. Chopin expressed his belief that duplication of effort should be eliminated and that the only way this goal could be accomplished was through external pressure. Like Dr. Hart, he was very pessimistic about cross-university cooperation. Chopin sounded much like the OSS people in maintaining that a total reorganization was necessary in order to break up the ingrained professional parochialism and vested interests of the various universities and colleges. Wall countered this argument by expressing his belief that reorganization merely shifts people from one box to another and does nothing to solve problems involving mutual trust and cooperation. Dr. Wall then asked Chopin if he would be willing to attend a "summit conference" with the people from SUM to see if a new relationship could be established. Chopin reluctantly agreed to a meeting of two representatives from each university.

In the next two weeks Lu and Wall had a number of informal meetings in order to set up the agenda for the summit meeting. Dr. Wall warned Lu that Chopin would need convincing arguments and a definite plan of action before he would be swayed toward their point of view. At their final meeting they agreed to propose an operational plan that would convince their presidents that cooperation was both imperative and feasible. The terms were expressed in the "Guidelines for Establishment of a SUM/SUR Coordinating Committee." As the guidelines set forth, the mutual relationships between SUR and SUM in any programs should be predicated upon the following principles:

1. The heads of the universities should be committed to a joint effort when it has been established that areas of overlapping interest exist. Such areas of overlap can only be determined by open discussion of the universities' missions, goals, and specific programs.
2. A coordinating committee consisting of high-level personnel (at the vice-president, dean, or department head level and their supporting staff) should be duly constituted to carry out the tasks of eliminating the overlap and mapping out areas of mutual responsibility.
3. Regular meetings should be scheduled that the principals (vice-presidents, deans, and department heads) should faithfully attend. These meetings should occur no less than once a month.
4. Support personnel should be designated by each vice-president, dean, or department head according to the needs of the programs under consideration.
5. A system of alternating chairpersonship should prevail and should be divided between the two universities.

6. Decision making should be in the hands of the coordinating committee so that agreement can be reached without clearing through channels.
7. The acting principals on the coordinating committee should be willing to go against self-interest such as departmental or disciplinary parochialism.
8. The focus of the meetings should be on problem solving and the resolution of disparate value orientations.
9. The meetings should generate a list of action items that would be realistically related to the mutual interests of both parties.
10. Follow-up on action items should be rigorously monitored.
11. Sanction of the coordinating committee should be conveyed to all academic and staff people in both universities outlining the purposes and objectives of the joint venture. This communication should be signed by the presidents of both universities.

Though both Harold Wall and Emma Lu felt that they had outlined a reasonable rationale and modus operandi for the proposed venture, Wall stated his concern that the proposed guidelines did not spell out the specific program areas. Lu convinced him that the specifics could only be delineated at actual working meetings of the proposed committee.

Lu, in turn, emphasized the need for rallying the two universities against the common enemy (OSS). Wall countered that mere slogans would not persuade Chopin and that some short-term benefits for both universities should be stressed at the meeting. Lu stated her belief that the short-term orientation of some nonacademic administrators worked against true cooperation. Wall was quick to point out that more than a third party persecutor would be needed to establish mutual trust and cooperation on a firm basis. He felt that stressing the victim role of the universities could be counterproductive. Wall thought that a more positive approach would be to demonstrate that competent cooperation and the elimination of overlapping functions would be the best road to prosperity for both universities. On that note they ended the meeting. The "summit conference" was scheduled for the following week.

QUESTIONS

1. What is the relationship between the goals of the individuals in this situation and those of their organizations?
2. How real a threat to the universities and colleges is Lu's theory of "territorial erosion" by executive and legislative groups?
3. Do you agree or disagree with Wall's belief that establishment of a "common enemy" is not the way to maintain the continuity of missions and goals of established programs?
4. How do you explain the contrast between the relationships of Lu and Wall with their superiors?
5. What are the strengths and weaknesses of the proposed guidelines?
6. If you were Lu or Wall, how would you prepare for the "summit meeting"? How, if at all, would you prepare if you were Dr. Hahn or Harvey Chopin?
7. How do you think the two presidents will react to the proposal?

THE INTERUNIVERSITY COORDINATING COMMITTEE (B)

INDIVIDUAL VS. ORGANIZATIONAL GOALS

The Summit Meeting

The meeting of the four principals took place on neutral territory at a small, isolated resort between the two universities. Both presidents had been persuaded that two days were necessary to discuss the guidelines, outline the plan, and set definite objectives.

The morning of the first day was devoted to discussion of the historical relationship between the two universities and analysis of pressures from the changing environment that already were affecting, or soon would affect, both groups. Harvey Chopin, SUR's president, seemed basically sympathetic to the plan devised by Wall and Lu, but pointedly remarked that "new wine poured into old bottles tasted just the same." Dr. Wall agreed with Chopin that efforts similar to those attempted in the past were doomed to failure and each new attempt had two strikes against it because of old wounds, but he went on to say that "today is different from yesterday, and there is good reason to think that cooperation can be achieved." He used the space effort as an ex-

ample of one case in which many scientific disciplines, and administrative and management people as well, were able to bridge the natural social distance between themselves and to collaborate on a system-based set of concrete tasks.

Dr. Hahn was silent during the early exchange of ideas and rebuttals among the three other participants. When he finally spoke, he prefaced his remarks by stating that altruism and the greater purpose that Dr. Wall talked about were not going to get the job done. What he wanted to know was what was the quid pro quo for SUM in joining forces with SUR. After all, he said, "We have the academic expertise to accomplish anything we want with no help from anyone." Hahn went on to stress the variety and quality of academics at SUM who he felt had good enough track records to beat down the boys from OSS in any fight.

Dr. Wall interjected that the crucial question was not, in his view, a matter of academic expertise but one of overlapping functions. Besides, he pointed out, SUR had some unique and extremely expensive facilities that could complement SUM's efforts. At that point Dr. Hahn reluctantly conceded that this kind of cooperation was sorely needed. He went on to agree to the joint effort but cautioned that he could see where the "tail might wag the dog just because SUR had the facilities." He wanted assurance of safeguards against any form of encroachment by SUR.

Emma Lu assured Dr. Hahn that she believed the guidelines constituted a viable contract that took all of his concerns into consideration. Harvey Chopin injected his belief that academic expertise had lost its currency in the present environment and that management of resources was the key to survival in the new environment.

"Frankly," Chopin said, "I came to this meeting ready to shoot down any efforts at cooperation. But right now I can see the beginnings of small but fruitful relationships. In many ways I differ from you, Dr. Wall, in that I am a professional manager and you are a professional scientist, but the concept of a quid pro quo for both groups appeals to me too."

The morning meeting ended on that note. The afternoon was devoted to detailed discussions of the guidelines for establishing a coordinating committee. The discussions were open and heated. A particular point of contention involved the potential conflicts and erosion of each university's prerogatives that was implicit and explicit in the guidelines document. For example, Chopin objected to item number 6 that put decision making power in the hands of the committee. He wanted to maintain this authority. After a long debate he conceded that such checks and balances as open minutes and feedback from the committee to all levels within the two universities would satisfy him on this point.

Dr. Wall felt that item number 7, the willingness to go against self-interest on the departmental or university level would be hard to accomplish at SUM and he wondered how this would be implemented. Emma Lu noted that a statement to all academic and staff people sanctioning the coordinating committee would be the first step in solving the prob-

lem. She went on to say that the rotation of various support personnel would be the best way of breaking down parochialism within both SUM and SUR.

These were but a few of the items of concern to representatives of the two universities. They spent the rest of the day and the next morning spelling out the composition of, and the specific charge to, the coordinating committee. They decided that the first task of the committee should be a careful scrutiny of their respective budgets in order to spot any overlaps.

The first meeting of the coordinating committee was set up for a month from the following Thursday. It was agreed that Emma Lu and Harold Wall would be alternating chairpersons and each university would have four other representatives at the meeting. Lu and Wall both agreed to start the process of disseminating information about the function of the committee to people at their respective institutions. The two presidents agreed that they would play a monitoring role but would not be active participants in the interuniversity committee. They reserved the prerogative, however, to call future summit meetings to assess the status of the détente.

QUESTIONS

1. Why is the professional versus nonprofessional, or academic versus nonacademic relationship a barrier to cooperative efforts?
2. Do you agree that academic expertise has lost currency in today's environment? Why?
3. Is it possible to go against self-interest on the departmental level or university level and still accomplish individual and group goals? What are the trade-offs?
4. What would you predict the reactions of some people back in the two universities might be to this committee?
5. Would you be willing to serve on such an interuniversity coordinating committee?

THE INTERUNIVERSITY COORDINATING COMMITTEE (C)

INDIVIDUAL VS. ORGANIZATIONAL GOALS

Epilogue 1 (two weeks later)

Some of the reactions of SUM and SUR people were recorded shortly after the plan to establish an interuniversity coordinating committee was announced in the two institutions.

At the State University at Metropole:
Phil Lawton, Ph.D., a metallurgist in the Engineering School: "I think that the whole proposal is a power play by SUR to take away as much of the legitimate role of SUM as possible. Before long all that we will have left will be a superorganization run by short-term bureaucrats who know nothing about the scientific process and the traditions of the engineering school. I'm going to continue to play my usual role right down the line according to my understanding of the situation."

Joan Handy, Nursing School: "Although our school is not directly involved with the interuniversity coordinating committee, I think it has great promise. Besides, I feel that the same concept can be used within the university; our relationships with the medical school point out the need for this kind of cooperation."

William Bates, Ph.D., a chemist in the College of Liberal Arts and Sciences: "I think that this coalition of SUR and SUM will help in obtaining some grants. I am certainly in favor of any joint scientific ventures. My one area of concern, however, is that the credit for the work on collaborative projects usually tends to work against the individual contributor. I am usually judged by my publication record. I hope we can work out a reasonable solution to this dilemma."

At the State University at Ruraltania:
Captain Flagg, chairman of the NROTC program: "I have been asked to participate on the interuniversity committee as a representative of SUR. For me personally this is not a new concept or a new role. I face this problem of working with professionals and civilians every day. As far as I am concerned, the give and take at these meetings will help to surface some constructive conflict and aid both universities in getting the job accomplished."

Sarad Salim, Ph. D., physicist: "The group over at SUM has been too autonomous for many years. I don't know if this will change the situation but at least it will bring out the conflicts. Sometimes group meetings only intensify the battle lines rather than rallying people together. I hope that it works. I understand that I will participate on the working committee in the near future; so as far as I am concerned the proof of the pudding will be in the eating."

Chelsea Ball, an administrative manager: "I have been dealing with professionals and academic types for years. You have your good guys and your bad guys. What you need is someone strong enough (or a group that is strong enough) to put things in place. I don't mean by bureaucratic edict but by strong purpose and authoritative persuasion. I hope this interuniversity committee will not be another talk show."

Epilogue 2 (two years later)

The Interuniversity Committee for Program Coordination has been in operation now for over two years. Since its inception as a bilateral instrument, a third institution, the State College at Exurbia (SCE), has been added to the membership roster. SCE has had overlapping functions with SUM and SUR on studies and grants in the traditional liberal arts and it was logical that it should be included in a new tripartite arrangement.

The first few meetings of the committee were rough-and-tumble affairs characterized by constant maneuvering for power. The joint leadership principle established in the guidelines helped avert real problems and at times the parties agreed to disagree and referred whatever problems they could not handle within the committee to higher levels. Basically, however, the first ten meetings were devoted to orientation, venting of pent-up hostilities, and establishing basic quid pro quos.

At least twenty action items have been brought before the committee for coordination of effort during the two year period. The actions include the following:

1. Office of Naval Research grants. SCE and SUR are collaborating on the analysis of psy-chological data gathered from Navy personnel. SCE will transfer some funds to SUR for research of existing data. SCE also worked with SUM on a planned program for summer activities.

2. SUR-SUM National Science Foundation grant. The results of a joint study effort on a recent major flood is now in press, and four other studies are in different states of preparation.

3. SUR and SUM have collaborated on a survey of earth observations from space under a contract from NASA.

4. SUR and SUM have agreed to jointly host several scientific workshops. The agreement involved a number of workshops on each campus that were attended by several federal agencies and 16 companies in addition to the usual number of academics from many other universities.

5. Collaboration has begun on a proposal for a Department of Defense grant for several baseline studies that will involve the coordination of SUM, SUR, and SCE activities. These studies involve the SUM engineering school, various science departments at SUR, and a group of psychologists at SCE. SCE will play a major role in drafting a memorandum of understanding. SUM has expressed a need to coordinate all relevant committee proposals and work with the Department of Defense in order to set priorities, determine funding, and identify ongoing programs and plans.

QUESTIONS

1. Can you explain why the Interuniversity Coordination Committee appears to be an effective working entity?

2. Do you think it will continue so to be? What influences might destroy its effectiveness in the future?

3. How significant are its accomplishments to date?

Joe Lane

In September, Joe Lane, senior analyst, was transferred to the headquarters staff of the International Banking Corporation (IBC) and assigned to the M Section of the Q Department. Lane started work for IBC sixteen years ago after graduation from Brown University with an BA in political science and had served in four overseas subsidiaries, all in analytic staff assignments. The M Section consisted of seven officers. All except the manager of the section, Cliff Kerr, were junior to Lane.

Cliff Kerr explained to Lane on his arrival that the vacancy he was filling carried a two-fold responsibility: first, he was to report regularly on certain aspects of the economic, financial, and monetary conditions in the areas of responsibility assigned to the M Section, and second, he was to supervise two other officers who were also assigned in this area. Kerr indicated his own duties and responsibilities were quite heavy and he would have to rely on Lane to handle the bulk of this analytic reporting. The section also contained two specialists and a trainee.

The two officers reporting to Lane were Jill Cook, a newly promoted associate senior analyst with a masters degree in money and banking from the University of Pennsylvania and a bachelors degree in economics from Cornell, and Ben Grant, a provisional junior analyst with a bachelors degree in economics from Columbia University who was working on his Ph.D. thesis in the same subject. Cook was in her mid-thirties, had come to IBC three years ago after six years with the Federal Reserve Bank in New York and two years with the First Pennsylvania Bank. Grant was twenty-four. Kerr told Lane that both Grant and Cook were thoroughly competent but tended to squabble.

At the time of Lane's arrival, the group was preparing an important report requested by the CEO's office containing detailed information on possible monetary reforms and devaluation of certain foreign currencies. Ben Grant was responsible for preparing the report; he had specifically asked Lane's predecessor for the assignment, partly because his workload had been light when the request was received and partly because the project interested him.

Lane was favorably impressed with Grant from the beginning. He seemed interested in his work, had a sound academic background, and was accurate and thorough; he became so engrossed in the monetary report that he frequently stayed at the office until late at night to work on it. During his first few months in the section, Lane had several long talks with Grant on subjects that interested them both. At the same time, he observed that Grant was not at ease in informal social situations in the office and tended to avoid them. On those few occasions when he did have coffee or lunch with someone in the office, he seemed tense and withdrawn.

Lane quickly observed the conflict between Grant and Cook. Cook openly criticized Grant's work, spoke unfavorably about him to the other officers, and frequently dropped thinly veiled hints to Lane about his incompetence. There were frequent, open flare-ups between the two. Once, for instance, Lane heard them arguing heatedly about the organization of the monetary report. When Grant came to his office to discuss it, Lane called Cook in to present her views. Lane refused to judge the issue. He said he believed it was something only the writer could judge at this point and that while Cook had been able to provide Grant with a great deal of valuable information and guidance, it was really Grant's responsibility to organize the report.

Shortly after the two had left the office, Cook returned to continue the discussion. She noted that she had spoken to Ben at least a dozen times about the organization of the report but he responded as if she had never spoken to him at all. She expressed concern that Grant was not following the format that was worked out before Lane arrived in the section, and the one Grant was using did not make sense to her. She asserted that Grant's format was inconsistent and confusing.

Lane responded that the content was more important than the organization of the material. Lane went on to observe that he felt Grant was very competent and would do a good job. In reflecting on the incident, Lane concluded that to ensure the development of Grant's best qualities, he should plan to shield him as far as possible from Cook.

At the end of January, the report was finished and submitted to the CEO's office. Shortly thereafter, Lane left on an extended trip to attend an important conference overseas. When he returned two weeks later, he learned from Cook that the report had come back accompanied by a sharply worded letter of criticism that stated that certain crucial facts were lacking. Cook had interpreted this as Grant's failure and had taken over the revision of the report herself. She had been backed up in this, she told Lane, by Kerr, to whom she had taken the matter in Lane's absence.

As soon as Cook left the office, Grant entered and requested that he be given responsibility for the revision of the monetary report. He expressed his concern that Cook, Kerr, and the CEO's office were blaming him for the incompleteness of the report. He observed that the missing information was very sensitive and extraordinarily difficult to deduce even from very confidential sources. He stated very emphatically that his reputation was a stake and he felt he should be given the opportunity to make the report more complete.

Lane tended to agree with Grant that the criticism from the CEO's office was unduly harsh. Information about sensitive monetary matters was not easy to obtain simply because of the nature of the information and the potential damage of leaks. Therefore, while it was true that information was lacking, he felt that Cook was not justified in assuming this to be due to incompetence on Grant's part. Nor had she, Lane felt, any right to take over the report herself. Accordingly, he agreed to restore it to Grant, though Cook protested strongly when he told her of this decision.

About a week later, Grant and Cook engaged in an argument so violent that Lane, heard them through the closed door of his own office and came out to investigate. As he approached them, Cook was loudly accusing Grant of incompetence and laziness; Grant was asserting that she had used the incident of the report to advance her own ends. Lane stopped the argument and sent them back to their desks. Later that afternoon, he had a talk with Grant and told him that he and Cook should try to avoid one another if they could not learn to work amicably together. Several days later, he called the first of what became a regular weekly staff meeting at which he stressed the importance of cordial office relations. He noted that it was important for the two of them to work together cooperatively because he, Lane, could not spend the time with them that he might like because of the two-fold nature of his job. In addition, he pointed out, they knew considerably more about the technical aspects of their work than he did. He wanted them to decide what was right with a cooperative and helpful set of attitudes.

Although the conflict did not stop, there was never again as serious an outbreak. Cook occasionally spoke to Lane, usually in a roundabout way, of what she regarded as Grant's shortcomings: his insolence, his incompetence, and his overconfidence. Lane felt she was trying to persuade him to discipline Grant by insinuating that he was a liability to the whole section.

Lane had great respect for Cook; he regarded her as an extremely competent woman with an extensive knowledge of economic and financial affairs who could be gracious and tactful in most situations. However, he also thought that Cook was given to strong and inflexible opinions and was jealous of Grant's ability. It was difficult for her to accept those views that differed from her own, especially those of Ben Grant. He spoke to Grant about this, feeling it was easier to expect self-control from him than from her, and explained to him what he thought were Cook's problems. Grant replied that he did his best to get along with her but that she had "double-crossed" him, gossiped about him in malicious ways, and taken advantage of his occasional confidences in her to the point where he no longer trusted her.

About this time, there was a story in the IBC Newspaper that the corporation was establishing a special training program at the IBC Institute (IBCI) for the concentrated study of foreign economic problems. Grant told Lane he would very much like to attend the training program and asked if Lane would support his request. Lane said he would think about it

adding that he wasn't sure Grant was ripe for such training. In ensuing weeks, Grant raised the subject of the training program frequently, to the point where Lane grew irritated when he heard about it.

In late April, the revision of the monetary report was submitted to the CEO's office and accepted in its entirety. Lane was gratified that his confidence in Grant seemed justified. His only wish now was that Grant could somehow work out a more satisfactory relationship with Cook.

A month or so later, Lane was preparing performance appraisals. Calling Grant into his office, he showed him his appraisal on which he had given him mid-range ratings. In the narrative portion, he had commented in detail on such factors as Grant's limited ability to get along with others, tactfulness, adaptability, cooperativeness, patience, and sense of humor. Lane noted that Grant had excellent potential and expressed his hope that Grant would not spoil his chances for advancement by refusing to improve himself in these areas. Lane felt Grant was somewhat opinionated and perhaps rather too critical of others. He thought Grant could work much more effectively with Cook if he were willing to make the effort. Lane noted that Cook had a lot of valuable experience that Grant could use to better advantage if he were not so intent on working independently. Lane also admonished Grant for asking for special favors (that is, to participate in the training program) before he had earned them.

After some further discussion with considerable argument from Grant, Lane removed a second appraisal from his desk drawer and showed it to Grant saying that this was the one he was going to submit. He had rated him a little less harshly in the second appraisal and had emphasized some of Grant's good points in the narrative portion. He had also given less weight to some of the criticisms. He spoke, for example, of Grant's studies and of his continued efforts to increase his familiarity with the area of his specialization.

Lane also called in Jill Cook and talked with her in somewhat more general terms about the necessity for getting along. He had rated her somewhat higher than Grant, and in the narrative portion he commented on Cook's excellent grasp of the sophisticated and complex issues with which the M Section dealt. He also alluded to opportunities to further improve her abilities to listen to the views of others and demonstrate flexibility regarding these views. Cook accepted the ratings, indicated her desire to improve, and then commented that it took two to get along and when one was immature, antisocial, biased, conceited, mistrustful, and devious, it makes it especially difficult.

Early in July, Lane received an urgent request from another department for projections on the gross national product of several countries for which the M Section was responsible. He showed the request to Grant. Grant stated that a proper job would require far more time than was available, that the information needed was much too difficult to obtain, and that it was needed too quickly to do justice to the requirements of such a study. In effect, he all but refused to accept it. Lane, therefore, assigned it to Cook and requested that Kerr assign the trainee to her for the three weeks necessary to get the report out. Kerr approved the assignment. Lane gave Jill and the trainee as much help as he could and thought that the report was quite good considering the time restraints. The report was accepted by the other department.

Lane was disappointed with Grant. He felt that Jill and the trainee had been willing to pitch in and do their best in an emergency, whereas Grant, with his unrealistically high standards, had made his special abilities unavailable to the section. Accordingly, in subsequent weeks, Lane made a point of denying Grant small personal favors that he requested, such as occasional afternoons off. He also formally disapproved a written request Grant submitted to him for attendance at the training program at IBCI.

Toward the end of August, another disturbing incident took place. Kerr, reading a report that Grant had submitted for transmittal to the CEO's office, questioned a passage in which the meaning and applicability seemed unclear. He telephoned Lane and asked him for his opinion. Lane knew little about the report since it was something for which he had assigned Grant full responsibility. He agreed with Kerr, however, that the passage should be clarified. He said he would discuss it with Grant.

When Lane asked Grant for an explanation of the passage, Grant became indignant that his work should be questioned. He maintained that he had used knowledge derived from his academic studies to shed light on the meaning of the material he was reporting. He asked Lane whether or not he had full responsibility for the work that was assigned him and why, if he had, his judgment could not be trusted.

Lane pointed out that it was not a question of trusting his judgment. Kerr had raised a question about the clarity of a statement and a response had to be made. Since Lane did not know as much about the subject as Grant did, he had come to him. Grant insisted that it was not possible to make the statement any clearer. Lane directed Grant to write an explanation of the statement immediately.

Grant wrote a memo restating his position that the paragraphs in question were as clear and as accurate as he could make them. Finally, Lane, unwilling to delay submission of the report, deleted the passage and sent the report back to Kerr.

Feeling that this relatively minor incident was symptomatic of a more basic problem, Lane sent Grant a memo detailing the nature of their disagreement. He asked Grant to think the situation over and to give him his views on the matter. If Grant felt Lane was wrong in deleting the passage or if there were some reason why the explanation should not have been given, then Grant should say so. Lane felt this memo might encourage Grant to think clearly and objectively about his relationship to his superiors and about his responsibilities as an analyst.

The following day, Lane left for a week to attend a conference. On his return, he looked for an answer from Grant but found none. A few days later, he asked Grant to have lunch with him and brought the matter up again. Grant argued that the subject was closed and that he did not wish to discuss it. When Lane insisted that they should talk the matter out, Grant became emphatic. He said that he was either responsible for the quality of his reports or he was not. He felt that unless it could be shown that he had been factually in error, no one should have the right to question his competence and his judgment once he had been given that responsibility. By the end of the lunch, both Lane and Grant were extremely angry and they returned to the office arguing heatedly. Grant, at one point, stated that he knew Lane was vindictive and had been saying unfavorable things about him behind his back. Lane, feeling that Grant was challenging his authority, ended by demanding that Grant give him an explanation of the criticized portion of the report. Grant refused.

Relations between the two were strained after that. A week after the incident, a phone call came for Grant while he was out of the office for the morning. It was a request from a subsidiary for certain information on a subject on which Grant had been working. In his absence, Lane took the call and tried to find the answer in the files. He couldn't find what he was looking for so he left a note on Grant's desk telling him of the request and his unsuccessful attempt to respond to it and asking him to take care of it when he returned.

When Grant found the note, he was outraged. Storming into Lane's office, he asserted that the subject was in his area and that Lane had no right to look in his files in his absence. Grant insisted he had that information at his fingertips, and could have given an answer immediately. Lane countered by observing that the subsidiary people were in a hurry and he thought it important to at least try to get an immediate answer.

Grant asserted that Lane should have told them he was out of the office and would return their call when he returned. Grant further asserted that Lane had no right to look in his files, that the subsidiary people had asked for him because the question was in his area. Lane insisted it was not *his* area and stated that even though it was something Grant had been working on that did *not* mean Grant had a separate jurisdiction all his own. Lane further insisted that, as a matter of policy, if anyone at IBC requests information that the M Section had, they had a right to get it regardless of who was or was not in the office.

Grant reiterated that Lane had no right to look in his files. Trying to control his anger, Lane pointed out that files were not personal property but were, instead, repositories for information for the office as a whole. Finally, after several more minutes of increasingly heated argument, Grant stormed out of Lane's office.

The following morning, Lane went to see Kerr, taking Grant with him to avoid any suspicion that he might be presenting the situation unfairly or talking behind Grant's back. He reported the several incidents between himself and Grant and ended by raising the main point as he saw it: the right of a supervisor to expect, at the very least, technical information from subordinates. He told Kerr that in his opinion, Grant's behavior amounted to insubordination.

Kerr avoided taking sides on the issue and did not support Lane as strongly as he had hoped. Kerr did discuss the problems with them for some time, dwelling on the functions of an analyst in the M Section, the contribution that each person makes to the discharge of those functions, and the need for cooperation and, most particularly, free communications among the members of the M Section team.

Later in the day, Lane saw Kerr privately and Kerr assured him that he supported him entirely on the issue but did not want to complicate relations with Grant. Kerr's desire, he noted, was to have easy communications between all levels. Lane learned later that immediately after he had left Kerr's office, Kerr had called Grant in and talked with him for nearly an hour.

After this incident, there were no more open clashes between the two. Grant avoided contact with Lane whenever possible and indeed had very little to do with any of the other officers. Relations were tense and strained and Lane felt that what had once been an atmosphere characterized by the free exchange of ideas had become one in which ideas were jealously guarded personal secrets. He still felt strongly that Grant was an exceptionally promising young analyst and it was with real regret that he watched his increasing inflexibility and inability to accept any challenge of his views.

QUESTIONS

1. Analyze and evaluate Ben Grant's behavior. If you had been in his position, what would you have done differently? Why?
2. Analyze and evaluate Jill Cook's behavior. If you had been in her position, what would you have done differently? Why?
3. Analyze and evaluate Joe Lane and Cliff Kerr's handling of Ben Grant. What could Grant have done to improve his impact on these two managers?
4. What would you do now if you were Joe Lane; Cliff Kerr; Jill Cook; Ben Grant?

KING INDUSTRIAL PRODUCTS COMPANY

Gail Green was sitting at her desk thinking about her research assignment for her Organizational Behavior class. The assignment was to analyze a problem situation in a work environment that she could do something to improve. She was sure the situation at her father's company would be a good case to analyze.

King Industrial Products Company (KIPC) is a small, family-owned company manufacturing industrial products. It was founded almost twenty years ago by Gail Green's father, George King. The company employs twelve men in the plant (including three plant supervisors) and four people in the office, three of whom are owners and family members. George is the president of the company. Gail's older sister, Joan, is the vice-president and has taken over most of the buying and selling for the company. Gail's mother, Helen, functions as the secretary and treasurer of KIPC. Kate Sims, who has worked for the family for 32 years, acts as office manager, secretary, and bookkeeper. (See Exhibit 1 for Gail Green's discriptions of the backgrounds of the key people at King Industrial Products Company and Exhibit 2 for a partial organizational chart.)

The company grew steadily since its founding and was quite prosperous in its first decade. After this, the company experienced a few lean years, including a loss one year, but then the company resumed its steady growth, becoming ever more prosperous. In more profitable years, the company issued substantial dividends to the owners, and although there is not a formal profit-sharing program, Kate and the plant supervisors receive bonuses as well.

Gail's family had been telling her that it was becoming increasingly difficult to maintain a productive work environment at the office. They felt Kate Sims had developed a very caustic personality. As evidence, they asserted that she had been rude to everyone in the office on occasion as well as to some of the plant workers and had become more critical of others. Over the past several years, Kate had given them the impression that she was becoming increasingly satisfied with just "getting by." It was the opinion of Gail's family that Kate's personality change began gradually at about

Source: This case was first prepared as a class project by Jon Eiche, Lynda Eiche, Charles Mitchell, Paula Norris Roney, and William Stone at the Jones Graduate School of Administration, Rice University. It has been edited and used here with their permission.

EXHIBIT 1

BACKGROUND AND DESCRIPTION OF OFFICE PERSONNEL AT KING INDUSTRIAL PRODUCTS COMPANY, AS SEEN BY GAIL GREEN

Gail Green is 26 years old. She grew up in the same area as her father, George King. She was always an extremely good student in all areas. Like her father, she is mathematically inclined. In college, she majored in Spanish and Economics. Studying literature as part of her Spanish major, she became aware of a whole other world, really a whole other side to herself, which was subjective and feeling. The nature of much of the literature helped her to appreciate liberalism; although, whether by nature, or upbringing, or both, she is conservative. She sometimes even wishes she was so kind as to be liberal. Still, she is conservative and figures that this must mean she is selfish. She can feel guilty at the drop of a hat. She put aside for awhile her intent to pursue business and got a master of arts degree in Spanish literature. She taught Spanish for two years, hoping she might help open someone else's eyes (as hers had been opened) and thought that teaching was a good way to contribute to the world. During that time, she married Bill Green, whom she had met in college (in Spanish class). He is very unlike her father, in that he is mild-tempered and easy-going. He is very unlike Gail, in that he dislikes rules and authority, loves risk, cooks creatively, and is very individualistic and independent (although they find that the longer they are married, the more alike they become). Gail worked for nine months for Bill's parents in one of their small grocery stores in a small town outside of Houston, Texas. Because she comes from a very sheltered background, the experience at the store helped her become aware of how seemingly very different people can have a great deal in common. Within the last year, she decided that although the subjective side of life is interesting it is too frustrating, given her basically objective nature, for her to make a career of teaching literature. Thus, she decided she should return to a more analytical area. She is now in business school. She hopes to do well after school, but worries that her motivation is not power or affiliation, but achievement, which may explain why she has been in school so much (where she knows she can do well) and not out doing something in the "real world." She has tremendous respect for the risk takers out there (like her family).

George King is 53 years old. He grew up in an affluent suburb of a medium-sized industrial southern city. His parents socialized and traveled a good bit, leaving him and his sister (who is one year older) in the care of a live-in cook/maid who worked for the family from the time George was born until he reached his mid-twenties. He is extremely intelligent, with a natural inclination for math and science. He graduated from Tulane University with a degree in engineering. Then, he took his ROTC commission in the Army Corps of Engineers, which he loved and wishes he had never left. After the army, he married Helen, whom he had met in college, and went to work for his father. By this time, his parents had settled down and taken an interest (an often domineering one) in their children's lives. George responded to their interest almost gratefully. George and Helen had three children, two daughters and then a son (who was born with Down's syndrome and died at age eight of a congenital heart defect associated with the syndrome). At work, George is very controlled emotionally and very lenient and softhearted with his employees. At home, he used to be very demanding and impatient, emphasized by a screaming temper. He also used to drink and smoke heavily, much as his father had done in his younger days. However, as he approached 50, George quit drinking (virtually coerced by his father, who in his old age no longer drinks or smokes). He also quit smoking, started working out daily, and developed a more mellow temperament. This year it was discovered that he had a large, inoperable malignant lung tumor. After three strong chemotherapy treatments and six weeks of radiation, the tumor is gone completely. The treatments reduced his stamina considerably, and only time will tell if he is truly cured. The whole experience seems to have mellowed him further, and he periodically considers selling his company. George's main complaint about Kate is that she doesn't do anything beyond what she feels she is supposed to do. For example, she will not stay 15 minutes late, or put sodas in the refrigerator, or take papers out to the plant when the workers out there are busy.

Helen King is 52 years old. She grew up in a small town in Louisiana. Her mother's family members were the town's doctors and lawyers. Her father and the other members of his family were entrepreneur types with a variety of business interests. Since both her mother's and father's families were very high status people in this small town, Helen was "a big fish in a small pond." She is very aware and proud of her family background (which is traced back to various houses of European royalty). She is a paradox because on one hand, she is very aware of class; on the other hand, she is an extremely kind and generous person. She is genuinely friendly and on a first-name basis with everyone, from the grocery checkers to the pharmacist to the service station boys. As a child, she would come home from school without her shoes, having given them to a child who had no shoes at all. She is truly sympathetic and concerned for less fortunate people; however, she seems to feel she is somehow inherently different from them. Her father died when she was eight years old. Her brother was 16 when their father died, but even as he got older, he did not fill the father's role at all. Helen's mother (Gail's grandmother), however, is a strong and unemotional type and handled her husband's death fairly well. Both Helen and her mother received considerable support (emotional, not financial) from their vast traditional southern family, in which even the most distant cousin is close kin. Helen married George after her junior year in college. She is very artistic and emotional and, in contrast to George, does not display an objective kind of common sense. Family is easily her top priority with no close second. She is an extremely loving mother and should have had a dozen children. She likes to paint and is a voracious reader, particularly of historical fiction. When her children were young she stayed home. As they got older she did a number of things, from selling real estate to painting seriously. Finally, seven years ago, she began doing secretarial work. She is the second largest stockholder after George. Her mother (whom she adores, although they are quite different) is crippled with arthritis and is in a nursing home, for which Helen has to pay some portion. Helen's main complaint about Kate, besides her occasional unpleasantness, is that Kate seems to pick one person to be down on, or (in Kate's words) "freeze out." For example, several years ago, a friend of George's worked in the office, too. Although all four other office members agreed that he contributed little to the company, it was Kate who kept the fire fueled, and eventually George dismissed him.

Joan King is 29 years old. She grew up in the same area as her father. When she went to college, she became very aware and appreciative of her family. She was an above average student. She majored in religion because she enjoys philosophy, not because she is extremely religious. Joan is a good cook and also likes to read. She enjoys contemporary fiction, especially by southern authors. During her junior and senior years in college, she was virtually engaged to a boyfriend from high school. It did not work out, and since then she has seemed a bit wary of men. Only now is she becoming interested again in a husband and family. She is a methodical person with a lot of routines; she is set in her ways in many respects. She has a dog, and is devoted to her family, much like her mother. She can be very critical of her father, both personally (for the way he caters to his parents and for his temper, which is much like her own) and professionally (claiming he really doesn't do anything at the office except read business journals and play with his computer). She has taken over most of the buying and selling for the company (done mainly over the phone in this business, with fairly regular suppliers and customers). She is tougher in business than George and more strict with employees. Helen and Gail tease her about being bossy; she laughs, but knows it is half true. She and Gail own equal portions of the company. She enjoys her work at KIPC but does not like the small, (to use her words) "redneck" town where it is located. Primarily for that reason, she hopes the company will be sold in the not-too-distant future. Joan's main complaint about Kate, besides her unpleasantness, is the way Kate dwells on others' mistakes but justifies her own.

Kate Sims is 62 years old. She grew up in a small, southern town with a population of about 5,000. She was the second of six children (five girls and one boy). Her brother (the third child, born shortly after Kate) died in his twenties, and she says that her father was never the same after that. She is closest to her youngest sister Mary, who is divorced from her abusive husband (both alcoholics), and whom she helps financially. Kate also felt close to her father (who died about eight years ago), and those who observed them together say they apparently did have a good relationship. Kate implies that she was his favorite child; however, she often contradicts this idea by saying, "I'm not good in math because my father always helped my older sister with her homework and not me." When asked about that sister, Kate says very little, except that she does not hear from her much. Kate has maintained a close relationship with her brother's widow and children. She also goes to see her mother about once every six weeks and takes her out to visit places or friends. Although Kate does not seem to mind, she does complain about being tired when she gets back. Kate finished high school, then she completed some secretarial training. She was married for a short time in her twenties. Her husband, who was in the army, cheated on her and abused her. She divorced him and, strangely, did not tell her family for quite a while. After her divorce, Kate worked as a secretary for a short time at an insurance company. She then went to work for George's father. He remembers her as being extremely "moody." He also says that she is "smart as a whip" and an efficient, hard worker. He seems to feel she has a subtle hostility toward men. He saw her as quick to form opinions where men were concerned and unwilling to tolerate any glibness from them. After working for George's father for one month, she told him that for $50 more a month, she could do the other secretary's work as well. Mr. King took her up on the offer and taught her how to do the bookkeeping. Since then, whenever other secretaries were hired, she would run them off, generally by being unfriendly and harping on their mistakes and shortcomings (such as occasional tardiness). Though quick to point out others' mistakes, Kate usually has an excuse for her own (for example, she was interrupted). In her thirties, Kate had a roommate. They were buddies and often went to the beach on weekends and to football games and other events. They seemed to not get along as well when the roommate acquired a boyfriend, whom she eventually married. Since then, Kate has lived alone. She likes to garden and read romance novels. Although Kate has no pets, she has several bird feeders, which she maintains religiously, and she is extremely knowledgeable about birds. Being a good cook, she enjoys good food. She smokes heavily and likes big cars. She is a Southern Baptist and attends church regularly, which is where she has met most of her friends. She is meticulously neat and appreciates that quality in other people. Being particular about her own appearance, she takes very good care of herself and dresses nicely.

Exhibit 2

King Industrial Products Company Organizational Chart

George King, President

Joan King, Vice-President

Helen King, Secretary/Treasurer

Kate Sims,
Office Manager

Jack, Billy, and Sam;
Plant Supervisors

the time Helen started helping out at the office, which was approximately seven years ago. Even though the family felt that Kate's personality was offensive, Gail Green's father felt that Kate should not be terminated because she had worked loyally for the family for so many years. Gail asked her family if they would allow her and her team of students at graduate school to do an analysis of the situation and make recommendations for improvement. The family members were all enthusiastic about the possibility of finding a solution to the problem.

Kate's official title at KIPC was office manager; however, her position had been more in the line of secretary/bookkeeper. She had been at KIPC since it was founded almost twenty years ago. Before that, she worked for George and his father for twelve years in a family-owned metal stamping business that was founded by George's grandfather during the Great Depression. She had complete access to the books, could write and sign checks, and had her own set of company keys.

The office employees took turns opening up the office for the plant workers. Gail had often heard her family say that they thought Kate resented having to open the office when it was her turn to do so. In fact, Kate often fell ill on these occasions or sometimes scheduled an unexpected vacation. On the days that she did come in early to open the office, Kate often left early in the afternoon, saying that she was ill or that she had to run errands.

Kate kept manual accounting ledgers for the company's finances. Everyone in the office had access to a computer, but Kate adamantly refused to use one. The books were meticulously maintained. Gail had often seen Kate take a ruler and carefully draw the lines on each new page. Kate was very proud of the condition in which she maintained the books and had been heard to say that not many people took pride in their work any more. George often used an accountant named Gary Knight to prepare his tax returns. Gary always complimented Kate on the accuracy and legibility of her books, and Helen and Joan noticed that Kate seemed very flattered when he did so. Kate always made it a point to dress up when she knew that Gary was going to be in the office; because of this, Helen and Joan seem to think that Kate had a crush on Gary.

Gail remembered her family describing one morning in particular. The family had planned a meeting that morning, so Helen had asked Kate if she would do the payroll. Many years ago, Kate had been responsible for the payroll, but that responsibility was turned over to Helen when she started working in the office. Doing the payroll had been a long and complicated process for Kate. Kate often said that she had never been good at math, and that her father had always helped her older sister with her math but not Kate. Helen had therefore given Kate a sheet of paper listing everyone's check amount.

As Kate was typing the checks, Jack (one of the plant supervisors) came in and asked Kate if she would type some papers for him. Helen noticed that Kate did not appear to notice Jack immediately. Kate often became irritated when she was interrupted. While Helen watched, Jack became increasingly irritated the longer he waited and he began to pace as if he were in a hurry.

When Kate finally looked up, Jack told her that he had three trucks backed up on the loading dock and he needed the papers typed right away. He asked her if she would type them immediately and take them out to the plant. Kate reluctantly agreed to stop what she was doing to type the papers, but then she adamantly refused to take them out to the plant.

At this point, Helen intervened and told Jack that she would take the papers out to the plant for him. Helen felt there were several reasons why Kate would not take papers out to the plant for the workers. First, in this instance, she and Jack had been arguing lately and that was a way to irritate him. Second, Kate was always dressed nicely and she didn't like going out to the plant because it was dirty there. Helen thought that a third reason, however, was because Kate liked to distance herself from the plant workers and disliked going into their work environment.

It was time for the meeting to start when Helen returned from the plant. Gail's sister, Joan, went over to Kate's desk and asked her to take messages for them while they were in the meeting. Kate responded, "Uh, huh." This sort of perfunctory response was common in conversations between Kate and Joan. Gail had often thought that her sister and Kate found it especially hard to get along.

During the meeting, George explained how he was thinking about hiring another secretary to reduce Kate's workload. He mentioned the fact that she would be retiring in a few years, and they would need to have someone trained to replace her.

Helen expressed reservations, noting that Kate had been driving off secretaries from the first month she started working for George's father over 32 years ago. Sometimes, Helen even felt that Kate was trying to run her off as well, except Kate knew that she couldn't turn George against his wife. George really thought a better alternative would be to buy an accounting software program for their computers that would automate the company records, but he knew from past experience that Kate wouldn't have anything to do with that idea. It wasn't that she didn't do her job well; he just thought a computer would make her job so much easier and faster. She wouldn't have to worry about transposing numbers and she wouldn't have to do all of the posting by hand. Joan commented (a bit nastily) that Kate had been doing her job for over 32 years and, thus, should be expected to do her job well.

While this meeting was taking place, Gail telephoned to talk to her family. Kate answered the phone. Whenever Gail called and Kate answered, Gail always took time to make small talk before asking to speak with a member of the family.

Gail: "Hi, Kate. How are you doing?"

Kate: "Oh fine, Gail. How are you?"

Gail: "Pretty good, but I'm really tired. I've been working hard in school. You sound a little hoarse. Are your sinuses bothering you again?"

Kate: "Yeah, but they always bother me. I'm used to it."

Gail: "How is everyone there feeling about Louisiana football?"

Kate: "Everybody's pretty disappointed."

Gail: "Me, too. Well is Daddy there?"

Kate: "Yeah, but he's in a meeting with your mom and your sister."

Gail: "What for?"

Kate: "I don't know. Your dad never tells me anything anymore. Do you want me to buzz him?"

Gail: "No, that's okay. I'm in between classes and just thought I would call. I'll call later. Thanks, Kate."

Kate: "Bye, Gail."

Gail: "Bye-bye, Kate."

Gail hung up the phone. She remembered how she and her sister used to go to the office to visit her father. Kate had seemed so friendly. She and her sister had always looked forward to seeing her. It seemed so strange how one's perceptions of people could change as a person grew older. Gail wondered what had happened over the years to change Kate's behavior so drastically.

Back at the meeting Helen wished George luck in bringing up the computer idea to Kate, as Kate had been in one of her moods lately. When George asked why, Joan said that she didn't know. She expressed frustration at the fact that all Kate ever seemed to say to her was "Uh, huh." Joan and Helen proceeded to dwell on how unpleasant Kate's attitude was until George interrupted, assuring them that she would get over it.

George mentioned that he had asked Gary to come to prepare his taxes again and asked Joan to make room for him in the spare office. Helen and Joan joked about Kate's crush on Gary. After that, the meeting broke up and they all went out into the main office.

Gail thought about Kate and her supposed crush on Gary, and wondered what Kate really felt for him. About ten years ago, Gail knew, Kate had had a relationship with a man who said he was with military intelligence. Gail felt that it was more likely that the man was married, and Kate was naive to believe this story. He came into town very sporadi-cally on the weekends, and after a couple of years, ended the relationship with Kate.

Helen called Gail several weeks after Gail had asked the family if they would allow her and her team to do an analysis of Kate's behavior. She told Gail that something had happened that day at work that might be useful in the analysis. The plant workers, who are unionized, had just completed renegotiating their contract with the company, and had received a substantial raise as part of the renegotiated package. Helen and Kate were working together, figuring out the differences in pay for each worker. A sense of camaraderie prevailed, and Kate observed that she and Helen should also get raises, since it had been over two years since they had been given a raise. Helen responded in a noncommittal manner. Helen then mentioned the fact that George wanted a new telephone line installed because he sometimes found himself having to wait for a phone line. Kate expressed surprise, saying that she hadn't heard him mention anything about it and; besides, when did he ever have to wait for a line? Helen was shocked, and just looked at Kate. Kate then seemed to remember who she was talking to and got up to take a break, going to look out the window with a frown on her face.

Gail was sure that something could be done to improve the work environment and efficiency of the office. She sat down at her word processor to draft up an outline of the case.

MAMMOTH INDUSTRIES, INC. (A)

MANAGING CHANGE

Looking back on nearly two years of concerted effort, Jo Sloan, vice-president for administration at the Houston subsidiary of Mammoth Industries, Incorporated (MII), believed that she was well on the way to successfully rebuilding, reorganizing, and rehabilitating a group that had, on her arrival, been characterized by extremely low morale, negativism, and ineffective performance.

Three months prior to Sloan's arrival in Houston, two very senior employees, one in the purchasing department and the other in the budgeting department, had been fired for malfeasance that involved kickbacks from suppliers and other dishonest acts. Both of the employees involved had been considered leaders among members of the staff, and their unmasking (which involved covert detective work by both corporate employees and various law enforcement officers) had shattered the morale of the entire group and also resulted in enduring feelings of mistrust and suspicion among the employees. These feelings were very evident to Sloan when she arrived, and it was generally agreed that they were still affecting the climate of the administrative group at the Houston subsidiary twenty months later.

Before coming to Houston, Sloan had twenty years of service with MII in various administrative positions, including personnel, accounting, planning, and purchasing. During her first month in Houston, she concluded that several of the managers reporting to her would have to be replaced before she could rebuild the administrative group. In addition, she felt that the subsidiary had strong endemic problems and that all systems needed to be questioned and decisions made as to whether to keep them, get rid of them entirely, or change them. She also felt that the employees needed to be brought into the decision-making process to a far greater extent than they had been to date.

Her initial effort was to try to work with the existing managers and employees. She attempted to set up a goal-setting exercise but discovered that no one wanted to participate. She also tried other means of involving both managers and employees in decision making, but soon saw these efforts stalled by a negative approach in almost every area. In an effort to modify this negativism, she greatly expanded her own involvement in daily operations. It quickly became clear to her that the only way to solve the problem was to replace several of the managers reporting to her.

The administrative group in Houston handled a large and relatively complex workload with a staff of twelve managers and seventy-five employees. Sloan's predecessor had been perceived by those who served under him as a low-key, almost retired, administrator who did not like to discipline people nor make changes in accustomed ways of doing things. Sloan believed that at least three of the managers reporting to her were simply unable to adjust to her own activist style of management and would have to be replaced before any meaningful changes could be implemented.

The deputy vice-president for administration, for instance, was doing an adequate job in the traditional sense but lacked imagination and seemed uninterested in changing what Sloan perceived as inefficient and costly ways of purchasing, handling accounts, and even dealing with a heavy load of both internal and external correspondence. Several months after Sloan arrived in Houston, George Grable, an assistant vice-president at MII's Dallas subsidiary, visited Houston for three days en route to a discussion on management improvement with a corporate support organization. Sloan had met Grable at several regional conferences and was aware of his reputation for successfully modernizing several of the administrative systems at the Dallas subsidiary. Grable had installed a network of personal computers connected to a new and larger mainframe and had modernized the entire budgeting and accounting process. At the same time, he had introduced an effective, highly participative, management-by-objectives program. Sloan knew Grable and was impressed with his knowledge, tenacity, and forceful, positive style. She asked if Grable might be interested in coming to Houston. Grable said that he would be pleased to do this but he did want to remain in Dallas for several more months to be sure the new systems were firmly established and operating smoothly.

Sloan was relatively satisfied with Sarah Cash, the personnel manager. She had been at the Houston subsidiary for a year when Sloan arrived, and she was the first personnel manager with previous corporate experience to serve in Houston in nearly a decade. Her long service and wide experience had resulted in a high degree of technical expertise at least in the traditional sense, Sloan discovered, but she was very resistant to new ways of doing things. This, combined with an aggressive and sometimes uncompromising approach, led to major confrontations between Cash and her superiors every few months.

Sloan appraised the purchasing manager as "a good manager in some ways but wrong for this subsidiary at this time." Fortunately, he informally sought a transfer after a serving two years in Houston and Sloan did not oppose his doing so. The planning and budget manager, on the other hand, Sloan perceived as a disaster and arranged with the corporate office for his immediate transfer even though it would take several months for corporate to arrange a suitable replacement. Her assistant, Sam Loud, the budget and fiscal manager, was a recent MBA graduate new to the job and inexperienced, but Sloan felt that she and Loud could take on the extra load for a few months.

As it turned out, Sloan found herself without a deputy or purchasing manager for two months before the new managers all arrived in September, fourteen months after her own arrival in Houston. She discovered she was working sixteen hours a day during July and August, partially because she was trying to lay the ground work for a personal computer network, purchasing equipment, and training three people to instruct the staff on how to use the network.

Bob Fowler, the very experienced new planning and budget manager, arrived in July and Larry Plant, the talented young purchasing manager arrived late in August. Sloan, exhausted, took a two weeks vacation. Shortly after her return, George Grable, her new deputy also arrived in Houston.

Looking back on this period six months later, Sloan saw several mistakes she had made. "For one thing, I wanted George, Larry, and Bob to take over all the things I had been doing. I tried to turn things over to them as fast as possible. But, apparently, none of them believed I wanted to. Maybe I did do the job myself too often instead of telling them to handle it.

"Then when George came, he landed too hard. He tried to do everything yesterday and everything he was doing represented a change from the way these people had always operated. Right away he established a real, highly participative, MBO system that seemed to scare the daylights out of everyone. I will say he does what I can't seem to do; he leaves people alone after goals are set. But everybody mistrusted him. They thought I was the nice person and he was the SOB. We've ended up with a real line of authority problem. People still come to me instead of to George. They seem to perceive him as a cold fish, but actually he may be more sensitive to people's needs than I am."

Sloan's appraisal of her senior staff after six months time was largely colored by their response to the changes being introduced, which included the following:

1. The PC network—"This proposal has caused the most controversy."
2. The MBO program—"A major departure; we have had three or four meetings with employees and ten meetings with the management staff trying to get them to set goals, but I seem to end up doing most of the talking."
3. Using the computer to automate some of the purchasing work—"We are trying to install an automated, integrated management system, which is very radical for MII."
4. The lead location for the new corporate facilities management system—"The facilities manager has a huge responsibility, but she

really has been using the PC network and turns out an incredible amount of work."

"Larry Plant, the purchasing manager, has really come around. He has a very big job and is handling it well. Bob Fowler, the planning and budget manager is excellent technically, but not really a manager. He is a traditional technician. Fortunately for the subsidiary, he is great at regularizing fiscal systems for us, but he hasn't developed his staff. He does everything himself.

"In spite of 20 to 30 hours of sessions with Sarah Cash, George and I have been unable to get anywhere with her. She simply won't change. Recently, I had to break one of my cardinal rules and overrule her. She wanted to terminate an employee who may have been abusing sick leave and sent out a letter to that effect when the employee went out sick for the third time in a few months. When I heard about it, I sent somebody out to retrieve the letter. The president of the Houston subsidiary had made it clear to us that he wanted to be personally involved in any action involving termination. When the executive vice-president suggested we cancel Sarah's letter, I agreed. Sarah said that I had completely destroyed her effectiveness. I told her that was nonsense. In fact, since this incident, she has done a very effective and long overdue job evaluation study that she had been staunchly opposing. The thing is, she is a leader; she comes on very strong, but doesn't realize it.

"My basic objective has been to implement a really meaningful change in a short time frame. I'm encouraged with the progress we've made, but there are still problems. We've had lots of conflict in the last one and a half years, but I've tried to manage it and I know performance has improved. Our customers certainly seem more satisfied with us. But George and I feel that we need to get the changes well established with the employees here; otherwise, if we happen to be transferred, it might revert to old bad habits. I hope in the next year here to be able to just tune up the new systems.

"In the meantime, George has really made me grow as a manager. He keeps feeding me articles and books on new management ideas and we discuss these together. Also, I recently attended the Corporate Advanced Management Program and that has sensitized me to the impact of my behavior."

QUESTIONS

1. How well is Jo Sloan managing the process of change within her group?
2. How do you assess the implications of her relationships with Sarah Cash, George Grable, and other senior staff managers?
3. How do you think the other senior staff managers feel about Sloan, Grable, and the changes they are trying to introduce?
4. What might Sloan have done differently? What should she try to do in the next year?

MAMMOTH INDUSTRIES, INC. (B)

REACTIONS TO CHANGE

Without exception and in varying degrees, the senior management staff people reporting to Jo Sloan, the vice-president for administration at the Houston subsidiary of Mammoth Industries Incorporated (MII) were resistant not so much to the changes being initiated by George Grable and Jo Sloan as to the way these changes had been introduced and implemented. They distrusted the motives of Grable especially, but to some extent the distrusted Sloan as well. They found it difficult to understand where the group as a whole was headed and why. Some of the employees reacted less strenuously than the managers, but they too expressed considerable concern.

Sarah Cash, Personnel Manager

Cash's first assignment after she joined MII was as a purchasing trainee at the Houston subsidiary. In the intervening fifteen years before returning to Houston, she had served at three other subsidiaries, the last two in personnel functions, finally rising to personnel manager. She had an assignment at corporate headquarters in the personnel department. At one or another of these assignments she had functioned informally in virtually every ad-ministrative area except accounting, budgeting, and planning.

"There is a new breed of senior managers in administration these days," Cash said. "They are full of new management techniques, which might be great at corporate headquarters or at some of the very large sophisticated subsidiaries, but they come out to the somewhat smaller, less sophisticated subsidiaries and the new broom starts sweeping without benefit to the people. We used to have managers who operated to benefit our customers, the corporation, and our employees. Now they are out for themselves and you go along with them or else.

"Here neither the vice-president for administration, her deputy, nor the purchasing manager have ever served at a subsidiary with an active personnel department functioning in accordance with corporate policies. A good vice-president for administration should know what everyone does. Ours doesn't, but tries to do everyone's job. She goes to the employees and gives them instructions and we managers don't know where we are. She came out of corporate headquarters to do a big job and doesn't know how to manage it.

"All of a sudden we have an influx of new equipment that gets rammed down our throats. PCs come in and no one knows how to use them and the result is chaos. The

399

attitude is 'this is the way it's going to be,' and as a result the employees are all shook up. These are things Jo Sloan wanted and she pulled every string you've ever heard of to get Grable here because he had put all this in elsewhere.

"There are three units without clerical assistance right now while they are all off being trained to deal with the PC network. For the past six months about all we've done is attend meetings, check out equipment, and try to set goals. But I can't get the file cabinet I need, the elevators in the building don't work properly, and the employees at the warehouse are complaining they are getting sick because the heating and air conditioning system is putting out polluted air.

"They are trying to do everything overnight and they don't even know what to put on the PCs or how to make them work. There's been no consultation with the people who are going to have to do the job. The equipment is just sitting there. What happens in the summer? We've got to expand and recondition our air conditioning system, which is going to cost a lot of money and we're not even sure we can do it.

"Jo Sloan should have had the courtesy to come to me and the others and say, 'This is what we want to do, this is what it will mean to you, and this is the training you should have.' Instead, she wants to be able to say, 'This is what I accomplished in two years.' As a result she is stepping all over everybody and the employees are saying, 'Well, here we go again; after two or three years this will all go in a drawer.' If this is effective management, I'm terribly out of date. Sloan sees to it that the president and executive vice-president get everything they want instantly. They appraise her performance. But they don't know the place is falling down around our ears. They don't hear what's happening.

"And then a few weeks ago, Sloan completely undercut my authority when I wanted to terminate an employee who was staying out sick for weeks at a time and whose supervisor wanted to get rid of her. Thank heaven I'm being transferred in a couple of months."

Larry Plant, Purchasing Manager

After many years of steady progression at various subsidiaries of MII, Larry had been assigned as manager of administration at a small overseas subsidiary. This was followed by an assignment as purchasing manager at the Tennessee subsidiary and now at the Houston subsidiary where his duties involve the supervision of two other managers and 60 employees.

"When I was told I was being transferred here, I didn't know whether it would be as purchasing manager or as deputy vice-president," Plant said. "I called Jo Sloan and she said she didn't know; the decision hadn't been made either at corporate headquarters or Houston. Twenty-four hours later I got the official fax announcing my transfer to the position of purchasing manager, which was O.K. with me. I didn't know either Sloan or Grable, but I did know this was one of the top purchasing jobs around. In the past seven months of long hours, and with the understanding of my wife, I'm just beginning to comprehend the full ramifications of the job.

"When I arrived, Jo was gone. She had told me she had to go on vacation or go crazy since she had been acting as purchasing manager *and* planning and budget manager and had been without a deputy for several months. She left me a 15-page memo on what to do. When she came back, we entered into what is still a very good working relationship.

"I found the purchasing employees here a disillusioned, do-nothing group. There were two reasons for this. First, the malfeasance situation was like a cancer; the group is still not over it. They thought everybody looked at them like second-class citizens who did nothing and were potentially dishonest. Then, secondly, my predecessor used to shout at them. Jo got him out of here as quickly as possible under the circumstances.

"I think I've turned this around since I've been here and the corporate staff people who just came through here confirmed this. I convinced the employees they could take responsibility. I also brought in Bert Harmon who was heading a special project study at the corporate office to be my purchasing supervisor. I turned them all loose and today they'll turn the world upside down for me. I'm proud of that. The group as a whole takes a lot of pride because their performance is way up and they know it.

"Jo wanted her own team and she broke every rule in the book to get George here. George knew what he was doing at his last assignment and Jo felt the same thing was needed here. I have no problem with the PC network. But, it's used as a scapegoat. The problem is the way the installation of these PCs and other machines was carried out. George has absolutely no human compassion. The employees have nicknamed him 'Mr. Mechano.' We all perceive him as not giving a damn about people as individuals; only how they can be useful to him. This is not necessarily true, but he is very ambitious and knows exactly what he wants to do. The resulting lack of trust is really a problem. Most of the senior managers in this group feel there is some diabolical plan known only to Jo and George as to what they are going to do.

"Jo is reasonable, relates to people, and is warm. But I don't trust her any more than I trust George, who is cold and can only talk about his systems. Bob Fowler controls the money for all this equipment in accordance with instructions from the corporate office, but he is fearful they are going to end run him and this puts him in a bad situation. What really bothers all of us is we don't know if there is a road map and if there is one, we don't know who knows what or who is on it besides Jo and George.

"Another aspect of this is that George is not doing his job as deputy vice-president for administration. He spends all his time negotiating for machines. He's good at that. He got a 50 percent reduction on the mainframe computer, but the rest of his job falls on us.

"Another thing he did that set people off was to come on too strong on MBO at the first staff meeting after he got here. He pushes too hard and confronts people in encounter fashion. The older people don't take too well to that. His style just lacks human skill. He is perceived as secretive and therefore dangerous and upsetting and he does nothing to dispel this belief. When I talk to George about these things he responds, 'Well, you've got me figured out and that's fine.' But it's not meaningful to him. He says, 'That's the way it is.'

"The result is we can't work with George. The staff is disorganized, discouraged, disjointed, and disgruntled. My productivity has suffered; everybody's has. Jo has said, 'Change always causes this; wait for a year and we'll all look back and laugh about it.' I don't believe that anymore."

Bob Fowler, Planning and Budget Manager

Fowler's service in Houston represented the eighth subsidiary to which he had been assigned during his 25 years at MII. Starting as an accounting clerk, he progressed to supervisor before entering MII's Management Training Program. He was a budget and fiscal manager before being transferred and promoted to planning and budget manager here at Houston.

"Most of the other places where I've worked were a lot better organized than here," said Fowler, "largely because of the continuity of the employees. Here, there is a lot of turnover. We are under constant pressure from Sloan and Grable and instead of correcting basic faults, they are going into new systems they don't know much about. All the first line managers are opposed to what they are doing. There is a very severe lack of communication. Jo said when I came here she wanted me to be frank with her but this has kind of worn off. She always has a better argument when you tell her something. She's not listening to me or the other managers.

"The whole administrative group is still demoralized by the scandal almost two years ago. In budget and fiscal I see some basic faults. For one thing, the employees don't consult the manuals so they don't know why they are doing what they do. Secondly, nobody knows how to do the budget and there is no senior employee to provide continuity in that function. Also, most employees have no concept of how to lay out the material.

"The lack of training by past budget and fiscal managers is the basic problem. I've been trying to train by example, but given the pressures from Grable, who has a thousand irons in the fire at all times, I just don't have time to train people. He and Sloan have ideas like automating the budget system. I don't think it can be done practically because there are too many variables and judgment calls. And besides, if it's going to be done, the corporate office ought to do it. Grable has a number of ideas about what should be done that are not practical. He doesn't know very much about budgets and fiscal affairs. It's virtually impossible to get my work done and also respond to new ideas that may take me three weeks to research. They want to go heavily into computerization, but some of this should come from the corporate office; we need to develop a compatible system so we can communicate with other subsidiaries and the Corporate office.

"Sloan and Grable are experienced managers, but even though they listen to us, they then do what they wanted to do in the first place. We were lying back a bit until the corporate staff people came and now George is going on vacation and then Jo will go, but when they both return in six weeks it will all hit the fan again! I'm afraid someone who comes after me will say, 'Good grief, why did you permit all this to happen?' They probably realized they almost had a revolution on their hands, at least from the three of us, and they've slowed down a bit.

"Basically, I don't trust George. He'll write any sort of paper to justify what he wants to do and he's a facile writer who makes figures lie for him. They're trying all kinds of new management approaches like MBO. They're buying and reading all these books. I don't know if I even like MBO. Basically, there have been too many changes in too short a time. They've bombarded us and don't realize the impact it has had. I've never seen such a flood of paper. George takes a dictating machine with him wherever he goes and working 12 hours a day he turns out memos to the rest of us by the bushel basket. And the trouble is, he's not doing the things a deputy vice-president for administration traditionally does. As a result, we don't have time to think. He bucks stuff down to us, by memo usually, while he's working on computerization. We've become purely reactive."

Sam Loud, Budget and Fiscal Manager

Like Sarah Cash, Loud also started his career at MII in Houston as an accounting clerk. He rose to supervisor and then was selected for MII's Management Training Program. In the last 13 years he has held positions at three other subsidiaries and at the corporate headquarters.

"Jo was here about two months before I arrived," Loud said, "so I got here about a year before George arrived and the automation and computerization process began in earnest. Mammoth Industries is certainly behind the times in those areas, but there is something to be said for both the old and new ways of doing things. It depends how you sell the new and there have certainly been some things shoved down our throats without any effort at selling.

"They are dealing with fear of the unknown. Bob Fowler, my boss, is an old-time budget and fiscal manager who has worked with the old ways for years. He's reluctant to change without seeing where it will all take us. I personally feel automation can do a lot for us, but the old-timers can be useful in telling us what will and won't work. The spirit here is full speed ahead and damn the torpedoes, and that worries Bob.

"We've had some false starts. They brought in two salespeople from Japan a few weeks ago to demonstrate their machines for us, but they didn't speak English well enough and had no way of showing us how to use them. The comment was, 'If they didn't want to sell us, they did a perfect job.' Even George agreed it was a flop. And two weeks ago the network was down for five days and they had to bring a specialist from California to fix it. Everything ground to a halt.

"If you spend all this money on equipment, you should show some savings on operations, but the feeling is we haven't saved anything with the PC network; we still have the same number of people. People say, 'Instead of pumping more money in, let's see what we have and how efficient we can make it.' Corporate headquarters has instructed us not to spend more than a certain amount, and our subsidiary has guidelines too, but concessions get made by phone and there's no official record of them.

"Nobody is against computerization and I don't think Bob and George are going to automate themselves into a bad situation. But it needs to be planned more carefully, people need to be consulted more fully, and it needs to be sold more astutely. We took ten years to get to the moon and did it very well."

Bert Harmon, Purchasing Supervisor

Harmon had been a section manager in the production control department here in Houston for many years. Several months after Larry Plant came in as purchasing manager, he asked Harmon, who had some experience with automated processes, to transfer to the purchasing department.

"Since I shifted to the purchasing department, about 70 percent of my time has been spent processing various computer-related equipment and supplies," Harmon said. "It has been hectic. There has been a rush to get the equipment on board. At the same time I had to get to know the people and learn the management job in purchasing. We were short of staff, so four new people came in at the same time we were being pushed to get the equipment.

"Grable literally bombarded me with computer literature so there would be a memory here when he and other managers get transferred. I've really been delighted in a way. I'm working hard and it's interesting. But it's also frustrating. We can't concentrate on anything but the masses of paper pouring over our desks, 60 percent of it from Grable. He expects me to absorb all the books, articles, and reports he sends me. I take something home every night. To a great extent I feel good about this, but too much is being crammed into a time frame without a planned progression.

"The contract and purchase-order files are a mess. Practically every one I take out of there has something wrong with it. There have been too many systems and not enough time. My predecessor told me he was on a merry-go-round. My new boss and I have at least revived the corpse; people like to work in our unit now because it is exciting and we are getting very efficient, but the contracts are still a mess. Five of us spent two days last week evaluating various computer equipment; the regular purchasing work gets delayed.

"We are getting positive feedback on our progress. It had been taking two weeks to get purchase orders out. George wanted us to get it down to 72 hours. We pressured the budget and fiscal people to get them to us and now we've got it down to 96 hours.

"Jo Sloan is a *real* manager. She was preceded by someone who changed nothing. The contrast is startling, Jo has changed everything; people, systems, even the partitions. This last caused a lot of unfavorable comments because people were used to having their own offices; now hardly anyone has. But it has resulted in a lot more interaction and relatedness among employees and has started some healthy competition. You see others putting out the work so—. Another thing, Jo regularly holds meetings and asks employees how things are going. That was never done before. Now, you realize she is trying to communicate."

QUESTIONS

[Refer back to the (A) case].

1. How accurate were your predictions regarding the feelings and reactions of the senior managers to the changes being introduced?
2. To what degree do you believe the feelings revealed in this case are normal reactions to change versus abnormal responses to the way Sloan and Grable are managing the change process?
3. What counsel would you give Sloan about what she should do now? What might you say to Grable if you were Sloan?

MAMMOTH INDUSTRIES, INC. (C)

GEORGE GRABLE: CHANGE AGENT

Looking back on his first six months in Houston, George Grable could identify a number of differences in both the situation he faced there and his own and other people's behavior as contrasted with what had happened in Dallas (his previous position), where he had successfully introduced many changes in the administrative group's systems and procedures.

The son of Baptist parents who were both teachers, Grable had been brought up in a family atmosphere that emphasized scholarship (both his parents and his two older brothers and sister all had advanced degrees), music (his mother was a gifted musician), and achievement. A history major in college, his major extracurricular activity was the Flying Club, and although he went on to graduate school in history, his primary ambition was to be an airline pilot. Two influential people helped change his mind. His fiancé voiced strong objection to the amount of time an airline pilot spends away from home and intimated that if he pursued that career path, she would have to reevaluate their engagement; and, while vacationing on Cape Cod, he met a management trainee from MII who suggested he apply for the program, which he did. A few months later, he was accepted into the man-

agement training program, and he started with MII some eleven years before his arrival in Houston.

In the intervening years Grable served as purchasing agent, purchasing supervisor, and budget and fiscal manager at three small subsidiaries, took a one year leave to work toward an MBA at Wharton, served two years as a personnel counsellor in corporate headquarters, and was transferred as assistant vice-president for administration to the small subsidiary in Dallas, where he served for two years before coming to Houston. During his assignment at corporate headquarters, he completed his work for an MS in administration with an emphasis on computer technology and successfully completed a paper-flow improvement study assigned him by the vice-president of personnel.

When assigned to the Dallas subsidiary, Grable had been led to believe he would find a group of skilled employees there who would make the job easy for him. He found quite the contrary to be true. The administrative group was being managed by crisis, there was no system of inventory control, the employees' skills were obsolete, and they were doing clerical work manually. On the other hand, the executive vice-president of the Dallas subsidiary, while conservative, appeared willing to give Grable a free hand in improving the operation of the group, although he insisted that Grable think through all the alternatives before taking action.

Feeling strongly that the employees had been poorly served in the past, Grable initiated a number of changes during his first year at Dallas. As a first step, he devised what he called "work requirements statements" to be developed with each employee as part of the performance appraisal process. These were statements of goals and objectives for each individual. (At the request of the case researcher who later interviewed him at Houston, Grable wrote a memo describing the philosophy behind the work requirements statements and how he used them [see Exhibit 1]. Note that these work requirement statements were used only with the employees of the Dallas subsidiary, while at Houston he used work requirements statements only with the five managers since he was not the direct supervisor of the employees there.)

Grable also instituted a program budgeting system at Dallas that allowed employees to spend money without his approval. He told the employees he was trying to make their jobs more meaningful and assured them that "if you don't make mistakes now and then, you aren't doing anything." He tried to get them to do away with services that were not really necessary and that involved a lot of clerical work instead of the "thoughtful work" he hoped they would begin to do. "It took them a long time to believe I was really serious about all this," Grable told the case researcher, "but they finally did and things started to improve."

Toward the end of his first year at Dallas, Grable realized that manual clerical functions were taking up a lot of the employees' time and he decided that a network of PCs targeted primarily at the employees was a logical solution. He held meetings with his staff, including the employees, to discuss possible applications, and then he began to implement the new system on an experimental basis. Beginning with his own secretary, he started training people throughout the subsidiary to use the PC network on an integrated basis. The Production Control Section installed the first equipment outside the administrative group and one of the sales managers, who was a friend of Grable's, also started using it in the sales department.

By the time Jo Sloan asked him to come to Houston, the PC network had been operating for nine months and Grable had also installed and integrated a mainframe computer to handle inventory control and other systems readily transferable to this kind of setup. While Grable was flattered by Sloan's offer, and by now almost evangelistic about the potential for PC networks at subsidiaries everywhere, he was loath to leave Dallas until the new systems were so firmly established that they would not fall into disuse when he left. He was also determined to get a good head start in Houston so that he and Sloan would have enough time to thoroughly integrate the new systems there. In order to accomplish both of these purposes, he remained at the Dallas subsidiary through the following summer, but communicated with Sloan about equipment to be ordered and people to be trained in Houston. By the time he arrived in September, most of the basic equipment for a PC network was on hand and three employees had been in training for several months. He and Sloan had PCs and one was also to be installed in the executive vice-president's office. A number of other PCs had been ordered for the Houston subsidiary but had not yet arrived.

To his dismay, Grable discovered that the PCs in place when he arrived, did not match the setup at Dallas, as he had instructed. He picked up the phone and asked for and got one-day service on delivery of the correct equipment. Unfortunately this cost considerably more than the setup that had been delivered and when the invoice came in, Bob Fowler, the planning and budget manager, was furious, as much because Grable had neglected to inform him about the change in the order as because the new equipment cost more.

EXHIBIT 1

MAMMOTH INDUSTRIES

MAILGRAM

From: George Grable
Subject: Work Requirements Statements

To establish performance objectives I generally spend three to six hours with my subordinates at our first meeting to discuss our mutual perceptions of what our relationship, job objectives, values, and so on are and what they should be. The discussion then moves into actually setting specific objectives (almost always accompanied by target dates). It is stated both orally and in writing that the objectives and dates are flexible; that is, as new events or priorities impact established objectives the latter can be changed to fit the new realities.

I generally attempt to have two in-depth review sessions during the year. This year has been an exception due to my arrival late in the performance year and the consequent delay in establishing the objectives.

The format of the review session is three phased.

Phase 1—The rated employee is asked to review the previously established work requirements statements. Both the employee and I have the copies of the statements in front of us. The purpose of this phase is twofold. First, I want to hear the employee's evaluation of the work requirements statement. This helps the employee to clarify his or her own thinking and to relate individual objectives into a coherent whole. Secondly, it allows for a calming period in which the employee has an opportunity to get over his or her nervousness.

Following the employee's review I then ask questions on any points I may have failed to understand. I generally do not like to interrupt during the employee's self-evaluation (even if she or he may be going astray) to ensure that I do not accidently steer the conversation in a direction it would not otherwise go and to get the employee relaxed. Following my review of the work requirements statements, I review my notes with the employee to be sure there has been no misunderstanding, asking for the employee's confirmation that my notes accurately reflect our discussion.

Phase 2—By this time the employee is sufficiently relaxed that I can move on to my appraisal of the employee's performance. I never begin this phase until he or she is completely relaxed (or as relaxed as appears likely to occur). I not only discuss the employee's performance, but go well beyond, discussing the employee's views on his or her relationships with subordinates, peers, other managers, me, and (in Houston) with Jo Sloan. As mentioned to you orally, many items are discussed that do not relate directly to the actual performance evaluation report, but that do, of course, relate to the employee's "whole being."

Phase 3—I call this the "rate-the-rating officer" review. I ask the employee to appraise my performance. I generally open by inquiring as to what areas in my personal or professional characteristics inhibit maximizing the performance of the subordinate. If I detect reticence, I try to throw out one or two examples that are obvious or that others in the past have cited. Generally this is all that is needed to get a reasonable discussion going. However, if I find the employee is still reluctant to bring up issues that others have been willing to, then I am frank and say to them, "I have heard from others that I need to pay attention to the following problem. What are your views on this?" This approach appears to remove most of the threat, if not all.

What I am particularly looking for during this phase is a common thread running through the comments of all my subordinates. If I find a common thread then I know I have a problem about which I have to make a decision. Do I wish to maintain my approach or behavior or do I wish to modify it? In some instances, I have chosen not to modify and to pay the obvious price that the trade-off calls for. When only one employee has a particular problem then it is a question of deciding how I want to deal with that particular problem. Some of the very best insights I have gained, however, have not come through the thread approach but rather from observations of a single, observant employee.

Some fairly interesting things do emerge from Phase 3 not only about myself but also about the rated employee. It gives me a much clearer picture of their inner values, many times values of which they, themselves, are not aware.

I have found my approach to work requirements statements to be quite time-consuming relative to the traditional MII approach to performance appraisal. The actual performance evaluation review generally takes from two to four hours. I consider these hours the most important hours I spend during the year. My experience has been that all except a handful of employees respond well to this type approach. I have had only two employees (one manager in Houston and one clerical employee at Dallas) who were unable to satisfactorily accomplish the work requirements statement. I have had only one who was emotionally unable to cope with the discussion engendered by this approach.

During his first two months at Houston, Grable concentrated on getting the PC network installed and in operation. He tended to communicate with others involved in the project by mailgram, a feature of the new PC network that allowed rapid dissemination of memos to all the recipients. Also, soon after his arrival, he called all the managers and employees together and informed them that the section would henceforth be managed by objectives and that work requirements statements would have to be prepared by all the managers. He pointed out that the only penalty associated with these statements would be imposed for failure to tell him in advance that schedules would not be met.

As the PC network became operational, Grable discovered that while many of the employees were using it heavily, only a few of the managers were. The new plant maintenance manager, for instance, had arrived in Houston recently to find a huge backlog of work and his secretary off being trained to use the PC network. He had quickly realized that his only recourse was to use the PC network and he had gotten his workload under control while using the new setup heavily. On the other hand, while the employees in the personnel unit were using the new setup extensively, Sarah Cash herself had hardly used it at all. Grable himself was far and away the leading individual user.

Looking back on the events of the past six months while talking to a case researcher, George Grable revealed a considerable capacity for introspection and an ability to perceive to some extent the reactions of others to his behavior since his arrival in Houston.

"My reputation proceeded me to Houston. Most people see me as a systems person, all caught up in computers and mechanization—a no-nonsense type guy. I think I'm sensitive to people, but I can't express it. I find it hard to give positive strokes to people, but at least I'm open about it. I want people to know my style, rather than pretend to be something I'm not. I think even my wife sees me as veiled because I don't talk shop at home although I work long hours. She thinks I neglect my family, and I do get pangs of guilt because I spend so little time with our daughter, who is a delight. Since childhood, I have known that my whole family has a strong drive to be very successful in worldly terms, and I guess you'd have to say I have a high need for achievement myself.

"When I came to Houston I was anxious not to make the same mistake I made at Dallas by waiting a year to get the new systems started and then moving so slowly that they were barely established when I was transferred. So by the time I got here, I walked into an already structured situation where three employees had been selected for training on the PC network and some of the equipment was on hand. I moved fast to get it installed and in operation. As a result, people here did not perceive that they had been informed about what was about to happen. I started using mailgrams to follow up on things but I was the only one who really knew how to use the system. Some people reacted; they said, 'Why is he picking on me?' Whereas I had many strong bonds with the employees at Dallas, here they know me only by reputation and it really made a difference in how they reacted.

"My relations with the unit managers have been influenced by a number of factors. First, I'm younger than they are. Second, this is my first experience with using work requirements statements with middle managers. At our first staff meeting I discussed my expectations of performance and how I intended to use the work statements, and their reactions ranged from feeling threatened to sheer terror, probably because of my reputation. I did this because I was so excited about the results achieved at Dallas and really had a strong belief in what I was doing. I still do. Next year I'd like our key employees to start having work statements. Then, third, many of my mailgrams went to the managers. I have an insatiable curiosity and want the answers to a lot of questions, and I was using the mailgrams to ask questions without seeing the potential negative consequences. Also, I was asking my secretary to follow up on things for me.

"I have tangled more than once with Bob Fowler. One time I asked him to do a special project and he wrote a mailgram saying he thought I should do it. I wrote a mailgram back saying he should arrange to have someone else do the job I'd assigned to him and he became outraged. He also gets upset when I go to his employees directly to ask for information. He is troubled by any discussion of computerization in his unit. He is very negative and says it won't work. He's an able man, but insecure and feels threatened by me. We've not been able to establish mutual trust. He thought the work statement was a club and only became easier about it when I told him I was planning to give him a good performance appraisal.

"In retrospect, I faced a very sophisticated personnel manager in Sarah Cash. She feels put out by our previous relationship. I was her personnel counsellor at corporate headquarters and she holds me responsible for her treatment in personnel. She was on vacation when I arrived, and she didn't like it that I asked her employees questions while she was away. Also, she feels I'm only interested in machines—not people. She refers to me as one of Jo's handpicked people and feels I will sacrifice anything to get ahead. She thinks I am close to Jo, but in fact my wife and I have never had the Sloans to our house, partly because we are not big entertainers. Maybe I'm trying to show her she is wrong or maybe I'm trying to be independent. In any case, I've changed my behavior here in Houston. Unlike the situation at Dallas, I don't have the ultimate responsibility—Jo does."

QUESTIONS

1. What critical differences do you see between the situation that existed for Grable at Dallas and the situation here in Houston?
2. How do you account for Grable's behavior as a change agent in Houston? How effective has he been?
3. Summarize what you have learned from this series of cases about the management of change.

JIM TATE'S SECRETARY

Jim Tate, a market analyst for the National Television Company (NTC) in New York, was angry with the situation in which he now found himself. He had just left a meeting with his boss, Ann Brook, at which he had insisted, perhaps more strongly than he should have, that his secretary, Sue Star, be fired immediately for incompetence and insubordination. Instead of the strong support he expected from Brook, all he got was a soothing set of questions and a promise to look into the matter.

Tate was proud of his record at NTC. He had demonstrated that a citizen from Little Rock, Arkansas, could do well in the sophisticated entertainment environment. He had graduated with a BS in business administration from the University of Arkansas just ten years ago. He had worked at two of the wholly owned television stations in marketing jobs and was recently promoted to his current job at NTC headquarters in New York.

What concerned Tate most was that this was his first job involving the supervision of a secretary and it was his misfortune to lose a good secretary seven months ago when she ran off and got married. Since then Tate had worked with nothing but "lemons," three of them; the most recent was Sue Star, the "Bennington Brat," as he called her.

After graduating from Bennington College, Sue Star went to secretarial school and then spent two years as a staff assistant to a water company executive. This was her first entertainment job. Star had been hired as a senior clerk and had been told she could expect to be promoted to secretary within a year. Tate's last two secretaries had been clerks. On her first day on the job Tate suspected trouble when Star said, "I'm *so* glad to be here in New York City. The entertainment business is so glamorous! It's going to be awfully exciting working here."

At the end of her first week, when Tate was trying to get out a very important report before a deadline, Star interrupted Tate to tell him she had just learned that a young and gifted singer had fired her agent and was in the process of looking for a new one. Since the singer was so popular with the teenage set, Star thought it might be a real coup if NTC could help her find a good agent.

Tate was angry at being interrupted and disturbed by her naiveté. He told Star to concentrate on her typing and get the report out. He observed that there were quite a few well-educated and experienced people at NTC whose job it was to be concerned about issues such as that, and they didn't need advice from a newly arrived senior clerk.

In the next several weeks, it became apparent to Tate that Star was demonstrating mediocre skills as a typist and a less than appropriate attitude toward him. He was particularly puzzled about the deterioration of Star's typing since she had turned out excellent work her first few days on the job; it was clear she could do the work if she wanted to. Tate had tried to motivate her by pointing to her Bennington education and suggesting that the school would not be proud of alumnae who made such obvious mistakes and took so little pride in the quality of her work.

Her smug attitude was particularly evident to Tate in the frequent encounters with her over spelling, grammar, and punctuation. Tate's first secretary had always corrected his spelling, grammar, and punctuation before bringing the rough drafts back to him for final rework. Star typed exactly what he had written in longhand. On one occasion, Tate had asked her if she read what she typed. He told Star it was her job to correct spelling and grammatical errors. "They did teach you those things at Bennington, didn't they?" he had asked.

She had snapped back, "They taught us just fine at Bennington, Mr. Tate. What did they teach you at Arkansas?"

Tate had reprimanded her for insolence and told her to do the drafts over, knowing that retyping them would probably make the reports late.

Tate had noticed recently that Star was spending more and more of her free time with the secretary to the sales manager across the hall. Then, this morning was the last straw. The sales manager casually mentioned that his secretary had told him that Star suggested that the department manager and his wife might like to visit the special exhibit of entertainment art on display at the Museum of Modern Art. Tate told the sales manager that the "Bennington Brat" was apparently more interested in doing the department manager's job than she was in doing the clerical work for which she had been hired.

Tate immediately went to his boss, Ann Brook, and insisted that Star be terminated. He told Brook that Star was incompetent as a senior clerk and insubordinate as well. Tate had shown Brook samples of Star's work, pointing out what he considered sloppy grammar, gross misspellings, and improper punctuation. Tate pointed out that Star was wasting time in the office across the hall making useless suggestions and doing nothing to improve her word processing skills. Tate stated that he would strongly oppose transferring her to another assignment at NTC and felt she should be fired for incompetence.

Brook agreed that Star's work did not seem very good. She pointedly asked Tate why Star seemed so disinterested in her work after she had been so enthusiastic at first. Finally, Brook agreed to "look into the matter."

Tate knew that the personnel office would most likely try to convince Brook to transfer Star to some other part of NTC. Tate felt the work he was doing was important and demanding but he was sure Star would not share that view. Tate wondered what effect his three "lemons" would have on his boss's assessment of his managerial skills on his next performance review. He knew Brook and the personnel office would speak with Star. He wondered what Star might say.

QUESTIONS

1. What motivates Sue Star?
2. What motivates Jim Tate?
3. If you had been Jim Tate, how would you have managed Sue Star?
4. What would you do now if you were:
   a. Jim Tate
   b. Ann Brook
   c. Sue Star

Up or Out

Terry Allan looked over previous internal audits as he considered the source of his discomfort. In the past year his career had changed dramatically, and, although he was enjoying the MBA program at Farina University, his new position as internal auditor for Texmarket was cause for concern.

Texmarket is a subsidiary of the Consolidated Group, a highly successful, privately owned French retailer. Last year, the Consolidated Group employed approximately 39,000 employees and had sales in excess of $10 billion. The Consolidated Group currently has 55 Consolidated Market stores in four countries. Forty of the stores are located in France. Each Consolidated Market generates between $100 and $250 million in sales annually. The stores are extremely large, often in excess of 250,000 square feet (almost six acres). The concept of the store is "everything you need under one roof," thus the stores sell everything from meat and produce to electronics, clothing, and hardware. Within a Consolidated Market, each department is operated as a separate profit center, and every location is encouraged to adapt to local markets. While the Consolidated Markets are considered the backbone of the business, the Consolidated Group also operates 150 restaurants and cafeterias, and 100 other specialty stores such as sporting good and electronics stores.

Texmarket was the Consolidated Market Group's first U.S. venture, and Houston was chosen as the most feasible site for its first store after two years of careful research and analysis. The Consolidated Market store opened in the fall two years ago. One other location was subsequently opened in Chicago as a second U.S. subsidiary, and Texmarket planned to open another store in Houston within four years. While the Consolidated Market concept is common in France, at the time the store opened, only three other stores of similar design existed in the United States. Texmarket's officers were Jean Beruard Destin, president, and Pierre Secoud, vice-president and treasurer (see the personal profiles in Exhibit 1). The present Texmarket corporate headquarters is located within the Houston Consolidated Market store.

The Houston store opened with five American division managers. However, after two years, only one of the five original American division managers remained in place (three had resigned within the first 18 months of operation). The four were replaced with French

Source: This case was first prepared as a class project by Cadmus Aholu, G.B. Frannea, Bryan Huchton, Troy Matherne, and Pablo Supkay at the Jones Graduate School of Administration, Rice University. It has been edited, revised, and used here with their permission.

EXHIBIT 1

PERSONAL PROFILES

JEAN BERUARD DESTIN, PRESIDENT, TEXMARKET

Destin has been with The Consolidated Group for 16 years. He was a highly successful store director for several locations within France. The job as Texmarket's president was a promotion and a highly visible opportunity. Destin had acquired a masters degree in human resource management from a French university. He has a reputation for returning profit from a new store within one year, important when the initial capital investment is over $30 million. The Houston store has not performed to that standard, but is well within the plan. He is French and is married with three children.

PIERRE SECOUD, VICE-PRESIDENT AND TREASURER, TEXMARKET

Secoud has been with The Consolidated Group for 22 years. He held the title of treasurer for the entire Consolidated Market Group prior to taking the position of vice-president and treasurer for Texmarket. Secoud indicated he accepted the new assignment because he wanted to live in the United States. He has a masters degree and the equivalent of a CPA. He is French and is married with four children.

Secoud works extended hours, often doing work that could be easily delegated. He is regarded as extremely intelligent, and most knowledgeable about the Consolidated Market business. People have expressed difficulty in working with Secoud because he works on multiple projects simultaneously, rarely indicating their importance or priority. It usually appears that all projects are a rush and are completed just in time.

BEUOÎT CRÈDIT, CONTROLLER, CONSOLIDATED MARKET

Crèdit was hired by Pierre Secoud two years ago to serve as his assistant and to coordinate special projects. He was also likely hired to begin training for the controllers position in future locations. Crèdit had just received his MBA with a concentration in finance from Purdue University when he was hired. He was given the responsibility of controller 18 months later, after the previous controller reached some sort of agreement with Secoud that would terminate his employment at that time. Crèdit was the third controller to work for Texmarket and the first French one.

Crèdit is married to an American and has just had his first child. He is very soft spoken and serious about his work. It has just been announced that Crèdit will take another, less stressful, position after the budgets are finished in January. The new controller will be from the French operation.

MARY JOHNSON, CHIEF INTERNAL AUDITOR, TEXMARKET

Johnson was hired by Texmarket three years ago to write software documentation for the data processing department. She has some college education, but may not have a degree. Johnson is a U.S. citizen, approximately 33 years old, and has just had her first child.

Johnson has no previous experience in the type of business Consolidated Market is in, although she worked for many years in the restaurant business. Her many jobs in that industry included writing policy and procedure manuals.

TERRY ALLAN, INTERNAL AUDITOR, TEXMARKET

Allan was born twenty-nine years ago in Louisiana. Two years later he and his family moved to a small gulf-coast town about eighty miles south of Houston, Texas. When Allan was eight years old, his parents divorced. His father, a chemical engineer for Dow Chemical, moved back to Louisiana, leaving his mother in Texas to begin a professional art career in order to support Allan and his three younger brothers. When Allan was eleven years old, his mother married a Dow Chemical research specialist who had two children of his own from a previous marriage, one boy and one girl, both younger than Allan. This marriage produced four more children, two boys and two girls. Just before he graduated from high school, Allan's mother and stepfather separated.

Allan began his working career at age 15 at the local supermarket. After high school, at age 18, Allan left home to attend the University of Houston. He arrived there with only enough money to pay the first semester's tuition and one month's rent. He quickly found a job and felt he was fully self-supported from age eighteen. He left school after three semesters to start his own company supplying inexpensive art for commercial buildings. As a result of this business, Allan traveled for months at a time to such cities as Washington, D.C., Philadelphia, New Orleans, and Birmingham. His own naive business practices and an economic recession forced Allan out of business.

Allan returned to the University of Houston at age 21 and at the same time began work for the Kroger company as a department manager. Before graduating with a B.S. degree in economics at age 25, Allan managed five different types of departments for the Kroger Company and served as assistant manager at one store. Allan was hired by Texmarket four years ago as a department manager. He is single.

managers. Pierre Secoud insisted he preferred American managers, but Terry Allan hypothesized that Jean Beruard Destin replaced the original managers with French division managers because of their experience with the Consolidated Market concept. Perhaps Destin believed that these managers would lend stability to the organization until qualified Americans were ready to take over. One of the American division managers who resigned told Allan that he and the others had left, because they felt their "opportunities for advancement were limited," and they "disagreed with upper management on how the store should be run."

Allan had been with the company for two years and, during that time, had been highly successful in his work. With eight years previous experience, he was hired as the manager for department A, the second largest in the company. Soon, however, Allan was transferred to run departments B and C after a resignation had been received at the critical time just before the opening of the store. Departments B and C were in the same division as A. Within six months, department A developed performance problems and, consequently, Allan was called back as its manager. Allan's assistant manager for departments B and C took over department B and department C was assigned to another manager. Within five months, Allan achieved a 120 percent increase in sales at department A and continued to run it as the single most profitable department in the Houston Consolidated Market. Sales in department A now accounted for almost 8 percent of total revenue and 20 percent of the profit for the Houston store.

Allan took the job as a department manager for Consolidated Market because of the autonomy he expected. As department head at other retail companies, Allan had limited ability to set policy. At Consolidated Market, however, Allan had complete control of the department. He hired his own employees, set product prices and promotions, and negotiated with vendors. Allan's division manager gave him free reign and exerted very little control. The division was regarded as the best within the store.

Allan felt he had good rapport with his coworkers and management. The diverse nature of the store brought together many people with different retail backgrounds. Only about 25 percent of Allan's fellow department managers had college degrees. The rest acquired their positions because of previous experience. Out of 35 department managers, all were American with the exception of two within Allan's division. Allan befriended one of the French department managers while in France training for the opening of the Houston location. He even served as a groomsman in this friend's wedding, soon after the store opened.

Allan's troubles began in the summer two years ago when, privately, he decided to further his education by pursuing an advanced degree. At first, he considered many possibilities, including a law degree, but he finally decided to work towards an MBA. While Allan had always thought that he would go back to school at some point, that decision was hastened when he heard Jean Beruard Destin tell another associate that he would only consider department managers for promotion after they had successfully run a department for at least two years. Allan found an excellent part-time program at Farina University that would allow him to continue working in some capacity at the company. However, Allan knew that he would not be able to continue his current duties if he attended the MBA program.

When Allan received an acceptance letter later that summer he reaffirmed his decision to attend graduate school. Now he was faced with the difficult task of notifying his superiors. Although he had mentioned the possibility of going back to school to some of his peers, he refrained from discussing it with his boss until his plans were solid.

Allan's secret was not well kept; before he had a chance to formally disclose his plans, he was approached by Jean Beruard Destin, the president. Destin inquired about the truth of a rumor he had heard concerning Allan's plan to go back to school. Allan confirmed it. In the course of the conversation Jean Beruard asked Allan if he would be interested in the position of division manager over ten departments. Allan told Destin, "At this time, I am not interested in the job of division manager, and that would not be the career path I would prefer to take with the company." He had already made a commitment to go to Farina, and he knew he could not juggle his current job and Farina, much less take on a position as a division manager.

Allan took the opportunity to indicate his desire to continue working with the company while in school, and he suggested the possibility of working under Pierre Secoud, the vice-president. Allan told Destin that Secoud's knowledge of finance would help supplement the school curriculum and would offer him an opportunity to become better acquainted with the financial side of the business. Up to this point Allan's contact with Pierre Secoud was very limited; Secoud's position was distinct from the operations side of the store.

Jean Beruard Destin agreed to find a position for Allan on the condition that Allan find a replacement for his position as department manager. One week later, it was announced that Allan's current American division manager would resign and be replaced by a division manager currently working in one of the French Consolidated Markets. Allan found a qualified manager to take his department head position, and then took a two-week vacation during the last weeks of the summer before school started.

Upon returning, Allan met with Pierre Secoud and was assigned the position of internal auditor, a position expressly created to accommodate Allan. Secoud told Allan, "You could best help the company in this capacity because it would provide the broadest overview of the company and allow your skills and knowledge of the commercial side of the business to be integrated with the corporate and financial side." Allan's duties included writing policies and procedures for Texmarket, sales and budget forecasting, and conducting audits of both commercial and financial operations.

After discussing these duties with Allan, Secoud mentioned that Allan's current salary was second only to the controller's, and the employees in the accounting department might question the basis for that. In order to work as an internal auditor, Allan would have to take a 20 percent cut in his base salary and give up the bonuses that accounted for 18 percent of his total income. Disconcerted, Allan chose not to accept or reject the offer immediately; instead, he told Secoud that he would think about it.

The start of school was one week away, leaving Allan no time to find a better paying job. Allan conceded, however, that even though he would be paid less, he would be working far fewer hours and would not have the burdens associated with supervising 30 employees and running one of the busiest departments in the store. He needed flexible hours and thought this job was a great opportunity to apply the financial skills he would learn in school. Allan told Secoud the following day that he would accept the position.

Being an internal auditor did not prove to be as challenging as Terry Allan had expected. Rather than working with Pierre Secoud, Allan was assigned to Mary Johnson, who had just been promoted to the position of head internal auditor. Like Allan, Johnson was in the process of learning her job and did not provide much guidance. Johnson did not assign Allan many challenging projects, but rather had him work on routine editing and compiling of procedures.

Two months after beginning school and assuming the responsibilities of internal auditor, Allan worked with Pierre Secoud and the controller on the preparation of the annual budgets and strategic plans. Allan enjoyed the challenging two-month project. When he resumed work under Johnson's direction, however, his duties seemed even more routine by comparison.

After completing his first semester of study at Farina, Allan was approached by Jean Beruard Destin at the annual Christmas party. Destin asked if Allan planned to stay with the company when he finished school. Conscious of the need to keep his options open Allan answered, "I would like to." Destin pointed out that the company will need a new controller in the future because of the plans for expansion in Houston. Privately, Allan thought the proposal exciting but wondered if that position would offer the pay and provide the opportunity that he was seeking.

During the Christmas break, Allan thought about school and his career. At the current pace, school would take three years to complete. The combination of three more years of studying and working at a job that was less than challenging did not appeal to him. Allan spoke to his adviser at school and discovered that it was possible to graduate in two years if he took full course loads the next three semesters and two courses during the upcoming summer. Having decided to do this, Allan then prepared himself for the reduced income from part-time work. He was not sure how Johnson or Secoud would respond, but was prepared for the worst when he asked to reduce his working hours to between 25 and 30.

One week after Christmas, Allan announced his intention to attend school full-time in order to graduate within two years. He presented Johnson with a detailed proposal outlining when he could work on a daily basis for the next year. Allan planned to work full-time during the summer and during any holidays from school. He also agreed to work extra hours during critical times such as the biannual inventories. Allan's plan was to work mornings on Mondays and Wednesdays and full days on Fridays and Saturdays to account for the minimum of 25 hours that was required to retain insurance benefits. Allan was surprised when Secoud readily agreed to the plan and proposed an hourly wage that was equivalent to his current weekly salary divided by forty.

Even though the full course load and work schedule allowed Allan very little time for any other activities, he was ecstatic about being able to complete school in two years. Allan's coworkers noticed that he wasn't around as much and frequently asked about his plans after graduation. Allan always responded that he would "take the best opportunity." Less frequently, but on occasion, he was asked by division and other top management whether he would remain with the company upon graduation. To these people, Allan always responded, "I would like to." Mary Johnson never asked him about his plans after graduation. Allan often got the feeling that

most people expected him to leave upon receiving his MBA.

While things were going well at school, Allan found his new work hours deprived him of being involved in important company decisions. It was very difficult to attend meetings because of his schedule, but Allan did not feel he could expect management to reschedule the meetings so he could attend. He approached Secoud on one occasion and expressed his desire to participate in "important" company activities and listed several areas in which his skills might be better utilized given his schedule. Secoud, however, stated that he realized Allan was busy with school, and he, therefore, did not want to give him too much work.

During March, the time for all annual salary reviews, Johnson was on maternity leave so Secoud performed Allan's review. Secoud focused most of the attention on Allan's previous job as a department manager since, as he told Allan, "You have not worked at this job very long and we don't have a good job description for the position." Consequently, Allan felt that the review did little to inform him of his immediate progress and was disappointed despite a 6 percent wage increase that was higher than most of his associates' raises.

Mary Johnson was on leave for two months after she had her child. During this time, Allan wrote policies and procedures for various areas of the store, including customer service and bookkeeping. Secoud also asked Allan to work with Jean Beruard Destin on a five-year plan for Texmarket, during which he learned more about the new location planned for next year. The president suggested Allan leave school and start training to be a controller. Allan declined Destin's offer, but reiterated that he would "like to stay with the company."

In May, several top executives from France visited the Houston location. They made it a point to stop and visit with Terry Allan, and ask about his ongoing education at Farina. They knew about Farina because of the upcoming Economic Summit in July, and they thought highly of the school. Allan took this opportunity to express his interest in working with the company in France, explaining that it would give him an opportunity to experience the larger company culture and operations.

In the summer, Allan worked 40 hours a week conducting audits and writing policies and procedures. He also took two classes to ensure that he would graduate by next May. The only highlight of the summer was when Pierre Secoud introduced Allan to Xavier de la Tour, the principal owner of The Consolidated Group. Allan recognized him from a recent article in *Forbes* magazine listing the world's billionaires. Xavier de la Tour was pleasant and asked a few questions, but because Secoud had to translate, the conversation was brief. In late August, Allan returned to a full-time school schedule and a part-time work schedule. When the time for annual budgeting arrived in October, Allan worked very closely with Secoud on the budgets for the commercial and service departments but did not participate in strategic planning decisions.

Allan had avoided discussing any plans to commit to Texmarket with Jean Beruard Destin, Pierre Secoud, and Mary Johnson because he wanted to find out about positions and salaries available at other firms. By postponing, Allan felt he could avoid an awkward situation of having to continue work should he turn down an offer. Allan needed to work to remain in school and did not want to jeopardize his pending graduation.

Allan also had doubts about where he would fit in the Texmarket operation and whether or not he would be happy as a controller. Although being a controller of a $150-million organization seemed prestigious, much of what Allan observed the current controller doing was routine accounting and budgeting. Allan knew he would not be happy doing that kind of work for long. On the other hand, there were management opportunities on the commercial side of the business, but Allan was not sure his MBA would be valued or used.

Allan also recognized that once the company expanded in Houston, the local Consolidated Market management would be much more independent from the Texmarket Corporate management. As it stood now, Jean Beruard Destin worked very closely with the store director and Pierre Secoud spent most of his time with the store controller and accounting manager. As he thought about all of this, Allan wondered if his dissatisfaction with his current job was obvious and if so, did this hurt his future chances with the company.

During the course of the labor budgeting for corporate staff the controller, Beuoît Crèdit, noted that Allan's salary for next year must be budgeted. This was especially true if Allan expected a large pay increase to coincide with the completion of his MBA program. Crèdit suggested to Allan that he speak to Secoud soon to make plans for the future. Allan, in turn, was not sure what the best course of action would be. Allan considered talking with Jean Beruard Destin, but wanted to postpone making this decision for as long as possible.

JACK WEBB (A)

Jack Webb returned from a week at an International Banking Corporation (IBC) executive education seminar determined to use his newly acquired management skills. Webb was discouraged about his career and his current assignment in the Advanced Studies and Projections Division (ASPD) of the Q department at IBC headquarters. He decided that as a first effort at using his new skills, he would try to understand better the people with whom he worked. Second, he would write an analysis and critique of the division organization, similar to the one he had seen prepared on the X department, in which many of the analysts perform functions similar to those in his division. Writing this critique, he felt, would also sharpen his analytic skills.

Webb decided to write down his impressions of the people with whom he worked and then add more information from time to time as his knowledge of them was modified. He recorded his initial impressions in his personal notebook, which he kept at home (Exhibit 1).

Three days after Webb had recorded his impressions of the people in the division, Peg Price came into his office visibly upset and expressed her dissatisfaction with the secretarial arrangements and Brian Foley's inability or unwillingness to do anything about it. She maintained that since the secretaries worked for all the analysts in the section including Foley, the section manager, there was no way of getting the work out. She felt the secretaries set their own priorities and ignored the requests of the analysts.

"There is absolutely no control of the secretarial situation here now. *You* seem to get along with them pretty well," Price observed. "Would you mind if I suggested to Foley that all the secretaries be assigned to report to you? Then you could give them some supervision and if any of us had a problem we could come to you with it and get some action. Of course, I don't know how the secretaries would react, but I would think having one boss instead of six would appeal to them. You act as section manager when Foley is away and all the secretarial work gets done well then. As the next most senior employee, you are informally Foley's deputy, if not formally, and it seems logical for you to supervise the secretaries all the time."

Webb told Price that he was flattered that she thought he could handle the situation but that he doubted Foley would approve such an arrangement. He volunteered to think about it and about how the situation might be improved. They agreed to discuss it again in about a week.

After Price left his office, Webb thought, "As far as the secretaries are concerned, Peg is right. I get all my work done in two or three days while it usually takes two or three weeks for the other analysts to get their work typed. The secretaries do all my filing but most of the other analysts do their own, including my

EXHIBIT 1

WHAT I KNOW ABOUT PEOPLE IN ASPD

My Bosses:

Gene Sears—Division manager (ASPD), age 56. BA, Whittier College. Married, now a grandfather. Both his sons on the West Coast. About two-thirds of his assignments have been in corporate headquarters in various analytical, staff, or advisory roles. Very likeable and pleasant; has no detractors as far as I know. (Perhaps too easy going.) Very research oriented. Seems to avoid situations he finds uncomfortable, particularly conflicts. When forced, he tends to waffle; prefers minimum loss compromise or papering over a problem. Reads and approves everything; seems to have a compulsion to change *something* on every piece of paper submitted, usually trivial. Not really *managing* the division, but is very concerned with the reception given to the output of ASPD at higher levels. Apparently doesn't see any connection between managing the division and the analytic output there-from. Seems far more academically than management oriented, appears to be ultra risk aversive, has no leadership but has good followership, and rigidly adheres to instructions from higher levels.

Ruth Robb—Deputy division manager (ASPD), age 62. BA, Bryn Mawr College. Married, no children. Husband retired lawyer. No line-operating experience. Clearly a working supervisor who prepares her own studies and projections. Sees ASPD as the conscience of Q department and seems to resent steady erosion of ASPD position and status; very deep dedication to ASPD. Perfectionist—everything she has anything to do with must be *perfect*; insists on being *very* thorough in her own work to the point of seeming to be very slow. (I wonder how easy it is for her to differentiate between the important and unimportant.) Appears to overwork herself; except for Brian Foley, she does more rewriting of staff papers than anyone else. Clearly more interested in documentation than line experience; verbalized her feelings that former line managers, including the division manager, are "too field oriented." Considers herself a flaming liberal but is very biased against Americans of Hispanic descent. This has created considerable problems with our secretaries.

Brian Foley—Section manager, age 50. BA and MA in economics from Cornell. Married, two daughters in college—Princeton, I think. Two-thirds of assignments in overseas sub-sidiaries or branches but both headquarters assignments in academically oriented staff functions involving analysis, studies, and projections. This is his fifth year in this head-quarters assignment. Former teacher of creative writing to freshmen at a community college. Appears to have been strongly influenced by Northern Irish Protestant parents; several uncles influential in Northern Ireland government and politics. Extremely impa-tient; very difficult to understand what he wants. Completely rewrites everything submit-ted to him by anyone to the point that sometimes every single word is changed but the meaning remains essentially the same with no noticeable improvement in clarity, readabil-ity, or anything else. Ted Ellis once resubmitted a study that Foley had rewritten three months earlier. Even though Foley had rewritten it once, it still came back with virtually every sentence changed and with nasty marginal notes. His managerial style has been called "the great put down"; he belittles the work of all those reporting to him, exercises no noticeable leadership, relies only on authority for power, and seems insecure. In the last year, four analysts left before their normal assignment was up—one volunteered to go to a very remote, sometimes dangerous, overseas branch to get out, two arranged for others to request their reassignments, and one was asked to leave. Personal idiosyncrasies: openly criticized the beard I grew on the camping trip I took two months ago (I thought it prudent to shave it off), openly objects to my playing tennis before work (I have stopped talking about it).

My Peers:

Jim Nance—Associate analyst, age 30. BA, MA, University of Virginia; Ph.D. candidate in international banking. Married, wife is quiet in the extreme. I can't even remember what she looks like. Two children, I think; I've never met them. A scholar's scholar, seems more interested in his academic pursuits than the problems of ASPD. Independently wealthy, truly a Virginia Gentleman from the landed aristocracy. His family raises horses and he is fond of fox hunting and polo, but his real hobby is genealogy. An avid family-tree man who is proud of his English ancestors, some of whom he says were Tory sympathizers during the American Revolution. He is a connoisseur of good food, wine, and tobacco (taught me all I know about fine tobacco). Seems to have enjoyed his two assignments in European branches—this is his first headquarters assignment. His office is adjacent to mine and he converses with me frequently, but then I have five years' operating experience in the area of the world for which he has analytic responsibility. I'm impressed with the way he picks my brain. He is not afraid to change his mind on an issue after he and I have discussed it. He can discuss a wide range of subjects and has a broad range of knowledge. He has a pleasant manner and seems popular with his peers in the office. In fact, he is surprisingly fascinating to talk to—not at all the bore I thought he might be.

Peg Price—Assistant analyst, age 40, single. BA, Smith College, MBA and Ph.D. candidate in banking and finance at the University of Pennsylvania. Only three years with IBC—this is her second headquarters assignment. She seems to do outstanding work professionally, has a good sense of humor, and is a good conversationalist. She makes it clear she wants to be treated as a professional colleague but does respond to male/female chemistry. She expects me to open doors and responds as if she enjoys it. She is very sensitive to women's liberation issues and considers herself a leader in the movement of "women in the world." She is highly involved in various social causes. Seems thoroughly competent professionally but very frustrated by our secretarial situation.

Steve Sand—Senior analyst (newly promoted), age 36. Married, three children. BA, Princeton. Socially conscious. Lives very close to the headquarters offices and walks to work all year long. Very intense, concerned more with substance than form. This is his first headquarters assignment in eleven years with IBC. Very loyal to the system and refuses to criticize it, but has been very critical of what he considers personal failures, as opposed to system failures which he refuses to acknowledge. Most of the problems in ASPD he attributes to a "lack of leadership—particularly on the part of the section manager." He is critical of Foley's unwillingness to stand up to those above him and fight for what he believes is correct. Sand seems professionally competent but very volatile. He screams and shouts at the secretaries, which makes them resent him. Recently engaged in a screaming contest with Foley. He screams in situations where I use charm. From what I understand, he is very good professionally and he is almost always right in his projections and studies. Although we interact when we meet at social functions, I prefer to mix with others. Sand and I have responsibilities in entirely different areas professionally and neither of us knows anything about what the other is doing. His office is as far from mine as it could be and still be in ASPD. We don't interact professionally.

Ted Ellis—Associate analyst, age 30, married, one child. BA, Columbia University. African-American descent. Former Peace Corps volunteer; spent two years as an economist with AID (Agency for International Development) before taking a job with IBC. Seems bright and professionally competent but aloof, almost secretive. Calm and cool but appears intimidated and certainly has withdrawn to the point where he is basically an observer to what happens in ASPD. He told me he was not at all sure he wants a career at IBC: "It's too anti-black." He dresses and acts conservatively and apparently has upper middle class values.

Jack Webb (me)—Senior analyst, age 40. Divorced, no children. BA, St. Bonaventure University. Catholic, but fallen from grace—haven't been to confession in twenty years. Worked my way through college laying and repairing railroad track part time. In army ROTC and served two years on active duty, one year overseas. Sixteen years with IBC, all but the last year at overseas subsidiaries or branches. Early experience as a small branch manager and as a loan officer in a large subsidiary. Have been a manager of corporate loan departments for ten years. At current pay level for three years. Apparently, I was punished for being right by the general manager at my last operating assignment and banished to my previous assignment at the Asian Economic Studies Subsidiary in Sumatra. Now doing additional penance here for the past ten months. Seem to have more operational experience than any of my peers and more management capability than anyone in our division. I see myself as 100 percent male—very virile and proud of it. I get along well with most people—both men and women but have been told by friends of both sexes that I am chauvinistic.

bosses Ruth Robb and Gene Sears. I kid and joke with the secretaries and they all seem to like it and return it, even Julie Cook. One of my friends who came into the office told me that Maria had been very rude to him when he first came into the office, but after he told her he wanted to see me her whole attitude changed and she started kidding and being friendly; she even came in to lock up my files because I had a visitor. I never saw her do that for anyone else."

Webb was intrigued by Price's suggestion and was convinced he could do the job. He was also convinced that Foley would instinctively oppose it as a reduction in his status. He wondered how the matter might be presented to increase the probability of a favorable response. To aid him in his analysis of the issue, he embarked on his planned analysis and critique of his division as an organization.

Over the weekend, he reflected on the way the division functioned. He felt that interpersonal relationships, both non-job-related as well as professional relationships, especially up and down the hierarchy, were strained at best and frequently dysfunctional, resulting in high frustration and low morale. The recent shouting match between Foley and Sand was a case in point. Foley used his authority to win the argument but analytically, Sand was correct. This incident reinforced mutual distrust.

Looking at non-job-related relationships, he knew that twice during the past summer their section had gone on outings: once on the evening excursion boat down the river and once on a Sunday afternoon picnic. In both instances, some spouses had come along. Peg Price had suggested both outings and generally organized them, though he and Nance had volunteered to provide the French bread,

Our Secretaries

Maria Martinez—Age about 65, divorced, no children. Secretarial skills minimal and declining. Active in Girl Scouts and other social organizations. Very religious. Has filed and won three discrimination cases against the company. Told me, "I have never been understood by *gringos*. You must be half Mexican." Can be very difficult if not impossible to deal with, sometimes rude when answering telephones but knows nearly everyone in the company and can get things done when she wants to. Does favors for me but for no one else in the office.

Lola Cardenas—Age 30, single. AA, St. Theresa Junior College. Puerto Rican descent. Maria Martinez apparently arranged for her to work in this office because she wanted someone she could talk to in Spanish. Is a good typist but now resents Maria and work in general; she tends to coast through the day. She is very attractive but doesn't flaunt it, wears provocative clothes and responds to masculinity. Apparently trying to come to grips with the liberated woman of Hispanic descent. Told me about her married Hispanic boyfriend. (Is she demonstrating or trying to prove her "womanhood"?) Deeply involved in Hispanic cultural movement and civil rights; an avid fan of all contact sports, particularly football, hockey, and boxing.

Julie Clark—Age 23, single. High-school diploma, Mrs. Hicks Secretarial School. Has lost dictation skills but good skills otherwise. Appears to enjoy being Ruth Robb's favorite and resents Maria. She has been promised a raise by Ruth Robb and expects to get it. She says funny things sometimes, and I think she adds humor to the office. She doesn't do anything for my "chemistry": she rejects her own femininity and therefore turns me off.

---

wines, cheeses and meats for the picnic. All the analysts and secretaries in their section had attended both outings except Brian Foley who claimed previous engagements. Peg Price had invited Gene Sears, the division manager, and Ruth Robb, the deputy division manager, and both of them had attended both outings. As Webb remembered it, everyone seemed to have had a genuinely enjoyable time. He thought these two outings were typical of the types of informal, non-job-related relationships.

Webb again reviewed the analysis and critique of the X Department (see Exhibit 2), which Webb had copied when a friend allowed him to read it. The document had been sent directly to the vice-president in charge of the X department and had resulted in the appointment of an ad hoc committee to correct deficiencies. The document had received very limited circulation and Webb was probably the only one outside the X department to have seen it, let alone have a copy.

Webb felt the critique applied generally to several organizations other than the X department, including the Advanced Studies and Projections Division. Webb prepared a cover letter addressed to Gene Sears stating that their division suffered from the same basic problems as the X department and that remedial efforts were needed as much in ASPD as they were in the X department.

Although Webb felt the letter was well written and accurately reflected his perceptions of the division, he began to have second thoughts about it. He was sure that Foley would be very hostile toward the letter if he ever found out about it. He wondered how Sears and Robb would react. He wondered if he should send it and, if he did, should he sign it?

EXHIBIT 2

EXCERPTS FROM THE X DEPARTMENT MEMO COPIED BY WEBB: THE CONTINUING CRISIS IN MORALE IN THE X DEPARTMENT

An employee coming from an assignment overseas into the X department discovers he or she has joined a group of bright, dedicated and highly motivated people who suffer from some of the worst morale found any place in IBC. This fact is readily admitted by many analysts in private conversations with their colleagues, most of whom hold theories about how this deplorable situation might be corrected.

This paper is an attempt to express some of the concerns, ideas, and suggestions discussed in a number of conversations with analysts from several different sections in the X department and bring them to the attention of the vice-president in charge. This is done in a spirit of constructive criticism based on a belief that there is an important role for the X department to play in the development of IBC. It is also written with the understanding that the various economic and political forces operating might affect IBC's business interests overseas or its policy decisions. It seems clear to many analysts that the X department is falling far short of its potential because of several serious problems. From the analysts' point of view these include lack of a clear definition of the role of the X department and the part the analysts play, the process of selecting analysts including the practice of assigning operationally oriented people into what are essentially analytical slots for a two year assignment, the poor utilization of secretarial staff, and the failure to produce a timely product, due in part to excessive supervisory editorial review.

WHAT IS THE ROLE OF THE X DEPARTMENT?

The role that the X department is supposed to play needs to be more clearly defined. No one would argue that the primary role of any department within IBC is to provide whatever services the president and other senior executives deem appropriate, but little effort has been made to ensure that the analysts understand just what that is.

Our department might best be described as a place where international banking experts, free from the demands of the daily grind, have a chance to study information in depth and produce studies and projections that help the president, the board of directors, and other senior executives to better understand current world wide economic and business conditions. . . .

While the analyst tries to meet all the demands of both current events and in-depth studies, it appears that the X department has never come completely to grips with establishing a system of priorities delineating the importance of each function in deciding how one's time is to be spent best.

During the time that the X department has taken on new responsibilities, it has faced a long progression of cuts in personnel and budget. As a result, analysts have to spread themselves increasingly thin trying to cover greater areas of responsibility. Both the quantity and the quality of the X department's product appear to have declined as a result.

A number of serious management problems need to be addressed as the neglect of sound, modern management principles contributes significantly to the inability of the department to fulfill its role with its present limitation of personnel.

STAFFING FOR EXCELLENCE

The Analyst—What Makes a Good One?

The majority of analysts now working in the department are on a two-year assignment. This differs greatly from the time when most of those in the X department were assigned there indefinitely and often stayed many years. The practice of placing operationally oriented mid-level people into these positions where there is no opportunity to use or develop management skills is open to serious question.

Developments in international banking over the last 30 years have forced IBC into an increasing recognition of the importance of management and personal relations skills for the success of the company. While ability to undertake in-depth studies is still required of an analyst, such a person finds in a developing career a growing emphasis on his ability to make contacts, to work closely with foreigners, businesspeople, and Americans in other companies and industries and to exercise a variety of other management skills. As a result, IBC people are becoming increasingly operationally oriented, both by force of circumstances and by choice. Some English banks are good at doing academically oriented in-depth studies and they do not attempt to bring back operational people and turn them into research analysts such as IBC does with the people assigned to the X department.

An employee with several years experience abroad usually finds he or she has considerable difficulty adjusting to work in the X Department. Used to responsibilities that emphasize dealing with others, developing information on the basis of personal contacts, and the first-hand study of a foreign culture, he or she quickly gets bored in this Department with the essentially academic nature of the work. As a result, many such people soon start to look for a way out of the assignment and a surprisingly large number have succeeded.

The Secretarial Staff

The X department shares with the banking community in this city a notorious reputation for the poor use of secretarial staff as well as a chronically unsound balance between analysts and secretarial personnel. Invariably when personnel cuts are required, the secretaries go first. Too often, the final result is that highly paid analysts spend a considerable portion of their time doing two-finger typing on their PCs (or worse—longhand writing), filing, handling of ordinary correspondence, sorting, answering telephones, and so on. All this represents an expensive misuse of analyst's time and contributes to the generally poor morale.

Expediting the Product—Timeliness

Nothing discourages an analyst more than the experience of preparing a timely analysis and then seeing several days to more than a few weeks pass by while the paper is edited, rewritten, reedited, and reworded through five or more levels of supervision. All this attention to editorial detail is, of course, meant to ensure that every item produced by the X department is a concisely written and brilliant piece of work, worthy to bear the name of the X department on the cover. Unfortunately, this emphasis on perfection often means that the piece, when it is finally produced, is about as useful as last week's newspaper.

One suggestion to improve this situation might be to identify and charge a specific level of supervision between the analyst and the vice-president, whose sole responsibility would be to edit and rewrite for content. This is not meant to suggest that branch, section, division, and department managers lose the final say in their group's product. However, it is suggested that supervisors at most levels limit themselves to either approving without comment, disapproving and returning the paper to the analyst, or adding a footnote or comment onto the paper.

QUESTIONS

1. Analyze Jack Webb. What are his values? His personality traits? His strengths? His weaknesses?

2. Analyze the people in this case (see Exhibit 1). What are their expectations, self-images, and personal characteristics including values, personality traits, strengths, and weaknesses? Predict spontaneous and reflective interactions based on your analysis.

3. How could the suggested change in secretarial reporting be successfully brought about? Evaluate all alternatives.

4. Evaluate Exhibit 2. What should Jack Webb do with it?

5. If you were Jack Webb, what would you do now about the situation in ASPD?

Jack Webb (B)

During the ten months that Jack Webb had been in ASPD, he had been repeatedly frustrated by the excessive corrections made in his papers by his supervisors [see Jack Webb (A)]. However, there had been some bright spots. On one occasion, when both of his supervisors, Brian Foley and Ruth Robb, were out of the office, Gene Sears, the office director, received an urgent request from the president's office for information about the business, economic, and political climate in the country of Arlena. He asked Webb to drop everything and work on it. Fortunately, the information was already included in a paper titled "Business Opportunities in Arlena" that Webb was just completing. Later that day, he took the paper to Sears and explained that it had been easier to complete the entire paper than to try to extract the specific information requested.

Sears seemed impressed and said the paper was very well done. After making one or two trivial changes, Sears took it to the president's office. Webb heard no more about it from any of his supervisors, but he did learn from a friend in the president's office that the paper had been very well received and the president himself had written a marginal note on it indicating how pleased he was with it.

Webb was mildly irritated that none of his supervisors commented on this since he was sure they knew about it. He wondered if maybe they were angry that the paper was good and indeed would have preferred that it be mediocre. "After all," he thought, "people will forgive you when you are wrong, but never when you are right."

Webb began to be a bit concerned as he recalled three previous incidents in which he had argued very strongly with Foley on technical issues in studies he had submitted. In all three instances he had been overruled by Foley and the conclusions were changed to conform with Foley's thoughts, only to have later events prove Webb correct. Webb never mentioned these to Foley but noted that in each instance, shortly after events proved him correct, the intensity of Foley's criticism of his work increased. Webb could not remember any instance in which Foley had overruled him and subsequent events had proved Foley correct.

On another issue, Webb also knew that in spite of their agreement to discuss it further and without his concurrence, his colleague, Peg Price, on her own, suggested to Foley that "all secretaries be assigned to Mr. Webb since he seems to get along with them so well." Price told Webb that the suggestion seemed to irritate Foley, and he not only dismissed the suggestion but insisted that any problem between the secretaries and Price was the fault of Price and *not* the secretaries. Webb was reasonably sure that some of Foley's irritation would be directed toward Webb.

Webb was also concerned that no one had said anything about the letter he had written enclosing the critique of the X bureau.

After preparation of this letter, he had decided not to submit it; but then, quite unexpectedly, Gene Sears, the division manager publicly announced his desire for ideas on how to improve the ASPD office and, under these circumstances, Webb decided to send the letter to him. Webb had signed the letter and attached the critique of the X bureau to make the letter more credible and reasonable, but had received no acknowledgement or other comment from Sears or anyone else in ASPD. Webb was relatively sure that if Foley heard about the letter, it would adversely affect his next performance appraisal.

It was while these issues were on Webb's mind that he was approached by Will Payne, the corporate liaison officer for the Arlena subsidiary. Payne told Webb that he had received an irresistible offer from a multinational oil company at three times the salary he was getting from IBC. Payne said he had submitted his resignation to IBC to be effective in one month. Payne went on to explain that it would be very difficult for the personnel department to find an immediately available and qualified banking officer for the important and sensitive job of maintaining liaison with the Arlena subsidiary. Payne suggested that Webb looked like an ideal candidate for the position, and indeed, the senior officers in the regional department were very impressed with Webb's paper on Arlena.

Webb was excited by this opportunity and readily acknowledged to Payne his interest in the job of liaison officer for the Arlena subsidiary. Webb had frequently attended meetings held by the vice-president for International Region II (Arlena was in this region), the liaison officer for the Arlena subsidiary, and others. Webb was invited to these meetings when the agenda included discussion of Arlena affairs. Webb felt he was thoroughly familiar with the business, economic, and political conditions under which the Arlena subsidiary functioned. Payne was a senior analyst and the liaison officer job would be slightly more than a lateral move. Webb thought the assignment would give his lagging career a real shot in the arm as well as get him out of his current awkward situation in ASPD.

Webb knew that the vice-resident was due to leave to become president of one of IBC's overseas subsidiaries within a week or two and that a new vice-president for International Region II had not yet been named. The assistant vice-president, Vic Root, had been in the job only two weeks. Webb had met him for the first time at the vice-president's meeting two weeks earlier. At Payne's suggestion, Webb went to see the vice-president and assistant vice-president. The vice-president assured Webb that if he were going to be in the job, he would be delighted to have Webb take the job as liaison officer for the Arlena subsidiary, but he also observed that since he was leaving, it would be up to the regional operations department and personnel department to fill the position.

The assistant vice-president, Vic Root, was clearly anxious to see the position filled since he had no previous experience in that part of the world and would need an experienced and knowledgeable person on board *before* Payne actually left. Root said the situation was compounded by the scheduled departure in three months of the only other experienced person in the office, the liaison officer for the Carmena, Doreena, and Irena (CDI) branches. Without making any commitment, Root indicated that he would be very happy to have Webb as liaison officer for the Arlena subsidiary.

Two weeks later, Payne telephoned and told Webb that he had discussed the possibility of Webb's taking the liaison officer's job with the regional operations department's senior assistant vice-president and the personnel specialist who handled most personnel matters within the regional operations department. Both people seemed impressed with Webb's qualifications. The sticky point was whether or not ASPD would release Webb quickly. Webb responded that he didn't think there would be a problem, that there had been a high turnover of bank officers in his branch, and that his immediate boss would probably be glad to see him leave. Payne asked if Webb would mind asking Foley if they would release him quickly and Webb agreed. Payne then indicated that Dave Katz, currently executive vice-president of the IBC subsidiary in Rondia, had been named the new vice-president and was expected to arrive in four or five weeks.

The next day, Webb found an opportunity to talk with Foley. He told him of Payne's resignation from IBC and was startled at Foley's expletives describing anyone who leaves IBC as a traitor. Webb went on to explain the transfer of the vice-president, the new assistant vice-president, the soon-to-depart liaison officer for the CDI branches and the severe need to find a liaison officer already familiar with the business, economic, and political conditions facing the Arlena subsidiary. He told Foley that he knew he was under consideration for the job and had been asked whether ASPD would release him quickly. Webb hurriedly went on to say that although he was not in a terribly good position to judge, he thought the bank's need for a liaison officer might be greater than its need for an officer to do in-depth studies.

Foley looked at Webb penetratingly for several seconds, turned to face the window and said, "Well, of course we would have to check it out with Mr. Sears, but I doubt ASPD would fight it if the personnel department decided to transfer you." Then he added, "Let me check into it a little further and call you." Webb thanked him and left his office.

Two hours later, Webb received a telephone call from Gene Sears. After some pleasantries and comments about "what a fine reflection on your reputation to be one of those considered for such an important job," Sears indicated that if a formal request were made to ASPD, Webb could be released immediately. Webb quickly called Vic Root, the now

acting vice-president, and passed on the information. Root said he was very pleased and would notify the regional operations senior vice-president.

Webb expected something to happen quickly, but it took two weeks before the personnel department telephoned him to tell him he was being reassigned to become the liaison officer for the Arlena subsidiary as soon as possible and that ASPD had already agreed to his immediate release. Webb quickly transferred the work he had pending to the other officers in the group, telephoned Root and Payne to say he would report for work the next day, and went in to say goodbye to Foley.

Webb arrived at his new job with enthusiasm and was greeted by Payne, who had agreed to continue for two weeks to ensure an orderly transfer of the job. They worked late for the next several days, and both Webb and Payne were pleased that Webb was picking up the work so quickly. Several days later the new vice-president, Dave Katz, arrived. When Payne introduced Webb as his replacement, Katz looked surprised but didn't say anything. A week later, Payne departed and Webb immersed himself in his new job with relish.

During the next four months, Webb enjoyed his operational responsibilities and the contacts he had throughout IBC and with other banks. Katz commented favorably about specific pieces of work on three occasions. The liaison officer for the CDI branches left and the office continued to hum to Webb's satisfaction.

The following month, Joe Max arrived from an assignment as manager of corporate loans at the Arlena subsidiary and took over as liaison officer for the CDI branches. Three days later, Katz asked Webb if he would mind coming in on Saturday morning to talk with him about "the way the office functions." Webb agreed and came in.

After going over a number of relatively minor things, Katz talked about how pleased he was to have Joe Max join the staff and how much confidence Katz had in him. He went on to talk about the outstanding work he had done as the manager of corporate loans in Arlena. "Jack," Katz said, "I know you are a fine bank officer and would always put the interests of IBC above personal interests just as I would. In view of Max's recent field experience in Arlena, I think for the good of the bank it would be better to have him as liaison officer for the Arlena subsidiary. I have every confidence that you will perform very well as liaison officer for the CDI branches. How about it?"

Webb was stunned. "But that's a job for a more junior officer; that's not only a demotion, it will be devastating in my personnel file!" Webb blurted.

Katz frowned and said, "Now don't react too quickly. I think this would be a good move for you. I certainly don't view it as a demotion of any kind. It's just a realignment of responsibilities in this office. As far as your personnel file is concerned, your performance appraisal is the important thing and I feel confident you can earn a better appraisal as liai-

son officer for the CDI branches. Why don't you think about it for a few days and we can talk again."

Webb left the Bank in a state of shock. "The liaison officer for the CDI branches is a nonjob," he thought, "and it has always been held by a junior officer. Katz has never given me any indication he was not perfectly happy with my performance as liaison officer for the Arlena subsidiary. I really enjoy my job now and I think I'm doing very well at it. What happened? How did I get into this mess? What can I do about it?"

QUESTIONS

1. If you were Webb, what would you do now?
2. Why do you think Katz wanted to make this move? Examine all alternatives.
3. If you had been Webb, what would you have done differently at the time you were being considered for the Arlena desk?
4. Evaluate the effect of the last four years on Jack Webb's future in IBC.

NOTE ON THE U.S. FOREIGN SERVICE AND THE STATE DEPARTMENT

Each year approximately 20,000 applicants take the Foreign Service Examination offered through the Educational Testing Service. Approximately the top 1,000 are selected to appear before a selection panel for an interview. Of these, about 100 are selected for entry into the Foreign Service. The Foreign Service is the "officer corps" of the State Department. Because of the selection process, it is sometimes accused of being elitist and sometimes its behavior leaves this impression with members of other government groups that have people overseas at some embassies. It should be noted that the U.S. Information Agency (USIA), which reports to the secretary of state but is a separate agency and not a part of the State Department, has a very similar process for selecting its new officers but has not acquired the elitist reputation.

The Foreign Service is, like the military, very competitive with a rank structure and an up-or-out philosophy. The rank structure very approximately can be compared to the military—a foreign service officer class 6 (FS-06) is equivalent to a second lieutenant, an FS-05 to a first lieutenant, an FS-04 to a captain, an FS-03 to a major, an FS-02 to a lieutenant colonel,

and an FS-01 to a colonel. There is also a senior foreign executive level similar to the general levels in the army with a foreign executive-officer counselor (FE-OC) equivalent to a brigadier general, a FE-CC (Career Counselor) to a major general, an FE-MC (minister/counselor) to a lieutenant general, an FE-CM (career minister) to a four-star general, and an FE-CA (career ambassador) to a five-star general. The above is intended to aid in class discussions and is not intended to describe the rank or salary schedules accurately.

The Foreign Service has four areas of specialization (or "cones"), each with a very specific status: the political specialty represents the highest status, the economic specialty is second in status, the administrative specialty is third, and the consular specialty is at the bottom of the professional ladder. There are also technical specialists that are equivalent to the enlisted ranks in the army, which include communicators, secretaries, and so forth. These latter, who are American citizens, may be supplemented by employees at embassies abroad who are citizens of the host country in which the embassy is located. USIA also has its officers in embassies abroad performing various public relations functions, such as press relations, cultural affairs, running the American library, and promoting travel to the United States.

Also serving in embassies abroad may be representatives of other agencies of the U.S. government, such as the Agriculture, Treasury, Commerce, and Defense Departments in addition to the Central Intelligence Agency (CIA), the Drug Enforcement Agency (DEA), NASA, and so on. The representatives of these agencies are usually attachés, but in some instances they may have other titles.

An embassy is headed by an ambassador, who is the president's representative to that country. About one-third of ambassadors are political appointees, and many of these are sent to the more prestigious countries such as Japan, Mexico, Canada, the countries of Europe, Australia, and New Zealand. The other two thirds of ambassadors are career appointments from the Foreign Service. Most of these appointments follow the status hierarchy described above in terms of the numbers from each specialty (that is, most are from the political specialty, some are from the economic specialty, a very few are from the administration specialty and, very rarely one will be from the consular specialty). The second ranking person at an embassy is the deputy chief of mission or DCM. Again, the people filling this position follow the same status hierarchy described above in terms of numbers.

The function of the political section is to report on all the various political activities going on in that country and to analyze these activities in order to better understand and potentially influence those countries' policies, United Nations votes, and so on.

The function of the economic section is to report on all the various economic activities going on in that country in the same way the political section reports on political affairs.

The administrative section provides all the support for the people at the embassy with respect to administrative activities such at housing, transportation, supplies, accounting, purchasing, maintenance, cashier services, commissary services, and so on. (The U.S. Marine Corps provides for embassy security and has a contingent of marines stationed at the embassy for this function.)

The consular section issues both immigrant and nonimmigrant visas, which in some countries is a major, time-consuming function, provides service to American citizens, such as the replacement of lost passports, visits those Americans being held by the local police, assists with social security, and so on.

All the other agencies that are represented at an embassy perform functions for their parent agency. They may be large enough to have their own section (for instance, the defense attaché's office may consist of army, navy and air force representatives with both officer and enlisted personnel; one of the officers may be the Defense Department representative as well and is designated as the defense attaché). Agencies that are considered large or important report to the ambassador or the DCM; smaller or less important agencies report through one of the State Department sections, usually the economic section.

Because the other agencies are usually better funded than the State Department and their people may be at a higher level in terms of status and salary, natural frictions have a tendency to evolve. These may be compounded by the perception of elitist attitudes. All the normal human behavioral problems that exist in organizations can be found in U.S. embassies, but these are often amplified because of the foreign environment and the pressures and strains imposed by being in a foreign culture.

It is often useful to examine Foreign Service cases because they are amplified in terms of the behavioral issues and are thus easier to identify and analyze. It is important to remember, however, that these same issues occur in other organizations and must be dealt with even when the symptoms are far less obvious and clear cut.

THE EMBASSY IN SABRINA

In mid-July, approximately one year after the new ambassador, Kay Ford, arrived at Lambda, capital of Sabrina, Kurt Law, an old friend of the ambassador and chief inspector for the recently completed inspection, was reflecting on the changes that had taken place at this embassy over the past several years. Kurt Law had remained in Lambda for the weekend to visit on a purely personal basis. As he sat by the pool watching the sun set, Law felt that, indeed, many changes had been brought about since the last inspection several years ago.

As he sipped his espresso, Law reflected on what he knew about the former ambassador, Chuck Howe. Howe had been a political appointee who had certainly increased the visibility of the U.S. presence in Sabrina, but he was somewhat controversial among Washington's bureaucrats, especially the career foreign service officers. Ambassador Howe owned a magazine publishing house and apparently viewed the role of ambassador as a dominantly public relations job in which the goal was to "sell" the United States. All who knew him acknowledged that in this regard he was excellent and had succeeded in this role very well indeed.

With respect to postmanagement, however, it was a different story. Howe tended to deal directly with all his section chiefs, insisted on signing *all* cables personally and had even remarked to the previous inspectors that he really didn't need a deputy chief of mission (DCM) and suggested the position be abolished. Kurt Law had talked with the previous inspectors before setting out on this trip and had learned from them that the staff of the embassy generally felt that Ambassador Howe didn't trust the Foreign Service; he seemed to get along well with all non-State Department agencies and USIA officers except one whose political sympathies put him at frequent odds with Howe.

The previous inspectors generally felt that Ambassador Howe tended not to rely on embassy personnel except for the most routine matters. They also felt that the DCM had lost the confidence of the ambassador, and indeed of the rest of the embassy as well. The other agencies effectively ignored the DCM. When he tried to involve himself in the work of the State Department sections, they would take the issues to the ambassador, who invariably would support the section chiefs. This was exemplified by the political counselor's statement that Ambassador Howe had told him, "You are my political counselor. I don't want the DCM mucking around in political affairs. If he gives you any trouble, you let me know!"

The previous inspectors felt that there was not only a complete breakdown in communications between Ambassador Howe and his DCM, but the ambassador had contempt for the DCM. For some reason, instead of replacing his DCM, the ambassador pushed him aside, leaving him nothing to do but general, area-wide political and economic reporting that did not conflict with the work of the sections. The ambassador's contempt for the DCM was evident in the daily staff meetings that the ambassador held. This was embarrassing, but gave the section chiefs more power, caused them to lose respect for the DCM, and contributed to easy aggravation when the DCM attempted to get involved in their work. In short, all sections became independent groups seen by the inspection team as "going their own way, doing their own thing, without any teamwork or coordination."

The previous chief inspector told Kurt Law that he thought the breakdown between Ambassador Howe and the DCM resulted from the DCM's lack of understanding of his role or the management function. The DCM apparently thought that he would be the brains and conscience of the embassy and would run the substantive side of the show. Politically, the DCM felt the Sabrina government was far too sympathetic to a Communist dictator in a nearby country, while the ambassador and most of the staff did not share this view. Some members of the Sabrina Foreign Ministry referred to the DCM as "Little Joe" (from the extreme anticommunist witch hunt activities of Senator Joseph McCarthy in the decade following World War II) because of his very suspicious view. This only exacerbated the ambassador's negative view of his DCM.

On the other hand, Law was told that Ambassador Howe's behavior contributed to the generally low morale and lack of a sense of self-worth that was felt by some foreign service officers. Howe tended to be very flamboyant, so much so that one member of the staff described him as a "huckster." He tended to react much more impetuously to events than a career diplomat would. Although he strongly supported U.S. positions in world affairs and was quick to criticize distortions of U.S. policy in the local press, there were a few issues in which he became strongly supportive of Sabrina government positions and attempted to sell these positions in Washington. This behavior tended to upset some of the embassy staff as well as the Washington bureaucrats.

Kurt Law knew that Ambassador Howe's DCM had become *chargé* (acting as chief of the mission temporarily) for several months prior to the arrival of Ambassador Ford. During the recent inspection, Law had been careful to obtain as much information as he could about the way the embassy functioned during the time the *chargé* was running it. The general consensus of the staff seemed to be that he knew he was in a caretaker role and he behaved that way. He continued the daily staff meetings but permitted the section chiefs to continue to operate independently, except that now the *chargé* signed all cables, although this was perceived to be automatic. He seemed to be deferring things or temporizing to avoid compromising the next ambassador. After the Sabrina government gave *agrément* for Ambassador Ford (that is, agreed to her appointment), he telephoned Washington frequently to ask Ambassador Ford for guidance even on small issues of protocol. The staff generally felt he wanted to stay on as DCM and, therefore, was not sticking his neck out. They also felt that both the embassy and the DCM would be better off if he left.

That afternoon, during a private poolside luncheon with Ambassador Ford, Kurt Law said, "I know you have made some significant changes in the way this embassy functions and of course I've learned a bit about how it operated before, but I'm curious: How did you manage to change things with such apparent ease and how did you know what to change?"

Ambassador Ford reflected for a few minutes and observed, "I suppose it has a lot to do with my previous experience when I was a DCM in the Middle East. I'm not sure I did any detailed analysis of the sort one learns in management school, or at least not consciously. As far as running the mission goes, I was determined to do it my way." Ford went on to explain that she had requested a full range of briefing appointments prior to coming to the post. In many of those briefings, she detected a tone of ambiguity toward Ambassador Howe. One agency had commented, "When you go out, we hope you remember which government you work for." Other agencies seemed satisfied with the product output from the embassy.

As for the way the post was run, Ambassador Ford said she had learned enough to conclude that the post was uncoordinated, that the DCM had lost the respect of the staff to such a degree that it would be disruptive to keep him, and that, in any event, the personality of the DCM did not seem compatible with her own. Therefore, she decided she wanted her own DCM, one who would supplement her own management skills and was willing to do the bulk of the management functions in addition to providing some additional insights on economic and personnel issues. She so advised the post and personnel. She said, "The key to what I wanted to do was reliant on the relationship I wanted with my DCM." She went on to explain that personnel never quite understood what she wanted and it was a real struggle to get the person she was looking for. Even then, personnel could not arrange for Lou Woods, the new DCM, to get to the post until several months after Ambassador Ford. For this reason, among others, Ambassador Ford determined not to change things until she had her new DCM and had a chance to make her own on-the-spot assessment of the post. "I left Washington feeling that what the embassy needed was quiet leadership and that I needed to go out and calm things down."

Ford went on to explain that after her arrival she made only two changes: she authorized all section chiefs to release their own cables, explaining that she and the DCM would review them after they had been sent; she also reduced the number of meetings from daily to three per week, and kept these short, usually less than an hour, compared with the two- or three-hour meetings that had been customary.

"How did the staff respond to signing their own cables?" asked Law.

"Pretty well," replied Ford. "I did that in my first week; I simply refused to sign all the cables and told the section chiefs to sign their own, except those involving policy or other issues that they felt I should see before they went out. They were to use their judgment in deciding whether I should see it before it was sent. Of course, I would continue to see all traffic, but after the fact. Some section chiefs went a little too far and I had to call them in on it, but it worked itself out after a few weeks. I also told them to stop using 'telegraphese'; that they should keep their messages short but should write complete sentences. This seemed to improve the quality of drafting. The outgoing DCM complained he didn't have a job, and he really didn't. I took away the last remnants of his old job as *chargé* and didn't see any point in giving him any new responsibilities since the staff had no respect for him. I wanted to wait for my DCM so he could get off on the right foot with the staff."

Ambassador Ford used the several months prior to the arrival of her secretary and new DCM to visit every element of the mission and get to know all of the people, Americans and Sabrina employees alike. She also hosted a reception for all employees and their spouses (including enlisted military, Sabrina employees, and staff personnel), which totaled some two hundred people. This reception was repeated at Christmastime and a few weeks ago, when the inspectors arrived.

"By the time my secretary and DCM arrived, I had concluded that the internal operations were a mess. Morale was low. The officers were playing games to see who could outscore each other, who could skirt the DCM most often. Several officers were not functioning up to their capabilities. There was not enough coordination. I sensed backbiting, individual hostilities, and certainly no team feeling. We also had the usual problems of American attitudes toward embassy employees who were Sabrinians. They were referred to as 'locals', with a generally colonial attitude. It's hard for any foreign service officer to recognize that host country nationals are people who want career opportunities, respect, and satisfaction just like they do."

Ambassador Ford then explained how she had sat down with Lou Woods, her DCM, and worked out very specifically what he should do and how he should behave as well as what he could expect from her (a good psychological contract). She told Woods that she wanted him, as DCM, to focus on management issues, such as embassy goals and objectives, coordination, budgeting, morale, and other behavioral aspects of the embassy. He was not to involve himself in any substantive areas that were the responsibility of the section chiefs. He was to concern himself with overall substantive policy issues in support of the ambassador. All the section chiefs were to go through the DCM, and he was to handle as many of the more routine matters as he felt comfortable doing. He *was* to keep the ambassador informed of all issues of significance and to act as the eyes and ears of the ambassador inside the embassy on a day-to-day basis. He was to visit all elements of the mission regularly and know *all* of the people in them and what they did. He was to build rapport with everyone, including the clerks, marines, drivers, charforce, (janitorial services) communicators, and secretaries. He was to build an environment in which everyone felt free to come to him with any issue, personal or business. In short, he was to support the ambassador by doing those things the ambassador would do if she had the time or was handling the issue. He was not to make decisions he thought best but rather decisions that the ambassador would think best. Finally, at the

ambassador's meetings, the DCM should sit anywhere he wanted except at the right hand of the ambassador or at the other end of the table. The ambassador explained that she preferred a less structured type of meeting and wanted people to sit in different seats at each meeting. For this reason, she wanted the DCM to shift around and set an example for the others to follow.

Ambassador Ford went on to note that after her discussion with her DCM, she announced to the staff that henceforth all matters should be taken through the DCM before being brought to the attention of the ambassador. Also, she announced that the ambassador would hold only two meetings each week, each to be kept short: a country team meeting and a staff meeting. In addition, the DCM would hold a meeting once a week with the section chiefs to deal with the issues that did not require the ambassador's attention or issues that needed more staff work prior to being brought to the ambassador's attention.

Ford reluctantly acknowledged that because she felt a strong need to maintain the high U.S. profile in Sabrina that had been initiated by Ambassador Howe, she still often dealt directly with her press attaché and the political counselor. She added that she did not feel that they were abusing their privilege of direct access and that the rest of the embassy staff generally understood this.

After a few refreshing laps around the pool, Kurt Law returned to his room at a nearby hotel to shower and dress for dinner. As he did so, he reviewed in his mind what he had learned during the inspection about Ambassador Ford's management style from various members of the embassy staff. Several comments stuck in his mind:

"I still have freedom in working with Lou Woods, our new DCM, to conduct my section as I had with his predecessor. On policy issues, I go through Lou direct to the ambassador."

"Ambassador Ford has a keen sense of how to use her DCM."

"Lou is very tolerant and easy to get along with. He has an ideal personality—just right for that job. He has the confidence of the ambassador and is savvy in lots of policy and procedural ways."

"Ambassador Ford is giving us a solid concept of management that we never had before. She is pulling this post together, using the DCM as an executive officer to keep things coordinated. Now people who need to know are kept involved."

"Lou's role here is that of manager. Although he has many good contacts with officials of the Sabrina government, he does not involve himself in the substantive work of the sections."

"In the clearing process, Lou may have an input, particularly where policy analysis or recommendations are involved, but he doesn't redraft it himself; he tells me his thoughts and I incorporate them."

"Ambassador Ford is being very strong about tying policy to our resources. Discretionary expenditures must be tied to specific goals and objectives, particularly representational funds."

"Ambassador Ford has been able to maintain the high visibility of the United States in Sabrina, but with an entirely different style than Ambassador Howe."

"Relations of the embassy (including the ambassador and DCM) with this office (a non-State group) are now excellent. This is quite a contrast to what we had before. Now we have a synergistic operation and are closely tied in with other elements in the embassy."

"Ambassador Ford knows management, substance, and diplomacy. Her style is more quiet and less flamboyant than Ambassador Howe's, but with considerably more humor."

"Ambassador Ford does not tolerate fools easily. She likes bright people and does not like plodders."

"The ambassador makes her unhappiness clear but is not cold or annoyed. She can look at herself and see and understand her own feelings and behavior."

"The ambassador has favorites like anyone else, and it's easy to see who they are."

"Both the Ambassador and DCM are good listeners. They do their homework. No more shooting from the hip. I think this embassy is beginning to have more influence, both here and at home."

"The ambassador is so smart it's scary. She really scares some people. Her warmth doesn't always come through. She is very fair, very friendly, has a good spirit, is quick-witted, and her meetings are often interspersed with humor."

"Under this ambassador and DCM, we get much better feedback. I am more diplomatically informed, but I find it hard to read the ambassador's moods."

"Professionally, the ambassador is brilliant, hard, cold, and calculating. She listens well and will change her mind. She can and sometimes does demolish a presentation and create an argument just to measure the people involved."

Kurt Law knew that some of the comments he had heard had been made by top-flight performers and some by those who were not quite so good. This post, like all others, had a distribution of talent; some performers were better than others. Kurt was not quite sure what to think about Lou Woods, the DCM. On the one hand, the DCM seemed very much in tune with the management functions, but law was uneasy about the apparent lack of any substantive economic or political reporting by the DCM except in policy areas.

Kurt Law sat down to review the notes on his interview with the DCM. Lou Woods had served in the economic section of another embassy when Kay Ford was political counselor. They had known each other, but on a relatively informal basis. The DCM told Law he was very flattered that Ambassador Ford had asked him to be her DCM, and that from his very first day at the embassy, the ambassador had made his role as DCM absolutely clear. The ambassador had held several management jobs in the department and saw the DCM's role as dominantly a management position. The ambassador had discussed in some depth the problems of the embassy and how she wanted them resolved. She discussed the staff with the DCM and explained what she saw as the strengths and weaknesses of each. The ambassador told the staff at a meeting what the new situation was, insofar as the role of the DCM was concerned, and then reinforced it in subsequent meetings by examples. The DCM had said to Law, "I had a better picture of what was expected of me than I have ever had. My purpose is not to be an extra layer between the ambassador and the staff but rather to optimize the ambassador's use of time."

As he reviewed his notes on his interview with Woods, Law thought there were a number of items of particular significance:

Almost immediately on my arrival at post, I started working with the ambassador on the goals and objectives for the embassy. This involved a major input from the ambassador but also involved all of the section chiefs. There was a lot of give and take in this process but, of course, the final decisions were the ambassador's.

After the goals and objectives were established to the ambassador's satisfaction, we started to relate our resources to these. The most important resource was the time of the people and the Ambassador made me responsible for coordinating so that everyone made the maximum contribution to each of the goals and objectives of the embassy and not limit their contribution to those goals and objectives that specifically related to their function. [See Exhibit 1: Goals and Objectives for Ambassador—Puritania (not Sabrina, but similar).]

Our first cut at our representational 'wish list' revealed that we wanted to do far more than we could afford but also that we did not have a very clear idea about how many of the things we wanted to do would contribute to the achievement of the goals and objectives of the embassy. We finally reduced our list to things that clearly related to goals and objectives. At my suggestion, the ambassador agreed to take our total representational funds and establish a reserve of a little over ten percent for unplanned or unforeseen opportunities. The balance was then allocated in accordance with our 'wish list,' with about half going to representational functions of the ambassador and the remainder to the sections.

Neither the ambassador nor I approve or disapprove each expenditure of the sections, but we do review guest lists and dollars spent quarterly and informally; each section chief tells us how each expenditure has contributed to the goals and objectives. . . .

I always take time to explain to the staff why I want something done a particular way. I will often raise an issue at my staff meeting so that everyone will know how he or she fits into the picture. . . .

Shortly after I arrived, there were a few times when a cable was sent out by one of the section chiefs that I thought I should have seen first. When this happened, I would go to his or her office and sit down to talk. I would say, 'Let me put myself in your shoes so that I can understand why you didn't think I should see this cable before it went out.' Usually the response was that since the subject was marginal, the section chief used his or her own judgment, based on the feeling that the ambassador wanted them to use their initiative. I responded that yes indeed, the ambassador *does* want the section chiefs to use their initiative but then went on to explain why, in this particular instance, I felt it should have been brought to me before being sent. This talk was not in any way a punishment or slap on the wrist, but rather a working out of our modus operandi. Within a few months, everyone understood what we expected to see

EXHIBIT I

GOAL AND OBJECTIVES FOR THE AMBASSADOR: PURITANIA

1. SUPPORT FOR THE PROCESS OF DEMOCRATIZATION

- Express support frequently, at high levels.
- Develop contacts and working relationships with the entire spectrum of legitimate political parties. Concentrate on principal opposition party where existing links are weak.
- Encourage high-level American officials to visit.
- Target exchange programs on young labor leaders and opposition politicians; look carefully at educational and cultural exchanges.
- Facilitate AFL-CIO programs with democratic labor unions.
- Encourage private exchange and cultural activities; seek to promote major cultural exchanges.

2. STRENGTHENING OF MILITARY RELATIONSHIPS

- Emphasize importance of U.S.-Puritanian Council (secretary of state and chairman, joints chiefs of staff, are our participants in twice-yearly meetings), not only as a symbol of our interest in Puritania but also of the importance of military cooperation.
- Work to improve military-to-military exchange programs, particularly by increasing the number of senior officer exchanges.

3. ENCOURAGEMENT OF PURITANIAN ECONOMIC STABILIZATION PROGRAM AND OF CLOSE PURITANIAN-AMERICAN ECONOMIC TIES

- Express our support for the economic stabilization program.
- Facilitate, as appropriate, Puritanian contacts with the International Monetary Fund (IMF), the Organization for Economic Cooperation and Developmment (OECD), and Western European governments.
- Undertake an assessment of the impediments of U.S.-Puritanian trade and investment relations imposed by needless regulations or inadequate understanding of administrative arrangements on both sides.
- Promote and facilitate direct contacts between U.S. and Puritanian cabinet officers responsible for finance and commerce.

4. IMPROVEMENT IN BILATERAL COOPERATION ON GLOBAL ISSUES

- Encourage, in a low-key way, Puritanian accession to the Non-Proliferation Treaty (NPT).

5. STRENGTHEN RESPECT FOR HUMAN RIGHTS

- Prior to important multilateral meetings, such as the U.N. General Assemblies, consult with Puritanian leaders on best tactics to further these goals.
- Encourage Puritanian leadership to press other countries to sign and ratify the American Convention on Human Rights.

before it was sent and what they should send on their own. . . .

In one instance shortly after I arrived, the embassy was asked to submit a major policy cable. When the drafter finished it, I was out of the embassy for the day and he took it directly to the ambassador. The ambassador asked if I had seen it and sent it back when she found out I hadn't. The drafter was upset and argued that this would cause a two or three day delay, but the ambassador insisted that on something that important she wanted my input. Of course, everyone in the embassy heard about this very quickly. I think this kind of support from the ambassador has made it easier for me to work out an effective set of relationships with the staff. In this instance, the ambassador told me later that she accepted several statements of mine in the cable that she might not have accepted from the drafter but stressed that she wanted to demonstrate support for me. . . .

As for cables, even though I prefer some words to others and have my own style, I do no drafting or redrafting. I make suggestions or maybe change a word or two where the meaning is likely to be misunderstood. When I do change something, I talk it over with the drafter and explain my feelings. I prefer to work with the drafting officers prior to the actual draft. Either the ambassador or I give oral direction and I'm concerned with direction, not details. I will often see an early draft or outline and work with the drafting officer before it is put together for clearance by anyone else. . . .

I'm a little concerned about one of our section chiefs. He telephoned me before I left Washington and called the ambassador by her first name. I did not think that was proper, but did not say so at the time. He still does this and I suppose I am going to have to tell

him I do not think it is proper; certainly I would never do it. He said he and the ambassador had discussed the staff at the embassy and could he tell me anything about the people. I said no, that I preferred to form my own impressions when I got there. I'm afraid he still thinks he is the DCM of the embassy annex, and of course he is not. This is less true now than it was in the beginning. If he didn't do such an excellent job, I might be more concerned. He sometimes comes on too strong and has offended people too much. Later, he sometimes recognizes this and says he shouldn't have said something or done something, so I think we are making progress. He just needs more experience. . . .

Law next reviewed his notes on his interview with the administrative counselor, who had been helpful on the subject of resource allocation:

While on home leave last year, I met with Ambassador Ford shortly after her appointment to Sabrina had been announced. We discussed her desire to tie policy objectives to our use of resources to the extent we could. She wanted a mechanism to rationalize what the embassy did.

The first step in this process was really in response to staff pressure. The previous ambassador had spent most of the representational funds directly on functions at the residence, including functions for various members of the embassy staff. Nevertheless, the staff felt constrained by this and telephoned the country director in Washington, requesting him to intercede with Ambassador Ford for them and suggest that representational funds should be allocated to each section. The ambassador and I discussed this and it was decided that after I returned to the embassy, each section should prepare a representational plan showing what they wanted to do, why, what they expected to gain and what it would cost.

I was also asked by the ambassador to initiate a complete review of staffing as a resource that could be allocated. I was to start by looking at where the embassy was and where the section chiefs thought it ought to be over the next several years. This forced us to look at policy and attempt to determine just what we were trying to accomplish. Goals and objectives were set for the administrative and consular functions and we were encouraged to involve ourselves in substantive discussions of policy review with the political and economic counselors as well as the other agencies. We were all asked to think in terms of how we could contribute to each other's goals and to coordinate with our new DCM, Lou Woods, in this regard.

Of course, our ability to reallocate resources is very limited, but the exercise is psychologically very valuable. We have thought about the way people spend their time and how each of us can contribute to the goals and objectives of the whole embassy. In addition, representation and travel funds are closely tied to our objectives, but these are rather small amounts of dollars. . . .

Kurt Law felt that Ambassador Ford had given the inspection team a good overall perspective of the resource allocation process.

I was asked to develop a set of goals and objectives for our embassy here in Lambda. After this was done, I was told that I was going to have ten percent less resources. Had I known this beforehand, I would have written different goals. I think it is inappropriate to tell each embassy they are going to have ten percent less. The cost of a ten percent cut in Sabrina may be far higher than the same cut elsewhere. I don't think across the board cuts make any sense.

The only real resource we have to allocate is people—the time of the people, what they do. We can enhance the effectiveness of the people by relating the controllable dollars to our goals and objectives. For example, consider my travel inside Sabrina. When I receive an invitation of some sort, we discuss it at a staff meeting to see what we can do with it, who else in the embassy may be able to benefit by going with me, and what such a trip might contribute to achievement of our goals and objectives. If the potential contributions seem high compared to the estimated cost, I will accept the invitation and assign a control officer to see that the embassy maximizes the benefit derived from the trip.

We recognize that not all benefits are tangible and that we must balance appropriately: time in the capital and time in the countryside; contacts with labor and management; military and educators; right, left, and middle of the road; bureaucrats and community leaders; news media and opinion leaders; and, of course, the American Friendship Organization. One of our goals is to maintain a high visibility for the United States presence in Sabrina and, therefore, we must evaluate the likelihood of getting good news coverage on each trip. On the last trip I took, we made the front page every day in one or another of the newspapers in Sabrina. We made many friends and created considerable goodwill.

"What is the value to the United States of goodwill, visibility, and good friends? It is very hard to measure the value of these things, but I feel intuitively that the U.S. gained a great deal. . . .

Several other comments from various people in the embassy stood out in Kurt Law's mind as he reviewed his notes.

Broadly speaking, I sense disparity between our objectives and the resources made available to me. Consequently, I can't do many things I think would be very worthwhile. There is no time for creative thinking or initiating our own reporting in potentially useful areas. . . .

I have participated fully in the process of setting goals and objectives. . . .

The goals and objectives are reached first, then we try to plan how we can meet them. . . .

Our cultural exchange program ties in with several of our embassy goals and objectives, not just the goals related to USIA. . . .

This is a synergistic operation. We are able to ride the ambassador's coattails. She allows us to go with her and through her get better access to some people than we might otherwise have. . . .

As he put his tie on for dinner, Kurt Law began to think about the additional questions he wanted to discuss with the ambassador. He then reread the letter he had received from Ambassador Ford before the inspection team had left Washington (see Exhibit 2).

QUESTIONS

1. Compare, analyze, and explain the way the embassy functioned under Ambassador Howe, the *chargé*, and Ambassador Ford.
2. What were the most significant changes introduced by Ambassador Ford and what impact did these have? Explain.
3. What suggestions or informal advice, if any, would you give to Ambassador Ford? The DCM?
4. What, if anything, can other DCM's learn and use from this case?

EXHIBIT 2

EXCERPTS FROM AMBASSADOR FORD'S LETTER TO CHIEF INSPECTOR LAW

As for your question about how we can use the budget process as a means of achieving effective resource allocation in line with our goals and objectives, well, I'm not sure we have such a process today and I'm not sure that any of the techniques tried or imposed fill the bill. I doubt that I can fully explain what troubles me, but let me try.

Our process starts with post goals and objectives. We are not then asked what resources we need to meet them. We are told, "Meet them with these resources but in the process don't change your goals and objectives." In my view, if the system were legitimate, it would start at a very high level with the question: What will be the quality of our diplomatic and consular presence abroad? What is, in fact, the base figure for a "standard presence"? What is a "standard presence"? Do the designations of embassies as classes I through IV reflect levels of importance to U.S. policy? (In my view, by the way, they don't; they provide a convenient way of deciding which embassy gets a Chrysler and which gets a Chevrolet.) If so, what we build on top of the standard presence ought to reflect policy, which in itself should reflect the magnitude of the U.S. interest. And, if we conclude that we have only a class III interest in a country, then it should have a level III staffing pattern and we ought not to impose upon the official Americans there the same requirements and expectations in terms of goals and objectives as we impose upon those at a class I post with a level I staffing pattern.

Let me use Florina and Sabrina as examples. Beta is a class I embassy; we, Lambda, are a class III. That ought to mean that the United States interest in Florina is larger than that in Sabrina and that, therefore, in addition to the Chrysler/Chevrolet distinction in automobiles, there is a Chrysler/Chevrolet distinction in goals and objectives. There is not, and we are as accountable for a drift in Sabrina-U.S. relations as Beta is for Florina-U.S. relations. We get the same requirements levied on us to consult regarding the United Nations, disarmament, the Organization for Economic Cooperation and Development, various trade issues, toxic substances, the General Agreements on Tariffs and Trade decisions, and a host of other topics. We are told we must pay the same amount of attention to youth and not be responsible for losing the next generation. We are supposed to have access to the same kinds of key leaders and officials and we are to win the battle of public diplomacy. The department acts as if class I means it takes more to do the *same* job than at a class III post, rather than more to do a *different* job.

And so I call the budget process unfortunate, or worse, misleading. Apparently, no one is prepared to take the responsibility for saying, first, *this* is the "standard presence" required of a world leader, and *this* is what is needed to reflect additional levels of policy importance; and if we don't get it, *these* are the countries we are prepared to treat as being of lesser importance, accepting the costs associated with such a conclusion, and *these* are the facts we will not ask our embassies in lesser posts to gather because we don't really care. And maybe, if someone were willing to relieve us of the responsibility for gathering all the facts just as if we were a class I post, we could be truly imaginative in some other areas and keep the losses to a minimum.

It should be clear that I'm angry about the whole subject and believe that the building blocks of the budget process in diplomacy are not embassies, but blocks of global and regional interests and blocks of standard presence, to which are added blocks of style (active or passive, policy influencing or fact gathering) and blocks of gains we wish to achieve minus blocks of losses (in current and long-term influence) we are willing to accept. To me, *that* is the Washington process, with the decisions consciously made at the secretary's level, and anything else is peripheral."

JIM SWEET (A)

Two weeks before Jim Sweet returned to Washington from his post as political counselor in a large embassy, he learned that he had been tentatively selected to be deputy chief of mission (DCM) at the embassy in Beta, capital of Florina (a Class I post). Sweet, FE-MC, had been in the Foreign Service for 25 years, chiefly filling political officer positions. When he was notified of his selection, he was also told that the new ambassador to Florina was a political one; the appointee, Harold Strong, had a long and distinguished career in American industry. Wealthy, socially and politically prominent and active, Strong had often visited Florina, where he had many influential friends in business and government. Sweet's name, along with two others, had been proposed to Strong as DCM candidates, and Sweet was flattered that he had been Strong's first choice, subject to reaffirmation after a meeting with him next week.

Jim Sweet had been hoping to be assigned DCM at an important embassy. In fact, he was inclined to view his years of Foreign Service assignments as preparation for just such a position. Now that he had been offered the job in Beta, however, he viewed the opportunity with misgivings. He was aware that he could refuse the assignment and that such a refusal would not be held against him. On the other hand, he knew that DCM assignments to important posts were not especially plentiful and there was no assurance that he would be assigned

as DCM at a different mission. Nonetheless, he wondered seriously if he should turn the assignment down.

Although many factors contributed to his misgivings, the principal factor was his reluctance to take on the DCM job under a politically appointed ambassador. Sweet viewed Foreign Service work as a profession; he believed that embassy affairs, in general, were better handled when the ambassador was a career Foreign Service officer. He had always felt that most political appointees were not especially competent as ambassadors. Yet he knew that, as DCM, his job would require unwavering loyalty to the ambassador even if he was a political appointee. Sweet was not entirely sure that he could provide such loyalty.

To help him reach his decision quickly, Sweet decided to have lunch with an old family friend in the State Department, Carroll McDonald, who had served as ambassador in three separate embassies. McDonald, in his sixties, was completing his final tour in the State Department and expected to retire soon. Sweet questioned McDonald on his experiences and asked for thoughts about how a DCM should approach his assignment.

"The major problems facing the DCM," McDonald began, "in any but the smallest posts, are managerial. You have to make sure the major issues are brought to the ambassador's attention. You have to assure adequate staffing and you must be good on detail. But, more than anything, you have to be good with people, to enlist their enthusiasm.

"As an ambassador, I wanted to know everything I needed to know and nothing else. If you pass all problems to the ambassador, you reduce the ambassador's flexibility and you increase his or her workload. Yet, if you handle a matter on your own and that matter later comes to the ambassador's attention, the ambassador may construe it as an attempt to bypass him or her, or as a case of poor judgment, or perhaps even disloyalty. I expected my DCM to give me his judgments and his reasoning for them, and to try to reduce my workload. Good judgment is the key. You have to be a good alter ego for the ambassador; you must act like the ambassador in his or her absence. I wanted to be able to say when I returned from a trip: 'I would not have done anything differently.' In fact, the ambassador should not be missed when he or she is away. And yet, the DCM mustn't give the impression that he or she is the ambassador when the ambassador is away. That's very bad!

"You have to understand what the ambassador wants to do and try to deduce what the ambassador feels is the proper way to implement our policy. To do that, you have to understand how the ambassador communicates. You should organize your work to fulfill the communications function."

Sweet interjected, "But didn't you sometimes have the feeling that your DCM knew more, or was better equipped to make certain decisions, than you were?"

"No, I never thought that, though I can understand why you ask that question," McDonald replied. "But an attitude of professional superiority is extremely dangerous. Remember that you must have absolute loyalty to the ambassador. The fundamental fact is that the ambassador serves the president, and as DCM, so do you. You are not elected; you carry out the policy of the president, not just that of the State Department. We

in the Foreign Service do not make foreign policy, we only carry it out. That's a hard insight to come by, but it's true. It also applies to all foreign service officers. If they can't be loyal and enthusiastically endorse whatever policies are handed down, they shouldn't be in the Foreign Service."

"But how about the situation I'm in?" asked Sweet. "You know that I came up through the political cone. I think I know a lot about political analysis. How can I use my knowledge as a professional and still keep happy a guy who may not know politics from botany?"

McDonald said, "What you're saying is that you're trained and the ambassador is not. Some DCMs expect to run the show and, in the process, they upstage the ambassador. They say to the staff, in effect, 'The ambassador doesn't count. I'll handle that problem.' Obviously, most ambassadors don't like this. You're in a particularly vulnerable position, Jim, because of your political experience. Many DCMs act as if they want to continue to run the political section. They oversupervise. They try to hold onto the political side too much.

"But your experience can be very useful. To use a homely example, the ambassador is like an orchestra leader. He wants to produce the music that the composer, the president, has in mind, and to do it, he has to understand all the instruments and what they can do. The DCM is the assistant conductor. He must understand all the agencies, how they function and what they do, to a greater degree and in more complete detail than the ambassador does. He must recognize the objectives of other agencies. The technical side must serve the policy side and so you must know AID [Agency for International Development], USIA [U.S. Information Agency], the military, the station and so forth, both technically and in the policy area. You have to know the language of engineering and marketing, so to speak, but the trick is to know all this and still maintain a strong sense of modesty. The DCM does *not* go in and divide duties with the ambassador. I wanted my DCM to come to me and discuss his problems, so we could thrash them out together. You'll find the ambassador, while not trained as you were, may have many good ideas. He's not totally dependent on foreign service careerists to run the show."

"What do you have to say about the relationships among the ambassador, the DCM, and the section chiefs?" Sweet asked. "I've witnessed situations in which the DCM was caught in the middle. Did you always work through your DCM when you had business with a section chief?"

"That's a ticklish question and I suppose the answer depends on the people involved. I liked to reserve the right to go directly to section chiefs for particular information; I wanted a DCM who was a good general manager, but I wanted to consult directly with my section chiefs on specialized matters. The real problem comes when the section chiefs persistently circumvent the DCM on matters the DCM needs to know. Circumvention by section chiefs creates more work for the ambassador. I found that if the DCM was involved, he could go over reports and suggest changes before I had to read them, thus saving me time. But the DCM must always be on guard against oversupervision. His tendency is to do it himself. Instead, he must delegate, and to delegate properly takes time and thought. I retained my right to go directly to my section chiefs and I didn't like DCMs who were thin-skinned about section chiefs dealing directly with me."

During lunch, Sweet discovered that McDonald took a rather hard line on the subject of foreign service officer qualifications. "Don't take this personally, Jim," he said, "but I think too many DCMs are picked from the political cone. It's not that important any more. In Western Europe, for example, foreign policy *starts* with trade and economic issues. I think our DCMs need a good economic background as much as they need a political one. For that matter, an administrative background would

be invaluable; the DCM position at most embassies is becoming more and more of a management job. However, I realize it's hard to change the current system.

"Further, in my view people ought to come into the Foreign Service only if they are protected by virtue of another profession or an advanced degree, such as a Ph.D., so if it's necessary or desirable for them to leave the Foreign Service, there'll be a place for them to go."

Sweet replied, "But if the system is to work, you can't keep changing the rules of the game. People make career decisions based on certain assumptions. You change them and then what happens?"

"Well, I agree, it's a problem," McDonald said, "but when you have highly placed officers in the embassies who are, to a great extent, confined by their foreign service experience, you can run into trouble. Poor relationships with other agencies develop. All too frequently, the problem with DCMs lies in their lack of concern for the work of other agencies. The DCM rarely devotes enough time to matters other than the traditional State Department affairs with which he or she is most familiar. The DCM should have broad experience, and I think we should see that he or she gets it."

Sweet remarked, "Well, I suppose, too, that any officer in the Foreign Service with professional or educational qualifications to fall back on wouldn't be so entirely dependent on the State Department. That officer would probably be more independent."

"Yes, I agree," McDonald said. "Such an officer wouldn't be so locked into the system. And that would do the system some good."

The next day, Jim Sweet had a luncheon meeting with another old friend who was then diplomat in residence at George Washington University, awaiting assignment to a mission. Martin Allen, FE-OC, had been DCM at an important medium-sized post in South America until four months earlier, when he was called home at the request of the ambassador, a political appointee. Sweet asked Allen how he felt about having held the DCM job under a politically appointed ambassador.

"I know this, Jim: the State Department *tends* to deal directly with the DCM when the ambassador is a political appointee. State really rides the DCM's back, almost without reference to the ambassador. Since the State Department assigned the DCM to the job to begin with, the DCM is forced to balance his or her loyalty between the ambassador and the State Department. This situation is exacerbated because the DCM grew up in, and has been loyal to, the State Department up to this assignment. On the other side of the coin, you have political ambassadors who are very suspicious of the State Department and of foreign service officers in general. They distrust the system. They resent it if the DCM has been *chargé*; you certainly should avoid arriving first if you can, by the way. The DCM has to work especially hard to build a relationship with the ambassador. I found that if I just watched and waited, I was able to make judgments that kept things running smoothly.

"One of the things I discovered was that it was difficult to learn exactly what the ambassador thought on some matters. I wasn't sure that he meant what he said. So, as I say, I just watched and waited. I didn't make too many decisions that way, but at least I kept the lid on things. The ambassador who claims to want a DCM to be his or her right arm probably doesn't mean it.

"My ambassador didn't understand the Foreign Service, nor did he understand that our primary function was political. He kept wanting me to get more involved with the other agencies such as AID, the military, and so forth. But after all, Jim, we're political officers and our main function is diplomacy. We don't run those other agencies. They certainly have enough staff of their own to run things without our being involved. And one thing's sure—our next assignment comes from the State Department and we are evaluated on what we do for *it*, not on what we do for USIA, AID, or the Department of Defense."

"Martin," Sweet said, "if you had to give a new DCM a few pieces of advice, what would you say?"

Allen thought for a moment and said, "The DCM should view the job as *not* important and should be humble. The DCM should be able to disagree privately with the ambassador without making the ambassador mad, and that requires humility. The DCM must be able to funnel information up *and* down. He or she should shield the ambassador from the rest of the staff. And there's one more thing."

"What's that, Martin?"

"He has to be able to take most of the --!"

Later that day, as he reflected on Martin Allen's indelicate but apt final remark, Jim Sweet realized ruefully that he was in a strange position. Here he was, half inclined to turn down a job for which he had been in preparation for 25 years. He was not at all enamored of the idea of working for a political ambassador, but knew that Carroll McDonald had been right in his observations about loyalty to the ambassador. Also, Martin Allen's experiences obviously hadn't turned out too well for him. How should he go about establishing a good relationship with Ambassador Strong and get things off to a good start? It seemed to be a very high-risk situation, yet it also represented a challenge. "Do I rise to it," he asked himself, "or do I sit this one out? What do I say when I meet with Ambassador Strong? What questions should I ask? What other advice should I seek?"

QUESTIONS

1. What is the role of a DCM? What difference does a politically appointed ambassador make?
2. Contrast the views of Ambassador McDonald with those of Martin Allen.
3. If you were Jim Sweet, what would you do?

JIM SWEET (B)

Shortly after Jim Sweet, the new DCM, arrived at the Florina embassy in the capital city of Beta, he was called in by Ambassador Harold Strong to discuss how they would divide responsibility for the conduct of embassy affairs [see Jim Sweet (A)]. Strong was a wealthy political appointee with a long and successful career in the steel industry. His frequent business trips to Florina had produced many friends who were influential in both business and government. Sweet, FE-MC, had been in the Foreign Service for 25 years, chiefly as political counselor at a large post immediately prior to his Florina assignment. The total complement of the American mission in Beta was numbered at about 300.

In his first discussion with Sweet, the new ambassador indicated that he knew the country fairly well. He knew many people who could be beneficial to the mission, but little about diplomatic protocol and even less about running an embassy. He felt it might be a mistake to assume that an embassy operates like a business. Therefore, he was going to rely on Sweet to guide him. Initially, at least, he wanted Sweet to run the embassy but to keep him informed about important problems and advise him on what actions should be taken. Later, he planned on assuming more control; he thought it was important that he and Sweet develop an open relationship that would encourage discussion of differing viewpoints on issues of importance to the mission.

The ambassador emphasized that he and Mrs. Strong would be doing a good deal of entertaining, probably once or twice a week, and that they preferred to invite people with common interests: bankers one night, businesspeople another, government officials on still another, and so on. The ambassador wanted some people from the embassy at these affairs to help them make important personal contacts and to broaden their viewpoints. He thought Sweet would be the best judge of whom to invite. After further discussion, it was agreed that the ambassador would send each guest list to Sweet with an indication of how many embassy people could be added, usually three or four embassy couples at a time. At the conclusion of this first discussion, Sweet felt relieved and gratified by the ambassador's apparent confidence in him.

In the following months, the ambassador's dinner parties became an important element in the social life of the embassy. Initially, Sweet arranged for invitations to be extended to the top officers in each of the major sections. With the passage of time, however, he tended to concentrate on officers in the political section. Soon, Sweet found that the guest list was being forwarded with a note indicating preferences as well, that is, embassy people whom either the ambassador or Mrs. Strong preferred. These preferences were generally three officers from socially prominent American families, two middle-ranking officers from the economics section, and a first-tour junior officer in the consular section.

Four months after Sweet's arrival at Beta, Dave Rex, the political counselor, casually mentioned to Sweet that George Hart, the administrative counselor, was concerned about the lack of invitations to other officers at the embassy who could benefit from the contacts made possible by the ambassador's parties. After some discussion, they concluded that the parties were indeed very helpful in making significant political contacts and that their size and makeup were about right. Both men recognized the potential value of the parties to other officers, but felt that except for the counselors themselves, the benefit to the political section was considerably greater than to other sections and that therefore, no change in the composition of the guest lists should be made.

Sweet and Rex then discussed the administrative counselor's apparent feeling that the parties were beginning to have a negative effect on morale. Rex mentioned that the economic counselor, Carl Mann, had given a cocktail party the same night as the ambassador's last dinner and had invited many officers on the embassy staff. Rex thought this might have bolstered the morale of those who had never received an invitation from the ambassador. He also felt it had provided a release of steam since he understood that some of the officers who never made the ambassador's guest list had been indiscreet enough to speak openly of their resentment at being left out. He noted that some friction seemed to have developed between the wives of the uninvited and invited officers and perhaps between couples who had never "made the grade." Rex observed that the problem was reflected to some extent in the day-to-day routine of the embassy; relationships between the officers of the political section who were invited and the officers of the other sections who were not invited seemed somewhat strained. Both agreed

to watch the situation and to encourage the senior officers in the other sections to follow Mann's example.

A month after Sweet's discussion with Rex, George Hart asked to see Sweet in order to discuss morale. After initial pleasantries, Hart indicated that he felt morale and efficiency at the embassy were declining rapidly. He was not criticizing the DCM in any way, but rather bringing to his attention a situation about which he might not be fully informed. Hart explained that the parties given by Mann and other senior officers had been dubbed "rump parties" by the officers at the embassy. Hart had attended these parties occasionally and noticed that the conversation almost always involved the personalities of mission members who were on the ambassador's guest list, that the tone of the talk was distinctly negative, and that the ambassador and Mrs. Stone came in for a number of barbed comments.

After further discussion, it became apparent that Sweet and Hart saw the situation in quite different terms. Sweet concluded the discussion by telling Hart, "The political section is the most vital part of our operations, George. Sure, there's bound to be some dissatisfaction, but the ambassador's parties have a real diplomatic purpose and I want to be sure that our political staff makes as many contacts as possible. That's what we're here for, after all. I don't see any point in loading these affairs with people who just want to have a good time and hobnob with the boss. You'll appreciate that the number of preferences Mrs. Strong adds to the list limits my choice even more. There's nothing I can do about that, but it makes it all the more important that I fill the few open spots left with our political people. The ambassador has made me responsible for this thing and this is the way I think it should be handled."

During the next several months, Sweet noticed that more and more preferences were showing up on the ambassador's guest list and he grew increasingly concerned about the small number of political officers that he could add to it. These preferences included a wider range of officers; most recently even the agricultural attaché, the labor attaché, and the commercial attaché had been invited. He had not previously seen their names on the guest lists, although he was aware that counterparts of these attachés in the host government sometimes attended ambassadorial functions. In fact, Sweet suspected that omission of their names from the ambassador's guest lists had produced an unusual effect: whenever Florina government officials representing agricultural, labor, or commercial functions wanted to contact the embassy on any matter, they usually made their contacts with him as DCM rather than directly with the attachés. He surmised that they contacted him because of his working relationship with the ambassador and because of his responsibility for the guest lists.

About the same time, Sweet began to notice that both the defense attaché and the station chief were discussing matters directly with the ambassador, in effect bypassing him. He learned this when, on several occasions, the ambassador spoke to him about DAO (Defense Attachés Office) or station matters, assuming that he was already familiar with the situations when, in fact, he was not. Sweet was not especially chagrined by these developments until Dave Rex, the political counselor, told him that he thought some of the functions of the political section were being usurped as a result of the station's direct pipeline to the ambassador. Rex particularly resented not being consulted on issues of significance to the section and not being given information that might be useful. He thought that Sweet should approach the ambassador about it.

QUESTIONS

1. What do you think of the way in which the DCM handled the ambassador's guest lists?
2. If you had been Sweet, what would you have done differently?
3. If you were Sweet at this point in time, what would you say to the ambassador?

JIM SWEET (C)

About eight months after Jim Sweet had assumed responsibility for the ambassador's guest lists, the ambassador's wife, Mrs. Strong, telephoned him to express her concern about some of the "less sophisticated" members of the staff who had recently been invited to the parties. [See Jim Sweet (A) and (B).] Sweet was surprised and said he had assumed those were her preferences. She indicated quite strongly that they were not. Jim promised to look into the matter and return her call. As he was pondering this information, Carl Mann, the economic counselor, came by his office with a complaint.

"Jim," he said, "I'm kind of upset about the allocation of representation funds. Personally, I did O.K., but some of my junior officers didn't get anywhere near what I thought they should have received. While I appreciate that the funds are limited, it seems to me that my junior officers really took a beating on this one."

Sweet said, "What allocation? The ambassador and I haven't had a chance to talk about representation funds yet."

Mann said, "Well, they've been allocated. George Hart came by today and told me how much we're getting."

"Well, I don't understand that," Sweet said. "Let me look into it, will you, Carl?"

"Okay, Jim. In case you're interested, I happen to know that Dave Rex is pretty upset too."

When Mann left, Sweet decided to check with Dave Rex, head of the political section, on the representation funds.

"Sure, Jim, they've been allocated. George Hart called to give me the figures and we got much less than we got last year and less than we expected to get this year. It makes me mad."

"What I don't understand," Jim said, "is that up to now, the ambassador and I have worked matters like that out together."

"Well, from what George told me," replied Rex, "he and the ambassador allocated the funds. Looks like George has been busy lately. A couple of people in my section have also told me that George has somehow managed to wangle a couple of places on the ambassador's guest list for people not in the political section. How they heard, or how George did it, I've no idea."

Sweet was surprised and rather embarrassed. Shortly after this conversation, Kate Grey, chief of the consular section, dropped by to thank him for the representation funds she had received. Sweet was annoyed, and he told her she shouldn't thank him for something on which he hadn't even been consulted. He recognized ruefully that of the section chiefs who had been given representation funds for the coming year, at least three were now aware that he had been essentially bypassed.

Sweet asked George Hart, the administrative counselor, to come to his office. In response to Sweet's question, Hart said, "Well,

Jim, the ambassador called me in late last week and consulted me on it, and together we worked out the allocations. I'm sorry if you haven't been informed about it until now but I assumed the ambassador had spoken to you."

"Well, he hasn't," Sweet said, "but I suppose it doesn't really matter, now that the funds have already been allocated. There's another thing too, George."

"What's that?" George asked.

Sweet told him about Mrs. Strong's call that morning. He added that someone had mentioned to him that the administrative counselor had somehow managed to have some new names added to the guest list.

Hart looked sheepish and said, "Well, I wanted to tell you about this but the ambassador said not to mention it to you." There was a long, embarrassing pause and finally Hart continued. "Look, Jim, my responsibilities involve matters of personnel morale and general welfare perhaps more than any other officer at this post. After you told me that you intended to keep only political section names on the ambassador's guest list, I exercised my right to see the ambassador and I gave him my side of the story. I told him exactly what I told you: in my opinion, morale was deteriorating and other embassy personnel should be invited. I

told him about our conversations and why you thought the political people should be given preference. The ambassador listened to me and said he was completely unaware of the whole situation. He told me he had intended to give *every* officer a chance to meet the local people and that he found the parties useful in many respects. Then he said that perhaps he hadn't been very wise in giving you the final word on the guest lists. He arranged for the list to be sent to me so I could add one or two names to it before it was typed and sent on to you for your selections."

Hart went on, "I had reservations about that kind of arrangement and told the ambassador so, but he said you'd never find out and that you would assume the names on the list were preferences of his or Mrs. Strong's. He specifically told me *not* to discuss it with you."

QUESTIONS

1. If you were Jim Sweet, how would you terminate the meeting with George Hart?
2. Why do you think the ambassador circumvented the DCM on both the guest list and on the allocation of representational funds?

JIM SWEET (D)

As Jim Sweet, the DCM at Beta, arrived at the embassy one morning, he met Ann Page, the public affairs officer, with a copy of the local newspaper in her hand.

"Well, that old battle ax has done it again!" she exclaimed.

"Now take it easy, Ann; sit down and tell me what happened," the DCM replied. Instinctively he knew it had something to do with Kate Grey, the consular officer. Lately, it seemed that Ann would not mention her name and was constantly referring to her as "the old battle ax."

"Here is a copy of the paper," Page began. "This editorial is even worse than those in the past. It claims that there is widespread fraud and bribery in our processing of visas."

"Now, you know that editor has always been anti-American," Sweet interrupted. "I'm not sure we can do anything about him."

At this point, Page produced copies of three more papers and continued: "These are all bad. They repeat in a softer tone the same charges and also argue that our people who process visas are racist. It's that old battle ax! She is so cold and detached, she treats these people like they were machines. Everybody who walks out of that office without a visa is infuriated by her behavior. It's really hurting our image with the local government." Sweet thanked her for bringing the matter to his attention and promised to look into it.

Later that morning as he made his usual rounds of the embassy, he walked into the consular area. He noticed with satisfaction that everything was running with quiet, cool efficiency. The work here, he thought, was quite routine, almost mechanical in nature, and he sensed a detached, impersonal atmosphere. Kate Grey ran a tight ship and Sweet knew she was thorough and hard working herself. She was a demanding supervisor, he thought, but all who worked for her produced at a high level.

Sweet walked into her office and after some small talk and pleasantries, he said, "Kate, I've been talking to Ann Page about the editorials in this morning's newspapers. They claim that we are racist and that there is fraud and bribery in our processing of visas. I know there isn't any fraud or bribery, but I was wondering what you think is behind the negative editorials about your operation."

"We both know that there is a strong desire on the part of many Florinian citizens to emigrate to the United States," the consular officer began. "Many of these people have a great desire to move to the United States and there are repercussions when applications are denied. I can assure you that the law is being applied fairly and equitably in this office. We are doing nothing to block legitimate applications."

"I'm sure that's true, Kate," responded Sweet. "I don't question the fact that we are applying the law fairly, but I am concerned about our reputation with the local people. I'd like you to give some thought to this subject over the next few days. Maybe there are some other reasons the newspapers are critical. Maybe there are some things we could do to improve our image." Sweet excused himself and continued his morning rounds.

There was no question in Sweet's mind concerning either Kate Grey's technical capability or Ann Page's knowledge of public affairs. He decided that the best course of action would be to allow things to simmer for a few days. This didn't seem to be the kind of problem which needed to be solved this minute, as long as he kept Page and Grey apart.

He stopped briefly in the economic section and immediately sensed genuine tension. He made a few innocuous remarks and left. On the way back to his office, he again reviewed the events that had led the new economic counselor, Steve Black, to request a transfer. Black had arrived at the embassy just a little over two weeks ago. Sweet knew that he had been hoping for a much better assignment and was disappointed to be sent to Beta as economic counselor. He was trying to hide his feelings but he wasn't very successful. Sweet took pride in the fact that he knew his people and he had made it his business to find out what he could about Black before he arrived. From a number of telephone calls to friends in Washington, he had determined that although Black appeared to have had a fairly good career, he was long overdue for promotion. This issue was obviously of considerable concern to Black, and to make matters worse, the latest promotion list had come out a few days before without Black's name on it.

Just a day after the promotion list came out, the ambassador had given a dinner to welcome a group of senior officers who had come to inspect the mission. Almost all of the foreign service officers at the embassy had been invited. During the evening, the ambassador had risen and proposed a toast to all those who had been promoted. Almost as an afterthought, he remarked that the quality of the Beta embassy was indicated by the fact that all his foreign service officers had been promoted within the past three years. There had been no comment or reaction at the time but after dinner, Mrs. Black turned to the ambassador and said that she was "sorry that he didn't consider them a part of the embassy or members of the Foreign Service." She had finished her speech and left before the ambassador could really respond. Her husband had followed her quickly and it had been difficult to determine his reaction. The ambassador had been embarrassed and upset. He asked Sweet to look into the problem and to explain that he hadn't meant to offend anyone.

The day after this incident, during his usual walk around the embassy, Sweet stopped in Black's office. After a brief exchange of small talk, Sweet had explained that the ambassador was a little upset and that he had asked Sweet to assure Black that there was no intention to offend him or his wife. Sweet said he thought it was just a harmless remark; that the ambassador felt proud of those who had been here for a while and wanted to toast them.

Sweet recalled that at that time, Black had seemed more embarrassed than upset. Black had stated that he understood the situation, that although his wife had become a little overwrought, he was sure she would get over it quickly and that there wasn't any real problem. They continued the discussion for a short time and Sweet then left, convinced the issue was closed. He so reported to the ambassador.

The next Monday morning, after telephoning to be sure Sweet was in, Black walked into the DCM's office and said he wanted a transfer. Black explained that he and his wife had spent the entire weekend discussing the situation and had concluded that the ambassador really wanted to insult them at the dinner. They felt that his remarks were intentional, malicious, and designed to embarrass them before other members of the foreign service community.

Sweet winced as he recalled how stunned he had been. He had tried to show

Black how illogical his feelings were. He pointed out that the ambassador wasn't the kind of person to hurt anyone intentionally. Sweet argued that Black was getting unduly emotional over a very minor slight. He praised Black's fine record in the Foreign Service and noted that the State Department had spent a lot of money sending Black to Florina. A request for transfer after only two or three weeks would not only look bad but could ruin his career. In his most sincere manner, Sweet pointed out that Black was very competent, that his current job was a good one for him, and that he was the only truly experienced senior economics officer at the mission. The mission valued and needed Black's skill and his transfer would be really disruptive. Sweet had finally added that if Black would stay, he would, after the political counselor's imminent departure, be acting DCM when Sweet was absent and that this would be very valuable experience.

Black had remained adamant for over an hour. At last, reluctantly, he had agreed to wait a few days to think it over more carefully, and

to look for another solution before formally requesting the transfer he was certain he wanted. As soon as Black left his office, Sweet had gone to the ambassador, only to learn that Black had already talked with him. While the ambassador hadn't been very specific about the content of his discussion with Black, it was quite clear to Sweet that he was upset. This was most unusual, as the ambassador rarely showed any emotion. After considerable persuasion by Sweet, the ambassador agreed to defer any action, but he made it clear that he would transfer Black if he persisted with his request.

QUESTIONS

1. How would you evaluate Sweet's actions in both situations? What would you have done differently?
2. Which problem is more important? Why?
3. If you were Sweet, what would you do now?
4. What do you think of Sweet's "usual walk around the embassy"?

JIM SWEET (E)

Captain Don Rock of the United States Navy, the defense attaché in the Beta embassy, stormed into DCM Jim Sweet's office in an obviously agitated state. "I want to get this issue squared away once and for all," he told Sweet.

"Hold on, Don, what is it?" Sweet replied softly. "I don't usually see you so excited."

Rock sat opposite Sweet's desk and said, "Cliff Green is interfering with my operation and I won't stand for it. Yesterday, in accordance with Green's instructions, the communications people delivered a message addressed to my office (DAO), to him as special assistant for political/military affairs, without a copy to me. This is the second such incident.

"Three days ago, I came to the embassy very early, before leaving on a tour of nearby military facilities. I wanted to send a cable reporting information I had heard the night before at a cocktail party. I drafted a message to our Defense Information Agency (DIA), signed it as releasing officer, and sent it to the communications center for immediate transmission. I then went on my tour and returned at 1700 and found a note to call Green. When I called him, he told me he had pulled my cable and prevented its being sent even though I signed it. He wanted me to come up to his office, he even tried to insist on it. I told him if he wanted to see me, he could come to my office. He is quite a bit junior to me and

shouldn't try to pull that nonsense. He made some lame excuse about classified material on his desk that he would have to lock up, and I told him that I had the same problem. Finally, he changed his tone and agreed to come to my office. I could tell that he had realized I wasn't going to take that nonsense from him.

"He came right down to my office and told me he had stopped the message because he didn't accept the information in it. I said that if I had signed my name to it, it was my responsibility. He tried to insist that any time he sees something wrong, he can hold a message even if it has been released by me. I told him he'd better not ever hold up my traffic again. He told me I was new here and that's not the way this embassy is run; that he handles all important matters concerning the military. I told him I wouldn't stand for it; that this embassy may be the communications center that services my traffic, but I control that traffic, not Green or anyone else in the embassy. I wanted to see you right then and there, but you had left for the day. At my insistence, the cable did go out. I later discovered that Green was correct about the information I had; it was wrong, so I sent another message saying so. But that doesn't change the fact that he has no right to interfere with my traffic.

"This morning, just three days later, I returned to my office after a one-day absence on another military tour and was met by the assistant army attaché, who told me excitedly that a message from DIA addressed to the DAO had been sent to Green as political/military assistant. I knew about the message because, while on tour, I was asked by the General in charge of the Military Assistance Group (MAG) how I planned to respond to it. I immediately called the communications people and demanded the message. They told me Green had notified them that anything of importance concerning the military was to go to him for action regardless of the nominal addressee. I again asked for the message in question and they told me they'd give me a copy. I told them I wanted the original. They said the original is for action by the political/military assistant. I asked if the addressee was the DAO or the embassy. They said it was the DAO. So I asked, 'Who pays the bill for that message?' and they said 'You do.' I said that I wasn't paying the bill *this* month because of their failure to deliver my traffic. They reiterated that they were under instructions to deliver important military messages to the political/military assistant. So I said, 'Fine. I'm not paying the bill. I suggest you tell the administrative counselor and also tell him why. Five minutes later, they called back and said they were transferring the original to me. They also said they had called Green's secretary and informed her that she should give the original message to the DAO's office because it was being transferred to DAO for action. I sent up an assistant to retrieve the message and Green's secretary handed it to him.

"When Green returned to his office, he discovered the message was gone and asked his secretary where it was. Apparently, she told him something like 'the assistant army attaché took it.' That must have set him off because my secretary told me he stormed all around saying we had 'stolen' the message. Then, just a few minutes ago when I was on my way to see the station chief, I stuck my head in Green's door and said, 'I hear you are saying we stole that message from your basket.' He said, 'That's right.' So I asked him if he had checked

with communications and had learned that the message had been officially transferred to DAO for action. 'That can't be,' he said, 'because all important messages concerning the military are sent to me as political/military officer.' I said, 'Not while I'm here. Let's go see the DCM and get this straightened out right now.' And he fired back, 'No, this is the way it's going to be and you'd better get used to it!'

"So, here I am and I want action *now*! I recognize that before I came to Beta, the defense attaché's office may have abdicated its responsibility and allowed its traffic to be stolen, and in so doing their necks were stuck out a mile. But I'm here now and I won't tolerate any interference in my operation, from Green or anyone else." Captain Rock paused, lit a cigar, leaned back in his chair and said, "Another thing, too, Jim. Green thinks he has functions that are really mine. When the foreign service inspector spoke to me about my job, he told me that Cliff Green, in his interview with the inspector, listed all *my* duties.

"Cliff has tried to be an obstacle in other ways, too. For example, during the recent military crisis in Clarina, I filed a report and cleared it with the political section. They told me that Green had a LIMDIS (Limited Distribution) file on it that I should read before sending my report. Green refused to let me see the whole file and made sure I got only those parts which *he* felt were relevant.

"This embassy is small enough to have really good coordination, but it doesn't. Green is the block. You know yourself that even the ambassador sometimes goes around him. Green doesn't use the chain of command. Sometimes he tries to give assignments directly to my junior officers. I've told them not to take any assignments from *anyone* except me, you, or the ambassador, and that if you or the ambassador give them an assignment they are to advise me immediately."

Jim Sweet said, "Well, I knew a little bit about the so-called stolen message because Cliff complained to me about it. As you said, he was storming around. I'll have to look into this. I want to carefully analyze the situation, alternatives, and various ramifications to determine how we can best handle this matter."

Captain Rock stood up, looked at Sweet coldly, and said, "You don't need to look into a damn thing. I'm going to be here three years unless you or the ambassador throw me out. All traffic addressed to me will be delivered to me, and all traffic I release will go out, or I won't pay any bills. Further, though it may be inconvenient, I will transfer all my traffic to the Military Assistance Group for processing. And another thing, let me make it crystal clear that if any officer of this embassy stops a message I release as defense attaché, or intercepts a message addressed to me or my office, I will personally guarantee him a punch in the nose!"

Jim Sweet said, "You are quite right. I'll explain that to Cliff right now." He called Green in and Captain Rock promptly excused himself. Green arrived red-faced and obviously angry. Sweet was able to obtain reluctant agreement from Green that traffic to or from the DAO should be respected in terms of both routings and release. But after Green left his office, Sweet knew that no fundamental problem had been solved.

Sweet mentally reviewed the circumstances leading to Green's appointment as political/military assistant. Some years before, due to a lessening of tensions and the increasing strength of the Florina defense forces, the military assistance program in Florina was reduced. This resulted in organizational changes in the Beta embassy. The embassy had once had a four-person military/political section, headed by an FE-MC. But then the military/political section had ceased to be a separate entity and its people and functions were merged with the political section. At the time, the head of the political section was transferred to another post and the FE-MC who had headed the military/political section was named political counselor. He had remained in the job for about six months, until he too

was transferred. Since the merged section was still overstaffed, no replacement officer had been sent.

The embassy had made the next ranking officer in the political section the new chief. He was a very sincere, strongly liberal man who had developed excellent relations with the left-wing government then in power in Florina. Six months later, however, this government had been overthrown in a bloodless military coup and the chief of the political section, who was violently opposed to any military regime, became publicly hostile to the new government. The embassy had found its relations with the new government deteriorating rapidly. Meanwhile, Cliff Green, an FO-02 who had arrived in Florina six months before the merger of the two sections, was the last remaining political/military officer. Because of the public hostility of the chief of the political section, Green was finding it very difficult to maintain effective contacts among senior military officers. To help alleviate this situation, Green had suggested to the ambassador (Strong's predecessor) that he be transferred from the political section and made a special assistant to the ambassador for political/military affairs. The ambassador had responded favorably to this suggestion and Green began reporting directly to the ambassador. Shortly before Jim Sweet and ambassador Strong had arrived in Florina, the chief of the political section had been transferred and replaced by Dave Rex, a man with extensive political as well as political/military experience.

As special assistant, Green was responsible for coordinating military and political affairs. He concerned himself with the remaining American Military Assistance Program, military sales, credit arrangements, the status of visiting U.S. forces and the activities of an American naval fleet that operated, in part, in waters off the Florina coast. He acted as principal embassy liaison with the Military Assistance Group and operating fleet groups. Green also stayed abreast of developments in the

Florina armed forces and provided the ambassador with analyses of the military situation. He maintained close contact with senior Florina military officers, particularly those involved in joint military exercises. When crises in nearby countries occurred, Green was especially busy because they sometimes called for use of Florina facilities. He played an active role in meeting with American visitors such as congressmen and representatives of the executive branch, and he was responsible for reporting "incidents" involving visiting United States military forces, sometimes amounting to 60 per month. Green handled traffic accidents and drug cases among military personnel if the person involved was on official duty. He also coordinated the negotiations involved in the sale of military hardware to Florina.

Although Jim Sweet knew the scope of Green's work, he recognized that Green's role as special assistant was no longer necessary or desirable and was adversely affecting the workability of the embassy organization. In fact, he knew that a very recent foreign service inspector's report had recommended the elimination of Green's job and the reintegration of his functions into the political section. In addition, Sweet was aware that Dave Rex, FE-OC, who had relieved the former head of the political section, objected strenuously to Green's special assistant status. Later that week he spoke to Dave Rex, since he knew that the problem, while temporarily smoothed over, still existed.

When Sweet asked him about it, Rex said, "I've done political/military work on earlier assignments and I think I have some clear ideas about what the political section should do here. It's obvious to me that most of Cliff Green's work now lies in the political area and it should be an integral part of the political section. I think Cliff has a chip on his shoulder. He had a falling-out with my predecessor. So, he asked to be special assistant and the ambassador acquiesced because of the open hostility of my

predecessor to the new military government. The thing is, I'm not sure even you are fully informed about what Green does. Green still doesn't clear everything with me. He tends to operate quite independently. The ambassador told him just last week that his work doesn't help anyone unless he gives the embassy staff the benefit of his thinking and knowledge. Admittedly, Green has good knowledge and good insight. But he still has a chip on his shoulder, even after all this time. I think he's a very insecure guy. He tries to keep everything to himself in order to become more indispensable and more secure. But, of course, it really works the other way around.

"Now it's getting worse because the foreign service inspector's report recommended flatly that Green's job be reintegrated into the political section. Green disagrees, of course. He was incensed by the inspection report. He maintains he needs special status to do his job. I don't believe it. I think work follows the individual who carries it out. You've read his memo, haven't you?" He was referring to a memorandum from Green to the ambassador (excerpts are reproduced in Exhibit 1).

Sweet nodded and said, "Yes, and apparently the ambassador found it persuasive because Green still has the job."

QUESTIONS

1. What do you think of the way Jim Sweet handled the problem of the DAO's message traffic?
2. Is any more action required on that problem?
3. As DCM, how would you handle the question of Cliff Green's job? Should it be reintegrated into the political section?
4. What additional information should Sweet attempt to obtain, and where and how should he get it?

EXHIBIT 1

EXCERPTS FROM CLIFF GREEN'S MEMO TO AMBASSADOR STRONG REGARDING THE FOREIGN SERVICE INSPECTOR'S REPORT

- In their recent report, the foreign service inspectors recommended that the political/ military function be reintegrated into the political section. I suggest that the embassy seriously consider all of the implications of this recommendation before concurrence is given. The arguments developed by the embassy in reaching the conclusion to establish this position in the Office of the Ambassador are not only still valid, but it seems to me, even more compelling. Implementation of the inspectors' recommendation would not result in "the more effective use of the resources that the embassy commands" as the report claims, but rather would have just the opposite effect.

- Events over the past several years have considerably enhanced the strategic importance of Florina in terms of United States national security interests. A proposal to station additional United States military personnel in Florina is already in the planning stages and actual negotiations for United States military bases will begin soon. The emergence of a third country in competition for sales of military equipment could weaken long-established United States/Florina ties.

- Paradoxically, the inspectors' report recommends reintegration of political/military activities into the political section "especially in view of the predominant role now being played by the Florina military on the political scene." On the contrary, it seems to me that this very fact argues for the presence of an experienced and independent political/ military section responsible directly to the ambassador.

- In terms of the establishment and maintenance of personal contacts with high-ranking military officers in both Florina and United States military forces, it is essential that the political/military officer operate as an authoritative and immediate representative of the ambassador. Absorption of the political/military function into another section with the consequent reduction of the position's status to that of "another political officer" would necessarily decrease the political/military officer's effectiveness in dealing with military officers of high rank. Consequently, confidence in the political/military officer would diminish and the officer's influence and effectiveness would suffer. Complicating this matter further is the traditional military distrust of civilian diplomats.

- The Florina officials are accustomed to acceptance of the political/military officer as the individual responsible for the full range of military subjects.

- A few examples of United States missions in which the political/military activity is maintained as an entity separate from the political section are Augusta, Bartonia, Estella, Hudsona, Martina and Teresa. It is hard to imagine that the United States interest in political/military affairs in Florina has decreased to such an extent that the inspectors' recommended staff change would be a true reflection of the degree of our interest.

- None of the foregoing is intended to indicate that the closest cooperation and collaboration between the political/military section and the political section is not both desirable and necessary. Quite the opposite is obviously the case. The intention of this memo is only to conclusively demonstrate the clear advantages of maintaining the political/ military function in a position that reflects its unique importance and responsibilities, and one that will allow the political/military officer to operate at maximum effectiveness. I strongly believe that it would be a very serious error to relegate the political/ military officer to a lesser slot in the political section. According to the report, the inspectors' recommendation is not to be implemented before the incumbent's departure in approximately eight months.

JIM SWEET (F)

"Jim, there is no mutual respect between the military people and the State Department people. That's the crux of the problem." So saying, Captain Don Rock of the United States Navy, the defense attaché at the Beta embassy, slapped his fingers firmly on the edge of Jim Sweet's desk for emphasis. Sweet, who was DCM at the embassy in Beta, capital of Florina, didn't respond directly but merely nodded.

Rock had been defense attaché at the embassy for several months. Florina was his first diplomatic post, but he had a long and distinguished military career including several assignments in staff positions. He came to Sweet's office to bring to the DCM's attention what he thought were dysfunctional conflicts between the fleet admiral operating in nearby coastal waters and the Beta embassy. Rock had received a personal letter from the admiral asking him why the ambassador had not responded to a message of two weeks earlier and raising questions about the embassy's relationship with the fleet. Rock wanted Sweet to be sure a reply was sent to the admiral's message, and he wanted advice on how he should answer the admiral's personal letter.

Rock began his remarks by refreshing Sweet's memory about the one-day special cruise on a U.S. aircraft carrier off the coast of Florina that had been requested by the ambassador. Rock pointed out that this cruise had been requested *four* times and the navy had arranged for it four times at considerable expense, only to have the ambassador cancel out at the last minute the first three times, and arrive over two hours late on the fourth. The ambassador's guests were four high-level Florina government officials and their wives plus six foreign ambassadors to Florina and their wives. Because of limited space, no other guests were permitted on the cruise. Even Rock didn't go; the admiral's aide acted as the ambassador's aide during the cruise.

The navy had been fully responsive to the ambassador's request, and the cruise had gone off quite well. An elaborate luncheon had been served in the admiral's quarters and the guests had been excited and impressed as they viewed flight operations from the admiral's bridge on the carrier. "Unfortunately, not only was the ambassador late but he insisted on being back so early that the carrier couldn't get very far offshore and these flight operations couldn't be completed until the carrier was very close to port, requiring our pilots to fly through the Beta commercial air traffic control zone. This resulted in the carrier receiving an official complaint from Beta Civil Air authorities," Rock stated.

Two weeks after the cruise, Rock had returned from fifteen days' leave and discovered that no formal message of gratitude had been sent to the admiral or the carrier's commanding officer. He thought that such a message should have been sent the day after the cruise. He checked with the ambassador's secretary and his aide to see if a letter had been sent and found that no such letter or official message was ever considered. Rock felt strongly that some form of thank you should be sent and took it upon himself to draft an appropriate message. Rock felt the message should be especially profuse in expressing appreciation, to compensate for its lateness. In his draft, he commented on the various details that had made the cruise such a success. Rock sent the message to the ambassador's office for clearance. The ambassador's aide felt it was much too long and he cut it down to one short paragraph and returned it to Rock, to whom the draft seemed terse and perfunctory. Rock took the matter up with Jim Sweet and a compromise draft was ultimately sent; fully 20 days had elapsed between the cruise and the date of the message.

During the negotiations on the compromise draft, Rock learned that all ten of the officials on the cruise had written thank-you messages or letters to the ambassador for his hospitality in arranging the cruise. Rock was the only member of the embassy staff who felt that these should be forwarded to the admiral. Several were in foreign languages and the ambassador's aide and the DCM argued that it would be expensive and difficult to have these translated, and that they were, after all, addressed to the ambassador. Rock remained adamant and it was finally agreed that the translations would be made and all ten sent to the admiral. This was done one month after the thank-you message.

Captain Rock told Jim Sweet that this was just one example of a pervasive insensitivity to the military and a lack of appreciation for what the military was able to do in maintaining friendly relations with host country officials and other notables. He said, "We gained a lot with Florina officials and those foreign ambassadors, but we lost a lot in relations between this embassy and the fleet."

Rock was even more upset by some recent developments that could have a bearing on the Florina government's willingness to allow the navy to establish a base on Florina soil. The navy had expressed interest in obtaining the Florina government's permission to establish a U.S. naval base, complete with docks, fuel supplies, and maintenance facilities. Most of the talks that had taken place with Florina officials had been conducted by embassy personnel, including the ambassador himself. A major obstacle to government approval was resistance by the local citizens of the communities near the proposed base, who feared conversion of their quiet villages into "sailor towns" with their associated bars, tattoo parlors, prostitution, and rowdy disturbances.

Admiral Barth, commander-in-chief of the Tenth Fleet, had told the ambassador he wished to participate in whatever way he could to help win the Florina government's approval of the plan. Yet, navy representatives had been excluded from most meetings and, in Captain Rock's opinion, the embassy's actions tended to suggest that the navy was not needed in the negotiations. Nonetheless, the admiral had actively sought participation in at least the peripheral activities associated with getting Florina approval. In an attempt to demonstrate the navy's good citizenship and community-mindedness and to gain local support and goodwill, the admiral had proposed to the ambassador that the fleet sponsor a variety show, produced entirely by the sailors and their dependents. He asked the embassy's assistance in publicizing the show. The ambassador had been very reluctant to lend his support to this type of activity but finally yielded to pressure from the admiral. Rock felt the ambassador had given in only as a means of keeping the admiral from getting involved in any other way.

The ambassador had invited a large number of senior Florina officials, a large contingent from the diplomatic corps and a few local officials from the communities near the proposed base to attend the first show. The remaining seats were filled by local citizens on a first-come basis. The ambassador left at the intermission and mentioned to those near him that he thought the show was unsophisticated and tasteless.

When word of his behavior reached Admiral Barth and his staff, they were livid. It was never intended to have a "sophisticated" show for high-level officials, but rather a down-to-earth, casual, perhaps even amateurish production for the local populace who, they thought, had responded enthusiastically to the show. The ambassador had invited the wrong people without even bothering to consult the admiral or his staff to find out what the show was about. Captain Rock knew that some of his navy colleagues had felt insulted by the ambassador's rebuff.

Admiral Barth wanted to schedule a repeat performance of the show to attract more of the local people. He sent a message to the embassy, again requesting help in publicizing it, but the message was not answered. A copy of this message was not forwarded to the defense attaché as might have been expected. When he received a personal letter from Admiral Barth, Rock learned about the admiral's message and that it had received no reply. The letter criticized the ambassador for not answering his message and for inviting an audience to the variety show for whom it was never intended. The navy had expected the embassy to publicize a free show in the local press of the communities involved and had not expected a diplomatic function. The admiral felt quite strongly that once the ambassador was there, he should not have left before the show ended, regardless of how "unsophisticated" he felt it was. The admiral thought his departure not only was rude and discourteous but damaged the image of the navy and the embassy in the eyes of the Florina citizens who were present. The admiral concluded his letter with the questions, "What the hell is going on over

there? Why can't we work together instead of against one another?"

"What should I tell the admiral? That the embassy doesn't think he is important enough to bother answering his messages? That we can't work together because officers in the Foreign Service feel they would be degrading themselves to associate with the military?" Captain Rock was growing more and more angry.

"The trouble with you State Department types is that you treat everyone else like second-class citizens. Your people give me the impression they think everyone who wears a uniform has a 'military mind,' which presumably means autocratic, right-wing, and uneducated. It may surprise you to know that most military officers are better educated than most foreign service officers. Among the attachés alone there are more advanced degrees proportionately than there are in the Foreign Service.

"You people act like a university faculty. Instead of acting forcefully at the right time, you put off decisions, hoping the problems will go away; instead of exercising vigorous leadership, you reduce clarity to obscurity as you grope for consensus; instead of terminating dead wood, you protect incompetence through your old boy network; instead of being concerned about contribution, you think about tenure.

"You even let your secretaries wear their bosses' rank. They will tell me 'No, Mr. X can't do that' without even *asking* Mr. X. They promise to call me when their boss is free—and never do. And another thing, I'm not too impressed with the nine-to-five syndrome among the foreign service officers. Sure, they go to lots of diplomatic functions. So do we. But we've also worked at least some part of the past nine weekends and there isn't a foreign service officer in sight around here on Saturday or Sunday. When I come here at 7:30 in the morning, the place is a morgue. Not that I think working weekends or coming to work early is necessarily something to strive for, but it does give me an indication of how dedicated people are.

"Well, now that I've shot my mouth off, I guess I have a duty to sit back and hear what you have to say. I suppose you're going to tell me that I just don't understand the highly complex functions of your profession—or should I say that to you?"

QUESTIONS

1. If you were Jim Sweet, how would you respond to Captain Rock?

2. What merit is there in Rock's arguments? What would you do about it?

3. What would you do about the unanswered message from the admiral?

4. What would you advise Rock to say when he answers the admiral's letter?

5. What would you recommend that Sweet do to help the ambassador understand that his behavior may not be aiding the goals and objectives assigned to the embassy?

6. If Sweet told you his relationship with the ambassador was distant and he suspected the ambassador was privately opposed to military bases in Florina and may be intentionally sabotaging the negotiations, what would you advise Sweet to do?

JIM SWEET (G)

Despite his personal desires to stay away from them, Jim Sweet, the DCM at Beta, capital city of Florina, found himself increasingly involved with narcotics problems. Ambassador Strong had designated Sweet chair of the Narcotics Coordinating Committee and had appointed as members George Scott, the CIA station chief; Dave Rex, the political counselor; Carl Mann, the economic counselor; and Chris Kane, the DEA (Drug Enforcement Administration) agent. Ambassador Strong had also designated Sweet chair of the Ad Hoc Drug Abuse Board, charged with handling any drug problems involving the embassy family or other official Americans. The administrative counselor, George Hart, and the consul, Kate Grey, were on this board along with Dave Rex and Carl Mann. Chris Kane was not a member.

Florina was one of the 59 countries sufficiently significant in drug-related issues for the United States to require that its embassy prepare a narcotics-control action plan. The DEA had assigned a narcotics attaché, Chris Kane, and three other agents to the embassy in Beta. All four were hard working and dedicated. They worked actively with the local police to encourage rigid enforcement of the existing Florina laws involving possession, dealing and trafficking in narcotics, and were advising appropriate host government officials on more effective drug-related legislation in accordance with the role DEA had assigned to them (see Exhibit 1).

Sweet had considerable respect for the dedication of the DEA people but felt they were sometimes overzealous. They actively participated in busts made by the local police, particularly those resulting from information obtained by the DEA. These activities were potentially embarrassing to the embassy and therefore both Sweet and the ambassador had found it necessary from time to time to restrain Kane and his agents in politically sensitive areas.

Another source of friction with the DEA people was the embassy policy with respect to members of the "official family" who were involved in the use of drugs. Both the ambassador and Sweet felt that it was politically prudent to get these people out of Florina as fast as possible and avoid any adverse publicity deriving from local prosecution. This was the generally accepted policy at U.S. embassies throughout the world and was tacitly approved by the State Department.

Chris Kane was strongly opposed to this policy and regarded it as lenient treatment of official Americans who had been charged with drug offenses. Kane was embarrassed by this double standard; one for official Americans, another for host country nationals. The local police complained to Kane that the Americans "talked out of both sides of their mouths." On one hand, the Americans urged the local police to enforce the rigid Florina drug laws where Florina nationals were

---

EXHIBIT I

INFORMAL DEA WORKING DOCUMENT

WHAT'S OUR ROLE IN FOREIGN COUNTRIES?

The advisory role of DEA in foreign countries is to stimulate coordinated action by foreign officials and guide the commitment of resources toward the most effective possible drug-control program within each country. The objectives in each country are tailored to its individual needs and capabilities, as well as the role it plays in the international traffic and the extent of domestic drug abuse by its population.

The advisory objectives of DEA will be accomplished through activity on several fronts:

1. Advise each country on passage of new legislation or more effective utilization of existing legislation for criminal and regulatory control.
2. Advise on setting an effective mechanism for the United Nations reporting requirements under the Single Convention and other United Nations agreements.
3. Advise on antidrug abuse campaigns.
4. Advise on the development of a Central Narcotics Unit. This unit would report to an important and trusted government official and receive specialized training from DEA. The DEA would continue its close liaison with this unit to critique and advise in its continuing development.
5. Advise on U.S./host country Drug Extradition Treaty.
6. Advise on the desired results of effective air and sea traffic control systems.
7. Advise on the feasibility and implementation of regional drug cooperation.
8. Advise embassy staff on narcotic policy and political action.
9. Periodically assist in advising appropriate host country officials of the state of the traffic by means of embassy-coordinated briefings.
10. Advise on eradication and crop substitution program studies where appropriate.
11. Advise on laboratory analysis and drug identification techniques.
12. Advise on the elimination of clandestine laboratories.
13. Advise national police organizations having jurisdiction in national narcotics enforcement.
14. Coordinate and advise host countries on current research and advanced technology in enforcement, prevention, detection, and rehabilitation programs.

---

involved and pressed for even more stringent penalties. On the other hand, the Americans used their considerable influence with high level Florina political figures to get their own people off.

One day, Sweet arrived in the office to find Bill Barney, the Peace Corps director, and George Scott, the station chief, waiting to see him.

"I need some fast action on this one, Mr. Sweet," Barney began. "I got a call at two o'clock this morning that three of my volunteers had been picked up for smoking pot and one of them had nine joints in his possession. They are all in that stinking jail and we've got to get them out of there. I'm afraid that there may be as many as ten or twelve of the volunteers who smoke pot, and I've heard rumors that one or two of them may be selling it; perhaps even to local Florina citizens. Perhaps I should have discussed it with you sooner, but I didn't have any firm evidence."

George Scott said, "I don't have any hard information either, but several of my contacts have given us data that strongly suggests Peace Corps volunteers are not only using the stuff but selling it as well. And it may be more than pot; we're not sure yet."

"Can you tell me who they are, George?" asked Barney. "I'll have them on a plane for home tomorrow. In fact, Mr. Sweet, I think we ought to send home all of those who are even suspected of smoking pot. The Peace Corps is a high-priority operation here in Florina and, so far, has maintained a good reputation. I'm sure the host government people like our work and want us to stay, but we can't put them in an embarrassing position. The sooner we get those involved out of Florina, the better off we'll all be. Before coming to your office, Mr. Sweet, I asked our consul to try to spring the kids who are in jail but she told me she was doubtful she could do anything through the local police. She said you might be able to work something out through the Foreign Ministry."

Scott assured Sweet that his information suggested that this was a case of naive kids getting in over their heads. He agreed that it would be best to get them out of Florina as quickly and as quietly as possible. Sweet then stated that he would look into the matter to see what might be done. As Scott and Barney were leaving, Scott turned, smiled and said: "Watch out for Kane. If you get those kids out, he isn't going to like it one damn bit."

Sweet returned the smile and thought to himself that Kane would indeed feel that the volunteers should be tried and punished right here in Florina. Sweet called the consul and asked her to find out whatever she could from the arrested volunteers and the local police as soon as possible, and to do what she could to get them released. He asked Grey to give him a report as soon as she returned from the police station.

As Sweet considered the options open to him, he recalled the very sticky situation that had occurred at another post last year. Sweet reflected that his Peace Corps problem seemed relatively easy compared to the one then faced by another DCM and old friend, Mary Weisner. Late the previous spring, Mary's administrative counselor had entered the DCM's office looking visibly shaken and said that they had a very serious drug situation at the International School, whereupon he had opened his briefcase, produced a package of about a half pound of marijuana and said: "This was found by the school principal in the ambassador's son's locker. The principal brought it to me and swore that no one else knows about it. What should we do?"

Weisner told Sweet that the police had raided the International School several times and had caught some students with drugs on them. These kids had been punished, but no American kids were caught. The principal, at the suggestion of the Committee of Concerned Parents and with the approval of the school board, had conducted a surprise inspection of school lockers. It was during that inspection that the marijuana had been found in the locker of the ambassador's son, who was a good student and had never been in trouble before.

Sweet thought the way Weisner had handled the situation was masterful. Weisner told her ambassador that apparently someone was trying to embarrass the ambassador and had planted a package of marijuana in his son's locker at school; that the package had been confiscated; that no one but the principal, the administrative counselor, and herself knew about it; and that she thought the best thing to do was to forget it. The ambassador had agreed, but immediately after the end of the school term several weeks later the ambassador had sent his son to a military boarding school in the States. Sweet reflected that he was glad he didn't have to face that situation.

Later that morning, Sweet had his regularly scheduled meeting of the Narcotics Coordinating Committee. The meeting got off to a fast start. Although it was common practice to go around the table to give each member a chance to report current events and any problems, Chris Kane obviously had a lot on his mind and dominated the meeting from the outset.

He turned first to Jim Sweet: "Mr. Sweet, I've been notified by the local police that they've got three Peace Corps volunteers locked up. I hope we're not going to have the usual rescue operation this time. These kids were caught red-handed and it's about time we made an example of some of them. Those Peace Corps kids think they can get away with anything over here, and they'll keep on thinking it until a few of them spend a few years in that lousy jail. Which reminds me," and Kane turned to the station chief, "George, the police think there are some pushers in that Peace Corps operation and I know your staff has been following it. Who are they? I'd like your cooperation on this one so we can get the solid evidence we need to convict."

"Chris, we don't have any evidence that would be useful to you and we can't risk exposing our informants or compromising our own operation to get it for you," the station chief responded. "I told Bill Barney this morning what little we know and he's working on it. You'll just have to leave it up to him to handle the situation."

Kane was visibly angry. "Yeah, I know what that means. The Americans get away with it again. Do you realize the flak I get from the local police when you people spring these kids? Look, the DEA is trying to do a job in Florina and we get blocked at every turn. It's bad enough having to deal with the local police and the Florina politicians without having to battle my own people and beg for some cooperation! But let's turn to more positive things," Kane smiled. "Now, we have an operation on for this afternoon that's going to kick these drug dealers where it hurts the most, and I hope you don't spoil this one for us."

Amid a dead silence from other members of the committee, Kane explained that members of his staff had been told by an informant that a transit shipment of ten kilograms of refined heroin was being stored somewhere in the large international transit warehouse at the airport. It was to be picked up by the first secretary of the Florina embassy in Washington, D.C., who was to put the stuff in diplomatic pouches and be the diplomatic courier. "We all know this playboy. He's the favorite cousin of the foreign minister and a frequent companion of the prime minister's daughter. Our informant in this case is totally reliable; he flew into Beta yesterday on the same plane with the stuff and whoever was bringing it in. DEA has been tracing this shipment from its origin in the Middle East, where our soon-to-be courier visited with the son of a member of parliament in Xenon who we know has over a thousand acres of poppies under cultivation. The grower arranged for shipment to a European processor and from there our informant accompanied the shipment here. DEA has kept us fully informed at each step of the way. Last night our playboy had a rendezvous with a girlfriend and talked too much. He told her he had to cover some heavy gambling debts and would have to leave today on the three o'clock flight to New York with his 'merchandise'. The girl mentioned it to another one of our informants, who passed it on to me. And one other thing, you'll have a hard time covering this one up because the major in charge of the local narcotics squad was with me when our informant passed the information to me. He knows it all."

George Scott, the station chief, broke in to say, "That sounds like so much fiction. We don't have any information that could possibly corroborate any part of that story. What we do know is that the local police are very cozy with the right-wing elements within the coalition government. Further, we know that the right-wing elements are trying to force the Prime Minister into stronger positions against the Liberal-Progressive party. How do we know this isn't a setup to embarrass the prime minister and force him to resign so that the right-wing elements can gain control of the coalition?"

Dave Rex added, "I know that the right-wing elements are gaining strength in the coalition in part because the prime minister has taken some slightly leftist positions in an attempt to reduce the voter appeal of the Liberal-Progressive party. Further, if the Liberal-Progressives should take power, the military bases we acquired a few years back could be abruptly shut down. If this bust is made and your information is correct, it would be very embarrassing indeed for the prime minister. He might be forced to call new elections, which I'm not sure he could win right now. If your information is false, the prime minister will be so furious that it wouldn't surprise me if he abolished the whole DEA operation in Florina. You and your staff could be thrown out."

Kane argued, "Look, we are talking about ten kilos of refined heroin! The plane makes two stops and one is in a country where we have no coverage. Therefore, we have no way of knowing whether he will have the stuff when he gets to New York. We strongly suspect he will transfer it to someone else at the airport where we have no coverage. And remember, this guy will be a diplomatic courier when he gets to New York. Ten kilos is a very large shipment that could set us back months if it ever gets to New York. We've got to make the bust here and the local police have asked us to go along. They feel they can withstand the political pressures easier if they can say we insisted on the bust. In fact, I strongly doubt they would make the bust without our participation, for the very reasons you cite. I can't tell my regional DEA people that we missed this one. It's too big. You can't call it off now!"

A heated argument ensued with Kane defending his planned bust from the attack by Dave Rex and George Scott. Sweet was relieved that Kane had not pursued the Peace Corps incident, but was increasingly disturbed by the possible implications of this other operation.

Sweet stated that he felt this issue was of sufficient importance that the ambassador would have to be informed immediately. He adjourned the meeting for thirty minutes.

Sweet recognized that there was considerable competition, rivalry, and perhaps professional jealousy among Rex, Kane, and Scott. He wondered if any one or all of them might be exaggerating their arguments because of this rivalry. Sweet knew from the ambassador, as well as his frequent contacts with Washington, that the drug program was a high priority one in Florina. He realized that he would have to take prompt action on both of the problems that had surfaced during the morning. After checking the ambassador's schedule and looking at his watch, he picked up the phone and dialed the ambassador's private line at the residence.

QUESTIONS

1. If you were Jim Sweet, what would you say to the ambassador when he answers the phone? What would you do if you were unsuccessful in reaching the ambassador?
2. Describe what you would recommend to the ambassador with regard to the two incidents in the case. Defend these recommendations. Are they based on win/lose or win/win assumptions?
3. What changes in embassy operations do you see as a result of the increasing attention being shown to the drug issue?
4. What conflicts do you see arising between narcotics control, the station, Defense Attaché? AID? Peace Corps? Trade relations? Political relations? How should Sweet resolve these?
5. Critique the informal DEA working document given in Exhibit 1.
6. How would you respond to Florina accusations that the United States "talks out of both sides of its mouth"?

ACTION PLANNING
EXERCISE 1

SETTING GOALS AND OBJECTIVES

Organizations, the various work units making up the organizational structure, and the individuals employed by those units all need a vision and a sense of direction—where are our opportunities and how can we capitalize on them? Ideally, this involves a process, with *opportunity identification and planning* at one end of the continuum and *performance leading to desired results* at the other. In between, the critical phases of the process involve the determination of organizational goals and defining work unit and individual objectives that stem from those goals.

Most of the literature on goal and objective setting treats the terms *goals* and *objectives* as interchangeable. This makes it difficult to differentiate between the strategic thinking and planning that defines the overall organizational vision and goals and the action planning that implements work unit and individual objectives. We have chosen to define a *goal* as a long-term vision of organizational strategy and an *objective* as a short-term target for implementing the long-range vision.

Those who are familiar with management by objectives will recognize the process described here as an expansion of the MBO concept in that it focuses on planning and developing psychological contracts as aids to goal and objective setting and the analyzing results of performance to reevaluate the goals and objectives previously determined. We note that the first step in the process, ordinarily the task of the top management group (with appropriate staff support), is a period of strategic thinking, resulting in an organizational vision and a set of long-term goals for the organization as a whole. Strategic thinking requires assessment of the market and consumer trends, technological innovations, unique organizational strengths, the culture and subcultures of the organization, the external competitive environment impacting the organization now and in the future, the internal resources, and the changes in cultures and performance required of the organization if it is to achieve desired results.

While many successful organizations in business, industry, and government have recognized the need for strategic thinking and the resulting vision and organizational goals, many, some successful and others not, have either done no such strategic thinking or have not communicated the resulting vision and goals down into the organization. Lacking a sense of direction from the top, managers and employees at lower levels have to set objectives based on their assumptions and perceptions rather than on a clearly-stated vision and specific organizational goals. This frequently leads to internal conflict, a lack of teamwork, and a negative impact on organizational culture.

Assuming that top management has devised and communicated a clear vision and the supporting organizational goals, the next important step is to filter these down to goals and objectives for various sublevels of the organization. The final step is to negotiate realistic expectations (psychological contracts) that support the vision, goals, and objectives identified at each level.

Prior to such negotiation, managers have found the role-mapping technique is useful preparation for discussions about expectations. Note that the work unit managers are not only setting objectives for their division, department, section, or branch, but also for themselves as individuals. The expectations or psychological contracts on which these objectives are based usually should include the responsibilities specified in formal position descriptions as well as the more informal expectations, including measurable standards, that are normally negotiated.

While setting objectives, it is important to meet certain criteria:

- Objectives should be keyed to the strengths and skills of the individual and to a realistic assessment of influential factors in the internal and external environment.
- Objectives should be achievable, subject to well-formulated action plans.
- Objectives should be within the control of the individual, that is, not subject to internal or external pressures that make it impossible for individuals to devise action plans to meet the objectives set, or at least they should be subject to revision to take these pressures into account.

- If practicable, performance levels based on these objectives should be measurable.
- If the objectives are met, the desired results will be achieved.
- The objectives and the action plans and performance requirements supporting them have interim, relatively short-term checkpoints (How am I doing so far? Is there need for changes in the plan or my behavior? Do I require additional resources, knowledge, or skill training?).

The stage is now set for a second round of highly relevant psychological contracts between work unit managers and the individuals who are based in those units. These contracts will be highly relevant because they will be based on known organizational goals and objectives already set for work units and their managers. Obviously, the process must work from the top down: managers of higher-level work units set objectives first and succeeding lower-level managers devise objectives that support those of their supervisors.

The next vital step in the process, action planning, is also the one many organizations and individuals fail to stress, usually resulting in unfocused performance and failed objectives. In order to devise a workable and realistic plan, each individual and work unit needs to answer an essential multifaceted question:

> What do I (we) need to do [activities] by when [timing] and how well do I (we) need to do it [performance] in order to achieve or surpass my (our) objectives?

The final step in the process involves feedback of results, reassessment of performance by individuals, and appraisal of results by management. On the basis of these analyses, the individual performers may wish to renegotiate their psychological contracts and reformulate their objectives and management can evaluate performance of individuals in light of results achieved. An important final step: based on their evaluations, management can initiate appropriate coaching and/or training opportunities for individuals.

ASSIGNMENT

1. Does your current organization or your last organization have a *vision*? If so, what is it?

2. List the three most important organizational goals of your present or previous organization.

3. List the three most important goals or objectives of the group for which you work or used to work.

4. List the three most important current objectives of the work unit supervised by your immediate boss.

Action Planning Exercise 2

Developing a Role Map: An Analytical Tool for Setting Goals and Objectives

The essence of negotiating a psychological contract or set of expectations revolves around the definition and clarification of the role or roles that one usually performs in relationship to other individuals.

A role is commonly defined as a *set of expectations* about *functional* or *appropriate* behaviors that people hold for someone in a particular position in a formal or informal organization. In other words, a role is defined and can be *mapped* by analyzing all of the psychological contracts or sets of expectations that influence the role as well as other factors, such as the required tasks to be performed (and related performance standards) or the social and career aspirations of the incumbent. The expectations of others, one's own expectations, and these other factors create a number of *demands* on the role of the incumbent.

Role ambiguity occurs when the various expectations and resulting demands are not clear to the incumbent or to important others.

Role conflict occurs when the expectations of the incumbent and/or important others differ in one or more instances.

By developing a role map, any ambiguities or conflicts can be clarified and goals and objectives developed to deal with them. A typical objective, for instance, might be the need to negotiate or renegotiate a psychological contract.

It should be noted that every individual plays multiple roles. Besides his or her job role, family roles (spouse, parent, relative), social, community, and political roles may be involved. Together these define a person's lifestyle and may or may not conflict with one another. While conflicts between roles can seriously impact the job role (the father who is never home or the working couple who have to juggle schedules to spend time together), this exercise will focus on developing a role map for one's job situation.

The following diagram (on page 475) is the skeleton of a typical role map. Like geographical maps, it is meant to define the *current* situation, which is of course subject to change over time. In fact, we construct the map to help us define the changes that may be needed.

The double-headed arrows in the diagram are meant to express the expectations (demands) on the role incumbent and, reciprocally, his or her expectations of other persons or of the tasks and the social and career aspirations involved.

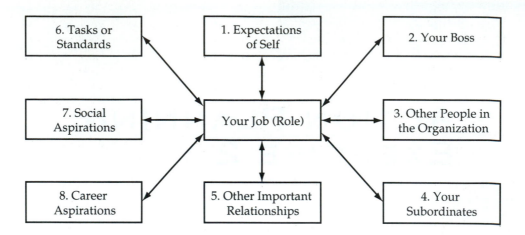

Before defining these eight sets of demands more exactly, let's take a more detailed look at the ambiguities and conflicts that can affect role relationships.

Role Ambiguity and Role Conflict

In most organizations today, most roles exist in a complex, highly uncertain, and dynamic environment. The most common resulting problem is that of ambiguity. Ambiguity occurs when the expectations held of a given role occupant are

1. not clearly sent by others
2. not clearly defined by others
3. not sent or defined by others
4. clearly misinterpreted by the receiver
5. partially misinterpreted by the receiver

If any of these conditions exist, the likelihood of any individual occupying a role position meeting expectations is seriously impaired.

There are three major sources of role conflict. First, an expectation one holds of oneself can conflict with an expectation someone else holds of the role incumbent. For instance, the boss may expect the incumbent to work overtime on frequent occasions while the incumbent, concerned about family relationships, expects to work overtime only in emergencies.

Second, the expectations two or more others have of the incumbent can be in conflict with each other. A frequent example occurs when the incumbent's boss has expectations that conflict with those of the incumbent's subordinates (resulting in the familiar "man in the middle" syndrome).

Finally, there may be a conflict between two or more of the other factors that make demands on the incumbent; for instance, a conflict between demands of the task and career aspirations or between social and career aspirations.

An additional source of role problems occurs when the total of all expectations creates a condition of overload in which the incumbent simply cannot meet all demands on him or her within the constraints of time, resources, energy and/or capabilities.

Defining the Relationships and Other Factors

While constructing your role map, you will need to consider your own expectations of the job you hold, as well as your expectations involving your relationships with others. The latter involve negotiation and renegotiation of psychological contracts, which also require analysis the expectations of others (your boss, subordinates, colleagues, and so on). While the demands made on your job role by the tasks and standards built into it and your social and career aspirations do not require psychological contracts, the demands, and conflicts between them and between them and your various psychological contracts, need to be factored into your role map.

Remember that you are constructing your role map in order to develop action-oriented goals and objectives that will help you improve your job performance and, it is hoped, deal with at least some of the ambiguities, conflicts, and overload that make it difficult for you to improve.

Probably the most important relationship you have on your job is with your boss. If the psychological contract is ambiguous or there is conflict between your expectations and those of the boss, your performance (and career aspirations) can suffer. In constructing your role map, be sure to pay special attention to the reciprocal expectations currently operative in this relationship and any consequent conflicts or ambiguities.

Relationships with your peers, colleagues, and subordinates (and resulting contracts, ambiguities, and conflicts) are also of obvious importance and should be mapped out. Do *not* try, in this exercise, to detail every expectation involved in every relationship you have. Do list the important ones and/or those involving need for renegotiation.

The "other important relationships" box included in our diagram refers to those mostly *outside the organization* relationships that are important to the role incumbent. In industry, these would include customers, suppliers, and financial interests. In government, other bureaus, agencies, or departments, Congress, the executive and judicial branches, and, of course, the public, all constitute other important relationships. Many jobs are not significantly affected by any of these, others by some or many. In your role map, include only those

relationships (and expectations) that, again, are really important or involve current or potential conflict.

The three "other factors" in our role map diagram (numbers 6–8) are each unique in the kinds of demands they exert on the role incumbent and in the way they relate to and/or conflict with each other and with the expectations of the incumbent and others involved with the role being mapped.

Consider, for instance, the impact on the role of tasks and associated performance standards that contribute heavily to an overload for the role incumbent. What needs to be done in renegotiation of psychological contracts with the boss, peers, and subordinates to relieve the overload?

Consider further the impact of a conflict between social and career aspirations and again the need for some action on the part of the role incumbent to resolve such conflicts. If, for instance, the incumbent desires to engage in expensive and time-consuming family and community-oriented activities but also wants to earn a promotion to an even more demanding job, what objectives does he or she need to set? What goals or aspirations does he or she need to rethink in order to resolve this conflict?

What Does a Role Map Look Like?

Referring to the diagram, a role map can be defined as follows:

1. A listing of your expectations regarding the job role you occupy.
2–5. A listing of important relationships (boss, people in other units, subordinates, etc.), in a two-column format:

My expectations   _____ expectations
  of _____   of me
a.   a.
b.   b.
c. etc.   c. etc.

6. A listing of important tasks or standards built into your job role.
7. A listing of important (to you) social aspirations such as family, community or political activities, dating, parties, sports, and so on.
8. A brief listing of your career goals, including alternatives you believe are realistically open to you.

Finally, going back over these lists, an analysis of any abiguities, conflicts, or overload situations that are apparent from the map you have developed is necessary.

ACTION PLANNING EXERCISE 3

SETTING INDIVIDUAL GOALS, OBJECTIVES, AND PRIORITIES

The basic objective of this course is to improve the managerial performance of the participants. It has been our experience, however, that translating the skills discussed and practiced in the class setting to the job environment back home is not easy. Doing so requires

- an analytical process (construction of a job role map);
- a goal, objective, and priority-setting process;
- an action planning process; and
- a sense of commitment to using the skills learned in the class to achieve the objectives set.

The job of any manager is to influence the behavior of others so they maximize their contribution to the goals and objectives of the organization. We emphasize individual development of managers attending this class and an important part of the process is the ability to translate the conceptual and people skills dealt with in the class to the on-the-job situations and relationships you will face when you go back to work.

This part of our Action Planning Exercise is targeted toward helping you to develop realistic goals, objectives, and priorities that you will want to try to achieve back on the job. It builds upon the role map you developed in Exercise 2, but extends beyond that to other objectives you may want to consider, based on some of the concepts and skills we have discussed.

A. Long-term goals relating to my social and career aspirations:

1.
2.
3.
4.
5.

B. Goals and objectives relating to the currently-assigned tasks and standards for my job:

1.
2.
3.
4.
5.

C. Objectives relating to *ambiguities* I have detected in my role map analysis:

1.
2.
3.
4.
5.

477

D. Objectives relating to *conflicts* I have detected in my role map analysis:

1.
2.
3.
4.
5.

E. Objectives relating to what I have learned about influencing people in organizations:

1.
2.
3.
4.
5.

F. Objectives relating to what I have learned about myself during this class:

1.
2.
3.
4.
5.

G. Given the goals and objectives noted above, how would I prioritize them? (Select the five you believe most important and list them in order of importance, #1 thru #5):

1.
2.
3.
4.
5.

ACTION PLANNING EXERCISE 4

WHAT WILL I DO TO ACHIEVE MY OBJECTIVES?

As we stated in Exercise 1, action planning is a vital step in the goal- and objective-setting process. Here we will make an additional point: unless the goal setter is *committed* to actually taking the action planned, the whole process collapses into futility. This means, among other things, that the action plan devised needs to be realistic; you need to be confident that you can accomplish your plan.

Base your action plan on your five high-priority objectives; obviously, prepare a separate plan for each one.

Be explicit: With *whom* will you interact? *What* will you say and do? *When* will you act (will you try to approach them when they are in a spontaneous or reflective mode)? Is your best strategy one or more one-on-one interactions or a group meeting? Do you have a back-up plan if the first one doesn't work? How confident are you that you can achieve this objective?

Your action plan should state explicit answers to each of these six questions for each of your five high-priority objectives.

ACTION PLANNING EXERCISE 5

How Am I Going to Use the Skills I've Acquired to Improve My Managerial Performance?

Experiential, contextual, and people skills are like body tone: it is hard work to get them and hard work to maintain them. These skills are developed and maintained by practice, on the job, over long periods of time.

During this course, you have been exposed to concepts and have begun to develop the skills to use them to improve your managerial performance. When you leave this simulated environment and return to the job, what are you going to do, specifically, to continue to develop (and maintain) these skills?

In the Jack Webb (A) case, we saw what one person did after returning to the job. What are the pros and cons of what he did? What additional things might he have done? This exercise is designed to help you focus on the skills you have acquired or want to acquire from this course, and what you are going to do on the job to further develop and maintain these skills.

The first step is to gather intelligence about all of the key people with whom you interact. Look at your role map as a starting point. It should contain the expectations for each of the key people. Try to develop for each of them what you know about their self-images and psychodynamic influences.

Write a scenario that could be a blueprint for your first week back on the job, given your personal goals and objectives, your action plan, the role map with expanded background and personality data, and the skills you have begun to develop in this course. Of course, this scenario will be an approximation that you will modify as additional data becomes available. Share your scenario with your colleagues in your study teams and discuss them. How are they similar? How are they different? What can you learn from what others are doing? How can you clarify your own thoughts?

This is essentially an open-ended exercise that will be shaped by your own style, sets of priorities, and the circumstances in your work unit. Use the curriculum outline as a checklist. Use each case study we have looked at to expand your checklist. Use your own knowledge and experiences as well as those of others to expand your checklist still further.

At the end of this exercise, you should have an outline of things you want to do and the commitment to get them done when you return to your job.

ACTION PLANNING EXERCISE 6

WHAT WILL I DO THE FIRST DAY?

First impressions usually have a profound effect on how we are perceived by other people. If we believe this general rule of perception, then we should put a great deal of thought into how others are going to perceive our behavior the first day in action. This first day could create momentum for future effectiveness, or possibly cause us to wish we had done it differently.

Although it is impossible to write a perfect script when we don't know all of the actors or circumstances, it is still possible to have a work game plan that will allow us to be reflective rather than spontaneous to the situation. The first step toward planning your first day is to gather intelligence about your immediate boss, your peers, your subordinates, and the organizational culture. Some of us will have some of this information while others will need to take steps to start the data gathering process.

The objective of this exercise is to have you write a scenario that could be the blueprint for your first day at a new job or when returning from educational leave. This scenario will, naturally, be a first approximation that will be modified when new data is collected. Another objective is to share these scenarios with colleagues for informational input (how I would do it), opinion seeking (others' reac-

tions to your plan), boot strapping (I never thought of that), and clarification (what and how). This exercise should allow us to focus on reflective behaviors that could ensure a favorable impression from the relevant people in the organization.

This is essentially an open-ended exercise that will be shaped by your own style, sets of priorities, and the circumstances in your organization. In order to guide you in constructing your scenario, a list of suggested considerations is presented below. Do not, however, feel constrained by this list. The list is not in any specific order and you should feel free to add to, subtract from, or modify any of the suggested considerations.

FACTORS TO BE CONSIDERED

1. Objectives you want to accomplish this first day.
2. Methods to achieve those objectives.
3. Topics to be covered and with whom.
4. Your encounter with your boss (include any encounter before the first full day).
5. Your encounters with your peers (include any encounters before the first full day).
6. Rituals to be performed.
7. Meetings to be held and with which groups and individuals.
8. Time management/flow of the day.

RESEARCH PROJECT (FOR FULL-TIME STUDENTS) AND ON-LINE PROBLEM-SOLVING PROJECT (FOR PART-TIME STUDENTS)

Purpose

This project is designed to assist you in the process of translating the skills you have acquired in this course to your on-the-job performance. To this end, you and your team should identify several problem situations from the experiences of your team members occurring at your level. Ideally, these would be *current*, *ongoing* situations that involve the issues that have been covered in this course or will be covered in the next several weeks. From these several problem situations your team should select one to be written up as a case study. In addition, you should prepare a written analysis of the case giving action recommendations (see also Chapter 3). Include the following criteria to select a case situation:

1. Are the relevant issues common to other situations in the organization?

2. How significant is this problem?
3. Is this problem mine (or a team member's) or partially mine (or a team member's)?
4. Does the problem involve the people-oriented issues from this course?
5. (For part-time students)—Will the problem still be current when the case is written and analyzed?

Typical of the problems that have been written in previous courses are listed below:

1. How to improve the relationship with a difficult boss, an important peer, or a recalcitrant subordinate.
2. Working across organizational lines.
3. Ethical dilemmas.
4. Improving the performance of an unproductive employee or group.
5. Taking over as a manager of a new group when several others in the group feel they should have been promoted.

6. Career development problems or opportunities.

Please do not feel constrained by these examples. The issues in this course have wide applications that extend far beyond the examples given above. If you have any concerns you wish to discuss, please talk to the instructor.

Overview

The problem you select should be written from the perspective of a person at your level (preferably a member of your team) who can do something to improve the situation. There are a number of case studies in this book that should help you see the many different ways a case can be constructed (see, for example, King Industrial Products Company and Up or Out). You can think of it as an anecdote or a short story, as a drama or a play, as a narrative history of a series of events, or in any other way you feel might be useful.

Data

Once you have selected a problem situation with which you or a member of your team are already familiar, the next step is to organize the information you have and identify what additional information you may need to get. This usually involves at least the following:

1. A clear and concise statement of the problems and issues as seen by the principle person around whom the case is written (for example, one of your team).
2. Identification of all relevant people, an explanation of why they are relevant (dependencies), and a description of their relationship to the principle person around whom the case is written.
3. A description of the background (history) and personality characteristics of all the relevant people including the person from whose perspective the case will be written. (These can be used as appendices to the case or included as text.)
4. A description of the environment and culture in which the incidents relevant to the problems and issues take place.
5. A sequential history of all relevant events up to the present.
6. Identification of existing or potential conflicts resulting from differences in perceptions, objectives, personalities, histories, and motivations.
7. Identification of power blocks (cliques or coalitions), allies, adversaries, and the differences between their public statements (reflective rationalizations) and private agendas (spontaneous, perhaps subconscious biases, desires, and so on).
8. A listing of the options for improving the situation that might be considered by the person around whom the case is written.

Outline

Sketch the case in outline form to see how it hangs together. There are many options you can use, such as a sequential narration, a statement of the current situation and a flashback to present the sequential narrative, or a delineation of a crisis ("the boss stormed out saying I don't care how you get it done, just do it") and alternatives with a rehash of all previous incidents that relate to the alternatives. It is often useful to prepare two or more outlines and then choose the one that seems most useful. For outline purposes you can use "bullet" statements.

The Case

After selecting the outline, write out in as much detail as possible what happened in each critical incident. Use quotes whenever you know exactly what was said but if you are uncertain or are making assumptions about what was meant, do not use quotes. (It is unlikely there would be many quotes unless the incident was recorded in some way.) As you write, think about what a movie camera might capture: the layout of the office, conference room, or work area; body language expressions, eye contact, facial expressions, and the assumptions or conclusions drawn from these signals such as concern, anger, sympathy; who said what to whom, what interpretation was given to this; and anything else you feel may have relevance, even if trivial. Sometimes it is useful to describe the alternatives the person around whom the case is written felt should be considered along with that person's assessments of the pros and cons of each.

You will probably find several rewrites are necessary before your team will feel that the problem, all relevant facts and incidents, together with alternatives have been spelled out in sufficient detail to permit analysis and discussion. Step back after each rewrite to be sure you have included *all* relevant information. Again, feel free to contact the instructor if you feel any assistance might be useful.

Finally, the case should be disguised. This is most simply done using a word processor through word substitution, that is, instruct the computer to substitute a generic name (such as "Ace Company") every time the name of the real organization appears. Do *not* try to get "fancy" or "cute" with the disguise to enhance its dramatic appeal (for example, do *not* change the sex, background, or motives of a person). Experience shows this may substantially alter the analysis and reduce the effectiveness of the project and minimize the ability to translate from the project and the course to your on the job performance.

When the case is finished to the satisfaction of the team, your last team meeting will be to discuss the case prior to deciding how your team will prepare the analysis and recommendations.

CAUTIONS

1. For this project to be of maximum benefit, you should select a problem that will most likely still be unresolved at the time it is written or that was unresolved when you left the organization.
2. Do not select a situation about which no one in the group has sufficient information (such as a situation in which no member of the team was directly involved).
3. The person from whose perception the case is written should be a member of your team and that person should have been, or still be, in a position to do something constructive about the situation. (That is, the situation should be occurring at the level of the team member from whose perspective the case is written.)
4. Think about what you are learning from this course as you select the situation, write the case study, and analyze the situation to reach action recommendations.

ANDERSON MANUFACTURING AND DEVELOPMENT CO.

"Ham" Wilson looked at the public relations man across his desk with irritation. Then, with his characteristic self-control in dealing with company colonels, he suppressed the quick words that were at his tongue.

It had been a rough morning—a morning of hard, disciplined argument over promotional copy for the new compacting machine. While Ham had become visibly upset and impatient to end the session, the PR man kept smiling, stubbornly fighting it out one point at a time. Ham disliked him intensely.

Although Anderson Manufacturing and Development had not had a PR man long, this guy was surely making up for lost time. Little by little he had taken under his wing everything that had anything to do with business development and promotion. He was young— somewhere in his early thirties, maybe four or five years older than Ham himself—and in spite of his smiling, driving assurance, technically ignorant. He didn't even understand what was basically new in the compactor, Ham thought with resentment.

Ham was proud of his compactor. He had directed its development from the beginning. The original concept had been tossed to him as a kind of challenge by his boss, the chief engineer, and Ham had given it long hours of exploratory thought and work on his own. And then he had become excited about it, sold it hard, and management had bought it. They had given him a tight budget and time schedule and he had made it. He felt damn good about that machine.

"You keep approaching this copy in the wrong way, Ham," the PR man was saying.

"This is aimed at the guys who are holding the money bags and you keep criticizing everything as though we were writing a technical report. I don't want to misrepresent your baby, believe me, but I'm trying to sell it. We've put a lot of money into its development and we're going to put a lot more into its promotion. Now we've got to sell it. I need good copy. Everybody upstairs wants good copy."

Ham was tempted to tell him what everybody upstairs could do, but checked

Source: This case was prepared by Mr. Walter Milne under the direction of Professors A. H. Rubenstein and H. A. Shepard for courses conducted at the Sloan School of Management, Massachusetts Institute of Technology, Cambridge, Massachusetts, and is used with permission.

himself again. He stared blankly at the copy, convinced that he was still right: it stunk. Worse, it seemed to border on dishonesty in some of its implications.

"What I would like to do," Ham finally said to PR, "is to have a chance to talk to the boss before we make a final decision on this. I don't want to let it go through as it stands on my own say-so."

"O.K., Ham," said PR, "but remember that I have to get final copy to the printer by the end of the week. I think what we've got right now is all right," he added, "but I certainly wouldn't want to see it watered down anymore."

PR left as he had come—smiling, self-sufficient and with hearty good words.

What a joker, Ham thought to himself. He wondered how a guy like that could live with himself, how he could do Anderson Manufacturing any real good. Apparently he did—at any rate he sat upstairs in a big room in executive row.

By way of contrast, Ham looked around his own little cubby. His battered desk and chair, and one visitor's chair, all but filled it. "The Conference Room" the boys called it. He laughed, and then lost his laugh when a knock at the door reminded him that he had asked Holden to see him as soon as PR had left.

Bill Holden came in, easy and relaxed as always, and slouched into the chair at Ham's desk. He was a bright, young D.Sc. (Doctor of Science) whom Ham himself had hired. But there were times when he wished he hadn't—and this was one of the times.

"Bill," Ham began, "I've just had a rough time with PR and I'm not going to beat around the bush. When your test results weren't in last Friday, you promised me—quite literally promised me—that we'd have 'em first thing this morning. And we don't have 'em. We practically rescheduled the whole program so that you could do some additional work with the physics group, and now you haven't made the new schedule. What are we going to do about it?"

"I know I promised to have them today, Ham," said Holden, "and believe me, I was shooting for it. The physics group work just took more time than I had expected. We're on some pretty fundamental stuff, and Dr. Maul asked me to do some library work on it. The whole thing just ran beyond our original expectations."

"Bill," snapped Ham, "your attitude confuses me; honestly, it does. I don't doubt that the physics group is doing important work, but you knew damn well that you were assigned part-time to my B project. And you know that when I juggled the schedule I was doing it to give you a break—you, personally. I never should have done it, but you practically pleaded with me and promised that you would come through on schedule. What do you think we're doing here anyway?"

Ham was flushed and angry, but Holden let it roll off easily.

"I suppose we're doing a lot of different things," Holden said in a tone that seemed half apology, half challenge. "The Chief was talking to me just the other day about the importance of the physics group work and about what a vital part I could play in it. You know it's pretty fundamental stuff, and frankly, that's why it appealed to me. It's well related to my previous experience—some of my doctoral work. I thought that's why you rearranged the schedule.

"Bill," said Ham, "you're talking nonsense and you know it. If all my men felt the way you do about the job, about fitting their work into the pattern, why the whole lab would fall apart."

"Well the whole thing seemed reasonable to me," said Holden. "After all, we're working for the same boss and good results in one place ought to be just as good as good results in another."

"Bill," said Ham in a rising voice, "you know damn well that's not so. Honestly, you're talking as though you were still a school boy and it didn't matter what you did—as though you didn't have responsibility to anyone else."

"But I've done good work," said Holden.

"I know it, and everybody knows it," interrupted Ham. "You've been here what—two, three years? During that time you've had more good ideas than anybody else on the lot. You're a good man, and the Chief has given you a pretty free rein. That's why I can't understand this. You try to run your affairs like a one-man band, but this lab is not being run the way you think it is."

Holden just kept looking at Ham.

"Everybody seems to think I've been doing O.K.," Holden repeated defensively. "I've always tried to do my best."

"Sure you have," said Ham, "but you run around this place as though we were subsidizing the Royal Academy. You know we're not subsidizing anything—we're organized to make money, and in order make money we've got to push the stuff out the door. It matters a hell of a lot to me whether we do or not, because if we don't it means my neck."

Ham looked at Holden and Holden looked at the floor and there was a long silence.

Ham liked Holden, but he was also a little envious of him, for Holden had the big degree. He also had brains. In fact, he had been good for the lab, Ham had to admit, even though he never worried much about meeting a schedule.

But hell, he said to himself as Holden looked up, I have to worry about a schedule even if Bill would rather be doing other things. Sometimes, he thought, I'd rather be doing other things myself.

"Bill," said Ham, finally cutting into the long silence, "I'm sorry I lost my temper. I've never blown my stack like this before. I was wrong in doing it now."

"I'm sorry too, Ham," said Holden. "You make me feel as though I've let you down personally. You've been very decent with me and I certainly didn't mean to let you down. If you want me to finish off the test runs . . ."

"No, no need," interrupted Ham, a little wearily.

"When I didn't have the final figures this morning, I took what you'd already done and passed it on to Porter. He's got one of his boys finishing it out. The Chief expected a report before this, but he hasn't been pressing me for it."

Ham doodled for a minute on his scratch pad, and then went on:

"This is no life and death matter as you well know, Bill, and I'm sorry I acted as though it were. The point is not so much that you fouled up this schedule, but that you've fouled up for still another time. Anybody can understand missing once in a while, but it never seems to bother you that you have a reputation for never worrying about time. It would bother me. Every time I miss a schedule it bothers me."

Ham doodled again.

"You certainly know the things I've been saying are right, Bill," he said. "I think we should forget it for now, but let's understand that something's got to be done. I'll speak to the Chief as soon as I can and we'll see what's to be done."

Holden backed out awkwardly, muttering apologies. As soon as he had left, Ham picked up the phone and called the Chief. The conversation was brief: Ham had a couple of problems he'd like to talk about; could he see the Chief sometime soon? "Sure" was the response—in about an hour, for lunch. Fine; done.

At lunch, the Chief characteristically opened right up with a hearty, "What's on your mind, Ham?" He asked it with a smile—a big, genuine, ready smile.

"Well, Chief, I had kind of a bad morning."

"I heard about it," said the Chief.

Ham didn't conceal his surprise. So PR had run to see the Chief, Ham thought. PR had tried to load the dice. That was a lousy trick.

"From PR?" Ham asked.

"No," said the Chief, looking hard at Ham, "from Holden. He was in to see me right after he left your office. He told me the whole story. And as a matter of fact, Ham, there's a part of the story you don't know: Holden's being assigned to Doc Maul's group as part of a general reorganization that's been approved by the Board."

Ham started, and he listened uneasily as the Chief began to explain. The reorganization was to involve the whole works. The Lab was to be split into three groups. The Chief was to have overall charge, but the company was going to appoint an assistant chief engineer who would be responsible for some 40 engineers and as many nonprofessionals. Doc Maul was going to direct a smaller group on some of the more fundamental work. This was going to be a low-pressure group.

"Maul's group may not work out at all," the Chief went on, "but we're going to give it a try. It won't be much different from the way the physics group has operated anyway.

"This is where Holden fits in. He's to be a research associate—which, as you know, is a new title with us—Maul's right-hand man. Holden knows about this and he's happy about it. I think one of the reasons he stopped into my office today was to check on whether you knew it, and course, you didn't.

"What happened was that Maul jumped the gun in telling Holden what his duties were to be and Holden jumped the gun in acting like a research associate. He realizes that and he's sorry."

The Chief looked at Ham with an apologetic smile.

"I was going to tell you all this at the end of the week, Ham, after the Executive Committee had formally approved our plans. But let's forget Holden and get right down to brass tacks. Let's see what this is going to mean on our side of things."

Ham's uneasiness increased as the Chief went over things in more detail.

Maul was to become Head Scientist, he said. The Chief himself was to pick up two assistants. One of the two was to have the title Assistant Chief Engineer. He would work in parallel with the Chief and have charge of about a third of the groups. The other new appointment was to be Assistant to the Chief Engineer—a kind of leg man for the Chief.

"Now how do you fit into all this, Ham?" the Chief asked rhetorically. Ham took a big bite of pie and gestured his curiosity.

"We have discussed this whole thing pretty thoroughly," the Chief went on, "and we've looked at all the men we've got and we've talked to some from outside in an exploratory way. After looking and talking, we're well decided we want you to be Assistant Chief Engineer."

Ham grinned. This felt good. Here he'd been working his fanny off and up to now, he thought, there hadn't been any gold stars on his report card. This really felt good.

"Actually, Ham," the Chief was saying, "you've been doing a big part of this job already. You know our procedures and you've proved you can keep on top of things. Whatever may have happened this morning I'd read as just a bad day. The record shows you work well with the men and keep them happy and push the stuff out."

Ham thought to himself that this was right. He had been doing part of this job all along. It had started nearly two years ago when Maul was out sick and the Chief began to dump things in his lap. And when Maul came back, the Lab started to grow and the Chief kept handing him things. There was no formal pattern—it was one of these things that had just developed.

Still, there had been plenty of time to participate in project work, too. Ham thought of the compactor. He had lived with that thing night and day. And that had been a good part of the setup as it was. Whenever something had come along that he had wanted to jump into, the Chief had always said to go ahead. And he had jumped into the compactor with both feet. That's the only way to do, Ham thought, when you really want to get something done.

The Chief was now talking specifics about the new job. It would mean a substantial raise—about 15%. Better still, it would mean participation in the bonus plan. It would mean a big new office. And it would mean a lot of little things: a private secretary, a membership in the executive's club, office expenses for journals and magazines—a whole new potful of the niceties of life.

Ham had an impulse to jump up and shake the Chief's hand and to rush out and call his wife, who had taken the youngsters on a two-week trip to her mother's, but the impulse was only a quick flash. It passed and was replaced by something like fear. This wasn't something Ham wanted to jump into—not just like that anyway.

As the Chief went through the slow, deliberate ritual of filling and lighting his pipe, Ham expressed his thanks for being considered for the position. But while he said the right things fully and fluently, he thought of reasons for delaying his decision.

He though of the reports, the judgments, the budgets, the people. He thought of sweating out one project while you were worrying about the next. And strangely enough, he though of PR.

He thought of PR because there was a guy he never wanted to be, a guy who was a kind of Mr. Management Merry-go-round in person. He wondered briefly if some day PR would wake up and realize he'd been running his whole life without ever catching up to anything. He wondered if some day after it was too late PR would wish he hadn't run so hard and so fast.

There was a pause during which the Chief looked searchingly at Ham.

"You're thinking this is a pretty big decision, Ham?" the Chief asked.

Ham nodded. "A very big decision," he said with emphasis.

"I agree," said the Chief, "and naturally no one wants you to make a snap judgment about it. The vice president told me to tell you to take your time. Personally, I want you to take a good hard look at it. We both know," the Chief added, "that you did a whale of a fine job with the compactor and it may be that that's the kind of thing you ought to stick with, that that's the kind of thing you really want. You've got to balance that equation for yourself, Ham. I emphasize this because if you do take the new appointment—and it's got a lot to offer—you ought to realize that you'll be completely away from the bench.

"When you sold me on the compactor," the Chief went on, "we arranged things so that you could see it through yourself. That wouldn't be likely to happen again. Of course, you'll sit on top of these things and you'll take pride in these accomplishments, but in a different way—an entirely different way."

The Chief stopped talking and scratched a match to re-light his pipe. Ham stirred his second cup of coffee.

"I understand what you're saying all right," said Ham, "and, believe me, I have very mixed feelings about it. I'm tempted by the new job, naturally, and I feel very flattered by the offer. But I do know that I like the purely technical side of things. And I know that if I took the new job I'd want to keep up in my field."

The Chief smiled at Ham as he waited for him to go on.

"I've enjoyed the courses I've been taking at the Institute," Ham continued, "and I'm satisfied that they've done me a lot of good. If I took this appointment, I'd keep working for my degree—just as I have been—one course at a time. And I'd probably sit in on some seminars. In fact I'd try to keep up technically in every way I could."

The Chief smiled again and then spoke quickly and earnestly: "You can sell yourself on that line of argument pretty easily, Ham," said the Chief, "because it makes so much good sense on the face of it. But I'll give you long odds that it won't work that way. I don't want to be discouraging, but the older you get the harder it is. It's hard to find the time—even harder to find the energy.

"Believe me," added the Chief with a wry smile, "I know. I went through it myself."

Ham thought about this. He thought of how little he really knew about the Chief. He did know he had been a top turbine man. And he knew the Chief had once won the Stalworthy medal "for outstanding contributions to turbine development." Not much of a medal, maybe, Ham thought, but still a medal—a symbol of achievement and recognition. Yet the Chief had traded this away for a stock-bonus deal with the Anderson Company. Ham wondered if he had any regrets. He wished he knew.

"The fact is," Ham heard himself saying a little apologetically, "I'd rather thought that this year I might have a go at the degree on a half-time basis. You remember that we talked about this last year and you said then that the company would sponsor me."

"I did say that, Ham," replied the Chief, "and I'm sure that we can still do it if that's what you want."

"Well, I'm not sure at all," said Ham, "but I have a tentative program worked out, and I've lined up a thesis."

"If this is what you want, Ham," returned the Chief, "I'd be the first to say Godspeed. My only advice would be to encourage you to pick a good thesis project. There are a lot of awfully facile theses written in that department and I wouldn't want to see you fall into that kind of trap."

"As a matter of fact," Ham answered quickly, "I've got a pretty exciting project in prospect. Werner wants me to work with him, and you know his work. This could mean a lot for me professionally. There's no denying I would like that. I think anybody would."

"Ham," said the Chief quietly, "I understand your feelings perfectly, and I won't try

to dissuade you if that's what you really want. You've got some good projects under your belt here, and a good job with Werner would never hurt you."

The Chief paused and brushed a few tobacco crumbs from the tablecloth to the floor.

"If I decide to finish up the degree on a half-time basis," Ham asked, "will I prejudice my chances here at the Lab?"

"Ham, you know better than that, I hope," replied the Chief. "I'm with you either way. And as far as the people upstairs go, forget it. There's no problem there."

The Chief brushed at a last elusive crumb of tobacco.

"No, you won't prejudice your future, Ham," he added, "but it will be a different kind of future."

The Chief looked at Ham for a minute. Then he knocked his pipe on the ashtray and looked at his watch. The lunch was over.

* * *

When Ham returned to his desk he sat down with the uneasy feeling that he hadn't been demonstrative enough in thanking the Chief for the opportunity he'd been offered. But he was interrupted by an unexpected call from Jack Masters, an old classmate and a fraternity brother of Ham's at the Institute. Jack was in town on business and their brief, hearty conversation quickly closed with arrangements for dinner at Ham's club.

As Ham cradled the phone, he let his mind savor past memories. He was glad Jack was in town, he decided. Jack was a real solid citizen. It would be good to see him.

During the next two hours Ham tried to put some final changes into his annual report, which was due next week. It was not until long past midafternoon that he became aware that only his hands were busy with the papers in front of him. His mind was still churning with confusion over the decision that lay ahead. With a gesture of disgust, he pushed the papers to the back of his desk and left the office. Without real purpose, he walked the length of A wing until he stopped at the cell where George Porter was finishing up the tests that Holden should have done. Porter and one of his technicians were running things with a quiet, easy competency. Ham liked George—everybody did.

"How are things going?" Ham called. Porter grinned and held up a finger asking him to wait a minute. Ham waved an O.K.

Ham never thought about George Porter much, but he thought about him now as he waited. He thought about him, because he suddenly realized that Porter wasn't so very much different from him. Of course he was twenty years older, but he had the same kind of background, the same kind of education. And Porter, Ham thought to himself, was a guy in a well-worn groove. For the first time, this realization worried him.

Back before the war, George Porter and one of the founders of Anderson Company had run a little one-horse shop. And there Porter had helped develop one of the basic patents that had brought Anderson Manufacturing into being. But Porter had never grown away from the first project. Not that he didn't keep improving it, for he did. Just last month, for instance, he had finished making changes that would let it be tied in with a computer-controlled line. A new series of Air Force contract orders had already come in on that development. That's the way Porter's baby was; high quality and custom-built, and the military kept it well fed.

"Just about winding up, Ham," said Porter, coming out of the open cell. "It all went very easily, no troubles at all. The data look good."

Ham took the clipboard and scanned the data, plotting them mentally against the earlier runs. "They do look good," he said.

Porter, pleased, turned back to his technician. "They look good, Al," he shouted, and the technician grinned.

Ham thrust his hands into his pockets and leaned back against the wall as Porter and the technician kept feeding in the adjustments on the last run. Ham thought about Porter some more. He thought about how helpful Porter had been to him when he first joined the Lab. Ham had been in Porter's group then and they had been quite close for a while.

Ham recalled his first visit to Porter's home. Porter lived in the country and he farmed a little. It wasn't much of a farm, Ham supposed: a couple of hundred chickens, a cow, a small garden. He remembered how impressed he'd been that first night that everything they'd eaten—from the very tasty salad to the peach dessert—had been grown right there. Ham hadn't seen much of the Porters recently, for Ham's wife ran their social life and she didn't care for the Porters. He was sorry, for he rather liked George and his raw-boned, easy-going wife.

Porter came out of the test cell and took the clipboard from Ham to record the data on the final run.

Funny, Porter's doing this job himself, Ham thought. After all, the tests were routine enough and a couple of technicians could have handled the job if company policy hadn't required that an engineer be present. But Porter could have covered this requisite by having one of his young engineers do the job. Yet he didn't, for that's the way Porter was—he never passed anything on to anybody else. He would worry, he once told Ham, that it wasn't being done right if he wasn't out there on the job. As Ham thought about this, he concluded that any worries Porter had were mighty little worries.

When the last run was completed, Ham took the clipboard again and looked at the final readings. They were right on the button.

"We'll all get the Anderson A of Approval for this one," Ham said, and Porter and the technician laughed at this reference to a standing company joke. Ham surprised himself by laughing, too.

"Flip you fellows for a Coke," he said, "odd man pays." Porter laughed again.

"You know, Ham," he said, "that's probably the thousandth time you've tried to match me for a Coke, and I've never taken you up on it. Not today, either."

Ham smiled, threw back a friendly insult, and then added that the Cokes were on him. While Ham was getting them, Porter and the technician shut down the machine. Then they all lounged back on the bench beside the test cell, drank their Cokes, and talked. They talked trivia, and Ham didn't say much. But Porter and the technician talked easily, sharing a rough kind of camaraderie.

Ham finished his bottle first, exchanged pleasantries with the two men, and walked on down the wing. As he turned the corner to his office, he looked back to see Porter and the technician closing down for the day. Although he couldn't tell for sure, he thought Porter was whistling. Ham watched him for a minute, and then almost imperceptibly shrugged his shoulders and walked slowly back to his office.

* * *

Ham met Jack Masters that evening in the lobby of the Engineer's Club. They exchanged quick greetings and went directly to the bar. It was a solid, comfortable bar, a good place to talk.

Over the first drink, Masters carried the conversation. He renewed old times, talked about new prospects. Masters was a good talker and Ham enjoyed listening to him. He hadn't changed much, Ham thought, except that he was a little heavier, a little less volatile.

Masters was with National Company and had been in their New York office for nearly two years. He talked objectively and happily about his job. It seemed like a good deal, and Ham said so two or three times.

"Believe me, Ham," Masters kept saying in self-deprecation, "I'm nobody in the company."

Over the second drink, Ham edged the talk around to his own prospects. Masters was immediately interested. He asked the right questions and drew out the right details. He understood Ham's doubts quickly enough and as quickly dismissed them.

"Hell, Ham," he said, as they went in to dinner, "you don't have a problem, you have an opportunity. You've been doing part of this job already and you like it well enough—that ought to be all you need. I had to cut a lot of bait before I got this kind of bite."

"What do you mean, you `had to cut bait'?" Ham asked. He was curious. And he was more than curious, for he was searching eagerly for any patterns of experience he might be able to match against his own.

Masters explained that after he'd been in National's Dallas operation for nearly three years, he began to have an almost panicky fear that he was stagnating. His jobs had become routine, and so had his raises. Masters had decided right then, as he put it, to fight his way out of the corner he was in. He did it by broadening himself technically. He did it by very deliberately avoiding getting stuck in the same kind of job too many times. He did it by smelling out every opportunity that was in the wind.

The break had come when his boss, an assistant to the chief engineer, went overseas to set up a new production facility in the Near East. This man's going left a kind of administrative vacuum which the company decided not to fill. But Masters flew into it and picked up every responsibility he could. He made himself a kind of communications center. And when the assistant's leave was extended Masters was appointed acting assistant in Dallas. Then, before the first man returned, he was transferred to Jersey and then to New York.

"Well, your story's something like mine in some ways," said Ham, "only I didn't consciously try to bring anything off the way you did."

"That may be," said Masters, "but I think we all do this kind of thinking, whether it's conscious or not. Personally, I like to plan things out quite deliberately, for then you have more control over them. That just seems like a matter of good sense to me."

"What you're saying," said Ham with a laugh "makes me feel a little like a country boy who's somehow getting along only because he's luckier than he ought to be. You're arguing that a guy has to be an opportunist to get ahead."

"Nothing opportunistic about it at all," Masters interrupted. "It's rather a question of creating opportunity, and certainly a question of taking opportunity whenever it comes along. Take this new job of yours—if you don't take it, somebody else will. That's the way I look at things."

"Maybe I'm just quibbling," said Ham, "so let's say I'm ready to buy your argument. This is not what really bothers me anyway. What bothers me is how do you know you ought to get out of technical work; how do you convince yourself that you ought to throw it all away?"

Masters explained it very readily in terms of money and in terms of status. He told Ham that he had analyzed National Company as thoroughly as though he were going to invest a couple of million dollars in it. This was only good sense, he said, for there he was investing his whole life in it. And his analysis showed that all the glory in National Company went to the guys in the management seats—all the glory, all the money and all the status. He also discovered that more than half the top men in National had come up out of research and development in the first place and so he decided that the odds were all in favor of his trying the same thing.

"Right now," Masters said, as though clinching the argument, "I'm making half again as much as the guys who came into the lab with me and stayed there. And I'm more flexible," he added. "I can do more things and I'm worth more to the company."

Ham bristled a bit at this. The implication was that the man on the bench was some inferior kind of character, and he found himself resenting it. The argument was also clearly something of a personal challenge.

"All this may have been pretty clear cut in your case, Jack," said Ham, "but I don't think it is in mine. You're with a big outfit— maybe that's where I should be, but I'm not— and I've got to look at my own situation. You fellows at National talk about millions the way we talk about thousands.

"Let's say I look at this thing pragmatically," Ham went on, "and I would agree with you that maybe this has been in my thinking all along. From a practical standpoint, I would say that you can afford to be secure and happy about your choice because your company is fat. If I were with National I might feel the same way. You don't have to worry about finding your next job."

"You don't mean that," said Masters. "You know darn well that if I didn't do my job today, I'd be out on my can tomorrow. We're not running a philanthropy any more than you are."

"No, that's not what I mean," Ham rejoined. "What I mean is that you're insulated from all the wear and tear that affects a guy like me. You're not going to mess your job and you're not going out on your can. But I might."

Ham was wound up now.

"When the Chief talked to me today, Jack," he said, "he quoted a lot of figures about the progress of the company. But I'll be frank with you—we run on government contracts— we couldn't keep our shop open six months without the military."

Ham disclosed that one of his own projects had had a prospective government contract cut right out from under it and some of the engineers had been let go. Ham worried that this might happen to the whole kit and caboodle. Then what would happen to the little guy low down on the management ladder, he asked?

"Would I go to you, to National Company, and say won't you please take me on? Would I say I'm a helluva good man even though I haven't any patents to prove it? Would I say I'm loyal and I need the work and if you take me on you'll never regret it?"

Ham was talking at Masters now rather than to him. He wasn't stopping for answers.

"The way I see it," he argued, "if I stick to the technical part of R&D, I've got money in the bank. I'm negotiable. I can go to anybody in the industry, and I can say here's what I've got and here's what I've done, and they can see it right away."

Ham stopped to sign the dinner checks and to order a second cup of coffee. He looked across at Masters again and apologized for his rush of words. He slowed himself down.

Maybe some of these arguments were pretty tenuous, he agreed, but there were other things. There was the plain and simple joy of accomplishment in good project work, for instance.

Ham had written Masters about the compactor and now he was speaking feelingly about it. That was the kind of thing a guy had to immerse himself in and that was one of the joys he was talking about. If you went into administration full time you kissed that sort of thing good-bye. And you lost something pretty substantial.

Ham let Masters chew over this point, while they finished their coffee. Then they went out to the reading room, where they sat in a couple of comfortable chairs and flicked their cigarette ashes into the fireplace.

After a while Ham said, "Jack, I've been thinking pretty seriously about going back for my doctorate on a half-time basis. The company will sponsor me and Professor Werner wants me to do my thesis under him."

"Well," said Masters, "I remember that you wrote me about a year ago to say that you were thinking about it. I wrote back and urged you to forget it, and I thought you had given it up."

Masters blew a few smoke rings and thoughtfully watched them flatten out and lose their shape.

"If you do go back on a half-time schedule, will you use your compactor for a thesis?" he asked Ham.

"No, I can't," said Ham, "the machine isn't really mine. I guess I didn't tell you that."

Ham explained that a friend of Bill Holden's—a local man—had come up with the basic concept. Holden had brought him around to see the Chief as a kind of personal favor.

"But believe me," Ham added quickly, "there was plenty wrong with that machine when we first saw it. The inventor didn't have a sound idea of the basic processes involved. In fact, the odds on this thing's paying off looked so slim that nobody really wanted to touch it. But then I came up with a process that made it look better and we worked like hell on it and now we've got something that's really good.

Masters took a last drag on his cigarette and flipped it into the fireplace.

"Suppose you do go back for this degree of yours on a half-time basis," he asked Ham, "what's going to come of it?"

"Why, just what I've been saying," said Ham. "In the first place I think it's a good move, just from a practical point of view."

"I don't," Masters countered. "I think you're kidding yourself." Look at this guy Holden, for example. He's already at where you're only going to be. And all the time you're sweating out the earn-while-you-learn routine, he'll be jogging along piling up points. And then when you come back full-time and give it the old college try to catch up, you'll find that all the heros have already been made."

"Well, maybe you're right," laughed Ham, "but why couldn't I look around just the way you did, only from an R&D point of view? I might just look around for the spot where the R&D man is well off and then I'd aim for that and try to hit it."

"You won't find it," said Masters with emphasis. "I laugh at this because I think of our annual report in which we say solemn things about basic R&D being the prime mover of everything that comes down the pike, and we publicly pat its little head, and sing hymns of praise. And I'm telling you—off the record and as a friend—that all of this is hypocritical as hell. It's like a bad scenario with half the lines stolen from `The Life of Louis Pasteur.' I don't know who we think we're kidding—unless it's all the sweet old ladies who own most of our stock."

"That's pretty typical of some high-powered wheel in public relations," Ham laughed. And he laughed again recalling his morning meeting with PR over the promotional piece on the compactor.

"And maybe," Ham added with a smile, "This is a pretty good `for instance' for my argument that by and large you'll find more honest substance in lab work than anywhere else on the lot."

"I won't argue that you won't find mutton-heads in management," said Masters, "but you know darn well that you find them in the lab, too."

Ham nodded his agreement.

"You take the guys on the bench," Masters went on, "and you can pick among them qualitatively. And you know that on any team you've got a few hands with damn good brains in them. But you know also that you've got some other good brains seeing things through. It's not just the turn of the wheel that sends one group up and another group down. There are guys seeing things through all along the line. And some of them take plenty of risks.

Ham thought that this was right, too. He had bought a risk, he thought, when he had sold the Chief on the compactor. They had looked at him and said, "O.K., it's your baby." It was a money down, win or lose proposition; luckily he'd won.

In contrast, Ham thought of Holden and Holden's new appointment. This was a different kind of deal. The company would carry Holden as a kind of overhead. It was like a sweeps ticket; maybe they'd get their money

back and maybe they wouldn't. The whole psychology of the thing was different.

Ham also thought of the pleasure he'd found in "seeing things through" for some of the men and some of the projects the Chief had assigned to him. There was a sense of accomplishment in this, too, he thought.

"Jack," Ham finally said, "I haven't been trying to give you an argument to deny what you might call the joys of management. I've tasted some of them, and I've found that I liked them. It's just that I have very mixed feelings, and I've been trying to see it from all sides.

"And you know," he added, "I honestly feel that I'm almost ready to decide to take the job."

Masters looked at Ham and smiled broadly with sheer delight.

"Ham," he said, "that's the most sensible thing your befuddled old brain has produced tonight. Let's have a nightcap on it before you lose it."

As they had their nightcap, they talked about their families and they made vague arrangements about getting together again "soon." When they had finished, Ham drove Masters back to his hotel. They were tired and they rode most of the way in silence. It was not until Masters shook hands on leaving that he returned again to Ham's decision.

"Ham," he said, "maybe I've got more faith in your company than you have, but I think it's a comer. And I think in this new job you've got a helluva fine opportunity to grow with it. Frankly, I think you'd be a sucker to do anything else. Do yourself a favor and take the job."

"Jack, I'm almost ready to think I will," said Ham, as he waved good-bye. And maybe I will, he thought as he drove the long fifteen miles to Cooperstown. He was glad he had seen Jack, he decided as he turned into his drive. It had been good to talk with him.

The next morning at the plant Ham sat for a long time with his annual report again.

And again he stared idly at the pages, thinking and worrying, especially worrying. He wished that he could avoid the decision altogether, that the Chief or somebody else would come up with some inevitabilities as to why it could go one way or another.

As Ham sat worrying, his mail arrived. It provided something of a diversion and he was grateful for its coming. He spotted among the usual run of internal mail a letter from the Society. He read it with mounting disbelief, and then read it again to make sure. There was no mistaking what it said; his paper on the compactor had won the Society's annual George Peabody Award for the best paper of the year by a young engineer. In stiff, formal phrases the letter sent congratulations from the president of the Society and outlined the Awards Night program at which the Peabody Medal would be presented.

Ham grinned, and the grin grew into a big bubble of elation. Quickly he tucked the letter in his pocket and hurried down the wing to see the Chief. The Chief was in, and he shared Ham's delight as he offered hearty congratulations. He also called the vice president with the news while Ham was still in the office. Ham could hear the vice president's voice gather enthusiasm and begin to dominate the conversation. He couldn't make out the words, but the sounds were friendly.

"He says that you're to make the Society's schedule," said the Chief as he hung up, "and that your wife is to go with you if she can. And he wants you to take any extra time you may need on either side of the meeting—all at company expense, of course."

Ham felt good. It was nice to have these guys in your corner.

"You're not to let the new job make the slightest bit of difference in planning your schedule around this award," the Chief added.

Ham's bubble burst. There was no escaping the thing.

"He also says," the Chief went on, "that he would like to have an answer by the twenty-seventh, if possible. Now that they've made up their minds to move on this, they want to go ahead as quickly as possible."

Ham felt a sudden emptiness in his stomach. "Sure, Chief," he said, "by the twenty-seventh. I ought to have an answer all right, I've already given it a lot of thought."

"And Ham," said the Chief, smiling, "one last thing: be sure to get in touch with PR on this award so that we can exploit it as fully as possible for the company."

Ham nodded and said he would. He added a few words of personal thanks to the Chief and left. He wanted to get back to his office as quickly as possible. He wanted to come to grips with this thing. He wanted to get it settled.

As he hurried past the physics lab, he saw Holden—cup of coffee in hand—sitting at one the tables, talking animatedly with Dr. Maul. As Ham neared his own cubby, he saw Porter lounging near the door, waiting for him with the formal report on yesterday's run. And as Ham drew nearer, he could hear that Porter was whistling.

THE ROAD TO HELL

John Baker, Chief Engineer of the Caribbean Bauxite Company of Barracania in the West Indies, was making his final preparations to leave the island. His promotion to production manager of Keso Mining Corporation near Winnipeg—one of Continental Ore's fast-expanding Canadian enterprises—had been announced a month before and now everything had been tidied up except the last vital interview with his successor—the able young Barracanian, Matthew Rennalls. It was vital that this interview be a success and that Rennalls should leave his office uplifted and encouraged to face the challenge of his new job. A touch on the bell would have brought Rennalls walking into the room but Baker delayed the moment and gazed thoughtfully through the window considering just exactly what he was going to say and, more particularly, how he was going to say it.

John Baker, an English expatriate, was 45 years old and had served his 23 years with Continental Ore in many different places: in the Far East, several countries of Africa, Europe, and, for the last two years, in the West Indies. He hadn't cared much for his previous assignment in Hamburg and was delighted when the West Indian appointment came through. Climate was not the only attraction. Baker had always preferred working overseas (in what were termed the developing countries) because he felt he had an innate knack—better than most other expatriates working for Continental Ore—of knowing just how to get on with regional staff. Twenty-four hours in Barracania, however, soon made him realise that he would need all of this "innate knack" if he was to deal effectively with the problems in this field that now awaited him.

At his first interview with Hutchins, the production manager, the whole problem of Rennalls and his future was discussed. There and then it was made quite clear to Baker that one of his most important tasks would be the "grooming" of Rennalls as his successor. Hutchins had pointed out that, not only was Rennalls one of the brightest Barracanian prospects on the staff of Caribbean Bauxite—at London University he had taken first-class honours in the B.Sc. Engineering Degree—but, being the son of the Minister of Finance and Economic Planning, he also had no small political pull.

The company had been particularly pleased when Rennalls decided to work for them rather than for the Government in which his father had such a prominent post. They ascribed his action to the effect of their vigorous and liberal regionalisation programme which, since the Second World War, had pro-

Source: This Case was written by Mr. Gareth Evans and is reproduced with permission.

duced eighteen Barracanians at mid-management level and given Caribbean Bauxite a good lead in this respect over all other international concerns operating in Barracania. The success of this timely regionalisation policy has led to excellent relations with the Government—a relationship which had been given an added importance when Barracania, three years later, became independent—an occasion which encouraged a critical and challenging attitude towards the role foreign interests would have to play in the new Barracania. Hutchins had therefore little difficulty in convincing Baker that the successful career development of Rennalls was of the first importance.

The interview with Hutchins was now two years old and Baker, leaning back in his office chair, reviewed just how successful he had been in the "grooming" of Rennalls. What aspects of the latter's character had helped and what had hindered? What about his own personality? How had that helped or hindered? The first item to go on the credit side would, without question, be the ability of Rennalls to master the technical aspects of his job. From the start he had shown keenness and enthusiasm and had often impressed Baker with his ability in tackling new assignments and the constructive comments he invariably made in departmental discussions. He was popular with all ranks of Barracanian staff and had an ease of manner which stood him in good stead when dealing with his expatriate seniors. These were all assets, but what about the debit side?

First and foremost, there was his racial consciousness. His four years at London University had accentuated this feeling and made him sensitive to any sign of condescension on the part of expatriates. It may have been to give expression to this sentiment that, as soon as he returned home from London, he threw himself into politics on behalf of the United Action Party who were later to win the preindependence elections and provide the country with its first Prime Minister.

The ambitions of Rennalls—and he certainly was ambitious—did not however, lie in politics for, staunch nationalist as he was, he saw that he could serve himself and his country best—for was not bauxite responsible for nearly half the value of Barracania's export trade?—by putting his engineering talent to the best use possible. On this account, Hutchins found that he had an unexpectedly easy task in persuading Rennalls to give up his political work before entering the production department as an assistant engineer.

It was, Baker knew, Rennalls' well repressed sense of race consciousness which had prevented their relationship from being as close as it should have been. On the surface, nothing could have seemed more agreeable. Formality between the two men was at a minimum; Baker was delighted to find that his assistant shared his own peculiar "shaggy dog" sense of humour so that jokes were continually being exchanged; they entertained each other at their houses and often played tennis together—and yet the barrier remained invisible, indefinable, but ever present. The existence of this "screen" between them was a constant source of frustration to Baker since it indicated a weakness which he was loath to accept. If successful with all other nationalities, why not with Rennalls?

But at least he had managed to "break through" to Rennalls more successfully than any other expatriate. In fact, it was the young Barracanian's attitude—sometimes overbearing, sometimes cynical—towards other company expatriates that had been one of the subjects Baker had raised last year when he discussed Rennalls' staff report with him. He knew too, that he would have to raise the same subject again in the forthcoming interview because Jackson, the senior draughtsman, had complained only yesterday about the rudeness of Rennalls. With this thought in mind, Baker leaned forward and spoke into the intercom. "Would you come in

Matt, please? I'd like a word with you," and later, "Do sit down," proffering the box, "have a cigarette." He paused while he held out his lighter and then went on.

"As you know, Matt, I'll be off to Canada in a few days' time, and before I go, I thought it would be useful if we could have a final chat together. It is indeed with some deference that I suggest I can be of help. You will shortly be sitting in this chair doing the job I am now doing, but I, on the other hand, am ten years older, so perhaps you can accept the idea that I may be able to give you the benefit of my longer experience."

Baker saw Rennalls stiffen slightly in his chair as he made this point so added in explanation, "You and I have attended enough company courses to remember those repeated requests by the personnel manager to tell people how they are getting on as often as the convenient moment arises and not just the automatic once a year' when, by regulation, staff reports have to be discussed.

Rennalls nodded his agreement so Baker went on, "I shall always remember the last job performance discussion I had with my previous boss back in Germany. He used what he called the "plus and minus" technique. His firm belief was that when a senior, by discussion, seeks to improve the work performance of his staff, his prime objective should be to make sure that the latter leaves the interview encouraged and inspired to improve. Any criticism must, therefore, be constructive and helpful. He said that one very good way to encourage a man—and I fully agree with him—is to tell him about his good points—the plus factors—as well as his weak ones—the minus factors—so I thought, Matt, it would be a good idea to run our discussion along these lines.

Rennalls offered no comment, so Baker continued, "Let me say, therefore, right away, that, as far as your own work performance is concerned, the plus far outweighs the minus. I have, for instance been most impressed with the way you have adapted your considerable theoretical knowledge to master the practical techniques of your job—that ingenious method you used to get air down to the fifth shaft level is a sufficient case in point—and at departmental meetings I have invariably found your comments well taken and helpful. In fact, you will be interested to know that only last week I reported to Mr. Hutchins that, from the technical point of view, he could not wish for a more able man to succeed to the position of chief engineer."

"That's very good indeed of you, John," cut in Rennalls with a smile of thanks, "My only worry now is how to live up to such a high recommendation."

"Of that I am quite sure," returned Baker, "especially if you can overcome the minus factor which I would like now to discuss with you. It is one which I have talked about before so I'll come straight to the point. I have noticed that you are more friendly and get on better with your fellow Barracanians than you do with Europeans. In point of fact, I had a complaint only yesterday from Mr. Jackson, who said you had been rude to him—and not for the first time either.

"There is, Matt, I am sure, no need for me to tell you how necessary it will be for you to get on well with expatriates because until the company has trained up sufficient men of your calibre, Europeans are bound to occupy senior positions here in Barracania. All this is vital to your future interests, so can I help you in any way?"

While Baker was speaking on this theme, Rennalls had sat tensed in his chair and it was some seconds before he replied.

"It is quite extraordinary, isn't it, how one can convey an impression to others so at variance with what one intends? I can only assure you once again that my disputes with Jackson—and you may remember also Godson—have had nothing at all to do with the colour of their skins. I promise you that if a

Barracanian had behaved in an equally peremptory manner I would have reacted in precisely the same way. And again, if I may say it within these four walls, I am sure I am not the only one who has found Jackson and Godson difficult. I could mention the names of several expatriates who have felt the same. However, I am really sorry to have created this impression of not being able to get on with Europeans—it is an entirely false one—and I quite realise that I must do all I can to correct it as quickly as possible. On your last point, regarding Europeans holding senior positions in the Company for some time to come, I quite accept the situation. I know that Caribbean Bauxite—as they have been doing, for many years now—will promote Barracanians as soon as their experience warrants it. And, finally, I would like to assure you, John—and my father thinks the same too—that I am very happy in my work here and hope to stay with the Company for many years to come."

Rennalls had spoken earnestly and, although not convinced by what he had heard, Baker did not think he could pursue the matter further except to say, "All right, Matt, my impression may be wrong, but I would like to remind you about the truth of that old saying, `What is important is not what is true but what is believed.' Let it rest at that."

But suddenly Baker knew that he didn't want to "let it rest at that." He was disappointed once again at not being able to "break through" to Rennalls and having yet again to listen to his bland denial that there was any racial prejudice in his makeup. Baker, who had intended ending the interview at this point, decided to try another tack.

"To return for a moment to the `plus and minus technique' I was telling you about just now, there is another plus factor I forgot to mention. I would like to congratulate you not only on the calibre of your work but also on the ability you have shown in overcoming a challenge which I, as a European, have never had to meet.

"Continental Ore is, as you know, a typical commercial enterprise—admittedly a big one—which is a product of the economic and social environment of the United States and Western Europe. My ancestors have all been brought up in this environment for the past two or three hundred years and I have, therefore, been able to live in a world in which commerce (as we know it today) has been part and parcel of my being. It has not been something revolutionary and new which has suddenly entered my life. In your case," went on Baker, "the situation is different because you and your forebears have only had some fifty or sixty years' experience of this commercial environment. You have had to face the challenge of bridging the gap between fifty and two or three hundred years. Again, Matt, let me congratulate you—and people like you—once again on having so successfully overcome this particular hurdle. It is for this very reason that I think the outlook for Barracania—and particularly Caribbean Bauxite—is so bright."

Rennalls had listened intently and when Baker finished, replied, "Well, once again, John, I have to thank you for what you have said, and, for my part, I can only say that it is gratifying to know that my own personal effort has been so much appreciated I hope that more people will soon come to think as you do."

There was a pause and, for a moment, Baker thought hopefully that he was about to achieve his long awaited "breakthrough," but Rennalls merely smiled back. The barrier remained unbreached. There remained some five minutes' cheerful conversation about the contrast between the Caribbean and Canadian climate and whether the West Indies had any hope of beating England in the Fifth Test before Baker drew the interview to a close. Although he was as far as ever from knowing the real Rennalls, he was nevertheless glad that the interview had run along in this friendly manner and, particularly, that it had ended on such a cheerful note.

This feeling, however, lasted only until the following morning. Baker had some farewells to make, so he arrived at the office considerably later than usual. He had no sooner sat down at his desk than his secretary walked into the room with a worried frown on her face. Her words came fast. "When I arrived this morning I found Mr. Rennalls already waiting at my door. He seemed very angry and told me in quite a peremptory manner that he had a vital letter to dictate which must be sent off without any delay. He was so worked up that he couldn't keep still and kept pacing about the room, which is most unlike him. He wouldn't even wait to read what he had dictated. Just signed the page where he thought the letter would end. It has been distributed and your copy is in your `in tray.'"

Puzzled and feeling vaguely uneasy, Baker opened the "Confidential" envelope and read the following letter:

From: Assistant Engineer
To: The Chief Engineer, Caribbean
    Bauxite Limited
14th August

ASSESSMENT OF INTERVIEW BETWEEN MESSRS. BAKER AND RENNALLS

It has always been my practice to respect the advice given me by seniors, so after our interview, I decided to give careful thought once again to its main points and to make sure that I had understood all that had been said. As I promised you at the time, I had every intention of putting your advice to the best effect.

It was not, therefore, until I had sat down quietly in my home yesterday evening to consider the interview objectively that its main purport became clear. Only then did the full enormity of what you said dawn on me. The more I thought about it, the more convinced I was that I had hit upon the real truth—and the more furious I became. With a facility in the English language which I—a poor Barracanian—cannot hope to match, you had the audacity to insult me (and through me every Barracanian worth his salt) by claiming that our knowledge of modern living is only a paltry fifty years old whilst yours goes back 200–300 years. As if your materialistic commercial environment could possibly be compared with the spiritual values of our culture. I'll have you know that if much of what I saw in London is representative of your most boasted culture, I hope fervently that it will never come to Barracania. By what right do you have the effrontery to condescend to us? At heart, all you Europeans think us barbarians, or, as you say amongst yourselves we are "just down from the trees."

Far into the night I discussed this matter with my father, and he is as disgusted as I. He agrees with me that any company whose senior staff think as you do is no place for any Barracanian proud of his culture and race—so much for all the company "clap-trap" and specious propaganda about regionalisation and Barracania for the Barracanians.

I feel ashamed and betrayed. Please accept this letter as my resignation which I wish to become effective immediately.

c.c. Production Manager
    Managing Director

RONDELL DATA CORPORATION

"God damn it, he's done it again!"

Frank Forbus threw the stack of prints and specifications down on his desk in disgust. The Model 802 wide-band modulator, released for production the previous Thursday had just come back to Frank's Engineering Services Department with a caustic note which began, "This one can't be produced, either..." It was the fourth time Production had kicked the design back.

Frank Forbus, director of engineering for Rondell Data Corp., was normally a quiet man. But the Model 802 was stretching his patience; it was beginning to look just like other new products which had hit delays and problems in the transition from design to production during the eight months Frank had worked for Rondell. These problems were nothing new at the sprawling, old Rondell factory; Frank's predecessor in the engineering job had run afoul of them too, and had finally been fired for protesting too vehemently about the other departments. But the Model 802 should have been different. Frank had met two months before (July 3, 1978) with the firm's president, Bill Hunt, and with Factory Superintendent Dave Schwab, to smooth the way for the new modulator design. He thought back to the meeting...

"Now, we all know there's a tight deadline on the 802," Bill Hunt said, "and Frank's done well to ask us to talk about its introduction. I'm counting on both of you to find any snags in the system, and to work together to get the first production run out by October second. Can you do it?"

"We can do it in Production if we get a clean design two weeks from now, as scheduled," answered Dave Schwab, the grizzled factory superintendent. "Frank and I have already talked about that, of course. I'm setting aside time in the card room and the machine shop, and we'll be ready. If the design goes over schedule, though, I'll have to fill in with other runs, and it will cost us a bundle to break in for the 802. How does it look in Engineering, Frank?"

"I've just reviewed the design for the second time," Frank replied. "If Ron Porter can keep the salesmen out of our hair, and avoid any more last minute changes, we've got a shot. I've pulled the draftsmen off of three other overdue jobs to get this one out, But Dave, that means we can't spring engineers

Source: Reproduced by permission of Dr. John A. Seeger, Professor, Bently College.

loose to confer with your production people on manufacturing problems."

"Well, Frank, most of those problems are caused by the engineers, and we need them to resolve the difficulties. We've all agreed that production bugs come from both of us bowing to sales pressure, and putting equipment into production before the designs are really ready. That's just what we're trying to avoid on the 802. But I can't have 500 people sitting on their hands waiting for an answer from your people. We'll have to have some engineering support."

Bill Hunt broke in, "So long as you two can talk calmly about the problem I'm confident you can resolve it. What a relief it is, Frank, to hear the way you're approaching this. With Kilmann (the previous director of engineering) this conversation would have been a shouting match. Right, Dave?" Dave nodded and smiled.

"Now there's one other thing you should both be aware of," Hunt continued. "Doc Reeves and I talked last night about a new filtering technique, one that might improve the signal-to-noise ratio of the 802 by a factor of two. There's a chance Doc can come up with it before the 802 reaches production, and if it's possible, I'd like to use the new filters. That would give us a real jump on the competition."

Four days after that meeting, Frank found that two of his key people on the 802 design had been called to Production for emergency consultation on a bug found in final assembly: two halves of a new data transmission interface wouldn't fit together, because recent changes in the front end required a different chassis design for the back end.

Another week later, Doc Reeves walked into Frank's office, proud as a new parent, with the new filter design. "This won't affect the other modules of the 802 much, "Doc had said. "Look, it takes three new cards, a few connectors, some changes in the wiring harness, and some new shielding, and that's all."

Frank had tried to resist the last-minute design changes, but Bill Hunt had stood firm. With a lot of overtime by the engineers and draftsmen, Engineering Services should still be able to finish the prints in time.

Two engineers and three draftsmen went onto twelve-hour days to get the 802 ready, but the prints were still five days late reaching Dave Schwab. Two days later, the prints came back to Frank, heavily annotated in red. Schwab had worked all day Saturday to review the job, and had found more than a dozen discrepancies in the prints—most of them caused by the new filter design and insufficient checking time before release. Correction of the design faults had brought on a new generation of discrepancies; Schwab's cover note on the second return of the prints indicated he'd had to release the machine capacity he'd been holding for the 802. On the third iteration, Schwab committed his photo and plating capacity to another rush job. The 802 would be at least one month late getting into production. Ron Porter, Vice President for Sales, was furious. His customer needed 100 units NOW, he said. Rondell was the customer's only late supplier.

"Here we go again," thought Frank Forbus.

Company History

Rondell Data Corp. traced its lineage through several generations of electronics technology. Its original founder, Bob Rondell, had set the firm up in 1920 as "Rondell Equipment Co.," to manufacture several electrical testing devices he had invented as an engineering faculty member at a large university. The firm branched into radio broadcasting equipment in 1947, and into data transmission equipment in the early 1960s. A well-established corps of direct sales people, mostly engineers, called on industrial, scientific and government accounts, but concentrated heavily on original equipment manufacturers. In this market,

Rondell had a long-standing reputation as a source of high-quality, innovative designs. The firm's salespeople fed a continual stream of challenging problems into the Engineering Department, where the creative genius of Ed "Doc" Reeves and several dozen other engineers "converted problems to solutions" (as the sales brochure bragged). Product design formed the spearhead of Rondell's growth.

By 1978, Rondell offered a wide range of products in its two major lines. Broadcast equipment sales had benefitted from the growth of UHF TV and FM radio; it now accounted for 35 percent of company sales. Data transmission had blossomed, and in this field an increasing number of orders called for unique specifications, ranging from specialized display panels to entirely untried designs.

The company had grown from 100 employees in 1947, to over 800 in 1978. Bill Hunt, who had been a student of the company's founder, had presided over most of that growth, and took great pride in preserving the "family spirit" of the old organization. Informal relationships between Rondell's veteran employees formed the backbone of the firm's day-to-day operations; all the managers relied on personal contact, and Hunt often insisted that the absence of bureaucratic red tape was a key factor in recruiting outstanding engineering talent. The personal management approach extended throughout the factory. All exempt employees were paid on a straight salary plus a share of the profits. Rondell boasted an extremely loyal group of senior employees, and very low turnover in nearly all areas of the company.

The highest turnover job in the firm was Frank Forbus's. Frank had joined Rondell in January of 1978, replacing Jim Kilmann, who had been director of engineering for only ten months. Kilmann, in turn, had replaced Tom MacLeod, a talented engineer who had made a promising start, but had taken to drink after a year in the job. MacLeod's predecessor had been a genial old timer, who retired at 70, after 30 years in charge of engineering. (Doc Reeves had refused the directorship in each of the recent changes, saying, "Hell, that's no promotion for a bench man like me. I'm no administrator.")

For several years, the firm had experienced a steadily increasing number of disputes between research, engineering, sales, and production people—disputes generally centered on the problem of new product introduction. Quarrels between departments became more numerous under MacLeod, Kilmann, and Forbus. Some managers associated those disputes with the company's recent decline in profitability—a decline which, in spite of higher sales and gross revenues, was beginning to bother people in 1977. President Bill Hunt commented:

Better cooperation, I'm sure, could increase our output by five to ten percent. I'd hoped Kilmann could solve the problems, but pretty obviously he was too young—too arrogant. People like him—that conflict type of personality bother me. I don't like strife, and with him it seemed I spent all my time smoothing out arguments. Kilmann tried to tell everyone else how to run their departments, without having his own house in order. That approach just wouldn't work, here at Rondell. Frank Forbus, now, seems much more in tune with our style of organization. I'm really hopeful now.

Still, we have just as many problems now as we did last year. Maybe even more. I hope Frank can get a handle on Engineering Services soon . . ."

The Engineering Department: Research

According to the organization chart (see Exhibits 1 and 2), Frank Forbus was in charge of both research (really the product development function) and engineering services (which provided engineering support). To Forbus, how-

EXHIBIT 1

RONDELL DATA CORPORATION
ORGANIZATION CHART—1978

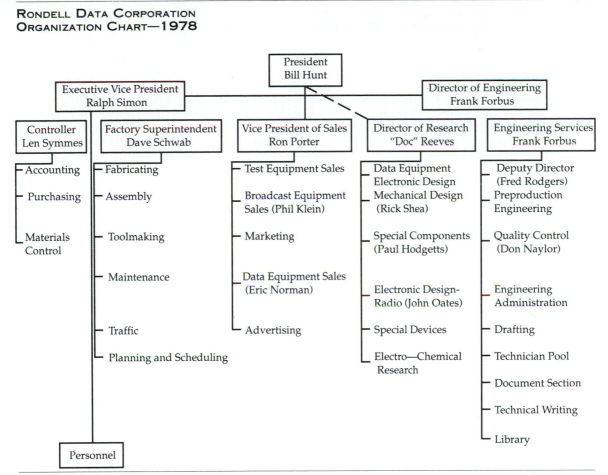

ever, the relationship with research was not so clear-cut:

"Doc Reeves is one of the world's unique people, and none of us would have it any other way. He's a creative genius. Sure, the chart says he works for me, but we all know Doc does his own thing. He's not the least bit interested in management routines, and I can't count on him to take any responsibility in scheduling projects, or checking budgets, or what-have-you. But as long as Doc is director of research, you can bet this company will keep on leading the field. He has more ideas per hour than most people have per year, and he keeps the whole engineering staff fired up.

Everybody loves Doc—and you can count me in on that, too. In a way, he works for me, sure. But that's not what's important."

"Doc" Reeves—unhurried, contemplative, casual, and candid—flipped his stool back against the wall of his research cubicle and talked about what was important:

"Development engineering. That's where the company's future rests. Either we have it there, or we don't have it.

"There's no kidding ourselves that we're anything but a bunch of Rube Goldbergs here. But that's where the biggest kicks come from—from solving development problems, and dreaming up new ways of doing things. That's

EXHIBIT 2

RONDELL DATA CORPORATION
BACKGROUND OF SELECTED EXECUTIVES

Bill Hunt

President, 63 years old. Engineering graduate of an Ivy League college. Joined company in 1946 as an engineer. Worked exclusively on development for over a year and then split his time between development and field sales work until he became Assistant to President in 1956. Became President in 1960. Hunt and Ralph Simon, together, held enough Rondell stock to command effective control of the company.

Ralph Simon

Executive Vice President, 65 years old. Joined company in 1945 as a traveling representative. In 1947 became Rondell's leading salesman for broadcast equipment. In 1954 was made Treasurer, but continued to spend time selling. In 1960 was appointed Executive Vice President with direct responsibility for financial matters and production.

Ron Porter

Vice President–Sales, 50 years old. B.S. in engineering. Joined company in 1957 as a salesman, was influential in the establishment of the data transmission product line and did early selling himself. In 1967 he was made Sales Manager. Extensive contacts in trade associations and industrial shows. Appointed Vice President–Sales in 1974.

Dave Schwab

Production Manager, 62 years old. Trade school graduate; veteran of both WWII and Korean conflict. Joined Rondell in 1955. Promoted to Production Manager seven months later after exposure of widespread irregularities in production and control departments. Reorganized production department and brought a new cadre of production specialists to the company.

Frank Forbus

Director of Engineering, 40 years old. Master's degree in engineering, previously division director of engineering in large industrial firm. Joined company in 1977 as Director of Engineering replacing employee who had been dismissed because of his inability to work with sales and production personnel. As Director of Engineering was responsible for administration of research personnel and had complete responsibility for engineering services.

Ed Reeves

Director of Research, 47 years old. Joined Rondell in 1960, working directly with Bill Hunt to develop major innovations in data transmission equipment. Appointed Director of Research in 1967.

Len Symmes

Controller, 43 years old. Joined company in 1955 while attending business colege. Held several jobs including production scheduling, accounting, and cost control. Named Controller in 1972.

why I so look forward to the special contracts we get involved in. We accept them not for the revenue they represent, but because they subsidize the basic development work which goes into all our basic products.

"This is a fantastic place to work. I have a great crew and they can really deliver when the chips are down. Why, Bill Hunt and I (he gestured toward the neighboring cubicle where the president's name hung over the door) are likely to find as many people here at work at ten P.M. as at three in the afternoon. The important thing here is the relationships between people; they're based on mutual respect, not on policies and procedures. Administrative red tape is a pain. It takes away from development time.

"Problems? Sure, there are problems now and then. There are power interests in production, where they sometimes resist change. But I'm not a fighting man, you know. I suppose if I were, I might go in there and push my weight around a little. But I'm an engineer, and can do more for Rondell sitting right here, or working with my own people. That's what brings results."

Other members of the Research Department echoed Doc's views and added some additional sources of satisfaction with their work. They were proud of the personal contacts they built up with customers' technical staffs—contacts which increasingly involved travel to the customers' factories to serve as expert advisors in preparation of overall system design specifications. The engineers were always delighted with the department's encouragement of their development, continuing education, and independence on the job.

But there were problems, too. Rick Shea, of the mechanical design section, noted:

"In the old days I really enjoyed the work and the people I worked with. But now there's a lot of irritation. I don't like someone breathing down my neck. You can be hurried into jeopardizing the design."

John Oates, head of the radio electronic design section, was another designer with definite views:

"Production engineering is almost non-existent in this company. Very little is done by the preproduction section in engineering services. Frank Forbus has been trying to get preproduction into the picture, but he won't succeed because you can't start from such an ambiguous position. There have been three directors of engineering in three years. Frank can't hold his own against the others in the company. Kilmann was too aggressive. Perhaps no amount of tact would have succeeded."

Paul Hodgetts was head of special components in the R&D department. Like the rest of the department he valued bench work. But he complained of engineering services.

"The services don't do things we want them to do. Instead, they tell us what they're going to do. I should probably go to Frank, but I don't get any decisions there. I know I should go through Frank, but this holds things up, so I often go direct."

The Engineering Department: Engineering Services

The Engineering Services Department provided ancillary services to R&D and served as liaison between engineering and the other Rondell departments. Among its main functions were drafting; management of the central technicians pool; scheduling and expediting engineering products; documentation and publication of parts lists and engineering orders; preproduction engineering (consisting of the final integration of individual design components into mechanically compatible packages); and quality control (which included inspection of incoming parts and materials, and final inspection of subassemblies and finished equipment). Top management's description of the department included the line, "ESD is responsible for maintaining cooperation with other departments, providing services to the development engineers, and freeing more valuable people in R&D from essential activities which are diversions from and beneath their main competence."

Many of Frank Forbus's 75 employees were located in other departments. Quality control people were scattered through the manufacturing and receiving areas, and technicians worked primarily in the research area or the prototype fabrication room. The remaining ESD personnel were assigned to leftover nooks and crannies near production or engineering sections.

Frank Forbus described his position:

"My biggest problem is getting acceptance from the people I work with. I've moved slowly rather than risk antagonism. I saw what happened to Kilmann, and I want to avoid that. But although his precipitate action had won over a few of the younger R&D people, he certainly didn't have the department's backing. Of course it was the resentment of other departments which eventually caused his discharge. People have been slow accepting me here. There's nothing really overt, but I get a negative reaction to my ideas.

"My role in the company has never been well defined, really. It's complicated by Doc's unique position, of course, and also by the fact that ESD sort of grew by itself over the years, as the design engineers concentrated more and more on the creative parts of product development. I wish I could be more involved in the technical side. That's been my training, and it's a lot of fun. But in our setup, the technical side is the least necessary for me to be involved in.

"Schwab (production head) is hard to get along with. Before I came and after Kilmann left, there were six months intervening when no one was really doing any scheduling. No work loads were figured, and unrealistic promises were made about releases. This puts us in

an awkward position. We've been scheduling way beyond our capacity to manufacture or engineer.

"Certain people within R&D, for instance John Oates, head of the radio electronic design section, understand scheduling well and meet project deadlines, but this is not generally true of the rest of the R&D department, especially the mechanical engineers who won't commit themselves. Most of the complaints come from sales and production department heads because items—like the 802—are going to production before they are fully developed, under pressure from sales to get out the unit and this snags the whole process. Somehow, engineering services should be able to intervene and resolve these complaints, but I haven't made much headway so far.

"I should be able to go to Hunt for help, but he's too busy most of the time, and his major interest is the design side of engineering, where he got his own start. Sometimes he talks as though he's the engineering director as well as president. I have to put my foot down; there are problems here that the front office just doesn't understand."

Sales people were often observed taking their problems directly to designers, while production frequently threw designs back at R&D, claiming they could not be produced and demanding the prompt attention of particular design engineers. The latter were frequently observed in conference with production supervisors on the assembly floor. Frank went on:

"The designers seem to feel they're losing something when one of us tries to help. They feel it's a reflection on them to have someone take over what they've been doing. They seem to want to carry a project right through to the final stages, particularly the mechanical people. Consequently, engineering services people are used below their capacity to contribute and our department is denied functions it should be performing. There's not as much use made of engineering services as there should be."

Frank Forbus's technician supervisor added his comments:

"Production picks out the engineer who'll be the "bum of the month." They pick on every little detail instead of using their heads and making the minor changes that have to be made. The fifteen to twenty year people shouldn't have to prove their ability any more, but they spend four hours defending themselves and four hours getting the job done. I have no one to go to when I need help. Frank Forbus is afraid. I'm trying to help him but he can't help me at this time. I'm responsible for fifty people and I've got to support them."

Fred Rodgers, who Frank had brought with him to the company as an assistant, gave another view of the situation:

"I try to get our people in preproduction to take responsibility but they're not used to it and people in other departments don't usually see them as best qualified to solve the problem. There's a real barrier for a newcomer here. Gaining people's confidence is hard. More and more, I'm wondering whether there really is a job for me here." (Rodgers left Rondell a month later.)

Another of Forbus's subordinates gave his view:

"If Doc gets a new product idea you can't argue. But he's too optimistic. He judges that others can do what he does, but there's only one Doc Reeves. We've had 900 production change orders this year—they changed 2,500 drawings. If I were in Frank's shoes I'd put my foot down on all this new development. I'd look at the reworking. I'd look at the reworking we're doing and get production set up the way I wanted it. Kilmann was fired when he was doing a good job. He was getting some system in the company's operations. Of course, it hurt some people. There is no denying that Doc is the most important person in the company. What gets overlooked is

that Hunt is a close second, not just politically but in terms of what he contributes technically and in customer relations."

This subordinate explained that he sometimes went out into the production department but that Schwab, the production head, resented this. Personnel in production said that Kilmann had failed to show respect for oldtimers and was always meddling in other departments' business. This was why he had been fired, they contended.

Don Naylor was in charge of quality control. He commented:

"I am now much more concerned with administration and less with work. It is one of the evils you get into. There is tremendous detail in this job. I listen to everyone's opinion. Everybody is important. There shouldn't be distinctions—distinctions between people. I'm not sure whether Frank has to be a fireball like Kilmann. I think the real question is whether Frank is getting the job done. I know my job is essential. I want to supply service to the more talented people and give them information so they can do their jobs better."

The Sales Department

Ron Porter was angry. His job was supposed to be selling, he said, but instead it had turned into settling disputes inside the plant and making excuses to waiting customers. He jabbed a finger toward his desk:

"You see that telephone? I'm actually afraid nowadays to hear it ring. Three times out of five, it will be a customer who's hurting because we've failed to deliver on schedule. The other two calls will be from production or ESD, telling me some schedule has slipped again.

The Model 802 is typical. Absolutely typical. We padded the delivery date by six weeks, to allow for contingencies. Within two months the slack had evaporated. Now it looks like we'll be lucky to ship it before Christmas. (It was now November 28.) We're ruining our reputation in the market. Why, just last week one of our best customers—people we've worked with for 15 years—tried to hang a penalty clause on their latest order.

"We shouldn't have to be after the engineers all the time. They should be able to see what problems they create without our telling them."

Phil Klein, head of broadcast sales under Porter, noted that many sales decisions were made by top management. Sales was understaffed, he thought, and had never really been able to get on top of the job.

"We have grown further and further away from engineering. The director of engineering does not pass on the information that we give him. We need better relationships there. It is very difficult for us to talk to customers about development problems without technical help. We need each other. The whole of engineering is now too isolated from the outside world. The morale of ESD is very low. They're in a bad spot—they're not well organized.

"People don't take much to outsiders here. Much of this is because the expectation is built up by top management that jobs will be filled from the bottom. So it's really tough when an outsider like Frank comes in."

Eric Norman, order and pricing coordinator for data equipment, talked about his own relationships with the production department:

"Actually, I get along with them fairly well. Oh, things could be better, of course, if they were more cooperative generally. They always seem to say, `It's my bat and my ball, and we're playing by my rules.' People are afraid to make Production mad; there's a lot of power in there.

"But you've got to understand that production has its own set of problems. And nobody in Rondell is working any harder than Dave Schwab to try to straighten things out."

The Production Department

Dave Schwab joined Rondell just after the Korean War, in which he had seen combat duty (at the Yalu River) and intelligence duty at Pyong Yang. Both experiences had been useful in his first year of civilian employment at Rondell, the wartime factory superintendent and several middle managers had been, apparently, indulging in highly questionable side deals with Rondell's suppliers. Dave Schwab had gathered evidence, revealed the situation to Bill Hunt, and had stood by the president in the ensuing unsavory situation. Seven months after joining the company, Dave was named Factory Superintendent.

His first move had been to replace the fallen managers with a new team from outside. This group did not share the traditional Rondell emphasis on informality and friendly personal relationships, and had worked long and hard to install systematic manufacturing methods and procedures. Before the reorganization, production had controlled purchasing, stock control, and final quality control (where final assembly of products in cabinets was accomplished). Because of the wartime events, management decided on a check-and-balance system of organization and removed these three departments from production jurisdiction. The new production managers felt they had been unjustly penalized by this reorganization, particularly since they had uncovered the behavior which was detrimental to the company in the first place.

By 1978, the production department had grown to 500 employees, of whom 60 percent worked in the assembly area—an unusually pleasant environment which had been commended by Factory magazine for its colorful decoration, cleanliness, and low noise level. An additional 30 percent of the work force, mostly skilled machinists, staffed the finishing and fabrication department. About 60 others performed scheduling, supervisory, and maintenance duties. Production workers were non-union, hourly—paid, and participated in both the liberal profit-sharing program and the stock purchase plan. Morale in production was traditionally high.

Dave Schwab commented:

"To be efficient, production has to be a self-contained department. We have to control what comes into the department and what goes out. That's why purchasing, inventory control, and quality ought to run out of this office. We'd eliminate a lot of problems with better control there. Why, even Don Naylor in QC would rather work for me than for ESD; he's said so himself. We understand his problems better.

"The other departments should be self-contained, too. That's why I always avoid the underlings, and go straight to the department heads with any questions. I always go down the line.

"I have to protect my people from outside disturbances. Look what would happen if I let unfinished, half-baked designs in here—there'd be chaos. The bugs have to be found before the drawings go into the shop, and it seems I'm the one who has to find them. Look at the 802, for example. (Dave had spent most of Thanksgiving Day [it was now November 28] red-pencilling the latest set of prints.) ESD should have found every one of those discrepancies. They just don't check drawings properly. They change most of the things I flag, but then they fail to trace through the impact of those changes on the rest of the design. I shouldn't have to do that.

"And those engineers are tolerance crazy. They want everything to a millionth of an inch. I'm the only one in the company who's had any experience with actually machining things to a millionth of an inch. We make sure that the things that engineers say on their drawings actually have to be that way and whether they're obtainable from the kind of raw material we buy.

"That shouldn't be production's responsibility, but I have to do it. Accepting bad prints wouldn't let us ship the order any quicker. We'd only make a lot of junk that had to be reworked. And that would take even longer.

"This way, I get to be known as the bad guy, but I guess that's just part of the job. (He paused with a wry smile.) Of course, what really gets them is that I don't even have a degree."

Dave had fewer bones to pick with the sales department because, he said, they trusted him.

"When *we* give Ron Porter a shipping date, he knows the equipment will be shipped *then*.

"You've got to recognize, though, that all of our new product problems stem from sales making absurd commitments on equipment that hasn't been fully developed. That always means trouble. Unfortunately, Hunt always backs sales up, even when they're wrong. He always favors them over us."

Ralph Simon, age 69, executive vice president of the company, had direct responsibility for Rondell's production department. He said:

"There shouldn't really be a dividing of departments among top management in the company. The president should be czar over all. The production people ask me to do something for them, and I really can't do it. It creates bad feelings between engineering and production, this special attention that they [R&D] get from Bill. But then Hunt likes to dabble in design. Schwab feels that production is treated like a poor relation."

The Executive Committee

At the executive committee meeting of December 6, it was duly recorded that Dave Schwab had accepted the prints and specifications for the Model 802 modulator, and had set Friday, December 29, as the shipping date for the first

10 pieces. Bill Hunt, in the chairperson's role, shook his head and changed the subject quickly when Frank tried to open the agenda to a discussion of interdepartmental coordination.

The executive committee itself was a brainchild of Rondell's controller, Len Symmes, who was well aware of the disputes which plagued the company. Symmes had convinced Bill Hunt and Ralph Simon to meet every two weeks with their department heads, and the meetings were formalized with Hunt, Simon, Ron Porter, Dave Schwab, Frank Forbus, Doc Reeves, Symmes, and the personnel director attending. Symmes explained his intent and the results:

"Doing things collectively and informally just doesn't work as well as it used to. Things have been gradually getting worse for at least two years now. We had to start thinking in terms of formal organization relationships. I did the first organization chart, and the executive committee was my idea too—but neither idea is contributing much help, I'm afraid. It takes top management to make an organization click. The rest of us can't act much differently until the top people see the need for us to change.

"I had hoped the committee especially would help get the department managers into a constructive planning process. It hasn't worked out that way, because Mr. Hunt really doesn't see the need for it. He uses the meetings as a place to pass on routine information."

Merry Christmas

"Frank, I didn't know whether to tell you now, or after the holiday." It was Friday, December 22, and Frank Forbus was standing awkwardly in front of Bill Hunt's desk.

"But, I figured you'd work right through Christmas Day if we didn't have this talk, and that just wouldn't have been fair to you. I can't understand why we have such poor luck in the engineering director's job lately. And I don't think it's entirely your fault. But . . ."

Frank only heard half of Hunt's words, and said nothing in response . . . He'd be paid through February 28 . . . He should use the time for searching . . . Hunt would help all he could . . . Jim Kilmann was supposed to be doing well at his own new job, and might need more help . . .

Frank cleaned out his desk, and numbly started home. The electronic carillion near his house was playing a Christmas carol. Frank thought again of Hunt's rationale: conflict still plagued Rondell—and Frank had not made it go away. Maybe somebody else could do it.

"And what did Santa Claus bring you, Frankie?" he asked himself.

"The sack. Only the empty sack."

HAUSSER FOOD PRODUCTS COMPANY

Brenda Cooper, the southeastern regional sales manager for the Hausser Food Products (HFP) Company, expressed her concern to a researcher from a well known eastern business school:

"I think during the past year I've begun to make some progress here, but the situation is a lot more difficult than I thought when I first arrived. Our current methods of selling products just are not adequate, and the people in the field don't seem interested in coming up with new ideas or approaches to selling."

Background

Hausser Food Products Company is a leading producer and marketer of infant foods in the United States. The company manufactures and markets a whole line of foods for the infant market, including strained meats, vegetables, fruits, and combination dishes. The product line includes foods that are completely strained, for infants, as well as foods that are partially strained or chopped, for children 6 months of age and older. HFP has traditionally been the leader in this field. The company has no other major product lines. Its products are known for their high quality and its name is well known to most consumers.

HFP owns its production and warehousing facilities. Its well-developed distribution network provides direct delivery of products to the warehouses and stores of most major food chains. The smallest segment of its market is composed of a limited number of institutions for children that purchase HFP products in bulk. HFP has had a long history in the infant food business. Traditionally the market leader, it has over the years maintained a market share of approximately 60 percent. During the 1960s, the firm experienced rapid expansion and growth. The number of different types of infant food products increased tremendously to keep up with increasing demand for a greater number of foods and a greater variety of products. From the mid-1960s to the mid-1970s, growth in sales approached 15 percent compounded yearly. During the past few years, HFP has faced a greatly changing market for infant foods. The sudden decrease in the birth rate brought about major changes in the whole infant food business, and projections of sales had to be altered drastically. In addition, the new concern about food additives, including

Source: Reprinted by permission of Dr. David A. Nadler.

flavorings, dyes, and preservatives, also had its impact on the baby food market. Many consumer advocates argued that mothers would be much safer in making their own baby foods, rather than purchasing the commercially prepared products, such as those manufactured by HFP. Finally, competition in the baby food market also increased with private brands competing on the basis of price against the nationally advertised brand names.

These changing conditions had been viewed with great alarm by the top management of HFP. The drop in growth of sales (to 3 percent in the most recent year) was accompanied by an even greater drop in earnings, as management found itself faced with unused plant and warehouse capacity. Management is currently concerned with looking for new ways to stimulate demand for HFP products as well as with the longer-range problem of finding other complementary products to develop and market.

Marketing Organization

In 1975 a researcher from a major business school became involved in studying the market organization of HFP as part of a larger-scale research project. His inquiries led him to look closely at the sales department and to investigate some of the problems that were being experienced there.

The marketing function at HFP is directed by a vice president for marketing, who reports directly to the president of HFP. The vice president for marketing has five functional directors reporting to him. Each director is responsible for one of the major areas of marketing activity, including market research, market planning, sales promotion, advertising, and sales. The sales department, which has been the focus of much recent concern, is headed by the director of sales. This person directs selling activities in the entire United States. The country is divided into seven major re-

gions, each of which has a regional sales manager. Regions are further divided into districts—each district may include a range of geographic areas, from several states to part of a city, depending upon the particular location. The district manager heads the HFP sales team for each district. The sales team has the ultimate job of selling HFP products to customers, offering promotions, maintaining contact with the customers, ensuring adequate shelf space, etc.

A key element in the marketing organization is the regional sales manager position. This position has been an entry position for many bright, aggressive, and well-trained young people who subsequently have risen to high-level positions within the company. The current president of the company, the vice president for marketing, and three of the five marketing directors began their careers at HFP as regional sales managers.

Brenda Cooper, the southeastern regional sales manager, is fairly typical of the kind of person placed in that position. Brenda entered an MBA program immediately after graduation from one of the best women's colleges in the country. Majoring in marketing, she did extremely well in business school and graduated near the top of her class. Upon graduation she received many job offers and took a position as an assistant production manager in a large nonfood consumer products company. During 4 years at that firm, she performed extremely well both in the management of existing products and in the launching of new products. By the end of her fourth year, however, she was becoming restless and, seeing no opportunities for quick advancement, decided to accept an offer to become a regional sales manager at HFP. The salary was attractive, and she would receive a potentially large bonus based on the profit performance of the entire company. What also attracted Brenda was the possibility of advancement within the company; she had heard that many of the senior staff had started in the regional manager position. At the end of her first year, Brenda is still very much concerned about doing well in her job; in particular, she is adjusting to her role as a manager, with six district managers reporting to her.

Much of the activity of the regional managers centers around the yearly sales plan. The sales plan is essentially a budget that includes projections of sales, expenses, and profit. It serves as the basic yardstick against which the performance of regional managers is measured. Each year the sales plan is developed through a multistage process, as follows:

1. The director of market planning projects sales for the coming year. At the same time, the director of sales asks the regional managers for their projections of sales for the next year. These projections are usually extrapolations of previous-year figures with adjustments for major changes in the market year, if any.
2. The directors of market planning and sales, along with their staffs, negotiate to resolve the differences that usually exist between their two projections (market planning always tends to be higher). Out of these negotiations emerges the sales plan for the coming year. This plan includes budgeted expenditures for promotions, advertising, expenses, and so forth, as well as projected sales volume and profit.
3. The sales director allocates portions of the sales plan to each of the regional managers, who are responsible for meeting the plan within their own region. Regional managers, in turn, allocate parts of the plan to each of their district sales managers and teams.
4. The district managers receive the plan in the form of sales targets and expense budgets for the coming year. The district manager typically receives a relatively low base salary combined with a relatively large yearly bonus, which is based entirely on the performance of the sales team, measured against the sales plan. At the end of the year, the district manager is also given a pool of bonus dollars, also based on team performance against plan, to be distributed to the individual salespeople. Salespeople look to their yearly bonuses as a major source of income.

Problems of Regional Sales Managers

As part of the investigation, the researcher visited Brenda Cooper in her Atlanta office. After describing the operations of her region, Brenda began to talk about some of her problems.

"We in HFP are currently wrestling with the problem of a very mature product line. Top management has begun to see the critical need to diversify, in other words to hedge our bets with some other lines of products which are not dependent upon a steadily increasing birth rate. They have been talking about some interesting and exciting things, but any new product is still a few years away from being introduced. In the meantime, it is the job of us out here in the field to come up with new ideas to help keep up sales of our existing product line. I think there must be better ways of selling our product and I am sure that there are new things that we can do to get much more performance out of the line than we are seeing now. The problem is that the best ideas usually come in from the field, from the salespeople themselves, and we really have had very little from our sales teams. They seem content to continue to let the products sell themselves and just keep the shelves stocked, as they have for years. I just don't get any new ideas or approaches from my sales teams."

Brenda and the researcher then reviewed the sales figures for her region, in particular the sales performance of the different areas. Brenda noted:

"Look here at Jay Boyar and his group in Florida. This is a prime example of the kind of problem I am facing. While we have been facing decreasing growth in sales, and actual drop off of sales some places, Jay's group consistently comes in at 10 percent above the sales plan. I've been down there and met with them and I've talked with Jay numerous times, but I can't figure out how they do it. They must be doing something that could be used in other places, but every time I ask how they do it I get very vague answers, such as, "Well, we work very hard down here" or "We work together as a group; that's how we are able to do well." I'm sure it must be more than that, but I can't seem to get them to open up."

Visit to the Florida Sales Team

Intrigued with the Florida figures, the researcher arranged an extensive visit (during January and February) with the Florida sales team. The researcher was given a letter of introduction from the vice president for marketing. This letter explained that the researcher was collecting background information for a major research project that would be of help to the company, that any information collected would be confidential, and that the sales team should provide any needed assistance. At first Jay Boyar and his group made no attempt to hide their suspicion of the researcher. Slowly, however, as the researcher spent numerous days in the field, riding the Florida roads with each salesperson, they began to trust him and reveal how they felt about their jobs and the company.

David Berz, the unofficial assistant team manager, talked at length about why he liked his job.

"What I really like is the freedom. I'm really my own boss most of the time. I don't have to be sitting in an office for the whole day, with some supervisor hanging over my shoulder and looking at all of my work. I get to be outside, here in the car, doing what I like

to be doing—being out in the world, talking to people, and making the sale."

Neil Portnow, who had been with the company longer than the other team members, commented on the group:

"This is really a great bunch of guys to work with. I've been with a couple of different groups, but this is the best. I've been together with Dave and Jay for about 15 years now and I wouldn't trade it for anything. Jay is really one of us; he knows that we know how to do our jobs and he doesn't try to put a lot of controls on us. We go about doing the job the way we know is best and that is OK with Jay.

"The guys are also good because they help you out. When I was sick last year, they all pitched in to cover my territory so that we could make our plan plus 10 percent without reporting my illness to the company. They can also be hard on someone who doesn't realize how things work here. A few years back, when one of the young guys, Fred, came on with us, he was all fired up. He was going to sell baby food to half the mothers in Florida, personally! He didn't realize that you have to take your time and not waste your effort for the company. The other guys gave him a little bit of a hard time at first—he found his orders getting lost and shipments being changed but when he finally came to his senses, they treated him great and showed him the ropes."

Picking up on the references to "the company," the researcher asked Neil to talk more about HFP as a place to work:

"It's all pretty simple: the company is out to screw the salespeople. Up in Atlanta and New York, all they are concerned about is the numbers, meeting the plan no matter what. The worst thing is you work hard, meet the plan, and then keep going so you can earn some decent money. Then they go and change the plan next year. They increase the sales quota so that you have to work harder just to earn the same money! It just doesn't pay to bust your ass...

"The people in Atlanta also want all kinds of paperwork: sales reports, call reports, all kinds of reports. If you filled out all of the things that they want you to fill out, you'd spend all your time doing paperwork and no time selling, looking for new accounts, making cold calls, or any of the things that a salesperson really is supposed to do if he's going to keep on top of his area."

As the researcher talked with the other salespeople, he found general agreement with Neil's views on the company.

Alby Siegel added:

"The biggest joke they got going is the suggestion plan. They want us to come up with new ideas about how the company should make more money. The joke of it is, if you come up with an idea that, for instance, makes the company a couple of hundred thousand in profit across the country, they are generous enough to give you $500. That's the top figure, $500 for your idea. That amount of money is an insult . . .

"One thing you have to remember is that in one way or another, we're all in this for the money. Despite what they say, it's not the greatest thing to be out on the road all of the time, staying in motels, fighting the competition. But it's worth it because I can earn more money doing this job than anything else I could do. I can live better than most "professionals" with all their college degrees. Jay is pretty good about the money thing too. He makes sure that we get our bonus, year in and year out, and he keeps the people in Atlanta from taking our bonus checks away from us. He's not management—he's one of us. You can really tell it during the team meetings. Once every 2 months we all meet in Tampa and spend a day going over the accounts and talking about ideas for selling. We spend the whole day in this hotel room, working, and then we go out and spend the whole night on the town, usually drinking. Jay is one of us. Many is the night that I've helped carry him back to the hotel."

After about 4 weeks with the team, the researcher participated in one of the bimonthly team meetings. During lunch, Jay came over to him and began to talk:

"Listen, I need talk over something with you before we start the afternoon meeting. We trust you so we're going to let you in on our little discovery. You may have noticed that we aren't doing so badly, and you're right. The reason is a little finding made by Alby about 3 years ago. He was out in one of the stores and he noticed that a lot of people buying our products were not mothers of young children, but old people! We started looking around and we began to notice that a lot of older people were buying HFP jars. We talked with some of them and it turns out that they like our stuff, particularly those people who have all kinds of teeth problems.

"Since then we've developed a very lucrative trade with a number of the old folks's homes, and we've been able to sell to them through some of the supermarkets who are located in areas where there is a large older population. It's a great new piece of the market: it takes the pressure off us to make plan, and we don't even have to push it very hard to keep making plan and about 10 percent.

"We've also been pretty successful in keeping Atlanta from finding out. If they knew, they'd up our plan, leaving us no time to sell, no time to develop new customers, no time to make cold calls, or anything. This way we use this new area as a little cushion, and it helps us to stay on top of our territory. I had to tell you because we'll be talking about the old people this afternoon. The boys seem to think you are OK, so I'm trusting you with it. I hope I'm not making a mistake telling you this."

Back in Atlanta

Soon after the Tampa meeting, the researcher left the Florida sales team and returned to New York. On the way back, he made a final brief visit with Brenda Cooper. He found her even more concerned about her problems:

"I'm getting all kinds of pressure from New York to jack up my sales in the region. They are pushing me to increase the plan for next year. I really am beginning to feel that my job is on the line on this one. If I can't come up with something that is good in the coming year, the future for me at HFP looks bleak.

"At the same time, I'm getting flack from my district managers. They all say that they're running flat out as is and they can't squeeze any more sales out of the district than they already are. Even Jay Boyar is complaining that he may not make plan if we have another increase next year. At the same time, he always seems to pull out his 10 percent extra by the end of the year; I wonder what they're really doing down there."

THE CASE OF THE MISSING TIME

At approximately 7:30 A.M. on Tuesday, June 23, 1959, Chet Craig, manager of the Norris Company's Central Plant, swung his car out of the driveway of his suburban home and headed toward the plant located some six miles away just inside the Midvale city limits. It was a beautiful day. The sun was shining brightly and a cool, fresh breeze was blowing. The trip to the plant took about 20 minutes and sometimes gave Chet an opportunity to think about plant problems without interruption.

The Norris Company owned and operated three quality printing plants. Norris enjoyed a nation-wide commercial business, specializing in quality color work. It was a closely held company with some 350 employees, nearly half of whom were employed at the Central Plant, the largest of the three Norris production operations. The company's main offices were also located in the Central Plant building.

Chet had started with the Norris Company as an expediter in its Eastern Plant in 1948, just after he graduated from Ohio State. After three years Chet was promoted to production supervisor and two years later was made assistant to the manager of the Eastern Plant. Early in 1957, he was transferred to the Central Plant as assistant to the plant manager and one month later was promoted to plant manager, when the former manager retired.

He began to run through the day's work, first one project, then another, trying to establish priorities. After a few minutes he decided that the open-end unit scheduling was probably the most important; certainly the most urgent. He frowned for a moment as he recalled that on Friday the vice president and general manger had casually asked him if he had given the project any further thought. Chet realized that he had not been giving it much thought lately. He had been meaning to get to work on this idea for over three months, but something else always seemed to crop up. "I haven't had much time to sit down and really work it out," he said to himself. "I'd better get going and hit this one today for sure." With that he began to break down the objectives, procedures, and installation steps of the project. He grinned as he reviewed the principles involved and calculated roughly the anticipated savings. "It's about time," he told himself. "This idea should have been followed up long ago." Chet remembered that he had first conceived of the open-end unit scheduling idea nearly a year and a half ago just prior to his leaving Norris's Eastern Plant. He had spoken to his boss, Jim Quince, manager of the Eastern Plant, about it then and both agreed that it was worth looking into. The idea was temporarily shelved when he was transferred to the Central Plant a month later.

A blast from a passing horn startled him but his thoughts quickly returned to other plant projects he was determined to get under way. He started to think through a procedure for simpler transport of dies to and from the Eastern Plant. Visualizing the notes on his desk he thought about the inventory analysis he needed to identify and eliminate some of the slow-moving stock items; the packing controls which needed revision; and the need to design a new special-order form. He also decided that this was the day to settle on a job printer to do the simple outside printing of office forms. There were a few other projects he couldn't recall offhand but he could tend to them after lunch if not before. "Yes sir," he said to himself, "this is the day to really get rolling."

Chet's thoughts were interrupted as he pulled into the company parking lot. When he entered the plant Chet knew something was wrong as he met Al Noren, the stockroom foreman, who appeared troubled. "A great morning, Al," Chet greeted him cheerfully.

"Not so good, Chet; my new man isn't in this morning," Noren growled.

"Have you heard from him?" asked Chet.

"No, I haven't," replied Al.

Chet frowned as he commented, "These stock handlers assume you take it for granted that if they're not here, they're not here, and they don't call in and verify it. Better ask Personnel to call him."

Al hesitated for a moment before replying. "Okay, Chet, but can you find me a man? I have two cars to unload today."

As Chet turned to leave he said, "I'll call you in half an hour, Al, and let you know."

Making a mental note of the situation Chet headed for his office. He greeted the group of workers huddled around Marilyn, the office manager, who was discussing the day's work schedule with them. As the meeting broke up Marilyn picked up a few samples from the clasper, showed them to Chet, and asked if they should be shipped that way or if it would be necessary to inspect them. Before he could answer, Marilyn went on to ask if he could suggest another clerical operator for the sealing machine to replace the regular operator who was home ill. She also told him that Gene, the industrial engineer, had called and was waiting to hear from Chet.

After telling Marilyn to go ahead and ship the samples, he made a note of the need for a sealer operator for the office and then called Gene. He agreed to stop by Gene's office before lunch and started on his routine morning tour of the plant. He asked each foreman the types and volumes of orders they were running, the number of people present, how the schedules were coming along, and the orders to be run next; helped the folding-room foreman find temporary storage space for consolidating a carload shipment; discussed quality control with a pressman who had been running poor work; arranged to transfer four people temporarily to different departments, including two for Al in the stockroom; talked to the shipping foreman about pickups and special orders to be delivered that day. As he continued through the plant, he saw to it that reserve stock was moved out of the forward stock area; talked to another pressman about his requested change of vacation schedule; had a "heart-to-heart" talk with a press helper who seemed to need frequent reassurance; approved two type and one color order okays for different pressmen.

Returning to his office, Chet reviewed the production reports on the larger orders against his initial projections and found that the plant was running behind schedule. He called in the folding-room foreman and together they went over the line-up of machines and made several necessary changes.

During this discussion, the composing-room foreman stopped in to cover several type changes and the routing foreman telephoned for approval of a revised printing schedule. The stockroom foreman called twice, first to inform him that two standard, fast-moving stock items were dangerously low; later to advise him that the paper stock for the urgent Dillion job had finally arrived. Chet made the necessary subsequent calls to inform those concerned.

He then began to put delivery dates on important and difficult inquiries received from customers and salesmen. (The routine inquiries were handled by Marilyn.) While he was doing this he was interrupted twice, once by a sales correspondent calling from the West Coast to ask for a better delivery date than originally scheduled; once by the personnel vice president asking him to set a time when he could hold an initial training and induction interview with a new employee.

After dating the customer and salesmen inquiries, Chet headed for his morning conference in the Executive Offices. At this meeting he answered the sales vice president's questions in connection with "hot" orders, complaints, the status of large-volume orders and potential new orders. He then met with the general manager to discuss a few ticklish policy matters and to answer "the old man's questions on several specific production and personnel problems." Before leaving the Executive Offices, he stopped at the office of the secretary-treasurer to inquire about delivery of cartons, paper, and boxes, and to place a new order for paper.

On the way back to his own office, Chet conferred with Gene about two current engineering projects concerning which he had called earlier. When he reached his desk, he lit a cigarette, and looked at his watch. It was 10 minutes before lunch, just time enough to make a few notes of the details he needed to check in order to answer knotty questions raised by the sales manager that morning.

After lunch Chet started again. He began by checking the previous day's production reports; did some rescheduling to get out urgent orders; placed appropriate delivery dates on new orders and inquiries received that morning; consulted with a foreman on a personal problem. He spent some 20 minutes at the TWX1[1] going over mutual problems with the Eastern Plant.

By midafternoon Chet had made another tour of the plant after which he met with the personnel director to review with him a touchy personal problem raised by one of the clerical employees; the vacation schedules submitted by his foremen; and the pending job evaluation program. Following this conference, Chet hurried back to his office to complete the special statistical report for Universal Waxing Corporation, one of Norris' best customers. As he finished the report he discovered that it was ten minutes after six and he was the only one left in the office. Chet was tired. He put on his coat and headed through the plant toward the parking lot; on the way he was stopped by both the night supervisor and night layout foreman for approval of type and layout changes.

With both eyes on the traffic, Chet reviewed the day he had just completed. "Busy?" he asked himself. "Too much so—but did I accomplish anything?" His mind raced over the day's activities. "Yes and no" seemed to be the answer. "There was the usual routine, the same as any other day. The plant kept going and I think it must have been a good production day. Any creative or special project-work done?" Chet grimaced as he reluctantly answered, "No."

With a feeling of guilt, he probed further. "Am I an executive? I'm paid like one, respected like one, and have a responsible assignment with the necessary authority to carry it out. Yet one of the greatest values a company derives from an executive is his creative thinking and accomplishments. What have I done about it? An executive needs some time

---

[1] Leased private telegram communication system using teletypewriter.

for thinking. Today was a typical day, just like most other days, and I did little, if any, creative work. The projects that I so enthusiastically planned to work on this morning are exactly as they were yesterday. What's more, I have no guarantee that tomorrow night or the next night will bring me any closer to their completion. This is a real problem and there must be an answer."

Chet continued, "Night work? Yes, occasionally. This is understood. But I've been doing too much of this lately. I owe my wife and family some of my time. When you come down to it, they are the people for whom I'm really working. If I am forced to spend much more time away from them, I'm not meeting my own personal objectives. What about church work? Should I eliminate that? I spend a lot of time on this, but I feel I owe God some time too. Besides, I believe I'm making a worthwhile contribution in this work. Perhaps I can

squeeze a little time from my fraternal activities. But where does recreation fit in?"

Chet groped for the solution. "Maybe I'm just rationalizing because I schedule my own work poorly. But I don't think so. I've studied my work habits carefully and I think I plan intelligently and delegate authority. Do I need an assistant? Possibly, but that's a long-time project and I don't believe I could justify the additional overhead expenditure. Anyway, I doubt whether it would solve the problem."

By this time Chet had turned off the highway onto the side street leading to his home—the problem still uppermost in his mind. "I guess I really don't know the answer," he told himself as he pulled into his driveway. "This morning everything seemed so simple but now..." His thoughts were interrupted as he saw his son running toward the car calling out, "Mommy, Daddy's home."

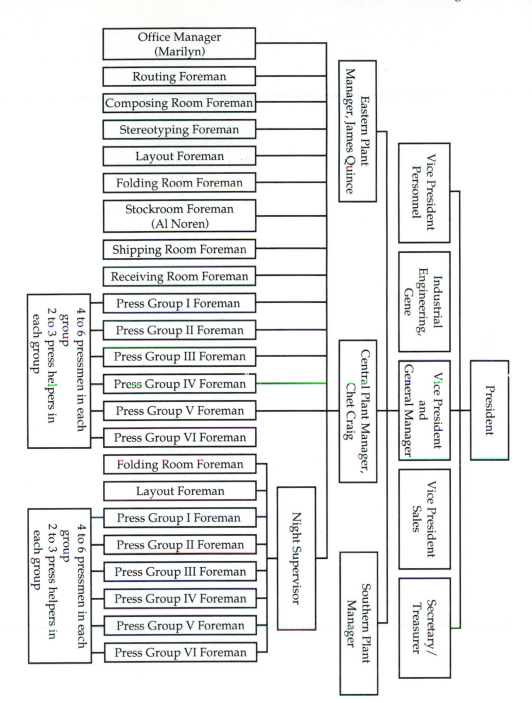

GLOSSARY

Achievement need. The desire to succeed or excel in a given area or endeavor.

Action steps. Process that must be followed to implement a plan.

Active listening. A technique employing verbal and nonverbal signals to demonstrate receptivity to what the speaker is trying to communicate.

Affiliation need. The desire for warm interpersonal relationships.

Affiliation power. Power that is borrowed from an authority through association, or wielded by a person acting as a surrogate for the authority figure.

Atomistic theories. School of thought that assumed a single cause can be found to explain behavior of people in organizations.

Attitudes. Evaluative responses to objects, people, or situations.

Attribution. The process by which we perceive people and the causes for their behavior.

Authority power. The right of a manager to give orders and expect them to be obeyed by his or her subordinates.

Behavior modification. The use of positive or negative reinforcement to elicit specific habitual behavior.

Behaviorally anchored rating scales (BARS). An employee performance rating system that utilizes a continuum of specific job-related behaviors.

Belief system. Judgments and values an individual or group brings to interactions with the environment and others.

Body language. Nonverbal communication, largely unconscious and spontaneous, including gestures, facial expressions, eye contact, and stance.

Brainstorming. A group technique encouraging the generation of ideas and solutions without fear of censure or criticism.

Case method. A process of learning through analysis, discussion, and skills development, utilizing case studies.

Case study. An accurate historical portrayal of an actual, usually multifaceted, situation with which a manager in a real organization has had to cope.

Change agent. An expert or consultant who encourages the reexamination of an organization's practices and problems, and who acts as a catalyst for organizational change.

Charisma. A leader's personal characteristics that command the loyalty and devotion of followers.

Climate. The interaction of personalities, attitudes, behaviors, and job requirements in the organization.

Coaching. A management technique based on knowledge about how and under what conditions employees improve and grow.

Coercion power. Physical or psychological injury meted out by a manager, such as a put-down, slight, or demotion, or even an actual physical attack.

Cohesiveness. The degree of closeness or unity in a group.

Communication. The exchange of information between a sender and a receiver.

Communication channel. The specific set of steps used by individuals or groups in an organization that result in the exchange of information.

Communication skills. Ability to listen to and express ideas.

Componential intelligence. Linear analysis or thinking, measurable by IQ tests.

Conceptual skills. The ability to analyze complex situations.

Conflict. Any functional or dysfunctional difference that exists within an individual, between individuals, or among groups.

Conflict avoidance. The tendency to seek consensus in problem solving.

Conflict management. The use of conflict as a motivator and catalyst for adaptive change, rather than as the cause of dysfunctional behavior.

Conflict resolution. Strategies aimed at minimizing interpersonal or group conflict.

Conformity. Aligning one's beliefs or behavior with those of a group.

Consensus.   Agreement by group members to support the decisions and actions of the group.

Content theories.   Concepts focusing on what factors motivate behavior.

Contextual intelligence.   Ability to read the environment and adjust to or manipulate it; sometimes referred to as "street smarts."

Contingency model of leadership.   As approach to leadership suggesting that effectiveness is determined by both situational factors and characteristics of the leader.

Coordinative organization.   An organization within an organization that integrates the traditional, vertical structure with the horizontal, task-oriented structure.

Creativity.   The ability to produce innovative and potentially useful ideas.

Critical evaluator.   One whose group role is to analyze and evaluate potential decisions.

Critical-incident technique. The evaluation of responses to critical incidents that relate to the skills needed for successful performance.

Defense mechanisms.   Reactive or protective behaviors evoked by stress, challenge, or change.

Delegation.   A complex process that involves the assignment of duties, the acquisition of power, and the assumption of responsibility.

Dissatisfiers.   In two-factor theory, the lower-level needs that, when unmet, become sources of dissatisfaction.

Distributive bargaining.   A negative situation that requires there be a winner and a loser.

Emergent system.   Informal patterns of group and group member behavior.

Empathetic listening.   Listening with an appreciation of another's perspective or frame of reference.

Environment.   Situations or events outside an organization that can affect the health and productivity of the organization.

Equity theory.   Workers' comparison of the fairness of job inputs and outcomes, often against those of other individuals or groups.

Evaluator.   Managerial role that includes periodic evaluations of employee performance.

Expectancy theory.   A motivational theory that states people, usually subconsciously, will put forth effort in proportion to the consequences they expect to occur.

Experiential thinking. Nonlinear or intuitive intelligence, or what we learn from experience.

Expert power.   Influence based on the possession of special expertise, knowledge, or ability.

Feedback.   Communicated response to the effectiveness of a worker's performance.

Fight-or-flight.   The physiological response to stress that arouses the body to action.

Filtering.   Process by which one's experiences, judgment, or expectations add or subtract from sensory input.

Forecasting.   The attempt by management to anticipate future circumstances that will affect organizational decision making.

Formal organization.   The formal design of an organization, including its hierarchy, information systems, pay systems, and personnel policies.

Frame of reference.   Point of view, reflecting one's perceptions and life experiences.

Gainsharing.   An incentive strategy in which employees who help achieve goals are rewarded by a share in the financial gains.

General Adaptive Syndrome (GAS).   The three stages of stress, identified by Selze as alarm, resistance, and exhaustion.

Goals.   Long-term expressions of organizational strategy.

Group culture.   Factors affecting the perceptions and behavior of the group, such as expectations, experiences, norms, roles, and required and emergent activities.

Group power.   Group interaction involving problem solving, conflict resolution, or creative brainstorming.

Groupthink.   Phenomenon of group decision making in which the consensus sought by members results in the inability or unwillingness to evaluate alternative courses of action.

Hawthorne effect.   Any managerial attention to workers that increases their productivity.

Hidden agenda.   Personal goals consciously or unconsciously pursued by group members, regardless of the group's agreed-upon task.

Hierarchy of needs. Maslow listed five distinct levels of human needs: physiological, safety, social, ego, and self-fulfillment.

Holistic theories. School of thought that assumes behavior results from many different forces operating simultaneously.

Human resources management. Managerial policies and decisions that provide the basis for the relationship between the organization and its people, such as personnel policies.

Hygiene factors. Herzberg's dissatisfiers or in Maslow's hierarchy of needs, the lower level needs that become sources of dissatisfaction if inadequately met.

Influence skills. The relative use of all types of influence, including directive, collaborative, and symbolic.

Information power. Influence based on access to information that is not public knowledge.

Innovators. People within the organization capable of applying new ideas to improve products, technology, or services.

Integrated motivational model. A model that ties together a number of motivation theories to show their interrelationships and to guide managers in the use of the various theories.

Integration. The process of bringing together to form a unified whole.

Integrative bargaining. Cooperative negotiations that seek a settlement in which both parties are winners.

Integrative devices. Devices, such as the control system, the reward system, the physical layout, and delegated authority, which help achieve integration of organizational efforts to complete a task.

Integrative units. Groups, such as committees, which integrate the activities of others who design and build a project.

Interaction. Any communication, including all verbal, nonverbal, and written exchanges of information.

Interpersonal skills. The ability to function effectively with peers, managers, and subordinates by using, in combination, componential, experiential, and contextual functions.

Intervention. The process by which someone intervenes in a situation for the purpose of changing or improving some aspect of it.

Jargon. Specialized language that allows a group the simple communication of complex meanings.

Job enrichment. Increasing job quality and employee satisfaction by designing jobs with greater opportunity for achievement, responsibility, and personal growth.

Knowledge-based approach. An extension of the critical-incident technique for the measurement of practical intelligence based on essential skills determined by gathering knowledge from experts and then applying Sternberg's classification of the three knowledge areas.

Management by objectives (MBO). A five-step managerial program involving the accomplishment of goals through the establishment of performance targets and progress checkpoints; individual and group meetings between superiors and subordinates; and assessment of the subordinates' efforts.

Manager. Individual whose function is to achieve organizational goals by influencing others.

Managerial grid. Theory of leadership that attempts to balance concern for people with concern for production.

Managing others. Knowledge of the work habits, strengths and weaknesses, and the goal orientation of subordinates and colleagues.

Managing self. Knowledge about how to manage oneself on a daily basis to maximize one's productiveness.

Matrix organization. A structure combining functional and coordinative concepts.

Mentor. An experienced person who establishes and maintains a developmental relationship with a protégé.

Motivation. Psychological forces that influence a person's persistence towards a goal.

Motivational approach. A measurement system focusing on motive patterns needed to manage successfully; using the managerial assessment of the needs of the employee for achievement, power, and affiliation.

Motivators. Those factors that influence behavior; in Herzberg's two-factor theory, those factors which satisfy social, ego, and self-fulfillment needs described by Maslow.

Multifunctional teams.   Work teams consisting of people performing many different functions in the organization.

Multiple influence model.   Theory that influence is an interdependent combination of expectations, self-concept, and intrinsic factors.

Negative reinforcement.   Reinforcement that weakens an undesirable behavior by providing a painful stimulus, thus encouraging the subject to avoid such undesirable behavior in the future.

Negotiation.   Bargaining process between two or more parties seeking to reach an agreement.

Nonverbal communication.   Messages conveyed through other than formal language, including body language and facial expressions.

Norms.   Unstated expectations of group and individual behavior, shared by the group members.

Objectives.   Short-term targets for implementing organizational strategy.

OD practitioner.   A person within the company or an outside consultant responsible for orchestrating changes necessary to improve an organization's efficiency, effectiveness, and health.

Open agenda.   The acknowledged task of a work group.

Operant conditioning.   The use of contingent cues and consequences to elicit desired behavior.

Opportunity finding.   The ability to survey the environment and focus on opportunities.

Organization.   A multivariate system that strives to achieve a common goal or goals through combination of its members' efforts.

Organizational behavior.   The study of individual and group influence on behavior or attitudes within organizations.

Organizational culture.   A consensus of shared values, expectations, rituals, and social ideas held by the organization members.

Organizational development (OD).   Changes made in an organization to improve the organization's effectiveness and the well-being of its employees.

Organizational effectiveness.   Ability of an organization to accomplish goals.

Organizational structure.   The formal pattern of people and tasks in an organization.

Participative management.   Theory Y-type management style, often more effective for tasks with high levels of complexity.

Pattern A decision making.   Behavior in group decision making that is thoughtful, rational, and mildly competitive.

Pattern B decision making.   Behavior in group decision making that is competitive first, thoughtful and rational second.

People-oriented manager.   One who consciously or intuitively utilizes good interpersonal skills in managing group performance.

Perception.   The process of receiving and interpreting sensory messages in order to give meaning to the environment.

Performance appraisal.   A periodic evaluation of employee performance.

Planned organizational change.   A specific series of interventions designed to influence the organization in the direction of greater effectiveness, efficiency, and health.

Politics.   Individual or group self-interest and behavior that may or may not correspond with the goals of the organization.

Positive reinforcement.   Reward for a behavior the manager wishes to be repeated.

Power.   The capacity to influence the behavior of others.

Power bases.   Tools managers use to influence others towards the goals of the organization.

Power need.   The need to have an impact on or influence the behavior or others.

Power skills.   Interpersonal skills a successful manager uses to influence others to work effectively.

Prediction.   Anticipating the outcome of behavior.

Problem finding.   An often intuitive ability to read the environment and subtle changes in the environment and their relationship to future events.

Problem solving.   The application of cognitive skills to classify a problem, seek and select solutions, then take action to resolve the problem.

Procedures.   Formal mechanisms for acquiring, sharing, and processing information, identifying alternatives, and making recommendations.

Psychological contract. Sometimes written but usually unwritten reciprocal expectations between two individuals or groups such as an employee and employer.

Pygmalion effect. A worker's performance is directly related to the positive or negative expectations others, such as a supervisor, may have.

Quality circle. A small group of volunteers who meet periodically to discuss and offer solutions to problems of product quality and cost.

Reference group. A group, such as a church, family, or profession, to which an individual may hold alliance.

Referent power. Influence based on admiration of and respect for the person in power; includes charisma, reciprocity, and track record.

Reflective behavior. Behavior influenced by the expectations the individual perceives others in the organization have of him or her, or the expectations the individual has of him or herself.

Reflective reiterative process. Strategy to handle conflict by turning it into an asset, with openness, individual risk-taking, and personal awareness.

Reinforcement theory. The belief that behavior is strengthened by positive consequences.

Relaxation response. The physiological and psychological opposite of the fight-or-flight response.

Required system. Activities and interactions that the group must carry out in order to remain a member of the larger organization and enjoy its benefits.

Reward power. A positive stroke, remuneration, or award that is seen as positive.

Risk-taking. The decision to take advantage of an opportunity or meet a challenge in the hope of achieving a goal with high rewards.

Role. A set of behaviors expected of an individual in a social unit.

Role conflict. A condition that exists when a person is confronted by different role expectations.

Satisfiers. Herzberg's term described in Maslow's hierarchy, as the higher needs: affiliation, self-esteem, and self-fulfillment.

Scientific management. Theory that stresses the use of systematic observation to find the most efficient methods to complete a task, then the systematic application of those procedures.

Scientific method. A systematic approach to research that includes observation of a phenomenon, developing a hypothesis about it, and testing the hypothesis through experimentation.

Self-concept. One's perception or mental picture of oneself.

Self-fulfilling prophecy. Expectations about likely behavior that actually causes the realization of those expectations.

Self-talk. Private evaluation of one's current situation.

Shared power. Concept that problem solving must involve

collaboration between all levels of an organization.

Simulation approach. Method used to assess job-related behavior through observation of performance in simulated situations.

Situational leadership. A theory that requires a leader to analyze the people and situation involved before settling on a particular leadership style.

Six-fold path model. Greiner's theory that change must involve collaboration between all levels of the organization.

Six-step performance appraisal review. An employee-manager partnership emphasizing the shared responsibility of discussing at different points in the employee's performance the best ways to utilize the employee's strengths and talents.

Spontaneous behavior. Instinctive and/or instantaneous behavior.

Status. One's position or rank in the social hierarchy.

Stereotyping. Attributing certain traits to an individual or group based on one's generalized expectations and set of beliefs.

Strategic plan. Program of action shaping an organization's movement towards long-term goals.

Street smarts. In cognitive functioning, the ability to read the environment and adjust to it.

Stress. An adaptive response to an action, event, or situation that causes a person physical or psychological distress.

Stress carrier. Individual who causes stress in others, either through incompetence, indecisiveness, demanding behavior, or personality traits over which the others have no control.

Stressors. External events or conditions that can cause physical or psychological harm.

Stress-prone (Type A) personality. Pattern of behavior characterized by chronic aggression, drive, impatience, and competitiveness.

Subculture. Culture within a culture, usually defined by physical separation or departmentalization within the organization.

Subordinate gamesmanship. Behavior pattern in which subordinates pass only positive information to top management while suppressing negative information for fear of reprisal.

Synergy. Influence that results when group members pool their efforts and encouragement and group results exceed the sum of the individual members contributions.

Task. A unit of work.

Team building. An intervention to increase work team effectiveness through clarification of goals, roles, procedures, and interpersonal relationships.

Technology. Tools and techniques used by the organization to complete tasks.

Theory X. Style of management that assumes people are generally lazy, dislike work, avoid responsibility, and must be coerced to achieve an organizational objective.

Theory Y. Style of management that assumes people find work as natural as play, can exercise self-control, and are self-directed in the service of objectives to which they are committed.

Time management. Determining priorities to maximize efficiency in accomplishing tasks in the time available.

Time, space, and things. Used to signal status or communicate nonverbal messages about ourselves and how we feel about others.

Total organization. The interdependence of an organization's social and formal structure, its procedures, systems, technology, tasks, and people.

Total Quality Management (TQM). Program in which every person in the organization focuses on producing the best product without any defects.

Traits. An individual's personal and psychological characteristics, including personality, social skills, and intellect.

Trait theories. Attempts to identify common individual characteristics leaders seem to possess.

Transformational leadership. Leadership characterized by charisma, inspiration, intellectual stimulation, and consideration for the individual used to transform an organization.

Two-factor theory. Herzberg postulated that hygiene factors and motivators cause worker satisfaction and dissatisfaction.

Value system. Set of values that an individual, group, or an organization consciously or unconsciously adopts.

Values. Beliefs that make a person choose one mode of conduct over another.

Vision. An imaginative view of where an organization can go in the future based on that organization's strengths and needs and its place in the environment. A shared vision gives a sense of direction to individual, group, or organizational endeavor.

Work group. A group formed to perform a particular task within an organization.

Work space. One's personal work area, the size, location, and accessibility of which communicate something of one's status in the organization.

Zero-sum bargaining. Negotiations in which there is a winner and a loser.

INDEX